ANIMAL EVOLUTION IN CHANGING ENVIRONMENTS

ANIMAL EVOLUTION IN CHANGING ENVIRONMENTS

WITH SPECIAL REFERENCE TO ABNORMAL METAMORPHOSIS

Ryuichi Matsuda

Biosystematics Research Institute
Agriculture Canada
Ottawa, Ontario

A WILEY-INTERSCIENCE PUBLICATION

JOHN WILEY & SONS

NEW YORK   CHICHESTER   BRISBANE   TORONTO   SINGAPORE

QH
371
M323
1987

Library of Congress Cataloging in Publication Data:

Matsuda, Ryuichi.
  Animal evolution in changing environments.

  "A Wiley-Interscience publication."
  Bibliography: p.
  Includes indexes.
  1. Evolution. 2. Metamorphosis. 3. Morphology
(Animals) 4. Abnormalities (Animals) I. Title.

QH371.M323 1986   591.3′8   86-15942
ISBN 0-471-87856-1

Printed in the United States of America

10 9 8 7 6 5 4 3 2 1

A NOTE TO THE READER

Dr. Ryuichi Matsuda was able to complete the manuscript for this book to his full satisfaction even though he unfortunately did not live to see it in print. Since leaving his hands the work has undergone only minor copy editing plus, of course, proofreading and indexing.

EDWARD C. BECKER
Ottawa, Ontario

ANNELLE R. SOPONIS
Tallahassee, Florida

It is very difficult to decide how far changed conditions, such as of climate, food, etc., have acted in a definite manner. There is reason to believe that in the course of time the effects have been greater than can be proved by clear evidence.

Charles Darwin, *The Origin of Species,* 6th edition, 1872, p. 139.

Preface

In this book an attempt is made to elucidate the evolutionary process of animals in more or less drastically changing environments. Metamorphosis appears to be highly relevant in considering the mechanism of conspicuous structural changes in changing environments during evolution, because the conspicuous structural changes in metamorphosis occur in tandem during postoval development, often in accordance with environmental changes. Sudden macroevolutionary structural changes could have occurred through essentially the same interaction between the genotype and changing environmental stimuli (and/or signals) as the one we see in the sequence of metamorphosis; the "genotype" as used in this work is, as defined by Mayr (1970), the totality of genetic factors that make up the genetic constitution of an animal.

As I (Matsuda 1979) attempted to show for arthropods, certain, well established modes of metamorphosis (such as the larva, pupa, and adult sequence in holometabolous insects) are often disturbed, resulting in various modes of abnormal metamorphosis (neoteny, halmatometamorphosis, caenogenesis, castes), and the consequence of abnormal metamorphosis is often a highly modified adult. Clear understanding of the mechanism of abnormal metamorphosis as well as that of normal metamorphosis, therefore, should enable us to gain insight into the mechanism of structural evolution of animals in general.

In analyzing the evolutionary process of animals involving abnormal metamorphosis, the effect of environmental factors on development, called the "proximate process," is considered first. The action of natural selection, or the ultimate process of evolution, is assessed after the proximate process has been analyzed. To understand the proximate process clearly, I have endeavored to integrate the ever-growing knowledge from endocrinology in the discussions of all animal groups concerned. The result shows that structural changes that occur during the proximate process appear to result from the interaction of the endocrine mechanism inherited from the ancestors and new environmental stimuli. Hence the structural modifications that resulted have, at least initially, nothing to do with natural selection. Often the latter is shown to have contributed merely to the improvement of the endocrine mechanism for such changes.

The data presented in Part Two: Special Discussion are those showing the effect of environmental changes on structural evolution. As might be expected, the data thus selected for different animal groups are never parallel, partly because of differences in organisms and their environments, and partly because of the difference in extent and intensity of studies that have been done for different groups. Homoiothermic vertebrates, that is, birds and mammals, and reptiles have not been studied, because they do not undergo appreciable metamorphosis in ontogeny and their growth and development are protected from environmental temperature fluctuation, which is probably the single most important factor affecting growth and development in other animals.

The question of how or whether environmentally modified phenotypes become genetically fixed is also a major concern in this work, as it was in my recent work (Matsuda 1982). Analysis of facts relevant to this problem has elucidated the nature of the so-called "inheritance of acquired characters" (Fig. 6) and of some evolutionary concepts such as Dollo's law and genetic polymorphism. As is repeatedly pointed out throughout the text, both the effect of environment on morphogenesis and that of natural selection on the morphogenetic consequence have been involved in producing the phenomena that we call here adaptive responses (Fig. 6). Indeed, many macroevolutionary changes mentioned in the text can be viewed as adaptive responses in new environments.

In explaining the evolutionary process in changing environments the most important group of animals to be considered is the Amphibia, not *Drosophila*. The action of hormones (not of their chemistry) is an integral part of the discussion, for it compels us to believe in the universal environmental effect on development (proximate process), which has been ignored in conventional neo-Darwinism. Also, as Fig. 6 shows, it is the genetic change involving the endocrine mechanism that could result in fixation of the newly formed phenotype. This approach of analysis of the evolutionary process is widely applicable and probably new to many readers, and it requires a bit of patience in reading the text.

RYUICHI MATSUDA

Ottawa, Canada
January, 1987

Acknowledgments

In completing Part Two: Special Discussion, I have received help from the following zoologists: L. Abele (Tallahassee, FL), R. Anderson (Ottawa, Ont.), E. R. Bousfield (Ottawa, Ont.), D. Calder (Toronto, Ont.), R. A. Cloney (Seattle, WA), F. R. Cook (Ottawa, Ont.), P. S. Cranston (London), K. G. Davey (Downsview, Ont.), R. Foottit (Ottawa, Ont.), R. Freeman (Toronto, Ont.), E. Frieden (Tallahassee, FL), W. H. Heard (Tallahassee, FL), G. Hendler (Washington, DC), M. J. Jones (Washington, DC), D. K. McE. Kevan (Ste. Anne de Bellevue, P.Q.), K. C. Kim (University Park, PA), E. Kirsteurer (New York), E. Lindquist (Ottawa, Ont.), D. E. McAlister (Ottawa, Ont.), S. Peck (Ottawa, Ont.), W. Peters (Tallahassee, FL), M. Rice (Fort Pierce, FL), R. M. Rieger (Chapel Hill, NC), F. Rosewater (Washington, DC), R. Short (Tallahassee, FL), A. Smetana (Ottawa, Ont.), C. Yoshimoto (Ottawa, Ont.), V. R. Vickery (Ste. Anne de Bellevue, P.Q.).

I thank them cordially for corrections to portions of early drafts of the manuscript and/or for additional information they provided.

I also would like to thank H. Ando (Sugadaira, Japan), A. Borkent (Ottawa, Ont.), C. Dondale (Ottawa, Ont.), R. Foottit (Ottawa, Ont.), E. Munroe (Ottawa, Ont.), J. Nagai (Ottawa, Ont.), R. Pearson (Toronto, Ont.), T. Saigusa (Fukuoka, Japan), A. Soponis (Tallahassee, FL), and K. Suzuki (Toyama, Japan) for constructive discussions during the prolonged course of this study. E. Munroe read Part One: General Discussion and gave cogent criticism.

Over the years I have been helped by library staffs, and I feel I owe thanks especially to E. Daniel and S. Gamman for their steady help in information retrieval. E. Krelina helped me in finishing the references.

Finally, my special thanks go to E. J. LeRoux for his approval and support of this research during my tenure at the Biosystematics Research Institute.

R. M.

Contents

ANIMAL EVOLUTION
IN CHANGING
ENVIRONMENTS

Part One

GENERAL DISCUSSION

1

Metamorphosis in the Metazoan Life Cycle

The prevalence and the physiological nature of the well-established cases of "normal metamorphosis" must be clearly understood so that the modes of derivation of abnormal metamorphosis can be understood. The normal pattern of metamorphosis represents a hereditarily determined norm of reaction of the genotype, and metamorphosis is here defined as the more or less conspicuous structural changes that occur during postoval development.

A. PREVALENCE OF METAMORPHOSIS IN METAZOA

Jägersten (1972) has shown, in his book on the evolution of the metazoan life cycle, that the pelago–benthic life cycle (pelagic larval and benthic adult stages separated by metamorphosis) occurs in no less than 17 phyla of marine invertebrates, which include Porifera, Cnidaria, Phoronida, Bryozoa, Brachiopoda, Platyhelmintha, Nemertinea, Entoprocta, Mollusca, Sipuncula, Myzostomida, Annelida, Arthropoda (Crustacea), Echinodermata, Pogonophora, Enteropneusta, and Prochordata. To this list should be added the Echiura. In these phyla, according to Jägersten (1972) and Chia and Rice (1978), pelagic larvae metamorphose into benthic adults upon settlement on the substratum of the seabottom; Jägersten called such larvae "primary larvae," and thus I call the metamorphosis of primary larvae into adults "primary metamorphosis." Primary larvae take various forms such as the trochophore, cyphonautes, pilidium, and veliger. When two or more larval forms occur in one ontogeny (e.g.,

3

the trochophore and the veliger in many gastropods) they are also regarded as primary larvae.

The ancient primary larval stage has been completely eliminated from the ontogeny of terrestrial arthropods. However, a new mode of metamorphosis has developed in many insects (called the Holometabola). It consists of the larval, pupal, and adult stages, and the larva thus formed differs considerably from the larva (called the nymph) in hemimetabolous insects (with a mild metamorphosis into the adult) in having (often) abdominal legs, usually more generalized mouthparts suited for their life, and so forth. These structures and many internal larval structures undergo histolysis and are replaced by developing adult counterparts in the pupa. Such an entirely new mode of metamorphosis is called "secondary metamorphosis." Secondary metamorphosis can occur in large numbers of species which constitute higher taxa (such as holometabolous insect orders). Thysanoptera (Sect. 23D17), scale insects (Sect. 23D18a), and whiteflies (Sect. 23D18a) also have secondary metamorphosis. A sequence of metamorphic changes that characterizes parasitic life cycles in Trematoda (Sect. 9B) and Cestoidea (Sect. 9C) is also secondary metamorphosis. Other examples of secondary metamorphosis include some nematode parasites (*Meloidogyne*, etc., Chap. 16), *Cupelopagis* in Rotifera (Chap. 15), some ctenophorans (Sect. 8B), and so on.

In the anuran *Rana pipiens* the larval stage consists of the earlier premetamorphic period, with little structural change, and the prometamorphic stage, characterized by differential growth of hind legs. During the later period of prometamorphosis certain morphological changes such as the resorption of the anal canal piece, the first sign of degeneration of the opercular skin over the gill chambers, and the emergence of forelegs and the loss of tadpole mouthparts mark the last phase of prometamorphosis and the beginning of the metamorphic climax. During the metamorphic climax body growth ceases and differentiation of frog structures proceeds extremely rapidly (cf. Etkin 1968). In fishes, associated with their aquatic life throughout their development, metamorphic changes are relatively slight. Balon (1975a) proposed the following terms for intervals in fish ontogeny: cleavage of the egg, embryo, eleutheroembryo, protopterygio larva, pterygio larva or alvin, juvenile, adult, and senescent adult.

B. ENDOCRINE BASIS OF METAMORPHOSIS

The reaction of the genotype that occurs during metamorphosis involves the alternation in the deployment of different sets of genes (sets of larval, pupal, and adult genes, to borrow the terms used for insects by Williams and Kafatos 1971) during metamorphosis. This alternation clearly represents gene regulation that occurs in a single ontogeny, and it is hormonally mediated. See Fig. 1.

In insects the so-called classic scheme of the endocrine control of postoval development and metamorphosis was established in early 1950. According to this scheme, neurosecretory cells (NSC) of the pars intercerebralis of the brain

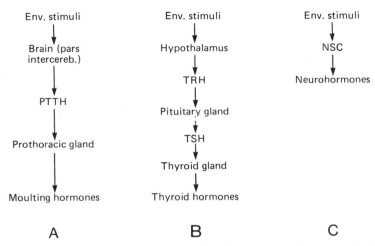

Figure 1. Diagram showing the sequence of the action of morphogenetic hormones for (A) insects, (B) amphibians, and (C) lower invertebrates.

release a brain hormone (prothoracicotropic hormone, PTTH) that stimulates the prothoracic glands, PG) to release molting hormone (MH), which then initiates the molt. The character of the molt, that is, larval–larval, larval–pupal, or pupal–adult, is determined by the titer of juvenile hormone (JH) (produced from the corpora allata, CA) at or before the molt. In the presence of a high titer of JH, MH elicits a larval molt and the presence of a reduced titer of JH evokes a pupal molt. Metamorphosis into the adult occurs in the absence of JH (Granger and Bollenbacher, 1981). Based on this classic scheme, Williams and Kafatos (1971) postulated a model of gene regulation in which JH controls the switch of the sets of genes (larval, pupal, and adult genes). However, the model was criticized by Nijhout and Wheeler (1982), who pointed out that the epidermal cells can secrete a composite cuticle after JH application such that cuticles have surface sculpturing characteristic of one metamorphic stage, but pigmentation of another. Hence, according to these authors, genes (or small groups of such genes) for different characters of a metamorphic stage are invidually sensitive to JH and can be on or off independently of one another. Earlier, Slama (1975) showed similar phenomena in *Pyrrhocoris* and *Galleria*. All these phenomena are a matter of tissue sensitivity, which is attributable to the presence or absence of the receptor for ecdysteroids; ecdysteroid receptors are known to occur in *Drosophila* (O'Connor et al. 1980, and Cherbas et al. 1980). Thus the classic scheme and the model by Williams and Kafatos do not hold strictly. Yet at the level of gross structures such as the mouthparts, wings, and genitalia the model does hold and is useful; hence it must be retained.

Other recently acquired knowledge is that there are three kinds of JH: JH I, JH II, and JH III, and two types of MH, ecdysone and 20-hydroxyecdysone, occurring in insects (they are collectively called ecdysteroids). In some orders (Blattaria, Orthoptera, some Lepidoptera, some Coleoptera, some Diptera, etc.) JHs also have a gonadotropic function in facilitating the entry of vitellogenin in developing oocytes. The synthesis of JHs in CA is controlled by both NSC and nervous mechanisms, but the details remain to be investigated (Granger and Bollenbacher 1981). Besides their role in molting, ecdysteroids have been known to trigger morphogenesis directly (puffing). In other major arthropod groups (Myriapoda, Crustacea, and Arachnida) the presence of ecdysteroids has now been well established and they appear to occur also in Nematoda (Chap. 16) and molluscs (Romer 1979, Whitehead and Sellheyer 1982), although their functions still remain obscure. In marine invertebrates hormones concerned with metamorphosis are known only scantily. Such a hormone appears to occur in *Aurelia* (Sect. 8A), and two antagonizing hormones for morphogenesis certainly occur in *Hydra* without the medusa stage (Sect. 8A). In prochordates the presence of thyroid hormones has been well established, and prolactin also appears to occur (Chap. 22). In *Nereis* (Sect. 10A) and *Lineus* (Chap. 13) a single hormone is known to control both reproduction and somatic development. In crustaceans androgenic hormone occurs widely (Sect. 23A), but among insects a comparable hormone is known to occur only in *Lampyris* (Sect. 23D21). Androgenic hormone occurs also in some molluscs (Chap. 21) and some oligochaetes (Sect. 10B). Regrettably, in the Mollusca and Echinodermata with profound metamorphosis, the presence of a morphogenetic hormone(s) remains unknown, although the existence of such a hormone(s) is highly probable.

In amphibians, as in insects, the presence of two major antagonizing hormones, thyroid hormone (thyroxine, T_4, and thyronine, T_3) and prolactin, has long been known. Thyroid hormones are, as MH is in insects, the immediate agents causing metamorphosis and differentiation of adult structures. Prolactin (produced from the anterior pituitary) is comparable with JH in insects in that it modulates the action of thyroid hormones during development.

Amphibian metamorphosis follows the control of the hypothalamus–pituitary–thyroid gland axis. Thyrotropin-releasing hormone, or TRH, stimulates the pituitary to release thyroid-stimulating hormone, or TSH, which in turn stimulates the thyroid gland. The thyroid gland has a trapping mechanism for excess iodine and can bind it chemically in the organic compounds T_4 and T_3 (see Fujita 1980 for details). Prolactin secretion appears to be under primary hypothalamic control, and TRH may also directly affect the prolactin cells (Bern 1983).

Etkin (1968) viewed anuran metamorphosis as a result of the shift in balance between T_4 and prolactin that is controlled by the hypothalamic TRH. In the early premetamorphic period the T_4 level is very low and remains so until just before prometamorphosis. At this time the hypothalamic TRH becomes sensitive to positive T_4 feedback. The increased TRH induces increased TSH release, which in turn results in increased T_4 level and consequent prometamorphosis. This positive feedback leads to the maximal activation of the pituitary–thyroid axis, thereby resulting in metamorphic climax.

During early premetamorphosis the level of prolactin is high. With the activation of the hypothalamus the production of prolactin drops (under the influence of inhibitory influence of hypothalamic activity), though T_4 production increases. During the premetamorphic period with abundant prolactin, larval growth continues and metamorphosis is inhibited by prolactin. With the shift in balance in favor of increased T_4, inhibition by prolactin diminishes, and eventually metamorphosis occurs in the presence of sufficient T_4 (and in the absence of prolactin).

Controversies arose over some details of the above model, as reviewed by Dodd and Dodd (1976), who themselves suggested that changing sensitivities of metamorphosing tissues determine the level of activity of the TRH–TSH–TH axis and that environmental factors affect the activity of the axis; in Etkin's model no environmental effect is suggested. Norris (1983) accepted Etkin's hypothesis as valid in principle and suggested the accommodation of new data into the model, which relied entirely on endogenous factors. At any rate, the essential TRH–TSH–TH control of the production of hormones and the involvement of prolactin and thyroid hormones remain as the underlying mechanism of amphibian metamorphosis. Tissue sensitivity depends on the presence or absence of hormone receptors, and sometimes it plays the decisive role in determining whether the tadpole does or does not metamorphose into the adult. The receptors for thyroid hormones have been studied in recent years (Sect.24B). Recent studies include also the change in tissue sensitivity to prolactin. White and Nicoll (1979), White et al. (1981), and Carr et al. (1981) showed that thyroid hormones induce the prolactin receptors in the tadpole kidney. Growth hormone is very similar chemically to prolactin but its function has not been well studied; it is known to promote the growth of hind legs in old tadpoles (Etkin and Gona 1967, Bern et al. 1967).

In fishes both prolactin and thyroid hormones occur. However, the action of thyroid hormones during metamorphosis is gradual and weak (Sect. 24A).

C. ENVIRONMENTAL EFFECTS ON ENDOCRINE ACTIVITY

Environmental signals are transmitted to the genes through the hierarchical endocrine system or through neurosecretion from NSC (in lower invertebrates). Many environmental factors, such as food, temperature, photoperiod, and population density, affect the endocrine activity. Of these, nutrition is most fundamental, because the organs or cells that produce and release hormones must grow to be functional. These environmental factors induce production and/or release of hormones. Demonstrations of the influence of environmental factors on endocrine activity are abundant in Part Two: Special Discussion, which deals with abnormal metamorphosis. Some more precisely known examples of environmental effect on endocrine activity are given below.

Among insects, Papillon et al. (1980) found that the decrease in temperature from 33° to 28° C results in much longer fourth and fifth nymphal stages in *Schistocerca*. At 28° C circulating levels of JHs, especially that of JH III, diminish from the middle of the fourth instar; the major peak of ecdysteroids is also delayed at 28° C, but the maximum value attained in the fifth instar is much higher than at 33° C. In *Schistocerca* the effects of starvation are the decline of JH synthesis and suppression of development (Tobe and Chapman 1979). A classic case of regulation of PTTH in *Rhodnius* shown by Wigglesworth (1934) was that abdominal stretch receptors stimulated by a blood meal promoted the synthesis and release of PTTH by acting either directly on the PTTH or NSC or indirectly via a circuit presynaptic to these NSC. Steel (1978) proposed a neural triggering of the release of NSC in this case. In *Manduca* the release of PTTH in each stage of postoval development occurs at a precise time of day established by a circadian clock (Truman 1972, Truman and Riddiford 1974).

The effect of diverse environmental factors on hormonal activity and the metamorphic pattern in amphibians is clear in Part Two; no further mention is necessary here. Rosenkilde (1972) found that the degree of dependence on the hypothalamus – pituitary – thyroid gland axis varies in different species of amphibians. Thus, according to Rosenkilde, the axis is rigidly maintained in *Bufo bufo*. In some other amphibians studied the thyroid function depends on the *pars distalis* of the pituitary, but the *pars distalis* does not depend on the contact with the central nervous system, and furthermore in *Triturus cristus* thyroid activity does not depend on thyrotropic stimulation (from the pituitary). These facts have been confirmed by later workers (Bull 1981), and they may show the trend of independence of the endocrine activity from environmental stimuli. However, the latter could possibly influence directly the thyroid gland or pituitary activity.

D. ORIGIN OF METAMORPHOSIS

The origin of primary metamorphosis must be ancient, judging from the wide occurrence of metamorphosing marine invertebrates during the period from the Precambrian to the Devonian through the Cambrian period. Concerning the mode of origin of primary metamorphosis there is a speculative theory by Jägersten (1955, 1959) called the "bilaterogastrea theory." According to this theory, ancient metazoans were originally pelagic and later they became benthic and bilaterally symmetrical as adults and pelagic only as juveniles. This splitting of the life cycle and adaptation to the respective biotopes resulted in metamorphosis. The two developmental stages diverged further, and the juvenile form became a larva. Jägersten surmised that the pelago – benthic life cycle is ancient and dates back to the ancestral forms of all metazoans. The association of metamorphosis with benthic settlement has been well established for many groups of marine invertebrates, as seen in the book edited by Chia and Rice (1978). As regards the physiological mechanism of primary metamorphosis, Chia (1978) maintained that the physiologically competent larvae must have acquired the chemical substance that effects metamorphosis. These larvae metamorphose in response to environmental cues that are generated as a result of benthic settlement. The chemical substance of Chia is presumably hormones. Thus according to Jägersten and Chia, primary metamorphosis required environmental triggering (benthic settlement), and the involvement of hormones during the origin of metamorphosis in primitive marine metazoans can be safely surmised, because hormones (steroid hormones and peptide hormones) are indeed ancient in origin, as Barrington's (1978) discussion indicates. Sandor and Mehdi (1979) postulated that steroids are very ancient biomolecules which evolved prior to the origin of eukaryotes and were even synthesized abiotically.

Of the several theories regarding the origin of secondary metamorphosis in insects, Handlirsch's (1906–1909) theory was mechanistic in maintaining that cold temperature during the Permian period induced holometabolism from the hemimetabolous insects polyphyletically. From the endocrinological viewpoint, this means that the hormonal programming for holometabolism (the classic scheme, Sect. 1B) has been derived from that in hemimetabolous insects. Such a hormonal reprogramming could have been possible under the persistent new environmental stimulus (cold temperature).

Crampton (1919) criticized Handlirsch's theory by pointing out that a high proportion of holometabolous orders occur in regions where warmer climates prevail. This criticism can now be answered in terms of later migration and continental drift. Once complete metamorphosis (holometabolism) had been genetically established and canalized, it would not be readily subject to changes in a new (warmer) environment. What apparently underlay Crampton's opposition was that he was enough of a Weismannian (as he said) to believe that environment could hardly cause metamorphosis (Crampton 1919, p. 38), and he considered environment only as a selective factor. As pointed out elsewhere (Sect. 4B), however, Weismann was actually a neo-Lamarckist who believed in the direct effect of environment on development and evolution. If the origin of metamorphosis was due to hormonal reprogramming as envisaged above, this could perhaps be tested by some experimental means. But such an experiment, involving the artificial production of the larva, pupa, and adult from hemimetabolous insects is admittedly very difficult.

According to Berlese (1913)–Jeschikov (1929) theory, the larva in Holometabola is essentially the embryo precociously hatched from small eggs. This theory was accepted by Imms (1937), but it was not acceptable to Hinton (1955, 1963, 1981), who claimed that the prolegs of larvae were a secondary formation, and this view was accepted by Snodgrass (1961). Matsuda (1976) showed, in an extensive survey of embryological data, that the prolegs were direct derivatives of embryonic abdominal legs, thereby supporting Berlese. As regards the alleged small eggs that enable deembryonization (early hatching), Anderson's (1972a,b) data showed the tendency (with some exceptions) for the eggs of the Holometabola to be smaller than those in Hemimetabola. However, Hinton (1981) disputed the data by showing that there is no significant difference in egg size between the Holometabola and the Hemimetabola. However, his data depended heavily on Coleoptera, which tend to have relatively large eggs; Anderson's data also show the same tendency for Coleoptera. Thus Berlese's theory appears to hold, as judged by the occurrence of ventral larval legs, which are probably the derivatives of embryonic legs. However, the claimed association of holometabolism with small eggs is far from conclusive. Even if such an association is proved (with the exception of Coleoptera), a further question still remains with regard to the mechanism of production of small eggs.

According to Ghilyarov (1949, 1957, 1969), both the Hemimetabola and Holometabola arose very early from the protohexapodans, which lived in moist soil. The Holometabola arose, as Berlese's theory dictates, from the protohexapodans with small eggs. They hatched earlier than the Hemimetabola, which emerged from yolk-rich eggs. Because of the earlier emergence, according to this theory, the difference between the larva and adult became so great in Holometabola that the pupal stage (for reconstruction of structures) became necessary. For other theories (such as the Hinton–Poyarkof and Henson theories) see Novak (1966). Handlirsch's theory seems to deserve serious consideration in the future development of the theory of insect metamorphosis.

Amphibian metamorphosis always accompanies the change of habitat from water to land, and therefore there has been no ecological theory to account for the origin of amphibian metamorphosis. Both prolactin and thyroid hormones, involved with amphibian metamorphosis, occur in fishes and prochordates. In fishes also the thyroid hormones are known to be the direct agent inducing metamorphosis, but their action is rather slow and indefinite. It appears highly probable, therefore, that in amphibians the endocrine mechanism has become highly efficient in achieving the definite and profound metamorphosis on land. Drastically different environmental stimuli presumably induced a stronger hormonal response and contributed to the induction of more clear-cut metamorphic changes. Presumably, natural selection has contributed to the improvement of the endocrine mechanism (see below).

Adaptive alterations of physiological functions of various organs and structures suited for terrestrial life have also accompanied the metamorphosis of externally visible structures. Frieden and Just (1970) summarized adaptive changes during metamorphosis as follows:

1. Tail regression and limb development leading to more powerful locomotion on land.
2. The shift from ammonotelism to urotelism reflecting the change in environmental water availability.
3. Change in hemoglobin reflecting the greater availability of oxygen to the frog.
4. Increase in serum proteins, particularly serum albumin, reflecting homeostasis and maintenance of the circulatory volume.

5. Changes in digestive enzymes and in intestinal design reflecting the necessary adjustment to a significant alteration of the diet.

Frieden and Just emphasized that all these changes were adaptive and that they
have been possible under the influence of thyroid hormones. To this list should
be added the land drive induced by elevated titers of thyroid hormones (Grant
and Cooper 1965); metamorphosis is completed in dry terrestrial environment.
It can be easily surmised that during the initial stage of evolution of amphibian
metamorphosis, the adaptive responses to the new environment (above) were
not as clear-cut as they are today. It appears highly probable that many individuals that failed to respond adaptively enough during this stage were eliminated,
and thereby natural selection has gradually perfected the mechanism of metamorphosis.

2

Abnormal Metamorphosis and Heterochrony

As the animals came to live in new (drastically different) environments (either passively as the ambient environmental conditions changed, or as they acquired the habit of exploring entirely new ecological niches such as parasitic environments, or as they got transferred to new habitats by some physical means such as wind, current, waves) some of them managed to adapt themselves by changing their developmental timing, by either acceleration or retardation in the onset of development of structures (heterochrony). Through such heterochronic changes the standard patterns of primary and secondary metamorphosis have been altered, resulting in disturbed patterns of metamorphosis which I (Matsuda 1979) called "abnormal metamorphosis." Abnormal metamorphosis applies also to disturbed development in animals normally without conspicuous metamorphosis.

A. KINDS OF ABNORMAL METAMORPHOSIS AND HETEROCHRONY

Halmatometamorphosis (halmato = jump) is the most pronounced metamorphic changes we see in some endoparasitic animals and some animals living in interstitial biotopes. It results in highly aberrant adult structures that are not comparable with any developmental stage or the adult of any free-living ancestral species. Comparably aberrant adult structures may also be produced through embryonization. The term *halmatomorphosis* is used in a broader sense to include the production of aberrant structures through halmatometa-morphosis as well as by other processes (if there are any). Halmatomorphosis is essentially the same as "archallaxis," which refers to the appearance of major novelty in early ontogeny (Chap. 6) and hence there is no parallel between ontogeny and phylogeny in halmatomorphosis.

Neoteny (or *paedomorphosis*) is the retention of structural organization of immature stages (larval and pupal stages) or the incompletely differentiated state of adult structures in reproductively functional individuals. These two distinct states of structural differentiation are recognized by observation of the definitive, neotenous adults, and it is practical to distinguish the two types of neoteny as larval (or pupal) neoteny and juvenile (essentially adult) neoteny, respectively. In metamorphosing animals both types of neoteny can easily occur. For instance, among amphibians neoteny in *Ambystoma* is larval neo-teny, whereas that in plethodontids is juvenile neoteny. The same applies to holometabolous insects. For instance, neoteny in some cecidomyiids is larval (or pupal) neoteny but many wing-reduced holometabolous insects (with some other neotenous features) are cases of juvenile neoteny; juvenile neoteny in insects may be called "nymphal neoteny."

Neoteny results from heterochrony, or the change in timing of development which results in either acceleration or retardation in appearance and rate of development (Gould 1977). Neoteny therefore can also be divided into two categories based on the heterochronic factors, that is, neoteny resulting from acceleration and that resulting from retardation. The former can be said to be progenetic neoteny and the latter metagenetic neoteny. The two subcategories based on the time factors here certainly do not correspond directly to the two kinds of neoteny based on the definitive adult states (larval and juvenile neo-teny). This is immediately clear from the example of larval neoteny in cecido-myiids being due to acceleration but that in *Ambystoma* to retardation.

Heterochrony can be easily recognized in the comparison of ecologically or geographically isolated populations of the genetically similar or identical (clones) of a species, such as gregarious and solitary locusts (Sect. 23D13), prolonged larval development in neotenous salamanders (Sect. 24B), winged and wingless morphs of aphids (Sect. 23D18a), and so on. However, the appli-cability of heterochrony as the criterion for determining the kinds of neoteny becomes limited and less reliable beyond the level of species, because the ancestral group(s) of neotenous higher taxa are often entirely unknown. The Rotifera, Grylloblattodea, and Strepsiptera are cases in point, and the heter-ochronic factor involved with realization of their neoteny is impossible to know, although Grylloblattodea have been regarded as an example of metagen-etic neoteny because of their extraordinarily prolonged nymphal developmen-tal stage (Sect. 23D8). Sometimes, however, the progenetic nature of neoteny was surmised by comparison of the much shorter developmental process of the neotenous taxa with the developmental process of their (presumed) ancestral group. Thus the Cladocera can be regarded as a case of progenetic neoteny derived from the Conchostraca by progenetic neoteny (Sect. 23A). Similarly, the Bathynellacea could have arisen by progenetic neoteny involving the truncation of the ancestral adult stage (Sect. 23A). It should be clearly borne in mind that the truncation of the ancestral adult stage does not always denote progenetic neoteny, for as already noted, the truncation of the adult stage in neotenous salamanders, for instance, is due to retardation. In embryonization larval stages (sometimes juvenile stages) tend to be obliterated or omitted, and therefore it is considered to result in acceleration of at least earlier developmental stages (Sect. 3B2). However, acceleration of larval stages may not necessarily be followed by accelerated juvenile development. When the juvenile stage is also shortened after embryonization (resulting in direct development) the resultant adult is often dwarf and neotenous.

Despite the limitations in applicability, the phenomena of progenetic and metagenetic neoteny must be taken seriously as the underlying mechanisms of dwarfism and gigantism in structural evolution of animals. In progenetic neoteny the body size tends to be smaller (dwarfism) regardless of the definitive adult state attained, larval or juvenile. In metagenetic neoteny the body size tends to be larger (gigantism) because of the prolonged larval stage, as seen in salamanders, or presumably because of greater growth ratios in such nymphal stage, as in Phasmida (Sect. 23D6). Without involving neoteny, the same appears to apply to the enlargement of the body in the tropical dragonfly species *Pantala flavescens* (Sect. 23D2). In fact, the tendency for gigantism and that for dwarfism seem to be fairly reliable criteria in distinguishing the two kinds of neoteny here in question. Without knowing their life histories, I predict the enlarged larval adults in salamanders to be metagenetic, and many tiny, neotenous marine invertebrates such as crustaceans to be often progenetic.

Progenetic neoteny and metagenetic neoteny correspond to the progenesis and neoteny of Gould (1977), and neoteny here is paedomorphosis in Gould's terminology. His proposal, made with some justifications, is not practical, however. First, the term neoteny has been in use to refer also to progenetic neoteny. Second, when four kinds of neoteny are recognized, the word "paedomorphosis" is too lengthy to use in each case. Third, progenetic neoteny and metagenetic neoteny are directly related to prothetely and metathetely (to be discussed), and this association is easy to remember. Some other terms relating to heterochrony and abnormal metamorphosis follow.

Hypermorphosis is a phyletic extension of ontogeny beyond the termination of the ancestral ontogeny, and *hypermetamorphosis* refers to conspicuous structural changes that occur during prolonged ontogeny by addition of new developmental stages (e.g., some parasitic copepods, Sect. 23A, meloid beetles, Sect. 23D21). *Peramorphosis*, a term proposed by Alberch et al. (1979), designates increasing differentiation of adult structures during the supposed phylogeny, and hence this is where Haeckelian recapitulation of the ancestral structural features is recognized in the ontogeny of descendants. Hypermorphosis may be involved with peramorphosis.

Caenogenesis is adapative embryonic and larval specialization and encompasses a large spectrum of cases. Caenogenesis must include social castes in ants

(Sect. 23D22), termites (Sect. 23D12), and some aphids (Sect. 23D18a). Other examples of caenogenesis referred to in this work include the glochidial larvae in Unionacea (Chap. 21), vitellaria larvae in echinoderms (Chap. 20) and the larvae of parasitic Hymenoptera (Sect. 23D22). These examples represent a very small fraction of the cases of caenogenesis known in the animal kingdom. For some other cases see Remane 1956, De Beer 1958, Matsuda 1976, and Gould 1977.

B. HORMONAL BASIS OF HETEROCHRONY AND ABNORMAL METAMORPHOSIS

The underlying hormonal basis of heterochrony and abnormal metamorphosis can be inferred from the phenomena of prothetely and metathetely, which are known in insect endocrinology. When JH activity ceases precociously (e.g. by CA removal or precocene treatment) precocious release of ecdysteroids may follow (i.e., prothetely) and the consequence may be the production of a neotenous, dwarf adult as seen in the experimentally induced prothetely in *Carausius* (Sect. 23D6), and in the progenetic neoteny in *Timema* spp. (Sect. 23D6) that results from prothetely in nature. When JH persists (as effected by application of JH to the larva or nymph at proper developmental stage(s)), the larval (nymphal) development is prolonged or supernumeral larval (or nymphal) stages result. The consequence is a more or less incompletely developed adult or it could even be larval (nymphal) in general facies; such a development resulting from retardation is called metathetely. When metathetely occurs in nature it is metagenetic neoteny (e.g., solitary locusts, Sect. 23D13).

In amphibians phenomena exactly paralleling prothetely and metathetely occur, although different hormones, prolactin and thyroid hormones, are involved. Thus, as discussed in Sect. 24B, the production of dwarf adults in *Eleutherodactylus* is due most probably to precocious cessation of prolactin activity, which is followed by the precocious action of thyroid hormones. Thus the production of the dwarf adult (progenetic neoteny) results from prothetely as in insects. When prolactin activity persists in salamanders, the larval stage tends to be prolonged and the larvae become larger (paralleling metathetely in insects); under some environmental conditions metamorphosis does not occur, thereby resulting in (larval) metagenetic neoteny (Sect. 24B).

Also in diverse groups in marine invertebrates acceleration (by embryonization) often results, as in insects and amphibians, in the production of dwarf adults (Sect. 3B2). Although in these animal groups morphogenetic hormones comparable with those in amphibians and insects have not yet been found, the existence of a similar endocrine mechanism is predictable at least in some of them, and the production of (juvenile) dwarf adults can be hypothesized as due to prothetely.

In endoparasitic animals (very) young larvae enter the host, where they soon undergo a drastic metamorphosis or halmatometamorphosis. Halmatometamorphosis therefore is expectea to occur even earlier than prothetely, and it can perhaps be viewed as an extreme prothetely where very early depletion of the larval hormones (comparable in action with JH or prolactin) results in the expression of an entirely new combination of genes for adult structures or for the structures in the succeeding developmental (metamorphosing) stage.

Excessive action of JH at certain stages of development results in the soldier caste in termites (Sect. 23D12) and ants (Sect. 23D22). These facts suggest that numerous cases of caenogenesis are most likely to be hormonally mediated.

It should be remembered that the unique hormonal actions resulting in heterochrony and consequent abnormal metamorphosis is most likely to have been induced by the unique environmental factors available in the new environments where the animals have come to live. It can be said therefore that heterochrony and abnormal metamorphosis are primarily the products of environmental influence on development (the proximate process) and natural selection has contributed in perfecting the physiogenetic mechanisms of heterochrony and abnormal metamorphosis.

3

The Process of Abnormal
Metamorphosis and Evolution

Abnormal metamorphosis occurs through two major types of environmental influence on development. One type of influence is that on postoval (usually called postembryonic*) development, and another is that on embryonization and some other egg-size-dependent developmental processes. Therefore, cases of abnormal metamorphosis produced through the two different processes are explained separately.

A. ABNORMAL METAMORPHOSIS AND EVOLUTION THROUGH ENVIRONMENTAL INFLUENCE ON POSTOVAL DEVELOPMENT

This is a widely recognized process that does not require a detailed explanation. Simply put, altered environmental stimuli induce alteration in the larval endocrine function to induce abnormal metamorphosis. As shown below, the degree of environmental impact on development and consequent abnormal metamorphosis depends roughly on how stressful is the environment in which animals live.

---

*When embryonization occurs, not only the intraoval embryonic stage of the (ancestral) free-living relatives but also varying numbers of normally extraoval larval stages are passed within the egg. Therefore the term "postoval" is more appropriate and more precise.

1. Parasitic Animals

In parasitic environments, especially endoparasitic ones, the animals have encountered the most drastic change in environmental stimuli on development, and the consequent developmental process has often been drastically altered, often resulting in halmatomorphosis. The effect of parasitism on the phenotype again varies depending on the nature of parasitism. When, for instance, animals are parasitic only as larvae and adults remain free-living, such as Unionacea and parasitic Hymenoptera, the parasitic environmental effect on the larval phenotype is caenogenetic, and their structural modifications as larvae would not affect adult structures (upon which the existing system of classification is based).

When the animals are parasites as adults, with a short free-living larval stage, and when they require only one host to complete their life cycle, the effect of the interaction between environmental stimuli and the genotype of the parasite is directly observed in (often) profound phenotypic modifications in adults. Myzostomida (Sect. 10C) are parasites of asteroids. Their trochophore larvae undergo a profound structural change on the hosts that may well be called halmatometamorphosis. In this case halmatometamorphosis has clearly resulted in the origin of a new class (or order). Similarly, in Podapolipidae (Sect. 23B) parasitism has resulted in the suppression of three nymphal stages and the resultant adult organization is halmatometamorphic. Both in Myzostomida and Podapolipidae the degree of halmatometamorphosis differs in different taxa (genera). The monogenean *Polystoma integerrimum* is dimorphic, depending on the site of infestation. Those infesting the gills of young tadpoles remain neotenous (progenetic), failing to develop vaginae and uterus. In some genera of Polystomidae the neotenous features appear to have been fixed. Among nematodes, plant parasites, *Meloidogyne* and some other genera, have the female conspicuously swollen.

Among insects, Arixeniina (Sect. 23D9) and Hemimerina (Sect. 23D9) may be regarded as parasitic suborders that arose through progenetic neoteny in which the number of nymphal instars might have been reduced to four. Similarly, the Mallophaga (Sect. 23D16) are a parasitic order that arose through progenetic neoteny in which the number of nymphal stages has been reduced from six to three. The Coccoidea are characterized chiefly by the wingless females, which are produced through progenetic neoteny (Sect. 23D18a). Strepsiptera are an order in which parasitic females of most species undergo halmatometamorphosis (Sect. 23D23); phylogenetic derivation of this order remains obscure. Siphonaptera, with pronounced adaptive, compensatory development (such as greatly developed hind legs for jumping to compensate for the loss of wings), represent an order whose phylogenetic derivation remains unclear. See also the discussion of Pupipara (Sect. 23D20), Polyctenidae (Sect. 23D18b) and Cimicidae (Sect. 23D18b).

Many other cases of parasitism requiring only one host include cryptogonochrism in crustaceans (Sect. 23A) and molluscs (Chap. 21), in which the male undergoes an extremely degenerative metamorphosis (halmatometamorphosis?), Fecampidae (Sect. 9A), *Salminicola* (Sect. 23A), *Cymbasoma* (Sect. 23A), *Paragnatha* (Sect. 23A), female rhizocephalans (Sect. 23D18a), *Bakerocoptes cynopteri* (Sect. 23B), and parasitic Ereynetidae (Sect. 23B).

There are also many parasitic animals that require two or more hosts to complete their life cycles. The digenetic Trematoda (Digenea) and Cestoidea are the best-known examples of parasites that require multiple hosts. In Cestoidea proglottidation, which can be called halmatomorphic, is apparently related to multiple hosts, because in Caryophylloidea with two or one hosts it does not occur; the absence of proglottidation is considered to be neotenous (Sect. 9C). In Digenea neoteny can be recognized in sexual maturation in the cercarial and metacercarial stages. Among isopods, Epicaridea often require two hosts and conspicuous metamorphosis and the change of sex occur (Sect. 23A). Nematodes may have two or more hosts in their life cycle, but they are not known to undergo a conspicuous metamorphosis within the hosts.

2. Interstitial Fauna

The degree of abnormal metamorphosis that occurs in the animals living in the interstitial biotope along the seacoast seems to be at least as pronounced as that occurring in the endoparasitic environment. Swedmark (1964) characterized the morphology of interstitial animals as:

1. Regressive evolution of body size and structure.
2. Elongation of the body leading to vermiformity.
3. Reinforcement of the body wall by development of the spicular skeleton and contractility.
4. Adhesion of organs such as epidermal glands.
5. Development of static organs which occur widely in interstitial animals.

Characteristic features of interstitial species given for some phyla (Turbellaria, Sect. 9A; Mollusca, Chap. 21; Polychaeta, Sect. 10A; Nemertinea, Chap. 13; Gnathostomulida, Chap. 14; Urochordata (Chap. 22) largely conform to the generalization by Swedmark. Combinations of these adaptive modifications could certainly result in halmatomorphosis.

Numerous higher taxa that have originated through abnormal metamorphosis in interstitial biotopes have been recognized and erected in major works by Remane (1933), Delamare-Deboutteville (1960), and Ax (1966), and many other separate papers. Gnathostomulida (Chap. 14) and Loricifera recently described by Kristensen (1983) are the new phyla that have been found in the interstitial biotope. Some interstitial taxa mentioned in Part Two: Special Discussion include *Psammodriloides faubeli,* which has arisen obviously through progenetic neoteny (Sect. 10A). Some new higher taxa mentioned appear to have arisen through more specialized developmental processes (exact modes of abnormal metamorphosis, whether they are halmatomorphic or they represent progenetic neoteny, must be left to specialists to decide). Such taxa include

Retronectidae (Sect. 9A), *Drepanilla limophila* (Sect. 9A), some interstitial polychaete genera (Sect. 10A), and Lobatocerebridae (Sect. 10B).

Swedmark (1964) and McIntyre (1969) listed three factors that determine the distribution of interstitial fauna. They are the grain size of the deposit, which affects the interstitial space; salinity, which varies in interstitial biotopes of the intertidal zone; and temperature in the surface layer of marine sand, which usually shows great variation. Of these, the last two act also as morphogenetic factors influencing development, and interstitial animals had to adapt themselves by changing their response mechanism to the interstitial environmental induction, which is unique.

It appears most probable that interstitial animals have undergone structural changes (initially nongenetically) in response to the change in environmental parameters, notably in salinity and temperature. Thiel (1963a) showed, in *Aurelia aurita,* that abnormal metamorphosis (scyphistoma) (a polyp bearing the statolith at the tip of tentacles and the polystrobila in which separation of the ephyra does not occur) can be induced most easily at or near the lowest tolerance limit of salinity (6 – 8‰) and near the lowest tolerable temperature of 1° C. It can therefore be surmised that low salinity, which must often obtain in the coastal interstitial habitats, could have been an important environmental factor inducing abnormal metamorphosis. In Cedar Key, Florida, fluctuating salinities obviously induce stunted development of many echinoderm species (Chap. 20).

Some other factors must also have induced abnormal metamorphosis. For instance, induction of progenetic neoteny in *Psammodriloides faubeli* is obviously related to the organic detritus where the animal has always been found (Sect. 10A). Similarly, Retronectidae occur where a high amount of organic detritus is available (Sect. 9A). Sometimes pollution could have contributed to the origin of new higher taxa. Thus, the typical biotope of Gnathostomulida is the hydrogen sulfide-rich substratum, and this suggests anaerobic metabolism. In this case such a metabolism might contribute to the enlargement of eggs and consequent abnormal metamorphosis (Chap. 14). *Drepanilla limophila* also lives in association with the sulfide system on subtidal flats. Abnormal metamorphosis of interstitial animals through embryonization is discussed later (Chap. 9A).

3. Other Animals

Most other animals treated in the Part Two: Special Discussion live in habitats less stressful than parasitic or interstitial environments, and halmatomorphosis does not occur. In fact, the environmental effect on development, resulting only in neoteny at the most, can be said to be much less in these animals than in parasitic and interstitial animals.

In certain cases, among noninsectan animals, smaller body sizes clearly represent progenetic neoteny, as seen in pauropods and some other myriapods in which substantial suppression of anamorphosis has occurred (Sect. 23C). A special kind of progenetic neoteny occurs in the male of *Emerita* (Sect. 23A), terrestrial talitrids (Sect. 23A), and *Bonellia* (Chap. 12), in which precocious activation of androgenic hormone (instead of ecdysteroids or thyroid hormones) occurs (at least in *Emerita* and the talitrids). In holopelagic Thaliacea (Chap. 22) and Larvacea (Chap. 22) the nature of their larval neoteny, whether metagenetic or progenetic, is not immediately clear. Similarly, the nature of neoteny through juvenile reproduction (dissogeny) in Ctenophora with holopelagic life cycle cannot be determined. Metagenetic neoteny has been recognized for salamanders, occurring under the influence of cold temperature and in some other stressful environments, and for the three-spined stickleback, which occurs in fresh water (Sect 24A). A very prolonged life cycle of amphioxides (with sexual maturation) (Chap. 22) probably must be considered as a case of metagenetic neoteny. For some other cases of neoteny (such as nereids, Sect. 10A) see Part Two: Special Discussion. Neotenous features in these cases certainly constitute important characters, distinguishing these animals at higher taxonomic levels.

In insects wing reduction is the best indicator of neoteny, because it is conspicuous and is easily recognizable. Wing reduction is usually a matter of degree, ranging from brachyptery to aptery through microptery, although it also takes other distinctive shapes such as stenoptery (in *Aradus cinnamomeus*) and others (in lygaeids). Reduction or loss of ocelli correlated with wing reduction occurs commonly, as has been known since Kalmus (1945). Often the reduction of some (or many) other structures accompanies wing reduction, rendering the insects more neotenous. However, compensatory development (i.e., enlargement) of some other structures such as the male genital segments or hind legs also may occur in wing-reduced insects.

Most cases of neoteny involving the reduction of wings and other structures are given in Table 1; this does not include similar tables on Lepidoptera and Diptera by Hackman (1964, 1966). It is seen that progenetic neoteny is fairly common in insects, although in many cases the environment–hormonally triggered heterochronic factors are unknown.

When JH has the dual function of antagonizing imaginal differentiation and promoting oogenesis, as in some groups of insects (Sect. 1B), neoteny appears to be more common in the female than in the male. In fact, female neoteny in cecidomyiids (Sect. 23D20), marine chironomids (Sect. 23D20), and psychid moths (Sect. 23D26) is highly conspicuous. Another characteristic feature known for insects is the group (population density) effect on wing development. When insects develop as a group they develop normal wings (macroptery), but when they develop in isolation or in a very low population density their wings do not develop fully, resulting in various degrees of reduction including total loss (aptery). This phenomenon, known as group effect, has been observed in many groups of insects including Blattaria (Sect. 23D10), Orthoptera (Sect. 23D13), Grylloptera (Sect. 23D14), Psocoptera (Sect. 23D15), auchenorrhynchous Homoptera (Sect. 23D18a), sternorrhynchous Homoptera (Sect. 23D18a), Coleoptera (Sect. 23D21), Diptera (Sect. 23D20), and Lepidoptera (Sect. 23D26).

TABLE 1. Neoteny in Insects

Taxa	Progenetic or Metagenetic	Environmental Factors, Conditions, etc.
Ephoron album and *Dolania americana*	Metagenetic?	
Perlodes microcephala and *Diura* spp.	Progenetic	Cold temperature
Wingless morph of *Zorotypus hubbardi*	Progenetic	Gregarious life
Grylloblattodea	Metagenetic?	Cold temperature
Anisolabis maritima and other Dermaptera	Progenetic, metagenetic	Genetically determined
Arixeniina	Progenetic?	Ectoparasitic
Hemimerina	Progenetic?	Ectoparasitic
Wing reduction in many cockroaches	Metagenetic	Isolation?
Attaphila spp.	Progenetic	Commensalism with ants
Eremiaphilidae	Progenetic	Desert life
Replacement reproductives in termites	Often progenetic	Deinhibition by removal of primitive reproductives
Solitary locusts *(Schistocerca* and *Locusta)*	Metagenetic	Isolation
Zonocerus variegatus	Metagenetic	Low population density and poor food
Metrioptera roeseli		
Tessellana vittata	Metagenetic?	Low population density or isolation
Stenopelmatidae		Underground galleries
Cooloolidae		Sandy moist soil
Cyphoderris		
Scapsipedes aspersus	Progenetic	Isolation?
Phasmida	Metagenetic?	High temperature?
Timema spp.	Progenetic	Cold temperature
Nemobius yezoensis	Metagenetic	Photoperiodic cycle in northern Japan
Psyllipsocus ramburi	Progenetic	Isolation
Archipsocus spp.	Progenetic	Life inside a web spun on trunk, etc.
Liposcelis granulicola	Progenetic	High humidity, domicolous

TABLE 1. (*Continued*)

Taxa	Progenetic or Metagenetic	Environmental Factors, Conditions, etc.
Embidopsocus enderleini	Progenetic	Under the bark of tree with high humidity
Mallophaga	Progenetic	Parasitism on birds
Seasonal brachyptery in *Anaphothrips obscurus*		Lower temperatures, shorter days, low population density
Nilaparvata lugens	Progenetic	Low population density
Prokelisia marginata		Low population density
Seasonal dimorphism in *Euscelis* spp.		Mainly photoperiod
Apterous morph in female aphids	Progenetic	Photoperiod, temperature, population density, food
Schizaphis graminum	Progenetic	Laboratory conditions
Female scale insects	Progenetic	Parasitism on plants
Wing-reduced Rhyparochrominae		Genetically determined?
Pyrrhocoris apterus		Mainly short days
Gerris spp.	Progenetic	Longer days and higher temperatures
Cimicidae		Ectoparasitism on birds and mammals
Polyctenidae	Progenetic	Parasitism on bats
Boreidae		Snow (cold temperature, etc.)
Apteropanorpa tasmaniae		Snow (cold temperature, etc.)
Panorpodes paradoxa		Higher altitude (cold temperature)
Brachypanorpa carolinensis and *B. jeffersoni*		Higher altitude (cold temperature)
Parthenogenetic generation of some cecidomyiid genera	Progenetic	Nutrition (mushroom), proper light, temperature, and low population density
Females of *Clunio* and *Pontomyia* spp.		Marine habitat
Oreadomyia albertae and other arctic chironomids		Cold temperature

23

TABLE 1. (*Continued*)

Taxa	Progenetic or Metagenetic	Environmental Factors, Conditions, etc.
Belgica antarctica and *Eretmoptera murphyi*		Cold temperature
Some simuliids		Cold temperature in the Arctic
Wing-reduced Tipulidae		Low-temperature environments
Chionea spp.		Snow surface (cold temperature)
Baenotidae		Taken from soil samples
Plastosciara perniciosa		Isolation
Some sciarids in Europe		Ground litter
Some sphaerocerids in Europe		Higher latitudes and in deeper soil
Leptocera spp. at higher altitudes in E. Africa		Low temperature and cryptozoic habitat (with high moisture)
Pupipara		Ectoparasites
Callosobruchus maculatus	Progenetic	Isolation
Micromalthus debilis (3 kinds of larval females)	Progenetic	High moisture
Wing polymorphism in Carabidae and Curculionidae		Genetically determined
Female *Rhipidius* and *Rhyzostylops*		Endoparasitism
Ergatogyne in ants	Progenetic	
Melittobia chalybii (wing-reduced forms)	Progenetic	Poor nutrition
Melittobia spp. from Caribbean (wing-reduced forms)		Low population density
Notomymar spp.		Cold temperature
Gelis corruptor (wing-reduced male)		Meager nutrition

TABLE 1. (*Continued*)

Taxa	Progenetic or Metagenetic	Environmental Factors, Conditions, etc.
Trichogramma sembilidis (wingless male)		When reared on *Sialis* eggs
Male Strepsiptera	Metagenetic?	
Females of non-Mengeniliid Strepsiptera	Halmatomorphic	
Siphonaptera		Ectoparasitism on mammals and birds
Dolophilodes distinctus and *Agrypnia pagetana* var. *hyperborea*		Cold temperature
Orgyia thyellina (brachypterous females)		Shorter days
Arctic Lepidoptera		Cold temperature
Areniscythris brachypteris		Coastal sand dune
Female Psychidae		Case dwelling

It should be noted that the hormones involved with neoteny in insects are those inherited from their ancestors. In Thysanura, which are primarily wingless and considered to be ancestral to the Pterygota, the presence of JHs is now evident (Madhavan et al. 1981) and ecdysteroid with molting function is known to occur (De la Paz et al. 1983). Ecdysteroid certainly occurs in crustaceans (Sect. 23A), myriapods (Sect. 23C), and arachnids (Sect. 23B).

Dwarfism is common in insects (an example is Ptiliidae, with fewer instars, Sect. 23D21), and this must have been possible by prothetely, which presumably occurred in diverse microhabitats that became available with the development of vegetation on land. Indeed, prothetely appears to have been a major hormonal preadaptation that has enabled insects to explore new microhabitats and hence achieve success on land. The concept of prothetely is likely to become important in the study of sympatric speciation.

B. ABNORMAL METAMORPHOSIS AND EVOLUTION THROUGH EMBRYONIZATION

Some animals produce large, yolk-rich eggs in changing environments (e.g., from sea to seacoast, to inland fresh water, then onto land, or directly from sea to land, or from temperate regions to polar regions). Nearly always during these transitions of habitats, eggs have become larger and richer in yolk content. Furthermore, when enlargement of eggs occurs, there is a marked tendency for intraoval development to be more or less modified, and free-living (swimming) larval stages in related species with smaller eggs are often passed within the egg and tend to become abortive. This phenomenon of larval stages becoming a part of intraoval development has been known as embryonization. The usage of this term has been well established in Russian literature (e.g., Sharov 1966, Zakhvatkin 1953, 1975), although it is uncommon in English literature. In fact, both De Beer (1958) and Gould (1977) failed to make this aspect of heterochrony which results in acceleration.

1. Process and Mechanism of Embryonization

An analysis of the process and mechanism of embryonization is attempted below. It should first be pointed out that embryonization nearly always occurs when the proximate causal factors inducing the enlargement of eggs are available; some examples of embryonization follow:

    1. Freshwater and saltwater habitats with lower salinities: *Cottus nozawae* and some other freshwater fishes; freshwater crab families Potamidae, Pseudothelphusidae, and Trichodactylidae (e.g., *Geothelphusa dehaani, Metopaulias depressus);* freshwater species of Palaemonidae, superorder Syncarida (*Anaspides tasmaniae,* order Bathynellacea); *Bonellia viridis;* some echinoderms (*Ophiolepis elegans,* Kirk's ophiuroid, etc.); some molluscs (*Brachystomia rissoides, Embletonia pallida, Turtonia minuta,* some aspects of Ascoglossa and Nudibranchia, freshwater pulmonates); some clitellates (Tubificidae, Lumbriculidae, Glossophonidae); the nemertean genus *Prostoma* and *Lineus desori;* most Rotifera and Neophora (Turbellaria); the cnidarian genus *Hydra;* and horseshoe crab *Tachypleus tridentatus.*

    2. In interstitial biotopes along the seacoast where salinity is relatively low or variable and some physicochemical environmental factors (temperature, oxygen tension, pH, etc.) are unique: Gnathostomulida, archiannelids *(Protodriloides symbioticus, P. chaetifer, Diurodrilus ankeli); Stygocapitella subterranea* and 11 other polychaete species; some cnidarians *(Halammohydra* spp., *Otohydra vagans, Protohydra leuckarti, Armorhydra janowiczi);* and the prosobranch *Caecum glabrum.*

    3. In the deep sea: the coelacanth *Latimeria chalumnae,* hagfishes, the crinoid *Comatilia iridometriformis,* echinothiuriid spp., and *Poriocidaris purpurata.*

    4. In polar regions with cold temperatures and an extreme annual photoperiodic cycle, or in conformity with Thorson's rule: Arctic fishes, some crustaceans (*Gammarus* spp.), many molluscs (Opistobranchia, Prosobranchia), many ophiuroid echinoderms, many holothurians and crinoids, many polychaetes, and a urochordate *(Molgula retorti formis).*

    5. In response to seasonal photoperiodic and temperature cues: the fish *Etheostoma spectabile,* the cladoceran *Bosmina longirostris,* Cephalopoda, the asteroid echinoderm *Echinaster* sp. and the opistobranch *Elysia cauze* (?).

6. On land where the ambient environmental factors differ drastically from those in their ancestral marine or freshwater habitat: amphibians (*Eleutherodactylus* spp., *Pelophryne* spp., South American frogs, *Arthroleptis* spp., and terrestrial plethodontids); crustaceans (talitrids, *Uca subcylindricus*); Neophora; Stylommatophora; Oligochaeta; reptiles; and birds (which are not studied in this work).

7. In tube and burrow dwellings: some polychaetes (most sabellariids, *Neanthes caudata*), the phoronid *Phoronis ovalis,* the sipunculan *Golfingia minuta.*

8. Brooding: some anurans (*Nectophrynoides* spp.); a fish genus *Labeotropheus;* some urochordates (ovoviviparous *Molgula* spp., *Polycarpa tinctor,* and holozoine genera *Distaplia* and *Sycozoa*); some ophiuroid echinoderms; and apoikogenic scorpions.

9. Brooding combined with high population density: compound ascidians, bryozoans.

10. By association with ants: the cricket genus *Myrmecophila.*

11. Cave dwelling: bathyscine beetles.

The environmental association of enlargement of eggs is not discernible for cnidarians (except for interstitial species). Some echinoderms, especially asteroids (e.g., *Pteraster tesselatus, Certonardoa semiregularis*) have large floating eggs. Conceivably, the production of large eggs could have become canalized in certain cases, and such eggs could be produced without a particular environment stimulus or a triggering.

The immediate cause of enlargement of eggs must be due, at least in part, to the increased yolk content (or the equivalent that serves as nutrients) within the egg, and this has occurred through different processes. Probably the increase in incorporation of the exogenous (heterosynthetic or secondary) yolk or yolk precursor into developing oocytes has often contributed to the enlargement of eggs. In the supralittoral talitrid *Orchestia gammarellus,* the egg is enlarged from 150 to 160 μm in diameter at the onset of secondary vitellogenesis to 800 μm at the time of egg laying (Sect. 23A), and the increase can be attributed to the entry of vitellogenin into developing oocytes. The amount of vitellogenin that enters in this species must be greater than in the ancestor, because the egg size has become obviously larger during evolution (Sect. 23A). Similarly, in the deep sea species of echinothiuriid species and *Poriocidaria purpurata* the oocyte grows to be 200–450 mm, at which stage vitellogenesis begins. Oocyte growth continues until a maximum size of 1.100–1.500 mm is attained by the entry of nutrient into oocytes (Tyler and Gage 1984).

Although the definitive egg size admittedly depends in part on the previtellogenetic oocyte development, the increased incorporation of yolk or yolk precursor into developing oocytes probably has contributed to the enlargement of eggs in other animals with the endocrine mechanism for secondary vitellogenesis as well. Among the animal groups here treated, the existence of such a mechanism has been well established for amphibians, fishes, molluscs, crustaceans, and insects, and appears to exist in echinoderms. The presence of a similar mechanism in Urochordata may be probable. In some polychaetes also heterosynthetic vitellogenesis occurs. In Rotifera and Neophora the vitellaria as the source of exogenous yolk (or yolk precursor) is well established. It appears most probable that the functioning of the endocrine mechanism has been altered by novel environmental stimuli in the new environments, and that the consequently altered pattern of vitellogenesis has resulted in the entry of a larger amount of yolk (or yolk precursor) into more limited numbers of eggs, so that the egg becomes larger. The fact that the enlarged eggs are yolk-rich reflects such entry of a large amount of yolk (yolk precursor).

At least for the amphibians and fishes with large eggs, it can be definitely said that the hormone for vitellogenesis, 17β-estradiol, has been the one inherited from their ancestors, because it occurs widely in Pisces, Amphibia, and even Echinodermata. The same may well be said for the molluscs and crustaceans that produce large eggs, for essentially the same endocrine mechanism appears to exist widely in their respective groups. Therefore, it is most probable that, in producing larger eggs in these animals, the endocrine mechanism for vitellogenesis inherited from their ancestors has responded to the novel environmental stimuli in their new habitats.

In some polychaetes such as *Nereis* and the nemertean *Lineus* a large amount of brain hormone has an inhibitory effect on oocyte development (including vitellogenesis). For the enlargement of eggs in the animals with this type of endocrine mechanism *(Prostoma* spp., *Lineus desori)* earlier deinhibition of oocyte development might have occurred, because new environmental stimuli could have caused earlier decline in secretion of the hormone.

In certain cases direct hormonal involvement with enlargement of eggs does not seem to occur. Thus in clitellates, which are protandrous hermaphrodites, only spermatogenesis is known to be hormonally controlled, and oogenesis, which follows, is an autodifferentiating process. Theoretically, therefore, precocious decline in secretion of the androgenic hormone could perhaps result in enlargement of eggs. Similarly, for cnidarians direct environmental influence on enlargement of eggs is inconceivable; environment – hormonal influence in these cases may be said to be only indirect, because in *Hydra,* for instance, the interstitial cells transforming into oocytes must be under the environment – hormonal control.

In *Hydra* absorption of neighboring oocytes occurs in producing a single large egg, and in *Diurodrilus* fusion of oocytes occurs in producing a single egg. Conceivably, various atypical oogeneses occur in producing fewer larger eggs in dwarfed interstitial invertebrates. Presumably in these animals an endocrine mechanism for vitellogenesis may often not be developed, as the pronounced arrest of development of other structures indicates. For the Sipuncula, Bryozoa, Phoronida, and Gnathostomulida the endocrine mechanism for reproduction has not yet been investigated.

Hydration (referred to in Chap. 20) might have been a contributing factor to the enlargement of eggs, as discussed by Prossor (1973) and Turner and Lawrence (1979). However, as has been consistently found in this work, production of large eggs in these animals has been always accompanied by the reduction in number of eggs produced, clearly indicating that the production of large eggs is determined within the mother's body. In fact, large eggs within the mother's body have been directly observed in certain cases (Sects. 8A, 10A). Therefore, the effect of hydration on egg size can be safely discounted, at least for most cases.

2. Embryonization and Consequent Developmental Modifications

Embryonization, or incorporation of free-swimming larval stages in related species with small eggs into the period of intraoval development in enlarged eggs, is a matter of degree, ranging from the incorporation of only the initial larval stage to that of all the larval stages within the egg. This trend of increasing suppression of free-living larval stage is considered here to result in acceleration in development. However, the reduction in number of larval stages does not necessarily result in the acceleration of the whole developmental process, which also includes embryonic and juvenile developmental stages. In certain cases embryonization involves juvenile stages only, because the animals in question (such as talitrids) are already without the ancestral larval stages. Acceleration in larval and juvenile stages and their resultant developmental modifications can be categorized as follows:

1. Acceleration in which early larval stages are passed within the egg; its immediate consequence is a shorter period of free-swimming larval stage without *known* neotenous features in the adult: South American frogs, *Nectophrynoides malcolmi* with lecithotrophic larvae, fishes in the Arctic, *Cottus nozawae. Caecobarbus geertsi* and *Anoptichthys jordani, Metopaulius depressus,* crustaceans at high latitudes, *Uca subcylindrica,* freshwater Palaemoninae, *Tachypleus tridentatus,* ovoviviparious *Molgula* spp., *Bonellia viridis,* some ophiuroids with nonpelagic and nonfeeding (vitellaria) larvae, *Amphioplus abditus,* many species of ophiuroid and echinoid species in Cedar Key, Florida, ecotype 2 of *Echinaster modestus,* populations of *Brachystomia rissoides* and *Embletonia pallida* living in brackish water, type 2 of opisthobranchs (of Thompson 1967) with lecithotrophic larvae, molluscs in the Arctic and Subarctic regions, some ascoglossans and nudibranchs with lecithotrophic larvae in Florida, many polychaetes with larger eggs, some polychaete species in Greenland, Tubularoidea with actinula larvae, scyphozoans with relatively yolk-rich eggs, some bryozoans with lecithotrophic larvae.

2. Acceleration that has resulted in direct development in which animals hatched from eggs are juveniles that are essentially adults in structural organization. Their juvenile developmental stage is often very short, becoming dwarf and neotenous adults: *Eleutherodactylus* spp., *Arthroleptis* spp., *Nectophrynoides vivipara* and *N. tornieri,* terrestrial plethodontids, *Labeotropheus* sp., *Latimeria chalumnae,* Neophora, *Geothelphusa dehaani* and other potamids, Anaspidacea, crustaceans at high latitudes, ovoviviparous *Polycarpa tinctor,* ophiuroids with large, yolky eggs, Kirk's ophiuroid, *Ophiolepis kieri, O. pauci-*

spina, Ophiomyxa flaccida, Comatlia iridometriformis (?), type 3 of opistho-branchs (of Thompson 1967) at high latitudes, nudibranchs and ascoglossans with large eggs in Florida, most freshwater pulmonates, many molluscs in the Subantarctic and Antarctic regions, many prosobranchs at high latitudes, Stylommatophora, Clitellata, some polychaetes from Greenland, an interstitial sabellid sp., 12 spp. of polychaetes with small adults, *Turtonia minuta, Hedylopsis riseri,* Cephalopoda, *Scoloplos armiger, Golfingia minuta, Themiste pyroides* and *Phascolion cryptus, Prostoma* spp., *Lineus desori,* Gnathostomulida, and *Phoronis ovalis* (with very short pelagic life).

3. Acceleration in which the ancestral juvenile stages (ancestral larval stages are absent in more immediate ancestors) have been shortened, resulting in neoteny: terrestrial talitrids.

4. Acceleration by truncation of the adult stage: Rotifera, Bathynellacea, *Neanthes caudata, Protohydra leuckarti, Hydra* spp.

The Actinulida and *Armorhydra* are chimeric in possessing the features of two or more developmental stages (Sect. 8A), and they are difficult to categorize.

In postulating the mechanism of suppression of larval (and juvenile) stages resulting in acceleration, we must consider the nature of intraoval environment in which the embryo–larva is forced to live. The enlarged egg is by itself a new environment that may be thousands times greater in volume than the ancestral egg. The question is how such a novel environment has influenced the development of the embryo–larva. Although the correlation between yolk-rich, large eggs and disturbance is early embryogenesis (such as the cleavage pattern) has been known in descriptive embryology, such eggs have been considered as an abundant source of nutrients for developing embryo–larvae, and this appears to be true when the enlargement of eggs is moderate (lecithotrophic larvae). As the above summary of acceleration indicates, however, in very enlarged eggs the presence of abundant yolk appears to hinder normal development of the embryo–larva. There have been attempts to relate biochemical components of the yolk — their distribution and change during oogenesis and embryogenesis — to different sizes of the egg (see the 1979 review by Turner and Lawrence for invertebrates). Yet a particular biochemical component or components acting as the direct causal agent of acceleration has not been demonstrated. More recently, Shakuntala and Reddy (1982) denied the generalization by Herring (1974) that in decapod crustaceans with variable egg sizes, larger eggs (which result in abbreviated development) have higher lipid content than smaller eggs.

In the absence (or the lack of knowledge) of a particular chemical stimulant(s) for acceleration and consequently modified development, the alternative hypothesis I propose is that the (very) enlarged eggs per se constitute highly stressful physicochemical environments, and that the new environmental stimuli that have become available within such eggs have, in bringing about acceleration and a consequently modified phenotype (abnormal metamorphosis), affected the morphogenetic endocrine mechanism of the developing embryo–larva. The cases of *Eleutherodactylus* and *Plethodon* (Sect. 24B) are explained by such a mechanism. In these amphibians precocious cessation of the prolactin secretion is followed by precocious action of thyroid hormones, thereby resulting in neoteny and small adults. Presumably, similar hormonal disturbances occur during acceleration and consequently modified development in the enlarged eggs of other animals.

Duration of juvenile development varies in different animals with direct development (categories 2 and 3 above). Diminution of the adult body size appears to be related to relatively short juvenile development, and this may well be due to precocious action of the hormone for metamorphosis still during the intraoval stage of development, as in *Eleutherodactylus* and *Plethodon;* earlier action of the hormone for metamorphosis might follow precocious depletion of the hormone for larval development (i.e., prothetely, discussed in Sect. 2B). Little is known directly, however, about such hormones in the invertebrates, although morphogenetic hormones do occur in Cnidaria, Crustacea, and ascidians. Besides *Eleutherodactylus,* examples of diminutive adults in category 2 above are *Arthroleptis crusculum, Polycarpa tinctor, Geothelphusa dehaani, Ophiolepis kieri, Turtonia minuta,* 12 spp. of polychaetes, Gnathostomulida, *Golfingia minuta, Phoronis ovalis,* and probably some others. These examples support the statement sometimes made in the literature of invertebrate zoology that small adults lay large eggs. It should be remembered, however, that the production of large eggs occurred most probably when the animals started living under new environmental conditions, before the new types of animals (including the diminutive ones) started emerging from such eggs. Evolutionarily speaking, therefore, it is more correct to say that production of new types of eggs (here, larger eggs) resulted in new types of animals (e.g., small adults). I would therefore say, in answer to the common conundrum "Which came first, the chicken or the egg?," that *the egg came first, then the chicken.*

Because the enlargement of eggs is essential for acceleration in development in the cases reviewed, genetic fixation must have often occurred at the level of egg size to ensure accelerated development and the consequent phenotype. When the yolk production is hormonally controlled it is probable that genetic fixation occurs through the process of genetic assimilation discussed by Matsuda (1982). It appears most probable that genetic fixation of a level or levels of the endocrine mechanism for vitellogenesis occurred to ensure the production of large enough eggs for accelerated development. Presumably, the accumulation of the genetic changes (probably mutations) fixing such an endocrine function has, under the pressure of natural selection, replaced the initially temporarily altered endocrine function by new environmental stimuli (genetic assimilation). According to Berven (1982), in higher-altitude (mountain) populations of *Rana sylvatica* the egg is larger and fewer eggs are laid (in comparison with low-altitude populations); the larger egg, which is related to delayed reproduction and larger adult size, is selectively advantageous in mountains. Berven's reciprocal transplant experiment of juveniles showed that the egg size and the egg number were determined solely according to the pattern of the original (parental) population, not by the effect of environment in which they mature.

This fact indicates that the egg size and egg number have been genetically fixed, presumably through the process of genetic assimilation.

3. Some Other Cases of Egg-Size-Dependent Developmental Modifications

Often in capsular development (in some annelids and gastropods) and in ovoviviparity the association of accelerated development with larger eggs is not pronounced. In capsular development eggs are laid in a mass of jelly or various forms of protective cocoons with rich nutrients, and larval development is sometimes maintained within the capsule even when the egg is large (e.g., *Protodriloides symbioticus*). Similarly, in ovoviviparous urochordates with large eggs (compound *Molgula* spp., *Distaplia,* and *Sycozoa*) development within the brood pouch is not direct, and the same may be true of some ovoviviparous echinoderm species. In Ascoglossa the capsule size is a more accurate predictor of development type than the egg size (Chap. 21). These facts indicate that as long as the larvae are protected, enlarged eggs do not necessarily result in pronounced accelerated development and this, in turn, appears to reflect the effect of natural selection in perfecting the mechanism of accelerated development (often direct development) in other animals that release large eggs outside the body.

Pechnik (1979) pointed out that in capsular development often the emerged worms are swimming larvae, although the larval stage is more or less shortened. He called such a development "mixed development," because it incorporates aspects of both direct and pelagic development, and suggested that even a short period of encapsulation can significantly reduce mortality during mixed development if daily mortality rates in the plankton are below critical levels. The question of the origin of capsular development remains. There seems to have been no stringent selection pressure for its origination and maintenance. As Pechnik (1979) pointed out, however, egg capsules and egg masses are structurally and chemically complex and the formation of gastropod egg capsules has required great morphological and physiological specializations in adults; the energy expenditure associated with encapsulation appears to be high as well. These facts suggest that encapsulation must have substantial selective value even in mixed development.

The extreme acceleration is what Jägersten (1972) called "adultation," which referred to the transfer of ancient adult structures to early stages of ontogeny (e.g., the shell and foot in the embryo of many molluscs). Jägersten (1972), on many occasions in his book, mentioned the relationship between yolk-rich eggs and modified developments such as shorter larval development and direct development. However, he says (p. 226),

> It is hardly probable that the quantity of yolk as such exerts real influence on adultation. . . . Total adultation has not occurred so very often, if by this we mean that a direct development no longer contains any trace of the primary larva.

The case of viviparous Phylactolaemata Jägersten discussed (1972, p. 31) appears to fit best the definition of adultation, because no trace of ancestral larval stage is expected to occur during ontogeny. In the Chaetognatha, which Jägersten thought to exhibit the best cases of adultation, both larval and juvenile stages occur, although the two stages are not separated by a metamorphic change (Reeve 1970).

Viviparity occurs, among the animal groups treated here, in Urochordata, Mollusca (the well-known case of *Paludina*), Polychaeta (*Nereis limnicola*, Smith 1958), Echinodermata (Fell 1945), Bryozoa (Chap. 18), some insects, the scorpion (Sect. 23B), Onychophora (Anderson and Manton 1972), some fishes (Wourms 1981 for a summary), some reptiles (Tinkle and Gibbons 1977, Shine 1983), and most mammals. Commonly, viviparity is associated with small yolkless or yolk-deficient eggs. In questioning the origin of viviparity a crucial question must be just how the deficiency in yolk content in the egg has occurred in nature. Here again, disorder in the endocrine mechanism for vitellogenesis has probably been involved. This question is not pursued further here, for it requires the study of animal groups that are not the primary concern of this work.

4. Natural Selection on Acceleration by Embryonization

In most cases treated here a new evolutionary process was initiated by new environmental stimuli that have induced egg-size enlargement and consequently accelerated development. As the following examples show, when this proximate evolutionary process is taken into account, the major role of natural selection has been to improve the structural and physiological changes that the animals have undergone during the proximate process.

Thorson's rule (Thorson 1936, 1950) states that at higher latitudes the frequency of planktonic larvae in fishes and invertebrates (echinoderms, crustaceans, polychaetes, molluscs, etc.) decreases. This phenomenon has been attributed to the scarcity of food and to low temperature, which act as a limiting factor for survival and distribution. However, this explanation does not apply fully to the invertebrates in the Subantarctic and the Antarctic regions, because the low frequency of planktonic larvae in these regions cannot be attributed to the scarcity of food which becomes very abundant seasonally. This inconsistency indicates, as repeatedly pointed out (Sect. 10A, Chap. 21, Sect. 24A), that it is primarily the local environmental factors in the polar regions and elsewhere, such as low temperature and unique annual photoperiodic cycle — not the abundance or scarcity of food — that induce the production of large eggs, which in turn results in embryonization and consequent decrease in planktonic larvae.

Clarke (1979), as already referred to (Sect. 23A), attributed certain features of reproduction and development in Antarctic invertebrates to the result of K selection. Clarke (1982) further maintained that slow rate of embryonic development in these animals is the result of large eggs, and not that of (low) temperature. However, the facts of "slow growth" he referred to occur in large embryonized eggs. As Clarke pointed out, the result of large (embryonized) eggs is that the young (larvae or juvenile) hatch late. This delayed hatching is, according to Clarke, a part of K strategies. It is certainly advantageous in the Antarctic for the young to emerge at a sufficiently advanced stage of development, so that they can be competitive at the time food is available. Presumably, these selective advantages have contributed to the maintenance and improvement of the physiological mechanism of embryonization, which was initially induced through the proximate process (i.e., through local temperature and photoperiodic effects). The important question Clarke failed to ask was how the large eggs were initially produced in the Antarctic. The kind of selection pressure Clarke envisaged does not seem to have a strong enough power alone to induce the production of large eggs.

Similarly, the enlargement of eggs and consequent abbreviation or omission of vulnerable larval stages (acceleration) in fresh water and on land, which have occurred in many animals, must have been largely fortuitous adaptive responses (by deploying the built-in endocrine mechanism) to new environmental stimuli. Larval stages in these animals must be highly vulnerable or useless in these habitats, and it is easily conceivable that the selection pressure for abbreviated development has resulted in the elimination of those individuals that failed to produce large enough eggs.

For settlement in the interstitial biotope, minute size must have been a very important prerequisite. It appears that as long as this condition was met, a wide variety of reaction of the genotype (and hence the change in the pattern of gene regulation) within the enlarged egg and of the resultant phenotypes has been allowed by natural selection in this biotope. Hence the frequent occurrence of animals with highly modified structural organizations in this biotope is conceivable. Further, when only limited numbers of eggs (sometimes only one) are laid at a time, competition cannot be high in the interstitial biotope, and predation also might not be very significant (McIntyre 1969). Thus the lack of intense biotic selection also might have contributed to the existence of the animals with so abnormally modified structures. Interstitial biotopes are unstable r environments where sands are unstable mechanically, salinity and temperature also fluctuate considerably (Swedmark 1964), and the production of large numbers of eggs is expected. However, the fact is quite contrary to what is expected, and therefore $r-K$ theory does not apply as a life history strategy to interstitial animals.

In several instances (see Sect. 3B4, Chap. 20, Chap. 21, Sect. 23A, Sect. 24A) where $r-K$ selection has been invoked, it has turned out that the theory often does not hold or its applicability is limited. The main reason for this is that the theory is a pure neo-Darwinian theory that ignores the proximate evolutionary process (which is an integral part of the evolutionary process of animals). In fact, the physiogenetic changes that occur during the proximate process often overwhelm the expected life history strategies (see also Boyce 1984 for a review of controversies over r and K selection as a life history strategy). Similarly in more recent discussions on reproductive strategies centering around the egg size, larval development and juvenile size in benthic marine invertebrates (Vance 1973, 1974, Underwood 1974, Strathmann 1978), the proximate cause of egg-size increase, which must affect larval and juvenile development, has not been taken into consideration. In changing environments, what Tinkle and Hadley (1975) called "reproductive effort" (referred to in Chap. 20, Sect. 23A) depends heavily on the animals' physiological response to new environmental stimuli.

As the preceding discussion clearly indicates, embryonization, which results in acceleration, is essentially an escape from time and space, as diapause and migration are in insects. Compared with the latter, however, embryonization has had far more profound evolutionary consequences, often entailing structural changes of a macroevolutionary magnitude, as discussed below.

5. Embryonization, Abnormal Metamorphosis, and the Origin of Taxa

Embryonization involving acceleration has often resulted in structural changes leading to the recognition of new taxa. The case of speciation of *Cottus nozawae* involves only mild acceleration of early larval stages. The origin of *Metopaulias* is related to a more abridged larval development.

Often, acceleration by direct development has not entailed a drastic structural change in the adult, the expression of adult genes having been largely unaffected by the omission or modification of the preceding larval and embryonic stages within the egg, and the result has often been a diminutive adult (Sect. 3B2). Of these, *Ophiolepis kieri* is distinguishable from its congeners by some more neotenous features. In *Phoronis ovalis* (Chap. 19), produced through embryonization, the degree of structural differentiation is much less (hence neotenous) than in other congeners with small eggs. Neoteny resulting from direct development and incomplete metamorphosis appears to have resulted in the origin of *Turtonia minuta,* which is the sole representative of the family Turtoniidae (Boss 1982). Terrestrial plethodontid genera are characterized by different degrees of incomplete metamorphosis of bone structures. A further contraction of direct development in terrestrial talitrids appears to be related to the origin of new taxa (genera and species). The origin of the genus *Prostoma* is clearly related to direct development that arose in the freshwater habitat. Direct development is also related to the origination of even higher taxa, such as the order Anaspidacea, class Clitellata, class Cephalopoda, and phylum Gnathostomulida. In these cases, however, it is difficult to see how much their unique structural organization has been due to alteration in the pattern of gene regulation (hence abnormal metamorphosis) involved with direct development, because their close relatives without direct development are unknown.

Sometimes embryonization has resulted in larval neoteny in which metamorphosis into the adult has been truncated. Sexual maturation occurs in the modified larva, and this has led to recognition of higher taxa. The family

Protohydridae and the phylum Rotifera have arisen through larval progenetic neoteny with some modifications. The order Bathynellacea also can be regarded as having arisen through progenetic neoteny. The order Actinulida, which comprises Otohydridae and Halammohydridae, is characterized by the possession of features characteristic of the polyp and the medusa and, in addition, has some larval features. Thus this order originated through a halmatomorphic change. Similarly the Armorhydridae, represented by a single species, resemble both a craspedete medusa and the ovoid polyp. Many other cases of embryonization discussed in this work must have contributed to the phylogenetic differentiation of structures. Evaluation of their taxonomic values, however, must be left to specialists.

Embryonization that has resulted in direct development has paved the way for further evolution of terrestrial molluscs, arthropods, and vertebrates. Our aquatic vertebrate ancestors must have acquired large eggs and consequent direct development on land, as the evolutionary history of modern terrestrial amphibians suggests. Similarly terrestrial talitrids may be said to be simulating the reproductive and developmental method used by earlier terrestrial arthropods which became such a successful group of animals later. Indeed, embryonization has had a far-reaching evolutionary consequence on land, and it should be remembered that the response of the endocrine mechanism for vitellogenesis, inherited from marine ancestors, to the new environmental stimuli on land played the key role in the further success of these animals on land.

4

Genetic Fixation (and Nonfixation) of the Environmentally Induced Phenotype (Abnormal Metamorphosis s. l.).

A. GENETIC FIXATION OF THE PHENOTYPE BY GENETIC ASSIMILATION

Environmentally induced, highly modified phenotypes often must have been genetically fixed, usually through the process of genetic assimilation (i.e., by accumulation of genocopies under the pressure of natural selection). It was shown that the process of genetic assimilation of neoteny in salamander species under the influence of cold temperature (which acts as the morphogenetic agent) was found to be comparable, phase by phase, with the process of genetic assimilation of modified wings in *Drosophila* by heat shock (Sect.24B).

For the genetic assimilation of neoteny in salamanders the evidence is complete at the levels of (1) the hormones (thyroid hormones, T_3 and T_4, and prolactin) concerned, (2) environmental factors (low temperature, pollution, darkness, etc.) affecting the hormonal activity and hormone receptors, (3) selective advantages of being neotenous at higher altitudes and in caves, (4) the mutant that copies the environmental induction of the thyroid hormone deficiency leading to neoteny, and (5) experimental facts showing the nature of endocrine malfunction resulting in neoteny (see Fig. 5).

The evidence for the (presumed) genetic assimilation of neoteny in other animals is much less complete. In *Rana* genetic fixation of the egg size in two localities can be surmised as due to genetic assimilation (Sect. 3B2). In *Dugesia gonocephala* asexuality, presumably induced by high temperatures initially, has been genetically assimilated in some populations (Sect.9A). In molluscs cases of presumed genetic assimilation of distorted shell shapes are known (Chap. 21). Among insects, experiments with *Callosobruchus* indicated that genetic assimilation of the experimentally (by isolation) induced flightless form could eventually come, because flight forms fly away from original populations (Sect. 23D21). Among butterflies, several cases of exceedingly stable color morphs in certain areas (such as high altitudes) are considered to have been derived through genetic assimilation (Sect. 23D26).

In the northeastern Japanese populations of the cricket *Nemobius yezoensis* genetic assimilation of microptery has been only partially completed; a population consists of genetically determined and only environmentally determined micropterous individuals, representing phase 2 of genetic assimilation (Sect. 23D14). Essentially the same situation appears to obtain in some high-altitude pierines *Tatochila* spp. (Sect. 23D26), and presumably in many other invertebrates (such as Stauromedusa, Sect. 8A; *Tessellana*, Sect. 23D13). It should also be remembered that apterous aphids can revert to their ancestral winged condition seasonally. In all these cases reversion of the phenotype to the ancestral condition may be said to violate Dollo's law. However, the occasional macropterous female of *Metrioptera roeseli* (which is usually brachypterous) is sterile. Therefore, a functional ancestral condition does not obtain in nature, and hence Dollo's law appears to hold (Sect. 4B). How frequently such a phenomenon occurs in other insects remains to be seen.

Reversion of the evolutionary process occurs rarely in the form of atavism in homoiothermic animals, as recent discussions on this topic (Lande 1978, Macbeth 1980, Blackburn 1984, Hall 1984) indicate. For instance, Lande (1978) asserts that a reversion may occur after a million generations. Because the objects of discussion were mostly warm-blooded animals whose physiology tends to remain relatively more resistant to environmental changes (especially temperature), reversion of structures to their ancestral condition by physiological change is not likely to occur as easily as in poikilothermic animals. This appears to account for, at least in part, the relative rarity of reversion of structure to the ancestral condition in higher vertebrates. It should be noted here, however, that reconstruction of eyes in snakes (poikilothermic), discussed by Blackburn (1984), is related to their change in habitat from burrow to surface living.

Complete genetic assimilation at phase 3 must have occurred in many cases, as seen, for instance, in permanently neotenous salamander species (Sect. 24B), and presumably in many permanently apterous insects such as Grylloblattodea (Sect. 23D8) and Mallophaga.

It should be remembered that the permanently modified, monomorphic taxa (often higher taxa, genus or above) have often been derived by fixation of a morph of initially environmentally induced di- or polymorphic species, as can be most clearly seen from the evolutionary process of neotenous salamanders. Various taxa of polystomatids appear to have arisen through the retention of the neotenous morph (Sect. 9B). Many cases of apterous or wing-reduced taxa in insects must have been derived through the fixation of the apterous individuals of the initially polymorphic species with respect to wing development. Accumulation of proper mutants (such as the one in *Ambystoma mexicanum*, Sect. 24B, a temperature-sensitive mutant *ecd* in *Drosophila*, and the like) would result in genetic assimilation the environmentally induced morph.

Seasonal morphs in butterflies are known to be induced by certain seasonal photoperiods and temperatures (Sect. 23D26). The ability to produce a certain definite color pattern in response to the photoperiodic and temperature cues must reflect the effect of natural selection and represents phase 1 of genetic assimilation; in the *Drosophila* experiment (Sect. 24B) a considerable selection was necessary before the steady modification of wings occurred by the heat shock. Rarely, one of the seasonal morphs could have become a distinct species by becoming univoltine. For instance, *Pieris virginiensis* may represent the spring form of *P. napi* that became isolated (T. Saigusa, personal communication).

In some animals permanent fixation of a modified morph never comes. In auchenorrhynchous Homoptera, among insects, environmentally induced wing-reduced morphs are never fixed genetically, and in female aphids production of winged and wingless morphs may alternate, according to environmental signals. In Homoptera there is no permanently wing-reduced taxon. This appears to be related to the fact that no homopteran has adapted to an extreme environment (such as subsoil environment). In migratory locusts the solitary stationary phase and the gregarious migratory phase alternate (Sect. 23D13). In *Gerris* spp. the appearance of wing reduction is seasonal. In some carabid beetles genetically determined wing reduction as well as full wing development occurs (Sect. 23D21). In these insects migration by the flight form is often an escape from unfavorable time and space, and it is an important life history strategy (Dingle 1978). Yet in the related species of these insects wing-reduced taxa occur (e.g., apterous gerrid genera, brachypterous orthopterous taxa).

Permanent fixation of the phenotype also depends on the morphogenetic plasticity of animals. Trematodes are usually not specific with regard to the final vertebrate host, and highly variable phenotypes produced in different hosts (as is the case with *Fasciola hepatica*) are perplexing to taxonomists (Sect. 9B). This is consonant with their capacity to add hosts, apparently endlessly, if the opportunity is presented. The Trematoda appear to be characterized by the presence of a great range of (host) environmentally induced variation at all taxonomic levels. It is difficult to conceive of genetic fixation of a particular phenotype, because the latter would easily change in the next host. Essentially the same nature of morphogenetic plasticity prevails in Cestoidea (Sect. 9C). Here proglottidation is often the indicator of morphogenetic plasticity. In *Hymenolepis diminuta* (Sect. 9C), which infests many species of insects belonging to five orders, the range of variation is great and is clearly associated with different hosts.

In cyclomorphosis in Rotifera (Chap. 15), Cladocera (Sect. 23A), and some Collembola (Sect. 23D1) great ranges of environmentally induced variation are perplexing to taxonomists, although certain features, such as the loss of the crest in *Daphnia* in the Arctic, appear to have been fixed. Sometimes the phenotypic modification after a long period of existence in a new environment has been called *Dauermodifikation*, or persistent modification. The modification of *Daphnia cucullata* transplanted in the new environment (in Italy) apparently became permanent (Woltereck 1934). However, this persistent modification reverted to the ancestral phenotype after 40 generations in the ancestral (older) environment (Sect. 23A). This phenomenon thus appears to parallel the phenomena exhibiting the violation of Dollo's law already discussed above. Thus the concept of persistent modification remains dubious, although it may sometimes represent nothing but phase 2 of genetic assimilation.

B. DENIAL OF THE "INHERITANCE OF ACQUIRED CHARACTERS"

Despite some apparent exceptions, it now has to be concluded that an environmentally modified phenotype could become heritable through the process of genetic assimilation, remaining at phase 1 or 2, or 3 of the latter. As I (Matsuda 1982) have discussed, the widely held belief that environmentally modified phenotypes are not heritable (and hence without evolutionary future) is misleading and it must be dismissed. The reason for the prevalence of this belief appears to have been a series of proposals and discoveries of important biological concepts that have confused biologists. Most prominently, the so-called Weismann theory was in accord with the idea of impossibility of inheritance of externally induced phenotypic changes. The theory states that only the germ plasm is continued from generation to generation, and therefore somatic (somatogenic of Weismann) modifications acquired during development by external influence cannot affect the germ plasm, and hence cannot be inherited. Against the possibility of transmission of somatic modification to the germ plasm, Weismann (1892, p. 393) asserted "we should have to assume the presence in all parts of the body a definite track along which somatic variation might be transferred back to the germ cells, in the germ plasm of which it would produce a corresponding change." This assertion was consistent with the Mendelian law of heredity that was discovered soon after, and the two theories together contributed to the development of neo-Darwinism, in which the external (environmental) influence on development is irrelevant to evolution.

Further, Weismann's theory was also consistent with the central dogma of modern molecular genetics in which the relationship between the genotype and phenotype (i.e., the DNA→RNA→protein→phenotype sequence) is unidirectional and there is no mechanism by which the process could be reversed, and later repudiations of the "inheritance of acquired characters" (Dobzhansky 1970, Mayr 1976, Ayala 1977) were based on this dogma. However, in these repudiations, as Matsuda (1982) pointed out, no distinction was made between the kinds of external agents causing modifications. In this connection, it is very important to point out here that Weismann (1892) actually recognized two kinds of somatogenic variations, namely, injuries and functional variations, and the variations depending on the so-called "influence of environment" which included mainly climatic variations. As his discussion shows, his refutation of the "inheritance of acquired characters" applied to the first two categories only.

As this work abundantly shows, environmentally acquired characters can become heritable through the process of genetic assimilation, without requiring the reversal of genetic transcription and translation. Weismann found, with regard to the climatic influence, that when the pupae of the German form of a lycaenid butterfly *Polymmatus phlaeas* was exposed to much higher temperatures, none of the emerged adults resembled the darkest form of southern variety *eleus*. Further, a reverse experiment was made by subjecting caterpillars of the Naples form to very low temperature in rearing. The result was that none was as light colored as the ordinary German form. From these results Weismann concluded that the German and Naples forms are constitutionally (genetically) distinct. Weismann (1892, p. 401) said,

> A somatogenic character is not inherited in this case, but the modifying influence — temperature — affects the primary consitituents of the wings in each individual, i.e. a part of the soma — as well as germplasm contained in the germ cells of animals.

Weismann (1892, p. 405) even went so far as to say, "In many animals and plants influences of temperature and environment may very possibly produce hereditary variations." Thus contrary to the prevailing belief, Weismann was a neo-Lamarckist, as Darwin was (1872, p. v). In 1904 Weismann again referred to *P. phlaeas* in the same context, although he also referred to cases in which environmental impacts such as nutrition and climatic factors have not affected the germ plasm (e.g., alpine plants, plant galls). In fact, Weismann's theory as a whole was not inconsistent with the Baldwin effect (discussed in Chap. 5). However, what happened later was that his general statement of refutation of the inheritance of acquired characters alone was taken seriously, and it provided a strong theoretical basis for the development of neo-Darwinism.

C. NATURE OF GENETIC POLYMORPHISM

In *Anisolabis* (Sect. 23D9), carabid beetles (Sect. 23D21), and *Paratettix* and *Apotettix* (Sect. 23D13) polymorphism is determined genetically, and no environmental influence is involved with morph determination. These cases appear to represent genetic polymorphism which Ford (1940, 1965) and others defined as "the occurrence together in the same habitat of two or more discontinuous morphs or phases of a species in such proportions that the result of them cannot be maintained by merely recurrent mutations." It excluded geographical races, seasonal forms, and continuous variation falling within a curve of normal distribution. According to Ford, the control of polymorphic forms may be imposed by segregation of a single major allele, or else by the corresponding members of a supergene, and polymorphism is maintained by the superiority of heterozygosity which results in balanced polymorphism.

As Clark's (1976) review showed, however, at least some of the cases of genetic polymorphism mentioned by Ford and many others are achieved by environmental influence. As seen in this work, the proximate process of the presumed genetic polymorphism in *Cepaea* (Chap. 21) and industrial melanism in Lepidoptera (Sect. 23D26) and others can be studied, although I fail to see a proximate process of mimicry in butterflies and other cases that are known to be induced purely by natural selection.

At any rate, there are cases of genetic polymorphism s. str. where the environmental influence is irrelevant or insignificant. Generally, nematodes have a highly rigid pattern of development (Chap. 16), and therefore the environmental influence on development and evolution (as a morphogenetic agent) can be largely discounted. The question is how this mechanism arose in evolution. Because the cases of truly genetic mechanism (independent of environmental influence) are rather rare as compared with the cases of environmentally induced polymorphism, it appears highly probable that they arose secondarily in evolution. Generally, the evolutionary future of genetic polymorphism, unlike that of environment–physiologically induced morphogenesis, appears to be highly limited. No clear case of speciation or beyond through isolation of genetically determined, adapted morph appears to be known.

5

A Historical Review and Reassessment of Neo-Lamarckism

The understanding and definition of neo-Lamarckism have, as my review (Matsuda 1982) showed, been different according to different authors in the past. More recent definitions (e.g., Jepsen et al. 1949, Gould 1977) emphasized the aspect of environmental influence on the development of organisms and consequent evolution. However, such definitions do not reflect the neo-Lamarckism that developed in the nineteenth century after Darwin (1859). Although even after Darwin environmental influence on evolution (through developmental alteration) was a dominant way of thinking among evolutionists, the important question was, as Romanes' (1896) review indicates, how to integrate Darwinian natural selection into their evolutionary thinking. Indeed, the combination of the two evolutionary mechanisms was accepted even by Darwin (1872, p.v) and Weismann (1892) who was later mistakenly considered as the founder of neo-Darwinism.

The theory of organic selection or the Baldwin effect, which was postulated independently and at about the same time by Baldwin (1896, 1902), Lloyd Morgan (1896, 1900), and Osborn (1896, 1897), was the attempt to compromise between Darwinian natural selection and Lamarckian inheritance of acquired characters (by environmental influence and use and disuse), and it appears to reflect the intellectual climate then prevalent among evolutionary biologists. The essence of the Baldwin effect may be defined as follows: characters acquired in individuals due to the influence of the environment they selected remain as they are when favored by natural selection (accommodation). Such modified characters may, under the influence of natural selection, become reinforced or replaced by similar hereditary characters (the coinciden-tal variations of Lloyd Morgan 1900 and Baldwin 1902). Thus the Baldwin effect differs from genetic assimilation only in the emphasis that animals select the environments that influence their development.

The Baldwin effect was primarily concerned with behavioral changes in evolution. Huxley (1948), citing examples mainly from the works by Thorpe (1930, 1940) on food plant preference in insects, emphasized the conditioning effect to a particular host plant as a nonhereditary barrier that may serve as the first stage in evolutionary divergence by the split of a population. He pointed out that the change is not impressed upon the germ cells, but holds the strain in an environment where mutations tending to the same direction are selected and incorporated into the constitution. An outstanding recent demonstration of the evolutionary process conforming to the Baldwin effect was sympatric specia-tion in some tephretid flies studied by Bush (1969, 1973), Huettel and Bush (1972), and others, which showed the chemically cued host selection, condi-tioning, and genetic changes during their evolutionary process. Similarly, Par-sons (1981) found that sympatric speciation occurs in some Australian *Dro-sophila* species, through selection (utilization) of microhabitats. As he contended, two aspects, selection of habitat and the direct genotypic response to environments, which may vary, must be studied perhaps simultaneously. He argued further that in the tropics environmental heterogeneity should promote habitat selection, resulting in the increase of species diversity.

To the above list I would add the case of psychid moths (Sect. 23D26), which build their habitats (cases) where they undergo conspicuous structural modifi-cations. Parasitism is also a case where Baldwin effect appears to apply, because parasites select hosts where they undergo modifications. For instance, miraci-dia larvae of trematodes are chemically attracted to the molluscan hosts where they become cercariae (Sect. 9B). In fact the Baldwin effect appears to represent a fundamental ecological principle which has evolutionary consequences.

Schmalhausen's (1949) scheme of evolution of developmental process roughly parallels the phases of genetic assimilation in which the environmen-tally modified phenotype is replaced, under the pressure of natural selection, by genocopies (Sect. 4A). The first and most primitive norm of development is "dependent morphogenesis," in which environmental stimuli determine pri-marily quantitative expression. The second norm of Schmalhausen is "autoreg-ulatory development," in which environmental stimuli trigger, at a definite intensity, adaptive responses, and this appears to correspond to phase 1 of genetic assimilation. Finally, "autonomous development" (which comprises autonomous mosaic and autonomous regulatory development) develops on the basis of autoregulatory processes through a definite change in the norm of reaction of the genotype. In autonomous development the role of external factor is more reduced than in autoregulatory development, and internal fac-tors of development now assume fundamental significance (phase 2 to phase 3).

In the above sequence of change from dependent developmental process to autonomous development, the development has become increasingly stabilized for normal morphogenesis. According to Schmalhausen, such a stabilized development has occurred mainly as a result of stabilizing selection, and it appears to correspond to the canalization of development of Waddington. A good example showing the sequence of evolutionary change in the developmental norm cited by Schmalhausen is the loss of leaves that becomes permanent. Thus shedding of leaves in certain seasons (during a drought and dry season in tropics) is adaptive because it protects the plants against the loss of water by transpiration through the leaves. In xerophytic plants and some others the loss of leaves is permanent, although young xerophytic plants may develop leaves (they then lose the leaves). In the course of further evolution, the shoots become expanded to form leaflike branches (phylloclades), and the shedding of leaves and the development of phylloclades are determined by autonomous or internal factors, not by drought. The compensatory development (phylloclades) is associated with the loss of foliage, and this phenomenon appears to represent a material compensation that abounds in the animal kingdom.

The Baldwin effect as applied to structural evolution was criticized by Simpson (1953b), who said that the works by Hovasse (1943, 1950), Gause (1947), and Schmalhausen (1949) had not shown an indubitable instance of evolutionary change that is explicable by their theories, which were the same or essentially the same as the Baldwin effect. However, Simpson (1953b) conceded the possibility of the prevalence of genocopy. Had Simpson seen the paper on genetic assimilation by Waddington that appeared in the same issue of the same journal, his conclusion might have been different.

Waddington (1961) and later Ho (1984, p. 457) objected to the Baldwin effect, mainly because they considered the initial adaptation to the new environment (by selection of habitats) as a nongenetic phenomenon on which selection has no effect, and Waddington even went so far as to say that this out-of-date speculation should be allowed to lapse back into oblivion. Actually, however, in many animals this behavior of habitat or host selection occurs before the process of genetic assimilation of modified structures starts in the new habitat (host). Hence the behavior is an integral part of genetic assimilation in these animals, and hence the rejection of the Baldwin effect is unjustified.

Thus the Baldwin effect, the concept proposed by Schmalhausen, and genetic assimilation of Waddington are the same in that they propose the proximate environmental effect on morphogenesis and the ultimate process by natural selection in the study of evolution, and they agree, in essence, with the evolutionary thinking in the late nineteenth century after Darwin (1859). I therefore call all these concepts "neo-Lamarckism." Neo-Lamarckism is a more complete theory of evolution than neo-Darwinism, in which the proximate process is ignored, and its methods should enable us to understand the evolutionary process more fully. It is perhaps important to point out further that, besides Huxley and Simpson already referred to, four other prominent evolutionists of our time, Dobzhansky, Rensch, Mayr, and De Beer, accepted or approved neo-Lamarckism. Dobzhansky (in Schmalhausen 1949), who edited the English translation of Schmalhausen's 1949 book, said that his logic was impeccable. De Beer (1958) accepted genocopy as the mechanism of (apparent) inheritance of acquired characters. Rensch (1959, p. 188) clearly approved of the Baldwin effect. Mayr (1959, 1976) accepted Waddington's demonstration of genetic assimilation of crossveinlessness by gradual accumulation of polygenes, and equated it to the threshold phenomenon, where numerous genes contribute to a certain phenotype but the potentiality for that phenotype is not pushed above the visible threshold until a sufficient number of genes have accumulated in the genotype.

6

Macroevolution, Adaptive Response, Monophyly Versus Polyphyly

As already summarized (Sects. 3A1, 3A2), in such stressful environments as parasitic environments and interstitial habitats along the seacoast, the magnitude of structural changes of the animals has often been truly remarkable (halmatomorphic), and the magnitude of structural changes can be said to be macroevolutionary. Another special environment is the enlarged eggs that, by themselves, constitute highly stressful environments for the developing embryo–larva, and the consequence of development in such an environment also has often been a macroevolutionary change in adult structures (Sect. 3B). The degrees of structural changes resulting from neoteny in the animals living in less stressful, freer environments can also be substantial (Sect. 3A3).

Judging from the structural changes that these animals undergo in extreme environments today, we can safely imagine some even greater morphological changes that could have occurred in the past (in association with environmental changes). Valentine and Campbell (1975) attributed the rapid evolution of the major metazoan phyla to major environmental changes some 570 million years ago. Jablonski et al. (1983) found that at two geological points (the Cambrian-Ordovician interval, 500 million years ago, and the Late Cretaceous, 60 million years ago) evolutionary novelties preferentially generated near shore (instead of offshore), and this implied that origination of evolutionary novelties tended to occur more in a stressful environment, just as this work abundantly shows the occurrence of such events in the transitional areas from sea to land.

It should be remembered that, in bringing about macroevolutionary changes, new environmental stimuli in the new (stressful) environments must have induced alteration in gene regulation pathways (proximate process) and natural selection must have cooperated in completing macroevolutionary changes (ultimate process). This cooperation of the proximate and ultimate processes has been pointed out many times in the name of adaptive response (pp. 70, 85, 86, 92, 108, 114, 126, 138, 162, 176, 182, 185, 193, 205, 206, 209, 215, 224, 231, and 247).

To repeat some examples (for the sake of emphasis): embryonization, which occurred as a result of interaction between new environmental stimuli and animals, was adaptive for the animals that migrated from water to land (e.g., plethodontids, pulmonates), because the resultant elimination of vulnerable larval stages (on land) was of definite advantage for survival, and natural selection must have contributed to perfect this proximate process by eliminating those individuals failing to produce large enough eggs. Similarly, neoteny of *Ambystoma* spp. has occurred at high altitudes in North America by the influence of cold temperature on the endocrine mechanism. The resultant neotenous morph was adaptive locally, and natural selection must have favored the individuals that could remain larval (neotenous). Thus in these instances what we see as "adaptive response" today is the product of intricate cooperation of the animals' genotypic response to new environmental stimuli and natural selection. Furthermore, it should be realized that the adaptive response often becomes genetically fixed (Fig. 5) and results in macroevolutionary changes of structures.

It is important to note further that what I call "adaptive response" was apparently the way Mivart (1871) understood evolution. Mivart was a saltationist who believed in the sudden origin of his "useful characters" (e.g., heads of flat fishes, baleen of whales, limbs of vertebrates. . . , and even many examples of mimicry) upon which later natural selection works. He believed that no mere survival of the fittest and minute variations can account for the incipient stages of the useful characters. Instead, he believed in the existence of the internal cause of remarkable changes (change in gene regulation?). As a neo-Lamarckist he believed that the internal force acts in cooperation with external influence and with natural selection (pp. 76, 259 and many other places in his book). Darwin (1872) was opposed to Mivart in his sixth edition of the Origin of Species (reviewed by Mayr 1959). Yet his opposition was, needless to say, without the knowledge of modern regulatory genetics.

Goldschmidt (1940) saw, as this work also demonstrates, the potentiality of macroevolutionary changes of structures in the norm of reaction of the genotype in animals and plants, which manifests itself in seasonal morphs of butterflies, habitat-dependent developmental changes in *Limnophila*, regulative activities of tissues known in experimental embryology, sexual dimorphism, and so on. He believed that developmental pathways for macroevolutionary changes exist in the genotype.

Very significantly, Goldschmidt (1940) maintained that hormones (and embryonic organizers) have, when called into action, immense morphogenetic effects of macroevolutionary order. He cited amphibian metamorphosis as an example that occurs as a hereditary mode of reaction of the genotype in the presence of thyroid hormones. He maintained that a single (and small) genetic change controlling the hormonal action or a genetically determined threshold condition (in tissue sensitivity) can produce the immense morphogenetic differences of macroevolutionary order between nonmetamorphosing and metamorphosing urodelans (pp. 273-274 in Goldschmidt 1940). This assertion is completely supported by this work (Sect. 24B). A mutant (a single genetic change of Goldschmidt) most probably affects the TSH function in the axolotl, resulting the deficiency of thyroid hormones* and consequent neoteny. Goldschmidt also cited some other similar examples showing the hormonally induced disturbance in the norm of reaction of the genotype in the abnormal phenotype (*Periophthalmus*, pathological types of giants and dwarfs in man, etc.). Goldschmidt believed, contrary to Darwinian thinking, that such macroevolutionary changes have not occurred by accumulation of small changes (microevolution).

However, his theory differed from the one presented here in two fundamental points. First, for Goldschmidt hormonal action was an autonomous action, independent of environmental stimuli. Presumably this aspect of environmental control of the endocrine activity was not firmly established as it is today, although Huxley (1929) was certainly aware of the effect of cold temperature on thyroid hormones, and Wigglesworth (1934) showed that food intake triggers the molting hormone activity. For Goldschmidt environmental changes had no relevance to evolution. In fact, he was vehemently opposed to the so-called Lamarckism that proposes an environmental effect on development and evolution.

The second difference was that for Goldschmidt evolution always starts with genetic determination of the phenotype. Therefore, a single hopeful monster resulting from a single macroevolutionary event was the initiator of the macroevolutionary change (and hence a new higher taxon). Such an origin is simply unrealistic, because the monster would, as pointed out by Mayr (1963) and many others, have difficulty in finding a mate. Actually, as the process of genetic assimilation of the neotenous morph in salamanders (Sect. 24B) clearly shows, initially monsters (the neotenous morph) arise by interaction between the animals' physiology and new environmental stimuli, and not by genetic determination. It is certainly not important selectively at this stage whether the newly formed monstrous morph is genetically determined or only environmentally induced. Goldschmidt (1938) was the founder of the concept of phenocopy, but he did not have the concept of genocopy which accumulates during the process of genetic assimilation.

Goldschmidt was revisited by Gould (1982), as well as by Harrison (1982), Bush (1982), Charlesworth (1982), and Templeton (1982), all showing the growing interest in Goldschmidt. None of them, however, appreciated or un-

---

*Such a gene should be considered a regulatory gene; Stebbins (1982) also called any gene that alters the metabolism of hormones that control gene action a regulatory gene.

derstood the nature of the "small genetic change for macroevolution" proposed by Goldschmidt.

Some early twentieth-century theories of macroevolution proposed autonomous force as the underlying mechanism. For instance, Schindewolf's (1936) theory of archallaxis, in which the change in early developmental stages results in discontinuous macroevolutionary changes, was free of both Darwinian selection and Lamarckian environmental influence on development. Simpson (1953a) and Rensch (1959) preferred intense natural selection and mutation as the mechanism of macroevolutionary changes to the autonomy of macroevolution.

Punctuated equilibrium proposed by Eldredge and Gould (1972) and Gould and Eldredge (1977) is sometimes considered to have a macroevolutionary implication. This theory, based on paleontological data, proposes a sudden origin of substantial structural change that results in speciation, and this is followed by gradual changes in succeeding geological times. Grant (1963, 1982), in criticizing punctuated equilibrium, recognized four general modes of evolutionary changes: (1) stasis, which is a bradytelic lineage associated with long continued stable environment; (2) slow phyletic evolution associated with slowly and progressively changing environment; (3) a trend progressing at moderate rates (mediated by a combination of speciational and phyletic changes) associated with moderately changing environment; and (4) a rapid evolutionary trend composed of a series of quantum speciational events which is associated with rapidly changing environment. This scheme, as Grant maintained, provides a broader diversity of macroevolutionary pattern than does the punctuational model. It should be remembered that in the Grant model environment is considered solely as the selective agent, although environment must act also as a morphogenetic agent.

A. MONOPHYLY VERSUS POLYPHYLY

Considering the high morphogenetic plasticity inherent in many animal species and the production of substantial evolutionary changes in structure as a result of adaptive response to new environments (see above), it can be suspected that existing higher taxa (each taxon can comprise many species) may not necessarily have been derived from a single common ancestor (monophyly). In the cases of animals that are known to have changed their habitat from sea to fresh water or onto land (terrestrial talitrids, hermit crabs, and oniscoid isopods, Sect. 23A, and the three spined stickleback, Sect. 24A) it is not likely that new higher taxa in the new habitats originated from a single ancestral species, for similar adaptive responses (changes) of certain characters could have occurred convergently in two or more species in the new habitats. Hence a possibility of their polyphyletic origin looms large in these cases (see especially Sect. 24A).

Another example is the polyphyletic origin of Mallophaga, which is discussed fully in Sect. 23D16. Because the morphogenetic plasticity in Psocoptera (from which the Mallophaga have been derived) is considerable, it is likely that during the long history of association of psocopterans with birds' nests some of them have become mallophagans and established as parasites of birds; the modifications that mallophagans have acquired are the result of adaptive responses that have become genetically fixed (presumably through the process of genetic assimilation). The phylogenetic process of this group of insects postulated by Hennig (1969, 1981) is consistent with his methodology in which homoplasy is negligible and specialization in common is regarded as synapomorphy for the sake of economy (parsimony) of hypothesis. However, such a phylogenetic process is certainly not supported by the biological facts, which strongly suggest the polyphyletic origin of this group of insects.

Hennig's preconception that in the modern system of insect classification no polyphyletic group (at the ordinal level) exists (Hennig 1969, p. 18; 1981, p. 5) is too optimistic and unfounded. Grylloptera (Kevan 1973) is an order that has been separated from Orthoptera since Hennig's statement (1969). Matsuda (1981) pointed out that Hennig's justification uniting the Ephemeroptera and Odonata into the Palaeoptera was based on dubious synapomorphy. Large orders or suborders such as Coleoptera and Homoptera are likely to be split into subgroups in the future, depending on the state of mind of taxonomists.

Although parsimony in determining synapomorphies and ancestors in the Hennigian methodology has been widely accepted in recent years (reviewed by Dupuis 1984), a cogent criticism was given by Gosliner and Ghiselin (1984), who showed the array of parallelism of characters recognized in the taxonomy of opistobranch molluscs. They question, as I do, the credibility of a system built up by the uncritical application of parsimony. The Hennigian method of examining specialization in common is certainly an advance. However, integration of various biological information is necessary before synapomorphy or homoplasy of characters can be determined.

7

Conclusion

It has now become clear that neo-Lamarckism has always been a reasonable theory, and it has stood the test of time for more than a century. Once some misunderstandings and inhibitions are removed, the theory can be regarded as a more complete theory (than neo-Darwinism) in that it analyzes the evolutionary process in terms of both the proximate and ultimate mechanisms, and in that it is especially suited for analyzing the origin of macroevolutionary change. Through the analysis of the proximate process we come to know the cause of variation and the presumed initial stage of evolution of the structures upon which natural selection has worked. In traditional neo-Darwinism natural selection is considered to be involved throughout the whole evolutionary process (of structures), which is indeed untrue, as Mivart (1871) already knew. In practice obvious cases of overextension of the theory of natural selection, which actually results from neglect of the proximate process, have often been criticized in terms of their falsifiability. Yet the critics have never offered a solution for this dilemma. Indeed, evolutionary biology has been in a state of constipation caused by the neo-Darwinian constraint that inhibits exploration of the proximate process of evolution. It should now be realized that such a worry will be over once we accept the neo-Lamarckian approach.

The application of the neo-Lamarckian analysis appears to resolve some outstanding problems and riddles in evolutionary biology. For instance, the problem of "inheritance of acquired characters" is now understood as the result of accumulation of genocopies. The age-old riddle of "Which came first, the chicken or the egg?" can now be answered from the evolutionary viewpoint

(Sect. 3B2). "Adaptive response" now must be restored as a fundamental evolutionary concept, though it has been neglected. All phenomena of abnormal metamorphosis (halmatomorphosis, neoteny, caenogenesis) resulting in macroevolutionary structural changes are now attributed primarily to environmentally induced alteration in the response of the genotype (alteration in gene regulation) during the proximate process. The study of the Baldwin effect as special cases of genetic assimilation must be encouraged.

It should be realized that all the above problems can be more clearly understood by inquiring into the hormonal mediation that becomes involved. Indeed, the environmentally induced hormonal intervention controlling gene action was the mechanism that was unknown to the nineteenth century neo-Lamarckists, and the lack of knowledge of such a mechanism might have hindered the acceptance of neo-Lamarckism.

A. PROPOSAL OF PAN-ENVIRONMENTALISM

In discussing the evolutionary process constant use of the term neo-Lamarckism has bothered my conscience, because the contribution by Darwin, that is, the part of the evolutionary process played by natural selection, becomes hidden under this term. More properly, therefore, neo-Lamarckism must be called "Lamarck-Darwinism." This again, however, does not convey properly what this work advocates, for both Lamarck and Darwin wrote of many things in addition to the environmental effect on development and evolution (Lamarck) and natural selection (Darwin). To resolve this dilemma and to provide a more precise meaning of what this work emphasizes, a new term, "pan-environmentalism," is proposed.

In pan-environmentalism, environment consists of both morphogenetic and selective factors. It is envisaged that the former induces, by response of the genotype, variation upon which the selective factor(s) works (Fig. 5). It follows, then, that there will be appreciable evolution with environmental changes. (Conversely, there will be no appreciable evolution without environmental change.)

Neo-Darwinism may be retained as a method of analysis of the evolutionary process where the effect of environmental change on development is minor or negligible.

Part Two

SPECIAL DISCUSSION

8

The Phylum Coelenterata

A. THE SUBPHYLUM CNIDARIA

Enlargement of eggs has occurred independently in different phylogenetic lines of the Cnidaria. In Scyphozoa, as seen in Berrill's (1949) analysis of the relationship between egg sizes and subsequent developments, the diameter of an egg varies from 0.03 mm in *Haliclystus* to 0.3 mm in *Pelagia*, a thousand-fold variation in volume. Types of gastrulation are correlated fairly closely with egg size, the smallest eggs gastrulating by unipolar ingression and the largest by complete or partial invagination, whereas eggs of intermediate sizes gastrulate by a combined process of ingression and invagination. The subsequent development is equally correlated with egg size and type of gastrulation: the smallest eggs become vermiform larvae incapable of constituting a polyp directly, the intermediate size eggs form planulae, which become polyps or scyphistomae, larger eggs may occasionally form actinula larvae, and the largest eggs develop directly into ephyra-medusae, omitting the scyphistoma stage entirely.

Two types of egg have been known to occur in *Aurelia*, very large yolky eggs that turn into actinula larvae and thence into ephyrae, and smaller eggs that turn into planulae first, and then into scyphistomae, which bud or strobilate. In this case ecological association with the egg-size differentiation appears to remain unknown. The habitats of *Pelagia* and *Aurelia*, which produce large eggs, do not seem to differ significantly from those in other scyphozoans.

Within the superfamily Tubularoidea (Hydrozoa), as summarized by Van der Vyver (1980), *Tubularia ceratogyne, T. indivisa, T. crocea, T. larynx, Condelabrum phrygium* (with fixed gonophores), *Hybocodon prolifer, Steenstrupia nutans*, and *Melagopsis haeckeli* (with a free medusa stage) have eggs containing a large amount of yolk, a completely irregular cleavage pattern, and no blastocoel. The blastula is a typical stereoblastula and is telolecithotrophic. The larval form in all species of *Capitata tubularoidea* (according to the list given by Van der Vyver 1980) and in *Zyzzyzus* species of Corymorphidae (D. Calder, personal communication) is an actinula larva with transitory tentacles which develops directly into the medusa; the large eggs released from the gonad are fertilized in the subumbrellar cavity and develop there into the polyp-like actinula larva, skipping the planula stage. As a rule, one such larva lives within a gonophore.

In hydras, also with large eggs, the medusa stage is completely suppressed, and its life cycle consists of asexual budding, which usually originates at the junction of the gastric and stalk regions, and syngamic reproduction, which usually occurs in autumn. During late cleavage (of syngamic reproduction) the embryo secretes a sclerotized yellowish shell, the embryonic theca, and then the whole embryo drops off the parent and sticks to the substrate, where the theca hardens. After a dormant period of 3 to 10 weeks or more, the theca softens and splits, permitting the exit of an embryo that already has a gastrovascular cavity and tentacles (characteristic of the polyp), and no further development ensues. Thus in hydras the postembryonic life cycle consists solely of the polyp stage, and hence the consequence is a progenetic neoteny.

Presumably, a very large egg in hydras itself has provided the necessary environmental stimulus for the suppression of the planula (Sect. 3B2) and the suppression of the medusa stage might have been effected by low salinities in the freshwater habitat where the polyp hydras had to live. Schaller et al. (1979) recognized four kinds of morphogenetic hormones controlling the head and foot formation in hydras. Such hormones might be involved with the suppression of the planula stage, but probably not of the medusa. Silverstone et al. (1978) showed that *Aurelia aurita* may synthesize thyroid hormone precursors, mono- and dithyrosine (MIT and DIT) (not thyroxine, as had been claimed), and they suggested that these substances may be the initiating agents of strobilation. It is therefore probable that permanent suppression of the medusa stage in hydras occurred as a result of inactivation of such morphogenetic hormones (presumably by lower salinities).

It is difficult to see from Reisa's (1973) discussion on the ecology of hydras, a stringent selection pressure under which their progenetic phenotype has become established in nature. Sessility of hydras in limnetic habitats, as Reisa felt, does not seem adaptive (although hydras may detach themselves from the substratum for dispersion). At any rate, genetic fixation (presumably through genetic assimilation) of the essentially polypoid phenotype in hydras appears to have occurred as a result of genetic fixation of the (presumed) endocrine function, which assures the suppression of planula and medusa stages.

Enlargement of eggs has occurred also in some cnidarians living in the interstitial biotope along the seacoast, and in these cases some unique environmental factors (such as low salinities) and large eggs are related. The consequences of enlarged eggs in these cnidarians are quite abnormal definitive adults. The Actinulida of Hydrozoa comprises two families, Halammohydridae, with eight species of *Halammohydra* (Clausen 1977), and Otohydridae, with one species, *Otohydra vagans*. They are free-living solitary hydrozoans inhabiting interstices of marine sands, and with characteristic tenacles borne on the aboral cone. Their body size ranges from less than 350 μm in *Otohydra vagans* to 0.3 – 1.3 mm in *Halammohydra* (Clausen 1971). The Actinulida have the features typical of both polyps and medusae and, in addition, they have larval features such as the complete cilia in the adult (Swedmark and Teissier 1966). This fact appears to reflect a profound modification in gene regulation pathway. Remane (1927), who first discovered *Halammohydra*, regarded it as an aberrant medusa and placed it within the Trachylina of the suborder Nacromedusae. Their development is direct. In two species of *Halammohydra* studied, sexes are separate and the fertilized egg develops, via an actinula stage, into a young animal (Swedmark and Teissier 1966). Eggs are yolk-rich and relatively voluminous; the diameter of an egg is 90 μm (Swedmark and Teissier 1957a). Females lay small numbers of eggs at a time, three to six in *H. schulzei* and one or two in *H. vermiformis* (Swedmark and Teissier 1966). *Otohydra vagans* is hermaphroditic. It incubates eggs that become (relatively) very voluminous (about 100 μm in diameter) (Swedmark and Teissier 1958a). This mode of development may be said to be ovoviviparity.

A hydrozoan genus *Protohydra*, represented by *P. leuckarti*, occurs in various biotopes such as diatomaceous mud and plant and animal detritus (Schulz 1950a). The species is a small solitary polyp (1.5 mm long) lacking tentacles. Eggs are yolk-rich and large, each measuring 0.25 x 0.14 mm in a somewhat contracted adult that is 0.5 mm long and 0.2 mm. wide, and development is probably direct (Westblad 1929). Both asexual and sexual reproduction occurs, and the former appears to be the major process for the increase of population. Each female produces only a single egg during sexual reproduction (Wehling 1976). This genus was assigned by Thiel (1962) to the independent family Protohydridae. Another hydrozoan genus *Armorhydra*, represented by *A. janowiczi*, resembles both a craspedote medusa and an ovoid polyp; there is a single whorl of tentacles near the oral end and the tentacles are differentiated into catching and adhesive tentacles (see Lacassagne 1968 for anatomy). The sexes are separate in *A. janowiczi*, and five to seven oocytes occur, each oocyte measuring 150 – 200 μm in diameter; such size must be considered large considering the adult size, which is 1.5 x 2 to 1 x 1.5 mm (Swedmark and Teissier 1958b). Based on this species Swedmark and Teissier erected a new genus and family, *Armorhydra* and Armorhydridae, but they were unable to assign these to a particular order of the Hydrozoa.

In the following examples the data on egg sizes are lacking, and in the last three examples reproduction is either sexual or asexual, or only the asexual mode of reproduction is known. Genus *Siphonohydra*, represented by *S. adriatica*, which is 0.75 – 1.2 mm long and has eight tentacles (four on each whorl), was assigned to Tubulariidae by Salvini Plawen (1966). Reproduction is sexual; the gonophore is formed. *Psammohydra*, represented by *P. nanna*, is another genus of Tubulariidae. It is the smallest known polyp, measuring 280–400 μm long (Schulz 1950b). Three to five short tentacles occur a little above the middle of the cylindrical body, and the swollen proboscis terminates in a distensible mouth. Gonads seem to be absent, and asexual reproduction by transverse fission was observed by Schulz (1950b). Genus *Stylocoronella*, represented by *S. riedli*, is a scyphozoan interstitial genus. The maximum size in *S. riedli* is 400 μm, of which the stalk makes up 150 μm. There are 24 tentacles surrounding the prominent proboscis, and only asexual reproduction is known. According to Salvini Plawen (1966), the assignment of this genus to a specific group of Scyphozoa cannot be determined. An interstitial anthozoan *Sphenotrochus* species, shown by Clausen (1971), attains a length of 2 mm. It is bipolar, with both upper and lower extremities, and with mouth and tentacle crown. The lower extremity generates a new polyp opposite to the upper extremity. The species is asexual (Rossi 1961). The genus *Sphenotrochus* belongs to Caryophylliidae (subfamily Turbinolinae) of the Madreporaria (Anthozoa).

In the cases of Tubularoidea and some scyphozoans (*Pelagia*, *Aurelia*), environmental influence on enlargement of eggs is apparently lacking, and this may be related to the absence of a specialized endocrine mechanism for vitellogenesis that responds to environmental signals; such a mechanism has not been found for these cnidarians. Environmental influence on morphogenesis, including oocyte development, must be effected through its influence on morphogens (hormones), which are known, in *Hydra*, to control differentiation of multipotential interstitial cells (Schaller et al. 1979). Derivation of oocytes from interstitial cells is known for *Corydendrium* (Glätzer 1971), *Obelia* (Aizenshtadt and Polteva 1982), and *Hydractinia* (Hertwig and Hündgen 1984). Thereafter, the process of yolk or nutrient deposition appears to vary significantly in different cnidarians (below).

Thus in *Hydra* each ovary contains a single egg of a size unusually large for the Hydrozoa. The oocytes situated in the center of each aggregation of syncytially connected cells (descendants of one interstitial cell) become the egg, whereas the other oocytes are absorbed by the egg. The absorbed oocytes constitute the main source of food for the embryo (Aizenshtadt 1978), and this ability to absorb neighboring cells exists also in *Tubularia crocea* (Boelsterli 1975). Spracklin (1978) reported that in each gonophore of *Tubularia larynx* thousands of nutritive oocytes, connected by a cytoplasmic bridge, synthesize and transfer yolk to a population of approximately 20 rapidly growing oocytes. In *Obelia* yolk synthesis is endogenous (autosynthetic); yolk proteins are synthesized in the endoplasmic reticulum, whereas yolk granules are formed in the Golgi apparatus (Aizenshtadt and Polteva 1982). In a species of *Trachylina* (Hydrozoa) intraooplasmic synthesis appears to constitute the major pathway for protein–carbohydrate yolk deposition (Kessel 1968). Wasserthal (1973) found that during vitellogenesis of *Eudendrium armatum* granular material — possibly glycogen — is transferred from the spadix to the growing oocytes. Thus the immediate proximate cause of enlargement of eggs in Cnidaria remains obscure, although the enlargement of eggs in interstitial cnidarians occurs in association with lower salinities and some other (unique) factors in their habitats.

Environmentally dependent postoval developmental plasticity in cnidarians has been observed in many experiments and in nature, and such a high plasticity may underlie macroevolutionary changes of structures under some environmental conditions. Some examples follow.

In many scyphozoans the polyp (scyphistoma) reproduces asexually by strobilation through budding, which results in the release of young medusae, called ephyrae. The process of strobilation, which is actually a metamorphosis (described by Spangenberg for *Aurelia*, 1966, 1968), is often affected by the change in environmental factors. Lambert (1935-1936) showed, after several years of observation of *Aurelia, Chrysaora*, and others in aquariums, that the conditions necessary for strobilation are (1) a heavy diet of suitable food, (2) a certain low critical temperature, and (3) food and oxygen supply at the critical period. Berrill (1949) concluded in his review that a relatively long nutritive preparation is a necessary condition for strobilation. An important role food supply plays for strobilation in *Aurelia aurita* is also clear in Thiel's (1962) observation, which showed that more individuals strobilate in the region of the Kiel Fjord where more food is available; during the second peak of strobilation later in the spring dense swarms of copepods and cladocerans (as food) are available. Thiel (1962) concluded that in Kiel Fjord the effect of temperature is presumably indirect. Spangenberg (1968) emphasized that the preconditioning to lower temperature is a necessary condition for strobilation. Borradaile et al. (1961) suggested that under certain conditions, such as uniformily high temperature, the scyphistoma would never strobilate and the gonad may mature, and that this onset of neoteny indicates a possible way in which the Stauromedusae (without the medusa stage) might have arisen. In a rhizostome *Cassiopea andromeda* (Stauromedusae) monodisk strobilation occurs when temperature is shifted from 20° to 24° C (Hofmann et al. 1978). In other rhizostomes strobilation was also induced by raising the temperature (Sugiura 1965, 1966). These facts indicate that the absence of the medusa stage in the Stauromedusae may (often) not have been genetically established.

With reference to the effect of light, Custance (1966) showed experimentally for *Aurelia aurita* that the presence of light of too high intensity inhibits strobilation. He therefore suggested that the progressive fall of illumination, which occurs in late autumn, might be a positive stimulus for the onset of strobilation. The effect of salinity on strobilation can be surmised from Thiel's (1963a) experiment, which induced abnormal scyphistomae failing to release ephyrae (polyp bearing the statolith at the tip of tentacles and the polystrobila in which separation of the ephyra does not occur). Thiel showed that the incidence of these abnormal scyphistomae can be significantly increased by lowering salinity from the normal 12–14.5‰; the result suggested an inhibitory effect of lower salinity on strobilation.

Crawford and Webb's (1972) observation indicated apparent involvement of neurohormone with strobilation in *Chrysaora quinquecirrha*. At the time of neck formation of this species the neurosecretory granules were most concentrated in the cell body, and at strobilation most of the neurosecretory product had disappeared from the axon. It is likely that the neurohormone first responds to environmental stimuli before strobilation starts. As already noted MIT and DIT might be the direct agents initiating strobilation.

In the Hydrozoa the most typical life cycle is characterized by "alternation of generations," in which hydroid colonies (polyps) give rise to free-swimming medusae, and fertilized eggs laid by medusae give rise to planula larvae that settle to form a new colony of polyps. A temperature effect on their life cycle is evident in many experiments and observations in nature. For instance, Werner (1963) showed, in *Coryne tubulosa*, that at 14°C the colony grows only by formation of new stolons and hydroids but at 2°C the hydroids of a colony are induced to reproduce by budding off medusae. Similarly, Werner showed that in the anthomedusan *Rathkea octopunctata* vegetative reproduction by budding off medusae is confined to low temperatures below the upper limit of 6°–7°C, and at higher temperatures reproduction occurs only sexually by germ cells.

As already discussed, the loss of the medusa stage in freshwater hydras is due in part to enlarged eggs, and in part to the freshwater environmental effect on postembryonic development. However, a freshwater species *Craspedacusta sowerbyi* has been known to have (sporadically) the medusa stage. In the order Trachylina, which comprises the suborders Trachomedusae and Narcomedusae, the medusoid develops directly from the egg and the polyp has either been reduced to a minute fixed individual or is represented by the planula larva which metamorphoses into a medusa (Borradaile et al. 1961).

Numerous environmental factors (carbon dioxide tension, population density, temperature, photoperiod, etc.) have been known to influence the growth and sexuality in hydras (Loomis 1957, 1959, Burnett and Diehl 1964, Burnett 1968, Schulz and Lesh 1970, Gurkewitz et al. 1980, Shostak 1981). These environmental factors affect the morphogenesis of hydras by influencing the activity of the four kinds of morphogens or hormones, which consist of an activator and inhibitor for head formation and an activator and inhibitor for foot formation; the two activators are peptides with molecular weights of about 1000, and the inhibitors have smaller molecular weights (500) (Schaller et al. 1979). It is important to point out further that mutants known to affect morphogenesis of hydras (*non-budding, aberrant, maxi, mini*, discovered by Schaller et al. 1977a,b,c) control the quantity of localized hormones (morphogens).

The morphogenetic plasticity in *Aurelia aurita* involving suppression of the medusa stage, observed both in nature and in the laboratory (Thiel 1963a,b), led Thiel (1963a, 1966) to postulate the secondary origin of the medusal stage in evolution of the Scyphozoa; in his phylogenetic scheme the Stauromedusae are a stem group of the Scyphozoa, in contrast to the idea of their neotenic origin by Borradaile et al. (already noted). Chapman (1966) also postulated that the polypoid preceded the medusoid stage in the evolution of Scyphozoa. Further,

Werner (1980) was of the opinion that the basic cnidarian was the sessile polyp and that the medusa represents a polyp that has detached and adapted to the free-swimming way of life; the polyp cannot be considered as larval. Thus according to Thiel, Chapman, Werner, and some earlier workers (Remane 1954; Jägersten 1955, 1959, 1972), metagenesis represents a secondary phenomenon of progressive evolution, and evolution proceeded through the Anthozoa – Scyphozoa – Hydrozoa sequence. On the other hand, some workers (Hyman 1940, Hand 1959, Uchida 1963) maintained that the phylogenetic direction is the opposite, from the Hydrozoa to Anthozoa via the Scyphozoa. Such a phylogenetic inference throughout the Cnidaria is inherently very difficult because of their environment-dependent, high morphogenetic plasticity, involving reversion, frequent abnormalities, and alternate pathways of reversion.

B. THE SUBPHYLUM CTENOPHORA

Except for the order Platyctenea, the life cycle of the Ctenophora is exclusively pelagic (holopelagic). Jägersten (1972) regarded the holopelagic life cycle as primary within the Ctenophora, and the pelago-benthic life cycle, in which the adult life is passed on the sea bottom, as secondary. Three types of life cycle were recognized by Jägersten: (1) the type in Cydippidea, in which the larvae hatched from eggs resemble adults in all essential features; (2) the type in the other orders of the class Tentaculata (Lobata, Cestidea, and Platyctenea) and Beroidea (class Atentaculata), in which the "cydippid larvae" undergo metamorphosis; and (3) the type in the genus *Gastrodes* (Platyctenea) in which the larvae (covered with cilia) parasitize *Salpa*.

In the Cydippidea type (type 1 above) development is direct, and it can either be a larval neoteny as in Rotifera, in which metamorphosis into the adult has been permanently suppressed, or a direct development in which the ancestral larval stages have been completely suppressed as in Nematoda. As Jägersten thought, the larvae in Cydippidea are probably not true larvae, the true planula-like primary larvae having been completely lost. Therefore, the "cydippid larvae" are essentially juveniles, as in nematodes. As a corollary, Jägersten called the larvae in type 2 "secondary larvae"; such larvae should compare with the larvae in holometabolous insects, which have been derived from hemimetabolous insects with juvenile (nymphal) postembryonic development. Jägersten regarded the ciliated condition in type 3 as secondary reversal to the ancestral condition. Jägersten attributed the direct development in Cydippidea to his mystical "adult pressure" which can be construed as an alteration in gene regulation, pushing back the juvenile stage to the initial stage of development.

The holopelagic life cycle in most ctenophorans might have been enabled, at least in part, by their unique ability to become sexually mature easily, as is reflected in the phenomenon of dissogony, in which reproduction can occur at different times (at larval–juvenile and adult stages). In fact, as Pianka (1974) summarized, larval reproduction occurs in *Bolinopsis* species and *Charistephane fugiens*, and neoteny (paedogenesis of Pianka) in the form of juvenile reproduction has been observed in several ctenophorans. Chun (1892) proposed innate fragility of pelagic ctenophorans (despite their regenerative ability) and extensive predation, especially by cannibalistic predation by *Beroe,* as the cause of dissogony, and Pianka (1974) suggested unpredictable food supply as a factor. The physiological mechanism of dissogony remains unknown.

9

The Phylum Platyhelmintha

A. THE CLASS TURBELLARIA

The trochophore type larva has been found in primitive groups, Polycladida, Catenulida, and perhaps Nemertodermatida (Ruppert 1978). The Polycladida is exclusively marine, with one exceptional species that is freshwater in habitat (Voge 1963). The larva of *Rhynchoscolex* species (Catenulida) was found to be freshwater pelagic (Reisinger 1924). In these primarily marine turbellarians, therefore, metamorphosis definitely occurs. However, in many other turbellarians direct development is the rule.

Ax (1963a) divided the Turbellaria into the Archophora, with uniform ovary and entolecithal egg production, and the Neophora, in which the female gonad is separated into germaria and vitellaria. The above-mentioned primarily marine groups with indirect development (with free-swimming trochophore larvae as in the Polycladida) belong to the Archophora. The Neophora are also characterized by ectolecithal, yolk-rich eggs and modified embryonic development in cleavage and gastrulation, and by direct development (embryonization); suppression of larval genes appears to occur within the yolk-rich egg. It can be reasonably suspected that embryonization probably occurred in freshwater and terrestrial habitats as the ancestors of neophorans migrated into these habitats. A specific endocrine mechanism for vitellogenesis is unknown, although in planarians neural secretion plays a role during the differentiation and maturation of gonads (Lender 1980). Such a knowledge of living planarians, however, does not help us directly to understand how the enlargement of eggs could have occurred after the transition from sea to fresh water and land.

The Turbellaria are primarily hermaphroditic. However, after having acquired direct development, some freshwater triclads (Dugesiidae and Planariidae) acquired an asexual mode of reproduction by fissioning (scissiparity); the genital apparatus remains undeveloped in these individuals. With reference to the mechanism of the origin and persistence of asexuality, Beveridge (1982) was inclined to believe in the environmental switch of chromosomal and genic changes for asexual reproduction. However, as discussed below, the transition from sexuality to asexuality can be accounted for in terms of genetic assimilation of the originally environmentally induced asexual reproduction.

Curtis (1902) found that the life cycle of *Dugesia tigrina* (= *Planaria maculata*) in the populations near Falmouth, Massachusetts, was variable. In one locality reproduction was exclusively asexual; in one location it was exclusively sexual; and in two other locations sexual and asexual generations alternated at different seasons, sexual during spring and summer, and asexual toward the end of August and in September. This observation was confirmed later by Curtis and Schulze (1924). In two localities near Falmouth, Massachusetts, and in two localities in Virginia, Kenk (1937) found that there were at least two kinds of population of *D. tigrina*. One type is asexual and another predominantly sexual in reproduction. Kenk failed to induce, by various experimental means, sexuality in the asexually reproducing population, although he found that temperature and nutrition significantly control the fission rate. Asexuality in these populations therefore appears to have been fixed permanently, presumably through the process of genetic assimilation. Similarly in a Japanese species *Dugesia japonica* (= *D. gonocephala*), according to Okugawa (1957), two types of reproduction occur, the Kyushu strain, which exhibits only asexual reproduction, and the Nishioji strain, in which sexual and asexual reproduction alternate (i.e., sexual reproduction in winter and spring and asexual reproduction in summer and early September). Here again sexuality could not be induced by any experimental means in the asexual Kyushu strain, indicating genetic fixation. In Europe also the existence of sexual and asexual populations has long been known for several species. In laboratory populations of *Dugesia gonocephala* s. lat. derived from different parts of Europe, Benazzi (1974) found that two populations were obligatorily asexual, five populations showed a tendency toward sexuality, and three populations clearly showed both modes of reproduction. Benazzi (1974) further found, by crossing 40 sexual individuals from a population in Corsica, that sexuality and asexuality appear to segregate in a simple Mendelian fashion.

During the initial stage of the (presumed) genetic assimilation of asexuality some sexual individuals must have responded to the environmental signal so that they became asexual in reproduction. In two populations Curtis studied and in the Nishioji strain sexual reproduction clearly depends on seasonal higher temperature. The dependence on higher temperatures for fissioning (and asexuality) was also demonstrated in the experiments by Kenk (1937), Hyman (1941), and Okugawa (1957). Even in Sri Lanka sexual reproduction of *Dugesia mannophalus* occurs only during colder months when temperature is below 24°C. Conversely, relatively high temperatures are necessary for asexual reproduction in this species (De Silva and De Silva 1980).

Presumably, the environmentally (notably by high temperature) induced asexuality has become, under continuous exposure to proper environmental stimuli and selection pressure, completely genetically assimilated. It has been known that neurosecretion from the brain and nerve cord is necessary for scissiparity (Lender 1974), and Webb and Friedel (1979) isolated a neurosecretory substance that stimulates RNA synthesis in regenerating asexual *Dugesia tigrina*. When the environmentally induced asexual reproduction becomes permanent, a genetic change or changes (mutations) must involve the function of a level or levels of the endocrine mechanism (including the brain neurohormone) that controls the activity of neoblasts and reproductive organs.

Genetic assimilation is considered to proceed under the pressure of natural selection. Reynoldson (1983) speculated that it is advantageous to be able to reproduce rapidly by sexual reproduction in streams where unpredictable spates occur frequently. Similarly Calow et al (1979) contended that fission is more efficient at converting food to offspring, and it is favored in ecological circumstances where food is always limiting. Despite the prevalence of asexuality, in no species of triclads is asexual reproduction the exclusive method of reproduction (Beveridge 1982).

INTERSTITIAL TURBELLARIANS. Swedmark (1964) characterized interstitial turbellarians (mainly Kalyptorhynchia and Otoplanidae) by (1) development of the tactile cilia and sensory hairs, particularly at the cephalic and caudal ends, (2) formation of the caudal appendix with sensory hairs, (3) body shape and type of motion suitable to the interstitial mode of life, (4) reinforcement or new formation of adhesive elements, (5) morphological specialization of the pharynx and its accessory organs and other adaptations concerned with nutrition. Character 2 was discussed in detail for many interstitial turbellarians by Ax (1963b). Bush (1968) discussed the evolution and the adaptive significance of elongation of the body in interstitial turbellarians. Otoplanidae, with 26 genera and more than 50 species, are exclusively interstitial (mesopsammal) in habitat (Ax 1966). Retronectidae, described by Sterrer and Rieger (1974) as a new family of the Catenulida, have the elongate body and are characterized by some degenerative features in physiology and structures (the lack of paratomy, ciliated pits or furrow, mouth, pharynx, or gut, etc.). As a rule, this family occurs in a rather sheltered environment represented by sand of varying grain sizes and containing a high amount of organic detritus. According to R. M. Rieger (personal communication), Retronectidae and Otoplanidae appear so far confined to interstitial environment, and he believes that it is a fair assumption that these groups have originated in the interstitial environment.

The abundance of "interstitial turbellarian species" is clear in the study of population dynamics and life cycle in interstitial Acoela and Macrostomida by Faubel (1976). Among more recently reported interstitial turbellarians, *Drepanilla limophila* (described as a new genus and species of Dalyellioidea by Ehlers 1979), living in association with the sulfide system on subtidal sand flats, is so modified that it does not show a clear phylogenetic relationship with any other dalyellioids.

PARASITIC TURBELLARIANS.   Each of the five orders of the Turbellaria contains families with representatives living in association with other animals. Of these, remarkably few genera are parasitic in that they apparently derive all their nourishment from the host. Their life cycle is simple in that they never require more than one host species. Structural modifications in parasitic turbellarians lie principally in the reduction of the gut and in a general tendency to increase the size and fecundity of the female part of the reproductive system (Jennings 1971).

Fecampidae with three genera (*Fecampia, Kronborgia,* and *Glanduloderma*) are the only family of turbellarians in which all members are parasitic to crustaceans and lack the mouthparts, the pharynx, and the intestine at least in the postlarval stage (Christensen 1981). In *Fecampia* species juveniles enter the crustacean hosts and settle in the hemocoel where they grow and become sexually mature, losing in the process the eyes, mouth, buccal tube, and pharynx. The mature *Fecampia* then leaves the host and produces bottle or flask-shaped cocoons that are attached to the substratum. The parent then dies. Each cocoon contains two eggs and masses of yolk cells, and eventually two ciliated larval forms develop, leave the cocoon, and become the motile juvenile stages (Jennings 1971). According to Christensen (1981), cocoon formation occurs also in *Kronborgia* (with four described species, which are dioecious), although the cocoon in the monotypic genus *Glanduloderma* remains unknown.

Paravortex cardii is a "viviparous" turbellarian in the digestive gland of the common cockle, *Cardium edule.* Adults are approximately 0.80 mm long and their tegument bears numerous cilia and microvilli. The embryos of *P. cardii* are enclosed in capsules in the parenchyma of the adult worms. Mature embryos break out of the capsules, migrate through the parenchyma, penetrate the intestinal epithelia of the adult, and are released through the mouth of the worm (MacKinnon and Burt 1982).

B. THE CLASS TREMATODA

In trematodes, as in cestoids, eggs are usually laid outside the mother's body (oviparous), and trematodes always have the initial free-living larval stage. In the host's body they undergo conspicuous metamorphosis, reflecting the (parasitic) environmental influence on morphogenesis.

MONOGENEA. The life cycle of (most) monogenean trematodes does not involve more than one host. The larvae, called oncomiracidia, transform into adults in the (final) host. Monogenean trematodes inhabit mainly the skin and gills of marine and freshwater fishes; polystomatids have become parasitic in vertebrates (including terrestrial ones) other than fishes. They show a high degree of host specificity, as shown by Hargis (1953, 1957) and several other later workers; Bychowsky (1957) pointed out that 711 out of 957 species of monogeneans were each confined to a single host species. Yamaguti (1968) examined 2,097 specimens of 122 fish species and found 71% of monogeneans to be restricted to one host species, 85% to one or two species, and only 8% occurring in more than one family of hosts. From the ecological viewpoint, Rohde (1977, 1979) concluded that strict restriction in microhabitat exists for each species of monogeneans, and that neither competition (such as seen in character displacement) nor reinforcement of reproductive barriers can be responsible for microhabitat restriction. Little is known, however, regarding the mechanism of larval attraction to a particular host. Kearn (1967) showed that larvae of *Entobdella soleae* respond strongly to isolated epidermis from the host, *Solea solea,* but the chemical nature of the substance involved in this process remains completely unknown (Kearn 1981).

In a well-known monogenean *Polystoma integerrimum,* which infests the common European frog *Rana temporaria,* two types of adult have been known to occur. The first type, called the bladder type, infests the bladder of adults and matures slowly in 3–4 years. The second type, called the branchial type, infests the gills of young larvae less than 8 days old and matures very rapidly in 5 weeks. According to Williams (1961), the female genital duct in the bladder type is complete, consisting of the oviducal chamber, uterus, and paired vaginae, but in the branchial type the uterus and vaginae fail to develop. Therefore, the branchial type is considered to represent a progenetic neoteny associated with acceleration.

The dimorphism in *P. integerrimum* clearly depends on the site of infestation and the age of the host, and reflects different reactions of the essentially same genotype to different environmental stimuli in different sites of infestation; presumably, gills and bladders provide different physicochemical stimuli (in temperature, nutrition, etc.). Gallien's (1935) observation indicated that the development of the neotenous branchial form is influenced by enough food (blood) taken from the young hosts. Stunkard (1959a) also showed that gametogenesis in *Polystoma stellai* can be induced by transplantation of the host's (*Hyla septentrionalis*) pituitaries. It should be noted, however, that neurosecretory cells are distributed in various parts of the body in *P. integerrimum* (Skowerska 1977), and it is likely that the neurosecretion from these cells is more directly involved with development.

Baer (1951) maintained that the dimorphism in *P. integerrimum* has the selective advantage in that the neotenous phase, which appears when the first tadpoles are themselves developing, enables the parasitic stage to spread over a much larger area, and consequently to infest a greater number of individual hosts, in which, finally, even more slowly developing larvae will become adults. Following such an explanation, dimorphism appears to represent a case of adaptive response.

Based on the incomplete formation of the female genital duct system and some other features, Williams (1961) inferred neoteny that has occurred in several phyletic lines of Polystomatidae. For instance, *Protopolystoma xenopi,* though occurring in the bladder, shares the neotenous features of *Polystoma integerrimum,* and neoteny may be permanent in this species. The absence of the true uterus in *Polystomoides, Neopolystoma,* and *Polystomoidella,* as well as perhaps the absence of vaginae in *Oculotrema,* may be a secondary simplification of the female genital duct resulting from neoteny. Furthermore, according to Williams (1961), the permanently neotenous condition appears to be correlated with an aquatic life of the host. She thought that the absence of the uterus is not an appreciable disadvantage to polystomes infesting the hosts constantly immersed in water, for the parasites are able to oviposit over an extended period. In the absence of a uterus, insemination through the ovovitelline duct is easily accomplished, and the reduction of vaginae would not be detrimental. It is possible (or probable) that in the permanently aquatic habitat the neotenous morph, which was intially induced only environmentally (as seen in *P. integerrimum*), has been genetically fixed, presumably through the process of genetic assimilation.

As reviewed by Llewellyn (1981), both ovoviviparity and viviparity occur within the Monogenea. In *Callorhynchicola multitesticulata* eggs are retained in the uterus and, moreover, undergo embryonic development and produce nonciliated larvae (ovoviviparity). Llewellyn contended that intrauterine embryonic development in thin-shelled capsules could well have been a step toward the complete loss of shells and hence to viviparity. In fact, viviparity accompanied by precocious intrauterine postoncomiracidial development has occurred in species of *Gyrodactylus.* Viviparity in Gyrodactylidae, to which *Gyrodactylus* belongs, has long been known, and a characteristic feature of this family is the vitellaria that are absent or united with the ovary (Price 1937). It is therefore most likely that the transfer of yolk to developing eggs does not occur or is limited, and the resultant small size of the egg may well be the immediate cause of the precocious development of adult structures (adultation) resulting in viviparity. In *Gyrodactylus gurleyi* the diameters of eggs are $23-27$ μm, and the adult sizes are proportionately small ($435-510$ μm long).

DIGENEA. In digenetic trematodes the life cycle consists of successive developmental stages that occur in association with alternation of hosts. The first intermediate host is usually snails, rarely lamellibranchs or scaphopods, and the final hosts are usually vertebrates. Most workers agree that digeneans have been derived from dalyellioid rhabdocoeles and that molluscs were the primary host, where the parasites formerly became sexually mature. Attraction of the first-stage larvae, miracidia, to molluscan hosts has long been known (see Cheng 1968 for references of earlier works), and some more recent studies (Chernin

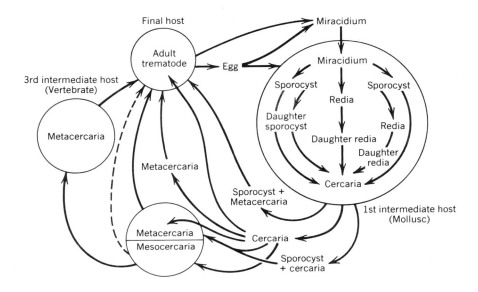

Figure 2. Diagram of the principal life cycles of digenetic trematodes (from Baer).

1970, Mason 1977, Roberts et al. 1979) also have shown conclusively that the miracidium of *Schistosoma* is attracted by snail-conditioned water. Enough constraints, however, appear to exist in achieving successful parasitization of molluscs (Cheng 1968).

A general scheme of life cycle of digenetic trematodes with two intermediate hosts (three hosts) is given in Figure 2. The ciliated miracidium larva hatches from the egg, either outside the final host or within the gut of the latter when the egg is swallowed. Within the first intermediate host (mollusc) a group of germ cells of the miracidium multiply to give rise to an elongate, sac-shaped sporocyst containing groups of cells derived from the original germ cells. These multiply rapidly and produce within the sporocyst either a second generation of sporocysts or a new type of the larva called the redia. Daughter sporocysts, rediae, or daughter rediae produce cercariae that appear in great numbers within these larvae. Cercariae are usually tailed, active forms that, in most cases, migrate out from the tissue of the mollusc, and finally escape into surrounding environment. The cercaria penetrates into an appropriate (invertebrate) host, loses its tail, and nearly always encysts. The larva, now known as the metacercaria, represents the infective stage, and when eaten by an appropriate vertebrate host, excysts and becomes adult in situ within the gut, or in some cases after migrating through the host's body (Baer 1951).

High plasticity in morphogenesis, as exhibited in the sequence of metamorphic changes in digeneans with three hosts (above), is evident further in "the tendencies in further evolution" discussed by Pearson (1972). They are:

1. Change from the early escape of the cercaria from the redia and completion of development in the mollusc's hemocoel, to full development of the cercaria within the redia/daughter sporocyst.
2. Progressive retardation of sexual development of the cercaria.
3. A small, short-lived primitive mother sporocyst that becomes larger and lives longer, producing more offspring.
4. An opposite tendency toward reduction of the mother sporocyst stage and production by it of a single redia.
5. Change from large eggs that embryonize and hatch in water, releasing short-lived miracidia, to small (more numerous?) eggs that hatch on ingestion by the molluscan host, thus increasing the infective life of the miracidium, and in the opposite direction.
6. Change to large, embryonized eggs that hatch on reaching the external environment.
7. Suppression of the redia/daughter sporocyst generation, and even of the suppression of both these generations and their replacement by modified stages of the adult generation.

These tendencies exhibit a wealth of cases of heterochrony (retardation and acceleration in development) that presumably have occurred, at least in part, in relation to environmental changes, although such an influence is not immediately clear in Pearson's generalization.

The three-host life cycle involving two intermediate hosts (already mentioned) is widespread, occurring in at least some members of 12 of the 18 major superfamilies (Pearson 1972). However, abridgement of the life cycle has also occurred as a result of (1) sexual maturity in the second host concomitant with the loss of the definitive host, (2) utilization of the definitive host as both second intermediate and definitive hosts, and (3) development of the metacercaria in the first intermediate host and loss of the second intermediate host (Pearson 1972). Modification in another direction is seen in the acquisition of the third intermediate host (Fig. 2) in certain strigeoids in which a new stage, the mesocercaria, is interpolated between the cercaria and metacercaria (Pearson 1959, 1972; Odening 1967). Here again heterochrony in sexual maturation and in the development of the metacercaria abounds, reflecting a high plasticity in morphogenesis.

When heterochrony is so common, a wide occurrence of (progenetic) neoteny is expected. Buttner (1950, 1951) in fact listed numerous cases (in some 20 genera distributing among a dozen families) in which reproductive maturation occurs or is likely to occur at the cercarial or metacercarial stage, although for Stunkard (1959b) these cases appeared to represent relicts, the survival of an earlier two-host (mollusc–invertebrate) cycle. Pearson (1972) rejected Stunkard's view because the occurrence of organs of attachment such as suckers in visceral parasites cannot be accounted for by Stunkard's theory.

An apparently well-founded case of neoteny is that of *Genarchella genar-*

chella (Hemiuridae). According to Szidat (1956, 1959), progenetic neoteny occurred in this species as a result of precocious sexual maturation in the cercaria and suppression of the cercaria–cystophora stage. These occurred, according to Szidat, as a consequence of the infestation of the definitive fish host (Charcinidae and Siluridae) by cercariae, eliminating the arthropodan intermediate hosts (*Cyclops,* etc.); the cercaria–cystophore stage occurs in the arthropodan intermediate hosts in the related species (*Halipegus ovocaudatus*). Szidat further hypothesized that in the new freshwater habitat the action of pituitary and thyroid glands was accelerated to produce more thyroxine, that this influenced the reproductive cells of the parasites in inducing neoteny of the latter, and that the neoteny has become genetically fixed as a result of *Dauermodifikation*. As discussed below, the induction of neoteny of parasites by the host's hormone is at the most indirect.

According to Van den Broek (1978), the life cycle of *Asymphylodora tincae* (Monorchiidae) in the region near Amsterdam includes a facultative progenetic neoteny; cercariae penetrating *Bithynia* species develop into metacercarial cysts or into progenetic neoteny. The incidence of the latter increases at higher temperatures, and hence is more common in summer than in winter. Van den Broek concluded that water temperature above 20° C may stimulate progenetic development in the animal.

External temperature also influences significantly the developmental process of *Fasciola gigantica*. As shown by Dinnik and Dinnik (1964), at 16°C or less rediae do not produce cercariae in this species. The first-generation rediae, developed from the sporocyst, and all the rediae of subsequent generations produce only daughter rediae and do not change over to the production of cercariae as long as the low temperatures of the cold season last. However, as soon as the cold season ends and the temperature of the water in the aquariums containing the infested snails rises to a mean maximum of 20°C, all the rediae switch to cercarial generation.

When, as Stunkard (1957) discussed, a trematode species is not specific with regard to the final vertebrate host, the highly variable phenotype produced would be perplexing for taxonomists. For instance, the liver fluke, *Fasciola hepatica,* has migrated to various parts of the world, and it matures in man, monkeys, sheeps, goats, cattle, buffalo, deer, camels, llamas, elephants, horses, asses, dogs, rabbits, guinea pigs, squirrels, beavers, and kangaroos. The size and morphology of these parasites are profoundly affected by the host species in which the worm develops, and the specimens from a cow, a rabbit, and a guinea pig manifest differences far greater than those usually employed to distinguish species. Similarly, many taxonomic characters in *Plagiorchis noblei* (Plagiorchiidae) induced by different vertebrate host species are highly variable, and hence they are not reliable taxonomically (Blankespoor 1974). It is hard to conceive of genetic fixation of these characters.

With reference to the hormonal influence on development, some earlier studies (Meade and Pratt 1966, Muftic 1969) indicated a possible influence of the snail's hormone on the earlier stages of development in trematodes. However, a recent study by Sluiters and Geraerts (1984) showed that the development of *Trichobilharzia ocellata,* which parasitizes the gastropod *Lymnaea stagnalis,* does not depend on the dorsal body hormone of the host (which stimulates vitellogenesis and differentiation of the female accessory organs). Many earlier works dealt with the effect of thyroid hormones on development. However, the effect appears to be only indirect. For instance, Abdel-Wahab et al. (1971) found that, in the case of murine schistosomiasis (*Schistosoma mansoni*), cercarial penetration was lower in the hypothyroid animals. The schistosomes in the hypothyroid animals were small, whereas those in hyperthyroid animals were large, matured earlier, and produced more eggs. Cornford (1974) found that in thyroxine-treated *Schistosomatium douthitti* oxygen consumption increased, and both males and females from hyperthyroid hosts were significantly larger than flukes from normal mice. The parasite *Fasciola hepatica* showed no sensitivity to various mammalian hormones including thyroxine (Hutton et al. 1972).

Thus the idea of direct effect of thyroid hormone in inducing neoteny in trematodes and cestodes, proposed by Szidat (1959), has not been proved in later works, although the host's hormone may affect the activity of neurosecretory cells in the parasites. The neurosecretory cells have been described in many trematode species since the earlier reports by Ude (1962), Dixon and Mercer (1965), and Silk and Spence (1969). It must be a neurohormone, or hormones, produced from these cells in the parasites that is directly responsible for gene regulation, enabling a sequence of metamorphic changes and presumably also sexual maturation. Thus far, however, the function of the neurosecretory cells has been very incompletely understood; Matsakis' (1970) study showed increased activity of the cells during noon hours in *Opisthodiscus diplodiscoides.*

C. THE CLASS CESTOIDEA

Although in some pseudophyllideans and trypanorhyncha a free-living, ciliated oncosphere, known as the coracidium, hatches from the egg, in all other tapeworms the oncosphere remains within the egg. In either case the oncosphere is ingested by an intermediate host. The paucity (or absence) of the data on host finding among cestoids in literature may be related to the relative scarcity of a free-living stage in their life cycle. According to Mueller (1959), in those groups where the free-living coracidium occurs, ingestion by suitable crustacean intermediate hosts appears to be entirely fortuitous. The cestodes employ arthropods as the first hosts, and parasitize all classes of vertebrates (Stunkard 1967).

Morphogenetic plasticity as reflected in metamorphoric changes during alternation of hosts appears to be somewhat more rigid than in the Trematoda, and this may be due to more restricted sites occupied by cestodes in intermediate and definitive hosts. The basic sequence of cestode development summarized by Freeman (1973) consists of (1) the monoecious (rarely dioecious) adult that produces (2) an ovum that develops into (3) an oncosphere, a six-hooked (hexacanth) larva that, once eaten by a suitable host—usually an invertebrate—migrates to a suitable parental site where it (4) metamorphoses and grows as a metacestode that includes all growth phases between oncosphere and first evidence of sexuality (i.e., when it has a fully differentiated scolex of adult size and a body showing proglottidation, or first sign of approaching sexual maturation), and (5) the sexually reproducing adult in the enteron. Two types of metacestode development have been recognized, namely, the primitive type, in which complete ontogeny occurs without a primary lacuna, and the neoteric (i.e., recent) type, in which a primary lacuna develops during ontogeny.

In the primitive development, following a sequence of metamorphic changes, the metacestode becomes a plerocercoid that varies with species. In *Dibothriocephallus latum* (Pseudophyllidae), for instance, the oncosphere within the egg hatches and becomes a free-swimming ciliated coracidium. Copepods eat the coracidia of *D. latum;* the cilia are shed and the young larvae migrate into the body cavity (hemocoel) there, metamorphosing into procercoids. The fish (salmon, trout, etc.) eat the copepods and the procercoids are freed in the intestine of the fish, but reenter a parenteral site where they become elongated plerocercoid metacestodes. Deviation from the developmental process in *D. latum* in other species is rather a rule, as seen in Table 1 of Freeman (1973). The number of hosts required to complete a life cycle in the species of Pseudophyllidea and Cyclophyllidea ranges from two to four. The procercoid does not occur in *Marsipometra hastata* with two hosts, in some species two stages of plerocercoid occur, etc. These facts indicate that heterochrony, partly associated with the number of hosts they acquired, has presumably been a dominant feature during their evolution; heterochrony in the strict sense (i.e., with reference to the ancestral species) is, however, not immediately clear. In neoteric development the oncosphere metamorphoses into a cysticercoid, cysticercus, or obvious derivatives (see Freeman 1973 or textbooks of parasitology).

Morphogenetic plasticity also manifests itself in infinite numbers of hosts they seem to be able to alternate. This is related to the fact that cestodes move up and down through the trophic level in the ecosystem, depending on the number of times they can be eaten. Actually, the maximum number of transfers is restricted to 4 or 5, and in terrestrial cestodes the number of trophic levels is usually restricted to 2 (Freeman 1973). As Baer (1951) and Joyeux and Baer (1961) suggested, the life cycle requiring two intermediate hosts (an arthropod and a vertebrate) was probably primary. However, reduction in the number of hosts has occurred in certain cases, resulting in acceleration. The evolution of Caryophyllidea discussed below appears to be a case in point, although some authors have regarded their life cycle as most primitive. It appears legitimate to regard the migration of caryophyllids to the freshwater habitat as secondary.

Following Mackiewicz (1981), the Caryophyllidea are regarded as an order derived from the multiproglottid ancestor. They are characterized most prominently by the lack of proglottidation. They have freshwater oligochaetes (Tubificidae and Naididae) as the first host; the oligochaetes eat the operculate eggs that liberate the oncosphere larvae, which metamorphose into the procercoids in the coelom or seminal vesicles of the host. The oligochaetes are eaten by various fishes (almost exclusively freshwater fishes); the procercoid loses the cercomer on digestion by the fish host and develops *in situ* into the plerocercoid and sexual maturation occurs. Thus, based on Mackiewicz's theory, the monozoic body plan acquired in the sexually mature plerocercoid adult in Caryophyllidea (except *Archigetes*) can be regarded as a case of progenetic neoteny in which the expression of ancestral genes for proglottidation has been suppressed. Thus their migration into the freshwater habitat has evidently resulted in the unique evolution. Some species of *Archigetes* require only the first oligochaete host to complete a life cycle, and sexual maturation occurs in the procercoid that develops in the host. Evidently, the degree of progenetic neoteny is more pronounced in *Archigetes* species than in other caryophyllids, even the plerocercoid stage having been suppressed in their ontogeny.

With reference to the cause of neoteny in caryophyllids, Szidat (1959) suggested that the hormonal activity of hosts increased as they migrated into fresh water, and that this induced neoteny of caryophyllids parasitizing the intestine. This idea was accepted as a testable hypothesis by Mackiewicz (1982). The effect of testosterone on the development of cestodes has been known for a long time. Addis (1946) showed that the reproductive development and growth of *Hymenolepis diminuta* stops in the castrated male rat, and that the treatment with testosterone restores this process. Among more recent studies, Novak (1975) showed that the application of testosterone increases the tetrathyridial population of *Mesocestoides corti* in gonadectomized mice of both sexes. These facts and many other similar experiments indicated that the host's sex hormone can influence the development of cestodes and the degree of infestation of parasites in nature. As discussed below, the host's hormone(s) might interact with the parasite's neurohormone(s).

More recent works, including Webb (1976), Webb and Davey (1976), and Specian et al. (1979), reported the presence of neurosecretory cells in *Hymenolepis* spp., and Gustafson and Wikgren (1981) reported the same in *Diphyllobothrium dendriticum*. There is also evidence that cestodes are capable of synthesizing and accumulating farnesols (insect juvenile hormone mimic) as Frayha and Fairbairn (1969) and Frayha (1974) reported. With reference to the mechanism of release of neurohormones, Tofts and Meerovitsch (1973) found that when farnesyl methyl ether (FME) is applied to *Hymenolepis diminuta* a significant decrease in weight gain (not in the number of proglottids) occurs. These workers also observed that the release of neurosecretory material from the neurosecretory cells in the rostellum was more advanced in time in the FME-treated worms than in the control, suggesting that application of FME acted as an environmental stimulus, which caused premature release of neurosecretion and consequent dwarfism. All these facts, however, constitute only indirect evidence, merely suggesting the endocrine involvement with development. It should be pointed out further that all these studies were based on adults, not on metacestodes.

When cestodes infest many species, as do some trematodes (Sect. 9B), the range of phenotypic variation is great. A well-known case is *Hymenolepis diminuta,* which infests many species of insects belonging to five orders. The phenotypic variation is clearly associated with different hosts, which most probably influence the development of the parasite. Consequently, in many instances varieties or races peculiar to certain hosts do not represent different species (Stunkard 1957).

The possibility of environmental induction of neoteny and concomitant origination of higher taxa can also be surmised from some experiments. Thus Smyth (1971) found, during in vitro culturing of *Echinococcus granulosus* from the protoscolex to the adult form, that a proportion of organisms (10%) in one culture developed sexually mature genitalia without becoming segmented (in fact *folded* without clear internal demarcation; see Melhorn et al. 1981) into proglottids. They were smaller than fully segmented specimens from dogs or from normal cultures. The resultant form actually represented an artificially induced progenetic neoteny, and it suggested independent control of germinal and somatic developments. Further, as Smyth thought, the production of such abnormal individuals appears to be due to environmental (i.e., experimental) induction rather than to mutation, for a series of worms ranging from nonsegmented (monozoic) to fully segmented worms appeared in the same condition. Similarly, Smyth and Davies (1975) were able to suppress proglottidation in some 70–80% of a population of *Echinococcus multilocularis* under axenic conditions (in either monophasic or diphasic media). The resultant worms were monozoic and asymmetric, with a lateral swelling produced by the cirrus sac. Smyth and Davies maintained that if such specimens had been recorded from a natural host rather than a cultural tube, the organism would undoubtedly have been classified as a member of a different subclass (the Cestodaria). Smyth and Davies presumed that some nutritional or physiochemical difference exists between the conditions provided by the cat or dog and those in their culture system, and that such a difference would enable polyzoic (but never monozoic) development to take place in the former, but mainly monozoic in the latter. The physiochemical difference must induce different activities of a morphogenetic hormone which, in turn, would induce different phenotypes. The occurrence of essentially monozoic tapeworms is apparently fairly widespread, as seen in the new class Cotyloda proposed by Wardle et al. (1974), which includes the Crayophyllidea and five other essentially progenetically neotenous orders.

10

The Phylum Annelida

A. THE CLASS POLYCHAETA

Although the Archiannelida with five families (Dinophilidae, Nerillidae, Poly-gordidae, Protodrilidae, Saccocirridae) are treated as a subclass of the Poly-chaeta, the consensus of a majority of recent workers (Dales 1962, Clark 1969, 1978, Orrhage 1974, Fauchald 1974) is that the Archiannelida are polyphyletic in origin, and this agrees essentially with Remane (1932), who regarded them as an assemblage of three or four lines of simplified polychaetes. Therefore, they are treated here concurrently with other polychaetes.

According to Hermans (1979), polychaetes with small oocyte volumes (e.g., *Armandia brevis, Hydroides uncinatus*) have trochophore larvae that are re-leased as planktonic forms. In slightly larger eggs the lecithotrophic trocho-phore-like stage is passed through within the egg; the worms develop several segments and become metatrochophores or nectochaetae before feeding com-mences. In the species with well-developed brood-protecting structures (such as tubes) eggs are very large, and there may be no free-living larval stage. Instead, a preadult may hatch from the egg and begin its independent existence in the benthic habitat of the adult. *Scoloplos armiger* emerges as a 12-segmented juvenile.

In *Neanthes caudata* (Nereidae), according to Reish (1957), the male incu-bates large eggs within a mucoid tube, and the egg measures 600 μm in diame-ter. The production of large eggs is related to the confined habitat (tube) in which the female lives. A ciliated embryonic stage is lacking and there is no larval planktonic stage, and the adult does not undergo metamorphosis into epitoky prior to sexual maturity; 55 segments are eventually formed. Thus this case can be regarded as progenetic neoteny associated with enlarged eggs and consequently accelerated development (embryonization); unique physico-chemical (environmental) factors within the tube can be considered as affecting oogenesis in producing the large eggs. Most sabellariids are also tubicolous and their eggs are relatively large (Berrill 1977).

Of the 35 species of polychaetes occurring in four locations near Godhavn, Greenland, according to Curtis (1977), 25 species produce directly developing or lecithotrophic larvae, showing varying degrees of embryonization; eight species produce planktonic larvae; and two produce asexually. His Table 3 indicates that the diameter of an oocyte is clearly larger in the species with direct development or with lecithotrophic larvae than in the species with planktonic larvae. Thus the dominance of abridged development in this Subarctic area is clear, as predicted by Thorson's rule, and presumably cold temperature is an important morphogenetic factor inducing the production of yolk-rich, large eggs and consequent embryonization.

Within the genus *Protodrilus* (Protodrilidae), which inhabits interstitial sands, some species (*P. rubropharyngeus, P. adhaerens, P. ciliatus*) described by Jägersten (1940a,b, 1952) are highly adapted for pelagic life as larvae, being provided with the funnel-shaped esophagus that serves to capture plankton. In *P. ciliatus* the female lays about 200 eggs (each 48 μm in diameter). In *P. adhaerens* the female lays smaller eggs (each 40–45 μm in diameter) in the cocoon fixed to sand grains, and consequently pelagic larval development is somewhat shortened (Jägersten 1952). Furthermore, Swedmark (1954) found that in *Protodriloides symbioticus* (described as *Protodrilus*) pelagic larval development has been completely eliminated. The species is only 2 mm long and smallest within the genus; it has segmental adhesive organs, and the glands for cocoon production occur in the female. Four to ten large eggs (100–110 μm in diameter each) are laid in the cocoon, and the larval stage comparable with the trochophore larva is spent in the cocoon; hence the pelagic larval stage does not occur. In this case large eggs have resulted in small adults, but not in the omission of the larval stage. In *Protodriloides chaetifer,* studied by Jouin (1962), the developmental process is similar to that of *P. symbioticus.* Eggs are large, ranging from 140 to 150 μm in diameter. Larval development proceeds in the cocoon and there is no pelagic larval phase.

In the interstitial polychaetes Westheide (1984) tabulated (his Table 1), the number of mature oocytes at a time and the diameter of a mature oocyte (egg) are clearly negatively correlated. For instance, *Protodrilus albicans* produces about 1200 eggs, and each egg is 30 μm in diameter, whereas in 12 species listed the diameter of an egg is 100 μm or greater, and the number of mature oocytes (at a time) is less than 15 (often one or two). His analysis also clearly shows that smaller adults tend to be produced from larger eggs. Furthermore, the mode of development is said to be direct in the species with large eggs. A case Westheide (1984) did not mention was an unidentified sabellid belonging to Fabricinae, which is dwarf as an adult (Berrill 1977). Here, dwarfism is clearly related to enlarged eggs. Its body length is 2.5 mm maximum, but the mature egg is approximately 140 μm in diameter, which may be more than half of the entire width of the worm, and only one egg is laid at a time; in many polychaetes with much larger sizes the diameter of an egg is 60–80 μm. Juvenile features (as seen in the number of thoracic and abdominal segments, in the number and nature of tentacles, abortive development of segmental blood vessels, etc.) are clearly retained, although the gonad is developed. Presumably, development is direct and the adult is neotenous in this sabellid species.

In some species of archiannelids large eggs are known to be produced through unusual developmental processes. In *Diurodrilus ankeli* fusion of paired oocyte rudiments in early stage of oogenesis results in an unpaired egg (Ax 1967). Jouin (1968) indicated the possibility that in *Mesonerilla* species small oocytes serve as nutrients for the development of few large eggs. In *Dinophilus gyrociliatus,* according to Grün (1972), two types of eggs occur: the smaller eggs that develop into males and are released into the cocoon early and larger ones that develop into females.

In polychaetes, as Eckelbarger's (1983) review shows, both extraovarian and intraovarian oogeneses are widespread, and yolk synthesis is carried out either within the oocyte (autosynthetic) or outside the oocyte (heterosynthetic, secondary); there are several routes of yolk precursor entry into developing oocytes (through oolemma, microvilli, nurse cells, endocytosis, etc.). Eckelbarger regarded heterosynthesis as a more derived process of vitellogenesis. Our knowledge of the endocrine mechanism for vitellogenesis in some polychaetes has become more complete in recent years. Olive (1976) found that there exists a brain vitellogenesis-promoting hormone in *Eulalia viridis,* and he (1979) suggested the occurrence of a wide range of gonadotropic hormones in Eunicidae, Phyllodocidae, Darvilleidae, Nephthyidae, and so on. Clark (1979) attributed synchronization in reproduction to the effect of environmental factors that trigger the action of the endocrine mechanism for vitellogenesis and other reproductive events in polychaete families. Furthermore, more recent studies by Olive and Bentley (1980) and Bentley (1982) indicated the presence of a gonadotropic hormone in the brain of *Nephthys hombergii,* and that concentration of the hormone increases to a high degree in November (Bentley and Olive 1982), indicating that the hormonal activity is seasonally controlled.

It seems reasonable to suppose that the presence of such an endocrine mechanism that responds to environmental signals (in temperature, photoperiod, etc.) during vitellogenesis is widespread within the Polychaeta, and that under some extreme environmental conditions and in some (or many) species the endocrine mechanism permits the entry of a greater quantity of yolk precursor into fewer developing oocytes, thereby resulting in the production of fewer yolk-rich eggs. However, this hypothesis does not apply to the unusual developmental processes of large eggs in some archiannelids (above), and presumably also not to some other very small species. The endocrine mechanism for vitellogenesis may not be sufficiently developed to be functional in the dwarfed interstitial polychaetes and archiannelids, in which the development of other structures also tends to be arrested. Yet the production of large eggs is related, at least, to unusual habitats (coastal interstitial habitats with lower salinities) in these cases.

In the following cases of evolutionary process of polychaetes changing environments appear to affect primarily postoval development. A large number of polychaete species migrate to the surface of the sea for spawning, and nearly all of them undergo some structural modifications or metamorphosis when they become sexually mature, to suit them for their brief pelagic existence; the metamorphosis of the immature worm into a special reproductive form is known as epitoky. Epitokal modifications include the development of foliaceous parapodial lamellae, the elongation of the dorsal and ventral cirri, the replacement of chaetae by specialized natatory chaetae, considerable development of the vascular system, particularly at the respiratory surface, histolysis of the body wall and reconstruction of much of the remaining musculature, histolysis of the gut and septa, the development of special sense organs on the cirri, and enlargement of the eyes (Clark 1961).

Most nereids undergo all these changes to a greater or lesser extent. A few members of 15 other families have been reported to migrate to the surface of the sea for spawning, but almost all of them undergo considerably less structural modification than nereids, and some apparently undergo no change at all (Clark 1961). Within the Nereidae again, however, suppression of epitoky has been reported for a number of cases. The nereids have made a substantial penetration into the freshwater habitat. In these freshwater nereids epitokal metamorphosis and spawning are rare, the pelagic larval phase is abbreviated or suppressed, and many of the freshwater species are known or believed to be viviparous (Clark 1961). Thus these freshwater species are neotenous (atokous), lacking the epitokal phase.

Nereis limnicola is a well-known such nereid that occurs in estuarine situations along the northwestern coast of the United States and in Merced Lake near San Francisco (which is a young post-Pleistocene freshwater lake). This species is atokous, hermaphroditic, and viviparous; fertilization occurs in the coelom, where development proceeds, and parturition occurs by rupture of the adult body (Smith 1958). As discussed below, the lower salinity in the estuarine situation appears to have induced atokous reproduction, by affecting the pattern of hormonal secretion.

In nereids a single hormone from the neurosecretory cells in the brain has been known to control somatic growth, regeneration, and gonadal development (Durchon 1952, Porchet 1976, Olive and Clark 1978, Olive 1979). It has been established that in the presence of sufficient amounts of the hormone somatic development occurs, and that reproductive development ensues under declining titers of the hormone; spermatogenesis occurs in the presence of reduced titers of the hormone, and oogenesis occurs at all levels of declining titers of the hormone. Furthermore, epitoky occurs in the absence of the hormone. When the reduced hormone secretion persists, therefore, epitokous metamorphosis would be prevented. In the meantime, reproductive development would ensue under reduced titers of the circulating hormone, and the atokous (neotenous) reproduction could result. It can be surmised that most likely the lower salinity in the habitat of this species has induced the necessary mode of hormonal secretion for the atokous reproduction, and the latter might have been genetically fixed (presumably through the process of genetic assimilation).

Because of the tendency for *N. limnicola* to be broken into isolated populations, Smith (1958) thought that the entire western population could not have arisen from a single self-fertilizing hermaphroditic ancestor. Rather, as he thought, a genetic tendency for internal self-fertilization and incipient viviparity may have been widespread throughout estuarine populations of the stock ancestral to *N. limnicola.* For reproduction in fresh water (or in water with reduced salinities) viviparity may be quite indispensable for the survival of a population deprived of a periodic access to more saline water; a widespread genetic tendency to viviparity, even if rarely expressed, in consecutively hermaphroditic cross-fertilization may have been rigorously selected for again and again in estuarine situations exposed to repeated drastic lowering of salinity for extended periods, and eventually the habit of viviparity became genetically established.

Nereid species are often polymorphic with respect to the stage of development at which reproductive maturation occurs. For instance, certain nereids are known to reproduce only by atoky, as seen in *Nereis diversicolor, Micronereis variegata,* and *Nereis caudata* (Durchon 1955); these species must be regarded as neotenous. In those nereids in which reproduction occurs as heteronereids (epitokous), portions of the body undergoing metamorphosis can vary in different species (Durchon 1955), and this may perhaps be attributed to different tissue sensitivities of different segments to the brain hormone, and in *Perinereis tenuisetis* atoky is more pronounced in the male than in the female. *Perinereis cultrifera* exhibits a geographical dimorphism. It is atokous in the Mediterranean and epitokous in the English Channel (Durchon 1955, 1965); this appears to reflect the effect of latitude (photoperiodic and/or temperature effects) on the phenotype. Durchon (1965) explained the atoky as due to the hormonal disturbance, which is genetically based. This situation can be reinterpreted that initially the production of atoky was environmentally induced (temperature and photoperiod), then the accumulation of genocopies (i.e., mutations inducing the proper endocrine functioning for atoky) has resulted in the occurrence of the permanent, genetically determined atokous phenotype (genetic assimilation).

INTERSTITIAL POLYCHAETES. Many polychaetes have established themselves in the interstitial biotope. According to Laubier (1967) and Westheide (1981), interstitial polychaetes occur in 16 families (Pisionidae, Phyllodocidae, Hesionidae, Syllidae, Sphaerodoridae, Nereidae, Nephytidae, Glyceridae, Goniadidae, Dorvilleidae, Orbinidae, Paraonidae, Cirratulidae, Ctenodrillidae, Stygocapitellidae, Psammodrilidae). To this list should be added Eunicidae (Dohle 1967), Sigalionidae (Laubier 1975), Sabellidae (Berrill 1977), as well as (Questidae and Acrocirridae) Westheide (1981) reported.

Hartmann-Schroeder (1964) found that in families apparently ecologically and morphologically preadapted to interstitial life (Glyceridae, Phyllodocidae, Goniadidae) interestitial species are rare. On the contrary, in the Syllidae, Hesionidae, and some others, which are neither ecologically nor morphologically preadapted for the interestitial habitat, there are more species predisposed to colonize interstitial biotopes. These facts appear to reflect the high morphological plasticity that manifests itself in interstitial habitats, and that the colonization of the interstitial habitats appears to be primarily a matter of opportunity.

The diminution of the body in interstitial polychaetes, which so often depends heavily on enlargement of eggs (see above), involves neotenous reduction of structures as emphasized by Westheide (1984). Earlier, Westheide (1981) recognized two types of evolution: (1) regressive evolution in body size and number of segments and setae and (2) modification of appendages in number and forms. Combinations of these tendencies result, according to Westheide (1981), in increased function of appendages as sense organs, development of extremely long filiform appendages that serve, perhaps, as adhesive organs, reduction to small, often tubercle-shaped tentacles and cirri, and finally the loss of all appendages.

In the following example the phylogenetic derivation of an interstitial species is clear. The genus *Psammodrilus* (Psammodrilidae) is characterized by the presence of an unique pharyngeal apparatus (derived from longitudinal muscles that develop at the stage when the worm is 1.00 mm long) (Swedmark 1955). Swedmark (1958) described a new genus and species, *Psammodriloides faubeli,* which closely resembles *Psammodrilus balanoglossoides;* the latter is much larger, the body volume being 25 times greater than *P. faubeli. P. faubeli* measures only 1 mm in body length and lacks the pharyngeal apparatus. It is therefore most likely that *P. faubeli* arose as a result of arrest of development of the pharyngeal apparatus that develops in *Psammodrilus.* Hence *Psammodriloides* is most probably a neotenous relative of *Psammodrilus.* In *P. faubeli* the egg is large; its diameter is about 110 μm, occupying almost 2/3 of the width of the abdomen, and a maximum of nine eggs is produced. In *P. balanoglossoides* also the diameter of an egg is 100–110 μm, although 75 eggs are produced. These facts indicate that progenetic (?) neoteny in *P. faubeli* is due not to the difference in egg size, but to a shorter juvenile development. *P. faubeli* has been found exclusively in organic sediments at a depth of 15–50 m, and presumably the ambient environmental stimuli in such a habitat have induced the precocious arrest of juvenile development. The trochophore larval stage is unknown for both *Psammodrilus* (Swedmark 1955) and *Psammodriloides* (Swedmark 1958), hence their development may be direct.

An extreme of the suppression of developmental stages appears to occur in *Pholoe swedmarki* discussed by Laubier (1975), in which an intra-elytral brooding involving internal fertilization may occur. Laubier found a juvenile with six setigerous segments underneath the elytra, and he hypothesized that this species may undergo a direct development involving the supression of trochophore, metatrochophore, and nectochete.

Recently, two neotenous interstitial dorvilleids have been described: *Ikosipodus carolinensis* was described as a new genus and species (Westheide 1982) and *Apodotrocha progenerans* also as a new genus and species (Westheide and Riser 1983). *A. progenerans* lay small numbers of large eggs (the number and the size were not given). Westheide and Riser thought, therefore, that the species has a direct development. The adult is only 0.6 mm long and has six trunk segments. It lacks parapods, setae, and fleshy appendages, but has three caudal cirri. The general habitus resembles a larval stage of the Dorvilleidae, and hence the neoteny of this species can be progenetic.

PARASITIC POLYCHAETES. Among polychaete parasites, a well-known case is *Ichthyotomus sanguinarius,* which is found fixed to the fin of an eel, *Myrus vulgaris.* The organ of attachment of this worm is two protrusible stylets located on the dorsal and ventral surfaces of the proboscis. The worm is known to be sexually mature when only 2 mm long with only 13 segments, although the worm grows to be a total length of 8–10 mm, with 70–100 segments. Baer (1951) regarded the peculiar mixture of larval and adult structures as neoteny. There are many eunicidians, mostly arabellids found inside the bodies of other worms (Pettibone 1957).

B. THE CLASS CLITELLATA

In the Clitellata the egg is often large. In tubificid and lumbriculid oligochaetes and glossiphoniid leeches, which are freshwater aquatic in habitat, large eggs range in different species from about 300 μm to 1.0 mm in diameter; smaller eggs in other clitellates, with the partial exception of Branchiobedellidae, are secondary (Anderson 1973). At any rate, such a range of egg sizes is clearly greater than that in most polychaetes. Eggs are laid in the cocoon where the worms hatch as juveniles. Early larval stages such as trochophore and metatrochophore present in the Polychaeta have been completely lost in their ontogeny, and therefore the development is direct; it should be recalled that in some polychaetes the larval stage is spent in the cocoon. Thus the origin of the Clitellata appears to have been related to enlarged, yolk-rich eggs laid in the cocoon; presumably, such environments have induced profound alteration in the pattern of gene regulation to produce characteristic features of the clitellates (see Sect. 3B2 for discussion).

Enlargement of eggs in oligochaetes must have occurred as their ancestors changed their habitat from sea to freshwater and terrestrial habitats, presumably by deploying the kind of endocrine mechanism for heterosynthetic vitellogenesis present in some polychaetes today. Some freshwater oligochaetes with large eggs may still have such an endocrine mechanism, although in no species has such a heterosynthetic vitellogenesis been reported so far. Thus in *Eisenia* the mechanism of gonad development is that a brain hormone stimulates the testicular androgenic hormone for spermatogenesis, and that oogenesis (including vitellogenesis) is an autodifferentiating system that occurs without direct hormonal intervention (Lattaud 1971, 1975, 1980, 1982). In *Erpobdella octoculata* a peptide hormone in a compartment of nerve cells in the supraesophageal ganglion stimulates spermatogenesis (Webb 1980) and in *Macrobdella decora* also brain hormone induces spermatogenesis (Webb and Omar 1981), although in *Poecilobdella viridis* the brain appears to play a role in oogenesis (Kulkarni and Nagabhushnam 1980). In most clitellates with protandric hermaphroditism, therefore, the androgenic hormone and perhaps also the brain hormone must cease their action (which is likely to be environmentally triggered) before autosynthetic oogenesis ensues, and in this sense the hormonal involvement with oocyte development may be said to be indirect.

At any event, the omission of vulnerable larval stages in the freshwater and terrestrial habitats, which occurred as a consequence of enlargement of eggs and concomital embryonization, must have been selectively advantageous. Presumably, therefore, natural selection has contributed to perfection of the mechanism of enlargement of eggs and consequent embryonization.

The cocoon, in which the eggs are laid in small batches, is secreted by a specialized part of the skin known as the clitellum. In lumbricids copulation has been known to induce cocoon production. The experiment of André et al. (1971) involving transplantation of the brain of the mated (and cocoon-producing) earthworm into the unmated earthworm also resulted in the production of cocoons. Marcel (1980) located the brain hormone for cocoon production which might be inhibitory in action. It should be remembered that cocoon production occurs in some polychaetes.

Hermaphroditism has been established within the Clitellata; in most oligochaetes hermaphroditism is simultaneous (Herlant-Meewis 1975). However, under some environmental conditions parthenogenesis appears to have arisen as a modification of the ancestral hermaphroditism. Thus, according to Jaenike and Selander (1979), 17 of 33 species of North American Lumbricidae reproduce primarily or exclusively by parthenogenesis. The parthenogenetic species occur in litter or decaying logs, and usually in upper or middle soil layers, in contrast to hermaphroditic species, which often occur in deeper, more stable layers. Because in *Eisenia* (belonging also to Lumbricidae), as already noted, only the male gonad development depends on the brain hormone and testicular androgenic hormone, parthenogenesis could occur when the endocrine system controlling the male gonad development is not functioning. It would seem to follow that when spermatogenesis does not occur, only oogenesis could occur ahormonally, and hence parthenogenesis results. The habitats in which the parthenogenetic species occur appear to provide necessary environmental stimuli for the endocrine malfunction.

The above interpretation is supported by some experiments. Thus Herlant-

Meewis (1975) observed that when adult worms of *Eisenia foetida* were raised on manure, instead of being reared on the older breeding grounds consisting of humus and rotting leaves, they lost their weight considerably for some generations. Anomalies in spermatogenesis were observed, whereas oogenesis was only slackened. The male genital duct became smaller, but ovisacs and oviducts remained normal. The seminal vesicles showed many spermatocytes blocked at meiosis, and in extreme cases they contained only spermatogonia and spermatozoa. This experiment clearly shows that the effect of rearing in an unusual environment (presumably involving the change in nutrition) was much more pronounced in the male than in the female, and the degree of development of gonads was similar to those obtained after the removal of the brain by Herlant-Meewis (1966). These results also paralleled the polymorphism in parthenogenesis as exhibited by various degrees of reduction of the male reproductive system in nature (observed by Jaenike and Selander 1979).

The habitats in which the parthenogenetic species occur are patchy, ephemeral ones in which *r* selection is expected. Rapid population growth and a greater colonizing ability in parthenogenetic species in such habitats are definitely selectively advantageous. Therefore, the coincidental induction of parthenogenetic individuals in such habitats by the local environmental stimuli on their physiology has been essentially a fortuitous adaptive response.

Possibly, genetic assimilation of parthenogenesis could occur. Such an hypothesis can be tested (theoretically) by altering the rearing condition of the "parthenogenetic strain."

INTERSTITIAL OLIGOCHAETES. Five families of oligochaetes are known to have representatives living in the marine meiobenthos (Lasserre 1971). Aeolosomatidae and Potamodrilidae are best adapted to intertidal environments. Typically, they live in underground water and they remain primitive structurally (Lasserre 1971).

Rieger (1980) erected a new family Lobatocerebridae based on single interstitial species *Lobatocerebrum psammicola*. He assigned the family provisionally to the order Oligochaeta, although the group cannot be aligned clearly with any class within the Annelida; this family also shows some superficial similarities to the Turbellaria. Rieger preferred the interpretation that this family has been derived from a larger noninterstitial form in the annelid line of evolution. No developmental data are available except the fact that two juveniles were collected along with 15 adults, which were designated as types.

C. THE CLASS MYZOSTOMIDA

Myzostomids are greatly modified parasitic annelids, principally associated with crinoids, and more rarely with asteroids and ophiuroids (Pettibone 1982). The aberrant body is small, flattened, oval, and disklike, lacking a distinct head and pygidium and without external segmentation. Although their systematic position has been disputed, in modern classification they are sometimes treated as a distinct class between the Polychaeta and Oligochaeta. Pettibone (1982) treated the Myzostomida as an order (with seven families) and assigned it to the Polychaeta.

In *Myzostomum* the trochophore larva is known to occur (Jägersten 1939). The larvae hatch from very small eggs that are poor in yolk content, and the eggs are already fertilized when discharged. Profound metamorphosis occurs on the hosts, resulting in highly modified adults (above). Within the Myzostomida, again, neoteny appears to have occurred in some of them. For instance, Baer (1951) pointed out that *Protomyzostomum polynephris* occurs within the coelomic cavity of an ophiuroid *Gorgonocephalus* and that this species possesses much more simplified and more distinctive larval features than other myzostomids; he thought that excessive nourishment has engendered neoteny.

11

The Phylum Sipuncula

According to Rice (1975, 1978, 1981), three species of sipunculans, *Golfingia minuta, Phascolion cryptus,* and *Themiste pyroides,* undergo direct development, the trochophore stage being completely suppressed during development. Three other types of development recognized by Rice have the following sequences of developmental stages: (1) egg–trochophore–worm, (2) egg–trochophore–lecithotrophic pelagosphera–worm, and (3) egg–trochophore–planktotrophic pelagosphera–worm. A close relationship is apparent between the yolk content of an egg and its subsequent development. The species with direct development and the species belonging to the first two types of the three above have eggs relatively higher in yolk content than those species in the last category, which have the smallest eggs (Rice 1975, 1976).

In the diminutive hermaphroditic species *Golfingia minuta,* with direct development, eggs are larger than in any other sipunculan, the size of each egg being (260–280) x (215–230) μm. Rice (1975) showed that eggs are enormously yolk rich and that the lecithotrophic stage lasts for 2 months. The increased yolk content in this species is associated with brooding by females within a burrow Åkesson 1958). Unique environmental factors in such a habitat can be suspected as having induced the production of such eggs. *Themiste pyroides* with large eggs (190 μm in diameter) and *Phascolion cryptus* with moderately large eggs (136 μm in diameter) undergo direct development within the jelly coat of the egg (Rice 1975). Although a hormone (or hormones) that may be involved with vitellogenesis remains unknown, the process of vitellogenesis has been studied for *Phascolosoma vulgare* (Gonse 1956a,b) and for other species by Rice (1973) and Sawada (1975). Sawada thought that nutrient uptake into oocytes takes place through short microvilli during early stages of oocyte development.

The consequence of enlargement of eggs appears to be increased suppression of genes for developmental stages, resulting in increasingly abbreviated development that culminates in direct development; the yolk-rich large egg per se must constitute a kind of environment which induces the suppression of developmental stages (see Sect. 3B2 for discussion).

12

The Phylum Echiura

Among echiurans, the family Bonellidae is of special interest in showing the environment-dependent sexual dimorphism; the male is a small neotenous form living in the uterus of the female. As Pilger's (1978) review shows, the extreme sexual dimorphism was first found by Baltzer (1912, 1914) to depend on the substratum larvae settle on; trochophore larvae remain sexually undifferentiated until settlement. Bonellids produce large yolky eggs (800 mm in diameter, Leutert 1974) and the larvae are lecithotrophic (Pilger 1978). According to Dawydoff (1959), the habitat of *Bonellia viridis* is seas with lower salinities. The production of large yolky eggs might well have been induced by the lower salinities, which influenced the endocrine mechanism of vitellogenesis. Yet the emerged larvae are essentially trochophores, though the larval life is much shorter than in other echiurans. They are not swimmers, and rather creep on the sea bottom (Dawydoff 1959, Gould-Somero 1975).

Baltzer's experiments with *Bonellia* (summarized by Pilger 1978) showed that most of the larvae (92%) that settled on clear substrate become females and that the rest become either intersexes or sterile females. On the other hand, 70% of those that settled on the proboscis of a female metamorphosed into males. Baltzer reasoned that development is possibly affected by a determining substance that diffuses from the proboscis of the female to the larvae. Baltzer (1925) further inferred that male determination may be the result of inhibited female development. Another possibility is the presence of an androgenic hormone for the male development. A determining substance (pheromone?) from the female proboscis might turn on the hypothetical "androgenic hormone" in inducing the development of larvae into dwarf, neotenous males, in the way dwarf males in some crustaceans are induced by darkness, which appears to turn on androgenic hormone (Sect. 23A). Or, when the "pheromone" inhibits the female development, the "male hormone" becomes activated.

Sex determination in *Bonellia* may not be totally phenotypic (i.e., reversible) as Baltzer's data (above) indicate. Furthermore, Leutert (1974) has shown, by culturing trochophore larvae of *B. viridis* both in pure seawater and in seawater containing intact or fragmented proboscis of an adult female, that when larvae are exposed to the action of the female proboscis, 76% of them become males. This result appears to indicate that in some individuals within a population the mechanism of sex determination is genetically controlled. Earlier, Wilczynski (1960, 1968) found that in the same species the male and female are already distinguishable cytologically during the egg and larval stages. However, Leutert's (1974) observation contradicted such results.

13

The Phylum Nemertinea

According to Jägersten (1972), the original division of life cycle into pelagic larval and benthic adult stages has been retained in all major groups of the Nemertinea. However, sometimes this division has been lost with emergence of direct development in some environments. In the freshwater hoplonemertine genus *Prostoma* eggs are yolk-rich and development is direct, and hence there is no pelagic larva. During embryogenesis of *P. graecense* a solid agglomeration of cells appears that Reinhardt (1941) (cf. Jägersten 1972) considered as equivalent to the blastodisc of the pilidial larva. Hence the direct development in this species involves a quick and precocious metamorphosis in which the development of the pilidial larva is compressed within the egg, and the production of yolky eggs and the consequent direct development are related to the freshwater habitat. Presumably, in the freshwater habitat lower salinities (among other environmental factors) have been the most significant factor that have effected the endocrine mechanism for vitellogenesis (see below). The consequent enlargement of (relatively few) eggs and loss of the larval stage (i.e., embryonization) in the less stable freshwater habitat must have been at a selective advantage, because by avoiding the exposure of vulnerable pilidial larvae to such habitat the chance of survival of the species must have increased. Furthermore, such selective advantage presumably has acted as the selective force in perfecting the mechanism of direct development involving the enlargement of eggs. The genus *Prostoma* comprises only freshwater species (six in number) (Gibson and Moore 1976, Gibson 1982), suggesting that the genus arose in the freshwater habitat.

Another example of direct development without a free-swimming larval stage is that of *Lineus desori* (described as *L. gesserensis-ruber* by Schmidt 1934). The egg size in this species measures 300–400 μm in diameter, in contrast to 180–220 μm in what Schmidt considered to be another type of *L. gesserensis-ruber.* According to Schmidt, this species occurs in the littoral zone where the up and down of the wave is pronounced. In such a habitat, as Schmidt thought, the absence of larval stage must be definitely advantageous. Compression of the pilidial larval stage inside the egg, however, must have occurred initially as a result of increased yolk content as in *Prostoma*. Here again, the production of larger eggs was clearly an adaptive response, and it is associated with the unusual habitat where the nemerteans may, according to Schmidt (1934), remain dried for hours.

As in nereid polychaetes, a single brain hormone has been known to control both somatic and reproductive development in *Lineus ruber* (Bierne 1964, 1966, 1970, 1973; Rué and Bierne 1979, 1980; Bierne and Rué 1979). In the presence of a significant amount of the hormone, reproductive development is suppressed both in males and females, and conversely with the decline of hormone secretion gametic development ensues. The hormone is therefore a gonad-inhibiting hormone (GIH). Rué and Bierne (1979) thought that GIH might be a regulatory hormone which would inhibit the secretion of sex-specific stimulating substances produced by the cells in the proximity of the gonad. Presumably, when the production of yolk-rich eggs has occurred in *Prostoma* and *Lineus,* unusual environmental factors (such as lower salinities) might have caused alteration in the function of endocrine mechanism, such as precocious cessation of GIH secretion.

Among the nemerteans inhabiting the interstices of marine sands, *Arenonemertes minutus* measures only 1 mm; it is the smallest described nemertean. Several of the other interstitial nemerteans are between 2 and 10 mm long and some species of Ototyphlonemerteans measures from 30 to 50 mm in length (Kirsteurer 1972). Kirsteurer (1972) listed 27 species of interstitial nemerteans, seven of which are paleonemerteans and the other 20 belong to the Hoplonemertina. Reduction of structures in the interstitial nemerteans includes the lack of ocelli that occurs in most of them, reduction in the digestive diverticula, and reduction in gonads, which occurs in smaller species. In large species of *Ototyphlonemertes* (with the body length 30–50 mm) the body is always extremely slender, with a diameter of not more than 500 μm, enabling them to move through the interstitial system without actively replacing the sand grains. For structural modifications in interstitial *Ototyphlonemertes* see Müller (1968). The development of interstitial nemerteans is assumed to be direct (Kirsteurer 1972). Precocious cessation of GIH might have been responsible for an overall reduction in body size and some somatic structures during the evolution of interstitial nemerteans.

14

The Phylum Gnathostomulida

The gnathostomulids are well recognized interstitial animals that constitute a phylum sharing some characteristics in common with the Platyhelmintha and Aschelmintha (Riedl 1969, Sterrer 1972, Rieger and Mainitz 1977); 20 genera and over 80 species were known to Sterrer (1982). They occur typically in the kind of biotope with a large amount of organic detritus. The aspect of their typical biotope (in which they reach a high population density), as well as their deep vertical distribution in hydrogen sulfide-rich substratum, suggests anaerobic metabolism (Sterrer 1982). Associated with such a biotope, eggs are large, the length of an egg measuring up to 300 μm, which may correspond to about 1/10 of the body length, and mature eggs seem to be yolk rich. Only one egg reaches maturity at a time, and development is direct; a juvenile hatches from the egg, and reproductive organs (both external and internal) develop during juvenile development (Müller and Ax 1971, Sterrer 1974). Probably the phylum Gnathostomulida arose in the above-mentioned biotope along the coast (R. M. Rieger, personal communication). It would seem, therefore that they owe their origin to a profound change in gene regulation that occurred in the developing embryo-larvae in the enlarged, yolk-rich eggs. The enlarged eggs, in turn, appear to have been induced by some unique environmental stimuli in their habitat (see Sect. 3A2 for discussion).

15

The Phylum Rotifera

In the Rotifera, which are predominantly freshwater interstitial in habitat, eggs are large and no metamorphosis occurs during postembryonic development, although the secondarily modified larva occurs in sessile rotifers such as *Cupelopagis*. The large vitellaria in most rotifers must provide sufficient yolk to developing oocytes, which become relatively large; in females of the marine genus *Seison* there is a pair of ovaries without a vitellarium (Nogrady 1982).

The question is the nature of postoval developmental stages. Remane (1963), based on their similarities to trochophore larvae, regarded them as modified trochophores, and hence they are neotenous (larval neoteny). It can be argued, in support of this theory, that as their ancestors migrated into fresh water, lower salinities affected the activity of vitellaria (or their precursors) and yolk-rich, large eggs were produced, and that concomital alteration in gene regulation in the embryo-larvae developing in such eggs resulted in the suppression of the ancestral adult structures. An alternative view that the postembryonic stages represent juvenile stages and hence the development is direct (by omission of larval stages) fails to account for their essential similarities to trochophore larvae. The phylum Rotifera are, based on their definitive structures, an isolated group and their phylogenetic relationship with other phyla remains completely obscure.

With reference to the mechanism of vitellogenesis, which must contribute to the enlargement of eggs, Clement et al. (1981) hypothesized that some physical environmental factors, notably photoperiod (as in *Notommata copeus,* Clement and Pourriot 1972), group effect, and others, probably stimulate the neurosecretory system through sensorial receptors before vitellogenesis starts. The hypothesis also suggests the direct influence of nutrition on vitellogenesis, and the possible effect of the waste that accumulates during the process of aging. Even if such a mechanism is proved, the question would still remain whether this mechanism (including the large vitellaria) is the one that was inherited from the marine ancestor and was instrumental in producing large eggs during their initial stage of settlement in the freshwater interstitial habitat.

The most conspicuous feature of rotiferan development is its environment-dependent morphogenetic plasticity. The typical environmentally controlled life cycle of the Monogononta, which produce three kinds of eggs, is as follows. During most of the year the females are all diploid, and produce amictic eggs, which develop into more diploid, amictic females without fertilization. The form of amictic females gradually changes during the year, undoubtedly in response to changing environmental conditions. At critical seasons, just before the species is to become quiescent or in response to striking environmental changes, the amictic eggs develop into diploid mictic females. Mictic females produce haploid mictic eggs which may develop parthenogenetically into haploid males, but if fertilized form a thick-walled case and remain dormant as diploid winter eggs until favorable environmental conditions return (Meglitsch 1967).

According to Clement et al.(1981), external factors influence the life cycle of monogononts at the level of the rate of reproduction of thelytokous partheno-genesis, of the appearance of mictic females, and of the eclosion of thick-walled eggs. Population density has been known to influence certain aspects of life cycle. Thus, for example, in *Asplanchna* the body wall growth, mixis, and fecundity are higher at higher population densities (Birky 1969), and in *Brachionus calyciflorus* the percentage of mictic females in the F_1 generation is higher when grouped in twos than in sixes (Pourriot and Rougier 1977). In *B. plicatilis* grouping increases the production of mictic females when the mothers feed on *Dunaliella,* but this effect disappears when they are fed with *Diogenes* (Pourriot and Rougier 1979). However, in *Notommata copeus* fecundity and the rate of reproduction are not modified by population density (Clement et al. 1981).

In *Notommata copeus* a long photoperiod has been known to be necessary to produce mictic females (Pourriot 1963, Pourriot and Clement 1973, Clement and Pourriot 1975, Pourriot et al. 1981), but the effect is modulated by popula-tion density (Clement and Pourriot 1975). Usually, population density and the quality of food modify the rate of appearance of mictic females by interacting with endogenous factors such as the genome and ages of parents and grandpar-ents (Clement et al. 1981).

In several species of *Asplanchna* dietary factors are known to regulate female polymorphism. Gilbert (1980) summarized the female polymorphism in *A. sieboldi* as follows: Three female morphs (saccate, cruciform, and campanu-late) are recognized in *A. sieboldi.* The saccate as the smallest in body size and always amictic, whereas the cruciform and campanulate may be either amictic or mictic. Thus the transformation of morphs is correlated with the mode of reproduction. Gilbert (1967, 1968) found that transformation of saccate into cruciform is caused by an active component of vitamin E, α-tocopherol contained in the lipid fraction of the algal cells that saccates ingest. The tocopherol molecule passes from the stomach into cavity and uterus, and then it is incorporated into the developing embryo in the uterus and induces the development of the body wall outgrowth. Thus the effect of tocopherol is direct. A more recent study with *A. brightwelli* by Gilbert (1983) showed that ingestion of one prey rotifer containing 0.02 pg tocopherol was sufficient to cause young amictic females to produce a high proportion of mictic daughters, and that population density modulates the effect of dietary induction of the mictic females. Induction of the campanulate morph is still poorly understood, although tocopherol appears to be necessary in addition to another mysterious dietary component.

As Gilbert (1980) emphasized, the three morphs can be expressed by individuals derived parthenogenetically from a single female, and hence have exactly the same genes. Therefore, the control of morph expression is due entirely to the influence of environmental factors during development, mainly tocopherol. According to Gilbert, saccate females have the potential for much more rapid numerical increase than other larger morphs and require much less food. Therefore, the function of this morph may be to facilitate population growth. Much greater size of cruciform females permits them to eat prey too large for saccate females to capture, and the body-wall outgrowth of cruciform females protects them from being eaten by other cruciforms or especially campanulates of their own species; furthermore, cruciforms are usually mictic, allowing them to initiate sexual reproduction and the formation of resting eggs. Campanulate forms are primarily adapted to eat large prey.

None of the above selective advantages, however, seems to constitute a stringent selection pressure in inducing the morphotypes, and thus the developmental polymorphism in *Asplanchna* appears to be largely a matter of response of their physiogenetic potency to changing environmental stimuli (i.e., mainly tocopherol). This interpretation is supported also by the fact there are intermediates between morphs. In the absence of a strong selection pressure, genetic fixation of a particular morphotype is not likely to occur in *A. sieboldi.*

16

The Phylum Nematoda

The Nematoda are mainly terrestrial in habitat, although they have secondarily invaded diverse biotas including the freshwater and marine habitats, and many of them have become parasites of animals and plants. In nematodes oogenesis does not seem to require deposition of exogenous yolk. In fact there seems to be no mechanism for a secondary vitellogenesis. The eggs of nematodes are remarkably similar in size, and as a rule the size ranges from 50 to 100 μm long and 20 to 50 μm wide, and this range in egg size is true also for *Placentonema gigantissima,* which measures as an adult 8 m long, although there are some exceptions to this rule (Maggenti 1981). Such sizes can definitely be said to be small as compared with the eggs in many other marine invertebrate groups, and the lack of secondary vitellogenesis is related to such small sizes.

Correlated with the yolkless small eggs, embryonic development is highly determinate; that is, each blastomere can be identified in embryogenesis as the stem cell of a particular organ or a part of an organ, and a theoretical first-stage larva would have 1024 cells at maturity (Maggenti 1981). Furthermore, in most nematodes postoval growth is effected without cell division, and this form of cell constancy from the first "larval" stage to the adult is called eutely. Typically, four so-called "larval stages" are recognized. However, they actually seem to represent juveniles, because these "larvae" do not undergo conspicuous metamorphosis to become adults. It is tempting to hypothesize that as their marine ancestors became terrestrial, eggs became smaller, possibly as a result of suppression of secondary vitellogenesis. Furthermore, in the small eggs the expression of ancestral larval genes became suppressed, and simultaneously precocious development of (juvenile) adult structures (i.e., adultation) occurred as in viviparous animals with very small eggs (Sect. 3B3).

The cell constancy from the first juvenile stage to the adult, or eutely, does not apply to the reproductive system, hypodermis, intestine, and body musculature in which the increase in cells occurs (Maggenti 1981). Another remarkable feature of postoval juvenile development of nematodes is the occurrence of molts in which the entire cuticle is shed; there are probably always four molts and the nematodes emerge from the fourth molt as adults, although somatic growth and reproductive development may continue after the last molt. Considerable increase in size is due to enlargement of cells, and prolonged growth even after maturation of the reproductive system is also a feature of nematodes. Conspicuous metamorphic changes occur only rarely. In plant parasites such as *Meloidogyne, Heterodera,* and *Naccobus* for instance, the female becomes very plump, eventually becoming pyriform or round, or lemon-shaped (Lamberti and Taylor 1979; B. Ebsary, personal communication).

The effect of environmental factors on body size and morphology have been known to be marked for some nematodes. Thus, for instance, *Dorylaimus thermae* measures 1.1 mm long in hot springs of Yosemite Park, Wyoming, whereas the same species from cold lakes in Utah ranges from 1.5 to 1.8 mm long (Hoeppli 1926). An experiment with *Rhabditis terrestris* by Stephenson (1942) showed that the increase of available food induces the increase in body length. As Thorne and Allen's (1959) review shows, nutritional and temperature effects on body size and gonadal development are also evident in some nematodes. Tarjan's (1967) review included cases of environmentally induced variation among plant and soil nematodes. Presumably, in all these cases the increase in size has occurred through enlargement of cells, not through cell division.

On record, at least, neoteny is not common in the Nematoda. However, when environmentally induced reduction in body size is accompanied by the arrest of growth of other structures and by maturation of gonads, the result would be neoteny. One well analyzed case of such a neoteny is that given for the genus *Rhabditis.* Within the subgenus *Rhabditis,* according to Osche (1952), the mouth cavity and associated structures, the female tail, and other characters are poorly developed in the stunted specimens induced by poor nutritional conditions. These poorly developed states obtain as normal ones in the subgenus *Telorhabditis* and *elongata* and *longicaudata* groups within the subgenus *Choriorhabditis,* and Osche regarded these species as neotenous (*partielle Neotenie*). The neotenous conditions that characterize the latter genera may reflect genetic assimilation of the originally environmentally induced modifications (i.e., neoteny) in the ancestor. Osche (1952) further pointed out that in subgenus *Rhabditis* no hermaphroditic or parthenogenetic species occurs, whereas within subgenus *Choriorhabditis* a considerable number of species are hermaphroditic. He suggested that this correlation is due to reappearance of the male conditioned by neoteny. A marine interstitial species *Astomonema jen-neri,* described by Ott et al. (1982) as a new genus and species, is mouthless and is provisionally assigned to Siphonolaimidae.

Despite the cases showing plasticity in morphogenesis mentioned above, nematodes are generally known to have a rigid development; as seen, first of all, in highly determinate embryonic development. The rigidity in morphogenesis during postoval development is reflected in some observations on parasitic nematodes. As Inglis (1965) maintained, free-living nematodes have under-gone little structural modification as a result of parasitism, and therefore the evolution of most groups of parasitic nematodes has been largely independent of hosts. Scolytid specific nematodes have undergone much less modification than their hosts (Rühm 1955). The fact that all parasitic groups within the Phasmodea can be traced back, more or less directly, to free-living Rhabditoi-dea (Osche 1963) also reflects conservation of their original rigid developmen-tal patterns in their free-living ancestors. In fact, there is no sharp distinction between aquatic and terrestrial species, and some of the same species occur in Dutch lowland and Austrian highlands (Meglitsch 1967); many similar exam-ples can be cited from the literature in taxonomic nematology.

Osche (1956) maintained that the saprobiotic biotopes that many terrestrial nematodes inhabit provide conditions under which free-living nematodes can live en masse. The ability to live in such environments has been obviously preadaptive to the parasitic life, and hence a significant structural modification was not necessary in their new parasitic environments. As discussed below, the built-in endocrine mechanism is likely to enable the parasites to dispense with a significant structural modification.

As Davey's (1976) review shows, the hormone secreted from neurosecretory cells in the anterior end of the head of *Phocanema* and *Haemonchus* acts on the very large excretory cell (excretory gland) in the posterior part of the body and permits the entry of water into the worm (concomitantly the water content of the excretory gland increases). This brings about activation of previously exist-ing stores of leucine aminopeptidase in the gland. The enzyme eats the old cuticle and then exsheathment, or ecdysis, ensues. The hormone definitely induces only exsheathment, not the formation of cuticle. It is probable that the altered environmental stimuli (notably temperature) and other stimuli such as carbon dioxide, hydrogen ion concentration, and digestive enzymes in the parasitic environment (Rogers and Sommerville 1968) would trigger the chain of the above endocrinological actions in inducing ecdysis, and thereby the parasitic nematodes would be permitted to grow primarily through enlarge-ment of cells. It is thus apparent that hormonally induced alteration in gene regulation pattern is not likely to occur in parasitic nematodes, and hence no conspicuous structural change occurs. The presence of ecdysteroids in female adults of the dog heartworm, *Dirofilaria immitis,* has been demonstrated (Mendis et al. 1983), although their function still remains unknown.

17

The Phylum Acanthocephala

All acanthocephalans are endoparasitic, and they are believed to attain sexual maturity in the alimentary tract of vertebrates. Their life cycles, where known, have been found to require arthropod intermediate hosts (Parshad and Crompton 1981). Oocytes develop within floating ovaries called the "ovarian balls" (see Parshad and Crompton 1981 for a review). Nicholas (1971) described acanthocephalan eggs as very small. Parshad and Crompton's (1981) summary shows that egg sizes range, among some 20 species studied, from the smallest in *Neoechinorhynchus emydis* (25 μm long and $18-22$ μm wide) to the largest in *Moniliformis dubius* ($112-120$ μm long and $56-60$ μm wide). Gastrulation in the strict sense does not occur during embryonic development, and it is said to be the distorted spiral type (Schmidt 1973). As in nematodes, postembryonic development is eutelic in that the cell division is completed very early during embryonic development except for gonads, and the tegument remains syncytial. Postembryonic development is accomplished by cell enlargement and cytodifferentiation as in nematodes.

The above facts of embryonic and postembryonic developments that parallel those in nematodes lead me to suspect that the "acanthor" larva that emerges from the egg is essentially a juvenile, the development of the ancestral (primary) larval stage having been completely suppressed in the yolkless, very small eggs. Unlike the nematodes, however, they require arthropod intermediate hosts for transformation, which is metamorphic. The acanthor larva emerged from the egg enters the body cavity of the intermediate host and changes through a series of acanthella stages to give rise to the final stages (cystacanths), which are involved with infection of the definitive hosts. During the transition the acanthor loses the hooks and inverts the proboscis, and the cystacanth differs from the acanthella mainly by a sexually more mature state. Both the male and female reproductive tracts develop during metamorphosis (summarized by Parshad and Crompton 1981).

18

The Phylum Bryozoa

Jägersten (1972) classified the correlation between the yolk content and methods of development in the Bryozoa into three categories: (1) small mass of yolk, freely discharged eggs, planktotrophy, and long pelagic life; (2) abundant yolk (in large eggs), brooding, lecithotrophy, and short pelagic life; (3) small mass of yolk, intimate brooding with supply of nutrients from the mother during embryogenesis, and short pelagic life. Type 1 must be most ancient, and the larvae are cyphonautes larvae. Type 2 represents a modification in embryonic development induced by (or associated with) the environmental factors in yolk-rich, large eggs (see Sect. 3B2), and such development may be called ovoviviparity; larvae are fully developed when hatched, but the common feature is the absence of a continuous digestive canal. Brooding, which may often result in ovoviviparity, is very common in Bryozoa, occuring both in Gymnolaemata, which are almost exclusively marine, and Phylactolaemata, which live only in fresh water (Meglitsch 1967). It is therefore difficult to associate ovoviviparity with a particular habitat. However, Bryozoa are also colonial, and this may be related to ovoviviparity, for nearly all compound (social) ascidians are ovoviviparous (Chap. 22). Type 3 is true viviparity, which arose independently several times within the Bryozoa. Remarkable features in viviparous Phylactolaemata are, according to Jägersten (1972), the absence of many organs (apical organs, pyriform organ, adhesive organ, and alimentary system) and early development of polypids during embryonic life. Jägersten (1972) regarded the early formation of polypids in small eggs as an example of adultation, that is, the shift in time of appearance of adult structures to the very early developmental stage (see Sect. 3B3 for discussion). As summarized by Ryland (1976), in viviparous *Bugula* spp. there is the mechanism of transfer of nutrients from the zooid to the embryo.

19

The Phylum Phoronida

In *Phoronis ovalis,* as shown by Silén (1954), development deviates from the primary life cycle of the Phoronida, which consists of the pelagic actinotrocha type larva with conspicuous tentacles and the benthic adult stage. The diameter of an egg is 125 μm, much larger in both absolute and relative (to the body size) sizes than in three other species of *Phoronis* Silén studied. The unique ecological association, which might have something to do with the production of large eggs, may be the retention of eggs in the parental tube (Emig 1974) and its living in coraligerous and detrital communities (Emig 1982). The emerged larva conspicuously differs from the actinotrocha in having the uniformly distributed ciliary covering of the body, and in the total lack of tentacles, alimentary canals, functional mouth, and anus; these features reflect profoundly altered gene regulation pathways associated with yolk-rich large eggs (see Sect. 3B2 for discussion). Thereafter, a short pelagic life follows. Metamorphic changes of structures appear to be highly limited. Abele et al.'s (1983) survey of 13 extant species of the Phoronida shows that *P. ovalis* is smallest in body size (6 – 11 mm long), fewest in number of tentacles (11 – 28 tentacles), and shortest in the length of tentacles (0.1 – 1.2 mm). Thus *P. ovalis* exhibits a clear case where the production of large eggs results in small adults with arrested (and hence neotenous) development of structures.

20

The Phylum Echinodermata

Abbreviated development occurs in all classes of the Echinodermata. Of the 61 species of British echinoderms, 70% of Holothuroidea, 63% of Asteroidea, 25% of Ophiuroidea, 14% of Echinoidea, and apparently all species of Crinoidea were said to have direct development (Fell 1946a). Actually, however, the percentages represent shortened development (G. Hendler, personal communication). Fell (1945, 1946a) divided ophiuroid development into three categories, mainly by association with egg sizes: Group 1 includes ophiuroids with small, yolk-deficient eggs (not greater than 0.1 mm in diameter) which undergo a long, indirect mode of development involving a pelagic ophiopluteus, followed by a pronounced metamorphosis. Group 2 includes ophiuroids with eggs of intermediate size (0.1–0.2 mm in diameter), in which nonpelagic and non-feeding larvae of different degrees occur in association with a moderate amount of yolk. Group 3 includes ophiuroids with large yolky eggs (from 0.4 mm upward in diameter) in which the mode of development is absolutely direct, without trace of a larval stage. Schoener (1972) found, mainly by literature survey, that in deep-sea ophiuroids direct development is positively correlated with larger eggs, and that there is a clear distinction between direct developers (2–2000 eggs in 29 species) and indirect developers (hundreds of thousands of eggs in six species Schoener counted).

Hendler's (1975) review indicates the existence of several kinds of abridged development within the Ophiuroidea. What Fell (1941) called "Kirk's ophiuroid" from New Zealand is absolutely direct, without a trace of larval development. Eggs are large and yolk-rich, with the diameter measuring 0.5 mm. They are laid in very rocky coastline. Apparently, low salinity along the coast is related to the enlargement of eggs in this species. As Fell (1941) has shown, embryonic development in yolk-rich eggs is quite abnormal and the animals that emerge from the eggs are juveniles.

Amphioplus abditus is, according to Hendler (1975), a burrowing, shallow-water amphiurid of the eastern U.S. coast. The species bypasses planktonic development and undergoes metamorphosis within the adhesive, demersal fertilization membrane. Therefore, this species has an abridged development, but such development is not direct. In this species the egg diameter ranges from 0.13–0.16 mm, and the number of eggs laid is 5000–30,000.

Another major type of abridged development in Ophiuroidea is what has been called "viviparous development." According to Hendler (1975), concurrent appearance of young in the genital bursae (brood sacs) and large yolky eggs have been adopted as the criteria of viviparity. However, Hendler's (1975) Table 1 on the size of viviparous eggs shows that in 22 species examined the value of egg diameter ranges from 0.1 to 0.9–1.0 mm. Apparently, viviparity associated with small eggs and what is here called ovoviviparity associated with large eggs are included in this "viviparity" category. In *Axiognathus japonicus* and *A. squamatus* the egg diameter ranges from 0.10–0.15 mm. They have a premetamorphosed "embryo" of 0.24 mm, which is attached to an "umbilicus" produced by the bursa. Thus by association with small eggs and attachment of the "embryo" to the bursal wall they appear to be viviparous. However, Fell (1946b) thought it highly improbable that the attaching organ in *A. squamatus* is used for the transfer of nutrient. Similarly, Oguro et al. (1982) reported that in *Axiognathus japonicus* the hatched embryo acquires a connection with the bursal wall, but they were also uncertain whether the connection conveys nutrients. Thus viviparity in the strict sense has not been conclusively proved in the Ophiuroidea. In many cases of "viviparity" eggs are large and the concurrent occurrence of juveniles may be regarded as the reflection of ovoviviparity, that is, hatching of juveniles from large eggs.

The majority of "viviparous" ophiuroid species occur in the Antarctic (Mortensen 1936, Fell 1945). Presumably, the ambient photoperiodic cycle and cold temperature have often induced the enlargement of eggs by affecting the endocrine mechanism for vitellogenesis (see below). Yet the retention of the (presumably) enlarged eggs within the mother's body (ovoviviparity) is definitely adaptive in this region, and the effect of natural selection must also be involved with such strategy; Dell (1972) thought it highly probable that the echinoderm species exhibiting "viviparity" (often ovoviviparity) would be at a selective advantage in Antarctic waters, where planktonic food material is extremely seasonal.

As shown by Stancyk (1973), an ophiuroid species *Ophiolepis elegans* produces large yolky eggs in the Cedar Key, Florida, area, where salinity fluctuates over the year (by 15–30%). The yolky eggs (0.25 mm in diameter) develop into vitellaria larvae with four ciliated bands, and the larvae nearly complete metamorphosis within 3 days. In this species the production of yolky eggs is apparently related to the fluctuating salinity, and its consequence is an abbreviated development of caenogenetically modified vitellaria larvae. Up to 75% of the ophiuroid and echinoid species in the euryhaline estuary at the Cedar Key area may have some developmental modifications that reduce larval exposure to the pelagic development (Stancyk 1973). Stancyk (1973) pointed out that the egg counts in two species with vitellaria larvae, *Ophiolepis elegans* (with 6720– 16,500 eggs) and *Ophioderma brevispinum* (with 785–1385) are intermediate to counts of eggs given by Schoener (1972, above) for the species with direct and indirect development. *Ophioderma brevispinum* is also known to produce large eggs (0.3 mm in diameter) (Brooks and Grave 1899).

According to Hendler (1979), three species of ophiuroids (*Ophiolepis kieri, Ophiolepis paucispina,* and *Ophiomyxa flaccida*) from shallow water in Portobelo, Panama, have direct development and are ovoviviparous (viviparous of Hendler). *O. flaccida* is gonochoristic and the egg diameter ranges from 0.70– 0.80 mm. *O. paucispina* is a synchronous hermaphrodite; its egg diameter is 0.35 mm. *O. kieri* is a protandrous hermaphrodite, and the egg diameter is also 0.35 mm. Thus direct development in all these cases is related to yolk-rich large eggs (larger than that in *O. elegans*), and the latter is most probably the cause of the former. The immediate cause of enlargement of eggs must be the altered function of the endocrine mechanism for vitellogenesis which, in turn, presumably has been induced by some unique (unidentified) environmental factors in their habitat (fringing coral reef, cf. G. Hendler). It should be noted that in these Panamanian species embryonization resulting in direct development is more pronounced than in *O. elegans* in Florida, and that this is related to the even yolkier and larger eggs they produce. It is thus apparent that the degree of embryonization is proportional to the size of the egg (see Sect. 3B2 for discussion).

Hendler (1979) noticed that certain features such as disk scalation are simplified in certain small species of ophiuroids. For instance, the scale pattern in small *O. kieri* approximates that of the juvenile of larger species, such as *O. impressa* and *O. pacifica,* with smaller eggs (0.2 mm in diameter). Thus *O. kieri* can be regarded as neotenous in reference to its congeners, and neoteny can be attributed, at least in part, to its larger eggs. Hendler (1979) pointed out that brooding and direct development in these Panamanian species mitigates the disadvantage of low fecundity associated with neoteny, because the chances of survival of juveniles would increase. However, such a selective advantage may be primarily a fortuitous by-product of the response of the built-in endocrine mechanism for vitellogenesis (discussed below) to new (unidentified) environmental stimuli associated with the reef habitat. The selective advantage attached to such development, however, may well have contributed to the perfection of such development in the offspring, while eliminating those individuals that failed to respond adaptively enough to the environmental stimuli (i.e., failing to produce large enough eggs).

Although developmental data are completely lacking, the case mentioned below parallels the neoteny by precocious, incomplete metamorphosis found in small *Ophiolepis* species. Sprinkle and Bell (1978) showed that three genera (with seven species) of the suborder Cyathocystina (Class Edrioasteroidea) from the Ordovician and Devonian are small as adults (5–8 mm in diameter versus 15–20 mm in most other isorophids), and their distinctive morphological features (five short and straight ambulacra, interambulacra with few plates, and proportionately large and modified peripheral rim with relatively few tightly sutured or fused plates) more closely resemble juveniles than adults of isorophids; it appears that cyathocystids evolved from one or more isorophids by neoteny. Bell's (1975, 1976) comparison of ontogeny of *Timeischytes casteri* (Cyathocystina) with *Isorophus* indicated that the adult stage in the former is roughly comparable with the terminal juvenile stage of the latter, reflecting earlier arrest of development (neoteny).

The brooding habit is also conspicuous among Antarctic holothurians. At least 15 species (out of the total fauna of 38) have large yolky eggs and brood their young (Pawson 1969). Over 50% of Antarctic comatulids (Crinoidea) brood their young. This percentage is very high, considering the fact that only about 1% of them are "viviparous" elsewhere (Dell 1972).

Comatilia iridometriformis (Class Crinoidea), living in deep water (250–700 m deep) off the southwestern United States is, according to Messing (1984), neotenous (paedomorphic) in retaining the attributes limited chiefly to juveniles of the species of Comasteridae (to which *C. iridometriformis* belongs). They are small in size, and with large radial ossicles, incomplete pinnulation, slender cirral ossicles, and coarse stereome. The species is also peculiar in being the only brooding member of the family. It is presumably an intraovarian brooder, for each of the swollen gonads (presumably ovaries) contains a single giant embryo or larva. Probably, this case can also be regarded as ovoviviparous. Here, this unique reproduction and consequent neoteny are related to colder temperatures ($< 10°C$ as compared with $> 20°C$ in the habitats of other species). Messing (1984) thought that the habitat of this species, which represents an almost unlimited area for colonization, could be regarded as an unstable habitat favoring rapid reproduction and large reproductive effort among so-called *r* selected organisms. However, the species produces only small number of progeny.

Among the asteroids, egg-size-related divergence in developmental process and phenotype is known for *Echinaster modestus* from the eastern Gulf of Mexico. Two ecotypes have been recognized in this species (the taxonomic status of this species has not been well established, cf. Schleibung and Lawrence 1982). Ecotype 1 has the egg volume somewhat smaller than ecotype 2 ($199.1 \times 10^6 \ \mu m$ versus $257.9 \times 10^6 \ \mu m$), and the biochemical composition is also different between the two (Turner and Lawrence 1979). Furthermore, according to Schleibung and Lawrence (1982), the two ecotypes differ in several other attributes: (1) type 1 broadcasts buoyant eggs in late May and June, and a brief period of planktonic life follows in this ecotype, whereas ecotype 2 deposits fewer, and larger, benthic eggs in late April; and (2) type 1 reaches sexual maturity at a larger size and expends a lower reproductive effort, but has a greater absolute reproductive output than ecotype 1. The adult size in ecotype 1 is greater than in ecotype 2 (35–70 mm in radius versus 16–20 mm in ecotype 2). Environmental stimuli inducing the divergence might be different temperatures in different months in which the two types of eggs are produced. The fact that smaller adults are formed in larger eggs (and vice versa) conforms with the general trend in marine invertebrates and amphibians. Ecological selective pressure operating on the two ecotypes remained unclear to Schleibung and Lawrence (1982).

In Asteroidea also, according to Hayashi and Komatsu (1971), eggs in brood-protecting species tend to be large (e.g., *Henricia sanguinolenta*). A more recent review by Strenger and Erber (1983) shows a clear correlation between increased lecithotrophy and suppressed development of larval stages in species of Asteroidea, with *Pteraster tesselatus* (reported by Chia 1966) as the extreme, in which the egg diameter is 1.46 mm (i.e., very large) and development is direct (without the feeding stage). Large eggs have often been found floating. Such floating large eggs include those of *Pteraster tesselatus* (above) and those of *Certonardoa semiregularis* described by Hayashi and Komatsu (1971). In these cases the environmental causation of enlargement of eggs, if it exists, remains unknown.

The production of the vitellaria larva, as we have seen, is related to larger eggs. Such larva is a caenogenetically modified one; it is a modified ophiopluteus in *Ophionereis annulata* (Hendler 1982). The vitellaria larva has the alleged tendency to remain near the bottom, and it has been found in crinoids, ophiuroids, echinoids, and holothurians (Williams and Anderson 1975, Hendler 1982).

The above cases of alteration in development, resulting in abridged development of various degrees, neoteny, and the caenogenetic vitellaria larva, are mainly the consequence of environmentally induced large, yolk-rich eggs. It now appears that the enlargement of eggs is due to an excessive secondary vitellogenesis. In five deep-sea species of echinothuriids and in *Poriocidaris purpurata,* as shown by Tyler and Gage (1984), the oocyte grows to be about 200–450 mm at which stage vitellogenesis begins. Oocyte growth continues until a maximum size of 1100–1500 μm is attained. Tyler and Gage thought that this increase is due to entry of nutrient into oocytes; periodic acid–Schiff(PAS)-positive tissue surrounding oocytes becomes vacuolated as oocytes grow, suggesting that there is a transfer of nutrients. Furthermore, the transfer of nutrients (vitellogenin) is likely to be mediated hormonally (below).

More recent studies have shown the presence of the vertebrate hormones concerned with vitellogenesis (progestrone and estrone) in ovaries, pyloric caeca and perivisceral fluid of *Asterias rubens* (Schoenmakers 1979), Dieleman and Schoenmakers 1979, Schoenmakers and Dieleman 1981). Furthermore, the studies by Schoenmakers and Voogt (1980) and Schoenmakers and Dieleman (1981) indicated that probably 17β-estradiol, after being converted into estrone by ovarian elements, affects the incorporation into oocytes of vitellogenin-like substances originating from the pyloric caeca, thereby resulting in the growth of oocytes. However, the treatment with 17β-estradiol by Van der Plas et al. (1982) did not stimulate the incorporation of the precursors of RNA, protein, and lipid in *Asterias rubens*. Thus the hormonal mechanism of secondary vitellogenesis still remains equivocal. Broertjes et al. (1984a,b) showed the chemical nature of the vitellogenin substance in *Asterias rubens*.

Although the detail of secondary vitellogenesis still remains to be elucidated, it appears reasonably certain now that the enlargement of eggs, which so often results in embryonization, is due to an excessive secondary vitellogenesis, which could occur in some stressful environments. It should further be borne in mind, as Turner and Lawrence (1979) discussed, that hydration may contribute to the enlargement of eggs in echinoderms. In the case of *Echinaster modestus* they maintained that the type 1 egg must have a low percentage of water. However, the marked negative correlation between the egg size and egg number produced within the body in echinioderms leads me to believe that hydration cannot contribute very significantly to the enlargement of eggs (see Sect. 3B1 for a discussion).

Apparently, sexual maturation never occurs during the free-swimming larval stages in echinoderms. They always metamorphose into a juvenile of the ancestral adult stage, and hence neoteny occurs when sexual maturation occurs in earlier adult (juvenile) stages.

21

The Phylum Mollusca

MOLLUSCA (EXCEPT CEPHALOPODA). Geographical variation in egg size observed for *Brachystomia rissoides* in four localities of Denmark (Rasmussen 1944, 1951) appears to reflect the influence of changing salinity on the egg size, because fewer but larger eggs and nonpelagic development occur in brackish water (with low salinities) populations. Similarly, Rasmussen (1944) observed that *Embletonia pallida* varies significantly in developmental processes in different localities. In the harbor of Copenhagen, with rather brackish water, fewer and larger eggs (each with a diameter of 0.13–0.15 mm versus 0.11 in the population from Iselfjord, with more saline water) are laid and the pelagic stage seems to be very short.

In the Opisthobranchia three distinct types of development were recognized by Thompson (1967): type 1, which occurs in those species with planktonic larvae that emerge from small eggs (40–170 μm in diameter); type 2, which occurs in those species with lecithotrophic larvae that hatch from larger eggs (110–170 μm in diameter) and have a short pelagic life; type 3, which includes those species with direct development in which veliger structures may be recognized before juveniles, hatching from larger eggs (205–400 μm). Thompson concluded that direct development is exhibited by species that have, in the main, small adult sizes and in species having a boreoarctic distribution, indicating that the trend conforms with Thorson's rule (below). Depending on the degree of condensation in development during embryogenesis, Bonar (1978) divided Thompson's type 3 into metamorphic development (with a typical larval stage) and ametamorphic development (with highly condensed develop-

ment). Bonar also pointed out, quite correctly, that the three types of development (which show increasing embryonization) seem to depend on the quantity
of yolk stored in the egg during oogenesis, and that extrinsic factors (salinity,
seasons, starvation) influence the quantity of yolk laid down in the egg.

Mileikovsky's (1971) analysis showed that Thorson's rule (Thorson 1936,
1950) — the marked tendency for higher frequency in abridged larval development at higher latitudes and in the deep sea — holds true for the Prosobranchia.
It shows that the percentages of the prosobranch species with pelagic development is 91% in South India and 85% in Bermuda, whereas the percentage
reaches zero in East Greenland, less than 5% in Baffin Island (Canadian Arctic),
and 6.9% in the southeastern Canadian Arctic. Similarly, the percentage of the
species with pelagic development in the Lamellibranchia is 79% in Denmark,
15% in East Greenland, and 13% in the eastern Canadian Arctic. These facts
clearly show that abridged development, which may result in direct development, increases in species occurring at higher latitudes. In these cases lower
temperatures (less than 4° C, cf. Thorson 1936) and presumably also an extreme annual photoperiodic cycle are likely to be the proximate environmental
factors inducing yolk-rich, large eggs and consequent abridged larval development by embryonization.

The validity of Thorson's rule has been questioned in more recent works on
molluscs. Thus Spight (1977) found that among rocky shore and oyster reef
muricacean prosobranchs in the temperature zone, all high-latitude species
hatch as young snails, whereas all tropical species hatch as veligers, clearly in
conformity with Thorson's rule. However, in the species from other habitats
(shallow-water sand bottoms, estuaries, and deep water) both types of development occur without clear correlation with latitudes. These facts appear to
indicate that in the final analysis it is the local ecological conditions (which
influence the pattern of yolk production and act also as selective agents) that
determine or strongly influence the types of development.

In Ascoglossa and Nudibranchia from a variety of shallow-water habitats in
southern Florida, as seen in Table 1 of Clark and Goetzfried (1979), there is
clear correlation between smaller eggs and planktonic type of development and
between larger eggs and lecithotrophic or direct development; when the egg size
is large, however, the number of eggs laid is not necessarily small. Clark and
Goetzfried pointed out that the Nudibranchia and Ascoglossa represent exceptions to Thorson's rule, for the incidence of direct development actually increases from the temperate zone to the tropics. These authors failed to note,
however, that eggs must become larger before direct development ensues, and
in fact in their material from Florida eggs are larger when lecithotrophy and
direct development occur. The question must be asked first how the eggs have
become larger in some species of Ascoglossa and Nudibranchia in Florida.
Lower salinities in the shallow-water habitats might well be a significant factor
inducing the enlargement of eggs as in some ophiuroid echinoderms in Florida
(Chap. 20). They attributed the higher incidence of lecithotrophy and direct
development in these habitats to the dominant role of trophic stability in the life

cycle of nudibranch molluscs. The proximate cause of enlargement of eggs must be elucidated before such selective explanation is presented.

Brooding that results in direct development and laying of egg cases is common in the Subantarctic molluscs (Arnaud 1974, Simpson 1977). Here again cold temperature and the unique annual photoperiodic cycle must be, as in the Arctic, the very important factors causing such development. However, the Antarctic Ocean is, unlike the Arctic Ocean, seasonally higher productive. Therefore, the idea of the scarcity of food as an underlying cause (which explains the scarcity of pelagic development and prevalence of abridged development in the Arctic) cannot be applied to explain the frequent occurrence of direct development in the Subantarctic and Antarctic regions. An important selective advantage of brooding must lie, as pointed out by Simpson (1977), in the fact that resultant juveniles can immediately find protected or specialized habitat. Such selective advantage must have contributed to the improvement of the physiological mechanism for direct development.

According to Picken (1979), 10 species of prosobranch gastropods occurring in the littoral or immediate sublittoral zones of Signy Island, South Orkney Islands (60°43'5 N, 45°38' W) are without a pelagic larva. The juveniles emerge from attached egg masses or capsules as crawling juveniles. Thus development is apparently direct and without the larval stage. A comparison of egg sizes between Arctic and Antarctic species of the same or closely related genera showed that they lay eggs of approximately the same size. Because the Arctic gastropods have been known to produce larger eggs than more southerly species, the Antarctic prossobranch must be considered as producing large eggs. Hence their direct development is apparently related to large eggs. Picken's (1979) list also shows that only 3 of the 17 species of prosobranchs known from the Arctic and Antarctic have a pelagic larva.

The subclass Pulmonata, most of which now occur in freshwater and terrestrial habitats, must have been derived from marine ancestors, probably before the Carboniferous (Morton 1955, 1958), and they have had an overall direction in change of habitat from water to land, although the reversal in direction from land to freshwater habitat occurred during the origination of the Basommatophora from their terrestrial stylommatophoran ancestors; Ellobiidae, which live in salt marshes and estuarine mud flats, are probably the ancestors of terrestrial stylommatophorans (Morton 1955). Pulmonate eggs are much larger and yolkier than those in opisthobranchs, which are nearly always marine, and free-living veliger larvae are released only in the primitive marine ellobiid genus *Melampus* (Russel-Hunter et al. 1972), *Amphibola crenata, Onchidium nigricans,* and various *Siphonaria* spp. (Raven 1975). Presumably, during the transition from sea to the freshwater habitat, lower salinities in the new habitat affected the pattern of vitellogenesis in producing larger eggs (Chap. 21). Calow (1978) argued that the enlargement of eggs and consequent telescoping of developmental stages (embryonization) has been the adaptive response to the challenge posed by inclement conditions in fresh water. It appears probable, however, that such adaptive response was initiated by the response of the built-in endocrine mechanism for vitellogenesis to new environmental stimuli in freshwater habitats (below). How much natural selection has been required later to perfect this response (while eliminating those that failed to produce large enough eggs) is certainly difficult or impossible to know.

Evidently, in the new terrestrial habitat further enlargement of eggs has occurred. In the terrestrial Stylommatophora eggs are, by comparison with other gastropods, fewer in number, extremely yolky, and sometimes very large (Morton 1958), and their development is direct. Shells are, when present, thinner and may be entirely lacking in slugs. It is easily conceivable that as their ancestors became terrestrial, entirely different environmental stimuli induced excessive incorporation of yolk per egg by altering the function of the endocrine mechanism for vitellogenesis (below). A profound alteration in gene regulation pathway that must have resulted in suppression of the larval stage is clearly related to the large eggs (see Sect. 3B2 for discussion). The suppression of the veliger larval stage, in turn, must have been selectively advantageous, for such larvae would be highly vulnerable and useless on land. Although the thin shell or the lack of it in terrestrial pulmonates is due mainly to the scarcity of calcium on land, it is also due to the loss of interest in calcium on the part of slugs. According to Boycott (1934), 45 species of the British pulmonates, including all 19 species of slugs, are indifferent to calcium. In addition, the resultant shell-lessness has enabled them to slide through narrow spaces or burrows to avoid predation.

Throughout the evolution of pulmonates outlined above, structural changes are attributable primarily to altered environmental effects on development in new habitats, although the resultant advantage of losing the larval stage must have acted as a selective force in perfecting direct development in these pulmonates. Indeed, during the course of evolution of slugs the environmental effect on development must have been truly overwhelming, because the effect is conceivable at two levels, that is, the enlargement of eggs and the loss (or great reduction) of shells.

Often in gastropods encapsulation of eggs occurs. It takes the form of gelatinous egg masses or firm, leathery egg capsules, and the larval stage is often passed within the capsule. Despite encapsulation, as already seen, eggs in many Antarctic prosobranch gastropods have become large and yolk-rich and development is direct. In Littorinidae with capsular development, however, the effect of environmental changes on egg size and consequent developmental pattern are not clear. Mileikovsky (1975) summarized the types of larval development in this family.

In Ascoglossa (Opisthobranchia), where a single embryo per egg capsule seems to be a general rule, the capsule size is a more accurate predictor of development type than egg size; that is, the greater the capsular volume, the more abridged is development (Clark and Jensen 1981). Type 3 development (direct development), recognized by Thompson (1967) and Bonar (1978), occurs, as Clark and Jensen's table shows, in the species (*Ascobulla ulla,* three species of *Elysia, Tridachia crispata, Costasiella lilianae, Limapontia cocksi*) producing large capsules, although in these species the egg diameter is also generally great with one exception *(Ascobulla ulla)*. Ecological association with the production of large egg capsules remains unclear in the study by Clark and Jensen (1981). In *Elysia cauze* (in Florida), according to Clark et al. (1979), the three types of development of Thompson (1967) occur seasonally within a single population; planktonic (type 1) in early spring, lecithotrophic (type 2) in summer, and direct development (type 3) in autumn and early winter. Thus the different developmental types appear to represent temperature–photoperiodically controlled seasonal trimorphism in development, although Clark et al. (1979) attributed the phenomenon to seasonal availability and unavailability (in winter and spring) of the food *Caulerpa* spp., which may control genetic expression of the developmental types.

In interstitial gastropods also, as shown below, capsular development is apparently common, and the developmental pattern appears to be variable. In the prosobranch species *Caecum glabrum* the diameter of an egg is 0.07 mm. One cocoon contains one egg from which a veliger larva emerges (Götze 1938), and hence development is not direct. In *Microhedyle lactea* and *Hedylopsis spiculifera* (Acochilidiacea) fewer than 50 yolk-rich eggs are laid in transparent, gelatinous cocoons which are attached to sand grains or fragments of shells. Within the cocoon veliger larvae hatch from the eggs (Swedmark 1968). In *Hedylopsis riseri* development was said to be direct (Morse 1976); the juvenile emerges from the capsule and the veliger larva development appears to be very reduced. Similarly, in *Philinoglossa* sp. (Philinoglossacea) the eggs, 50 or so in number, are spawned in spherical cocoons which are attached to sand grains. They pass through the typical cleavage and develop into veliger larvae in the cocoons (Swedmark 1968). In the aeolid species *Pseudovermis axi* a couple of dozen of eggs are spawned in transparent, stalked, gelatinous cocoons, and veliger larvae hatch from the eggs; the diameter of an egg is 70 μm (Swedmark 1968).

In the bivalve *Turtonia minuta,* according to Ockelmann (1964), the few large eggs laid are rich in yolk and embryos develop directly into the adult. The adult resembles a spat (juvenile). Yet the species becomes sexually mature before the formation of inhalant siphon and outer demibranchs. Hence the species has a direct development and represents a progenetic neoteny; specialized features of this species are related to its attached mode of life in the intertidal zone, very shallow water, and its mode of reproduction. Thus it would appear that lower (or fluctuating) salinities in the intertidal zone induced the production of yolk-rich eggs and consequent direct development and neoteny. Ockelmann explained that the evolution of this species took place in response to the conditions which rendered the dispersal of progeny of the ancestral species disadvantageous, and that this brought about the type of reproduction found in this species. Such selection pressure must have contributed to the improvement of the mechanism for neoteny (including the enlargement of eggs) which initially resulted through the proximate process.

In the freshwater pulmonate *Lymnaea stagnalis* neurosecretory cells in the lateral lobes produce a hormone that stimulates four dorsal bodies attached to the cerebral ganglia. Then the dorsal body hormone stimulates vitellogenesis and growth of the female accessory glands (Geraerts 1976a,b, Geraerts and Alegra 1976, Roubos et al. 1980); no gonadal hormone has been found thus far. Furthermore, the growth and reproduction are influenced by photoperiod (Bohlken 1977, Van Minnen and Reichelt 1980, Bohlken and Josse 1982) which presumably affects the activity of the lateral lobes. In a terrestrial stylommatophoran *Agriolimax reticulatus* also dorsal bodies produce a hormone that promotes maturation of oocytes (hence vitellogenesis) and the differentiation of the female sex organs (Wijdenes and Runham 1976). It is probably safe to assume that such an endocrine mechanism for vitellogenesis occurs widely within the Mollusca. Presumably, in producing large yolk-rich eggs, altered environmental stimuli (lower salinities, lower temperatures, extreme annual photoperiodic cycle, environmental stimuli on land) have induced the alteration in functioning of the above endocrine mechanism for vitellogenesis (which responds to environmental signals). Hormone(s) concerned with somatic growth and metamorphosis has not been found for the Mollusca, although the existence of such hormone(s) is highly probable. Acceleration in development in enlarged eggs must have involved the alteration in the action of morphogenetic hormones (see Sect. 3B2 for discussion).

CEPHALOPODA. The cephalopods are generally known to have large eggs; the largest one in *Octopus bimaculoides* measures 9.5×17.5 mm (Fioroni 1982). Associated with large eggs, their development is direct, although it has sometimes been said to be indirect because of the transitory larval organs recognized during intraoval development.

As was first shown by Wells and Wells (1959) for *Octopus vulgaris,* ovarial maturation is determined by secretion of gonadotropin from the optic glands which can be held in check by an inhibitory nerve supply from the subpedunculate lobes. D'Or and Wells (1973, 1975) showed further that the gonadotropin accelerates several maturational stages of both male and female gametes, and that the yolk protein synthesis by follicle cells around oocytes during vitellogenesis depends on the gonadotropin. The conclusion that the optic glands, released from nervous inhibition, secrete gonadotropin was confirmed for the cuttlefish *Sepia officinalis* (Durchon and Richard 1967, Richard 1970a). In the squid *Illex illecebrosus* also the optic gland gonadotropin stimulates protein synthesis in the ovary (Rowe and Idler 1977). Selman and Arnold's (1977) study with *Loligo pealei* indicated heterosynthetic (secondary) yolk production and the synthesis of the secondary envelope or chorion by the follicular syncytium, and Selman and Wallace (1978) concluded that the follicular syncytium is the sole source of heterosynthetic yolk production.

Richard (1966, 1970b) showed that in *Sepia officinalis* the increase in temperature to 20° C accelerates gonadal development. The same author (1967, 1970b) also reported that decreased day length (long night) accelerates gonad maturation by activating the optic gland. D'Or et al.'s (1977) experiment, however, showed that in *Illex illecebrosus* female maturation occurs under increased day length (from 10.5 to 15.5 hrs and from 12.5 to 15.5 hr), apparently contradicting the result reported by Richard (1967, 1970b). Nevertheless, it is clear that environmental factors such as photoperiod and temperature control yolk synthesis. Most probably, the environmental signals are transmitted to the subpedunculate lobes, and thereafter inhibiton or deinhibition of gonadotropin ensues.

Often, the life cycle is pelago–benthic in cephalopods, and generally benthic development is associated with increased yolk content in the egg (Fioroni 1982). The consequence of yolk content is highly divergent embryonic development and suppression of most parts of larval development, thereby resulting in direct development. The Cephalopoda, as judged by adult structures, are an isolated group, and their phylogenetic derivation remains totally unclear.

The question of how such an efficient mechanism for yolk production has been produced in evolution is difficult to see in terms of altered environmental effects on physiology in a new environment, for cephalopods must have been always marine in habitat; that is, they have not changed their habitat drastically in their evolution. Thus in the lack of definite evidence for the proximate cause, the (presumed) effect of natural selection on the evolution of endocrine mechanism for vitellogenesis (i.e., the ultimate cause of evolution) in cephalopods is considered below.

Packard (1972) pointed out resemblances between cephalopods and fishes in some important physiological mechanisms (locomotory system, hydrostatic control system, etc.), behavior, and growth of the brain. He considered that cephalopods and fishes have adopted the same broad adaptive zone, and presented the evidence that the convergence is not due merely to similar physical demands of the marine environment, but also to dynamic interactions (avoidance of predation, competition) between cephalopods and fishes from the late Paleozoic onward. It can be imagined that, under such selection pressure, cephalopods had to change their structures and physiology substantially; loss of the shell, for instance, must have been essential to increase the speed of their locomotion. Such changes must have been possible only by a profound alteration in gene regulation pathways, which could occur in very yolk-rich, large eggs.

Under the strong pressure to produce large enough, yolk-rich eggs, the mechanism of neural inhibition and deinhibition of gonadotropin appears to have arisen as a highly efficient mechanism for yolk production; certainly nervous control must be faster and more precise than the neurohumoral control, and hence it is more efficient. As already seen in *Lymnaea* and other molluscs, essentially the same endocrine mechanism for vitellogenesis occurs. It is therefore reasonable to suppose that in cephalopods the endocrine mechanism inherited from their ancestors has been improved under the pressure of natural selection, mainly by replacing the neurohumoral control of gonadotropin by neural control.

In his review of reproductive strategies in cephalopods Boletzky (1981) found that the $r-K$ selection model for reproduction is applicable in part only to Octopodidae, and pointed out that a combination of both r and K features is noted in all cephalopods. According to Naef (1923, 1928, cf. Boletzky 1981), nektonic forms of cephalopods produce large numbers of juveniles from smaller eggs (1.0–2.0 mm in diameter), whereas benthic cephalopods produce fewer but much larger eggs, from which relatively large juveniles emerge. This difference within the Cephalopoda may indicate that colder temperature in the benthos may induce the production of larger and yolkier eggs.

The following discussions of environmental effects on evolution of molluscs do not include the effect of egg size.

The Mileikovsky (1975) survey of larval development of Littorinidae (Prosobranchia) showed that 32 of the 39 species reviewed have pelagic development, invalidating an earlier generalization regarding the types of larval development and different tidal levels the animals inhabit. Streif and Le Breton (1970) showed that the development of the penis in the sexual female of *Littorina littorea* can be induced by the action of a hormonal substance from the right ocular tentacle in the sexual male, and that regression of the penis in the sexual female is affected by the hormonal substance produced from the pediopleural complex in the female. These demonstrations of physiological effects should help us to understand seasonal changes of the penis and other reproductive modes in *Littorina* (Bergerard 1975, Bergerard and Caugant 1981), which are important in the taxonomy of the Littorinidae (Heller 1975, Raffaeli 1979). Also in *Crepidula* development of the whole male genital duct including the penis is subject to cyclic changes. A pedal morphogenetic factor (hormone) and a pleural regressive factor are responsible for the differentiation of the male tract (Le Gall 1981, Le Gall and Feral 1982).

Generally, the growth of the shell in land pulmonates depends heavily on the availability of calcium; land pulmonates have a calcium store in the digestive glands upon which they draw for shell building. Therefore, the shell can become very thin in certain environments. An example is a Pleistocene land snail *Poecilozonites bermudensis,* which exhibits the decrease in shell thickness associated with lime-free soil that served as substrate (Gould 1977). The shells in these populations are paper thin, scaled-up replicas of early ontogenetic stages in the main lineage. In this case the thinness of the shell, which Gould regarded as paedomorphosis, probably resulted from the extreme scarcity of lime. Apparently, the selective advantage of such a thin shell remains unknown, or is absent.

A well-known environmental effect observed in nature is the effect of wave action in stunting shell size in freshwater molluscs (see Berry 1943, Miller 1978 for summaries). *Lymnaea stagnalis* normally has an elongate shell. However, according to Piaget (1929, cited in Waddington 1975), shorter varieties known as *lacustris* and *bodamica* occur in Switzerland and Sweden, in fairly shallow water where the lake bed is flat, stony, and much exposed to wind and wave action. Piaget was able to show experimentally that a similar phenotype can be produced as a physiological adaptation to wave action. During the growth period, until it attains the adult form with six or seven gyres, snails tend to contract their columnar muscles to hold themselves firmly to the bottom whenever a wave or disturbance threatens to dislodge them, and as a consequence of this continued contraction the shell develops with a shorter form. Contracted forms collected in nature still retained the contracted phenotype through many generations, even when bred in still water in laboratory tanks. Waddington's (1975) interpretation was that the contracted form, which originated as a physiological reaction to the stress of wave action, has been converted, presumably through selection, into a genetically assimilated condition and has developed independently of a particular precipitating stress, and the altered developmental (epigenetic) process has been canalized.

Similarly, Boycott (1938) worked with varieties of *Lymnaea peregra,* known as *involuta, burnetti,* and *lacustris,* all of which have shell shapes very different from the normal type. In the laboratory offspring of var. *lacustris* reverted to normality in a single generation. On the other hand, the F_5 generation of var. *burnetti* was still identical to the parent population, and the relatively pale, speckled mantle of *L. involuta* from Lough Cricanam was equally persistent, indicating the genetic determination of the phenotype.

Photoperiodic effect on shell increment is evident in the experiment with *Argopecten irradians* by Wrenn (1972) and in the one with *Helisoma duryi* by Kunigelis and Saleuddin (1978). Oosterhoff (1977) showed experimentally that various environmental factors (temperature, photoperiod, humidity, calcium) affect shell growth in *Cepaea nemoralis.*

Shell enlargement starts at the mantle edge, with the formation of new proteinaceous periostracum by the mantle edge gland (Saleuddin 1979, Saleuddin and Kunigelis 1984). This periostracum serves as a substratum on which the crystalline layer (calcium carbonate) is deposited (Wilbur 1976, Saleuddin 1979). As shown by Clark (1974), the formation of a growth increment in the bivalve *Pecten diegensis* (as observed by time-lapse and scanning electromicroscopy) involves the deposition of crystals by the mantle on the periostracum attached to it, followed by mantle withdrawal, reextension, and outward curvature. It has now become apparent that in *Lymnaea stagnalis* a growth hormone from the light green neurosecretory cells acts specifically on the mantle edge; it stimulates the formation of the crystalline layer and probably also the periostracum (Dogterom et al. 1979, Dogterom and Jentjens 1980). Kunigelis and Saleuddin (1978) showed that, in *Helisoma,* injection of brain homogenates from the fast-growing individuals (of *Helisoma*) stimulate shell deposition in slow-growing individuals. These facts clearly indicate that there exists an endocrine mechanism for shell growth that responds to environmental signals (see Saleuddin and Kunigelis 1984 for more discussion), and genetic assimilation of the deformed shells could occur, in part, by accumulation of the mutants that induce the necessary endocrine functioning for deformation of the shell.

Some species of the terrestrial snail genus *Cepaea (C. hortensis, C. nemo-*

ralis, etc.) are polymorphic with respect to the shell color and banding pattern, and they are known to be controlled by supergenes (Murray 1975, Murray and Clarke 1976, and others). The frequency of morphs has been attributed primarily to visual predation, notably by the thrush (songbird) and others (Jones et al. 1977). Another important cause of polymorphism is what has been called "climatic selection." Different shell morphs are known to have different rates of heating in sunshine (Emberton and Bradbury 1963, Heath 1975). Therefore, different morphs are expected to have selective advantages, depending on the climatic conditions. However, both Jones et al. (1977) and Clarke et al. (1978) found that many patterns of variation attributed to climatic selection are inconsistent, and Clarke et al. (1978) had to conclude that the evidence for climatic selection may be regarded as weak. Jones et al. (1977) gathered facts indicating that the production of the brown morph of *C. nemoralis,* which absorbs more heat than other morphs, is associated with accumulation of cold air or with cold climate. It appears to me possible that initially cold temperature physiologically induces the dark morph which could be selectively advantageous. This hypothesis is similar to that for the production of the dark form of *Pieris* butterflies in cold, mountainous areas (Sect. 23D26) and to the hypothesis with regard to the melanic moths in industrialized areas (Sect. 23D26).

INTERSTITIAL MOLLUSCS. Interstitial molluscs, as summarized by Swedmark (1968), include the species of *Solenogastres,* a few prosobranch gastropods, and, most numerous, opisthobranchs with more than a dozen species belonging to Acochilidiacea, which are shellless and which have great contractility. Swedmark (1968) characterized interstitial molluscs as follows: (1) Small size (0.8 – 4.0 mm). (2) Regressive anatomical characteristics that may affect many organ systems; all are without the shell, but the larval shell occurs. (3) Specialized features in body shape and anatomy, such as the vermiform tendency, strong development of spicules, and mucus-producing epidermal glands. (4) More pronounced extension of the body cilia than in noninterstitial molluscs. (5) Striking adhesive ability. (6) Striking contractility, especially in species without cutaneous differentiation for mechanical contraction. (7) Limited production of gametes, which is compensated for by prolonged period of reproduction; some other adaptive features of reproduction (hermaphroditism, cutaneous fertilization, etc.); and tendencies toward stationary larval development.

Of these seven characteristics, 1 and 2 are simple structural reduction, characteristic of neoteny; 3 and 4 appear to represent compensatory developments, which often accompany structural reduction in neoteny and halmatometamorphosis; 5 and 6 appear to be the consequence of the shelllessness. Combinations of these characteristics certainly make their relationships with other molluscan groups obscure. For instance, Odhner (1937) erected the Acochilidiacea (Opisthobranchia) — which are characterized by highly regressive features and cutaneous reproduction — and regarded it as the derivative of more primitive Diaphanidae, but there is as yet no generally accepted opinion with regard to their natural systematic position (Swedmark 1971). In interstitial gastropods capsular development is apparently common (above).

The "dwarfed fauna" in the Maquokata formation (Upper Ordovician), in which molluscs are dominant, had been attributed to the action of certain environmental factors, such as oxygen deficiency, abnormal salinity, and deficient food supply. Snyder and Bretzky (1971) interpreted the dwarfism in two species of bivalves (*Palaeoneilo fecunda* and *Nuculites neglectus*) as paedomorphic species produced by an active adaptive strategies by *r* selection. Such an adaptationist's view disregards the high probability that stressful environments (which might have been the coastal interstitial habitats) initially induced physiologically the paedomorphic phenotype.

PARASITIC MOLLUSCS. Two kinds of parasitism occur in the Mollusca: (1) parasitism resorted to by the larval stage only, adults remaining free-living, and (2) parasitism in which only the adult is parasitic and the larva is free. The first kind of parasitism is called "protelian parasitism," and it occurs in the freshwater bivalve superfamily, Unionacea. The modified (i.e., caenogenetic) parasitic larva is called the "glochidium," which consists of two thin hinged valves. Females incubate their eggs within variably modified brood pouches within the gill in producing the glochidial larvae, which are variable in body size, ranging from 0.05 to 0.4 mm (Kat 1984). The glochidia drawn in by the respiratory movements of the fish are distributed over the gills or outer parts of the body. When the parasites are completely enclosed within the epidermis of their hosts, the larvae undergo a complete metamorphosis, which consists of disintegration of body parts and formation of new structures (such as the intestine, heart, liver, gills, foot, and others) which replace the embryonic organs. The tiny mussel produced through the metamorphosis breaks through the epidermis of the host and falls to the bottom, where it burrows in the mud and grows into an adult clam (Baer 1951). With a single exception, all unionaceans are parasites of fishes (Kat 1984). Kat (1984) postulated that parasitism in unionaceans is advantageous mainly in terms of predictability of dispersal by habitat-specific hosts.

The well-known case of molluscan endoparasitism during the adult stage is that of the prosobranch family Entoconchidae, which comprises four genera *(Entocolax, Entoconcha, Enteroxenos, Thyonicola);* they are all parasites of holothurians and are dioecious (Lützen 1968). The female is generally oblong or vermiform and has no shell (except in the larval stage), and the dwarf male is found in the pseudophalial cavity (central cavity) of the female (Lützen 1968). As the larvae enter the host metamorphosis ensues. During the first phase of metamorphosis of *Enteroxenos oestergreni* (an endoparasite of the holothurian *Stichopus tremulus*), according to Lützen (1968, 1979), the shell and operculum are cast off. The second phase proceeds at different sites in the two sexes. In the female metamorphosis takes place in the host's esophagus; the details are unknown. In the male metamorphosis occurs in the female's central cavity, and it is completed in the epithelial petiole (male receptacle) in the female's central cavity. The larva's epidermis is lost and replaced by extroverted intestinal cells, and the larva is absorbed into the tissue of the receptacle. Later, the young male loses all its tissue except for rudimentary testes, which expand considerably, and a small area that develops into the small vas deferens. This degenerative process in metamorphosis of the male within the female, which results in nothing but the production of the male reproductive system, is clearly comparable with cryptogonochorism that occurs in the copepod *Aphanodomus terebellae* (Sect. 23A).

The small limpet-like prosobranch *Thyca crystalina* is an ectoparasite of the asteroid starfish *Linckia laevigata*. All the attached parasites are females, and most of the large females have a dwarf male, one-tenth their length, attached under the mantle, at the anterior end (Elder 1979). The dwarf male attached to the underside of the mantle is essentially neotenous and is comparable with the dwarf male attached to the underside of the mantle in some parasitic cirripeds and *Emerita* (Sect. 23A). It appears probable that, as in the crustaceans, precocious action of the androgenic hormonal factor — known to be produced in the brain of *Helix* (Guyard 1971), *Crepidula* (Le Gall and Streif 1975, Le Gall 1981), and probably in many other molluscs — is involved with the production of dwarf males in some protandrous, hermaphroditic molluscs.

22

The Phylum Prochordata

THE UROCHORDATA. According to Cloney (1978) all ascidian species have lecithotrophic larvae. In general, small eggs and oviparity are characteristic of solitary ascidians, although a few are ovoviviparous; nearly all compound (social) ascidians have relatively large eggs and are ovoviviparous. Within molgulids, as seen in Table 1 of Berrill (1931), the diameters of eggs in seven species of *Molgula* and two species of *Eugyra* with oviparous development are all 0.11 mm; in *M. retortiformis* with oviparous development, which occurs in the Arctic and in Subarctic regions, the egg diameter is 0.18 mm. On the other hand, in all species with ovoviviparous development (i.e., developing in the protective atrial cavity) the diameter of an egg is much greater, ranging from 0.14 to 0.25 mm, with the exception of *M. platei,* in which the egg diameter measures 0.10 mm. Thus it may be said that in these genera there is a marked tendency for ovoviviparous species to have larger eggs. For the production of large eggs in *M. retortiformis,* however, low temperatures and local photoperiodic cycles might well be responsible for the increased yolk incorporation per egg, as in other invertebrates and fishes occurring in the circum-Arctic region. The emerged larvae are large, apparently reflecting a certain degree of embryonization.

Compared with the tadpole larvae of oviparous molgulid species, according to Berrill (1931), those of ovoviviparous species are not only larger and therefore faster swimmers, but at the time of hatching they have already developed more; they possess both branchial and atrial invaginations, and the first beginning of the respiratory ampullae, all of which do not appear in the development of oviparous forms until the tail has been resorbed. A more recent review by Cloney (1982) also shows that the larvae of compound ascidians (which are ovoviviparous) are usually more complex structurally than those of solitary ascidians; prospective juvenile organs are usually in an advanced state of differentiation. All these facts indicate clearly that in larger eggs with more nutrients larvae are allowed to stay longer, and differentiation of juvenile structures proceeds further beyond the level of differentiation in the larvae of solitary, oviparous species, indicating a moderate degree of embryonization. In those ovoviviparous molgulids with larger eggs and larvae, however, the average size of the adult is definitely smaller (3–12 mm long) than those in the molgulids with oviparous development (13–40 mm) (Berrill 1931). Thus, in producing smaller adults in ovoviviparous species, earlier sexual maturation appears to occur, and such small adults may be regarded as neotenous. It should be noted that some *Molgula* spp. undergo direct development (called "anural development"). Of the nine sand-flat species, eight have anural development (Berrill 1975).

In *Polycarpa tinctor* (Styelidae) an excessively enlarged egg attains 0.73 mm in diameter, and acceleration in development is extreme. In this species the egg develops, within the atrial cavity, directly into a miniature adult that measures 2.2 mm in the mature oozooid, and no larval stage was found (Millar 1962). This sand-dwelling ascidian is known only from shallow coastal waters in New South Wales. Therefore, the enlargement of eggs and consequent embryonization may be related to the habitats where salinity can be relatively low.

In all species of Holozoinae recorded from Australia, New Zealand, and Japan, according to Brewin (1956), there is a marked tendency for the egg size to increase at the expense of the egg number. In the ovoviviparous genera *Distaplia* and *Sycozoa* eggs are heavily yolked and comparatively large (280–520 μm in diameter). In each genus the species with the smallest eggs has the largest number of embryos (which appear to be "larvae" of Millar 1971, p. 15) per brood pouch [*Distaplia taylori*, egg diameter 290 μm, average number of embryos (= larvae) 3; *Sycozoa sigillinoides*, egg diameter 280 μm, average number of embryos (= larvae) 6;]; in the species with eggs of large diameters (*Distaplia stylifera* 520 μm; *D. australensis*, 480 μm; *Sycozoa cerebriformis* 370 μm) the number of embryos (= larvae) in the brood pouch does not exceed 1, though more than one egg is present in the ovary. In these species once the first ovum is liberated from the ovary, development of the remaining ova is suppressed. In *Hypsistozoa fasmeriana* of the same subfamily viviparity occurs (Brewin 1956). In this ascidian a very small egg, 25 μm in diameter, develops into a large larva in an oviducal brood pouch, there receiving nourishment through a pair of larval endodermal tubes. During the whole developmental period of 5½ months, attachment to the parental zooid is maintained. The resulting larva that is released is very complex, with numerous buds that must facilitate metamorphosis. Brewin (1956) speculated that coldness of the environment has been a contributory factor in the establishment of viviparity in *H. fasmeriana,* because low temperatures are often associated with large yolk-rich eggs and accompanying ovoviviparity or viviparity in marine animals.

When the enlargement of fewer eggs occurs at the expense of other oocytes, an excessive amount of exogenous yolk (or yolk precursor) must enter a limited number of developing oocytes. The endocrine mechanism for vitellogenesis in urochordates, however, remains unknown, except for the fact that in *Symplegma reptans* ganglionic neurosecretory cells might function as gonadotropin in sexual reproduction (Sugimoto and Watanabe 1980). It is possible that, as in echinoderms and vertebrates, estrogens might well be involved with vitellogenesis. Earlier, Berrill (1931) contended that ovoviviparity preceded accumulation of large amounts of yolk. Because, according to Berrill, the chance of any egg surviving to maturity increases with its store of yolk, there has been, in ovoviviparous forms, every inducement for egg size to increase at the expense of egg number; he regarded the small egg in *Molgula platei* as primary. Thus, following Berrill, the larger eggs in all other species of *Molgula* must have been produced purely as a result of the kind of selection pressure he envisaged. However, when the switching on of sudden production of larger eggs by a built-in endocrine mechanism in some (new) environments becomes conceivable, the production of such eggs, which happened to be selectively advantageous, now can be seen as a fortuitous adaptive response to the new environmental stimuli. Presumably, natural selection has contributed toward the improvement of such an endocrine mechanism for this adaptive response, while eliminating those individuals that failed to respond adaptively (i.e., failed to produce large enough eggs).

Precocious sexual maturation and differentiation of adult structures in the smaller ascidians, such as seen in ovoviviparous molgulids with large eggs (above), might result from precocious release of hormones for somatic differentiation (metamorphosis), as in *Eleutherodactylus* (Sect. 24B). With reference to the hormone for metamorphosis, the presence of thyroid hormones (T_3 and T_4) in the endostyle of adult ascidians has now become evident (Thorpe et al. 1972, Thorpe and Thorndike 1975, Dunn 1980a,b). Furthermore, Patricolo et al. (1981) found that L-thyroxine stimulates metamorphosis in *Ascidia molaca.* However, as Cloney (1982) pointed out, there is as yet no evidence that ascidian larvae actually produce thyroid hormones. Furthermore, Pestarino (1984) found, in *Styela plicata,* acidophile cell types in the neural gland that appeared to be homologous to prolactin in the mammalian pituitary. Their function remains unknown, though they may possibly be involved with metamorphic events as in ascidians.

During the settlement of larval ascidians for metamorphosis (see Cloney 1978), sensory organs, the unicellular otolith and multicellular ocellus, enable them to detect a proper substratum for settlement. Molgulid tadpoles lack the ocellus, although the otolith as the sole directive organ of the larva is present. Berrill (1955) maintained that the absence of the ocellus resulted in elimination of the shadow response and thus prevented the tadpole from turning selectively toward the shaded rock surface favored by the tadpoles of other families. The molgulids consequently settle submerged in sand and mud flats. The loss of the ocellus thus appears to have resulted in the selection of a new kind of habitat for development.

According to Monniot (1966, 1971), dwarfed interstitial ascidians occur in shallow water as well as in the deep sea. They are 1 – 3 mm long, and the body form is either flat (in Phlebobranchia) or elongated (Stolidobranchia). In Phlebobranchia larval stages occur in the mother's body. The larval body is often so reduced that the heart and the kidney are often difficult to distinguish; all these features are due to the arrest of development and hence they are neotenous. Interstitial ascidians can easily be assigned to families, but it is difficult to place them in proper genera (Monniot 1971).

The life cycle of the cycle of the class Thaliacea, which comprises the orders Doliolida, Salpida, and Pyrosomida, is holopelagic, and these organisms are generally considered to be the derivatives of sessile ascidians. In *Doliolum* (Doliolida) the sexual gonozoid generation alternates with the asexual oozoid generation. It lacks the ocellus, although a statocyst occurs on each side of the body in the oozoid generation. The residual tail occurs, although it does not persist. Berrill (1955) interpreted this to mean that *Doliolum* is an ascidian that lost the larval sense organs while retaining the larval tail, and that it has converted the bands of muscles normally associated with closing and opening the ascidian siphon into contractile locomotor bands for the creation of internal water current. Associated with their failure to find a suitable site for attachment, metamorphosis is more or less inhibited, resulting theoretically in a larval neoteny. For the summaries of highly specialized modes of development in *Salpa* and *Pyrosoma* refer to Berrill (1955, 1975).

The class Larvacea, which comprises a few genera, is essentially larval in structural organization and is holopelagic. These organisms have been considered as derivatives of ascidian larvae or of thaliacean doliolids (Garstang 1928, Berrill 1955). They lack the ocellus and the otolith. In *Oikopleura* eggs are small, each measuring 0.085 mm in diameter (Berrill 1955). They are fertilized and develop free in water. Settlement does not occur in the absence of the sensory organs, and hence there is no metamorphosis; their morphology definitely represents a larval neoteny. Compensatory developments in these neotenous animals are the statolith, which has nothing to do developmentally either with the ocellus or with the otolith; the well-developed, twisted tail, which is used for drawing water; and the "house," which serves as an efficient food trap.

It is now apparent that during the evolution of the Urochordata, the loss of the larval sense organs often has resulted in the failure to settle on the proper substratum for metamorphosis (holopelagic), and the further consequence of such events appears to have been the origination of higher taxa with neotenous features.

THE CEPHALOCHORDATA. In cephalochordates two types of larva, the amphioxus and amphioxoides types, have been recognized. According to Wickstead (1964), an amphioxoides larva has three main characteristics that distinguish it from the amphioxus type larva: (1) a greater size, (2) more numerous gill slits, and (3) a pharynx that is divided by a longitudinal plica into a dorsal pars nutritoria and a ventral pars respiratoria. Clearly, the increased differentiation of these structures in the amphioxoides is correlated with its larger body. Wickstead (1964) thought that this occurred under the pressure of food requirement and that the increase in gill slits and the division of the pharynx into two functional units would occur in any larval species if it grows large enough, and the gonad would develop while maintaining larval features (neoteny). Wickstead (1964, 1975) suggested further that under some circumstances (such as the deep sea) normal amphioxus larvae may lose contact with the bottom, where metamorphosis occurs (Wickstead 1967). Without the contact with the bottom, as Wickstead (1964, 1975), thought malfunction of the endostyle (producing T_3 and T_4?) could result and there would be no metamorphosis. Monaco et al. (1981) demonstrated the presence of thyroid hormones in thyroglobulin included in the endostyle of *Branchiostoma lanceolatum*. Fredriksson et al. (1984) contended that the endostyle in *Branchiostoma* has iodinizing capability.

23

The Phylum Arthropoda

A. THE CLASS CRUSTACEA

The Crustacea are primarily marine. Some of them later became freshwater in habitat, and relatively few of them have come to be adapted to life on land. A majority of crustaceans have the nauplius as the first larval stage; the occurrence of this stage is probably primary for crustaceans. Some branchiopods successively add new segments after the nauplius stage until the definitive numbers of segments and appendages are attained. In many crustaceans, however, metamorphosis has been superimposed on this essentially anamorphic development. For instance, in copepods the nauplius is usually followed by the copepodid stage, and in cirripeds the nauplius metamorphoses into the cypris. In many decapods the first larva is the zoea, which is followed by the megalopa before it metamorphoses into the adult, the nauplius stage having been lost. In amphipods development is epimorphic (direct development) as in insects and myriapods. As shown below, abbreviation of larval stages, which culminate in epimorphic development, has occurred primarily as a result of the enlargement of eggs that occurred in the newly acquired habitats.

As Bliss's (1968) review shows, marine decapods produce large numbers of small eggs during spawning. For instance, *Penaeus setiferus* lays 500,000–1,000,000 eggs, each measuring less than 0.4 mm in diameter (A.B. Williams 1965, Anderson 1966). Furthermore, in semiterrestrial and terrestrial decapods that return to the sea for spawning the numbers and sizes of eggs also compare with those in marine decapods. However, freshwater crabs of the families

Potamidae, Pseudothelphusidae, and Trichodactylidae, which are for some or much of the year terrestrial but seek fresh water to release their eggs, show the reduction in number and increase in size of eggs that are characteristic of freshwater decapods lacking a terrestrial life. In these crab families the diameter of each egg ranges from 2.5 to 7.0 mm (Bliss 1968). For instance, *Geothelphusa dehaani,* according to Koba (1936), lays no more than 53 eggs, and each egg is 2.5–2.8 mm in diameter. Diminutive juveniles (3.5 mm long) hatch directly from such eggs, omitting the larval stage. Hence the development is direct; the juveniles are essentially the same as adults and they grow somewhat thereafter. Many of the species of Potamidae, to which *G. dehaani* belongs, are known to have direct development (Kaestner 1967).

Metopaulias depressus, a graspid that inhabits fresh water, collecting among leaf bases of large tank bromeliads in Jamaica, carries 60–100 eggs, each about 1.5 mm in diameter (Hartnoll 1963). Hartnoll found that the egg size has increased in this habitat and the developmental process has been abbreviated. In this species no prezoeal stage occurs; a first zoea can swim only feebly and does not eat; two zoeal stages last only for 3 days and are succeeded by a megalopa which, having only rudimentary pleopods, is unable to swim and is thus confined to a benthic existence. It is apparent that the origination of this monotypic genus is related to the alteration in life cycle in this unique habitat, where salinity must be low.

Uca subcylindrica (Ocypodidae), a fiddler crab, is endemic to southern Texas and northwestern Mexico. In contrast to other primarily intertidal members of the family, according to Rabalais and Cameron (1983), this species is found in supralittoral areas several meters to several kilometers from permanent bodies of water. Preferred habitats of *U. subcylindrica* are the banks of ephemeral ponds and intermittently flowing streams, the vegetated areas on the periphery of expansive salt flats, and the shorelines of bays and lagoons subject to hypersalinity and/or fresh water following tropical storms. Associated with such unique habitats, the species lays relatively few ($\bar{x} = 580$) large ($\bar{x} = 106$ mm in diameter) eggs, and development is abbreviated. Late zoeae hatch from eggs in an advanced developmental condition. Within as little as $2\frac{1}{2}$ days most zoeae metamorphose into advanced megalopae. Then most of the megalopae complete metamorphosis into the first crabs in 8 days. According to Rabalais and Cameron, adaptive advantages with such abbreviated development include the avoidance of predation and suboptimal conditions for growth and development, reduced dispersal from specialized and restricted adult habitats, and reduced critical molt periods.

The table given by Dobkins (1969) shows that in 18 freshwater species of Palaemoninae egg sizes range from 1.0 to 3.7 mm, and these species undergo abbreviated development (embryonization); two to five larval stages occur in them. In the *Palaemonetes varians* complex, according to Gurney (1942), the egg size and consequent development differ, depending on where the eggs are laid. In the populations living in brackish water eggs are small, whereas in those inhabiting fresh water in the Mediterranean region eggs are very large. In the larvae hatched from the large eggs adult appendages are already present, but those from small eggs are normal. However, despite the differences in egg size and larval development, adults in the two populations are similar (poecilogony). The genus *Palaemonetes* contains species occupying a wide variety of habitats that includes both marine conditions and fresh water. Some species have large numbers of larval (zoeal) molts before metamorphosis. For instance, *P. vulgaris* and *P. pugio* have 7 – 11 molts (Hubschman 1975). Because a larval stage can be skipped under altered rearing conditions (in temperature), as shown by Gore (1979), and because other experiments (Costlow et al. 1960 and many others) showed varying effects of different salinities and temperatures on larval development in crustaceans, substantial reduction in number of larval stages in freshwater *Palaemonetes* spp. might also have been due, in part, to environmental effects on (postoval) larval development that have accumulated during the course of their evolution.

In *Palaemon paucidens,* occurring in the Sagami River, Japan, according to Mashiko (1982), two types of reproduction occur. In the adjacent lake and pool of the upper stream the eggs spawned are smaller (0.47 mm^3 in volume) than those laid in lower (running) stream (0.89 mm^3 in volume). Larger larvae hatch from the larger eggs, although there is no significant difference in the body size between the two populations. As Mashiko thought, larger eggs might settle better. Yet the proximate causative agent inducing the difference in egg volume is unknown, although the production of smaller and larger eggs is related to stagnant water and running water, respectively.

The superorder Syncardia, considered to be a primitive malacostracan group without the carapace, comprises two orders, the Anaspidacea and the Bathynellacea. The marine ancestors must have migrated into the inland freshwater habitat and from there they further invaded subsoil groundwater; the evidence indicates that the two orders migrated into the new habitat at different times (Schminke 1981). *Anaspides tasmaniae* (Anaspidacea) occurs in Tasmania. It is large, measuring about 5 cm in body length, and the average diameter of an egg is 1 mm (Hickman 1937). Hickman's (1937) embryological study showed clearly that the nauplius stage (egg nauplius of Hickman) is passed within the egg, and this stage is followed by additional stages before the (juvenile) adult hatches from the egg. Thus the development is, as in some decapods with yolk-rich eggs, direct. According to W. D. Williams (1965), the typical habitats of *A. tasmaniae* are small upland streams and moorland pools. The species is most frequent at the altitudinal range of 915 – 1066 m above sea level, and the upper limit of thermal tolerance is 15 – 20°C. These facts suggest that relatively low temperatures in the habitats have induced the production of large, yolk-rich eggs and consequent direct development.

The order Bathynellacea is much smaller than Anaspidacea in body size, the largest species, *Bathynella magna,* measuring only 5.4 mm long (Kaestner 1967). However, the egg is relatively large for the small body size, as in some other small invertebrates; in *B. varians* the egg is yolk rich, measuring 0.11 mm in diameter (Jacobi 1954). Schminke's (1981) analysis of developmental data

(Bartok 1944, Chappuis 1948, Miura and Morimoto 1953, Jacobi 1954, Chappuis and Delamare-Deboutteville 1954) revealed that a nauplius stage (nauploid stage of Jacobi) is passed within the egg. Two postembryonic stages were called by Jacobi (1969) "postembryonic (i.e., larval) phase" and "preadult (juvenile) phase," respectively. Schminke (1981) pointed out that some species hatch as larvae and some as juveniles. Thus embryonization has occurred to varying degrees within the Bathynellacea, but not as extensively as in *Anaspides*. Schminke pointed out that the postembryonic stage corresponds to the protozoea and the adult stage (called the bathynellid) to the zoea in Penaeidea. Thus the adult has, in comparison with the Penaeidea, essentially larval fascies, and Schminke concluded that the Bathynellacea are neotenous (larval neoteny). Following this interpretation, the ancestral stage has been truncated. The case may be called progenetic neoteny, because it is related to embryonization (i.e., acceleration). Yet the environmental influence on postoval development in inducing neoteny cannot be ignored in this case. Bathynellacea, hatching from the egg as relatively small larva or juvenile, have adopted the strategy of entering interstices of sands, and thereby they have avoided the danger of being swept downstream; their diminutive sizes certainly fit the life in sand interstices.

In the Talitroidea with direct development (as in other amphipods) the number of eggs laid is relatively low. Sexton (1924) attempted to show the tendency for the number of eggs to decrease in littoral species (as compared with marine species) of *Gammarus*. The marine species *G. locusta* had up to 143 eggs; the brackish-water species *G. chevreuxi,* 30–40; the freshwater *G. pulex,* 8–12; and a littoral species of *Gammarus,* also 8–12. Furthermore, as shown by Hurley (1968), there is a great reduction in number of eggs in supralittoral species. In the littoral species *Allorchestes novizealandiae* a female taken at random had 161 eggs; in most terrestrial talitrids the number varied from 1 to 10, and in *Talitrus sylvaticus* the average was between 3 and 4. In *Orchestia platensis* the number of eggs laid is 1–47, and the long axis of an egg is 0.59 mm (in September) to 0.70 mm (in April) (Morino 1978). Bulycheva (1957, cf. Hurley 1968) found that most supralittoral species carried 10–20 eggs and Amphithoidae had 50 or more — *Amphithoe tarasovi* up to 226. She concluded that terrestrial talitrids had developed larger eggs with a greater reserve of nutrients. In these cases the enlargement of eggs is related to the terrestrial environment where the immediate ambient medium is air instead of water. The endocrine mechanism for the secondary vitellogenesis has been well investigated for supralittoral *Orchestia gammarellus* (below). Therefore, the idea that the enlargement of eggs is due to (environmentally related) altered endocrine function that results in incorporation of excessive amount of vitellogenin per oocyte (Sect. 3B1) applies directly to this case.

Hurley (1968) concluded that the eggs are larger and fewer in terrestrial talitrids than in marine talitrids, but the young (juvenile) emerges larger and more fully developed, reflecting embryonization by telescoping early juvenile stages into the egg. Wildish (1972) found that the small size of *O. remyi rof-*

fensis, which occurs at the highest level of the supralittoral zone, is due solely to the decrease in molting frequency. These facts suggest that embryonization of early juvenile stages in enlarged eggs has had a significant influence on late juvenile development, and consequent neoteny involved mainly the reduction of certain structures such as the male gnathopods, pleopods, and other appendages (discussed by Matsuda 1982). Conceivably, the resultant shorter period of juvenile development would be advantageous on land, because more vulnerable earlier juvenile stages are passed within the egg, and the opportunity for mating would increase.

Gurney (1942) and Makarov (1968) maintained that Thorson's rule applies to crustaceans, because the frequency of abbreviated development increases in the Arctic and Antarctic. Gurney pointed out several examples of abridged or completely suppressed larval development in Hypolytidae and Crangonidae, and referred to Thorson (1936), who maintained that a restriction of larval life is necessary because the period of production of phytoplankton in Arctic regions is very short. According to Makarov (1968), pelagic larvae of crustaceans have never been found in the Antarctic.

In five species of *Gammarus* in the northwestern Atlantic, according to Steele and Steele (1973), the duration of embryonic development is correlated with egg size, and temperature influences the duration. *G. setosus* produces the largest egg (0.690 mm in diameter) and has the most northern distribution. Its embryonic (i.e., intraoval) development lasts for 117 days at 0° C and 35 days at 10° C, whereas in *G. lawrencianus* with the smallest eggs (0.409 mm in diameter), the duration of embryonic development is 82 days at 0° C and 17 days at 10° C. Clearly, the production of the largest eggs is correlated with the highest latitudes. Steele and Steele (1977) further showed that the northern species (*G. wilkitzkii* and *G. setosus* with large eggs) produce a single, larger egg, and a well-timed young is released within the shortest period of the optimum condition. The medium-sized species produce medium-sized broods that spread through the longer optimum season. The small southern species can produce a large number of small broods per female and higher temperatures allow more than one generation in a season.

According to Clarke (1979), two Antarctic species of the caridean decapods (*Chorismus antarcticus* and *Notocrangon antarctica*) have, in contrast to two comparable species from temperate zones, low fecundity coupled with large, yolk-rich eggs from which relatively advanced larvae hatch. Brood sizes are smaller compared with the temperate species and measurable individual reproductive effort is also less in the polar species. Clarke regarded these features as *K* strategies. Very stable cold temperature and highly predictable primary production in the Antarctic appeared to fit Southwood's (1977) criteria for selection favoring the evolution of *K* strategies (discussed in Sect. 3B4). This interpretation does not apply to the essentially same developmental pattern that occurs in Arctic crustaceans and other invertebrates, because food is nearly always scarce in this region.

The seasonal change in egg size is a part of cyclomorphosis in some cladocerans. As shown by Kerfoot (1974), the female of *Bosmina longirostris,* which is parthenogenetic and has direct development, carries small eggs during the summer (123 μm long in July), then switches to large eggs in late fall (179 μm long in December); more than doubling of the enclosed yolk occurs during the winter. Kerfoot (1974) attributed this change to changing pattern of predation, without enquiring into the proximate cause of the egg enlargement.

Many facts mentioned above clearly show that enlargement of eggs has occurred as the crustaceans migrated into new habitats, such as fresh water where salinity is bound to be lower (than in their ancestral marine habitat), the cryptozoic habitat on land where the immediate surrounding medium is air instead of water and the exposure to light is limited, and polar regions where temperature is low and the annual range of photoperiod differs considerably from that in temperate zones, etc. It appears most probable that the new environmental stimuli in the new habitats have induced the enlargement of eggs by incorporation of more yolk per egg. The presence of a hormonal mechanism for vitellogenesis, which must have responded to the new environmental stimuli, has now become increasingly clear in recent years (below).

In *Orchestia gammarellus* the fat body is the site of vitellogenin synthesis (Junera et al. 1977, Croisille and Junera 1980, Zerbib and Meusy 1981); Picaud (1980) reported vitellogenin synthesis also in the fat body of *Porcellio dilatatus.* The result of cauterization of the antemedian area of the protocerebrum in *O. gammarellus* by Blanchet-Tournier et al. (1980) indicated that a hormone in this area promotes the secretion of vitellogenin-stimulating hormone (VSH) in the follicular cells of oocytes. VSH then stimulates the subepidermal fat body to produce vitellogenin, which enters the developing oocytes (described by Zerbib and Mustel 1984); this synthesis requires the presence of ecdysteroid (Blanchet-Tournier 1982). The contribution of this secondary (heterosynthetic) vitellogenesis to enlargement of eggs is considerable in *O. gammarellus.* According to Meusy (1980), the oocyte diameter increases from 150 – 160 μm at the onset of secondary vitellogenesis to about 800 μm at the time of egg laying. It should be remembered that secondary vitellogenesis occurs also in other malacostracans (e.g., De Leersnyder et al. 1980, Faure et al. 1981); the uptake of vitellogenin by oocytes occurs during the secondary folliculogenesis (Charniaux-Cotton 1982). On the other hand, many destalking experiments have also clearly indicated the presence of gonad-inhibiting hormones (GIH) in the eyestalk of decapods; in *Palaemon* the medulla externa of the X-organ slows down the GIH production during the reproductive season (Faure et al. 1981). Secondary vitellogenesis occurs also in a copepod *Centropages typicus* (Arnaud et al. 1982).

Although the details of hormonal mechanism may differ in different crustaceans, secondary vitellogenesis appears to occur widely in response to environmental stimuli. The fact that secondary vitellogenesis occurs only seasonally indicates that it occurs only in response to certain environmental signals (such as a certain range of temperatures and photoperiods). It is easily imaginable that under some extreme environments the function of endocrine mechanism for vitellogenesis would be altered, and the consequently altered pattern of secondary vitellogenesis would, at least in part, be responsible for the entry of an excessive amount of vitellogenin into fewer developing oocytes, resulting in the production of fewer but larger eggs. Furthermore, abortive larval development in enlarged eggs can be attributed, in part, to the altered action of ecdysteroid, which is now known to be involved with larval development (McConaugha 1980, Chang and Bruce 1981) and even with embryogenesis (Chaix and De Reggi 1982). The altered action of ecdysteroid must be due to new environmental stimuli that became available within the enlarged eggs (discussed in Sect. 23B).

As already seen, the juveniles of talitrids that emerged from enlarged eggs are relatively large and more fully developed, and continuous living on the supralittoral zone appears to have contributed to a further contraction of developmental stages. Adaptive structural modifications that arose in association with such developmental processes were relatively weak; these included the shortlening of urosome segments 2 and 3, and strengthening of the pereipods 5–7 and uropods 1 and 2 for jumping (Hurley 1968). Obviously, more pronounced structural modifications have occurred in terrestrial talitrids, which live under leaf mold in forests along the seashore, or even grassland considerably (15 km) away from the seashore. Characteristic structural features of terrestrial talitrids, summarized by Matsuda (1982), are:

1. The reduction of the male gnathopods; in some terrestrial species of *Orchestia* they are strikingly like those in stages of development of the male gnathopod in supralittoral species.
2. A trend toward the loss of pleopods; in *Orchestia patersoni* and a cavernicolous blind species of *Speleorchestia kolona* three pairs of vestigial stumps occur, and in others one or two pairs of pleopods may be lacking.
3. Considerable development and proliferation of the gill surface.
4. A trend toward slender, finely shaped legs, antennae, and mouthparts.
5. Development of relatively translucent, thin, and smooth exoskeleton.
6. Reduction in size and marginal setation of the brood plate.

All the above characters except 3 appear to represent the precocious arrest of development, characteristic of neoteny as suggested by Hurley (1959), and 3 appears to represent a compensatory development that often accompanies the reduction of other structures in neoteny (Matsuda 1982). This interpretation of the features as representing neoteny is supported further by the fact that body sizes in terrestrial talitrids from New Zealand are much smaller than eulittoral and supralittoral talitrids from New Zealand and Europe (exceptions being the supralittoral *O. remyi remyi* and *O. r. roffensis,* Wildish 1979); this strongly suggests precocious arrest of somatic development in terrestrial talitrids, as in *O. r. roffensis,* which occurs at the highest level of the supralittoral zone with decreased molting frequency. Furthermore, sexual maturity in this species occurs at a molt much earlier than in eulittoral species *O. mediterranea* (Wildish 1979). It is therefore highly probable that smaller body sizes in terrestrial talitrids are due to decrease in molting frequency and to precocious sexual maturation as in *O. r. roffensis.*

Bousfield (1968) recognized two types of terrestrial talitrids. In one type, apparently derived directly from regional seashore species, the sexually dimorphic body form of amplexing type amphipods is still retained. In the second type of terrestrial talitrids, which are (apparently) not closely related to the seashore species, sexual dimorphism is nearly totally suppressed. At least, the second type is clearly due to precocious arrest of development of secondary sexual characters (such as highly modified male second gnathopods, male pereiopods, and the female oostegite), and is plainly indicative of neoteny. Furthermore, the presence of the two types of talitrids indicates that neoteny is a matter of degree within the terrestrial talitrids, the second type representing a more pronounced one.

The evidence supporting the idea of neoteny in terrestrial talitrids is now incontestable; the next question is how the environmental stimuli in the leaf-mold zone on land could have influenced the endocrine activity to induce neoteny. It has now been well established, as Charniaux-Cotton's reviews (1972, 1975, 1976) show, that the gland located at the posterior end of the stomodaeal genital duct in *Orchestia* and others produces an androgenic hormone necessary for spermatogenesis and for the production of secondary male sexual characters. Also, this androgenic gland is under the control of a hormone from the X organ–sinus gland in the eyestalk; the light sensitive hormone is essentially inhibitory in function and moderates the activity of the androgenic gland. Furthermore, it is well known that another hormone from the X organ–sinus gland also inhibits the activity of the Y organ, which produces ecdysone for molting (see Highnam and Hill 1977). These are the hormones that appear to be involved directly with neoteny in terrestrial talitrids (Fig. 3).

Under leaf mold the 24-hr average light intensity must be considerably less than that of the exposed littoral zone. Thus the talitrids living under leaf mold would receive less light and other stimuli than they would receive on the seashore,* and an immediate consequence of the lack of these environmental stimuli could be a much lowered release of the androgenic gland-controlling hormone in the X organ–sinus gland; this, in turn, is expected to result in deinhibition of the action of androgenic gland (Fig. 3). The titer of androgenic hormone in the terrestrial talitrids would then become significantly higher than that in eulittoral and supralittoral species, spermatogenesis would be accelerated, and the production of male characters would ensue. Thus the precocious development of the male gonad and the male characters (which are incompletely formed) in terrestrial talitrids may result mainly from the lack of sufficient light, and this condition is comparable to the accelerated spermatogenesis in destalking experiments (i.e., the removal of the effect of light on the hormone

---

*In two species of New Zealand *Orchestia* the annual rhythm of adaptation is not vertical (Hurley 1968), and hence this statement does not seem to apply to them.

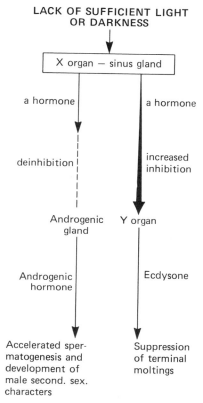

Figure 3. A simplified hypothesis suggesting changes in hormonal actions and evolutionary consequences in the terrestrial environment during the evolution of male talitrids (from Matsuda).

in the X organ–sinus gland controlling the androgenic hormone activity; see Highnam and Hill 1977 for a summary of such experiments). Therefore, the above interpretation may be said to be consistent with the experimental results.

Under leaf mold, deinhibition of a hormone controlling the Y organ (which produces ecdysone) may also be expected to occur. However, the fact of decreased molting frequency appears to indicate that inhibition of ecdysone release from the Y organ becomes even enhanced. In parallel with this phenomenon, suppression of molting is known to occur both under constant exposure to light and constant darkness in *Gecarcinus* (Bliss 1954a,b) and in the complete darkness in *Cambarus* (Stephens 1955). All these facts suggest that inhibition of the Y organ by a hormone from the X organ–sinus gland becomes intensified in extreme regimes of light, and this appears to be the underlying mechanism of the suppression of later molts in the talitrids living under leaf mold (Fig. 3). It should also be borne in mind that there are other hormones known to be involved with the molting cycle in Crustacea (Highnam and Hill 1977). Association of male neoteny with darkness is apparent also in some other crustaceans as seen, for instance, in *Peltogaster,* in which the dwarf male fixes itself to the female's mantle opening (Reinhard 1942), and the dwarf neotenous male of *Emerita,* which remains attached to the ventral surface of the female (below).

Regardless of the adaptive significance of structural physiological, and behavioral changes [see Williamson (1951) and Hurley (1959, 1968) for the behavioral change], however, it is important to point out that the hormones concerned with such changes were preexisting ones. Thus ecdysone for molting has been known to occur throughout the Crustacea. The gland producing androgenic hormone has been found in species belonging to all superorders and orders, and most of the suborders, of Malacostraca (Charniaux-Cotton 1972). The brain hormone stimulating the ovary development is present as in decapods (Adiyodi and Adiyodi 1970), and the occurrence of this hormone is probably widespread within the Malacostraca. Therefore, the changes in terrestrial talitrids can be said to have occurred as a result of response of these preexisting hormones to the new environmental stimulus on land. Presumably, the role of natural selection has been to eliminate the individuals that failed to respond (change) adaptively enough, in physiology and structure, in the new habitat.

It is reasonable to suppose further that colonization of the supralittoral zone by talitrids was accomplished repeatedly (and in rather rapid seccession) by populations, because migration along the seashore must depend heavily on the rise and fall of sea level; a group of individuals could often have been washed away, by the fall of sea level, onto the supralittoral zone. Similarly, invasion of the terrestrial zone might well have been done by many individuals of one or more species, simultaneously or in rapid succession, for in many lands the forest reaches right to the sea's edge, or borders streams running to the sea. Adaptive responses must have occurred in the new habitats before these populations eventually established themselves as new taxa. This mode of origin of terrestrial talitrids as a population in similar to that of the neotenous taxa in salamanders (Chap. 6). Another idea implicit in the above discussion is that a new taxon of terrestrial talitrids could have arisen polyphyletically and independently; this idea is probably supported by the fact that the distribution of terrestrial species is noticeably localized, although littoral species tend to be cosmopolitan (Hurley 1959, 1968).

Those isopods that are now terrestrial constitute the suborder Oniscoidea. As in Amphipoda, both marine and terrestrial isopods have direct development. Commonly, they possess oostegites, forming the brood pouch within which the eggs develop, and in this way the Oniscoidea have been fully emancipated from water (Edney 1960). Besides dorsoventral compression in some members and the walking habit, oostegites must have facilitated their adaptation to the terrestrial habitat, and the modification of the pleopod into the pseudotracheae is associated with respiration in dry air (Edney 1968). On some morphological grounds, Vandel (1943, 1965b) believed that the Oniscoidea are triphyletic in origin, each having been derived from a separate marine ancestor.

Hermit crabs, which are commonly intertidal and well known for their use of gastropod shells as their shelters, comprise more than 800 species in 86 genera and six families. Of these, only 12 species are semiterrestrial (McLaughlin 1983). Based on larval morphology, they were considered by Macdonald et al. (1957) as consisting of two independent lineages, Coenobitoidea and Paguroidea. However, McLaughlin, based on the five characters which she thought to be synapomorphic, reunited all related families under the superfamily Paguroidea, implying that the hermit crabs are monophyletic in origin. Other terrestrial crustaceans are some harpacticoids found underneath fallen leaves (Klie 1943, Menzel 1946), an ostracod genus *Mesocypris* (Harding 1958, Chapman 1961), and a cladoceran genus *Byrospilus* which comprises two species (Frey 1980).

The adult size of the brine shrimp *Artemia* has been known to vary inversely with the salinity of the external medium (see Gilchrist 1960 for a review of earlier works). In *Artemia salina* Voronov (1979) showed morphological difference (sizes and proportion of different body parts) between populations in salt lakes in Crimea and in Balkash territory. Although the total salinity of the waters is similar, they differ in specific salt composition. However, it is now known that temperature also affects the growth and maturation (Voronov 1982). Baid (1964) found that *A. salina* from a lake in India transformed into a form more or less identical with *A. malhauseni* (which is smaller in body size) when the concentration of chloride in the medium was raised to saturation point. Baid interpreted that *A. salina* is a neotenous form of *A. malhauseni*. However, the degree of morphological differentiation (such as the number of visible abdominal segments and of setae on cercopods) is more advanced in *A. salina* than in *A. malhauseni* (or transformed *malhauseni*-like individuals). It can therefore be said that *A. malhauseni* is neotenous in comparison with *A. salina*. Neurosecretory cells in *Artemia,* which are presumably involved with osmoregulation and morphogenesis, have been described by Hentschel (1964), Kulakovsky (1976), and Van den Bosch de Aguilar (1976); the X organ – sinus gland complex is absent.

In most species of the anomuran genus *Emerita,* as shown by Efford (1967), the male is known to be much smaller than the female. The juvenile adults are certainly precociously mature, retaining (in *E. talpoida* and *E. emeritus*) some larval features such as the stumps of the pleopods, which are normally present in the zoeae, megalopae, and the females. Efford therefore concluded that they are neotenous, and the neoteny is progenetic. The small males are attached to the posterior side of the proximal segment of the third walking legs close to the genital pore, in *E. rathbunae,* and elsewhere, such as the ventral side of the female or in the "gill chamber" clamped between the coxae of the thoracic appendages in other species of *Emerita* (Efford 1967). It is apparent that, in producing the neotenous males, androgenic hormone is turned on by darkness where they attach themselves. Subramoniam (1981) observed, however, that the neotenous males of *E. asiaticus* (3.5 mm in carapace length) continue to grow, gradually lose male functions, and reverse sex at around 19 mm in carapace length. Androgenic glands, active in neotenous males, show signs of degeneration in larger males, and disappear in the intersexes.

Margalef (1949) mentioned several cases of ecologically related forms or subspecies in copepods and amphipods that are neotenous. *Diacyclops bicus-pidatus* var. *lubbocki* has 14-segmented antennae, instead of the normal 17 segments for this species, and it occurs in salt water. *Megacyclops viridis,* with normally 17-segmented antennae, also has a form *M. v. claudi* with 11-segmented antennae that occurs in very deep waters; colder temperatures in such a habitat appear to have induced the antennal reduction. *Gammarus pulex* subsp. *fossarum,* whose center of distribution is the Alps and which has spread through France as far as Normandy, shows certain characters of immature stages (smaller sizes, simpler and fewer setae, smaller numbers of "calceola") of *G. p. pulex,* which occurs in fresh water in most parts of Europe but not in high mountains. Here again, the effect of colder temperatures appears to have been involved with its development. In comparison with marine *Gammarus locusta,* the brackish water form *G. l. aequicauda* is neotenous in having fewer antennal segments and in having uropod branches that are uniform; the case appears to have been induced by lower salinities. A parallel is another closely related freshwater or brackish-water species, *G. zaddachi,* which is also smaller, with fewer antennal segments and less developed carapace and telson.

Among cladocerans cyclomorphosis, or seasonal change in morphology, is well known, especially for the females of limnetic species, such as *Daphnia* spp. Characteristically, a population of a cyclomorphic species has a normal or roundheaded form during the late fall and early spring. As the water temperature becomes warmer, there is commonly a progessive elongation of the head and the appearance of a "helmet." The helmet becomes fully developed by midsummer. Beginning in the late summer or early autumn, the shape of the head progressively reverts to the normal head condition. Cyclomorphosis may also involve the size of the eyes, the length of the posterior spine, and the egg size (above).

The change in form in cyclomorphosis is the function of a combination of external conditions and inherent physiological conditions. Among the proximate factors of cyclomorphosis, temperature has been shown to be the most significant factor (Wesenberg-Lund 1908, Coker and Addelstone 1938, Brooks 1966a,b, Green 1963); relatively high temperatures have been found to induce helmet development. For instance, Coker and Addelstone (1938) found, in *Daphnia longispina,* that at a temperature of 10° C or below (during the last one-third of the period of the first juvenile instar in the brood chamber) all had round heads; 15% of those raised at 12° C had pointed heads; 32% at 13° C, 87% at 14° C, and all of those at 16° C had pointed heads. This and other similar results have indicated that temperature can often be the dominant factor in inducing cyclomorphosis. Other proximate factors for cyclomorphosis involving the helmet growth are turbulence (Jacobs 1961, Axelson 1961, Brooks 1966a,b) light combined with turbulence (Hazelwood 1966), and nutrition.

Most of the more recent works on cladoceran cyclomorphosis have been concerned with the effect of predation as the selective agent, nearly to the point of total disregard of the proximate causes of cyclomorphosis. Thus Dodson (1974) proposed that various appurtenances (helmet, horns, or spines) are induced to grow by some prey species as an anti-lock-and-key mechanism to foil invertebrate predators. The larger prey species reduce the visible parts of the body to reduce vertebrate predation and elaborate hyaline appurtenances to foil invertebrates. Temporally, maximum development of appurtenances is best correlated with the presence of predator species. Dodson dared to propose that the proximate environmental cues (temperature, etc.) for cyclomorphosis may act as environmental cues, if they are sufficiently correlated with the advent of intense invertebrate predation; cyclomorphosis therefore should be correlated with fluctuation in predator density, and not necessarily with any environmental parameters. Wong (1981) observed that individuals of *Bosmina longirostris* underwent an increase in mucro length during the summer at a time when adults of the predaceous copepod *Epischura lacustris* appeared. Wong's (1981) predation experiment demonstrated further that *Bosmina longirostris* individuals with enlarged mucrones were less susceptible to copepod predation than similar-sized prey without such adaptation. Thus Wong thought that the results supported Dodson's theory of adaptation against size-selective invertebrate predators. Furthermore, Kerfoot (1975) showed that polymorphism in two adjacent populations of *Bosmina longirostris* in Seattle, Washington, is maintained by two different kinds of predators (fish and copepod). According to Kerfoot, not only do the fishes directly affect the morph composition by differentially removing the more conspicuous morphs, but also they indirectly control the magnitude of counterselective forces by regulating the abundance of predatory copepods. A more recent review of life history strategies in *Daphnia* by Schwartz (1984) also ignores the proximate process of polymorphism. Earlier, Zaret (1969, 1972) and Green (1967, 1971) showed that predation results in polymorphism in tropical cladocerans.

Contrary to the adaptationists' claim in recent years, Herbert (1978) pointed out the following:

1. *Ctenodaphnia* spp. with the most prominent crests inhabit intermittent environments in which vertebrate predators are absent. Therefore, the predator avoidance hypothesis does not explain this phenomenon and the fact that many *Daphnia* species never produce crests, and why even the cyclomorphic species produce crests only when food levels and temperature are high.

2. The Dodson theory also fails to explain the origin of striking association between low temperature and the absence of crests, for there is evidence to suggest that predator pressure is inordinately low in cool environments. The Arctic species *D. middendorffiana* always lacks a crest, yet populations of this species often coexist with extremely high density populations of the copepod species.

3. Dodson's suggestion that *Daphnia* lacking crests produce more progeny than those with crests is invalid in the light of his actual observation.

The above-mentioned facts presented by adaptationists show that selective predation at two levels (copepods and fishes) contribute to polymorphism. Yet the fundamental fact of direct environmental effect on development resulting in polymorphism cannot be denied. It appears, then, that both the proximate and ultimate (predation) processes contribute to polymorphism, and the degree of contribution of each one of these must vary in different species, and it may depend on the environmental conditions under which they live.

According to Herbert (1978), also, all four species of *Daphnia* present in the North American Arctic have small heads, which are maintained even if the species are cultured at high temperatures. Furthermore, the only *Daphnia* species (*D. cephalata, D. barbata*) with permanent cephalic crests are restricted to tropical and subtropical areas. These facts appear to indicate that in the Arctic the cold temperature-induced small headedness has become genetically fixed and that the warmer temperature-induced crested head has also become genetically fixed. Earlier, Woltereck (1934) introduced a race of *D. cucullata* from Denmark into a lake in south Italy uninhabited by the species, and found after a number of generations a changed form. This new form persisted through generations under experimental conditions (more limited nutrition and lower temperatures). However, the form became gradually lost and after 40 generations had reverted to the ancestral form. Woltereck (1934) regarded this phenomenon as "*Dauermodifikation*" (persistent modification). Persistent modification can occur, according to Woltereck, through the maternal effect, and it can revert by a counterinduction.

The switch to sexual reproduction in cladocerans is accompanied by the formation of dormant eggs enclosed within the thickened, pigmented portion of the brood chamber, the ephippium. Interactions between various environmental factors (such as photoperiod, temperature, population density, water quality, and food availability) has been shown to induce sexual reproduction and the (usually) concomitant ephippium production (Stross 1965, 1969a,b; Stross and Hill 1968; Bunner and Halcrow 1977). Attempts to show the relationship between the activity of neurosecretory cells and the ephippium production (Angel 1967; Van den Bosch de Aguilar 1969, 1972; Bunner and Halcrow 1977) remained equivocal. Bunner and Halcrow (1977) pointed out that the production of the ephippium does not depend on the production of eggs, and suggested that they are under separate hormonal (neurosecretory) controls.

A continuous series of reduction of structures in a presumed phylogenetic sequence has been recognized for certain groups of Crustacea. An outstanding case of such neoteny (a phylogenetic neoteny) is seen in the evolution of the Conchostraca–Cladocera complex. In the Conchostraca the number of trunk limbs is variable, being 10–32 pairs; of these, 1–16 are postgenital. In the Conchostracha the number of naupliar stages in known to be five (Kaestner 1967). After the nauplius stage, molting occurs many times. In all Cladocera except for two species, on the other hand, the naupliar stages are passed within the egg; they hatch as juveniles with six (or five) pairs of functional trunk limbs, and no more trunk limbs are added during subsequent growth and development (Anderson 1973).

In a conchostracan species, *Cyclestheria hislopi*, embryonization of naupliar stages occurs, and the young conchostracan hatches from the egg with six pairs of functional trunk limbs, as in most cladocerans. Thereafter, however, larval development continues in the usual way, with the addition of further trunk segments and limbs. It is apparent, therefore, that the Cladocera arose from a *Cyclestheria*-like ancestor(s), and suppression of anamorphosis occurred, resulting in acceleration of development (De Beer 1958, Tasch 1963, Anderson 1973). Schminke (1981) pointed out that the lengthy discussion on phylogeny of the Cladocera by Eriksson (1934) indicated polyphyletic origin of cladocerans from various conchostracan ancestors at different times. It is difficult to see immediately the effect of environmental changes associated with such polyphyletic origins, because both conchostracans and cladocerans are not marine in most species. Only eight species of cladocerans are marine; their life cycle, which includes parthenogenesis, was summarized by Onbe (1978).

INTERSTITIAL CRUSTACEANS. Although structural modifications in interstitial crustaceans are generally not as pronounced as in the interstitial forms of other invertebrate phyla, some are the so-called *"Lebensformtypen."* According to Hartmann (1973), marine interstitial ostracods inhabiting the supralittoral waters and the coral rubbles are characterized by (1) reduction in body size, which seldom exceeds 0.5 mm in length, (2) reduction of eyes, even the nauplius eyes being absent, (3) reduction in number of segments, which very commonly occurs in Polycopidae (Cladocopa) (with only five head segments with appendages, instead of seven to eight in related families), and (4) reduction of both external and internal genital organs in Polycopidae (in which the copulatory organ is unpaired) and Parvocytheridae. Often, concomitant modifications of structures also occur in the shell shape, and the modification of appendages is especially pronounced in those species living in association with coral rubbles. The latter involves the reduction in number of bristles and concomitant transformation of remaining bristles into strong claws. Several families of ostracods occur in limnetic subsoil water, but they are not *Lebensformtypen* (Hartmann 1973).

Numerous cases of interstitial copepods have been described, especially for Harpacticoidea. According to Noodt (1974), interstitial forms of the Harpacticoidea have arisen convergently, through wormlike stretching of the body, reduction in body size, and specialization of appendages. These modifications must have resulted from neoteny, proposed by Serban (1960). In the harpacticoid genera inhabiting phreatic water the body size is sometimes less than 0.3 mm (the size smaller than many protozoans) and the body form is cylindrical. Serban (1960) attributed these features to suppression of a larval stage; the majority of harpacticoids are known to have all developmental stages. The copepod *Cycloporella eximia,* described as a new genus and species by Monchenko (1981), lives in the interstitial biotope in the Black Sea; it is characterized by reduction of arms (p_5) and oligomerization of maxillipeds, etc., although certain characters remain primitive.

Another well-known case of interstitial crustaceans is the subphylum Mystacocarida (with 12–13 species in two genera, Renaud-Mornant and Delamare-Deboutteville 1976), which has been considered to be primitive and/or neotenous since the description of *Derocheilocaris typicus* as the type species of Mystacocarida by Pennak and Zinn (1943). In *D. typicus* from North America and *D. remanei* from Europe the first postembryonic stage is the metanauplius (Cals and Cals-Usciati 1982), which presumably hatches from rather large eggs (Fize 1963, Hessler 1971). Postembryonic development is characteristic in that certain appendages (A$_2$ and Md) remain virtually unchanged until the adult stage is reached (i.e., without a metamorphic change) and Renaud-Mornant and Delamare-Deboutteville thought this feature to be neoteny. Hessler and Newman (1975) suggested that the Mystacocarida evolved through neoteny from a malacostracan ancestor. Lombardi and Ruppert (1982) suggested that the biramous structure of the A$_2$ and Md of the nauplius or metanauplius larva permitted the animals to move into confined interstitial spaces.

The interstitial isopod *Angeliera phreaticola* has undergone, besides reduction in body size, elongation of body shape, blindness, and profound modifications in nervous, digestive, and reproductive systems; the last has been greatly reduced in both sexes and the female lays a single egg at a time (Renaud-Mornant and Coineau 1978). Schminke (1978) regarded the interstitial Stygocarididae as a neotenous family of the order Anaspidacea that retain some juvenile features of the Anaspidacea as adult structures.

The suborder Ingolfiellidea (Amphipoda), with 27 species in three genera allocated to two families (Stock 1979), is a clear example of emigration from the sea to fresh water, apparently without conspicuous structural changes. Some members of Gammaridea (Amphipoda) also have colonized interstitial habitats. Their adaptive changes are slight, so that their relationship to free-living relatives is often clear (Stock 1973).

PARASITIC CRUSTACEANS. There are normally six naupliar instars in the free-living cyclopoid copepods (Elgmork and Langeland 1970); the typical nauplius (as in *Cyclops*) hatched from the egg is followed by the second naupliar instar and four metanaupliar instars. In the metanauplius instars the body lengthens, and three pairs of appendages (including the maxilliped and two pairs of legs) are added beyond the mandibles. At the next molt, the larva begins to assume a form with adult structures called the "copepodid." After six copepodid instars it becomes the sexually mature adult; the number of thoracic legs added during this period varies in different copepods from three to five (Kaestner 1967). In parasitic copepods the naupliar and metanaupliar stages are often passed within the egg (embryonization), and it is usually the first copepodid that finds the host for parasitization. Some are ectoparasitic, undergoing relatively small structural changes. However, some are endoparasitic and their structural transformation is profound (halmatometamorphosis). Furthermore, some of them require two hosts. Examples follow.

Salminicola californiensis (Lernaeopodidae), described by Kabata and Cousens (1973), is an ectoparasite of the sockeye salmon (*Onchorhynchus nerka*); the metamorphic changes are relatively small. The free-swimming copepodid hatched from the egg becomes attached to the host and transforms into four successive chalimus stages. Major structural changes during this transformation begin with evagination of the filament from the anterior margin of the head upon contact with the host. Each successive chalimus stage reattaches the filament during molting. Degeneration and eventual loss of the trunk appendages occurs, and further development and elaboration of the second maxilla and maxilliped occur thereafter.

Cymbasoma rigidum (Monstrillidae) exhibits a case where the adult becomes free swiming after undergoing a profound metamorphosis within the host (Malaquin 1901, Snodgrass 1956). The nauplius of this species is provided with curved hooks on the mandibles that are used for attaching itself to the host (the serpulid worm *Salmacina dysteri*). The nauplius enters the host's body after casting off its cuticle and appendages. Within the host it becomes a shrunken oval mass of undifferentiated cells. In this form the parasite traverses the coelom of the host and makes its way into the ventral blood cells, where it secretes new cuticles and then from its ventral side anteriorly there grow two armlike processes that serve as food (blood)-absorbing organs. As Snodgrass (1956) said, here we see a metamorphic development adapting the parasite to its life in the host that had no counterpart in the presumed free-living ancestors of its species; (hence this is halmatometamorphosis). As the larva grows, the nutritive arms increase in length, a rostrum is formed in front, and the posterior part of the body becomes encircled with spines. The organs of the future adult now gradually develop within the cuticle of the larva. Eventually, the adult with one pair of antennae and four pairs of swimming legs emerges. Thus the parasite undergoes metamorphosis in its life cycle.

The life cycle of the female of *Lernaeocera branchialis* (Lernaeopodidae) requires two hosts (summarized by Snodgrass 1956). The first-stage larva that hatches from the yolk-rich egg is the metanauplius, which directly develops into the copepodid (Kohler 1976). The copepodid larva (in both sexes) molts into the chalimus in the gills of the flounder; the chalimus becomes fixed to the host by a filament secreted by a gland in the head. The chalimus undergoes gradual change in form and structure and becomes the adult at the fourth instar after the copepodid stage. The male undergoes no further transformation. The female, still not sexually mature, begins her metamorphosis upon reaching the second host, which should be the cod. The curious transformation of the female in the second host involves the production of large, branching hornlike structures of the head as anchoring devices and lengthening of the abdomen, particularly the genital segment, which grows out in a twisted wormlike form; then the abdomen becomes long and straight and eventually swells into a great, elongate twisted bag; this stage is known as the penella stage.

As shown by Bresciani and Lutzen (1974), *Aphanodomus terebellae* (Xenocoelomidae) is a parasite of the polychaete *Thelepus cincinnatus*. The male, after undergoing a degenerative metamorphosis, settles itself in the receptaculum masculinum of the female (cryptogonochorism). The female is cucumbershaped and unsegmented, and it is attached to the external wall of the host's gut;

its early developmental cycle and the manner of entry into the host remain unknown. The female develops the receptaculum masculinum consisting of the bipartite receptaculum seminis and establishes communication with the exterior through a pore. The planktonic phase of the male consists at least of the nauplius and the copepodid stages. The copepodid enters the female atrium through the pore, where it transforms into a simple vesicular body that is conveyed to the receptaculum masculinum, then the vesicular body develops into the male reproductive organs (testis and testis commissure).

Bouligand (1966) summarized the facts on the copepods parasitic on anthozoans; semi-free (ectoparasitic) families include Asterocheridae and Lichomolgidae, and some are endoparasitic and generally greatly deformed. Furthermore, Gotto (1979) published a comprehensive summary of the association of copepods with marine invertebrates, and Kabata (1981) summarized the more recent works on copepods associated with fishes.

Peltogaster paguri (Rhizocephala, Cirripedia) is the parasite of the hermit crab *Pagurus pubescens* and, as shown by Reinhard (1942), the male is nothing but a sexually mature cypris larva (neotenous). Reinhard found that the male fixes itself to the opening of the mantle of the female, and expels a material that consists of spermatogenic elements and "nurse cells." The material migrates through the cavity of the mantle to enter the so-called "testis," which Reinhard found to be a sperm receptacle. Likewise, Ichikawa and Yanagimachi (1958, 1960) demonstrated that in *Peltogasterella socialis, Peltogaster paguri,* and *Sacculina senta* the cypris larva injects the male material into the receptacle, and that it is the sole source of spermatozoa. Reinhard and Evans (1951) found that in *Mycetomorpha vancouverensis* the cypris male attached to the mantle undergoes a degenerative metamorphosis to become a mere spermatophore. Veillet (1962) observed spermatogenesis in the cement secreted by colleterial glands in *Sylon hippolytes,* which had been thought to reproduce parthenogenetically. Yanagimachi and Fujimaki (1967) noted the extremely transformed cypris male residing in the mantle of the female of *Thompsonia japonica.* Thus the nature of the male in these rhizocephalans is essentially the same as that in the copepod *Aphanodomus,* that is, an example of cryptogonochorism. Furthermore, it seems possible that the neoteny of the male is enabled by precocious deployment of androgenic hormone (under some environmental conditions such as the attachment to the mantle).

The females of rhizocephalans undergo profound metamorphosis (halmatometamorphosis), as exemplified by the well-known case of *Sacculina* (established by Delage 1884 and summarized by Snodgrass 1956). The free-swimming female cypris larvae, upon attachment to antennules of the young crab, undergo degenerative metamorphosis, shedding the thorax along with the legs and the abdomen and most of the internal tissues, leaving only a mass of cells containing the reproductive elements. The latter contracts to a sac walled by the ectoderm. From this sac is formed a larva called the "kentrogon" with a dart at the anterior end. The dart pierces the integument of the crab and the larval tissues penetrate into the crab's body through a narrow channel of the dart.

Inside the crab the parasite (i.e., the larval tissue) becomes a small body consisting of a mass of cells enclosed within the ectodermal epithelium, attaches to the ventral side of the crab's intestine, and forms rootlike processes (rhizai) through which nourishment is absorbed. The parsite at this stage consists of the reproductive organ (ovary) and the food-absorbing fungus-like structures. At the next molt of the crab the body of *Sacculina* becomes external. The external parasite consists of the ovary, the sperm receptacle, and the mantle that encloses the peripheral brood chamber. Rubiliani et al. (1982) provided some additional information regarding the parasitic life cycle of *Sacculina*.

As shown by Bocquet-Verdine (1969) and Bocquet-Verdine and Parent (1972), *Boschmaella balani* is a parasite of the cirriped *Balanus improvisus*, which has no pelagic larval stage; the larvae emerge as blind cyprids that immediately reinfest. The radicular system of this species bears a unique sac that undergoes asexual reproduction, presumably by budding. *Chthamalophilus delagei*, described by Bocquet-Verdine (1961), has a life history similar to that of *Boschmaella balani*.

Parasitic isopods require either one host (either as the larva or adult) or two. An example of the former is *Paragnatha formica*, which is parasitic in its larval stage on fishes. The relatively small metamorphic change that occurs upon establishment on a fish is mainly the lengthening of the thorax, which is accompanied by swelling of the last three thoracic segments (Monod 1926, Snodgrass 1956).

All species of the suborder Epicaridea are parasitic on other crustaceans (Kaestner 1967) and often require two hosts. The larva that hatches from the egg is known as an epicaridium. The larvae attach themselves to the surface of swimming copepods, where they undergo six successive molts, and pass through two distinct larval stages known as the microniscus and cryptoniscus stages. The cryptoniscus larva abandons the copepod and goes in search of a decapod (Baer 1951). However, in most bopyrids the epicarid larva may directly develop into the cryptoniscus (Hiraiwa 1936). In *Danalia curvata* (Smith 1906, Caullery 1908, Snodgrass 1956) the cryptoniscus becomes a functional male before it seeks out a crab parasitized by a sexually mature female of his own species. After accomplishing insemination of the female the larval male undergoes a radical change in structure within the cryptoniscus cuticle and becomes a small cylindrical sac. The testes now degenerate and ovaries begin to develop, to change into a functional female. Similarly, in *Ione thoracica*, according to Reverberi and Pitotti (1942) and Reverberi (1947), cryptonisci that attach to the female become males. In *Stegophryxus hyptius*, as shown by Reinhard (1949), sexes are already distinct during the cryptoniscus stage; cryptonisci destined to become functional males are those found attached to young or mature females as in *Ione*. Reinhard assumed that, as in *Bonellia*, the female secretes a specific masculinizing substance. Sexual changes and concomitant development of sexual characters must involve the action of androgenic hormone, which has been rather extensively studied for isopods (Hasegawa and Katakura 1981 and Raimond and Juchault 1983, among more recent works).

B. THE CLASS CHELICERATA

Varying degrees of acceleration in intraoval and extraoval developmental stages have occurred in the Chelicerata. As Francke's (1982) review on the developmental pattern in scorpions has revealed, apoikogenic scorpions (which have simple ovariuteri without diverticula) have relatively large, yolk-rich eggs (0.4×0.2 to 1.20×0.83 mm) and they are considered as ovoviviparous, whereas katoikogenic scorpions (which have ovariuteri with numerous diverticula) have small alecithal eggs and they are considered as viviparous. Embryonic nutrition is provided in the former by yolk and supplemented by a diffuse placenta, and in the latter by specialized cells (located at the apices of the diverticula) leading into the oral cavity of the embryo. Despite the distinction in egg size and in some other features, all scorpion embryos derive some nutrients directly from the mother during development. Therefore, Francke (1982) considered that all scorpions are viviparous. In Scorpiones postoval development is prolonged. After the first molt the young acquires the typical scorpionlike appearance. The total number of molts may be variable, but it is believed that there are eight stadia in *Palamnaeus* and seven in *Androctonus australis* (Cloudsley-Thompson 1958).

In the Japanese horseshoe crab *Tachypleus tridentatus,* according to Sekiguchi et al. (1984), molting occurs four times intraovally, and at the end of the third molt the "embryo" presents the appearance of a trilobite. The number of molts after hatching remains unknown, although in the American horseshoe crab *Limulus polyphemus* it is known to be 15, which occur in 9–11 years (Shuster 1960). Sekiguchi et al. attributed this extreme embryonization to the increase in yolk content during evolution. They thought that probably only the first instar passed within the egg initially. The increase in yolk content could possibly have occurred after acquisition of the new shallow water habitat along the coast, where the crab's endocrine function for vitellogenesis could have been altered (for the increase). An inner membrane (or embryonic envelope) is developed under the chorion after the blastula stage. This membrane is expanded by the influx of water into the inside of the membrane, followed by the rupture of chorion. Afterward, the subsequent swelling of the inner membrane provides the developing embryo an adequate space to repeat embryonic molting four times (Sekiguchi 1970, Sugita and Sekiguchi 1982).

Within the Acari, which are considered to have been derived from the Opiliones with five to seven postembryonic stages (Cloudsley-Thompson 1958 and Kaestner 1963), the maximum number of postembryonic developmental stages is six, which consist of the prelarva, larva, protonymph, deutonymph, tritonymph, and adult (Travé 1976). However, acceleration in development by omission of stages has occurred frequently, especially in association with parasitism. The consequence of acceleration has often been a highly modified structural organization in the adult, resulting in the origination of distinct taxa. An outstanding example is the Podapolipidae, which parasitize wing bases, spiracles, etc., of insects (mainly Orthoptera and Coleoptera). In this family the female adults emerge from the larval exuviae (Regenfuss 1968, Baker and

Eickwort 1975, Eickwort 1976), and the active nymphal stages are eliminated from their ontogeny. In the male the adult hatches from the egg, skipping the larva (Regenfuss 1968).

The female adult that emerges from the larva varies greatly in degree of adult (imaginal) differentiaton in different species; it is especially conspicuous in the number of legs it acquires. Thus *Eutarsopolipus, Ovacarus, Dorsipes,* and *Tarsopolipus* have three pairs of legs; *Tetrapolipus* spp. have two pairs; *Bakerpolipus, Podapolipoides, Lacustacrus,* and *Podapolipus* have one pair; and *Archipolipus* is completely legless (Regenfuss 1968, 1973). *Chrysomelobia* is more generalized in that four pairs of adult legs are produced as in the plesiomorphic related family Tarsonemidae, although the fourth pair is somewhat reduced and modified (Regenfuss 1968, 1973; Eickwort 1976). Reduction of other structures such as tergites is pronounced in the podapolipids with one or two pairs of legs, and displacement of the male copulatory organ onto the dorsum or even to the anterior end of the body occurs in these mites. The development of all these structures is clearly related to the omission of nymphal stages, and reflects a profound alteration in gene regulation that occurred in association with suppression of the nymphal genes. The adults with fewer pairs of legs are so unique, that the cases of Podapolipidae can be safely regarded as halmatomorphosis. Regenfuss (1973) proposed that the acquisition of the habit of precopulation, in which the male copulates with the larval female, created a new selection pressure for the reduction in leg numbers and displacement of the male copulatory organs.

Bakerocoptes cynopteri, which represented a new subfamily Bakerocoptinae of Teinocoptidae (Fain 1962), is a parasite of bats, with six-legged adult mites in both sexes. The adult male closely resembles the larva, being distinguishable from the latter by longer hairs, the presence of the second solenidion on the first tarsus, and the voluminous penis. Therefore, the adult is essentially a six-legged protonymph that is sexually mature. Hence the case is a progenetic neoteny.

Neotenogynium malkini was described by Kethley (1974) as representing a new family Neotenogyniidae. The species is associated with spirostrepid millipeds, and postembryonic development consists of the larva, protonymph, deutonymph, and adult. Many features (essentially larval setation on palpal femur, gena, and tibia; eyes; etc.) are neotenous.

In Ereynetidae both free-living species and endoparasitic species occur, and the latter must have been derived directly from the free-living species; no ectoparasites occur (Fain 1969, 1972). In the free-living subfamily Ereynetinae the developmental cycle consists of egg – larva – protonymph – deutonymph – tritonymph – adult. However, in Lawrencarinae, parasitizing the nasal cavities of frogs and toads, the active tritonymph stage does not occur. Furthermore, in Speleognathinae, which parasitize the nasal cavities of birds and mammals, no nymphal stage occurs, and the adult emerges directly from the larval exuviae; nymphal stages are represented by vestigial chitinous and membranous structures (Fain 1963, 1972).

As has been repeatedly pointed out by Fain (1969, 1977, 1979), structural modifications in parasitic mites involve both regressive and constructive changes (material compensation) that can be attributed primarily to altered gene regulation induced in the parasitic environment. The hormonal mechanism that must be involved with this alteration in gene regulation can now be surmised (below).

The presence of ecdysteroids (ecdysone and ecdysterone) is now known directly for several groups of arachnids including the ticks (Winget and Herman 1976, Bonaric and De Reggi 1977, Delbecque et al. 1978, Germond et al. 1982, Diehl 1982, Dees et al. 1984). In the tick *Dermacentor variabilis* Germond et al. (1982) found, by radioimmunoassay, that apolysis and formation of the exuvial space occurred as the ecdysteroid rose and as the highest ecdysteroid concentrations were observed during the deposition of cuticle; a similar observation was also reported for *Amblyomma hebraeum* by Diehl et al. (1982). Thus these results clearly showed a parallel to the ecdysteroid-induced molting events in insects. Most probably, therefore, acceleration involving the suppression of nymphal instars (both inside and outside eggs) has involved the altered (presumably lowered) action of ecdysteroid in the parasitic environment. However, the presence of JH, which antagonizes the action of ecdysteroids in insects, has not been proven directly for any chelicerate, although the involvement of this or a similar hormone is probable. Alteration in gene regulation leading to the progressive and regressive developments of structures (material compensation), including the suppression of nymphal stages in parasitic mites, must involve disturbance in hormonal activity, which is likely to be induced in the parasitic environment.

Natural selection appears to have worked mainly on constructive developments, which are clearly adaptive. Attaching organs, for instance, must have been the "sine qua non" condition for the beginning of parasitic life, and various elaborations of the organs have occurred in diverse parasitic mites (Fain 1969). In discussing coevolution of fur mites (Myobiidae) with mammalian hosts, Fain (1977, 1979) maintained that the immune system is most perfected in the most evolved hosts (Rodentia) and the myobiid parasites are most regressed, so regressed that the attaching claws are absent. He therefore thought that the reduction of the structures in these parasites is a result of natural selection, which tends to favor the less antigenic and therefore most regressed phenotype. This interpretation is not compelling, lacking experimental support, and the idea may be based on the too much faith in natural selection as the agent of evolution.

In Mesostigmata, according to Lindquist (1965), there are two types of setal deficiency: (1) the chaetotaxy of the larva is deficient and the deficiencies are retained in the adult and (2) the larval chaetotaxy is complete (holotrichous), but some of the setae usually added to the larval component in the protonymph and deutonymph are suppressed. Lindquist (1965) showed how, in *Hoploseius tenuis* (Blattiscidae), the deficiency of setal pattern occurs in conformity with these general tendencies, resulting in localized neoteny. No suppression of developmental stage is involved with this process, and the case may represent a metagenetic neoteny. The species was collected from the pores of coniferous bracket fungi at elevations of about 7500–9000 ft in Mexico. Relatively low temperature may be the proximate cause that induces the localized (partial) neoteny.

The deficiency in setal pattern resulting in localized neoteny has been known also for some pseudoscorpions. For instance, the chetae of the posterior row of the cephalothorax in the adult of *Chthonius orthodactylus* are identical to those in the tritonymph of *C. ischnochelae,* and in some other species of *Chthonius* the protonymphal chaetotaxy of the first and second tergites may be retained in the adult (Gabbutt and Vachon 1963). Similar cases of retention of the nymphal trichobothrial pattern in the adult of some other pseudoscorpions were noted by Weygoldt (1969). In these cases the (presumed) ecological association is not immediately clear.

C. THE CLASS MYRIAPODA

In myriapods the young that hatched from eggs must be considered as juveniles, because the presumed larval stage in the marine ancestors has been completely eliminated. In Lithobiomorpha and Scutigeromorpha (of the Chilopoda), Diplopoda, Symphyla, and Pauropoda postoval development proceeds by anamorphosis, that is, by the increase in number of abdominal segments (often bearing legs) that occurs by splitting of the preanal zone of proliferation or of the growth zone; one or more segments are formed at each molt. The number of antennal segments also increases at each molt (Scheffel 1969). When the reduction in number of abdominal and antennal segments occurs in these myriapods, it must be due to suppression of the anamorphic process, and such reduced conditions can be regarded as neotenous.

Furthermore, as the review by Anderson (1973) indicated, much of the evolutionary modification of intraoval development has been related to the secondary reduction in yolk content (and hence egg size) and associated precocious hatching with only a few segments, as seen in Diplopoda, Pauropoda, and Symphyla. In *Pauropus sylvaticus* the egg size, measuring 0.09–0.11 mm in diameter, was described as minute by Tiegs (1947). Its embryonic development is highly modified, being characterized mainly by its simplicity, and the size of the juvenile (called the larva) rarely exceeds 1.1 mm. Three juvenile stages were recognized and the third-stage juvenile molts into the adult with nine pairs of legs; during this process the short fifth and sixth trunk segments are demarcated in front of the growth zone (anamorphosis) (Tiegs 1947). At any rate, the consequences of simplified embryonic development in the minute egg and of anamorphosis result in a highly reduced number of trunk segments and the loss of the circulatory system (or no tracheae or other differentiated organs of respiration) (Snodgrass 1952). No special environmental factor(s) that might have induced the reduction in egg size and a significant suppression of anamorphosis is conceivable at the present. Highly simplified adult structures are due to accelerated development, and the case may be regarded as progenetic neoteny.

Reduction in number of trunk segments has occurred repeatedly during the evolution of myriapods with anamorphosis, and the trend has been highly pronounced in diplopods. Demange (1968, 1974) recognizd two types of reduction, one ecologically related and another genetically determined. He regarded the reduction in number of trunk segments and the loss of ocelli as neotenous features. In diplopods the definitive number of trunk segments depends on the number of molt and that of the apodous segments produced at each molt, and Demange (1974) postulated the following tendencies:

1. In the diplopods with relatively few segments the segment number is fixed (e.g., Craspedosomoidea with the order of 30) or relatively fixed (e.g., Polydesmoidea with the order of 20), and in the subclass Pentazonia the segment number is 12. On the contrary, in the diplopods with high numbers of segments (Julidae) the segment number is highly variable.

2. The number of diplosegments acquired at each molt is relatively small in the more fixed forms, and it is greater in the species with large numbers of segments.

The above sequence of increasing (genetic) fixation of segments appears to have involved the alteration in functioning of the morphogenetic endocrine mechanism comparable with that in insects (below). Because the molting has been known to be induced by ecdysteroids since the experiments with *Lithobius* by Joly (1964, 1966), Scheffel (1969), and Scheffel et al. (1974), production of fewer segments in the fixed form must have occurred as a result of alteration in functioning of the ecdysteroid-producing organs (Lymphstränge of Scheffel 1969, or the glandula ecdysalis of Seifert and Rosenberg 1974 and Rosenberg 1979), which are comparable with the prothoracic glands in insects. Furthermore, as Scheffel (1969) first concluded, the ecdysial glands must be under the inhibitory control of the frontal lobe – cerebral glands.

As Joly (1977) has shown, temperature and starvation are the most important factors controlling the activity of the cerebral glands; light does not seem to be an effective environmental factor, for the animals are cryptozoic. Joly (1977) showed that low temperature (5° C) and starvation seem at first to stimulate the activity of the cerebral glandular activity and the release of the elaborated product. Subsequently, cellular injuries appear and the activity decreases. Joly thought that inhibition of molting may first be related to an increase in glandular activity (which influences the activity of the ecdysial glands) and later comes essentially from a metabolic action. The effect of environment on molting cycle was shown also by Joly (1966) and Scheffel (1977), and its influence on gametogenesis is also known (Descamps 1981, Herbaut 1975).

The ecologically related variation in trunk segment number (Demange 1968, 1974; Seifert 1966) must be due to the altered environmental influence on the cerebral glands – ecdysial glands axis. It can further be surmised that under the influence of continued unfavorable environmental influences (such as low temperature and poor food supply) some myriapods have presumably decreased the molting frequency and the number of segments they form at each molt; such effects could have accumulated under continued unfavorable conditions, resulting in the genetic fixation of the reduced number of trunk segments (through the process of genetic assimilation).

Geophilus carpophagus, belonging to the Geophilomorpha, is epimorphic in that the number of trunk segments is determined within the egg. Yet, as shown by Eason (1979), the number of trunk segments formed apparent depends on environmental conditions. In the natural habitat of Britain the number of segments is 47–49 in most male individuals, rarely 45, and never 51 or more. In females, the number is 49–51, rarely 47 or 51, and very rarely (2%) 53. However, in urban and suburban districts the corresponding numbers are 53 in the male (based on only one individual), and 55–57 in the female. In northern European countries the populations of *G. carpophagus* seem to be close to the urban/suburban populations in the number of trunk segments. Furthermore, in *Pachymerium ferrugineum,* according to the summary by Eason, the modal number of trunk segments for females in the Finnish population is 45, whereas in North Africa it is 55. Eason therefore preferred the interpretation that this difference is due to phenotypic plasticity, which is reversible, and thought that temperature is likely to be the important environmental factor that induces such plasticity. Because the species is epimorphic, Eason believed that environment must act either at the time of fertilization of the ovum or some time during embryonic development before the formation of the peripatoid larva (the stage that succeeds the last embryonic stage). Eason was not concerned with the ultimate selective factor that might be involved with the temperature-dependent plasticity in trunk-segment formation.

In the above case the difference in yolk content in the egg might well be related to the differing numbers of trunk segments formed. It can perhaps be hypothesized that the larger the eggs (with more yolks), the longer the embryo stays within the egg and the more segments formed. Herbaut (1975) showed that in *Lithobius forficatus* the pars intercerebralis activates the growth of oocytes and that its action appears to be of a metabolic nature. The same author (Herbaut 1976) showed that oogenesis is assured by the neurosecretion in the frontal lobes–cerebral glands complex control of vitellogenesis. The action of the frontal lobes–cerebral glands complex may well be influenced by the pars intercerebralis as Joly and Jamault-Navaro (1978) indicated. The entry of exogenous vitelline into developing oocytes, however, has not been directly observed thus far. In *Jonespeltis* (Diplopoda) connective tissues attached to the lateral esophageal connectives control oocyte development including vitellogenesis (Nair 1981).

D. THE CLASS INSECTA

1. The Order Collembola

The number of juvenile molts varies with different species of Collembola; molting occurs even after sexual maturation (Hale 1965); the largest number of molts known appears to be 45 in *Orchesella* (Lindenmann 1950). Betsch and Vannier (1977) showed that juvenile development in Collembola Symphypleona consists of two phases that are separated by significant structural differences, especially by those of integumentary structures and the tracheal system, which differentiate in phase 2. Betsch and Vannier (1977) contended that such structural modifications have enabled these organisms to exploit ecological niches on the surface of soil, and thought that the developmental process and its consequences in the Collembola Symphypleona are analogous to complete metamorphosis in winged insects. In the Collembola Arthropleona both juveniles and adults live together in the same subsoil habitat throughout their life.

In some collembolans structures are highly susceptible to modification by environmental changes, and the morphogenetic plasticity that expresses itself in changing environments has been known by two different terms, cyclomorphosis and ecomorphosis, which are essentially the same phenomenon; it occurs in Hypogastruridae and Isotomidae (Najt 1983). Cyclomorphosis, known since Folsom (1902), is the seasonal change of structures in which the effect of changing temperature (and presumably also of changing photoperiod) on development must be involved. Among more recent works, Fjellberg (1976) found, in laboratory rearing and field observation in Norway, that *Isotoma mucronota* (with slender and long apical teeth in the mucro) and *I. hiemalis* (with a short-toothed mucro) are different morphotypes of one species. Transformation from *I. mucronota* to *I. hiemalis* was observed in early November, and the reverse transformation occurred at the end of February. Fjellberg therefore concluded that they are temperature-induced seasonal morphs, or a case of cyclomorphosis. Furthermore, Fjellberg (1978) found, during the period of October–April, that an apparently undescribed species of *Vertagopus* occurs together with *Isotoma nivea* and that, by a single molting, typical features of *Isotoma* develop in the *Vertagopus* species. He therefore suggested the possibility that the genus *Vertagopus* arose through retention of the winter form of cyclomorphic *Isotoma*. In *Hypogastrura socialis,* as shown by Leinaas (1981a), the shape of the furca undergoes seasonal change; during the winter fully grown juveniles have large teeth on the dens, and in summer both juveniles and adults have much smaller teeth. The mucro becomes more heavily sclerotized in winter. Transformation occurs through one molt in September–October and in May. Leinaas thought that the enlargement of teeth and the more robust mucro in winter are adaptations for jumping on the slippery snow. Furthermore, Leinaas (1981b) found that *Hypogastrura frigida* represents the winter form of *H. lapponica.*

Transitory structural changes (in Hypogastruridae and Isotomidae) that occur in response to change in temperature have been studied in terms of "ecomorphosis" by Cassagnau (1955) and later workers in France. Cassagnau (1955) found that in *Hypogastrura purpuracens* the optimum temperature for "normal development" obtains in the midwinter in France. By raising the temperature to 20° C, Cassagnau obtained an aberrant form and observed that it increases at higher temperatures; the latter acquires anal spines characteristic of the genus *Ancistracenthella*. More recent studies on ecomorphosis include those by Cassagnau (1958), Cassagnau and Raynal (1964), Cassagnau and Fabres (1968), Cassagnau and Dalens (1976), Najt (1979), Lauga-Reyrel (1979), and Dalens and Vannier (1983). Profound effect of temperature and humidity on morphology and life cycle is also clear in an experiment with a tropical species *Lobella maxillaris* by Choudhuri et al. (1979). Najt (1983) discussed structural modifications related to ecomorphosis in Isotomidae and Hypogatruridae. Environmental-related morphogenetic plasticity is, as shown by Christiansen (1961), also reflected in abundant occurrence of convergence and parallelism in cave-dwelling collembolans *Sinella* and *Pseudosinella* (Entomobryinae), which are patently polyphyletic groups. Christiansen distinguished the cave-dependent characters that result in parallelism and convergence from the more stable, cave-independent characters.

As in other insects, molting appears to be mediated by ecdysteroids. In *Folsomia,* they are known to induce both apolysis and secretion of new cuticle during molting cycles (Palevody et al. 1977). JH appears to be involved with vitellogenesis in *Folsomia* (Palevody and Grimal 1976). Furthermore, Lauga-Reyrel (1984) showed, in his experiment involving precocene treatment and JH injection, that in *Hypogastrura tullbergi,* ecomorphosis results clearly from the decline of JH titer. This appears to mean that during ecomorphosis a certain temperature regime suppresses CA activity and induces the release of ecdysteroid, and then primitive morphogenesis (of Lauga-Reyrel) ensues. For a comprehensive review of the neuroendocrine structure in Collembola see Cassagnau and Juberthie (1983).

2. The Order Odonata

Rather conspicuous metamorphosis of structures (such as the mouthparts) occurs during the last nymphal molt into the adult (see Snodgrass 1954 for a summary). As in other insects, metamorphosis is effected by ecdysteroids, as has been known since Deroux-Stralla (1948), and it can be prevented or disturbed by injection of JH 1 (Andries 1979) and JHA (Schaller and Defossez 1974). However, neoteny involving the reduction of wings (which is an excellent indicator of neoteny in other insects) has never occurred in Odonata. In Odonata the wings can never be folded back on the dorsum because of the unique flight mechanism (Tannert 1958, Matsuda 1970, 1981). They must be either held vertically or spread horizontally, and consequently dragonflies always had to be free-flying as adults. Apparently, natural selection has consistently eliminated those that failed to develop functional wings by some hormonal disturbance (which could have occurred, judging from the above-mentioned control mechanism).

The developmental basis of the increase (or decrease) in body size in evolution was discussed by St. Quentin (1969) for two related species of libellulids. In *Nannothemis bella* from North America, which is small (14 mm long in the adult), the number of molts is 11 or 12, and 674–1037 days (interrupted by diapause) are required to complete the nymphal development. In another related but much larger species, *Pantala flavescens* from the tropics (39 mm long), molts also occur 10–12 times, but it takes only 55–101 days to complete nymphal development. Thus the number of molts is about the same in the two species, and the differences are shorter intermolt period and much faster growth rate in the latter.

3. The Order Ephemeroptera

Molting of the reproductively mature subimago into the adult (imago) in mayflies is probably a primitive feature, because it is comparable with the molting of sexually mature individuals in Thysanura. Schaefer (1975) contended that such primitive development has been retained in modern mayflies with a very short adult life, for the simultaneity of sexual maturity and the completion of somatic development, which occurred in other insects, has not been necessary in mayflies with such a short subimago–imaginal period. Presumably, according to Schaefer, the adult life of modern mayflies has been even more shortened than in their ancestors; this would protect them effectively from predation.

Further abbreviation in completing the life cycle has been established for some mayflies. Probably in all of the subfamily Oligoneuriinae of the Oligoneuriidae, according to Edmunds (1956), only partial exuviation occurs before the nuptial flight; that is, the subimaginal skin is shed from all parts of the body except the wings, and such incomplete metamorphosis can be a metagenetic neoteny. In some mayflies such as *Ephoron album* (Edmunds et al. 1956) and *Dolania americana* (Peters and Peters 1977) females do not molt into the adult, owing perhaps to persistent action of JH (discussed below), resulting in a metagenetic neoteny.

In Ephemeroptera, as in other orders, the ventral glands (=prothoracic glands) disintegrate rapidly during the subimaginal stages (Kaiser 1978), suggesting that ecdysteroids are involved with metamorphosis. CA (corpora allata) in mayflies have been observed since Nabert (1913) and Hanström (1940). More recently, Kaiser (1980) described them electron microscopically. Yet the presence of JHs has not been directly demonstrated by modern assay methods, although their presence is most probable. It appears that the absence of the subimaginal molt is due probably to disturbance in the balance between ecdysteroids and JHs, which results in the persistent action of JHs, which in turn reduces the effect of ecdysteroids during the final molt.

Reduction of hind wings is highly conspicuous in genera of several families (e.g., Baetidae, Leptophlebiidae, and Tricorythidae), and they have been entirely lost in many genera (e.g., *Hagenulodes* and *Isca* in Leptophlebiidae, *Pseudocloeon* in Baetidae, *Tricorythodes* in Tricorythidae, and *Caenis* in Caenidae) (W. Peters, personal communication). Peters also indicates that at least one genus in many phyletic lines of the Leptophlebiidae has independently lost the hind wings. In *Leptophyphes* (family Tricorythidae) the hind wings are present in the male but absent in the female (Edmunds et al. 1976). The total loss of wings has never occurred in Ephemeroptera, most probably because the nuptial flight is such a vital part of their life history. Natural selection, therefore, has allowed only the flight form. Mayflies, as in Odonata, also cannot fold their wings on the back of their abdomen; however, females of several species of

Baetis crumple their wings against the abdomen while ovipositing under water (Thew 1957, Leonard and Leonard 1962).

Remarkable caenogenesis involving posterior extension of the promesonotum has been known for *Prosopistoma* (Vayssiere 1934, Pescador and Peters 1974). Poecilogony—dissimilar nymphs and similar adults—is apparently common in mayflies, as summarized by Verrier (1950). The production of dissimilar nymphs is apparently correlated with different ecological conditions (such as different altitudes and stagnant vs. torrential water).

4. The Order Plecoptera

The oldest fossils of Plecoptera are known from the lower Permian (Illies 1965). They were aquatic as nymphs and they seem to have had large numbers of molts; the number of nymphal stages in modern stoneflies is known to range from 22 to over 30 (Richards and Davies 1964). Wing reduction to various degrees (aptery, microptery, brachyptery) has been reported for some plecopterans, especially for those occurring at high altitudes in northern parts of both eastern and western hemispheres (Hynes 1941; Brinck 1949; Nebeker and Gaufin 1967; Lillehammer 1974, 1976; Müller and Mendl 1978; Donald and Patriquin 1983). The wing reduction itself and structural changes in the genitalia, reduction in body size, and so on can be regarded as neotenous features. In certain cases (*Leuctra* and others) reduction of wings and that of the body size occur together, although in others only the wings may be reduced.

Major proximate environmental factors responsible for wing reduction are lower temperatures, certain photoperiods, and presumably the scarcity of food that may prevail at higher altitudes. Khoo's (1964) experiment indicated that a combination of the effect of lengthening days and that of lower temperatures would cause the production of short wings in small adults in *Capnia bifrons.* In nature, at least, cold temperatures appear to be responsible for the reduction in wings and body size, as seen from the fact that adults of *Perlodes microcephala* were smaller than usual after a severe winter (Elliott 1967) and that adults of *Diura* from very cold lakes tend to be exceptionally small (Hynes 1976). These cases appear to represent progenetic neoteny resulting from prothetely (below).

As Nebeker's (1971) observation on adult emergence in the Rocky Mountains indicated, there are probably three groups of species, which differ in response to photoperiodic and temperature cues: (1) those species in which temperature is the main stimulus, although photoperiod may provide the initial stimulus; (2) those for which photoperiod is the main influence *(Nemoura besametsa);* and (3) those in which photoperiod is the main influence but whose emergence may be delayed by lower temperatures at high elevations.

In Norwegian stoneflies (*Diura bicaudata, Nemoura arctica, Capnia atra,* and *Amphinemura standfussi*), according to Lillehammer (1976), increase in wing reduction, which is often not accompanied by reduction in body length, occurs at higher altitudes. He attributed this tendency to low temperature, isolation, and some other factors. Similarly, in the lake populations of three species of Capniidae on the Continental Divide in Alberta, British Columbia, and Montana, substantial wing reduction occurs in the female. Donald and Patriquin (1983) found a clear tendency toward functional winglessness (as measured by the wing length/head capsule ratio) to be greater in the lakes at higher altitudes. However, they were inclined to think that cold temperature alone cannot influence the wing length. They attributed the wing reduction in lakes to continuous selection for brachyptery, because the latter would reduce dispersion, which would be advantageous (Brinck 1949, Hynes 1976). The occurrence of apterous species *Utacapnia tahoensis* and highly wing-reduced populations of *U. confusa* and *U. trava* in colder lakes (50,000 to 100,000 years old) is consistent with their theory, reflecting a long continuous selection against long wings. It appears to me, however, that initially cold temperature (and perhaps also meager food resources) acted as the proximate causal agent inducing the production of short-winged stoneflies, and natural selection has encouraged further wing reduction.

Although nothing is known directly about the hormonal control of development in Plecoptera when short-winged, small adults emerge (as shown above); this is due probably to environmentally induced prothetely, where precocious action of ecdysteroids on imaginal differentiation follows precocious cessation of JH activity.

Stoneflies are known to crawl out of water onto land for emergence of adults (Hynes 1976). Presumably, by analogy to amphibians, an elevated titer of ecdysteroids might induce land drive, just as an elevated thyroxine titer induces land drive in amphibians. Metamorphosis then follows in the drier environment. A similar situation obtains also for the Diptera, which require dryness for the release of an elevated titer of ecdysteroids and consequent pupation (Sect. 23D20).

A puzzling phenomenon is the tendency for wing reduction to be more pronounced in the male than in the female (Aubert 1945, Brinck 1949, Nebeker and Gaufin 1967). In Sweden the males emerge earlier in spring than females (Brinck 1949). These facts lead us to suspect that wing-reduced males might undergo fewer molts than the females. The underlying physiological basis is not at all clear; in most other insect groups wing reduction tends to be more pronounced in the female than in the male.

5. The Order Embioptera

The Embioptera appear to have been derived from plecopteroid ancestors (Rohdendorf 1961, Ross 1970, Matsuda 1970); possibly, some of the Miomoptera (an order within the Plecopteroidea) fossils actually represent early Embioptera (Ross 1970). They are terrestrial and live within a silk gallery formed between cracks and crevices of barks, etc.

In all living Embioptera the female is wingless, and females exhibit the anatomy of an early instar nymph before the appearance of even a trace of wing pads. During nymphal development females merely increase in size while maturing their internal reproductive organs (Ross 1970). Hence the female may represent a metagenetic neoteny (below). How this female neoteny could have originated in the (presumed) winged ancestors can only be speculated on, and explained on the assumption that in the ancestors JHs had the dual function of suppressing imaginal molt and the gonadotropic function in the female. It can be imagined that the new environmental factors that became available within the gallery so upset the activity of the CA that an excessive secretion of JHs occurred. Because the hormones were gonadotropic in facilitating the deposition of yolk in developing oocytes, the female nymphs could have become sexually mature while the same hormones were suppressing further nymphal development. Because winglessness is definitely advantageous in gallery living, a sex-linked mutation inducing female aptery (which must act on the endocrine mechanism) has accumulated (genetic assimilation).

JHs have no gonadotropic function in the male. Therefore, neoteny must have occurred with more difficulty in the male than in the female. Dispersal by flight must have been usually essential in their life history, so that the full development of wings, at least for the male, must have been favored by natural selection. Yet according to Ross (1970), aptery or brachyptery of various degrees occurs frequently in the males of the species inhabiting arid regions or locations with a long dry season. Ross (1984) described many new wing-reduced taxa from Mexico, including a nymphoform new genus *Pelorembia.*

6. The Order Phasmida

If we assume, as Crampton (1916) and Matsuda (1970) maintained, that the Phasmida have been derived from amphibious plecopterous ancestors, their enlarged body and very frequent aptery are related to their acquisition of the fully terrestrial habit throughout their life. With a stretch of imagination, it can be envisaged that more persistent secretion of JHs (metathetely) occurred on land in producing these features that represent metagenetic neoteny. Possible effects of high temperature on the pattern of JH secretion must be considered, because the distribution of phasmids is confined to the temperate – tropical areas (Günther 1953); high temperature is known to promote the secretion of JHs in *Rhodnius* (Sect. 23D18b).

Within the Phasmida progenetic neoteny has occurred in the genus *Timema* (Timematidae). *Timema californicum* is a very tiny phasmid measuring only 16 – 17 mm long in the male and 21 – 25 mm in the female. The species emerges in spring or summer, and has a vertical distribution from 1000 to 6500 ft in the Chaparral, California, area (Henry 1937). The insect has three-segmented tarsi, instead of the five-segmented tarsi of other phasmids (Günther 1953), and the female ovipositor mechanism and the posterior abdominal segments show some juvenile features (though they copulate) (Matsuda 1976). All these features represent incomplete metamorphosis, which appears to result from precocious emergence of the adult, as the following experiments indicate.

Pflugfelder (1937a) showed that when CA are removed from the third- or fourth-instar nymph of *Carausius (=Dixippus),* the nymphs molt only twice and become sexually mature. Berthold (1973) found that the removal of CA from the fourth-instar nymph of *Carausius* results in premature molt, the nymph developing into a dwarf adult; the control nymphs develop until the seventh stage (adult). In these cases early exhaustion of JHs as a result of the removal of CA was apparently followed by precocious action of ecdysteroid (i.e., prothetely) for imaginal differentiation. It is therefore probable that the dwarf adult of *Timema californicum* also most likely results from prothetely, which has been induced by relatively cold temperature in their habitat. The genus *Timema* comprises nine species (Kevan 1982). In other species also the body size is small. In *T. dorotheae* it is 14.5 mm in the male and 24 mm in the female (Strohecker 1966) and in parthenogenetic females of *T. genevieval* the body length is 23.7–24.1 mm (Rentz 1978). These species also must represent progenetic neoteny.

In Phasmida JH has no gonadotropic function, as has been known since Pflugfelder (1937b). Application of JHA to the last instar nymph of *Carausius* suppressed the follicular epithelial differentiation (Socha 1974). In *Clitumnus extradentatus,* which lays eggs continuously, oocyte development does not require hormonal intervention; an inhibitory substance from one oocyte to another regulates oocyte development (Mesnier 1980). In *Carausius* Giorgi and Macchi (1980) established vitellogenin synthesis in various tissues and found that both synthesis and uptake of vitellogenin by oocytes occur, irrespective of the hormonal control. Therefore, the early depletion of JHs during progenetic neoteny in *Timema* should not hinder oogenesis, as long as oocyte maturation occurs through some other means.

7. The Order Zoraptera

The Zoraptera comprises one family, Zorotypidae, with one genus *Zorotypus,* of more than 20 known species (Brown 1982). These occur on four continents, inhabiting sawdust, decaying wood and leaves, and so forth. The order has been known to be polymorphic. Gurney (1938) distinguished two major morphs in *Zorotypus hubbardi,* the winged and wingless adults. In wingless adults ocelli are lacking and the traces of degenerate compound eyes are visible in occasional individuals, although antennae are nine-segmented as in winged adults and the male genitalia do not differ from those of winged males. The wingless adult, therefore, exhibits neotenous features.

According to Gurney (1938), the last nymphal instars of the winged individuals have, in addition to the wing pads, eight-segmented antennae, small compound eyes, and ocelli, whereas the last-instar nymphs of the wingless form have eight-segmented antennae and lack eyes, ocelli, and wing pads. It is apparent, therefore, that the divergence into the two morphs occurs at the penultimate nymphal molt, and the penultimate stage is the third nymphal stage, judging from the presence of four nymphal stages (Riegel and Eytalis 1974). Thus the neoteny of the wingless morph may be metagenetic. Further, crowding does not seem to result in the production of winged insects (group effect) as in some other insects (Shetlar 1978). However, Shetlar reported individuals intermediate between winged and wingless forms in which the caudolateral extensions (presumably wing pads) occur in the meso- and metanota.

Occasional observations that a polymorphic population of *Zorotypus* occurs in association with termite nests led to the claim that they are social, although true sociality in *Zorotypus* was denied by Gurney (1938) and Delamare-Deboutteville (1948). As Shetlar (1978) concluded, they are definitely gregarious although not social; when they are reared in isolation they soon die (Riegel and Eytalis 1974).

8. The Order Grylloblattodea

The genus *Grylloblatta* in North America and the genus *Galloisiana* in Japan and Korea inhabit the alpine areas where relatively low temperatures prevail, and the areas of their distribution are considered to be relics of Pleistocene glaciation (Kamp 1979, Rentz 1982, Yamasaki 1982). They live under stones, crevices, fallen leaves, and sometimes in caves where a certain amount of humidity is available.

The nymphal development in these insects has been known to be very prolonged. In *Grylloblatta campodeiformis* it presumably lasts for 5 years (Walker 1937), and in *Galloisiana nipponensis* it probably takes $3\frac{1}{2}$–8 years to complete nymphal development, which consists of eight stages (Nagashima et al. 1982). We do not know whether the eight stages have resulted from reduction or increase in number of stages in evolution, for their phylogeny remains totally unknown (discussed below). The prolonged intermolt stages probably mean persistent circulation of JHs, which presumably has been induced by relatively constant, low temperature in their habitats. *Galloisiana nipponensis* is essentially solitary during development (Nagashima et al. 1982), and hence the lack of group effect also might have contributed to such a pattern of JH secretion.

The consequence of prolonged nymphal development is the retention of many juvenile features that presumably has resulted from excessive inhibitory action of JHs. Besides the total suppression of wing development, other so-called "primitive features" appear to represent the retention of juvenile features due to arrest of development, and hence they are neotenous (Matsuda 1970, 1979). Such features include the retention of the metathoracic spina and the first abdominal sternum, which usually become lost during development; the subanal lobes, which are distinct from the 10th abdominal sternum (usually they become indistinguishably fused); the absence of ocelli, which usually form very late during nymphal development; the absence of the subgenital plate, owing probably to developmental arrest; paired penes which do not undergo further division; arrested development of the tubular accessory glands; and eyes that are poorly developed, consisting only of 40 ommatidia in *G. nipponensis* (Gokan et al. 1982). Retention of the dorsal longitudinal muscles (for flight) appears to indicate that the wing reduction arose relatively recently; this muscle is lost in other secondarily wingless insects (Matsuda 1970). At least some of these features, such as the poorly developed eyes and winglessness, are selectively advantageous in the alpine, cryptozoic habitats. Yet these features are essentially adaptive responses of the initially environmentally induced developmental arrest.

Persistent action of JH appears to underlie the very prolonged nymphal stages and consequent arrest of development of many imaginal structures, and these features probably justify the interpretation of neoteny in this order as metagenetic. At any rate, the array of neotenous features makes it difficult to analyze their phylogenetic derivation. Very confused controversies over their phylogenetic relationships were recently reviewed by Rentz (1982).

9. The Order Dermaptera

In *Anisolabis maritima,* according to Ozeki (1958a), nymphs at different developmental stages (ranging from the fourth to sixth) metamorphose into adults with fully developed external genitalia in both sexes, and they acquire different numbers of antennal segments: those that molted into adults at the sixth nymphal stage acquired 25 – 35 segments, and those that molted at the fifth and fourth stages acquired 23 – 31, and 21 – 27 segments, respectively. Furthermore, the removal of the CA – CC from nymphs at different stages by Ozeki (1958a) resulted in metamorphosis into the adult at the next molt (prothetely). In these adults the degree of development of the male efferent system (ejaculatory ducts, seminal vesicles, etc.) was vastly different, depending on the stage at which the operation was made; the earlier the insects were operated on, the less the system was developed, especially the ejaculatory ducts. Conversely, when the CA – CC complex was implanted in these nymphs by Ozeki (1958a), an abnormal efferent system with juvenile features was obtained. Ozeki (1958a) was also able to produce adultoids and nymphoids in the female by removal and transplantation of the CA – CC complex, and found that the last-stage nymph elaborates only the principle promoting yolk deposition. Furthermore, participation of the ventral glands (producing ecdysteroids) in molting and the development of the internal reproductive organs was also clear in another experiment involving decapitation of the head (Ozeki 1959).

The above facts indicate that the nymphal development in *Anisolabis* is mediated by the shift in balance between JHs and ecdysteroids as in other insects, and that *Anisolabis* is highly labile in morphogenesis, easily resulting in polymorphism in certain structures such as antennal segments, the male efferent system, and others. No particular environmental triggering is apparently involved in producing polymorphism. The material Ozeki studied was derived from females collected on the campus of a university and reared in a laboratory at 27° C. Hence the hormonally controlled polymorphism is apparently genetically biased or determined. The great variability in the development of antennal segments and the male efferent system exhibited in *Anisolabis* appears to underlie, in fact, the great variation in number of antennal segments within the Dermaptera, which ranges from 10 to 50 (Chopard 1949b), and in the degree of development of the male efferent system, notably the length of the ejaculatory ducts, which varies greatly in different species of Dermaptera (summarized by Matsuda 1976).

Furthermore, the above interpretation is consistent with the conclusion reached by Lamb (1976) with regard to the polymorphism in males of the European earwig, *Forficula auricularia.* Lamb (1976) found that polymorphism in body weight, head width, and cercus length and width of the adult male were polymorphic (there are four morphs) in both field-collected and laboratory-reared samples, and discounted the earlier claims that the polymorphism (mainly in the cercus) is environmentally induced. It may well be, however, that the polymorphism found by Lamb (1976) and others (Ollason 1972 and some earlier workers) is associated with the different nymphal stages at which they metamorphose into the adult (as in *Anisolabis*). The adaptive significance of the (apparent) genetic polymorphism (involving the hormonal function) remains unknown; apparently, natural selection does not seem to prefer any particular morph. Dimorphism in the cercus is also known for *Pseudochelidura sinuata* (Gadeau de Kerville 1930).

Reduction and loss of wings have occurred in some Dermaptera. La Greca (1954) classified the wing reduction into three categories, as follows:

A. Typical elytra (1) with hind wings normally developed (*Forficula auricularia* type), (2) with hind wings shortened (*Forficula decolyi* type), and (3) with hind wings vestigial (*Forficula decipiens* type).

B. Reduced elytra (1) with elytra slightly shorter and hind wings vestigial and lobate, but not distinct from the metanotum (*Psalis gagatina* type), and (2) with elytra lobate and hind wings absent *(Euborellia moesta).*

C. Elytra and hind wings absent (*Anisolabis* type).

Ecological association with wing reduction is not immediately clear. According to La Greca (1954), it is not rare to find macropterous individuals in the species that are normally brachypterous. The hormonal basis of reduction of antennal segments and the male ejaculatory duct found in *Anisolabis* presumably apply to the reduction of wings; the inhibitory effect of JHs might well have been involved with the cases of wing reduction here listed. When a JHA was applied to the nymphs of *Labidura riparia,* reproductively capable supernumerary nymphs resulted, and such nymphs possessed modified fore and hind wings (Srihari et al. 1975). JH 3 is a gonadotropic hormone (Caussanel et al. 1979) and vitellogenesis is associated with the rise of JH 3 titer in the hemolymph (Baehr et al. 1982). These facts indicate that wing reduction and maturation of the female gonad can occur together, resulting in neoteny in the female.

The suborder Arixeniina and the suborder Hemimerina are ectoparasitic. Each contains one family, two genera, and less than a dozen species. They are always wingless, blind (or nearly so) and have slightly modified cerci. In superficial appearance they bear little resemblance to most of the free-living earwigs (Nakata and Maa 1974). Arixeniina have been found from caves and hollow trees in the Malaysian and Philippine subregions. They are parasitic on bats *(Cheiromeles);* most of their time is spent on or in guano and on the walls or ceilings of bat roosts; they go onto host bats probably for feeding. Both genera, *Xeniaria* and *Arixenia,* are considered to pass through four nymphal stages (Cloudsley-Thompson 1957, Giles 1961). The Hemimerina (comprising *Araeomerus* and *Hemimerus*) are ectoparasites of rats in eastern and western Africa. *Hemimerus* is gregarious and probably spends most of its time on the body of the host, and it passes through four nymphal stages (see Nakata and Maa 1974 for a summary). In *Hemimerus,* which is viviparous, eggs are without chorion and yolk. A placenta-like structure (pseudoplacenta of Hagan 1951) is formed in the ovariole, and the embryo develops fully before it emerges as a young (Heymons 1909, 1912; Hagan 1951). Taxonomic treatment of these parasitic suborders has been disputed (see Popham 1973 and Giles 1974). It is not clear whether four nymphal stages in these suborders represent reduction in nymphal stages. Hincks (1949) recorded four nymphal instars in each of five British Dermaptera, although six instars occur in *Anisolabis* (above).

10. The Order Blattaria

In Blattaria wing reduction occurs more frequently in the female than in the male. Hence many cockroach species are dimorphic with respect to wing development. For instance, in *Blatta orientalis* the female is brachypterous and the male is macropterous, and in *Polyphaga aegyptica* the male is macropterous although the female is apterous (La Greca 1954). Similarly, in *Ectobius panzeri* the female has greatly reduced wings, although in the male wings are well developed (Cornwell 1968). *Cryptocercus punctulatus* is wingless in both sexes. Reduction or loss of other structures such as ocelli, compound eyes, antennal and cercal segments, and some integumental structures such as sensilla (Lefeuvre and Sellier 1970, Bullière and Bullière 1975) may accompany wing reduction.

Environmental association with wing reduction has not been clearly understood, although population density can be an important factor in wing development. In cockroaches, as in some other insects, fecal aggregation pheromone(s) has been known to occur since its first demonstration by Ishii and Kuwahara (1967, 1968), and in aggregated populations accelerated (or normal) growth occurs. In contrast, as various isolation experiments since Landowski (1938) and Petit (1940) have shown, isolation retards development. Wharton et al. (1968) found that *Periplaneta americana* when reared in isolation, has a longer duration of nymphal development and larger adult size than when reared in groups. Similarly, Woodhead and Paulson (1983) found that *Diploptera punctata* has a longer duration of nymphal development when reared in isolation than when reared in pairs or groups, and that the greater adult weight of isolated animals is a result of their longer duration of nymphal development; males have either three or four instars, and when isolated the four-instar type increases in proportion. Although these experiments have not shown the effect on wing development (this feature was not studied), the prolonged nymphal development may result in larger adults with reduced wings. Rivault (1983) suggested the possibility of continuous density-dependent polymorphism in cockroaches, which would be comparable with that in locusts (Sect. 23D13). It appears highly probable, at any rate, that prolonged nymphal development is due to more persistent activity of JHs (metathetely). As shown below, JH and JHA injection and CA implantation resulted in retardation of nymphal development, and the morphogenetic effect of such experiments was clear in partial arrest of wings.

Thus Lefeuvre (1971) found that implantation of CA from the seventh-stage nymph of *Blabera craniifer* into the last instar results either in an imaginal molt or an extra (supernumerary) nymph that metamorphoses into a giant adult (metathetely). Furthermore, depending on the time of implantation of CA a "pseudoimago" may result, this in turn undergoes a second molt, and the resultant adult often lacks the hind wings. Radwan and Sehnal (1974) found that JHA injection into the nymphs of *Nauphoeta cinerea* at different days after the last ecdysis and into nymphs results in all degrees of abnormal development including giant supernymphs with considerably reduced wings. An experiment involving implantation into and extirpation of CA from nymphs in *Periplaneta americana* by Fraser and Pipa (1977) showed that supernymphs were a direct consequence of CA activation. A similar experiment involving the injection of JHs in the last instar nymph and the female adult of *Nauphoeta cinerea* by Lanzrein (1979) showed various juvenilizing effects including various degrees of arrest of fore and hind wing development.

Thus both isolation experiments and the experiments enhancing JH action caused prolonged nymphal development. It appears safe to hypothesize, therefore, that in nature isolation would result in a more persistent action of JHs and this in turn could result in wing reduction in cockroaches, illustrating a case of metagenetic neoteny by metathetely in nature: in some Orthoptera the degree of JH-mediated wing reduction is considerable in isolated populations (Sect. 23D13). It is probably worth mentioning here that a dispersion-inducing substance has been discovered in *B. germanica* (Suto and Kumada 1981, Nakayama et al. 1984); it is secreted from the saliva when a population becomes overpopulated. Deployment of this or a similar substance might have occurred under some environmental conditions, resulting in isolation and consequent wing reduction.

Other environmental factors also must have contributed to wing reduction. By rearing the nymphs of four species of cockroaches under varying temperatures, Tsuji and Mizuno (1972) induced retardation under relatively low temperatures. Solomon et al. (1977) found that increased exposure to illumination results in decreased longevity and a significant acceleration of nymphal development.

The tendency for the wing reduction to be more pronounced in the female than in the male appears to be related to the well established fact of JH-mediated vitellogenesis in cockroaches (Engelmann 1970, Sams and Bell 1977, Lanzrein 1979); the experimental fact that topical application of farnesol evokes precocious vitellogenesis in *Blabera* (Brousse-Gaury et al. 1979) supports this interpretation. When abundant JHs are available during prolonged nymphal development, they accelerate maturation of oocytes while suppressing wing development, whereas such an acceleration of the male gonad can not occur. Hence the reproductively functional, wing-reduced female would be more readily produced than the wing-reduced functional male.

Acceleration in development could also have occurred during the evolution of cockroaches. Allatectomy performed on the nymphs of (macropterous) *Blabera craniifer* by Lefeuvre (1971) resulted in dwarf adults with fully developed wings, pseudo-dwarf adults in which the wings are reduced, and adultoids with extremely reduced wings, which look more like the nymph than the adult. Presumably in these cases, precocious action of ecdysteroids followed the depletion of JHs as a result of allatectomy (prothetely). These facts indicate that when the reduction of body size occurred, it could often have been accompanied by reduction in wings and other structures, thereby resulting in progenetic neoteny. According to Lefeuvre (1971), some wing-reduced species have fewer numbers of nymphal stages than their macropterous relatives. The genus *Attaphila,* which comprises 15 species (Brossut 1976), is the sole representative of the family Attaphilidae; these species are commensals of ants. *A. fungicola,* first described by Wheeler (1900), is a small (3 mm long), wingless insect with the eye consisting only of 70 ommatidia (instead of 1800 in *Blatta orientalis*) (Brossut 1976). These features, especially the small size, suggest that the case probably represents progenetic neoteny produced through acceleration in development. Other cockroach species with highly specialized habitats and behavior also tend to be apterous or micropterous. For instance, termitophilous *Sphecophila termitium,* cavernicolous *Alluandellina,* and fossorial *Nymphrytria mirabilis* are apterous (Chopard 1938).

Presumably, when the apterous or micropterous phenotype became permanent, this has often been effected by genetic fixation of the nymphal stage at which the insect molts into the functional adult. Kunkel (1981) was able to canalize, by a genetic selection, a particular stage of instar (in *Blattella germanica*) at which metamorphosis occurs, indicating that in nature natural selection could induce canalization of the developmental stage at which the insect molts into the wing-reduced adult.

11. The Order Mantodea

In the family Eremiaphilidae, which occurs in the desert of North Africa, wings are strongly reduced. Hence the family can be regarded as neotenous. In *Eremiaphila* the tarsus is five segmented in all legs. In *Heteronutarsus* of the same family, however, the tarsus is four segmented in the front legs, and three segmented in the other pairs of legs (Beier 1968a). These reduced conditions of the tarsi must result from developmental arrest, and the degree of neoteny is more advanced in this genus (progenetic neoteny?).

Brunneria borealis (Mantidae) is almost apterous. It occurs in Texas and is known to be diploid parthenogenetic (White 1948). In other species of *Brunneria* in South America the male is macropterous and the female is brachypterous (Hebard 1942). Both the strong wing reduction and diploidy in *B. borealis* can perhaps be attributed to JH-induced disturbance. It remains completely unclear under what kind of environmental conditions in Texas such cytological and somatic abnormalities have occurred.

12. The Order Isoptera

The Isoptera, or termites, are close relatives of the Blattaria. Anatomical and paleontological evidence points to their probable derivation from late Paleozoic to early Mesozoic cockroaches (see Wilson 1971 for a further discussion). Termites are eusocial; nymphs at different stages of development and various castes occur together within a colony. The kinds of young and castes that have been recognized (cf. Miller 1969 and Noirot 1969) are *larva*, which specifies early nymphs without wing buds; *nymph*, which designates older nymphs with wing buds; *pseudergate*, which has regressed from a nymphal stage by a molt(s) that reduces or eliminates wing buds, or derived from a larva by a stationary molt; *soldier*, which is a highly modified nymph with defense function; *worker*, which is essentially larval and whose function is to build the nest and provide food; *primary reproductive*, which is fully winged; *second-form reproductive*, which is a functional male or female with wing buds; and *third-form reproductive (ergatoid)*, which is a functional male or female without wing buds. Second- and third-form reproductives are often called replacement or supplementary reproductives.

Despite the apparent complexity, the modes of structural differentiation are comparable with those in nonsocial insects. First, the distinction between the "larva" and "nymph" is purely arbitrary, designating different stages of nymphal development. The soldier caste represents quite clearly a caenogenesis or nymphal (larval) adaptive specialization; the adaptive development includes the conspicuously enlarged head, which is armed with a frontal gland (through which a white liquid is sprayed) in some families (Rhinotermitidae, Serritermitidae, and most Termitidae). Unlike the caenogenetic larva or nymph in other insects, however, the soldier does not molt, and it remains sterile. The worker caste is also caenogenetic. In Termitidae the entirely wingless worker is also characterized by the reduced pterothorax, loss or great reduction of ocelli and eyes, the voluminous head with powerful mandibular muscles, and so on (Noirot 1969). Although sometimes workers molt into soldiers, they never become reproductively functional. The two kinds of replacement reproductives are neotenous adults.

The fact that, as seen in Figure 4 the larva, nymph, and pseudergate can develop into any one of developmental stages and castes reflects a high mor-

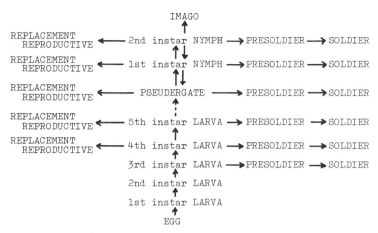

Figure 4. Diagram showing possible developmental pathways of the larva, pseudergate and nymph in *Kalotermes flavicollis* (from M. Lüscher).

phogenetic plasticity in *Kalotermes flavicollis.* Watson and Sewell (1981) pointed out another (major) developmental pathway seen in *Mastotermes darwinensis* in which two distinct lines of differentiative molts start at the end of the first instar, producing worker and alate lines. According to these authors, this type occurs at least in Mastotermitidae, Kalotermitidae (but not *Kalotermes flavicollis*), Hodotermitidae, Rhinotermitidae, and Termitidae, and is the primitive pattern in termites, although the straight line type in *Kalotermes flavicollis* deviates less from the pattern in other Hemimetabola. Developmental pathways are known to be different in different groups and species of termites, but they are not mentioned here.

The diverse developmental pathways during the caste differentiation in termites are controlled by environmental factors and are mediated hormonally. The most important environmental factor for caste differentiation in some termites (such as *K. flavicollis*) may be the presumed pheromonal involvement in controlling the JH activity within the colony. It is assumed that the pheromone of soldiers stimulates the development of the primary reproductives by suppressing JH activity (Springhetti 1971 and Lüscher 1975). During the final nymphal molt into the primary reproductive the total absence of JH in the last instar is necessary (Wanyonyi 1974, Yin and Gillott 1975). It is apparent that depletion of JH (as a result of suppression by soldier?) is followed by the activity of ecdysteroids which induce molting and expression of adult genes as in other insects. JH activity appears to increase after the molt into the reproductive, in association with gonadotropic requirement (Lüscher 1963). The gonadotropic function of JH in termites has become increasingly apparent in recent studies (Vieau and Lebrun 1981, Sieber and Leuthold 1982, Sieber 1982) and presumably secondary vitellogenesis occurs in termites (Greenberg et al. 1978, Greenberg 1979) as in Blattaria.

The primary reproductive is supposed to produce a pheromone that inhibits, through fecal feeding, the differentiation of pseudergates into reproductives (primary and secondary) (Lüscher 1976 and earlier; Springhetti 1970, 1971). Lüscher (1975) assumed that the pheromone of the reproductives stimulates the CA of the larva to produce more JH for soldier development, and it inhibits the production of the reproductives at the same time. Removal of the primary reproductives from a colony therefore results in the development of supplementary reproductives, because of the absence of extra JH (for soldier development) (Lüscher 1963, 1972; Wanyonyi 1974; Yin and Gillott 1975). Greenberg and Stuart (1982) showed, in *Zootermopsis angusticollis,* that in the absence of a functional reproductive pair, neotenic molts begin in the apterous larvae during the third to fourth weeks after isolation from a parent colony. This experiment suggests the potential for neoteny in termites, and agrees essentially with the result of the JHA-influence experiment by Wanyonyi (1974), which showed that replacement reproductive development can arise not only from the last instar, but also from younger nymphs and larvae. The replacement reproductive can often represent progenetic neoteny. Ergatoids originate from workers through two successive molts in *Nasutitermes corniger* and some others, although rarely one molt occurs in the formation of ergatoids (Thorne and Noirot 1982).

Lüscher (1958) first discovered that implanted CA from the reproductive could induce soldier development. In many later works presoldier and soldier development have been shown to be induced by JH and JHA. Among higher termites, soldier development was induced by JHA in *Macrotermes* (Okot-Kotber 1980). It is apparent that the unusually increased JH titer underlies the production of the soldier caste. As already seen, the pheromone from the reproductive appears to stimulate the development by inducing the increase in JH titer. As shown by Okot-Kotber (1983), ecdysteroids are certainly involved with molting and worker and soldier differentiation in *Macrotermes.* It is apparent that the high JH titer modifies the activity of ecdysteroids suitable for soldier development. The proportion of soldiers within a colony varies significantly in different species; in some species it is around 30% or more, and in many others it is about 1% or less (Haverty 1977).

Possibility of blastogenic determination of castes also must be taken into account. Lüscher (1976) found that JH content in the egg is highly variable in different colonies of *Macrotermes subhyalinus,* and suggested that only those eggs with a low JH titer may be competent for the development of the nymph. Delbecque et al. (1978) found that eggs collected from different colonies of *Macrotermes* spp. have different titers of ecdysteroids. Thus the relative concentrations of JH and ecdysteroids in the eggs can influence the determination of castes. Conceivably, however, such a blastogenically determined balance would be subject to modification during postoval development by environmental factors (such as the population density and structure of a colony, temperature, photoperiod, and quality of food).

The currently accepted hypothesis with regard to the origin of eusociality in termites is that it is a consequence of their dependence on symbiotic intestinal flagellates (Cleveland et al. 1934, Wilson 1971). At the initial stage of sociality the aggregation pheromone(s) inherited from the blattarian ancestors might have contributed in keeping the developing nymphs together as a colony. The division of labor by different castes has been perfected later, presumably under the pressure of ergonomic efficiency of a colony (Oster and Wilson 1978). The real nature of the pheromones concerned with caste differentiation (their molecular constitution, their phylogenetic origin, etc.) remains to be discovered.

Compared with Blattaria, as discussed by Matsuda (1979), many structures in primary reproductives have undergone reduction that can confidently be attributed to the increased effect of JH on development. Thus, for instance, the female ovipositor has become lost, except in a primitive genus *Mastotermes,* and the penis has become completely lost in the winged Isoptera. The seven kinds of exocrine glands of the head in Blattaria have become reduced to two or one (Brossut 1973). Within the Isoptera, as shown by Jucci and Springhetti (1952) and Springhetti (1964), four types of the male seminal vesicles– accessory gland complex are recognized in the male primary reproductives, and they represent four stages of evolutionary reduction. Of these, only the most primitive type in *Mastotermes* is comparable with that in Blattaria.

13. The Order Orthoptera

In Orthoptera environmentally induced variation may often be continuous and reversible, as is well known for the population density-dependent polymorphism in locusts (*Locusta migratoria, Schistocerca gregaria,* and others). The two extremes of this polymorphism, known since Uvarov (1921), consist of *gregaria* and *solitaria* phases, which differ in developmental process, certain morphometric characters, coloration, physiology, and behavior (discussed below).

As was first shown by Hunter-Jones (1958), eggs are larger and darker in gregaria than in solitaria. In *Schistocerca gregaria* smaller solitaria nymphs, hatching from paler and smaller eggs, usually undergo an extra nymphal molt (i.e., six molts total) before becoming adults. A more recent isolation experiment with *Schistocerca* by Injeyan and Tobe (1981a) confirmed these tendencies. They showed that in six generations the extra molt increases to 94% in the female F_6 and to a maximum of 78% in the male. The ovariole number also increased from 110 to about 150 in the F_4 and later generations in solitaria. Further, the increase in ovariole number was also correlated with the decrease in the size of mature oocytes (8.2 mm long in gregaria versus 6.6 mm in solitaria 12 days after oviposition); the entry of vitellogenin (which is controlled by JH and synthesized in the fat body, Chen et al. 1978, 1979; Reid and Chen 1981) into oocytes does not influence the final size of the oocyte (Injeyan and Tobe 1981b).

In *Melanoplus differentialis* the ovariole development starts after blastokinesis (Nelsen 1934). In *Dociostaurus maroccanus* the number of newly hatched nymphs is comparable with that in the adult (Jannone 1939). As discussed below, hormonal influence appears to be involved with embryonic development of ovarioles in these cases and other Orthoptera.

Lagueux et al. (1977) found that in *Locusta* ecdysteroid synthesis occurs in the follicle cells surrounding the oocytes, and that the newly synthesized ecdysteroids pass into the ooplasm where they become progressively converted into the ooplasm. More recent studies (Lagueux et al. 1979, Gande et al. 1979, Sall et al. 1983) have shown unequivocally that the conjugated intraoval ecdysteroids in the early stages become progressively hydrolyzed to free ecdysteroids in later post-blastokinetic stages, and that they are able to exert morphogenetic function. These facts indicate that intraoval embryonic development is likely to be influenced by exogenous ecdysteroid, exhibiting a maternal effect. Because the ecdysteroid synthesis in the follicle cell epithelium is probably stimulated by brain neurosecretion (Charlet et al. 1979), the ecdysteroid that passes into oocytes is likely to be controlled by environmental factors such as population density (which is known to determine phase polymorphism). Hence the postulated maternal effect on the embryonic ovariole development can be attributed to environmental control.

The next question is how eggs get larger (in gregaria) or smaller (in solitaria). Because vitellogenin incorporation into oocytes does not effect the final egg size (Albrecht et al. 1959, Injeyan and Tobe 1981b), it is difficult to conceive of the exogenous influence on the egg size. Injeyan and Tobe (1981b) attributed the difference in egg size between the two phases to postvitellogenic growth, possibly hydration. At any rate, the size of each egg is clearly inversely proportional to the number of eggs formed, and this is likely to happen because the total metabolites available for the ovariole development are presumably much the same in both phases. An examination of the populations from six different geographical areas (Africa, Australia, Turkey, etc.) showed that in certain populations the number of ovarioles and that of eggs do not change under different rearing conditions (isolated or crowded, or at three different temperature regimes) (Khouaidjia and Fuzeau-Braesch 1982), indicating that the developments of the features are canalized (presumably through the process of genetic assimilation).

The newly hatched solitaria nymph is smaller in size than the gregaria nymph, and there are some other differences including the ovariole numbers. Lauga (1977a) attributed such differences to the different amount of hormones impregnated into the egg. However, a more important reason appears to lie in the fact that the solitaria nymph hatches earlier, mainly because of the more limited supply of food (yolk), and hence is smaller.

During the process of phase differentiation in developing nymphs environmental stimuli are supposed to activate the chain of neuroendocrine activity. In locusts, according to Girardie (1976), neurosecretion from the median neurosecretory cells (MNSC) of the pars intercerebralis (PI) stimulates prothoracic glands (PG), and AB cells in PI act on CA as an anti-allata (inhibitory) factor, and the C cells in PI stimulate CA. Lateral neurosecretory cells (LNSC) appear to have the same function as AB and C cells. Charlet et al. (1979) observed that MNSC stimulate the ecdysone synthesis in the epithelium of follicle cells.

Nolte (1968) and Nolte et al. (1970) reported that a pheromone produced in the crops of gregarious nymphs is excreted through feces, and maintained that it stimulates gregarization; the pheromone was later called "locustol" (Nolte et al. 1973). Gillett and Philips (1977) and Gillett (1983) confirmed the existence of a pheromonal factor in the feces of crowded nymphs which induces solitary-reared nymphs to acquire gregarious behavior and pigmentation. Furthermore, these authors found that the feces in the crowded adults contain a factor that stimulates solitary-reared nymphs to become more solitaria-like. Gillett (1983) further showed that antennae perceive the pheromonal stimulus and contradicted the assertion by Nolte (1974) that reception of the airborne pheromone occurs through the spiracles. *Ceuthophilus* secretes a pheromone for gregarization; the abdomen appears to be the site of pheromonal production and antennae receive the pheromonal stimulus (Nagel and Cade 1983).

Effects of other environmental factors (such as photoperiod, temperature, nutrition, and humidity) on development and reproduction have been known for a long time (see Mordue et al. 1970, Joly 1972 for reviews of earlier works). Among more recent studies, Albrecht and Lauga (1978) showed that increasing day length and high temperatures have a solitarizing effect in gregarious *Schistocerca*. Some studies show the direct effect of environmental changes on hormonal activity, which results in the change in development and reproduction (Sect. 1C).

The underlying hormonal basis for the differentiation of phases in *Locusta*, shown by Joly and Joly (1974), is as seen in Figure 5. In the solitary phase the titer of JH sharply increases after the drop in the early fifth instar. In gregaria, on the other hand, JH becomes nearly completely depleted as it becomes the fifth-instar nymph, and this condition continues until the sixth day of adult life, then JH sharply increases. Injeyan and Tobe's (1981b) study with *Schistocerca* also showed early onset of relatively high JH titer in solitary females. It is likely that the high titer of JH in the fifth-instar nymph (as already seen) causes earlier synthesis of vitellogenin and early entry of the latter into oocytes, while limiting the action of ecdysteroids for imaginal differentiation; in solitaria *Schistocerca* early onset of vitellogenin synthesis and uptake actually occur (Injeyan and Tobe 1981b). As a consequence of such a pattern of JH secretion the solitaria adult would tend to become neotenous. In gregaria of *Locusta* (Fig. 5) and *Schistocerca*, on the other hand, ecdysteroids would be allowed to act in the presence of very low titer (or in the absence) of JH during the fifth nymphal stage and early postimaginal development. Consequently, adult structures would be more fully differentiated, and the ovaries would become mature after the fifth day of the adult life as the JH titer increases sharply. In fact, the pattern of hormonal secretion, as well as its morphological and reprodutive consequences in gregaria, is typical of the Hemimetabola with normally developed structures (including wings). The JH-controlled postoval development (including metamorphosis) in locusts was evident also in earlier allatectomy and CA

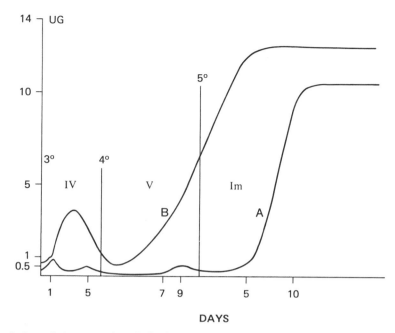

Figure 5. Juvenile hormone titers during late developmental stages in the gregarious phase (A) and solitarious phase (B) of *Locusta migratoria* (from Joly and Joly).

transplantation experiments (e.g., Joly 1962) and in a more recent CA implantation experiment with *Zonocerus* (discussed below).

The long recognized phase differences in the adult are some morphometric characteristics such as E/F ratio (elytra/hind femur), F/C ratio (hind femur/head). Dirsch (1953) found that in *Schistocerca* the F/C ratio is greater in the solitary phase and the E/F ratio greater in the gregarious phase (i.e., the wings are relatively a little shorter in solitaria). Later, more complicated and more informative statistical analyses were employed in discriminating the phase characteristics (Lauga 1977b, Pener 1983). Color polymorphism is another conspicuous feature that is often phase dependent (see Rowell 1971 and Pener 1983 for summaries). In solitaria retention of the prothoracic glands during the adult molt occurs under humid conditions (Fain-Maurel and Cassier 1969, Cassier and Fain-Maurel 1970), and this feature may be regarded as neotenous.

Both in *Locusta* and *Schistocerca* appreciable reduction of the wing does not occur during the solitary phase. In some grasshopper species, however, there is a marked difference in wing development between the two phases. In all three geographic regions in southeastern Australia *Phaulacridium vittatum* exhibits dimorphism with respect to wing size (and color pattern): one is macropterous and another brachypterous. A rearing experiment with this species by Nicolas et al. (1982) clearly showed that under high population density macroptery can be induced in brachypterous insects. Similarly, in Nigeria *Zonocerus variegatus* exists in two forms, one with relatively long wings (with well-developed flight muscles) and the other with relatively short wings (with less developed flight muscles) (Chapman et al. 1978). McCaffery and Page (1978) found that increased food and crowding promote the production of the long-winged adult of *Zonocerus variegatus.* The results of allatectomy and implantation of CA into the fifth- and sixth-instar hoppers and the injection of JHA into sixth-instar hoppers indicated that the absence of JH in the last-instar nymph results in the formation of long-winged adults and that extra JH results in the formation of short-winged adults. It was therefore apparent that environmental stimuli influence the JH activity, which determines the wing morphs. The insect has either five or six nymphal instars, and the wing length is not clearly related to the number or duration of the nymphal instars. However, a significantly greater proportion of long-winged adults are produced in the insects with five instars than those with six instars.

Dirsch's (1965) monograph on the African Acridoidea shows that there are impressively large numbers of genera that are wing-reduced in varying degrees, and the wing reduction is clearly more pronounced in the female than in the male. Modifications of other structures (such as the hind legs and the pronotal lobe) are especially pronounced in apterous genera.

Metrioptera roeseli (Tettigoniidae) is normally brachypterous and rarely macropterous in nature. Ramme (1931) found that in all macropterous females the ovariole tubes are completely reduced and contain only small, weakly developed eggs, although the sperm in macropterous males are normally developed. Ramme associated the emergence of macropterous individuals with more or less humid soils and low soil temperature, which are associated with very rich vegetation. Judging from what we know about the hormonal balance in macropterous *Zonocerus* (above), abnormally early depletion (for this species) of circulating JH probably results in the occasional appearance of the macropterous form; the abnormal JH activity is presumably induced by the environmental stimuli in the microhabitat. Despite the normal wings, such a form without functional reproductive organs can no longer establish itself in nature, and only the brachypterous form would be allowed to exist. Ramme therefore thought that Dollo's law of irreversibility of evolutionary process is applicable to this case.

The genus *Tessellana* is another (usually) short-winged genus in which macroptery occurs sporadically in nature. As reported by Sänger (1976), however, macroptery occurs abundantly in *T. vittata* in laboratory, and Sänger recognized the existence of an intermediate form (mesoptera of Sänger) between the normal micropterous form and the secondary macropterous form. Furthermore, Sänger (1984) showed that crowding beyond the fourth nymphal instar results in increasing numbers of macropterous adults in correlation with the length of time *T. vittata* nymphs spend under high population densities.

In Stenopelmatidae, which live in underground galleries, wings are usually lacking or highly reduced and some other structures remain juvenile (Chopard

1949a); hence the family is neotenous. Thus in the genus *Hemiandrus* the stylus is retained as in the soldier caste in termites, and the ovipositor is also incompletely developed. Furthermore, in this genus the degree of fusion of abdominal ganglia is much less marked than in other Orthoptera (Snodgrass 1937, Matsuda 1976). In another stenopelmatid genus, *Oryctopus,* wings (at least in the female) and ocelli are absent, eyes are greatly reduced, and antennae are short. However, the front and hind legs are greatly developed and curiously modified in adaptation to their subterranean habitat (Chopard 1938). Cooloolidae, described as a new family of Ensifera (Rentz 1980), is represented by a single species, *Cooloola propator,* which lives in the sandy moist soil in southwest Queensland. The male is micropterous and the female is micropterous or apterous. Eyes are reduced and legs are robust in adaptation to the burrowing habit. Each antenna consists of only 10 segments as in *Oryctopus. Cyphoderris* (Phalangopsidae) is brachypterous or micropterous. Its neotenous features include a multilobed penis and lack of the male accessory glands (Snodgrass 1937).

La Greca (1946) pointed out that in Orthoptera wing reduction tends to be more pronounced in the female than in the male, as seen, for instance, in *Chrysochraon dispar* and *Metrioptera roeseli,* and that in some Orthoptera *(Porthetis, Lamarckiana, Saussurea)* the male is winged and the female is wingless. A simple hypothesis to account for this tendency is that an excessive titer of JH would cause precocious sexual maturation in the female because of its gonadotropic function and simultaneously the excessive JH would suppress the development of wings; the gonadotropic function of JH in the female Orthoptera has been well established (above).

Two mechanisms of color change — one induced by physiochemical environmental factors and another that occurs as homochromic response to match the background color — are operating in Orthoptera. The color change associated with the change from solitary to gregarious phase, or vice versa in *Locusta* and *Schistocerca,* is hormonally controlled. It has been known that elevated titers of JHs induce green pigmentation, as earlier CA implantation experiments indicated (see Rowell 1971 for a summary), and that this is regulated by AB NSC in pars intercerebralis which have an inhibitory function on the CA activity (Girardie 1967). Black pigmentation in the gregarious phase is induced by C NSC (Girardie 1967). Crowded males of *Locusta* and both sexes of gregarious *Schistocerca* become yellow with sexual maturation; increasing titer of JH during the adult stage appears to induce yellow pigmentation. These observations are supported by the fact that allatectomy leads to the absence of yellow color (Pener 1976) and that both JH I and JH III in high doses are effective in inducing yellowing under crowded conditions, with JH I being the more potent of the two hormones (Amerasinghe 1978).

Phase-dependent color polymorphism occurs in many grasshopper species besides *Locusta* and *Schistocerca* (see Rowell 1971). Examples of green–brown dimorphism that responds to environmental changes (such as relative humidity, temperature, habitat change from green vegetated to brown terrestrial area) are also numerous. According to Rowell (1971), among the East African acridoids comprising 180 species and 107 genera, a green–brown polymorphism is known to occur in 85 and 43 of these, respectively. Rowell (1971) contended that cryptic coloration is the only aspect on which selection acts and that differential predation also occurs depending on colors. According to Rowell (1971), there are no data that show that grasshoppers select brown or green environment according to their own morph. However, he thought, by referring to Albrecht's (1964) experiment, which showed the induction of the green morph by high humidity (and conversely low humidity induction of the brown morph), that they would select an appropriate humidity, which is apparently the dominant environmental factor regulating polymorphism. It appears to me probable that those accidentally moved to drier areas become brown as a result of the physiological response to the new environmental stimulus. Generally, in drier environments without (or with less) green vegetation the brown coloration would be selectively advantageous. Hence such a physiological response is adaptive and fortuitous. A study with three species of grasshoppers (*Syrbula admirabilis, Dichromorpha viridis,* and *Chotophaga viridifasciata*) by Otte and Williams (1972) shows that green morphs are more frequent in green habitats and brown morphs are more abundant in dry, brown habitats. Their feeding experiment showed that the color change is causally related to water uptake (through food) and water loss in *S. admirabilis.*

Homochromic response, which involves the migration of pigment granules (ommochromes) to the interior of the hypodermic cells of the integument, occurs in response to the change in background color (Levita 1970; Rowell 1971; Helfert 1977, 1978). Rowell (1971) listed six subfamilies of Acrididae in which homochromic response is known to occur. Helfert (1978) showed that in *Chorthippus biguttatus* six color variations (green, yellow, brown, black, gray, and purple) occur. Of these, yellow, brown, black, and gray variation (*Parallelochrom* of Ramme 1951) depend on the color of background, and not on the climatic parameters (temperature, humidity). Helfert (1978) found further that the occurrence of green and purple variations is not affected by the color of substrate, temperature, or relative humidity, indicating that these colors are genetically determined. Thus both environmentally (background) and genetically determined colors can occur simultaneously. With reference to the endocrine control mechanism of homochromy, Morteau-Levita (1972a,b) and Morteau (1975) found that in *Oedipoda coerulescens* with homochromic response, secretion from the median NSC, passing through CC, activates pigments; CA do not seem to be involved with this process.

An outstanding natural case that leads us to suspect homochromic response is the observation that grasshopper populations of recently burnt vegetation are predominantly black; the dark coloration is cryptic and adaptive in such habitat. Rowell (1971) thought that three mechanisms underlie cryptic coloration in the burnt vegetation: (1) differential predation, (2) selection of the habitat by the individuals with matching coloration, and (3) homochromic response. Cox and Cox's (1974) observation shows that in *Circotettix rabula* selective preda-tion (1 above) on mismatched nymphs on both red and gray substrates in fact occurs. The second mechanism is not likely. Rowell thought that these factors are not mutually exclusive, and maintained that the third, homochromic re-sponse, would have little or no selective value unless individuals thereafter settle on their habitat for ground color.

Genetic fixation of color morphs has been reported in a number of cases. The case of *Paratettix texanus* and *Apotettix eurycephala,* studied by Nabours (1929) for more than 60 generations in more than 20 years, provides the most reliable source of information regarding the genetic determination of color patterns. In *Paratettix* at least 18 factors influencing the color and pattern were identified. None of the environmental factors (excessive humidity, tempera-ture, aridity, acidity, and numerous others) was found to influence coloration. Rowell (1971) called this case quite legitimately "genetic polymorphism" (in the sense of Ford; see Sect. 4C). Fisher (1930b, 1939) proposed, based on the data in *Apotettix,* the theory that the diversity of the genotype is maintained by selection against the homozygous dominant. Among more recent workers, Dearn (1981) reported that in *Phaulacridium vittatum* three color patterns are controlled at a single autosomal locus with a striped phenotype dominant. In many cases of claimed genetic determination of color pattern, however, ac-cording to Rowell (1971), the evidence for genetic determination is less com-plete or such mechanism may easily be influenced by environments. For in-stance, in *Chortoicetes terminifera* the response to high humidity is a green pigmentation that obscures the genetically determined patterning.

14. The Order Grylloptera*

Some species of crickets (*Gryllus, Acheta, Gryllodes,* etc.) are known to be polymorphic with respect to wing development, both in laboratory experi-ments and in field observations. Effects of various environmental factors (pho-toperiod, temperature, population density, food) on wing development have been studied in laboratories. In *Gryllodes sigillatus* from Canada, which is micropterous in both sexes, Ghouri and McFarlane (1958) found that the optimal level (for both growth and wing development) is 20% protein in the food. They failed to see the group effect in producing macroptery (probably because of the unfavorable photoperiod). Mathad and McFarlane (1968) found that the exposure of the nymphs to a 10-hr photoperiod suppresses wing devel-opment completely, and that a 14-hr exposure is optimal for wing develop-ment. They found further that adults exposed to a 14-hr photoperiod produce more winged progeny than adults exposed to an 18-hr photoperiod. In the same species from Japan, however, Arai (1978) found that the macropterous form appears even in the isolated condition. He showed various photoperiodic effects at different temperatures. Thus all three factors, photoperiod, temperature, and population density influence wing development in *Gryllodes sigillatus.* Of

*Kevan (1973).

these, photoperiod appears to be a more important factor than the others.

In several species of *Gryllus* and *Scapsipedus* Fuzeau-Braesch (1961) found that isolation and grouping in rearing have the following consequences: In *Gryllus assimilis* macroptery is 100% whether they are reared in isolation or as a group; *G. desertus* adults are always brachypterous whether isolated or grouped in rearing; in *G. capitatus* 2 of 27 individuals became macropterous when grouped; and in *G. argentinus* and *Scapsipedus marginatus* significant numbers of macropterous individuals were produced by grouping, although in isolation *S. marginatus* is always brachypterous (as in *Nemobius yezoensis* discussed below), and in *G. argentinus* most of the individuals are brachypterous.

In *Scapsipedus aspersus* Saeki (1966a) showed a clear group effect and photoperiodic influence on wing development. Under a 16-hr photoperiod and when nymphs are reared together, 80% of them became macropterous, and the number of molts to achieving macroptery at the same time also increases (many of them eight stages instead of seven), regardless of the rearing conditions, whether isolated or grouped; this contrasts with the case of *Nemobius yezoensis* (Masaki and Oyama 1963), in which the duration of nymphal stage becomes shorter and the body size larger in becoming macropterous. This appears to mean, in turn, that the macropterous ancestor of *S. aspersus* probably had eight nymphal stages and that the neotenous brachypterous form has resulted from the omission of a nymphal stage (prothetely resulting in progenetic neoteny). Saeki (1966b) further found that the occurrence of the macropterous form is highest when four nymphs are reared together, and that macroptery results from direct contact between insects by antennae; when antennae are removed the insects become brachypterous. Earlier, Fuzeau-Braesch (1960) showed that in *Gryllus bimaculatus* the group effect manifests itself in color change, from dark in isolation to yellowish brown in groups, and that tactile stimulation by antennae and cerci is more important than the other stimuli (olfactory, visual) in causing the color change. Presumably, as he thought, such stimuli modify the physiological mechanism in inducing the color change.

Nemobius yezoensis occurs in the northern half of Japan and is always micropterous. However, Masaki and Oyama (1963) succeeded by a photoperiodic treatment (14-hr, in group), in inducing macroptery in more than two-thirds of the individuals tested. This showed that genetic determination of microptery is far from being complete in northern Japan. It is highly probable that initially the prevailing photoperiodic cycle and some other factor such as colder temperature in northern Japan induced microptery by affecting the endocrine mechanism (presumably in favor of more persistent JH secretion), and that in some of them canalization of development for microptery has occurred, most probably through the process of genetic assimilation. It follows, then, that in northern Japan microptery of this species is in phase 2 of genetic assimilation. Masaki and Oyama (1963) failed to see the selective advantage of microptery in this species. In the French population of *Gryllus dessertus* the brachypterous morph is genetically determined (phase 3 of genetic assimilation), although in eastern Europe this species is brachypterous (Fuzeau-Braesch 1961).

In *Gryllus campestris,* as shown by Cousin (1938), neotenous features are recognized (in addition to the reduced wings) also in some other structures, such as the poorly developed ovipositor and accessory glands of the spermathecae, and the absence of the male accessory glands. Similar studies certainly must be done for other wing-reduced species or populations of this order.

The cavernicolous Grylloptera comprise many genera, which include several genera that belong to Phalangopsida (Vandel 1965a). The majority of cavernicolous Grylloptera are characterized by paler body color, reduced eyes and ocelli, reduction or loss of wings, and short elytra (Vandel 1965a). These features are neotenous. *Luzongryllus* is a recently described new genus of Phalangopsidae that is cave dwelling and without wings, though with reduced elytra (Yamasaki 1978).

Myrmecophilidae, which comprises 5 genera and 45 species, are always associated with ants and are wingless in both sexes. They are minute, seldom surpassing 2 mm in length. Their eggs are relatively very large and with prolonged intraoval development (more than a year) (Kevan 1982). Thus the production of minute, neotenous (wingless) adults is associated with embryonization, as in some marine invertebrates, which results in minute neotenous adults (Sect. 3B2). *Apteronemobius,* which comprises two species, is apterous and inhabits only mangrove forests and swamp (Yamasaki 1979).

Recent endocrinological studies of crickets [Bradley and Simpson (1981)] on the brain neurosecretion have revealed that the endocrine mechanisms of growth and development and of reproduction nearly parallel those of locusts, Chudakova (1981), Chudakova and Delbecque (1983), Renucci and Strambi (1983), and Loher et al. (1983) on JH and analogues; Romer and Eisenbeis (1978), Renucci and Strambi (1981), Hoffmann and Behrens (1982), Hoffmann et al. (1981), and Behrens and Hoffmann (1983) on ecdysteroids. It is most probable that environmental signals are mediated by the endocrine mechanism, as Hoffmann et al. (1981) emphasized. Abnormal development resulting in wing reduction in crickets therefore must result from the altered activity of the brain neurohormone, as Mathad and McFarlane (1970) observed in connection with the development of the micropterous form in *Gryllodes sigillatus.* The works by Chudakova (1981) and Chudakova and Delbecque (1983), introducing JHA to the last instar of *Acheta domestica,* indicated that wing reduction is probably due to increased titer of circulating JHs, which limits the action of ecdysteroids toward the end of development.

15. The Order Psocoptera

In Psocoptera wing reduction takes the form of brachyptery, microptery, and aptery. Although some taxa are always brachypterous, most species of *Liposcelis* are apterous. Mockford's (1965) survey shows that wing polymorphism occurs in 16 of 27 families of Psocoptera and in 88 species of about 1400 described species. Furthermore, there is no tendency for wing reduction to be more pronounced in one sex than in another (Mockford 1956, 1965).

Structural modifications in wing-reduced (and hence neotenous) forms include ocelli that are poorly developed in the brachypterous form and vestigial or absent in the apterous form; compound eyes that are less developed in the brachypterous form and least developed in the apterous form (Kalmus 1945; Mockford 1956, 1965; Schneider 1977); obliteration of the trilobed condition of the mesonotum, the narrower precoxal bridge, and the poor development or loss of the ctenidia on the ventral surface of each proximal tarsal segment (Mockford 1965); two tarsal segments instead of three in neotenous females of some species (Smithers 1972, Lienhard 1975); and retention of the styli and the absence of the penis (Klier 1956). An apparent compensatory development that has accompanied wing reduction in domicolous Trogiomorpha is the increase in number of antennal segments (to 22 – 50) and in the total length of antennae (Schneider 1977).

According to Badonnel (1951) and Mockford (1956), the primitive number of nymphal stages (for macroptery) in Psocoptera is six, although in *Cerobasis* (*Hyperetes*) *questfalicus* with fully developed wings five nymphal stages occur (Jentsch 1939). Variable numbers of nymphal stages are required to produce the above-mentioned neotenous features, including wing reduction. Badonnel (1938, 1948) reported five or six nymphal instars for the development of micropfery in the parthenogenetic species *Psyllipsocus ramburi*. However, the duration of nymphal stages in micropterous individuals is, according to Badonnel (1959), definitely shorter than in macropterous individuals (36 – 40 versus 43 – 53 days in six instars). Hence, micropfery is progenetic neoteny. In *Archipsocus* spp., which live within a web they spin on trunk, twigs, branches, and other places, adult males are all micropterous or apterous, and they have four to six (usually five) instars (Mockford 1956); clearly in this genus the degree of neoteny (nymphoid and adultoid of Mockford) is more pronounced in the male than in the female. At any rate, fewer nymphal stages indicate that wing reduction is progenetic neoteny in this genus.

Broadhead and Hobby (1944) reported four nymphal instars for *Liposcelis granulicola*, which is apterous and domicolous. In another liposcelid, *Embidopsocus enderleini*, which occurs under the bark of trees in England, Broadhead (1947) found four nymphal instars for apterous females and three nymphal instars for apterous males. These cases are progenetic neoteny. The adult of *E. enderleini* produced through this process is tiny, measuring 1.7 mm in females and 1.2 mm in males (Broadhead 1947). Liposcelidae have been recorded from a variety of habitats — under bark, in vegetable litter, in stored products, insect collections, human dwellings, and so on. All these habitats provide fairly high humidity (Broadhead 1950). Thus high humidity could be suspected as a major physical environmental factor inducing prothetely (and progenetic neoteny) in this family.

Badonnel's (1938, 1948) experiments on the group effect with parthenogenetic *Psyllipsocus ramburi* showed that the larger the number of nymphs grouped in rearing, the higher the frequency of macroptery. When fewer nymphs are grouped, micropterous and apterous adults result, and when the nymph is isolated it never develops into a macropterous adult. Furthermore, according to Badonnel (1949), temperatures above 23° C cancel the effect of grouping; at 25–27° C no macropterous individual is formed even with grouping. It is thus apparent that temperature effect can often overwhelm the group effect in nature. Because the species experimented with is parthenogenetic, the effects produced in the above experiments represent purely those induced environmentally, without involving genetic differences.

Apart from the existence of the prothoracic glands (Badonnel 1970), nothing is directly known about the endocrinology of Psocoptera. Yet Badonnel (1959) hypothesized that the stimulus produced by grouping controls the activity of ecdysteroids (molting hormones). It appears most probable, at any rate, that polymorphism in wing development and associated structures results from a disturbance in hormonal balance. Micropery and aptery in these taxa (such as atropids, *Liposcelis*) must have been derived from ancestral polymorphism in wing development that was reversible initially. Accumulation of genocopies of micropterous and apterous phenotypes (involving a change or changes of the levels of the endocrine mechanism concerned with wing development) must have occurred during their evolution, resulting in genetic assimilation of the phenotypes. Badonnel (1951) referred to an unpublished work that shows genetic fixation of brachyptery by a single dominant allele in the female *Peripsocus parvulus.* He thought that in some species reduced wings are inherited (e.g., *Neopsocus rhenanus*), but in some they are *"accomodata";* that is, they are the temporarily modified phenotype.

Mesopsocus unipunctatus is dimorphic in abdominal color (dark and light) in northern England. According to Popescu (1979), the light form is common in rural areas, whereas the dark, industrial melanic form is common and highly cryptic in urban areas on dark barks without epiphytic growth. Selective predation of the color morphs was also found to be significant in maintaining the color dimorphism. The (presumed) proximate physiological process involved with melanism remains to be seen.

16. The Orders Mallophaga and Anoplura

Mallophagans are all ectoparasites of birds and mammals, and anoplurans are exclusively parasites of mammals. It is unanimously agreed that they are related to Psocoptera and that mallophagans are direct descendants of the Psocoptera. All developmental stages are passed on one host, and three nymphal stages are known to occur (Richards and Davies 1964, Kim and Ludwig 1978). This is a substantial reduction in number of nymphal stages, considering that their psocopteran ancestor presumably had six nymphal stages (see Sect. 23D 15). The consequence of such accelerated development in parasitic environments has been profound. The total loss of wings and the strong tendency for body parts to become consolidated are the external features common to all groups of the Mallophaga–Anoplura complex (Matsuda 1970). Other well-recognized regressive features include reduced eyes, loss of ocelli, and reduced numbers of tarsal and antennal segments. Mouthparts are of a modified biting type in Mallophaga and of a piercing–sucking type in Anoplura. A shift ventrad of the mouthparts and development of various structures on legs for attachment to the host are also adaptive modifications. It can safely be said that the unique adaptive structural organization (both regressive and constructive) of the Mallophaga, which has resulted from acceleration in development, represents progenetic neoteny.

It appears most probable that as the psocopterous ancestors of mallophagans settled in parasitic environments, varying degrees of reduction in nymphal development and concomitant reduction in wings and other structures (such as eyes and ocelli) occurred, as we see today in some polymorphic psocopterans (see Sect. 23D15). It can be easily imagined that the physical environmental factors available in the warm-blooded hosts were unique and strong enough to induce the developmental changes. It is most likely, furthermore, that at least the absence of wings and concomitant reduction in eyes and the loss of ocelli were definitely advantageous in the new parasitic environments, that natural selection allowed only those individuals with such neotenous features to stay initially, and that later some other adaptive modifications evolved, presumably under the pressure of natural selection. It is most likely that, sooner or later, genetic fixation of the mallophagan phenotypes came through the process of genetic assimilation.

What is of special interest here is the presumed ecological mode of the origin of the Mallophaga, which can be surmised from what we know about the close association of psocopterans with birds' nests. For Kéler (1957), as it was for Handlirsch (1908), the nidicolous condition of the psocopterans was the precondition for the origin of Mallophaga as parasites of birds. Kéler (1957) referred to Nordberg (1936), who reported the findings of 13 species of Psocoptera in the nests of 56 bird species in Finland. The 13 species represented about 20% of Psocoptera known from Finland and they were distributed in 11 genera. This close ecological association leads us, indeed, to suspect their occasional success in achieving parasitism on birds, and the probable polyphyletic origin of the Mallophaga. Considering, in fact, the high morphogenetic plasticity exhibited by psocopterans today, it is very difficult to believe that only one psocopteran species ever had, in their long history of association with birds, the chance to become parasites.

The possibility of polyphyletic origin of Mallophaga can also be surmised from their high host specificity. It has been known that usually one group of Mallophaga occurs in a certain particular group of birds (Harrison 1914, Wilson 1934, Zlotorzycka 1967). Hence they cannot settle successfully in distantly related host birds (Wilson 1934). This indicates that parasitism by different groups of ancestral (psocopterous) Mallophaga occurred independently, and it is least likely that an ancestral mallophagan species (as monophyly presupposes) has spread onto many different groups of birds, each time changing their structures substantially. As Zlotorzycka (1967) pointed out, mallophagan parasitism is complicated by the fact that one host species may have two or more groups of Mallophaga as parasites. This mode of parasitism can be accounted for by assuming that different groups of psocopterous ancestors succeeded in parasitizing one host species at different times, although the possibility exists that this is due to a secondary shift of host.

In more recent discussions of the origin of Mallophaga the possibility of their polyphyletic origin has been ignored. Thus according to Königsmann (1960), the Amblycera, on the one hand, and three other groups (Ischnocera, Anoplura, Rhynchophthirina), on the other hand, arose independently within the hypothetical Phthiraptera, which is characterized by winglessness and some other features (flattened head, short antennae, etc.). Clay (1970) accepted the "Phthiraptera" as well as Königsmann's classification of the Phthiraptera into two major groups. According to Hennig (1969, 1981), a species younger than the stem species of the Psocoptera gave rise to the Phthiraptera as well as some psocopterans (paraphyly). This phylogenetic argument is certainly consistent with this methodology in which, for the sake of parsimony of hypothesis, only a single species is assumed to be ancestral to the recognized group. Needless to say, however, such a formalism completely ignores the biological information upon which the idea of polyphyletic origins of the Mallophaga is based.

Kim and Ludwig (1978) rejected the concept of Phthiraptera, as the characters used for the erection of the "Phthiraptera" are related primarily to the parasitic mode of life and the result of parasitism. They replaced the "Phthiraptera" by the "parasitic ancestral Psocodea" which, according to them, gave rise to the Amblycera lineage and later also the Protoanoplura and the Ischnocera–Rhynchophthirina stock. Yet Lyal (1985) suggests that the common ancestor of the monophyletic (holophyletic) group Phthiraptera was parasitic.

17. The Order Thysanoptera

Postoval development of the Terebrantia passes through nymphal (sometimes called larval) instars I and II, a prepupal stage, and one pupal stage; in Tubulifera there are two pupal stages —pupa I and pupa II after the prepupa (Ananthakrishnan 1984). The prepupal and pupal stages are quiescent and externally not greatly different from the preceding stages (except in wing development), although metamorphosis of internal organs is comparable with that of holometabolous insects during these stages (Snodgrass 1954a).

In many genera of Thysanoptera wing polymorphism occurs, and different morphs are called macroptery, brachyptery, hemimacroptery, and aptery, depending on the degree of wing reduction. According to Ananthakrishnan (1969), in truly apterous forms eyes are reduced to a few ommatidia, ocelli are absent, sense cones are shorter, the pterothorax is considerably reduced, and in the Tubulifera the sigmoid setae are absent; these features are neotenous. Totally wingless species are known in very few genera such as *Leptogastrothrips* and *Emprosthiothrips* (Ananthakrishnan 1984), although, as Ananthakrishnan

(1969) pointed out, winged morphs have often been recorded later in the species that had been considered to be apterous. In the apterous male of *Rhopalandrothrips annulicornis* the maxillary palpus is two segmented, although it is three segmented in the macropterous female of the same species (Pesson 1951, Dyadechko 1977).

Köppa (1970) found that the macropterous form of *Anaphothrips obscurus* increases in number when exposed to long days, and that short days inhibit the production of macropterous individuals. These results were correlated with the field observation that the proportion of brachypterous individuals increases toward autumn; here the effect of lower temperatures may also be involved. Kamm's (1972) experiment on the photoperiodic effect with the same species agreed with the results obtained by Köppa. Kamm also found that higher population densities induce the increase in macropterous individuals (group effect). Köppa's (1970) experiment also showed that the kinds of food also affect the determination of wing morphs. All these facts showing the environmentally related morphogenetic plasticity must underlie neoteny in Thysanoptera.

18. The Order Hemiptera

a. The Suborder Homoptera

THE AUCHENORRHYNCHA: Wing dimorphism consisting of macroptery and brachyptery is known for some auchenorrhynchous Homoptera. Kisimoto (1957) found, in the brachypterous forms of *Nilaparvata lugens, Sogata furcifera,* and *Delphacodes striatella,* that (1) the forewings are short and hind wings are rudimentary, (2) the scutellum is shorter than in the macropterous form, (3) the lengths of the hind femur and tibia and the ovipositor are greater than in the macropterous form, and (4) the body color is paler and the preovipositional period is shorter than in the macropterous form. Of these, 1 and 2 are most probably due to developmental arrest, and 3 may be interpreted as a case of compensatory development. The number of nymphal stages does not seem to differ between the two forms in the species studied. However, in the achievement of brachyptery in *N. lugens* the total length of the nymphal stages appears to have been shortened (Kisimoto 1956a,b). Hence brachyptery in this species can be regarded as progenetic neoteny.

Nilaparvata lugens is a serious pest of the rice plant in Asia. This species arrives at the paddy field in Japan in June by migration, presumably from southern China, and they are naturally macropterous as they reach Japan. However, brachypterous females appear soon afterward and increase in number during the summer and autumn. Brachypterous males appear in late summer and autumn, and they are less frequent than females. By late summer when the rice plant ripens, the macropterous form (in both sexes) becomes abundant again.

Kisimoto (1956a,b) studied the group effect on the wing morph production in *N. lugens.* His experiments showed that at the lowest population density (i.e., isolation of each individual) all emerged females were brachypterous and, surprisingly, males were all macropterous. With increasing density female macroptery increased and most females became macropterous at the maximum experimental density (i.e., 20 individuals in a test tube). In the male, on the other hand, the brachypterous form (71.4% of them) emerged in the middle range of density, although no brachypterous individual emerged when isolated individually; short day lengths and lower temperatures promote brachyptery in the male (Johno 1963). In the male, as in the female, however, the frequency of brachyptery declined and most of them became macropterous at the maximum density. Kisimoto (1956a,b) found that the quality of food plant is also important in determination of wing morphs; the wilting of host plants and other factors contribute to the production of macroptery.

The above experimental results indicate that the seasonal fluctuation in wing dimorphism in *N. lugens* probably depends largely on population density, especially in the female. The hoppers disperse individually in the paddy field after their arrival in Japan, and the resultant lower population densities appear to underlie the emergence of brachypterous females during the summer and autumn. The emergence of macropterous individuals that occurs later appears to be related to the increase in population density that coincides with the ripening of the rice plant. At least, most of the macropterous individuals produced at the end of the autumn migrate away from Japan (Kisimoto 1975), and thus macroptery at this season is of selective advantage, enabling them to fly away from the unfavorable (winter) environments.

In the Philippines climatic factors such as photoperiod and temperature are not important for the determination of the wing morphs in *Nilaparvata lugens*. Instead, as shown by Saxena et al. (1981), changes in the physiological status of the host plant have a profound effect on the wing morph determination. Saxena et al. observed a significant increase in macroptery in progeny reared on senescent hosts, and they attributed this to the decline in the host's nutritional condition. Saxena et al. explained that atarvation inhibits JH release, suppressing brachyptery and expressing macroptery, and referred to Nasu (1969), who showed that in this species CA appeared to be inactive in the macropterous form, but appeared to be active in the brachypterous form.

In *Javesella pellucida* the percentage of macropterous adults (in both sexes) is higher in crowded conditions (Mochida 1973; Ammar 1973). In *Laodelphax stratellus* also, wing morphs are determined by the quality and quantity of food and by crowding (Mahmud 1980). Mahmud found further that the production of the macropterous form is greater when the lines of macropterous form are crossed, and claimed that possibly genetic factors have some influence in wing dimorphism.

More recent ecologists view wing dimorphism in planthoppers as a life history strategy. Denno (1978) maintained that brachyptery in delphacids must be predominant in more stable habitats (in terms of food resources, oviposition space, overwintering sites), such as salt-marsh lands, and that macroptery enables the insects to explore new niches when the environments deteriorate or become unstable. In fact, Denno's (1978) survey shows impressively high percentages of brachyptery (often reaching 100%) in most of the delphacids inhabiting the tidal salt-marsh habitat. Undoubtedly, emigration of macropterous individuals has contributed to the realization of such a high frequency of brachypterous individuals in the habitats. Yet it is not necessarily due solely to emigration and selection pressure. It is probable, or at least it can be suspected, that the chemical quality of food in the halophytous plants in the these habitats must differ significantly from that in other habitats, and the intake of such nutrition affects the development of nymphs, resulting perhaps in higher frequency of brachyptery. As already seen, the quality of food affects the wing morph determination, and some aphids infesting halophytic plants have shorter antennae (Hille Ris Lambers 1966). Some other proximate factors must affect the wing morph determination.

As Strong and Stiling (1983) pointed out, the mechanism of wing morph determination in *Prokelisia marginata* is complex, and diverse environmental cues are involved. They found that when the experimental population of *P. marginata* is caged to prevent emigration, the incidence of macroptery suddenly increases dramatically in October–November, although in controls and in the field no winged form is observed at this season. This appears to indicate the effect of shortening day length and lowering temperature on wing development. The effect of higher populations also might have to be considered in such an experiment. It is possible that in the field macropters produced during this season emigrate quickly to some overwintering sites.

In the leafhopper genus *Euscelis* also environmentally induced dimorphism occurs. Müller (1954) found, by extensive examination of specimens and repeated experiments, that *E. plebejus* and *E. incisus* in Europe actually represent seasonal dimorphism of a single species *E. plebejus,* the former occurring in the summer and the latter in the spring. They are distinguishable by darker and lighter colorations, larger and smaller sizes of wings, and different shapes of the apical end of the aedeagus. The short-winged condition and other characters can be considered neotenous. Müller (1957) found further, based especially on the shape of the aedeagus, similar relations between the West European species *E. lineolatus, E. stictopterus, E. bilobatus,* and four related but undescribed forms, all being seasonal modifications of a single species *E. lineolatus.* He showed that the *lineolatus* and *superlineolatus* forms result from exposure to a photoperiod of 8 hr/day, and that *bilobatus, dubius, substictopterus, stictopterus,* and *superstictopterus* result from long days (16 hr or more of light per day). By such photoperiodic manipulation Müller was able to produce either the *incisus* or *plebejus* form, and either the *lineolatus* or *bilobatus* form, respectively. Müller's experiment further showed that temperature only modifies but does not cancel the effect of photoperiod, and that the quality of food also slightly influences the photoperiodic effect on the aedeagus size in *E. plebejus* and *E. lineolatus.*

In Auchenorrhyncha no apterous taxon seems to have been recognized. In fact, as the preceding discussion shows, wing reduction is moderate when wing dimorphism occurs; only brachyptery, never microptery or aptery, occurs in the examples discussed. This may be related to their freer ways of living than in apterous taxa in other groups (such as some Heteroptera). When wing dimorphism occurs the macropterous form is the colonizer of new habitats.

Geographic variation in color pattern polymorphism in *Philaenus spumarius* has been investigated in Fennoscandia and eastern Europe (Halkka et al. 1975, 1980, and others) and in Britain (Hutchinson 1963, Lees et al. 1983, and others). Of special interest here is a case of industrial melanism of this species. Lees and Dent (1983) reported that a striking relationship exists between the eight dark melanic morphs and proximity to a factory in the Cynon valley of South Wales; maximum melanic phenotype frequencies greater than 95% occur in both sexes immediately adjacent to it. Lees and Dent suggested that the relationship is due to the selective effects of the local air pollution from the factory, although the exact nature of the selection involved was unknown

THE STERNORRHYNCHA. Female aphids are dimorphic in wing development. They are either winged (called "alate" in aphidology) or wingless (apterous), and the male is usually alate. The alate or apterous condition in the female is associated with various reproductive morphs that are produced at different seasons of the year, although in primitive aphids the alate condition occurs more frequently (Hille Ris Lambers 1966). Commonly recognized morphs include the fundatrix (viviparous parthenogenetic females developing from a fertilized egg), the virginopara (viviparous parthenogenetic female producing only other parthenogentic viviparae), the oviparous female or ovipara (female that lays hibernating eggs), the gynopara (vivipara that produces only oviparae), and the sexupara (vivipara that produces oviparae and males). Usually in temperate regions parthenogenetic generations (morphs) occur in spring and summer, and they are followed by a single sexual generation (morph).

Each of the morphs is not the same in the presence or absence of wings in different species. For instance, the fundatrix is either alate or apterous, depending on the species. When the apterous viviparous female occurs in a life cycle of a species, the fundatrix is usually apterous, and conversely when no apterous viviparous female occurs in later generations the fundatrices are alate (Hille Ris Lambers 1966). The presence or absence of wings in particular morphs is also related to their life cycle, whether they are monoecious (with a single host plant) or alternate hosts.

It is well known in taxonomic aphidology that in the apterous morph of the fundatrix, parthenogenetic vivipara, and ovipara the degree of differentiation of structures is generally much less than in the alate morph, as seen in shorter antennae with fewer rhinaria, smaller compound eyes, the lack of ocelli, and so on. These features, along with the absence of wings, definitely represent neotenous conditions that result from the arrest of development. As Lees' (1961) observation with *Megoura viciae* showed, certain structures such as the associated complex structures in the pterothorax are simply not formed through metamorphosis in the apterous adult, and some structures such as antennal sensilla are only incompletely formed, reflecting developmental arrest. Furthermore, the degree of neoteny in apterous fundatrices is more pronounced than in apterous viviparous females, as seen in more reduced conditions of sensilla, length of antennae (often in number of antennal segments), and length of legs, sipunculi, and cauda (Hille Ris Lambers 1966). Lees' (1983) reservation for regarding the lack of wings and less differentiated states of some adult structures as neoteny was based on the concept of neoteny that refers only to the retention of juvenile structures.

In aphids the apterous form appears to require a shorter time to complete its nymphal development. Kennedy and Stroyan (1959) state that apterous virginoparae have a shorter generation time than winged virginoparae. In *Aphis craccivora* Johnson (1959) found that both forms have four nymphal instars, but winged forms spend one more day in the last instar. The occurrence of progenetic neoteny in *Schizaphis graminum* was reported by Wood and Starks (1975). This species usually undergoes five molts from birth to maturity. Under laboratory conditions, 1.8% of greenbugs were found to reproduce precociously. In the test 13 insects reproduced 1 day before molting into alata, four reproduced 2 days before molting to alata, and one reproduced 3 days before the final molt.

Diverse environmental factors (photoperiod, temperature, population density, and food) have been known to influence the production of different morphs. Although these factors appear to act jointly, one factor could well be more important than others, depending on the species and under different conditions. Photoperiod and temperature are usually interrelated, one factor modulating the effect of the others. In the monoecious species *Megoura viciae*, for instance, the type of female progeny is controlled by photoperiod and temperature to which the developing parent is exposed. With daily photoperiods shorter than 14 hr and 55 min and at a moderate temperature (15°C), only oviparae are produced. With longer photoperiods and at higher temperatures the daughters are exclusively virginoparae (Lees 1961). A group of NSC (the group I cells), located in the protocerebrum, are mediators of the photoperiodic response (Steel and Lees 1977, Hardie et al. 1981, Hardie and Lees 1983).

Bonnemaison (1951) first discovered the importance of crowding (group effect) on wing development in virginoparae, and distinguished the direct effects of higher density from indirect effects of poor nutrition (which by itself tends to result in the production of the alate form) under crowded conditions. Later works with *Aphis craccivora* (Johnson 1965), and *Acyrthosiphon pisum* (Sutherland 1969), and *Megoura viciae* (Lees 1961, 1966, 1967) also showed the group effect on wing development in virginoparae, and the effect appeared to depend on tactile stimulation. In *Megoura viciae* Lees (1961, 1967) found that progenies of adult aphids isolated after a brief crowding experience continue to produce alate offsprings for many days, sometimes even throughout the whole reproductive period. In some aphid species the proportion of nymphs developing into alate adults is a function of the density at which nymphs are reared (see Harrison 1980 for references).

It is a common observation that alate aphids are produced more abundantly on mature, old, and wilting plant tissues than on seedlings or growing shoots (Bonnemaison 1952). In *Aphis craccivorae* Johnson (1966) observed that prolonged starvation results in an increase in aptera production. Mittler (1973) had to conclude that the dietary influence on aphid polymorphism is extremely varied, as varied as the many facets of nutrition and the various morphs in which aphids can exist.

With reference the hormonal control of wing development and morphs, many earlier works showed the juvenilizing effect of JH and its analogues (reviewed by Matsuda 1979), and the JH control of the alate and apterous morphs was apparent in the correlated decrease and increase of CA size during the development of *Bryocoryne brassicae* (Hales 1976). An experiment by Hardie (1981) showed that all naturally occuring JHs (JH I, JH II, JH III) have a juvenilizing effect, though they differ in potency. The precocene analogue treatment with adult *Myzus persicae* resulted in precocious metamorphosis in the offspring; the precocious aphids became adultoids in the third or fourth instar (Hales and Mittler 1981). Furthermore, when precocene II was applied to the newly molted alate adult and apterous virginoparae of *Macrosiphum euphorbiae* the production of alate virginoparae increased in a generally dose-dependent manner (Delisle et al. 1983).

Although the nature of endogenous JH in aphids still remains to be identified, Hardie (1980) found that in *Aphis fabae* larger doses of JH I, when applied to the first instar of the presumptive alate gynoparae, closely mimics the photoperiodic apterization (by long-day conditions). Hardie inferred that long-day conditions induce the increase of endogenous level of JH in *A. fabae*, and maintained that low titers of endogenous JH induced by short-day conditions would promote both wing development and embryonic development of oviparae. It appears most probable that the suppression (or cessation) of JH secretion by short days is followed by the secretion of ecdysteroids, which more directly induces the development of wings. Hardie (1981) further showed that when JHs are topically applied to the fourth instar, oviparous/viviparous intermediates emerge in the progeny.

Despite an isolated report by Applebaum et al. (1975) that β-ecdysone has no effect on wing development, involvement of ecdysteroids with aphid morphogenesis is highly probable. For instance, the maternal factor, which appears to be profoundly involved with wing development and such a related phenomenon as the interval timer, may turn out to be the ecdysteroids incorporated into the eggs as in locusts (Sect. 23D13), termites (Sect 23D12), Hymenoptera (Sect. 23D22), and others. It is significant to point out here that in the diapausing egg of the scale insect *Lepidosaphes ulmi*, ecdysteriod was identified by Gharib et al. (1981).

The group I NSC in the brain of *Megoura viciae* were first shown by Steel (1976) to secrete a factor that induces virginoparae under the influence of long days (reviewed by Kats 1984).

Because the lability in developmental cycle and morphogenesis depends on triggering by environmental parameters, suppression of certain morphs is expected to occur in the absence of proper environmental induction. *Myzus persicae*, which is distributed worldwide, is a case in point. Thus, as Blackman's (1974) review revealed, holocycly of *M. persicae* with sexual reproduction and overwintering eggs on *Prunus* occurs in temperate regions of every continent. However, anholocycly without overwintering eggs is widespread in warm climate (although there are indications that the potential for sexual reproduction may be retained). Probably this can be attributed to the lack of proper photoperiodic induction for development of oviparae. However, another equally important factor is temperature; the temperature threshold above which the sexual morph production is inhibited is around 22°C in *M. persicae* (Bonnemaison 1951). Blackman attempted to correlate the global pattern of life cycle variation with temperature differences between regions.

Although a genetically isolated anholocyclic biotype presumably exists, in temperate regions where both anholocycly and holocycly occur together, the anholocyclic biotype (of Blackman 1972) could be the principal source of parthenogenetic overwinterer (Blackman 1974); the anholocyclic condition is induced by a recessive switch gene that completely suppresses male production (Blackman 1972). Müller (1966) showed that *Toxoptera auranti, Macrosiphoniella sanborni* and *Rhopalosiphum malis,* with an anholocyclic life history in subtropical and tropical regions, can persist in regions with cold winters only when suitable plants are present in greenhouses. Whether anholocycly has been established genetically in warmer regions has not been investigated (Müller 1966, Blackman 1972). At any rate, the production of hibernating eggs must be advantageous in temperate regions where food may be scarce or absent in winter. However, in the tropics and subtropics, where food is available throughout the year, anholocycly with parthenogenetic generations would enable propagation throughout the year. Seen in this light, anholocycly in warmer climate originated as an adaptive response to the unique environmental stimuli (e.g., higher regimes of temperature).

The case of the spotted alfafa aphid *Therioaphis trifolii* that has invaded North America illustrates how viviparous parthenogenesis combined with high plasticity in development could have enabled aphids to survive and further propagate in new environments (summarized by Blackman 1981). *T. trifolii* first appeared on alfalfa in North America in 1953–1954, probably starting in New Mexico, and by 1956 it had spread through most southern states of the United States. For several years after its introduction they apparently reproduced solely by parthenogenesis. All evidence (such as a narrow morphological variation) strongly suggested a single clone, perhaps resulting from the introduction of just one female (founder effect related to parthenogenesis). It can further be surmised that they became anholocyclic as a result of environmental (photoperiodic and temperature) suppression of the sexual generation in the southern United States. Thereafter, the aphids started invading alfalfa in some more northerly states. In the autumn of 1960 a population in the center of Nebraska suddenly started to reproduce viable sexual morphs, and passed the winter successfully in the egg stage. Evidently, they deployed the potential for sexual reproduction in response to the local environmental stimuli in Nebraska. Today, the spotted alfalfa aphid is found throughout the United States, and sexual reproduction with overwintering eggs occur over most of the northern part.

As the preceding discussions show, environmentally induced morphogenesis in aphids is highly labile in that it is reversible as in Auchenorrhyncha (see above), and the reversible wing dimorphism in most Homoptera is unique.

As shown by Hille Ris Lambers (1966), caenogenetic modification of the nymphal stages occurs in some aphids. For instance, in three or four European species of *Periphyllus* aestivating larvae have extremely long hairs on the dorsal surface of the body, whereas in another group of species of *Periphyllus* from Europe, North America, and eastern Asia aestivating nymphs have very short dorsal hairs. However, they are provided with lateral lobes arising from the posterolateral angles of the metanotum and abdominal segments, and even from the anterior margin of the pronotum. These lobes are veined as the tracheal gills in nymphal mayflies and appear to represent the expression of archaic genes that are normally hidden.

Another interesting case of caenogenesis is the occurrence of a "soldier caste" in some aphids. As Aoki (1977) first showed, in *Colophina clematis* two types of nymphs are produced from apterous viviparae, one normal type and a second type with a short rostrum and enlarged forelegs and middle legs. Aoki discovered that the second type does not molt and that it attacks intruders to defend the colony. Hence it is comparable with soldier caste in termites and ants. Aoki (1982) summarized three types of the soldier caste: (1) pseudoscorpion-like first-instar soldiers of *Colophina* spp. (Pemphiginae, Eriosomatini), which clutch at a predatory intruder such as a syrphid larva and sting it with their stylets; (2) pseudoscorpion-like first-instar soldiers of *Pseudoregma* spp. and *Ceratovacuna japonica* (Hormaphidinae; Ceratophidini), which clutch at a predatory intruder with their thickened forelegs and pierce it with their acute frontal horns; and (3) second-instar soldiers of *Astegopteryx styracicola* (Hormaphidinae, Ceratophidini), which sting not only insect predators but also human skin with their stylets and cause itching.

Associated with plant parasitism, female scale insects have fewer nymphal instars than males, and the wings are not formed in the female. The first female nymphal instar (crawler) is provided with three pairs of legs that ensure its dispersal. However, the subsequent developmental process differs considerably in different groups of female coccids. In a more primitive family, Pseudococcidae (mealybugs), two nymphal stages are known to follow the first nymphal instar, and the adult female emerges from the third-stage nymph. The adult female of this family usually maintains three pairs of legs, an exception being *Antonina* spp., which are apodous and some of which have (only) two segmented antennae (McKenzie 1967). Constructive developments in the female adult of mealybugs comprise various types of pores, some of which are believed to produce filamentous ovisacs, and more numerous trilocular pores engaged in the production of the white powdery secretion. Furthermore, two pairs of ostioles, located submarginally on the seventh segment and on the head secrete globules of the body fluid as a defense mechanism (McKenzie 1967). The lack of wings and the compensatory production of these pores and ostioles are neotenous features of the female mealybugs. Because the third male nymphal instar becomes the fourth instar before emerging as an adult from the latter, the female mealybugs clearly undergo one less molt than the male mealybugs, and therefore the female mealybugs represent progenetic neoteny.

Börner (1910) showed that the male *Aulacaspis rosae* (Diaspinae) exhibits dimorphism in juvenile stages, the last two preimaginal stages being pupa-like and distinct from the first three stages that precede. The first-stage "pupa" develops into the second "pupa" with some further structural changes before the latter metamorphosis into the adult male. Such a metamorphic change is comparable with that in Holometabola, and Börner called it *Parametabolie.* The female diaspines become adult after the first three nymphal stages. Within the male, again, the degree of forewing development varies in different species. Some are brachypterous and some are even micropterous. Greatly reduced hind wings are haltere-like, or the hind legs are absent. Thus neoteny seems to have occurred also within the male.

The accelerated development of female scale insects is clearly related to their existence as plant parasites, and the nutrition they obtain might induce acceleration and consequent neoteny. The effect of hosts on behavior, morphology, and speciation in scale insects is well known. Miller and Kosztarab (1979) thought that divergent morphologies on different hosts are caused by different chemical nature or physiology of parts of the host plant. Thus examples of host-related (determined) modifications include a very considerable diversity in structures associated with different hosts in *Lecanium corni,* which has been known since Ferris (1920) and Ebeling (1938); *Aspidiotus ancylus,* which develops into its typical form on the twigs of trees and matures on elm and sugar maple leaves, has distinct forms formerly known as *howardi* and *comstocki* (Stannard 1965), etc. Furthermore, Cox (1983) showed experimentally that many female structures (length of appendages and setae, number of wax-producing pores and ducts, etc.) in *Planococcus citri* are greatly affected when the bugs are reared at different temperatures. Rieux (1975) developed a hypothesis relating to the host influence on scale insect speciation. Species of *Matsucoccus* are restricted to specific groups *Pinus.* Therefore Rieux concluded that such trophic affinities are probably the result of concomitant speciation of *Pinus* and *Matsucoccus.* Thus, as in aphids (Eastop 1973), host specificity can be the major cause of speciation in scale insects.

Differential activity of CA between sexes is apparent in an observation on *Lecanium* by Pflugfelder (1936), which showed that the CA are very much larger in the female than in the male, although they are nearly equal during earlier nymphal stages. It is obvious, therefore, that the CA grow in volume much faster in the female than in the male. This can be interpreted that more JH is secreted (presumably an excessive secretion) in the female than in the male, resulting in the suppression of imaginal structures and concomitant maturation of oocytes because of its gonadotropic function. Such a difference in JH activity must result, at least in part, from different environmental (including nutritional) stimuli different sexes receive, because the female nymphs are sessile (and covered by the wax material) and the male nymphs are free-living.

Among the Aleuroidea, seasonal dimorphism in *Aleurochiton complanatus* infesting *Acer platanoides* has been known since Haupt (1934) and Müller (1962a,b,c). The species is bivoltine and dimorphism occurs in the "pupa" (puparium) which is formed after three nymphal (called "larval") stages. In the summer morph the puparium is almost colorless and the winter form, which enters diapause, is dark colored with a white wax pattern. Later, more structural differences (in development of gonads and of wing rudiments, musculature, oenocytes, mycetocytes, egg sizes, and lengths of wings in adults) between the two morphs were recognized by Bährmann (1973, 1974a, 1978). Müller (1962b) showed that at a photoperiod of less than 17–18 hr/day the winter pupa emerges, and at a photoperiod longer than 17–18 hr the paler summer form. He also showed the influence of the physiological state of the host plant on the production of seasonal forms. Bährmann (1979) maintained that the overwintering darkly pigmented puparia, which are found in decaying leaves on the ground, are heavily waxed and hence protective. Bährmann (1974b) also reported seasonal, photoperiodically induced dimorphism in *Neobemisia paveli;* under short-day conditions (8/16) or lower light intensity (25–150 lx) during the photophase of 14, 16, 17, or 18 hr light/day, dark puparia are produced.

The taxonomy of the Aleuroidea has often been confused because of their morphogenetic plasticity associated with host plants. Russell (1948) deduced that the pupa (the fourth nymphal instar) of *Trialeurodes vaporariorum* could vary considerably in its structure, matching the structure of the host leaf; that is, on hairy leaves the pupal case bears large papillae and long setae, and on glabrous leaves, small papillae and short setae. This host-related ecomorphic variation led to the proposal of many new species, and Russell (1957) synonymized several described species of *Bemisia* from the tropics with *B. tabaci*. Mound's (1963) experiment substantiated the synonymy of Russell (1957). In the experiment several forms were raised from a single virgin female whitefly by allowing her progeny to develop on different plant species (cassava, tobacco, *Dolichos* bean, cotton, etc.). It was found that each resultant phenotype derived from each different host plant was similar to that found in the same host plant in nature. These host-dependent adaptive variations are apparently induced directly by different host plant environments. How the mechanism for this instantaneous adaptive response has ever evolved in nature remains a mystery.

Photoperiodic control of imaginal (ovarial) diapause has been known for psyllids, and certain wing lengths are correlated with diapause (Bonnemaison and Missonier 1955, Oldfield 1970, Thanh-Xuan 1972, Mustafa and Hodgson 1984). In *Psylla peregrina,* according to Sutton (1983), seasonal color change (from green or yellow to dark brown) is related to sexual maturation in autumn; upon maturation the insects migrate. Sutton reasoned that this correlated change might be hormonally (possibly by JH) regulated, and that the dark coloration might serve cryptic function.

b. The Suborder Heteroptera

Wing reduction has occurred in many groups of Heteroptera, and aptery sometimes became permanent. Southwood (1961), after reviewing the facts then available, postulated a theory of the cold temperature–hormonally induced wing reduction in Heteroptera. The theory was based on the endocrinological facts brought forward in the studies of *Rhodnius* by Wigglesworth (1952, 1954). Its essential points were as follows: the short-wingedness is a juvenile character and is likely to arise through the change in the concentration of JH that is necessary for the long-winged adults. This change could be brought about either one of the two ways: (1) by excessive influence of JH leading to juvenile characters — metathetely, or (2) by depression of the influence of JH (and thus the loss of the prothoracic glands and thus failure of molting hormone), leading to adult characters in the nymph (larva of Southwood) — prothetely. This view of regarding wing reduction as an aspect either of metathetely (leading to metagenetic neoteny) or of prothetely (leading to progenetic neoteny) has turned out to serve as a very important concept that can be extended to explain the two kinds of neoteny in insects as well as in other animals (Sect. 2B).

Southwood failed to refer to the action of ecdysteroids (molting hormones) that must be involved with metathetely and prothetely. As Brinkhurst (1963) pointed out, the juvenile wings (characters) of Southwood are actually incompletely formed imaginal wings in *Gerris*, and here a subnormal action of ecdysteroids is apparently involved as a result of excessive influence of JH leading to metathetely (as in solitary locusts, Sect. 23D13). Presumably, in prothetely, precocious morphogenetic action of ecdysteroids occurs. Diverse environmental factors influence the hormonal activity, and it is certainly not the cold temperature alone (as claimed by Southwood) that influences JH activity and consequent wing reduction.

In Heteroptera, as Southwood (1961) pointed out, the loss of ocelli correlated with wing reduction is uncommon. According to Southwood, wing reduction in *Gerris* spp., *Nabis ferus, Bryocoris pteridis,* and *Trapezonotus* spp. is due to metathetely induced by cold temperatures that acted on the hormonal balance. His examples of prothetely (progenetic neoteny) included *Dolichonabis limbatus,* which has four nymphal instars instead of the normal five in cold mountainous conditions, and some apterous *Microvelia* spp., with four nymphal stages. Furthermore, according to Southwood, there is little association of sex and wing morphs, although in many Miridae and all Microphysidae the male is generally fully winged and the female is always or usually brachypterous.

In subsequent studies on wing polymorphism in Heteroptera, as discussed below, cold temperature – hormonal induction of wing reduction has not been properly appreciated. In fact, Slater (1977) denied Southwood's hormonal theory on the ground that there are all gradations of wing reduction in Lygaeidae and that they are not similar to the experimentally induced reduced wings in *Rhodnius*. The experimentally induced reduced wings are not expected to correspond exactly to the graded series of wing reduction in nature, because the former depends on the JH dose applied and on the stage at which JH is applied or JH effect is removed (by the removal of CA or precocene application). The resultant hormonal milieu in the insects of the experiment cannot be the same as that occurring in nature. The main thing is that JH controls wing development. In fact, JH involvement in wing reduction has become even more apparent in recent experiments applying precocene to lygaeids (Bowers et al. 1976, Masner et al. 1979, Unnithan and Nair 1979, Belles and Baldellou 1983), which resulted in precocious metamorphosis with some disorders. Topical application of 0.1 mg JHA resulted in significantly earlier emergence of adults, which were nymph – adult intermediates (Smith and Nijhout 1981). It must be assumed that if the wing reduction is genetically determined, as Slater was inclined to believe, the genes concerned must affect or control the hormonal activity.

The discovery by Klausner et al. (1981) of a mutant causing wing reduction in *Oncopeltus* is of special interest, for such a discovery tends to give strong support to Slater's idea. It is safe to assume here that such a mutant affects hormonal activity in causing wing reduction. Klausner et al. found short-winged individuals in laboratory cultures of *Oncopeltus fasciatus* (Lygaeidae) derived from the island of Guadeloupe of the Caribbean. Crossing of them showed that a single recessive Mendelian unit can cause brachyptery. There were, however, modifiers involved with the phenotypic expression, because the brachyptery was characterized by considerable variation. Neither temperature nor photoperiod had any effect on the expression of the brachypterous trait in the homozygous short genotype. Furthermore, short-wingedness was not sex related.

In *Oncopeltus fasciatus* wing reduction does not occur in nature (Klausner et al. 1981). Apparently, therefore, the mutant for wing reduction has not been allowed to exist by selection. However, if such a mutant is allowed to exist, either one of two processes would occur. One is that it would replace the environmentally induced short-wingedness (genetic assimilation). Another possibility is that wing reduction starts out with mutation, and that under the pressure of natural selection such a mutant gradually accumulates in a given population as in carabids (Sect. 23D21). Because the cases of wing reduction in lygaeids discussed by Sweet (1964) and Slater (1977) are related to environmental changes, and because they have not yet shown the genetic mechanism of wing morphs by crossing, I attempt below tentatively to interpret the cases in terms of the first alternative, in the hope that it will stimulate further studies.

Sweet (1964) found that 51% of Rhyparochrominae from New England have reduced wings with various modifications (micropterous, brachypterous, submacropterous, coleopteroid type brachyptery, etc). Because all the rhyparochromines Sweet studied have five nymphal instars, these wing-reduced species may represent metagenetic neoteny (by metathetely). The wing reduction was found to be highly correlated with northern distribution and these boreal species were found in sericlimax habitat, usually in hot summer; vegetation of such habitats is very sparse and low and represents a low biomass productivity. Thus at least colder temperatures and, presumably, more northerly photoperiodic cycle appear to have acted as proximate environmental causes in inducing wing reduction. Because the resultant short-winged individuals were unable to migrate a long distance, they were forced to stay in the area where they were born and the frequency of brachyptery must have increased over the generations. Sweet ignored the proximate cause of wing reduction, and interpreted that selection induced a close relation between brachyptery and habitat permanency. An interesting result Sweet obtained in his laboratory was that in *Carpilis consimilis* high population density in rearing appeared to promote, as in Homoptera and other orders, the production of macroptery.

Slater (1977) found that, among the South African lygaeids, geophilous species of Rhyparochrominae and some Geocorinae show a strong tendency to develop flightlessness with various types of modification of wings, although aptery does not occur; aptery has not been found in Lygaeidae (Slater 1975). The same tendency was found to hold true with Blissinae, which are laminophilous (i.e., living in a closely appressed space between the stem and leaf sheath of various types of monocotyledonous plants). Arboreal lygaeids, which pass most of their life cycle above the ground on trees, shrubs, or herbaceous vegetation, are fully winged. Because, as Slater (1977) maintained, geophilous and laminophilous species have been derived from arboreal species, it is safe to regard that wing reduction has occurred secondarily as these insects started becoming geophilous and laminophilous, respectively. Slater related the wing reduction to the permanence of habitats; that is, the longer the geophilous and laminophilous conditions persisted, the higher the frequency of wing-reduced forms. Probably in these cases, again, the influence of new environmental stimuli in the new habitats on development resulted the wing reduction, and the permanence of the new habitats contributed to the increase and permanence of wing reduction, which has been advantageous. The wing-reduced individuals have a limited vagility and would tend to remain where they were born, and the wing-reduced condition must have been selectively advantageous, enabling them to burrow or glide through more restricted spaces in their habitats.

A laboratory experiment of two brachypterous, geophilous species of *Neosuris* (Lygaeidae) under different temperature, nutritional, and crowding conditions by Sweet (1977) did not yield a macropterous individual, although Barber (1911) collected a few macropterous individuals in Arizona. These facts may indicate that genetic determination (presumably by genetic assimilation) of brachyptery has been completed in some populations, but not in some others.

Rankin and Jackle (1980) found no evidence for the participation of JH with vitellogenin synthesis in *Oncopeltus fasciatus,* although injection of ecdysteroids induced both vitellogenin A and B in the hemolymph. This lack of gonadotropic function of JH may underlie the equal occurrence of wing reduction in both sexes in Lygaeidae.

The effect of photoperiod on wing polymorphism (macroptery, brachyptery, and microptery) in *Pyrrhocoris apterus* is evident in an experiment by Honek (1974), which showed that under a long-day condition (18 hr) some of the progeny from brachypterous parents became macropterous, whereas under a short day length (8 hr) virtually no macropterous individual was produced. Honek (1976) further showed that this photoperiodic effect becomes modified significantly by temperature, and that isolation probably modifies the physiology so that brachyptery can occur. JH control of metamorphosis including wing development in *P. apterus* has long been known (Slama 1964, 1965) and brachyptery in nature must be due to environmentally induced disturbance in the endocrine function for metamorphosis. An experiment involving the application of precocene II indicated the lack of the gonadotropic function of JH (Hodkova and Socha 1982). Hence the wing-reduced functional adult could occur equally in both sexes.

The effect of host plants on wing morphs is clearly seen in an interesting discovery of the "paper factor" by Slama and Williams (1965). When the European species *P. apterus* was reared in the United States, the nymph failed to undergo metamorphosis, and all nymphs molted into sixth instars or into adultoid forms, preserving many nymphal characters. The cause of this phenomenon was soon traced to exposure to the active principle present in a certain towel that had been placed in the rearing jars. The towel was made from an American pulp tree, the balsam fir *(Abies balsamea).* It was found that this active material readily penetrates the cuticle and is distributed throughout the insect, exerting its juvenilizing effect at the time the endogenous JH becomes depleted before metamorphosis, with a consequent abnormally prolonged nymphal stage. Slama and Williams (1965) further showed that the extracts of *Abies balsamea, Tsuga canadensis,* and *Taxus brevifolia* have high JH activity, whereas those from other trees have intermediate or barely detectable activity. Furthermore, the most active extracts were found to be without any detectable effect when applied to some other insects. These findings indicate that wing reduction could depend on host plants.

Winglessness (aptery) has occurred in 107 genera (50% of the world total) and in seven out of eight subfamilies of Aradidae (Monteith 1982). In the temperate region most of them are macropterous (only occasionally brachypterous or stenopterous) and they inhabit the appressed space between loose bark of dead trees (subcortical). In the tropics they are often apterous and live outside the bark. These apterous aradids are heavily sclerotized and strongly sculptured and they may assume bizarre shapes; they have diverged at least at the generic level (see Usinger and Matsuda 1959). Warmer temperatures in the tropics can be suspected as an environmental agent that has induced aptery in these taxa. In *Rhodnius prolixus* high temperature up to 36°C has been known to delay molting (Wigglesworth 1952 and Okasha 1968). Presumably, continuous exposure to high temperatures in the tropics has tended to delay their metamorphosis, thereby resulting in adultoids. In fact, many apterous genera are large in body size, and this could have occurred through metathetely.

Wing reduction is rare in Pentatomidae. Only two brachypterous ochlerine pentatomids are known from the Western Hemisphere (Rolston 1982). Photoperiod is known to affect the coloration and the shoulder shape in *Euschistus* (McPherson 1974, 1979), and color and pubescence in *Thyanta* (McPherson 1978).

In British Corixidae polymorphism occurs in flight ability which results from varying development of flight muscles during teneral development (Young 1965a). Young (1965b) discovered that 22 species (belonging to *Sigara, Corixa* and others) are polymorphic in the development of flight musculature; another four species are polymorphic in wing development as well. Only seven species appeared to lack flight polymorphism. Furthermore, among the species polymorphic in flight muscles, according to Young (1965c), the point at which the new generation arises in summer may be divided into three periods on the basis of the morph being developed. During the first period, lasting up to 4 weeks, production of the early, light-pigmented flightless form predominates; in the second, the main normal form is produced; and in the third the main normal form, the main flightless form, or both are developed. Young's (1965c) experiment with temperature (20 and 28°C) indicated that higher temperatures are usually effective in causing nymphs to develop into the normal flight form; these results were in accord with the change observed in field populations in relation to habitat conditions. For instance, Young found that all nymphs molting into adults in the temporary pool gave the normal flight form, whereas those molting in the lake were flightless. This difference was found to be correlated with ambient temperature; the pool temperature was 31°C and in the lake temperature ranged from 21°C at the bottom to 24°C at the lake margin. Starvation was also found to be a stimulus for muscle growth.

It seems highly probable, as Young (1965c) concluded, that the development of the flight morph depends on ambient environmental factors such as temperature and amount of food. Because indirect flight muscles in the flightless form of *Cenocorixa bifida* are due to developmental arrest, presumably induced hormonally (Scudder 1971), the environmental factors probably influence endocrine activity in producing flight polymorphism. A discussion of the adaptive significance of flight polymorphism by Young (1965c) was not conclusive. For instance, between flight and flightless forms there seemed to be no marked difference in the ability to overwinter or in longevity. It appears then that frequency of wing morphs depends mainly on the accidental environmental effects on development, and natural selection does not seem to have been an effective agent regulating flight polymorphism. Young (1970) further found essentially the same pattern of flight polymorphism in New Zealand Corixidae and Notonectidae; normal bugs develop in early and mid summer and the flightless one predominantly toward the end of the summer.

In European species of *Gerris* (Gerridae, water striders) also seasonal dimorphism or polymorphism has long been known. In Britain, according to Brinkhurst (1959), bivoltine species are seasonally either dimorphic or polymorphic. In dimorphic species *(Gerris odontogaster, G. argentatus, G. palludum, G. thoracicus)* the wing-reduced form appears in July and August, apparently under the influence of lengthening days and warming temperatures, and the second generation consists solely of macropters that fly away for hibernation sites on land. In the bivoltine polymorphic species *G. lacustris* all degrees of wing reduction are observed. Photoperiod operates as a switch mechanism in seasonal dimorphism in Finland (Vepsälainen 1971, 1974).

Vepsälainen (1973) proposed the following relationships between the habitat and wing length for the Finnish species of *Gerris:* (1) unstable habitat with potential risk of water drying up — macropterous when univoltine, dimorphic when bivoltine; (2) stable habitat with the risk of drying up negligible for many years — univoltine and polymorphic (*G. lacustris* and *G. lateralis*); (3) very stable permanent and isolated habitat — almost wholly apterous, with rare macropters *(G. najas).* As Vepsälainen (1971) maintained, macroptery in temporary habitats is of selective advantage, because it enables the insects to fly away to find overwintering sites. As Southwood (1962) predicted, immobility of apterous species (3 above) is linked to permanent habitat, and the ability to fly is associated with temporary habitat (1 above). Vepsälainen also referred to similar ideas with regard to the connection between the permanence (or nonpermanence) of the habitat to flight morphs proposed earlier by Lindroth (1949), Brown (1951), and Young (1970).

The proximate cause of the abundance of macropters in temporary habitats and that of wing-reduced (sometimes apterous) species in permanent habitats have not been studied. It is important to remember in this connection that water temperature differs significantly between temporary ponds and permanent lakes in Britain (see above). It can be hypothesized, therefore, that lower temperatures in large permanent lakes and streams have been the dominant factor that induced wing reduction (2 and 3), and that higher temperatures in more temporary waters (1 above) tended to induce macroptery. Because the wing-reduced individuals cannot fly away so easily, they tended to stay where they were born, and sooner or later the wing-reduced phenotype became genetically assimilated. The wing-reduced individuals may have enhanced reproductive activity as suggested by Brinkhurst (1963). Further, the nymphal life of short-winged forms is shorter than that of long-winged ones (Poisson 1924). These advantages might have facilitated the processes of (presumed) genetic assimilation. The fact that macropterous form occurs rarely in the population of *G. najas* Vepsälainen studied appears to indicate that genetic assimilation of aptery has not been completed, remaining in phase 2 of the latter.

Permanent dimorphism in *G. lacustris, G. lateralis,* and *G. asper* was considered to be genetically determined by Vepsälainen (1973, 1974). Vepsälainen (1974), as did Poisson (1924), proposed that in *G. lacustris* genetic switch operates through one locus, with one allele for brachyptery being completely dominant. However, Matsuda (1979) pointed out that most of the data do not show a clear-cut Mendelian segregation of alleles, because the morph determination is strongly influenced by photoperiod. In fact, Vepsälainen and Krajewski (1974) showed that the Polish population of *G. lacustris* is seasonally dimorphic. Zera et al. (1983) further showed, in their carefully controlled experiment, that the wing morph determination in *Limnoporus (= Gerris) canaliculatus* from the United States was inconsistent, with a single-locus, two-alleles mode of inheritance.

Aptery is so common in the tropical gerrids that the classification and phylogenetic inference of higher taxa must be based primarily on apterous species (Matsuda 1960; Calabrese 1980, 1982). Warmer temperatures in the tropics could have been the proximate causative agent that has induced aptery.

Cimicidae are, associated with ectoparasitism, without functional wings; these are represented by hemelytral pads. However, because of the temporary nature of the parasitism the cimicids lack the modified tarsi and combs characteristic of many ectoparasites of birds and mammals. There are five nymphal instars, and there seems to have been no acceleration. Usinger (1966) speculated that *Cimex lectularius* became permanently associated with man during the period of movement of man from cave to village and to city. Polyctenidae are also parasites of bats in tropical and subtropical regions of both the Old and New Worlds (Maa 1964), and the family is presented by 5 genera with 31 species (Slater 1982). Forewings are represented by short, nonarticulated coriaceous scales and hind wings are absent. They are viviparous, and early instars are nourished by females through a pseudoplacental mechanism. The young are born in an advanced state and there are two molts after birth (Slater 1982).

19. The Orders Mecoptera and Neuroptera

In Boreidae, which emerge on the snow, the female is wingless, and the reduced wings in the male are forceps-like and form an ovoid pseudoovipositor. The ocelli are absent, as in many other wing-reduced insects. The family comprises three genera and 24 species (Russell 1979). The genus *Apteropanorpa* is monotypic, being represented by the apterous species *A. tasmaniae* (Carpenter 1941), and it is now assigned to Apteromorphidae (Byers and Thornhill 1983). In this species the eyes are small and there are no ocelli, and the long antenna consists of 60 segments (or rings). The species occurs in the mountains of Tasmania and has been found on the snow as in Boreidae. These examples indicate that the modifications induced by cold temperatures and other factors related to the snow (which must have acted both as the proximate morphogenetic agent inducing abnormal development and as the ultimate selective agent) have reached a magnitude such that these insects are now recognized as a distinct family (Boreidae).

Panorpodes paradoxa is macropterous at lower altitudes in Japan, but the female is brachypterous at higher altitudes (H. Ando and A. Mutuura, personal communication). *Brachypanorpa carolinensis* with short wings occur in the southern Appalachians at middle to high elevations (2500–6600 ft) and *B.*

jeffersoni, with highly reduced wings, occurs in North Carolina at elevations over 4200 ft (Byers 1976). All these cases of wing reduction also appear to have been induced by cold temperatures.

Complete winglessness and the relatively large body size in *Apterobittacus apterus* can probably be attributed to metathetely that might have occurred in association with their burrowing habit. Byers and Thornhill (1983) thought that *Apterobittacus* in the United States and apterous *Anomalobittacus* in southern-most Africa may have evolved from winged ancestors within the genus *Bittacus* somewhere near their present ranges of distribution.

In Neuroptera wing reduction is extremely rare. However, the hind wings of *Psectra diptera* can be micropterous in both sexes (Killington 1946).

20. The Order Diptera

Wing reduction of various degrees, including total loss (aptery), is not uncom-mon in Diptera. The first comprehensive survey of this phenomenon was that of Bezzi (1916), who observed and listed 339 such cases of Diptera. The next important summary is that of Hackman (1964) which showed the predomi-nance of wing reduction in the female and some general features associated with it. The more valuable part of Hackman's work was his classification of wing reduction based on ecological associations, which is transcribed below.

  I. Terricolous habitats. . . . Sciaridae (several species) and Cecidomyii-dae (few spp.)
   a. Secretive habitats (in litter), under stones or in hypogenous habitats and among low-density population. . . . Phoridae (in the female) Sciaridae (few spp.), Cecidomyiidae (few spp.), Empididae (few spp.), Ephydridae (several spp.),Borboridae (several genera and numerous spp.), Chloropidae (several species), Bibionidae — *Penthetria,* Limoniidae — *Molophilus* (1 spp.)
   b. Cold habitats or nival mating ground. . . . Tipulidae (few spp.), Limoniidae (*Chionea*), Borboridae (few species)
   c. Deep-boring mode of oviposition. . . . Tipulidae (numerous spp.), Limoniidae (numerous spp.)
 II. Marine and littoral habitats
   a. Littoral, near water line. . . . Chironomidae (several spp.), Coelopi-dae (few spp.), Ephydridae (few spp.), Heleomyzidae (few spp.)
   b. Marine. . . . Chironomidae (*Clunio, Pontomyia*)
III. In nests of social insects
   a. Myrmecophilous or termitophilous. . . . Phoridae (numerous gen-era and very numerous spp.)
   b. Commensals of honey bees. . . . Braulidae (*Braula*)
IV. Ectoparasites
   a. On insects. . . . Ceratopogonidae, Phasmidohelea
   b. On some warm-blooded animals. . . . Hippoboscidae (several spp.), Nycteribiidae (all species)

Perhaps the best-known case of the loss of wings is that associated with "paedogenesis" in some cecidomyiid flies, or gall midges, in which the bisexual generation with fully developed wings alternates with a parthenogenetic, wingless generation. The latter clearly involves progenetic neoteny in which immature, ovoviviparous adults (either larval or pupal) reproduce parthenogenetically; such reproduction is called "paedogenesis" in the study of biology of these cecidomyiid flies.

The stage at which paedogenesis occurs varies in different groups of cecidomyiids (Nikolei 1961; Wyatt 1961, 1963, 1964, 1967). Thus in *Henria psalliotae* paedogenesis occurs after the third larval instar; the pupal adult thus formed has peculiarly formed spiracles, and it is called the "hemipupa." Within the hemipupa the "embryos" grow very rapidly and appear to undergo a normal embryological development (Wyatt 1961). In Micromyini the evolutionary trend has been toward larval paedogenesis. In *Micophila nikoleii*, for instance, the hemipupal stage has been eliminated, but three larval stages are retained (Nikolei 1961), and *M. speyersi* completes paedogenesis in the second larval instar (Wyatt 1964). For more variations in the life cycle of paedogenetic cecidomyiids refer to Nikolei (1961) and Wyatt (1967).

During paedogenesis of *Heteropeza pygmaea,* which has been most intensively studied, female- and male-determined follicles (each consisting of the oocyte–nurse chamber complex and an enveloping epithelium) produced from larval ovaries are released into the hemocoel of the larva. Soon the oocytes pass through one equational meiotic division in the female-determined eggs, and two meiotic divisions in the male-determined eggs. The reserve material in mature eggs, accumulated during the short period of egg formation, contains mainly fatty yolk and no protein yolk (Ivanova-Kazas 1965) and a chorion is not formed. The increase in size of the eggs in the course of embryonic development is about 200 times (Went 1979, Camenzind 1982). Thus the embryo develops without normal vitellogenesis, starting its development long before the usual processes of oocyte growth have been terminated or even initiated.

Experiments (Went 1979, Went et al. 1984) indicated that ecdysone would accelerate the formation of follicles during paedogenetic development; ecdysone does not seem to be released from the prothoracic glands (Treiblmayr et al. 1981). Went maintained, by referring to Furtado (1977), that ecdysone may determine the mode of oogenesis in *H. pygmaea* by causing the meiotic block (i.e., by promoting or inhibiting the completion of meiosis) to which paedogenetic development is directly related. Furtado (1977, 1979), in fact, showed that in *Panstrongylus megistus* (Heteroptera) two groups of NSC in the pars intercerebralis are involved with mitosis and meiosis. He suggested that one group acts directly and another indirectly, by acting on thoracic glands. Robert (1979) also showed that the brain controls meiosis in *Roscius* spp.

Paedogenetic larvae of *H. pygmaea* hatching from such abnormal eggs (above), do not develop beyond the third larval stage, although an incompletely formed pupa (hemipupa) is hidden beneath the larval skin (Went 1979). Kaiser (1974) observed that the CA are enlarged in the third-stage larva of *H. pygmaea,* and he interpreted this as indication of heightened release of JH, and that progenetic neoteny (called Metathetelie in error?) is attributable to this excessive action of JH. In this case, however, the enlarged CA is more likely to be the sign of accumulation of synthesized JH rather than the release of it. The precocious cessation of JH secretion appears to result in a modest amount of ecdysone secretion which, in turn, induces the production of the hemipupa. This is the hormonal explanation of the highly conspicuous progenetic neoteny in some cecidomyiid flies. Such an explanation, however, still appears to be very incomplete. Some modern assay methods (such as RIA) are likely to elucidate the matter more readily and perhaps more decisively.

Paedogenesis has been known to be induced by various environmental stimuli. Good nutrition has been known to induce paedogenesis; bisexual reproduction depends mainly on uninhabitable mushrooms (Ulrich 1936). However, paedogenesis can also be induced by starving the larvae taken from a well-nourished mother; many later works on paedogenesis have been based on starved larvae (Kaiser 1969). Other factors that influence the alternation of generations are light and temperature, which were considered to be important by earlier workers, and high population densities which result in fully winged sexual forms (Wyatt 1964, 1967). Kaiser (1969) found that paedogenesis can occur only under low oxygen tension, and further that glycogen derived from the mushroom mycelium seems to be the source of energy during paedogenesis. Kaiser (1974) found that even injury and intoxication can result in paedogenesis. Most probably, these environmental factors influence the endocrine activity before the larvae enter either one of the alternative developmental pathways, paedogenetic or bisexual development.

Ibrahim and Gad (1975) reported a case of paedogenesis in *Eristalis* larvae (Syrphidae) comparable with that in Cecidomyiidae; small larvae were found, both in field and laboratory observations, to emerge from larvae.

Some chironomids have succeeded in a variety of intertidal environments. Undoubtedly, intertidal chironomids are polyphyletic in origin. They have adapted from freshwater habitats *(Chironomus, Halocladius)* or terrestrial habitats (Telmatogetoninae and the *Clunio* group) to intertidal environments independently on a number of occasions (Neumann 1976). In some of these genera, notably *Clunio* and *Pontomyia,* the female has lost the wings, and some other structures such as antennae, palps, halteres, and legs have undergone reduction. Such females still hatch from the pupae and the incompletely differentiated condition of adult structures may represent metagenetic neoteny due to metathetely. Hashimoto (1971, 1981) summarized the neotenous features as follows: In *Clunio,* besides the absence of wings, reduction is clear in eyes, legs, and antennae. The degree of reduction is least pronounced in *C. marinus* and most pronounced in *C. takahashii.* For instance, the antenna is seven segmented in *C. marinus,* and with one segment in *C. takahashii;* the hind tarsus is five segmented in *C. marinus,* though two segmented in *takahashii.* The number of ommatidia per eye is 21–23 in *C. marinus* and zero in *takahashii.* Furthermore, in *C. marinus* vestiges of wings occur although no trace of wings is recognized in other species of *Clunio*. Other species of *Clunio* exhibit intermediate conditions in the degree of reduction of structures (such as eyes, antennae, and tarsal segments). Four species of *Pontomyia* are known (Hashimoto 1981). Their larvae live in the nest formed at the base of marine algae, for example, and hence they are benthic. In the male the forewings and hind legs are modified into "oars" for skating on the sea surface. The female is completely wingless, the legs are vestigial or completely absent in the female, and other structures (antennae, mouthparts, eyes) are also reduced. The whole female body is therefore little more than a bag containing eggs, and clearly the structural reduction is more advanced than in *Clunio*.

In none of these cases of female neoteny, however, is the number of larval stages known. Yet disruption of the normal hormonal balance (probably resulting in persistent action of JHs) probably has been induced in the marine habitat, and this underlies the suppression (and consequent reduction) of the female imaginal structures. It can be hypothesized further that an abundant supply of JH expedited the maturation of eggs in these chironomids before the completion of normal somatic metamorphosis, because Laufer and Greenwood (1969) showed that injection of JH into the prepupa of *Chironomus thummi* results in precocious maturation. This explanation certainly does not apply to the males, which are normal, or at least more normal, dipterans.

Neoteny is known to occur also in other chironomids. In species of the *Stylotanytarsus* group of Tanytarsini, larviform females are known to produce eggs (Wesenberg-Lund 1943). Hinton (1946) found that the supposed paedogenetic (pupal) adult of *Tanypus bohemensis* was in fact the pharate adult that failed to shed the effete cuticle. Examples of neoteny associated with cold climate include a micropterous *Oreadomyia albertae* known from Alberta, Canada (Oliver 1981), and many brachypterous species that occur in the Arctic (Downes 1965). *Belgica antarctica*, occurring in the Antarctic Peninsula, is characterized by having the wing reduced to a short strip (Sugg et al. 1983). Similarly, the Antarctic *Eretmoptera murphyi* shows wing reduction and, additionally, it is parthenogenetic (Cranston 1985). Both species have four larval stages.

Metagenetic neoteny might have occurred in some simuliids. According to Downes (1965), in eight of nine species of the simuliids occurring in the Arctic area the female is nonfeeding. The mouthparts are weak and cannot pierce the skin. The eggs start developing before the adult emerges from the pupal cuticle, and in at least two species they are mature at that time. Downes thought that this implies a considerable reorganization of the hormonal control of metamorphosis and ovarian development. The lower temperatures in the area must certainly have been the dominant factor causing the hormonal imbalance, probably in favor of increased JH activity.

Byers (1969a) pointed out that in Tipulidae wing reduction occurs in low-temperature environments such as the Arctic and Antarctic areas, at high altitudes, and on islands with cold climates (but not on islands with warmer climates, such as Hawaii). These facts suggested that wing reduction is due to the effect of cold temperature (in the adaptive sense), and contradicted the theory that wing reduction on islands (regardless of prevailing temperatures) is adaptive, because wing-reduced forms would not be blown away by wind. Byers thought that wing reduction is an adaptation to cold. It appears to me, however, that cold affected their hormonal balance first, perhaps in favor of more persistent JH action, which results in an incomplete metamorphosis with reduced wings, and presumably such reduced wings have been preadapted in colder areas (adaptive response). The higher frequency of wing reduction in the female than in the male can be accounted for by assuming that JH has the gonadotropic function by inducing vitellogenin synthesis as in some other insects, and that the persistent JH would tend to promote oocyte development, but not the development of the male gonad. This hypothesis must be tested directly for tipulids, because the hormonal involvement with vitellogenin synthesis and its incorporation into oocytes is by no means the same throughout the Diptera (see Hagedorn 1980).

Byers (1982) found a subapterous (strongly reduced wings) new species, *Limosina (Dicranomyia) sabroskyana,* from Hawaii. The discovery of this wing-reduced form in the tropics was unexpected. Byers suspected that this might be related to the peculiar larval habitat; the related species *L. (D.) kauaiensis* is a leaf miner in its larval stage.

The genus *Chionea* or snowfly (Tipulidae) has only vestigial forewings, although the halteres and legs are well developed. The haltere appears to have some sensory function and the male hypopygium is large (Byers 1983). They are found on the snow surface, although their habitat is underground burrows constructed by other animals. Nearly the entire distributional range of *C. vulga* in North America is the formerly glaciated regions (Byers 1983), suggesting that initially cold temperature induced aptery.

A unique, wingless female dipteron, which Byers (1969b) described as a new species and genus, *Baenotus microps* belonging to a new family Baenotidae, was recovered by Berlese funnel extraction from a soil sample taken just beneath the leaf litter in montane oak forest in Virginia. In this species appendages are apparently well differentiated. However, the abdomen is enlarged and indistinctly segmented, and without sclerites. The ecology of this species remains unknown.

In some sciarids wing reduction occurs, resulting in di- or polymorphism; other structures are also reduced in the wing-reduced forms. In laboratory rearing of *Plastosciara perniciosa*, Steffan (1973, 1975) found that when a gravid macropterous female was isolated on a fresh agar plate or in a vial, F_1 was always micropterous (in both sexes), and the macropterous form was produced only when colonies were maintained. The micropterous morph differs profoundly from the macropterous form, in that all head structures (antennae, eyes, ocelli, maxillary palpi, proboscis) and thoracic sclerites and structures (legs, halteres, wings) are reduced, and in the abdomen no discrete sclerite is recognized, although the genitalia are similar to those in the macropterous form. Thus a switch mechanism is clearly at work, and this mechanism appears to depend on population density, as in some other insects (group effect). As Steffan thought, such a switch will be effected by mediation of the endocrine mechanism. Steffan maintained further that micropterous individuals, their larvae remaining under the surface of the substratum, are protected from the danger of predation and from inability to find the food source and to find a mate. Thus the switch of morphs is adaptive. How much the effect of natural selection has been involved with this adaptive response can never be known.

Wing reduction in other sciarids has also been reported by Mohrig (1978), Mohrig and Mamaev (1970a,b, 1974, 1978), Mohrig et al. (1978, 1980), and Mamaev and Mohrig (1975). These wing-reduced species have been found in the ground litter in Europe. Wing reduction in these sciarids often occurs only in the female. When wing reduction occurs in both sexes, it is more pronounced in the female than in the male. The brachypterous female of *Hesperinus imbecillus* (Hesperinidae) was described by Mohrig et al. (1975).

Wing reduction is not uncommon in Sphaeroceridae. In the European species *Leptocera* (*Pteremis*) *fenestralis,* according to Roháček (1975), brachyptery is rare in Europe, frequent in Britain, and so frequent in northern Finland that the insect is recognized as *L.* (*P.*) *fenestralis* f. *subaptera.* In this case brachyptery is clearly related to latitude, and the differences in temperature and photoperiod appear to be underlying proximate causative agents, inducing different frequencies of brachyptery. In *Limosina pullula* usually the brachypterous form occurs in nature, although the macropterous form has been found rarely. Roháček (1975) found that in Czechoslovakia the frequency of brachyptery is correlated with the depth of the biotope. He found that only macropterous individuals exist at the upper zone and that the frequency of brachyptery increases at deeper levels. Thus the situation appears to compare with wing dimorphism in *Plastosciara.*

At high altitudes in the eastern African mountains, according to Richards (1954, 1957, 1963), *Leptocera* spp. are brachypterous and some other genera of Sphaeroceridae (*Paraptilotus, Ocellipsis, Mesaptilotus,* etc.) are apterous or have greatly reduced wings. They live among dead leaves or in humus, or in burrows, as do the European brachypterous sphaerocerids. Richards (1957, 1963) thought that they arose where they are now found by extensive sympatric speciation. Here the wing reduction is related to high altitudes with lower temperatures and cryptobiotic habitat. An additional new brachypterous genus *Gobersa* was described by De Coninck (1983) from central Africa. De Coninck (1983) further maintained that all central African Sphaeroceridae are confined to damp habitats.

Although population density (as in Sciaridae) and some other physical environmental factors such as cold temperature must be the major factors involved with wing polymorphism, humidity appears to be the factor controlling the timing of pupation in many Diptera. Ohtaki (1966) showed that when the larvae of *Sarcophaga peregrina* are kept in a wet condition the larvae do not pupate, but when they are kept dry they pupate by releasing ecdysone; this finding is consistent with observations that many kinds of dipterous larvae leave wet environments to pupate (G. Byers, personal communication). Similarly, Zdarek and Fraenkel (1970) found that moisture controls the release of ecdysone in *Sarcophaga,* and suggested that inhibition of pupation by moisture has arisen in many Diptera as an adaptation to unfavorable conditions.

The above experimentally known facts appear to indicate that the release of proper amount of ecdysteroids at proper times is probably important in producing the normal wing morph. The fact that fully winged individuals occur in the surface layer of a population (in sciarids and sphaerocerids above) may well be due to drier environmental conditions where the release of ecdysteroids occurs synchronously. Conversely, in deeper layers the release of ecdysteroids may sometimes be unduly disturbed, and might contribute to wing reduction.

In *Drosophila* genetics mutants affecting the morphogenetic hormone are known. A temperature-sensitive mutant *ecd* becomes deficient in ecdysone by the temperature shift from 20 to 29 °C; at 29 °C the larva does not pupate (Garen et al. 1977). Another mutant is ap^4(apterous), which affects the JH activity, which in turn results in abnormal development of many structures including the loss of wings (Wilson 1981a,b). It is imaginable, therefore, that when genetic fixation (assimilation) of hormonally induced wing reduction occurs, accumulation of such mutatants is likely to occur.

The parasitic Diptera, called the Pupipara (within the Cyclorrhapha), comprises Hippoboscidae, which are ectoparasites of birds and large mammals, and two other families, Nycteribiidae and Streblidae, which are ectoparasites only of bats. Wings are often absent or reduced in these parasites, and characteristically claws are highly developed. Highly characteristic dorsoventrally compressed structural modifications of the body, especially of the thorax in such genera as *Basilia* (Nycterbiidae, studied by Nussbaum 1960) and *Trichobius* (Streblidae, studied by Zeve and Howell 1963) present difficulties in establishing homologies of parts (discussed by Matsuda 1970). Both Nycteribiidae and Streblidae are larviporous (larvae develop adenotrophically inside the uterus of the mother). Larvae are deposited as prepuparia on the host. It appears that the highly modified structural organization in these families is related mainly to processes associated with parasitism.

21. The Order Coleoptera

In this highly heterogeneous order no general trend with regard to the morphogenetic plasticity or rigidity is discernible. Utida's studies on density-dependent polymorphism in the southern cowpea weevil *Callosobruchus maculatus* (summarized in 1970 and 1972 by Utida were important in showing clearly how both proximate and ultimate causes contribute to the increase in flightless forms, and how the genetic fixation (presumably through the process of genetic assimilation) of the flightless form could proceed in nature. This species is dimorphic with respect to the size of wings and some other associated structures (such as the presence or absence of pubescence, general shape of the body, pygidial length, some physiological and behavioral features). The wing size difference must account for the difference in flight ability.

In 1946 in Kyoto, Japan, the insect started infesting the cow beans released by the U.S. Army. It soon became noticeable that the emergence of the flight form of this insect was decreasing rapidly, as reported by Utida (1954). The processes of Utida's routine rearings of this species were summarized as follows: The rearing was carried out at 30° C and at 8 light hr/day, and the relative humidity was kept at 60–80%. Experiment 1 was started with five populations, each consisting of eight males and eight females which were flightless. After 15 generations the frequency of the flight form dropped to 0–4.8%. Experiment 2 was started with two populations, each consisting also of eight males and eight females. Here again the percentage of the flight form dropped drastically to 4.7–7.9% after 15 generations of rearing. Experiment 3 was started with 32 flightless males and the same number of flightless females derived from the progeny of experiment 1. After an additional 15 generations the frequency of the flight form dropped to 0% in one population, and 0% in the male and 6.2% in the female in another population.

During the experiment no selection, that is, no artificial removal of flight individuals, was made. The flight individuals that emerged simply flew away and lived on leguminous plants outdoors, and only the flightless individuals (with higher fecundity) remained in the bean heap. These experiments show that a new phenotypic modification can, under some new environmental conditions, become predominant and perhaps permanent; Utida (1970) suggested "genetic assimilation" of Waddington (1953) as a possible underlying mechanism of permanent modification. Compared with genetic assimilation experiments, however, the experimental conditions for *Callosobruchus* were far more similar to what occurs in nature, without requiring either a heat shock or artifical selection. The migration of flight forms in these experiments was a natural selection comparable to the flying away (aided by winds) of flight forms that may occur during the origin of flightless beetles on islands (e.g., Darwin 1859).

According to Utida (1954, 1956), no flight individual emerges when only one larva develops in each bean, but the percentage of the flight form increases as the number of larvae per bean increases. Thus the group effect is at work in producing the flight form in both sexes. This fact clearly indicates that in the newly created bean heap environment, isolation of larval stages also could have contributed to the increase in flightless forms. Utida attributed the group effect to higher temperatures, which are generated by crowding, because it is known for other stored-product beetles that when the density of larval population is high, the temperature in heaps of beans rises far beyond the air temperature. Sano (1967) supported the idea by showing that when the beans containing one or two larvae (second larval instars) were transferred to high-temperature cabinets (from 20–25 to 35° C) the percentage of the flight form was the highest. Low water content in the bean was also found to contribute to the production of the flight form. Continuous light or darkness was also found to increase the percentage of the flight form. However, such extreme photoperiodic regimes do not actually exist during the life cycle of the cowpea weevil. Utida (1972) summarized these studies dealing mainly with the proximate causes of wing dimorphism.

The selective advantage of the flightless form is higher fecundity. Flightless individuals lay more eggs (a maximum of 80 instead of fewer than 40 eggs in the flight form) and earlier, and have a shorter developmental period (Utida 1956). Because the history of infestation of the cowpea bean started very recently, it is unlikely that a significant selective pressure has been at work in provoking such adaptive responses. Rather, it appears safe to interpret that the latter have been fortuitous consequences of the physiological response of the weevil to the new environmental stimuli.

Ptiliidae, or featherwing beetles, are among the tiniest insects, measuring usually less than 1 mm long. Dimorphism in wing development and in other features has been known for *Ptinellodes, Ptinella,* and several other genera (Dybas 1978). Two strongly differentiated morphs occur in both sexes, a normal morph with normal wings, eyes, and pigmentation and a flightless (vestigial) morph, in which wings and eyes are reduced and some other structures are also reduced or absent (Dybas 1978). The neotenous flightless form far outnumbers the flight form; more than 90% of *Ptinellodes* are flightless (Dybas 1978).

Dybas was inclined to think that the dimorphism is due to environmental switch. He had the impression that large populations under bark in early stages of long succession often consist entirely of flightless forms. When a great majority of individuals are already flightless, genetic fixation of the flightless morph might have occurred in some of them, perhaps through the process of genetic assimilation; the latter is possible if the populations under bark have continuously existed long enough. In *Ptinella* spp., as shown by Taylor (1981), the frequency of the flight form increases in warmer months (reaching over 30% in *P. errabunda* in August), although no flight form may occur in colder months. This fact again suggests that only a certain proportion of individuals still respond to environmental stimuli and that in a majority of them flightlessness might have been genetically determined. Her laboratory experiment also suggested that the emergence of the flight form is temperature dependent, and suggested the presence of an inherited component in the control of polymorphism or some form of the maternal effect.

In Ptiliidae the ovary carries only one egg and thelytokous parthenogenesis is associated with wing reduction. Dybas (1978) considered that one mature egg at a time is the consequence of the extreme reduction in body size, and that therefore any change that effectively increases fecundity (e.g., by parthenogenesis) will be favored by natural selection. However, Taylor (1981) showed that the total fecundity of the parthenogenon *P. errabunda* is significantly lower than that of bisexual species (*P. apterae* and *P. taylorae*).

The single egg that matures at a time is relatively huge. In *Bambara* the egg is about 0.32 mm long, or nearly half the length of the female (Dybas 1966), and the developmental period is presumably short in this family; in *Acrotrichis fascicularis* it requires only about 3 weeks from egg to adult (Hinton 1941). The number of larval instars is not known for any species of Ptiliidae. All these facts lead me to suspect that embryonization of early larval stages has occurred in the enormously enlarged egg (acceleration), and the result appears to be a contracted larval stage and the small adult (progenetic neoteny), as in some dwarf animals producing large eggs (Sect. 3B2).

Contraction of larval developmental stages associated with large yolk-rich eggs is known to occur in the cavernicolous catopid subfamily Bathyscinae. As shown by Deleurance-Glacon (1963), the maximum number of larval stages in this subfamily is three, instead of the typical four in Coleoptera. Within the Bathyscinae some of them lay small eggs and one to three larval stages (commonly two or three) occur. Another group of Bathyscinae *(Speonomus* spp., *Antrocharis querilhaei, Troglodromus bucheti gaveti)* lay large, yolk-rich eggs and usually one larval stage ensues; the larva does not eat. Clearly, therefore, suppression of larval stages within the large eggs has occurred in the second group (embryonization). In most cases the intraoval developmental stage in larger eggs lasts twice as long as in the smaller eggs; presumably the abortive larval stage(s) is passed within the yolk-rich, large eggs. Consequently, the free-living larval stage is much shorter than in the bathyscines with small eggs, although the duration of life in the pupal chamber is very much prolonged. The shorterning of the free-living larval stage is, at any rate, advantageous in the environment where the food resources tend to be highly limited.

Deleurance and Charpin (1972) noted the difference in the state and abundance of the smooth reticulum cells of the CA between the species laying large eggs and those laying small eggs. They suggested that such a difference may be due to different actions of CA during vitellogenesis (assuming that CA, through JH secretion, has a function in vitellogenesis); a longer duration of such action must occur in producing larger eggs. If this hypothesis is proved by a more reliable assay method the enlargement of eggs can be attributed to the abnormal functioning of the endocrine mechanism for vitellogenesis, which has been induced by new environmental stimuli in the caves (such as darkness, scarcity of food) to which early bathyscines migrated. Vandel (1965) pointed out that Bathyscinae have been preadapted to cavernicolous life, because their lucicolous members already show hypogenous characteristics.

An extraordinarily labile morphogenetic plasticity is exhibited by the wood-boring species *Micromalthus debilis* (Micromalthidae) in which five kinds of adult occur (Barber 1913a,b; Scott 1936, 1938, 1941; Kühne 1972). They are the winged male, thelytokous (female-producing) larval female, arrhenotokous (male-producing) larval female, amphoterokous (male- and female-producing) larval female, and winged female. The three kinds of larval females are paedogenetic and their development is by progenetic neoteny as in some cecidomyiids. The winged male is derived from the progenetic male producer by haploid parthenogenesis, and the female producer gives rise to the female by diploid parthenogenesis. The amphoterokous progenetic female is essentially a male producer in which the development of the male is arrested and the female-producing eggs develop secondarily (Scott 1938).

Barber (1913a,b) thought that drier and warmer environments might be favorable for the development of the winged male and female. When Scott (1938) brought wood into the laboratory the great majority of forms developed into adult females, male producers, and their male offspring. He thought that relative dryness is an important factor associated with the development of these forms. According to Scott (1938), further, the thelytokous progenetic mother is frequently found in wood of relatively high moisture content. Kühne's (1972) experiment failed to confirm Scott's hypothesis, and his ecdysone treatment also had no effect in inducing pupation.

In some Cantharoidea the adult female is apterous and is apparently larviform. During postembryonic development of *Lampyris noctiluca* according to Naisse (1966a), the male undergoes four larval molts, one pupal molt and one imaginal molt. On the other hand, the female undergoes five larval molts before the pupal molt. Clearly the female undergoes one extra molt, which accounts for her larger size.

At the level of neuroendocrine activity, Naisse (1966b) found the following differences in producing sexual dimorphism. In the male the small granular NSC in the brain start their secretion at the time of sexual differentiation, that is, after the third molt, and the secretion continues up to the imaginal molt. The CA remain inactive during the pupal and adult stages, and the prothoracic glands (PG) degenerate in the pupa. In the female, on the other hand, the neurosecretion from the small granular NSC starts after the fourth molt and has three periods of interruption. The CA are active in both the pupa and adult, although inactive at the pupal and imaginal molts; the PG remain active until the end of the pupal stage and degenerate after the imaginal molt. Clearly, the activities of CA and PG in the male are abnormal, although they are normal in the female.

Naisse (1966b,c, 1969) discovered further that in the male neurosecretion from the small granule NSC induces the mesodermal apical cells of the gonad to secrete androgenous hormone, and that the hormone induces the development of the normal male structures, including the wings and the genitalia; implantation of testicules into female larvae resulted in masculinization, and this was probably due to the hormonal action of the apical tissue of the testicules (Naisse 1966a). Clearly, during the pupal stage, the apical tissue replaces the morphogenetic function of the CA and PG which become inactive or degenerate. Although the presence of the androgenous hormones appears to be universal within the Crustacea, its occurrence (which may differ chemically) in *Lampyris* is unique in the Insecta.

In the female of *Lampyris* the activity of the CA and that of PG are more comparable with those in the other insects with fully developed wings, and the absence of wings does not seem to be due to hormonal suppression of wing rudiments, which are apparently never present during postembryonic development. In fact, Davydova's (1967) CA – CC removal experiment with the same species failed to cause the development of wings. It is therefore probable that the absence of wings in the female is determined by a sex-linked gene or genes. Because of the lack of wings, the adult female of *Lampyris* appears to be larviform. However, other structures and the integument are quite normal and imaginal.

In Carabidae wing dimorphism has been known to be inherited through Mendelian segregation of two alleles of a single gene. Lindroth (1946) first demonstrated, in his crossing experiments of *Pterostichus anthracinus* (macropterous ♂ × macropterous ♀, brachypterous ♂ × brachyterous ♀, macropterous ♀ × brachypterous ♂, macropterous ♂ × brachypterous ♀) showed that (1) the wing dimorphism has a hereditary basis; (2) brachyptery is dominant, and the macropterous individuals are homozygotes; and (3) inheritance takes place in a simple Mendelian fashion. A more recent crossing experiment with *Calathus mollis erythroderus* by Aukema (in Den Boer et al. 1980) strongly supported the above conclusion by Lindroth (1946). Many field observations on wing dimorphism in Carabidae appear to have been consistent with the hereditary mechanism of wing morphs.

Darlington (1936, 1943, 1971) reported that hind wing reduction occurs in Carabidae inhabiting mountainous areas. For instance, at low altitudes in New Guinea only 4% of carabids have reduced wings. However, the percentage of wing reduction rises to 32% in the carabids living at 500–1000 ms, and to 95% in those living at an altitude of 3000 m and higher. Because, however, wing reduction does not occur seasonally and because its occurrence is usually not confined to certain geographical areas, Darlington (1943, 1971) thought that the wing reduction had been induced by recurrent mutations, and he denied the effect of cold temperature as a proximate cause of reduced wing development. He proposed that three selective factors are important in favoring wing atrophy and flightlessness in the mountains: (1) an indirect effect of cold temperature which reduces the ease and usefulness of flight, (2) intensity of competition with ants correlated with altitudes, and (3) the limitation of area in higher altitudes. A study on wing polymorphism in *Agonum retractum* in Alberta, Canada, by Carter (1976) and that in *Notiophilus biguttatus* in Bohemia by Honek (1981) also indicated genetic determination of wing morphs; no particular environmental factor associated with wing polymorphism was discernible.

Den Boer et al. (1980) emphasized migration of the flight forms away from stable sites as an important mechanism of evolution of flightless carabids, as did Darwin (1859), Darlington (1943, 1971), Palmén (1944), and Utida (1970). Migration of flight forms would gradually result in separation of fully winged populations in unstable habitats from the populations with reduced wings in more stable habitats. The difference from the case of *Callosobruchus* (Chap. 9) is that in carabids wing morphs are determined genetically, and hence the environmental effect on wing morph determination is not expected to occur. However, an important complication Den Boer et al. (1980) reported was the discordance in degree of development of wings and that of flight muscles. As these authors have shown, flight muscles may not be developed even when wings are fully developed; the difference in the evolutionary rate between musculature and associated exoskeletal structures is a widespread phenomenon in insects (Matsuda 1970, 1976). Thus flight muscle development is not necessarily determined genetically. It might, as in Corixidae (Sect. 23D18b), depend on the environmental factors such as temperature.

Among the macropterous monomorphic species of carabids, *Amara plebeja* develops flight muscles in May; the muscles become reduced in June with the start of reproduction, and they develop again after reproduction. This syndrome is connected with the change of habitat from deciduous trees during hibernation to grass vegetation during reproduction (Van Huizen 1977, Den Boer et al. 1980). Various deviations from the oogenesis–flight syndrome exhibited by *A. plebeja* occur in other species; in some species flight muscles develop only in limited number of individuals, exhibiting dimorphism in flight muscle development. In *Hippodamia convergens* (Coccinellidae) JH appears to stimulate migratory flight behavior along with the ovarian development (Rankin and Rankin 1980).

Genetic determination of wing morphs was also shown experimentally for Curculionidae (Jackson 1928, Stein 1973). The results showed a simple Mendelian segregation of alleles at a locus, and were essentially the same as that found in *Pterostichus* (see above). In the Israeli populations of *Longitarsus* spp. (Chrysomelidae) there is no evidence that intraspecific wing length polymorphism is environmentally induced. Therefore, the polymorphism is probably genetically controlled (Furth 1979). Shute (1980) also found that in British species of *Longitarsus* wing morphs are not correlated with sex, geographical distribution, temporal difference, or host association, suggesting that the wing morphs are genetically determined. Wing reduction occurs also in desert *Trox* spp. (Trogidae). Moisture control of subelytral cavity formed as a result of wing atrophy and sealed elytra is probably the overriding factor favoring the wing reduction in desert-living *Trox* spp. (Scholtz 1981).

Hypermetamorphosis is known to occur in Rhipiphoridae, Meloidae, some Carabidae, and some Staphylinidae. Of these, that of Meloidae is the best known. Postembryonic development in Meloidae consists of polymorphic larval stages, and it exhibits environment-dependent high plasticity which manifests itself in skipping or reversing four larval stages that are morphologically and behaviorally distinct. The first larval stage in this developmental cycle is the triungulin larva, with well-developed thoracic legs. Triungulin larvae disperse from the eclosion site. Those that find appropriate food (the provisions of bees or grasshopper eggs) engorge themselves and molt into the first grub phase which consists of three, four, or five instars (sometimes six instars in *Epicauta*, Selander and Weddle 1969); the larva is robust, its head somewhat hypognathous, and its legs short. Subsequently, the first grubs enter an inactive coarctate phase at the next molt, thereby losing the grublike features (such as further reduction of legs), and enter diapause in most groups. With resumption of development the larvae undergo ecdysis and enter the second grub phase. The latter excavate pupal chambers in the soil or may remain within the ruptured *(Meloe)* or intact (Nemognathinae) coarctate exuviae (Selander and Weddle 1969). The pupal and adult stages then follow. Deviant developmental sequences involving omission, reversion, or repetition of stages have been known. Pupation of the grub larva into the pupa by omission of the coarctate and second larval stages has been shown in number of studies (Horsfall 1943, Selander and Mathieu 1964). In all these cases association with high temperatures (both in field observation and laboratory experiments) was clear. Further, diapause of *E. segmenta* is also temperature dependent; chilling for 90 days at 15° C resulted in 100% diapause (Selander and Weddle 1972). It is most probable that temperature-dependent deviations in the developmental sequence are hormonally mediated (though it has not yet been investigated). It appears probable that persistent or deviant JH action is involved with hypermetamorphosis, as can be surmised from the experiments on *"Dauerlarven"* (below).

Retrogression in larval development was shown by Beck (1971a,b, 1972) for *Trogoderma glabra* (Dermestidae), which may have five or six larval stadia under optimal rearing conditions. When deprived of the food and water, and under continuous darkness, the larvae of this species may survive from one to several years, during which period they undergo periodic ecdyses; postecdysal insects continue to be larval in form but they are of progressively less weight and smaller linear dimensions (Beck 1971a). Such *Dauerlarven* can also be induced by adding JH to diet (Beck 1972); 21 molts were induced without pupation. Such a highly labile larval developmental potency may underlie hypermetamorphosis in Meloidae and others. This experiment also suggests that the effect of food could be significantly involved with the process of hypermetamorphosis.

Rhipiphoridae is another family with hypermetamorphosis, the first-stage larva being the triungulin for dispersal. The family is unique among the beetle families in being endoparasitic at least part of its life cycle. The adult females of several species of *Rhipidius* and that of *Rhyzostylops* are apterous and distinctly larviform (Clausen 1940). In the anomalous genus *Rhyzostylops* (first described by Silvestri 1905), the adult females bear a marked resemblance to those of the genera *Mengenilla* and *Eoxenos* (Strepsiptera).

Adalia bipunctata (Coccinellidae) is highly polymorphic in color pattern. It has been known to be under the control of a number of alleles at a single locus, with the black morph being dominant to the red morphs. The black morph is very frequent in industrial areas in Britain and northern Europe. The cause of melanism has always been explained in terms of the ultimate selective cause. Creed (1971) suggested that some unidentified components of the polluted atmosphere was less toxic to the melanics than to the typicals. Muggleton et al. (1975) challenged this view by proposing that melanic morphs will have a selective advantage over the nonmelanics because of the greater ability to absorb solar radiation, and this advantage may be important in cooler and less sunny conditions, including those where smoke reduces sunshine levels; his experiment showed that the melanic morphs have higher internal temperatures. The data of Muggleton et al. could be read the other way around. In northern Europe and less sunny industrial areas lower temperatures initially could have induced melanism, and the resultant melanism was a fortuitous adaptive response enabling them to absorb heat more easily.

22. The Order Hymenoptera

In some Hymenoptera polymorphic castes occur in association with their social life. Of these, ants are the most conspicuous in degree of structural differentiations between castes, which include the queen, haploid male, soldier, worker, and ergatogyne. The queen and the male are provided with deciduous wings, but all others are apterous; imaginal disks for wings never inflate and become lost into the thoracic wall in the apterous castes (Brian 1959, 1965). The worker is an individual diverted from the normal female (queen) course of development by having part of its adult system shut down. The workers within a colony are produced through various degrees of arrest of allometric growth of structural dimensions in different individuals (Wilson 1953), and hence the body sizes and structures are often continuous. A discontinuity in variation among workers may denote the soldier caste with (usually) disproportionately large head and mandibles; the soldier caste has the defense function of the nest and is comparable with the soldier in termites. The ergatogyne or ergatomorph is the intermediate between the worker and queen, and in some species it replaces the queen entirely and is not connected to the worker by a graded series. The ergatogyne with the extremely enlarged abdomen is called "dichtadiiform ergatogyne."

Caste determination seems to be determined largely within the egg (blastogenic). For instance, eggs in *Pheidole pallidula* may be (largely) predetermined to become either queens or workers within the egg. As shown by Passera and Suzzoni (1979), all developmental stages in this species — oocyte development, embryogenesis, and larval development — respond positively to JH application by producing sexual larvae, and workers fed on JH-injected mealworms or the larvae produced by the queens that were deprived of JH are unable to sexualize eggs. These facts indicated that eggs are caste biased in the queen already during oogenesis, and that this depends on the JH rate in the queen during oogenesis. Furthermore, Suzzoni et al. (1980) found that the ecdysteroid level is higher in worker-biased eggs than in queen-biased eggs; the intraoval ecdysteroids are probably exogenous as in Orthoptera, Isoptera, and others. At any rate, it is apparent that the proportion of JH and ecdysteroids within the egg is important in determining which developmental course the developing embryo takes.

As these experiments indicated, higher titers of JH (relative to ecdysteroids) during early developmental stages tends to result in queen development (which must be normal for Hymenoptera). It is apparent that differential impregnation of ecdysteroids into developing oocytes influences the proportion of the two hormones and consequent developmental pathway into either the queen or the worker. Another factor that must be considered is the egg size, which may vary significantly; in *Myrmica rubra* the first ones laid are larger (Brian and Hibbie

1964); the degree of embryonic differentiation would tend to differ in eggs with different sizes. Furthermore, it is even more important to remember that egg maturation is controlled by the brain NSC JH (Barker 1978), and Passera and Suzzoni (1979) suggested the entry of exogenous JH into oocytes. Thus our understanding of the mechanism of blastogenic determination of developmental pathways awaits further precision.

What is unique with ants is not the production of the reproductive queen that is a normal hymenopteron, but the production of workers in which the balance between JH and ecdysteroids has been upset in favor of higher ecdysteroid level during development. It is therefore possible, as suggested by Brian (1959), that worker production could result from prothetely in which early depletion of JH is followed by precocious morphogenetic action of ecdysteroids. As already seen, the ecdysteroid level is higher in worker-biased eggs than in queen-biased eggs. The question is therefore how such a hormonal proportion (favorable for the worker production) is produced in nature. It is, as in *Apis,* presumably the food factor that induces such a hormonal mechanism during larval development, but this is not yet definitely known.

In some ants the queen has been known to have an inhibitory function through its pheromone, although the details of its action and the site of the pheromone production and secretion remain inconclusive (Passera 1980). Passera (1980) demonstrated, in *Plagiolepis pygmaea,* that the inhibitory effect is exerted by preventing egg-laying by workers and by inhibiting the differentiation of queen larvae. Passera showed that the inhibitory pheromone is passed on by licking.

In the absence of queen inhibition, workers produce unfertilized eggs that usually develop into winged males (arrhenotokous parthenogenesis) which are haploid, as seen, for instance, in *Myrmica* (Brian 1969, Smeeton 1980). In *Cataglyphis cursor,* however, thelytokous parthenogenesis occurs in the absence of queen inhibition, giving rise to queens; in the worker of this species the spermatheca is not developed (Suzzoni and Cagniant 1975).

In *Pheidole bicarinata* the worker caste is completely dimorphic. It consists of the soldier and the minor worker in the absence of the media worker. Wheeler and Nijhout (1981) found, by manipulation in topical application of JH at 27° C, that the soldier determination occurs during the last larval instar as a result of the shift upward of the body size at which metamorphosis takes place. Topical application of JHA to the third-instar larvae dramatically increased the soldier production in a dose-dependent manner. Earlier, Passera (1974) found, in *Pheidole pallidula,* that soldiers are produced only when larvae are fed a highly proteinaceous diet (insect bodies) and at 24° C. It appears, then, that in nature a nutritional factor induces the production of an excessive amount of JH. Thus the soldier caste in ants, as termite soldiers, appears to be produced by excessive secretion of JH. Furthermore, adult soldiers can suppress the development of soldiers, presumably through a contact pheromone (Wheeler and Nijhout 1984). Soldiers assume the defensive function with the caenogenetically enlarged head.

Ergatogynes are the sole reproductive form in a high percentage of the endemic species of New Caledonia, belonging to such phylogenetically advanced genera as *Chelaner, Lordomyrma, Prodicroaspis,* and *Promeranoplus* (Wilson 1971). Wilson (1971) thought that ergatogeny in these ants correspond to the flightlessness found commonly among the endemic species of birds and insects on oceanic islands. In *Harpagoxenus* the development of female larvae into ergatoid or alate females is determined by a genetic mechanism (Buschinger 1975, 1978).

The honey bee, *Apis mellifera,* is trimorphic: the male, the queen, and the worker. The male emerges from unfertilized, haploid eggs as in other Hymenoptera. Workers sometimes lay eggs, from which the male emerges. As in ants, workers are essentially sterile females. However, they are winged, and the structural divergence between the queen and the worker is much less than in ants. According to Michener (1974), the differences include: (1) 2–12 ovarioles per ovary in the worker bee and 150–180 ovarioles per ovary in the queen; (2) the larger spermatheca in the queen; (3) the presence of the wax gland and Nassanov's gland in the worker and their absence in the queen; (4) the proboscis, which is longer in the worker than in the queen; (5) the presence of the corbicula in the worker and its absence in the queen; (6) the pollen pores, which are present in the worker and absent in the queen; and (7) some other structures (relative of the antennal surface, chemoreceptive plates per antenna, number of facets of compound eyes, antennal lobes of the brain, hypopharyngeal lobes, and so on) that are better developed in the worker than in the queen.

Differentiation of the larvae into either queens or workers starts during the fourth day of larval life, although queen development can still be induced after a critical period of $4\frac{1}{2}$ days (Dietz et al. 1979). The duration of the last (fifth) larval instar of the queen is 1 day shorter, and that of the pupal stage 4 days less than in the worker (de Wilde 1976). The queen bee must be considered as the normal female of the Hymenoptera, and the production of the worker caste is clearly secondary. The worker caste cannot be considered as neotenous, because it has no reproductive function. Its developmental cycle is longer than in the queen, and some structures are more differentiated or present only in the worker, although the development of internal reproductive organs is arrested. Thus the development of the honeybee worker can be regarded as metathetelous.

Higher concentration of JH most probably contributes to queen production (Wirtz and Beetsma 1972, Wirtz 1973, Zdarek and Haragsim 1974, Lensky et al. 1978, Dietz et al. 1979, Asencot and Lensky 1984). Ecdysone titer is also higher in the queen than in the worker bee during larval and early pupal stages (Lensky et al. 1978). However, in the worker the ecdysone titer increases very significantly toward the end of the pupal stage, which lasts 4 days longer than in the queen. Apparently, more constructive (and compensatory) development of some structures (three to seven) is related to this prolonged action of ecdysone during the pupal stage. In the queen JH has been known to be involved with regulation of vitellogenesis. However, Ramamurty and Engels (1977) found that vitellogenin synthesis and yolk incorporation are only slightly affected by allaiectomy, and that vitellogenin synthesis by JH is dose-dependent. They therefore suggested that the queen may have another source of JH, or neurohormone may compensate for the lack of JH. Furthermore, Fluri et al. (1981) found no correlation between the titers of JH, protein, and vitellogenin in queens. Thus the mechanism underlying the differential ovary development, which distinguishes the two castes, remains equivocal.

Caste differentiation is indirectly controlled by differential food regimes,which induce differential JH secretion. Royal jelly, considered to be the specific food of the queen larvae by Rembold et al. (1974a,b), is no longer believed to be the specific food necessary for queen development. Dietz et al. (1979) found that $4\frac{1}{2}$-day-old worker larvae can still develop into queens with the worker jelly fortified with sugar. They therefore contended that only those larvae that follow normal food intake sequence, that is, moderate during the first 3–4 days or so, will develop into queens, and that the food intake restriction that worker larvae normally encounter in the hive probably results in cessation of CA activity and hence the lower JH titer for the worker development. Asencot and Lensky (1984) also established the fact that larvae reared on worker jelly differentiate into queens when JH I is topically applied. Inhibition of the queen larvae differentiation by the queen pheromone, known to occur in some ants and bumblebees, is not known to occur in the honeybee.

In the bumblebee, *Bombus hypnorum,* the queen–worker differentiation is only physiological. According to Röseler (1970), queens are produced of the larvae that are fed with a sufficient amount of food; production of intermediates (in body size) between the worker and the queen can occur, depending on the amount of food taken by larvae. Experimentally, larvae were induced to develop into queens by JH application during the fourth larval instar (Röseler and Röseler 1974).

In *Bombus terrestris* the queen and the worker are structurally differentiated (Röseler 1970). Larvae are determined alternatively to be either workers or queens in the first $3\frac{1}{2}$ days of development and here again an optimal amount of food is necessary for the development of queens. Furthermore, an experiment with feces indicated the presence of the queen pheromone which inhibits the differentiation of workers into queens (Röseler 1970). The CA activity (i.e., JH synthesis and release) in queenless workers is strikingly higher than in the queenright workers. It is therefore likely that the CA activity depends on the presence or absence of the queen pheromone (Röseler and Röseler 1978). Röseler et al. (1981) further found that the pheromone is produced in the mandibular glands, and that it inhibits the activity of the worker CA. Röseler (1977) showed that in queenless workers, in the absence of the pheromonal inhibition, the JH production is stimulated on the first day of adult emergence, and eggs are rapidly formed. Röseler (1977) also showed that JH promotes oocyte development (including vitellogenin synthesis) in a dosage-dependent manner.

The production of castes (worker and queen) in the stingless bee genus *Melipona* has been shown to be genetically biased (Kerr 1950, Kerr et al. 1975, de Camargo et al. 1976); no intermediate between the queen and the worker occurs. According to this theory, only the doubly heterozygous (xa^1/xa^2; xb^1/xb^2) larvae can develop into queens, provided that they are reared with the proper amount of food. With the optimal amount of food both workers and queens emerge in the expected ratio; in many cases 25% of them are queens. When the quantity of food given is below certain limits, however, the result is confusing because all larvae may become workers. Kerr et al. (1975) found that queen development is correlated with a greater CA activity as in *Apis*. Velthuis and Velthuis-Kluppel (1975) found that JH application is most effective in producing the queen when applied to the prepupal stage; most larvae treated this way became queens. It appears, then, that in producing the queen, the presumed genetic mechanism expresses itself more or less fully only within the optimal range of the hormonal balance.

Darchen and Delage-Darchen (1971, 1974a,b, 1975, 1977) consistently found, in their studies of Trigonini from Mexico and Africa, that caste differentiation depends purely on the quantity of the food taken; slightly more nutrition results in the production of the queen. However, Velthuis and Velthuis-Kluppel (1975) and Velthuis (1976) seriously criticized the method of these studies. The difference in conclusion regarding the mechanism of caste differentiation between the two schools may be due in part to different species of the stingless bees studied. Yet a genetic mechanism that has penetrated as poorly as found in *Melipona* might not be worth taking so seriously.

Among the parasitic Chalcidoidea wing polymorphism has been well known for *Melittobia* (Eulophidae). In *M. chalybii* wing reduction occurs, as shown by Schmieder (1933), in two forms, the type form and the short-lived second form in both sexes. In the male of the type form wings are already considerably reduced, and in the second they are even smaller. In the female the second form differs from the type form in brighter color, in their failure to spread their shorter wings upon emerging from the pupa, and in the larger swollen abdomen that is full of eggs at the time of emergence. Reduction of ocelli and eyes is correlated with the reduction of wings. The large compound eyes present in the female of both types are aborted in the male of both forms. In the male of the type form three dorsal ocelli are present, though they may be absent in some individuals of the second form.

Schmieder (1933) found that those larvae that are the first to feed on a given host *(Trypoxylon)* ingest the blood, becoming the second type, whereas those that begin feeding somewhat later ingest to a large extent the remaining available tissues, and they become the type form. The duration of larval and pupal stages is much shorter in the second type (14 days versus 90 days in type form), which is less completely differentiated structurally (progenetic neoteny).

In another species of *Melittobia* from the Caribbean and Central America studied by Freeman and Ittyeipe (1982), and males, which constituted only 5% of the progeny, had morphs with and without ocelli. In the female brachypterous, negatively phototactic "crawlers" correspond to the second form in *M. chalybii*. Two other forms of females are macropterous; of these one of them (jumpers) corresponds to the intermediate form in *M. chalybii*. Interestingly, Freeman and Ittyeipe found that macropterous females developed only under crowded conditions. Conversely, there was a marked tendency for the increase in the brachypterous form as the density of eggs decreased. Their experiments demonstrated that the proportion of the three morphs emerging were unrelated to the sequence in which the eggs were laid, to the species of the host, and to the quality and absolute amount of food given, but related only to the density experienced by the young. Thus in this species the group effect occurs.

The apterous genus *Notomymar* (Mymaridae), described by Doutt and Yoshimoto (1970) from the subantarctic region (South Georgia Island), represents a case of island wing reduction where natural selection must favor flightless forms. In this case cold temperature and perhaps also malnutrition might also have contributed as causative proximate agents to the wing reduction. *Kleidotoma (Pentakleidota) subantarcticana,* described by Yoshimoto (1964), from Campbell Island (Subantarctic) has strongly narrowed wings, and the scutellar disk tends to be smooth.

The ichneumonid parasite *Gelis corruptor* exhibits wing trimorphism. Females are invariably apterous, and males may be either macropterous or micropterous; the sex-limited female aptery is apparently genetically determined. The male, as shown by Salt (1952), can be either macropterous or micropterous, depending on trophic conditions. On a host insect *(Apanteles)* providing adequate nourishment, male larvae develop into macropterous males, and on a host providing meager nourishment, the male larvae develop into the micropterous males. Salt found that when eggs or young larvae were transferred from a small to a large host, they developed into macropterous males, and that larvae removed from large hosts before they had finished feeding developed into micropterous males. Two males are quite distinct and therefore such a difference may be determined by Mendelian genetic factors as in *Melipona;* the expression of such a genetic mechanism, if it exists, depends on nourishment.

In the chalcidoid genus *Trichogramma,* parasitizing insect eggs, the male is dimorphic, either macropterous or apterous, although the female is always fully winged. In *T. semblidis* males reared on *Sialis* eggs are always apterous; those reared on three species of Lepidoptera are macropterous (Salt 1937). In *T. evanescens* Salt (1940) discovered that the sizes of adults are positively correlated with the sizes of eggs from which they emerge. He further showed that when the amount of food is insufficient to allow complete development the so-called "runt" (with stunted development of many structures, including the failure of wings to develop) is sometimes produced.

Wing reduction is common in Proctrupoidea. High percentages of wing reduction obtain in Scelionidae, Diapriidae, and Ceraphronidae, and the reduction occurs usually in the female, rarely in the male or both (L. Masner, personal communication). Reid (1941) summarized the cases of wing reduction and consequent thoracic modifications in Hymenoptera then known. He pointed out the frequent reduction of ocelli and eyes that accompanied the wing reduction. He also pointed out the enlargement of legs in some families (Sclerogibbidae, scolioids, Bethylidae, Agaonidae, some ants) with reduced wings. These modifications are, as suggested by Reid, adaptive for particular modes of life, such as that of burrowing. Permanently apterous taxa are rare in Hymenoptera. According to Reid (1941), the occurrence of aptery among the males as well as females in some species of Pompilidae is a rather exceptional feature; in a great majority of cases wing reduction occurs in the female only in Hymenoptera.

Typical parasitic species of Hymenoptera are entomophagous and are parasites only during the larval stages (parasitoids). The first-stage larvae vary greatly in their structural organization, and some of them are obviously caenogenetic (e.g., sacciform, caudate, encyrtiform, teleaform). However, the development thereafter tends toward a convergence to the hymenopteriform development (Clausen 1940).

23. The Order Strepsiptera

In Strepsiptera the first-stage larva is a free-living triungulid larva for dispersal. After reaching the hosts (Thysanura, Homoptera, Heteroptera, and Hymenoptera) it becomes the secondary parasitic larva, which undergoes variable further larval molts, and the last larval instar may be morphologically distinguishable from the preceding instars; in Mengenillidae such a larva is called the tertiary larva (Kinzelbach 1971b). *Mengenilla* and *Eoxenos,* which belong to Mengenillidae, are parasites of Thysanura. The final instar larvae leave the host and pupate under stones. A pupa is formed both in the male and female. The female, though wingless, is free-living, with functional eyes and antennae. The unpaired brood canal opens between the seventh and eighth abdominal sterna where the primary gonopore opens in the other orders of insects (Ulrich 1943, Askew 1971, Kinzelbach 1971a).

In other Strepsiptera the female spends her life inside the body of the host (Hymenoptera, Orthoptera, Hemiptera) and only the fused head and thorax protrude from the host. There is no obvious pupal stage, and the female body undergoes profound modifications (halmatometamorphosis). The anterior half of the body is fused to form a cephalothorax. Although the mandible is retained, only rarely are the maxillae, antennae, and eyes retained (Kinzelbach 1971b). The normal genital opening is absent. Instead, several brood canals, through which larvae emerge, are formed on the anterior abdomen. These female Strepsiptera are essentially caenogenetically modified, reproductively functional larvae.

The male larvae undergo pupation in all Strepsiptera. As Kinzelbach (1971a) pointed out, various structures in the adult male appear to be paedomorphic, in retaining some larval features: the trochanterofemur of the first and second pairs of legs, which are comparable with those of the secondary larvae; the apparent reduction of sternal articulation of the mesothoracic legs, which represents the larval condition; the less differentiated antennae that occupy the larval position; the highly reduced mandibles in some groups; the highly simplified maxillae; the peculiar compound eyes in which ommatidia are widely spaced from one another; and some internal organs (some nerves, etc.) all can be interpreted as paedomorphic. The retention of these larval features appears to reflect persistent action of JH, combined with more limited action of ecdysteroid during imaginal development.

In the adult male the forewings are greatly reduced, and Crowson (1955) homologized them with elytra in Coleoptera. Crowson pointed out that their reduction can be correlated with the fact that almost the entire life of the male *Stylops* is spent in flight (by means of well-developed hind wings).

24. The Order Siphonaptera

The Siphonaptera, or fleas, are parasitic as adults on mammals and birds. Only 6% of the fleas are parasites of birds, and they are clearly the derivatives of mammal fleas (Smit 1972). The eggs are laid loosely on the bodies of hosts and they drop off on the floor of host's burrow or nest. Varying degrees of association of the adult with the host have developed later, which range from only a short period of visiting on the host to the sedentary existence on the skin of the host, remaining imprisoned until death.

Structural changes involving the suppression of wing rudiments [which are present in the pupa (Sharif 1935, 1937; Poenicke 1969)], enlargement of legs, formation of ctenidia, and so on are related to the host's burrow and bird's nest, where necessary environmental factors (both as morphogenetic and as selective factors) must have been available for the production of these structures.

Morphogenetic plasticity related to environmental changes within the order Siphonaptera is apparent in some cases. For instance, *Glaciopsyllus antarcticus,* found in the nests of the silver gray petrel and the snow petrel on two small islands just off the coast of the Antarctic mainland, lacks the ctenidia (Smit and Dunnet 1962), and this is related to cold temperature; the biotope where the immature stage of this flea develops is buried under a meter or more of snow for most of the year. Some fleas are primarily nest dwellers, seldom traveling upon the host's body. Such fleas — belonging to various taxonomic groups — tend to have structural similarities, for example, reduced eyes, reduced thoraces, and weak legs that permit crawling but not jumping (Holland 1964).

The spines and bristles of fleas serve to help maintain a hold on the host (Rothschild 1917, Traub 1980), and hence the specialized chaetotaxy has selective value, and they have evolved convergently. Because the specialized chaetotaxy and overall traits of the host are so profoundly associated, Traub (1980) thought it possible to glance at a new genus or species of fleas and make a correct statement about some characteristic attributes of its hosts.

25. The Order Trichoptera

Among Trichoptera, the female with greatly reduced wings occurs in the winter generation of *Dolophilodes* (= *Tretonius*) *distinctus* (Ross 1944); this case is apparently induced by cold temperature. *Agrypnia pagetana* var. *hyperborea* is brachypterous in colder areas or at high altitudes (La Greca 1954). In the female of *Enoicycla pusilla* both forewings and hind wings are completely lacking (Schmid 1951). Less marked wing reduction occurs in both sexes of *Baicalina reducta* and *Thaumastes dipterus* (F. Schmid, personal communication).

26. The Order Lepidoptera

Hackman (1966) classified the cases of reduction (and loss) of wings in Lepidoptera in terms of their ecological associations, and summarized below.

1. Species at high altitudes—flightless females of numerous Geometridae, Bombyces, Arctiina, and some Microlepidoptera.
2. Cold-season species in a temperate climate at lower altitudes—Geometridae (e.g., *Apocheima hispidaria*), Oecophoridae.
3. Arctic species—Some examples given by Downes (discussed below).
4. Species of xerothermic habitats (in mountains and deserts)—mainly Bombyces and Arctiina (e.g., *Chondrostega, Somabrachys, Ocnogyna, Mallocephala*).
5. Species from oceanic islands—Pyralidina, Tortricina, and Tineina on low, exposed subantarctic islands.
6. Aquatic species—*Acentropus niveus* living in brackish water in the Baltic.
7. Some cases of wing reduction that cannot be associated with a particular ecological condition.—Psychidae and Teleoporiidae, which occur in very varied habitats and even at lower altitudes in the tropics.

The case of Psychidae (7 above) is related to their peculiar behavior (discussed in detail below). *Acentropus niveus* is macropterous when it occurs in fresh water (Palmén 1953).

Structural modifications associated with (or consequent to) wing reduction were summarized by Hackman (1966). They are, as a rule: (1) a strong tendency for wing reduction to occur in the female, an exception being a slight reduction of the forewing in *Dismorphia* (Pieridae); (2) the correlated reduction that occurs in the mouthparts and the tympanic organs; and (3) physogastry. A review of more recent works follows.

Orgyia thyellina has been known to be seasonally as well as sexually dimorphic in wing development. In northern Japan the first generation emerging in summer has normal wings in both sexes. However, those females emerging in autumn are brachypterous. Kimura and Masaki (1977) have shown that all the 90 females reared as larvae in the short photoperiod were brachypterous, whereas brachyptery occurred in 3 out of 72 females when reared under long photoperiod; they were kept at 22° C during rearing. The brachypterous females lay much larger and darker diapause eggs (as compared with those laid by macropterous females) and the pupa is also darker. Presumably, in nature, temperature effect is also involved with the production of brachyptery. Thus the seasonal dimorphism of this moth appears to result primarily from the insect's physiogenetic response to changing environmental stimuli (in photoperiod and temperature).

Selective advantages of the female brachyptery suggested by Kimura and Masaki were that the flying ability of females is useless at least for increasing the chance for mating, and that in cold weather flight tends to be hampered. At least these advantages do not seem to constitute a strong enough selective force to induce female brachyptery initially. Rather, they seem to be fortuitous selective advantages that resulted from the altered physiological (presumably involving JH activity which may have the dual function, Sect. 3A3) reaction of the moth during the cold season which, in turn, could result in wing reduction in the female.

In the Egyptian species *Orgyia dubia* the adult females never leave the cocoon and they are brachypterous (Hafez and El-Said 1970). Similarly, an extreme wing reduction in *O. antigua* is related to the fact that females never leave the cocoon (Paul 1937).

In central Europe, according to Dierl and Reichholf (1977), 33 species of Lepidoptera are wing reduced. Of these, 23 are active during the winter, 4 of them are alpine, and 19 of them belong to Geometridae. Dierl and Reichholf interpreted that wing reduction saves the loss of energy from the wing surface, especially in Geometridae, with large wings and small body. Another example of cold temperature-related wing reduction is the Arctic Lepidoptera. Downes (1965) showed that in this area brachyptery combined with physogastry (the enlarged abdomen containing excessively developed ovaries) is common and listed 11 such species (*Aspilates orciferarius, Psodos coracina,* etc.). He also showed examples of reduced eyes in several species of Arctic Lepidoptera, and pointed out their long larval life and the tendency for melanism (either in the female alone or in both sexes). In the subantarctic islands only three species of Lepidoptera are known to occur. Two of them *(Pringleophaga kergulensis, Embryonopsis halticella)* are flightless species with reduced wings, and the other is a flying species that is nonendemic (Gressitt 1970).

Areniscythris brachypteris (Scythrididae), discovered by Powell (1977) from coastal sand dunes in California, is brachypterous and has enlarged hind tibiae and elongated tarsi in both sexes. Larvae are extraordinarily elongate and thin, living in sand-covered silken tubes attached to buried, green parts of various green plant species at the margin of the active, moving sand dunes.

Wing reduction associated with case dwelling of larvae is highly pronounced in Psychidae. For the Japanese species of this family Saigusa (1961) recognized four types (degrees) of wing reduction, which apparently depend on modes of case dwelling: Type A with fully developed wings and legs (five genera including *Diplodoma*), in which the pupa exposes the anterior half of the body outside the case in hatching into the adult; type B without wings and with legs (three genera including *Teleporia* and *Solenbia*) in which also the adult hatches from the pupa which exposes its anterior half of the body; type C without wings and with legs *(Bacotia, Fumea, Brundia, Proutia)* in which females hatch within the cocoon; and type D, which is wingless and legless and hatches from the pupa inside the case (10 genera including *Clania, Nipponopsyche, Oiketicoides*). Compensatory development (by elongation and enlargement) of the ovipositor and associated apophyses, which has accompanied the reduction of wings and legs, is noted in the species belonging to types B and C. In type D species wings are completely absent in the female, legs are represented by protuberances or absent, and the ovipositor and associated apophyses are also very short.

It appears most likely that the rather profound structural modifications these psychid moths undergo are primarily the direct consequence of the unique environmental stimuli (within the case) on the physiological mechanism (especially of the endocrine mechanism) of the developing moths within the cases; the reduction and compensatory development of structures appear to depend largely on their sojourn as pupa and adult within the case. It should be remembered that the cases, in which the whole larval and pupal stages are spent, are built by the first-stage larvae of these psychid moths. In other words, the larvae create the environments that induce profound structural modifications during their subsequent development. The cases of psychids therefore perfectly fit the definition of the "Baldwin effect," the evolutionary significance of which has not been properly appreciated (Chap. 5).

The environment–hormonal basis of wing reduction and some other neotenous features in Lepidoptera discussed above can be explained more fully as follows: Because decerebration experiments with the silkworm *Bombyx mori* by Kobayashi (1956) and Maury (1962, cited by Bounhiol 1970) resulted in the production of small wings, a brain factor appeared to be involved with wing reduction. This brain factor has turned out to be a prothoracicotropic hormone (PTTH) which activates the prothoracic glands (PG) to secrete ecdysteroids for metamorphosis including the development of wings in *Galleria* (Oberlander 1969, 1972); in *Manduca* (and presumably others) PTTH is regarded as a photosensitive clock during a specific portion of the light–dark cycle (Truman and Riddiford 1974). During the normal development secretion of JH, which inhibits the action of PTTH, stops so that the PTTH–PG axis becomes active. For the arrest of development (leading to wing reduction) the action of the PTTH–PG axis must be limited, and this is probably effected by a prolonged inhibitory action of JH secreted from CA. The prolonged action of CA, in turn, presumably occurs when unusual (or new) environmental factors excessively activate the median neurosecretory cells (MNSC) in the pars intercerebralis, which secretes allatotropic hormone (Bhaskaran and Jones 1980). Some experiments involving JH or JHA application to the last larval instars of Lepidoptera (Hintze-Podufal 1975, Sehnal et al. 1976, Srivastava and Prasad 1982) resulted in various degrees of development affecting larval-pupal or pupal-adult metamorphosis. The results of such experiments are exaggerated, yet they indicate excessive involvement of JH in wing reduction.

In some Lepidoptera such as *Polygonia* (Endo 1972), *Papilio* (Fukuda and Kondo 1965), *Manduca* (Sroka and Gilbert 1974), *Pieris* (Karlinsky 1967), *Nymphalis* (Herman and Bennett 1975), and *Vanessa* (Herman and Dallmann

1981), JH is involved with vitellogenin synthesis. Therefore, the presence of an excessive amount of JH may expedite the maturation of ovaries, even before the completion of somatic development (including wings), and physogastry may also accompany wing reduction. In some Lepidoptera such as *Bombyx mori* and saturnid silkworm, ecdysteroids are essentially for ovary maturation (Chatani and Ohnishi 1976). In such Lepidoptera neotenous females with reduced wings may not occur, or may not occur so easily.

Substantial wing reduction never occurs in butterflies. However, seasonal polymorphism (or polyphenism) in color pattern and to some extent the shape of wings in the temperature-zone butterflies is common. As discussed below, seasonal polymorphism also appears to be induced environmentally– hormonally, and genetic fixation of a particular morph may eventually occur. The production of alternative seasonal wing morphs is determined mainly by the seasonal photoperiod and temperature. Earlier, as Shapiro's (1976) review clearly indicated, photoperiod was not known to be a very important factor for the determination of seasonal morphs in butterflies, although the temperature effect was known (e.g., many chilling experiments, which are especially effective for nymphalids, and temperature experiments with lycaenids by Weismann 1892, 1896, etc.; see Sect. 4B).

In *Polygonia c-aureum* photoperiod appears to control seasonal morphs (summer and autumn morphs). In this species, according to Endo (1972), the MNSC of the pars intercerebralis ultimately control the wing morph and reproductive maturation. He found that MNSC in the summer form stimulate the CA about 30 hr after pupation by way of the nervi corporis cardiaci, and the activiated CA promote ovarian maturation throughout the ovarian development. In the autumn form, on the other hand, the MNSC are inactive and fail to activate CA. Consequently, CA have no influence on ovarian development. An important fact is that color morphs and reproductive maturation are coupled; that is, wing morphs are also related to JH activity. Scheller and Wohlfahrt (1981) found that in *Iphiclides podalirius* (Papilionidae) ecdysteroid concentration is about three times higher in the spring generation than in the summer generation. Ultimately, it may be found that a divergent balance of ecydsteroids and JH during development results in the production of seasonal morphs. Thus much of the hormonal mechanism of seasonal morphs in butterflies still remains to be studied.

Some butterflies are monomorphic, and the monomorphism could have been derived from polymorphic ancestors. For instance, in the hesperid *Polites sabuleti* the montane subspecies *tecumseh* continued to produce its usual phenotype, and did not produce an "aestival" phenotype comparable to that produced by multivoltine, low-elevation nominate *sabuleti* when reared under identical conditions, suggesting the canalization of development and consequent fixation of the phenotype (Shapiro 1975). *Reliquia santamarta* (Pieridae) collected at an altitude of 3950–4000 m in Colombia produced only its usual dark-veined type when reared under continuous light at $26.5 \pm 2°$ C, without showing a latent polymorphism (Shapiro 1977). Another high-altitude pierine species from the northern Andes, *Tatochila xanthodice,* is multivoltine but monomorphic; it has lost plasticity and the phenotype is exceedingly stable. Shapiro (1978) failed to induce conspicuous modification by photoperiodic and temperature manipulations. Apparently, in all these cases, presistent low temperatures have induced the stable monomorphic phenotype. A puzzling example is *Nymphalis antiopa,* which has a wide distribution in both the Old and New Worlds. In this species seasonal variation is nonexistent, although it is very susceptible to modification by temperature shock on the pupa (Shapiro 1981).

In the above cases monomorphism appears to have been genetically fixed. Shapiro (1975, 1980b) suggested the selection of modifiers affecting the developmental threshold for expression of a major gene (as in genetic assimilation of Waddington 1953, 1961) as the mechanism of genetic fixation. Shapiro (1980a) compared these cases with permanent neoteny in some salamanders *(Proteus, Necturus).* In the latter case the proximate and ultimate causes as well as the process of genetic assimilation are known (Matsuda 1982 and Sect. 24B). The same details must eventually be elucidated for the cases of monomorphism in butterflies. It is interesting to learn that genetic fixation of an environmentally modified phenotype in butterflies was already known to Weismann (1892), as was clear in his conclusion of the experiment with a lycaenid butterfly (Sect. 4B).

According to Shapiro (1980a), furthermore, some of the temperate, mid-latitude *Tatochila* spp. of South America are polymorphic, and Shapiro considered them as having been derived from the monophenic ancestor of *Tatochila* distributing further north. It is conceivable that genetic assimilation of monomorphism was not complete in the ancestors (Phase 2 of genetic assimilation). As they migrated southward, where seasonal change in photoperiod and temperature occurs, some of them (which were not genetically assimilated, though monomorphic phenotypically) could have responded to the annually variable environmental parameters, and hence show polymorphism.

Several butterfly species are known to exhibit seasonal pigment polymorphism that is photoperiodically controlled. In *Colias eurytheme* melanin deposition occurs on the ventral surface of hind wings during the short days of spring and fall (Ae 1957, Hoffmann 1973), and the darker hind wings in *Colias* spp. absorb more radiant energy, allowing the insect to reach the thoracic temperature needed for flight (Watt 1968, 1969). Similarly, in another pierine, *Nathalis iole,* Douglas and Grula (1978) found, by rearing larvae under different photoperiods, that short photoperiods induced dark adult forms with melanic scales, whereas long photoperiods induced the development of immaculate adult forms with few melanic forms; these two forms corresponded to seasonal dimorphism in natural population. They also found that the melanic form absorbs solar radiation more efficiently. This photoperiodic control of thermoregulatory melanin deposition enables these forms to undertake extensive migration in winter. Probably the effect of lower temperatures correlated with shorter days cannot be excluded, because the melanism in *Tatochila* (above) occurs at colder temperatures in mountains. In *Phyciodes tharos* (Nymphalidae) the photoperiod similar to that of early summer induces the paler *"morpheus"* form, and the photoperiod regime similar to that of late summer induces the darker *"marcia"* form (Oliver 1976).

Population density-dependent phase variation, comparable with that in locusts, occurs in larval Lepidoptera. In *Leucania separata* and some others, as shown by Iwao (1962, 1968, and others), divergence in some morphological, physiological, and behavioral features occurs, depending on the number of larvae reared together. In the larva of *L. separata* low-density type larvae are green to brown with a whitish band, whereas those reared under gregarious conditions are velvety black, with white and reddish bands. In the adult wing loading is heavier in those reared at low density than in those reared in high density. Developmental rate (both pupa and adult) is slow and variable in low density and in some species (e.g., *Euproctis pseudoconspersa*) the low-density reared larvae tend to undergo extra molts, and so on.

Ikemoto (1983) found that topical application of JH and JHA to the crowded larvae of *Cephanodes hylas* caused pale pigmentation of the solitary phase at the next instar. As Ikemoto suggested, JH might inhibit the formation of cuticle melanin and epidermal ommochromes (which are responsible for dark pigmentation) in the larvae of *Cephanodes*. Earlier, Truman et al. (1973) also found that in *Manduca* larvae JH inhibits melanization. Curtis et al. (1984) found that in *Manduca* the absence of JH at the time of head cap slippage during the last larval molt causes deposition of premelanin granules, and their melanization is regulated by declining ecdysteroid titer.

Industrial melanism in moths is a stronghold of neo-Darwinism, in which the proximate process has been ignored. As seen above, melanization certainly can occur under some environmental conditions. It is therefore reasonable to suppose that industrial melanism could be induced through some proximate processes. Kettlewell's (1973) demonstration of preferential predation of light forms by birds is convincing, and it would certainly contribute to the increase in frequency of melanic forms afield. However, as Heslop-Harrison (1956) pointed out, the development and progress of melanism in the Lepidoptera may take place quite independently of the bird attack, through the proximate process.

24

The Phylum Vertebrata

A. THE CLASS PISCES

As shown by Marshall (1953) in his summary, Arctic, Antarctic, and deep-sea fishes produce large, yolky eggs. The number of such eggs produced is relatively few, and the larvae hatch at more advanced stages of development. Marshall pointed out that the production of large eggs is correlated with sparse concentrations of planktonic food in oceanic and polar inshore waters. In the latter environment the advantage of larger larvae is a smaller food requirement combined with increased power of swimming, leading to a widening of the range in search for suitable food. Marshall further thought that in deep-sea fishes also the advantages of producing as large a larva as possible are mainly increased swimming speed and relatively reduced food requirements.

Dealing with the same problem, Rass (1941, 1977; cf. Marshall 1953) emphasized the temperature effect on egg size. In a series of related species the size of eggs is inversely proportional to the temperature of the medium at the moment of egg laying; that is, the eggs are larger the nearer the habitat of the species lies to the pole. Rass (1977) pointed out that in *Liparis* the adult size gets smaller as its egg gets bigger. This appears to reflect the effect of compressed development in larger eggs on the adult size as in terrestrial amphibians (see Sect. 24B for discussion), although Rass related it simply to the quantity of food for embryonic development. The effect of cold temperature on the egg size is also clear in the size variation in central Texas populations of *Etheostoma spectabile* (Percidae). In this species, as shown by Marsh (1984), increase and decrease in egg diameter are seasonal. Eggs are in general heaviest when water temperatures are coldest. Thus what Rass and Marsh pointed out was the proximate process of egg enlargement, and what Marshall emphasized was the ultimate process of evolution of egg size by natural selection.

Alteration in the pattern of vitellogenesis must have been involved with enlargement of eggs during the proximate evolutionary process of the above-mentioned fishes. The endocrine mechanism of vitellogenesis in fishes, which is essentially the same as that in amphibians (Sect. 24B), has now become increasingly clear in recent works on salmonids (e.g., Idler and Campbell 1980, Van Bohemen et al. 1982, Bromage et al. 1982) and others (mentioned below). Bromage et al. (1982) investigated the effects of seasonally changing photoperiodic regimes on the level of serum gonadotropin, 17β-estradiol, and vitellogenin in the developing rainbow trout *(Salmo gairdneri)*. They have found, under both control and experimental regimes (in which the increasing and decreasing components of photoperiod were maintained but compressed into a 6 – 9-month period), that the primary change was an increase in serum level of gonadotropin during the early stage of ovarian development, and that the levels were reduced thereafter. This was followed by the increased 17β-estradiol level, which became particularly pronounced during the period of exogenous (heterosynthetic) vitellogenesis. However, minor modifications were noted in the experimental population. For instance, much higher levels of gonadotropin were produced more under the 6-month regimes than in the other cycles, presumably in response to the increased intensity of light to which the fish had been exposed. This experiment suggests that the pattern of gonadotropin production and consequent vitellogenesis could become altered in some geographical areas such as the Arctic and Antarctic areas, where very considerable seasonal fluctuation in photoperiod occurs, and the consequence could be the production of larger (but fewer) eggs. In these areas cold temperature also probably affects jointly the endocrine mechanism of vitellogenesis.

A case of speciation resulting from egg-size differentiation is known for two closely related species of *Cottus*, *C. nozawae*, and *C. amblystomopsis*, which occur in the rivers of Hokkaido, Japan. The two species had been regarded as two populations of *C. nozawae* until Goto (1980) assigned the downstream population to *C. amblystomopsis* which occurs in Saghalin, and hence the name *C. nozawae* applies only to the upstream population. The results of a series of studies by Goto since 1975 were summarized by Goto (1982) and Maekawa and Goto (1982) as follows: In *C. nozawae*, which lives upstream and is landlocked, egg sizes range from 2.6 to 3.0 mm in diameter and 100 – 700 eggs are laid at a time, whereas in *C. amblystomopsis*, which lives downstream and is anadromous, eggs are less than 2 mm in diameter and 600 – 3000 eggs are laid at a time. In *C. nozawae*, with larger eggs, the embryonic development lasts 2 – 3 days longer than in *C. amblystomopsis*. Living in gentle currents along the bank, where food is available and predation is negligible, is certainly advantageous for the larvae and juveniles of *C. nozawae*. Here the question remains as to how strongly such advantages have acted as selective forces in producing larger eggs. It appears certain that initially the production of large eggs and consequent abbreviation of larval stages in *C. nozawae* occurred as a result of the response of the built-in physiogenetic mechanism to new environmental stimuli (such as colder temperature?) and without selection pressure, as the animals became isolated (landlocked) upstream. Therefore, the emergence of larger larvae, which suited the local living condition, was mainly a fortuitous adaptive response in which little, if any, immediate effect of natural selection appears to have been involved, and later selection may reinforce these events. Furthermore, as pointed out by Maekawa and Goto (1982), the production of fewer large eggs in the generally more precarious upstream environment cannot be explained by the theory of r – K selection.

According to Balon (1977), development of *Labeotropheus* takes place in the buccal pouch of the female until such time as juveniles are formed; in all known cases this group of mouth-brooders produces a clutch of a few but large eggs. Hatching from the vitelline membrane occurs early, after 6 days of incubation, and the eleutheroembryos develop, without a metamorphic stage, into juveniles. Apparently, such a hiding strategy occurred independently in various taxa such as salmonids, liparids, acheilognathinids, and others (Balon 1977). The omission of the larval stage is most probably the consequence of large eggs, with which the suppression of larval genes occurs, and it would certainly contribute to additional safety of the fish. Balon attributed the enlargement of eggs and consequent acceleration in development solely to such adaptive advantage. However, the fish under study lives in a freshwater habitat, where salinity must be relatively low as in the habitat of *C. nozawae*. It is imaginable that eggs were already fairly large before the fish developed such mouth-brooding behavior, and that the advantage attached to the accelerated development has acted as a selective force in inducing the production of even larger eggs.

The hagfishes, most of which occur in the deep sea, produce large, yolk-rich eggs. The length of an egg in *Myxine* varies, ranging from 14 to 25 mm. (Walvig 1963). In *Eptatretus burgeri*, which regularly migrates into shallow water in colder months and into colder water in warmer months (Kobayashi et al. 1972), the egg length is 24 mm, and about 165 eggs are expected to be formed (Patzner 1978). Associated with the larger eggs, development is direct, lacking the larval stage (Gorbman 1983). Because in *Eptatretus stouti* vitellogenin synthesis can be induced by estrogen (Yu et al. 1981, Turner et al. 1981) and because the site of vitellogenin synthesis is known to be the liver (Yu et al. 1980, Turner et al. 1981), enlargement of eggs must occur through an altered pattern of vitellogenin synthesis in the deep sea, where the pattern of estrogen release would be affected by cold temperature. The absence of the larval phase must be adaptive in the deep sea, for the planktonic food would be difficult to obtain by weak, usually degenerate larvae (D. E. McAllister, personal communication).

Enlargement of eggs and the consequent direct development associated with the deep-sea habitat is apparently true also of the living coelacanth, *Latimeria chalumnae*. Smith and Rand (1975) reported juveniles with large yolk sacs lying free in the right oviduct. Because large eggs (measuring 8.5 – 9 mm in diameter) had been known to occur in this fish, Smith and Rand (1975) proposed that *Latimeria chalumnae* is ovoviviparous (and is presumably without the larval stage). The proximate and ultimate processes of egg-size enlargement and consequent ovoviviparity are essentially the same as those of egg-size enlargement and direct development in hagfishes. Speleophilous fishes (such as troglodytes *Caecobarbus geertsi* and *Anoptichthys jordani*) produce only a few large eggs. Their embryonic period is extended, and well-developed larvae or juveniles probably emerge from these large eggs (Balon 1975b).

The three-spined stickleback, *Gasterosteus aculeatus*, is trimorphic. In the marine anadromous form a row of lateral plates, beginning posterior to the head, terminate on the caudal peduncle, and such a morph is called the complete morph. In freshwater populations the row is often incomplete, being represented by the partial morph (in which a row of plates on the abdomen is separated from a row on the caudal peduncle by an unplated region) and the low morph (with only the abdominal row), although the occurrence of the partial morph in the marine habitat has been known. Bell (1981) showed that the partial and low morphs correspond to the ontogenetic stages of the complete morph, and therefore he regarded them to be paedomorphic (neotenous) and derived from the complete morph by developmental arrest. Because the alternative alleles at one or two loci have been known to specify the complete and low morphs (Munzing 1963, Hagen and Gilbertson 1973, Avise 1976), Bell proposed that the change of one or two genes regulates the lateral plate ossification, and alluded to Tompkins (1978), who found that in the paedomorphic Mexican axolotl *Ambystoma mexicanum* one gene controls the physiological process of metamorphosis (presumably the TSH function; see Sect. 24B).

The above facts appear to indicate that initially neoteny in the stickleback arose as a consequence of migration of the ancestral complete morph population(s) into the freshwater habitat, where they became isolated and the development of the lateral plates became arrested by the new environmental factors (lower salinities must have been one of the most important). Thereafter, as Bell's interpretation indicates, a mutation or mutations affecting the endocrine mechanism for ossification might have replaced the environment – hormonally induced arrested ossification (i.e., genetic assimilation). In fact, such an evolutionary process closely parallels the evolution of neoteny in *Ambystoma* by the process of genetic assimilation.

In his attempt to fit the definitions of the kinds of paedomorphosis (neoteny) proposed by Gould (1977), Bell faced a dilemma, because he discovered that 7.6% of the difference between complete and low morph in plate number is caused by termination of plate development (progenesis of Gould) and the remainder results from a reduced rate of plate ossification (neoteny of Gould). Yet paedomorphosis of lateral plates has evolved primarily by neoteny (of Gould). Furthermore, Gould's association of his neoteny with predictable environments (*K*-selection) was not fully applicable here, because the freshwater habitat, where these neotenous morphs occur, is not necessarily more predictable than the marine habitat where the complete morph occurs.

Recurrence of incomplete and low morphs in related stickleback genera associated with freshwater habitats in different geographical areas in the northern Holarctic and islands led Bell (1974, 1981) to postulate their polyphyletic origin derived from the complete morph which reached these habitats. Bell (1981) thought that this may be a common mechanism for differentiation of peripheral freshwater fishes from their immediate marine or anadromous ancestors (Bell 1974, 1979; Vladykov and Kott 1979).

Cases of neoteny in the lamprey have also been known. Zanandrea (1957) found sexually mature ammocoetes of the brook lamprey *Lampetra zanandreai* in northern Italy. In 12 individuals the ovaries were well developed, as were the secondary sexual characters in one individual (two enlarged dorsal fins that are fused, development of the anal pseudofin, and the transparent body wall). The endostyle was intact. Because the endostyle has been known to undergo transformation into the thyroid gland during metamorphosis (Wright and Youson 1976, 1980; Youson 1980, and more recent works) the presence of an intact endostyle is a neotenous feature. The only environmental peculiarity that could have induced neoteny was the tannery pollution. Zanandrea (1957) thought that the neoteny may represent an extreme of the tendency toward precocious sexuality in nonparasitic forms in which there is no growth period interpolated between metamorphosis and assumption of full sexual maturity.

Another example of lamprey neoteny is that of *Lampetra lethophaga* from some locations in the United States (most strikingly in Full River in the Pitt River system in California) (reported by Hubbs 1971); maturity apparently occurs in all individuals of both sexes in the prenuptial conditions: They have passed through the ordinary prejuvenile metamorphosis and some are in a full maturity, yet none has developed the ordinary nuptial attributes (melanistic pigmentation and the principal secondary sexual characters). The physical causative agent of neoteny in this case is unknown; cold temperature at the type locality does not seem to be a factor suppressing nuptial development. Similarly, Walsh and Burr (1981) found in Kentucky sexually mature but neotenous males and females of *Lampetra aepyptera* that lack the nuptial attributes. They tentatively attributed the failure of this population to develop normal, secondary characters to limited food supply during the ammocoete stage.

As Youson (1980) concluded in his review, the factor(s) controlling the lamprey metamorphosis remains unknown. Numerous attempts to induce metamorphosis by artificial means (involving the thyroid hormonal manipulation) failed. More recent observations by Suzuki (1982) and Lintlop and Youson (1983) showed that T_3 and T_4 sharply decline soon after metamorphosis. All this information does not help us to account for the hormonal mechanism of neoteny in the lamprey either. Botticelli et al. (1963) isolated 17β-estradiol, estrone, and progestrone from mature ovaries of *Petromyzon marinus*, supposed to be produced in the follicle cells. Therefore, for the precocious maturation of the ovary in the neotenous forms of lampreys, altered functioning of these hormones is presumably involved.

Smoltification in many species of Salmonidae (belonging to the genera *On-*

chorhynchus, Salmo, Savelinus) refers to the spectrum of simultaneous or consecutive morphological, behavioral changes that transform the darkly pigmented, bottom-dwelling parr into a pelagic, silvery smolt prepared for the transition into seawater; deposition of guanine in the scale and skin gives the fish a silvery color that obscures the dark parr marks. This silvering is the major index of metamorphosis (smoltification) in salmonids (for other characters that accompany this transformation see Gorbman et al. 1983).

During smoltification the environmental factors appear to affect the activity of thyroid glands, as was first suggested by Hoar (1939). White and Henderson (1977), Dickhoff and Folmar (1978), Dickhoff et al. (1978, 1982), and Nishikawa et al. (1979) found the distinct thyroid hormonal surge in mid-spring at the time the day length is increasing, and Grau et al. (1981, 1982) found that the trend of increasing T_4 concentration coincides with the time of the new moon. The effect of water temperature on smoltification also has been known (Folmar and Dickhoff 1980).

As Dickhoff and Folmar (1978) pointed out, the occurrence of a distinct thyroid hormonal surge during smoltification of salmonids can be compared with the similar thyroid hormonal surge during the amphibian metamorphosis. In amphibians the thyroid hormonal surge causes migration of the tadpoles onto land (land drive), where metamorphosis is completed, whereas in the young salmon the thyroxine surge causes the migration from the freshwater habitat to the seawater habitat. Another important difference is that the anuran thyroidal surge lasts about 6 days and the morphological effect is drastic. In the parr–molt transformation (metamorphosis) the surge lasts about 30–60 days, and the morphological change is much more gradual. Furthermore, smoltification is of finite duration, and if the smolted fish are prevented from migrating to seawater, they will revert (desmoltify) to immature parrs. Presumed involvement of prolactin, which is expected to antagonize the action of thyroid hormones during metamorphosis (by analogy to amphibians), is not yet known directly, although its presence and osmoregulatory function in freshwater fishes has been known (Pickford and Philips 1959, Grau et al. 1984).

In North American salmonids, as shown by Rounsefell (1958) and Hoar (1976), there is a gradation in types from the most extreme of the obligatory anadromous forms to the (nearly always) wholly freshwater forms through the optionally anadromous forms. Yet there are numerous species of the salmon that complete their life cycle in fresh water, but none that is strictly marine (Tchernavin 1939, cf. Hoar 1976). Moreover, according to Hoar (1976), there are very few species that, in their native haunts, do not sometimes complete their life cycle (including smoltification) in fresh water, and none that cannot. These facts appear to indicate that the difference in salinity, unlike the case for three-spined sticklebacks (and lampreys?), has no effect on morphogenesis. In fact, as already seen, day length, temperature, and lunar periodicity are the factors that control smoltification. This (relative?) insensitivity to the salinity difference during morphogenesis does not contradict the currently accepted theory (Tchernavin 1939, Rounsefell 1958, Hoar 1976, Maekawa and Goto 1982, etc.) that proposes the freshwater origin of the salmonids.

Salangidae (Salmonoidei) are small fishes (with 6 genera and 12 species) that occur in the Far East, and they are considered to be neotenous. They live typically in brackish water, but most of them are acclimatized to fresh water. During the spawning season, they come in swarm toward the coast to lay their eggs, which are small and adhesive (Wakiya and Takahashi 1937).

Some higher fishes have found a way to live on land temporarily, as seen in lungfishes (Dipnoi) and the mudskipper *Periophthalmus* (Gobiidae). The Devonian crossopterygian fishes, the close relatives of lungfishes, are believed to have given rise to the Amphibia. Some recent workers have proposed that the Dipnoi or the lungfishes themselves gave rise to the Amphibia (Gardiner 1983). In these cases altered thyroid hormone action might have caused land drive (as in amphibians, but not as in salmonids), and the consequent adaptive changes in structures and physiology could have been substantial, as the thyroxine experiment with *Periophthalmus* by Harms (1934) indicated.

The lungfishes or Dipnoi have remained essentially freshwater animals. *Protopterus* and *Lepidosiren* live in an environment where oxygen is in short supply and a high concentration of carbon dioxide occurs (Thompson 1969). What is of interest here is that neoteny has played a pervasive role in the evolution of Dipnoi. According to Bemis (1981, 1984), recent lungfishes have protocercal tails, suppression of endocondral ossification, and greatly reduced fin rays. More recent studies on the physiological adaptation of the mudskipper (*Periophthalmus*) include those by Gordon et al. (1969, 1978) and Morii et al. (1978, 1979).

The stalk-eyed fish (*Idiacanthus*) has sexually dimorphic neoteny that is very marked; the mature males are less than one-sixth the length of the females and are larvoid (Gibbs 1964). Similarly, in ceratioid fishes, living in deeper layers of oceanic water, the male, which becomes attached to the female, is dwarf (Bertelsen 1951).

B. THE CLASS AMPHIBIA

Usually, in both anurans and urodelans, eggs are large and yolk-rich when they are laid out of water, and the consequence is often direct development without the tadpole stage (Noble 1931, Lutz 1948, Dent 1968, Lamotte 1977). An outstanding example is *Eleutherodactylus* (a widely distributed genus of Leptodactylidae with many species in South and Central America), in which most, even the water-loving ones, lay their eggs out of water, and eggs are large and yolky, the diameter of each egg ranging from 3.0 to 5.0 mm (Lynn and Peadon 1955, Lynn 1961); in *E. jasperi* from Puerto Rico, however, developed "embryos" are located prior to birth in a distended section of the reproductive tract (Drewry and Jones 1976), and the case was called "ovoviviparity." The egg size was not reported.

Most probably, altered functioning of the endocrine mechanism for vitellogenesis is at least partly responsible for the enlargement of eggs in *Eleutherodactylus* (and some other amphibians). In *Xenopus* it has now been established that the environmental stimuli, transmitted through the hypothalamo–pituitary complex, induces the release of estrogenic hormone from follicle cells of the ovaries. The hormone (17β-estradiol) reaches the liver, where it turns on vitellogenin genes. The vitellogenin (yolk precursor) thus produced is carried by the blood to enter developing oocytes (Tata 1976, Tata and Smith 1979). It can be surmised that in producing large eggs in *Eleutherodactylus* the new environmental stimuli available on the dry terrestrial habitat, which certainly must differ drastically from those in their ancestral aquatic habitat (e.g., now the immediate surrounding medium is air, instead of water), have induced alterations in the endocrine function for vitellogenesis, so that an excessive amount of yolk precursor enters more limited number of eggs. It should be remembered that essentially the same endocrine mechanism for vitellogenesis exists in fishes (Sect. 24A) and echinoderms (Chap. 20). Therefore, the essential features of the mechanism can be said to have been inherited from their ancestors; its existence has not been induced by natural selection.

Embryonic development of *Eleutherodactylus* within the yolk-rich egg is quite atypical, as shown by Lynn (1942) and several later workers. During intraoval development the embryo develops a short, highly vascular tail with exaggerated dorsal and ventral fins. Simple external gills may appear transiently in some species, although they are lacking in others. No gill slit of internal gills occurs. Fore and hind limbs appear almost simultaneously. Tadpole-like mouthparts and the characteristic lateral line system of the tadpole are absent. In short, many of the familiar features of an aquatic tadpole larva are either completely lacking or only slightly represented. A significant caenogenetic feature is the tail, which functions as the larval respiratory organ. The animal that hatches from the egg is an adult, larval development being obliterated within the egg, and thus development is direct. The adult is miniature, reaching some 5 mm in length about 8 hrs after hatching in *E. nubicola*; *Eleutherodactylus* spp. are certainly among the smallest tetrapods (Hughes 1966).

The abortive larval development within the egg and highly accelerated differentiation of adult structures, which are accompanied by precocious maturation of gonads, clearly reflect a profound alteration in gene regulation pathways. It is probable that the yolk-rich, large egg itself constitutes not only an abundant source of nutrition for the developing embryo–larva, but also it must provide the kind of environmental stimuli for the induction of abnormal hormonal activity (discussed below). Furthermore, the abnormal hormonal activity must induce alteration in the gene regulation pathway, thereby resulting in their abnormal developmental process.

By reference to the well established pattern of the balance between prolactin and thyroid hormones (T_3 and T_4) for amphibian metamorphosis known since Etkin (1968) (Sect. 1B), the abortive larval development and consequently accelerated development of adult structures within the egg of *Eleutherodactylus* can be attributed only to precocious cessation of prolactin secretion and consequently accelerated action of thyroid hormones. Conceivably, such hormonal balance can occur in the embryo–larva living in the very yolk-rich, large egg where the physicochemical environmental stimuli on the endocrine activity must be highly unique (see Sect. 3B2 for more discussion). Some experiments with *Eleutherodactylus* tend to support (or at least do not contradict) this interpretation. Thus application of thyroid inhibitors (phenylthiourea and thiourea) to the "embryos" of *E. martinicensis* by Lynn and Peadon (1955) did not result in larval development, although it did result in the production of a larval stage in *Plethodon* (see below); prolactin for larval development must have been depleted at the time the drug was applied. The experiment merely showed that the development of certain features depends on thyroid hormones. Hughes and Reier (1972) found that when the "embryo" of *E. ricordii* (not later than the early digit stages of limbs) is treated with prolactin, delay in the loss of certain features including the tail occurs, and the tail length compares with that obtained after thyroidectomy (Hughes 1966).

The genus *Arthroleptis* (Ranidae) in tropical Africa also has direct development. For instance, *A. crusculum* is, as are *Eleutherodactylus* spp., terrestrial (living on the crests of hills or abrupt slopes where water does not accumulate) and produces about a dozen large, yolk-rich eggs (3.5 mm in diameter) laid in humid soil, and the adult size is diminutive (20 mm long) (Lamotte and Xavier 1972, Lamotte 1977). Within the African bufonid genus *Nectophrynoides* ovoviviparity and viviparity occur in addition to oviparity. *N. vivipara* and *N. tornieri* are ovoviviparous and they produce large yolk-rich eggs to ensure the completion of (abortive) larval development within the egg, resulting in direct development; in *N. vivipara* about 100 small juveniles occur in the female genital duct (Lamotte and Xavier 1972). During the development of *N. tornieri* a few important characters do not develop; there is no indication of adhesive organs, labial teeth, or horny beaks in the material Orton (1949) studied. An interesting case is *N. malcolmi*, from a high altitude in Ethiopia, first described by Grandison (1978) and later redescribed by Wake (1980). In this species diameters of fully yolked eggs measure 2.7–3.9 mm. Tadpoles are mouthless (as in ovoviviparous *N. tornieri*) and they cannot swim when placed in water. As Wake (1980) thought, feeding is obviated because of the considerable amount of yolk present throughout development. All these features are also shared by lecithotrophic larvae in many invertebrate species with moderately large eggs. Therefore, perhaps the larva in this amphibian species can also be called the "lecithotrophic larva" (direct development of Wake). In truly viviparous *N. occidentalis* eggs are small in size (550 μm in diameter) and poor in yolk content (Lamotte and Xavier 1972). For many other cases of direct development in the Anura, refer to Lamotte and Xavier (1972) and Lamotte (1977). According to Lamotte (1977), direct development has occurred independently in Leptodactylidae, Ranidae, Rhacophoridae, and Microhylidae.

In South American frogs, as shown by Lutz (1948, Table 3), there is a clear negative correlation between the egg size and the number of eggs laid. In those species laying their eggs on the backs of females, bromeliads, and on banks of the earth, the egg diameters are decidedly greater than those in frogs that lay eggs in standing water or on leaves, and the period of intraoval development is very much prolonged (embryonization). She also observed that in developing clutches of large yolk-rich eggs there are often a few small ones that do not develop. The tropical genus *Pelophryne* also shows increasing terrestriality, and egg sizes of this genus are also proportionately enormous (1.5–2.5 mm in diameter). Furthermore, their clutch sizes are small, ranging from four to six, in contrast to *Bufo* which has approximately 75–80 ova per ovary (Inger 1960).

Among urodelans, the family Plethodontidae show the evolutionary trend in the direction of abandonment of aquatic larval stages, and many of them are truly terrestrial and undergo direct development. Within the genus *Desmognathus* (Desmognathinae) some are still aquatic and have the larval stage, and some are terrestrial and development is direct. As Dowling and Duellman (1978, Table 16.2) show, in the terrestrial genera *Aneides, Batrachoseps, Bolitoglossa, Chiropterotriton, Ensatina, Hydromantes, Parvimolge, Plethodon* and *Pseudoeurycea*, all belonging to Plethodontidae, no larva occurs, and hence they must be considered as having direct development. In some terrestrial genera (*Lineatriton, Phaeognathus, Oedipina, Thorius*) the aquatic larva is unknown and, these may also have direct development. Presumably, in these terrestrial plethodontids eggs are larger than those in their aquatic ancestors, because in anurans enlargement of eggs is correlated with their terrestrial life and direct development. The egg size in *Plethodon cinereus*, a common terrestrial salamander in the eastern United States, was described as large by Noble (1931), who was seriously concerned with the relation between the egg size and development and consequent amphibian evolution. Thiourea and phenylthiourea treatments of the eggs of *Plethodon cinereus* by Lynn (1947) resulted in the production of a larval stage, indicating that direct development in this species and other terrestrial plethodontids (discussed below) might well be due, as in *Eleutherodactylus* (see below), to precocious cessation of the prolactin secretion and concomitant, precocious action of thyroid hormones. Earlier, Dent (1942) suspected that early hypertrophy of the thyroid may be responsible for the lack of the true larval stage in this species.

The pattern of neoteny, which is marked in terrestrial plethodontids with direct development, is what Wake (1966) called "differential metamorphosis." In differential metamorphosis, some elements (of bones) complete metamorphosis early, others very late, and some do not metamorphose at all. Differential metamorphosis through direct development, therefore, appears to reflect differential effects of the thyroid hormones that were released precociously. According to Wake (1966), differential metamorphosis resulting in (progenetic) neoteny is clearer in bolitoglossines than in other plethodontids, and he described different patterns of development of osteological characters for each genus. Within the largest genus, *Bolitoglossa*, as later works by Wake and Brame (1969), Wake and Lynch (1976), Alberch (1981), and Alberch and Alberch (1981) have revealed, neotenous clines in some morphological features (relatively short tail, more fully webbed hands and feet, reduction and loss of phalanges, fusion of carpals and tarsals, absence of prefrontal bones, reduction in skull ossification) are associated with reduction in body size.

Among the terrestrial plethodontids, according to Wake et al. (1983), *Aneides lugubris* has the most prolonged ontogeny. Until the end of the second year its osteological ontogeny is similar to that of other species, but beyond that point ossification of long bones continues throughout life and is never finished. Elements such as pelvic plates ossify, though never completely, mesopodial elements remain cartilaginous throughout life, and dramatic changes occur in structures related to the feeding system. Wake et al. (1983) believed that all plethodontids can be considered as paedomorphic relative to ancient amphibians, and that the paedomorphic process appears to have been reversed in this species. For the plethodontids, which are already terrestrial, the environmental factors that might cause prolongation or reduction of the juvenile development remains unknown.

As Lutz (1948) contended, prolonged intraoval development of (more or less suppressed) larvae in frogs, which may result in direct development, alleviates the danger from predation and drying, and the competition in securing food on land. It is therefore apparent that diminutive adult sizes that often result from direct development are not the direct target of natural selection, the latter working primarily on the developmental process per se.

As we have already seen, direct development resulting from the production of large eggs has resulted initially from the response of animals' physiological potential, inherited from their ancestors, to environmental stimuli on land. Thereafter, the endocrine functioning for the production of large eggs and consequent direct development must have been improved or reinforced by natural selection because of the selective advantages of direct development on land. Conceivably, many individuals lacking the ability to produce sufficiently large and yolk-rich eggs for direct development were eliminated during the initial stage of colonization of land by early plethodontids and others.

In salamanders larval metagenetic neoteny has often occurred as they changed their habitats. It has commonly occurred at higher altitudes in North America, where lower temperatures are the main physical environmental factors inducing neoteny. In montane Colorado, according to Sexton and Bizer (1978), three life history patterns are recognized for the populations of *Ambystoma tigrinum*: the standard life history, with only one size of larvae; a life history with two size classes of larvae, and metamorphosis occurring in the second season (neotenic life history of Sexton and Bizer); and a life history with three or four size classes of larvae, in which either metamorphosis or neoteny (paedogenesis of Sexton and Bizer) occurs in the third or later warm seasons. Their study showed that the third type of life history increases at higher altitudes with lower temperatures, and in some lakes at the highest altitudes the life history is solely neoteny (Sexton and Bizer 1978, Bizer 1978).

These facts are consistent with the long established fact that in amphibians the effects of low temperatures are the slowing of growth and the inhibition of metamorphosis, and temperature certainly appears to be a major controlling factor determining alternative life history in this case, as Bizer (1978) contended. The retardation in development at colder temperatures has often been attributed to the tendency for tissues to lose, at colder temperatures, their sensitivity to thyroid hormones (T_3 and T_4), which are immediate agents for metamorphosis (Huxley 1929, Frieden et al. 1965, Ashley et al. 1968, Tata 1970, Griswold et al. 1972, Norris and Platt 1974, etc.); the loss of tissue sensitivity at colder temperatures appears to involve the malfunction of receptors for thyroid hormones (Griswold et al. 1972). The presence of receptors for binding thyroid hormones has been known (Tata 1970, Samuel and Tsai 1973, Kistler et al. 1975, Galton 1979, 1984). Thus there seems to be a mechanism through which loss of tissue sensitivity to thyroid hormones can occur at high altitudes and results in neoteny in *Ambystoma tigrinum.*

However, it is also known that it is the relative proportion of circulating prolactin (which promotes the growth of larval structures, such as the gills and tadpole tails, and is concerned with osmoregulation) to thyroid hormones for metamorphosis that determine whether metamorphosis will take place in amphibians. Therefore, another possible mechanism of neoteny in *A. tigrinum* is the overproduction of prolactin that could result in the persistence of larval structures, as suggested for neoteny in *Necturus* (Bern et al. 1967). Furthermore, Norris' (1978) data show that synthetic mammalian TRH (thyrotropin-releasing hormone) has no effect on metamorphic events when administered hypothalamically to neotenes of this species, suggesting that neoteny in this species might result from the loss of sensitivity of the pituitary to TRH and consequent deficiency in TSH (thyroid-stimulating hormone). One or a combination of the two such causes is presumably involved with the production of the neotenous morph. It should be remembered that the hormones directly concerned here with neoteny (prolactin and thyroid hormones) must have been inherited from their ancestors (Sect. 1D).

For *Ambystoma* spp. the aquatic habitat is definitely advantageous at high altitudes, where unusually harsh conditions, such as severe temperature fluctuation, lack of cover or food, and low humidity exist on land, provided that lakes are permanent and fish as predators are absent or rare (Sprules 1974a), as in montane Colorado (Sexton and Bizer 1978). The ability of *A. tigrinum* to become neotenous and aquatic at higher altitudes in montane Colorado is therefore adaptive. Such an adaptive response has been possible by deploying the hormones inherited from the ancestor, and it must have been the result of continued selection on genetic variation with respect to the ability (in the pattern of hormone secretion, or tissue sensitivity, or both) to respond to lower temperatures; those individuals that failed to respond adaptively enough (by becoming neotenous) must have been eliminated. It should be admitted, however, that the neotenous populations at higher (especially at the highest) altitudes in Colorado may contain individuals in which neoteny is genetically determined (as a result of genetic assimilation, to be discussed below).

Sprules (1947b) found, in laboratory experiments, that sampled populations of *Ambystoma gracile* appeared to be made up of at least three types of individuals: (a) those that always metamorphose regardless of environmental conditions; (b) those that are always neotenous; and (c) those that may or may not metamorphose, depending on conditions. Therefore, Sprules contended that predictably neoteny in *A. gracile* would be more common in permanent, cold, and unproductive ponds, because all individuals belonging to type c would become neotenous by the effect of cold temperatures (on the endocrine system) and by the local selection pressure already noted. This prediction was in accord with the finding by Snyder (1956), which showed that the incidence of neoteny in this species, is higher at higher altitudes. Furthermore, the response of larvae to thyroxine treatment at 48°F and the occurrence of metamorphosis (Snyder 1956) indicate that the temporary loss of ability to secrete thyroid hormones occurs in type c individuals at higher altitudes (thereby resulting in neoteny), although the loss of tissue sensitivity to thyroid hormones is also likely to occur at lower temperatures. Eagleson (1976) showed that the incidence of metamorphosis in the sample from Lost Lake, British Columbia (100 m above sea level), is 88%, compared with 23.5% in the sample from Goldie Lake, British Columbia (1300 m above sea level). This clearly reflects the increase of genetically determined neoteous individuals (type b) as a result of natural selection at higher altitudes.

Laboratory populations of *Ambystoma mexicanum* represent a case of almost obligatory neoteny, because the animal very seldom undergoes metamorphosis. TRH treatment by Taurog et al. (1974) failed to induce metamorphosis in this species. Furthermore, because pituitaries from this species incubated in vitro with TRH did not stimulate the release of TSH, they suggested that its neoteny might be due to insensitivity of the pituitary to TRH from the hypothalamus. Schulthuis (1960) suggested that either the production or releasing rate of thyrotropin (TRH) is too low to cause sufficient secretion of thyroid hormones for the induction of metamorphosis. Whatever the precise mechanism may be, however, the neoteny in *A. mexicanum* most probably results from the deficiency in thyroid hormones, which in turn results from the functional failure of the pituitary; injection of ovine TSH induces complete metamorphosis (Taurog 1974), supporting this interpretation. It is therefore highly probable that a genetic change, presumably a mutation affecting the pituitary level (Fig. 3), is responsible for the almost obligatory neoteny in this species. In fact, such a gene exists. According to Tompkins (1978), neoteny in *A. mexicanum* is caused by homozygosity for a single recessive gene. Although the site of action of the gene was unknown to Tompkins, it is most likely to affect the pituitary in one way or another, as the endocrinological studies indicate.

This genetic mechanism, which presumably has been inherited from *Ambystoma* ancestors in Mexico, appears to have increased in frequency in laboratories. In their natural habitats near Mexico City, according to Malacinski (1978), spontaneous metamorphosis of this species may reach 75%. Malacinski (1978) attributed the very high percentage of neoteny in laboratories to inadvertently performed selection of inbred lines since 1864; this can occur because neotenous individuals are easier to handle in rearing. Recurrence of the mutant for neoteny (above) also must be considered here.

Deficiency in thyroid hormones, whatever its underlying mechanism may be, is also probably the cause of neoteny in *Eurycea tyrenensis* and *Eurycea neotenes*, because a complete metamorphosis was brought about within 18 days after immersion in a 1:500,000 solution of thyroxine (Kezer 1952). Dent (1968) referred to some other neotenous salamander species (in nature) in which metamorphosis can be brought about by thyroxine treatment. In these species tissues are, as in *A. mexicanum*, competent to respond to thyroid hormones. Therefore, their neoteny might result also from hypofunction of the pituitary gland.

In some salamander species permanent neoteny apparently has resulted from the loss of tissue sensitivity to thyroid hormones. Among the cave-dwelling plethodontids examined, *Haideotriton* is most resistant to thyroxine treatment; it undergoes only few integumentary changes and loses only a single bone, the coronoid (Dundee 1961). Dent (1968) gave other examples of what he called permanent larvae (*Siren, Pseudobranchus, Cryptobranchus, Amphiuma, Proteus*), in which thyroxine treatment has been shown to have very limited effects on metamorphosis. In all these cases, therefore, a genetic change (presumably mutation) appears to have affected the level of tissue sensitivity to thyroid hormones, and hence that of gene regulation (Fig. 6B). In normally metamorphosing amphibians, as already noted, the tissue sensitivity to thyroid hormones tend to become lost at cold temperatures, and this phenomenon appears to have become genetically fixed in these salamanders. It appears probable, therefore, that these taxa (or many of these taxa) arose in cold environments, presumably under the kind of selection pressure *Ambystoma tigrinum* and *A. gracile* have today.

These cases of neoteny can be classified into three phases as follows:

1. The case of *A. tigrinum*, in which neoteny depends on environmental stimulus (cold temperature) and selection, although genetic fixation of neoteny might have occurred in some individuals at higher altitudes (phase 1).

2. Cases of *A. gracile* and *A. mexicanum*, in which genetically determined neotenous individuals have increased as a result of selection (phase 2); a genetic change (presumably a mutation) affecting the secretion of thyroid hormones has resulted in genetically determined neoteny.

3. Other cases of neoteny in which genetically determined neoteny occurs in all individuals of a population as a result of selection (phase 3); a genetic change (presumably a mutation) either at the level of secretion of thyroid hormones and/or at that of tissue sensitivity to thyroid hormones has resulted in genetically determined, permanent neoteny.

Matsuda (1982) has shown that the transition from phase 1 to 3 in genetic fixation of the neotenous morph in salamanders (above) is paralleled by genetic assimilation of the crossveinless phenotype in the experiment with *Drosophila* by Waddington (1953).

In Waddington's (1953) heat-shock experiment (at 40° C for 4 hr, 17–23 hr after puparium formation) it was found that some individuals of the population exhibited an abnormal phenotype, which took the form of the breaking of the posterior crossvein on the wings upon treatment. When selection was applied by choosing for further breeding only those individuals with the broken crossvein, the frequency of crossveinlessness increased from generation to generation of upward selection. After a dozen further generations of upward selection, well over 90% of the individuals developed broken crossveins following the temperature treatment. In each generation of upward selection a fair number of untreated pupae were examined. No crossveinless individual was found among these until generation 14, when a few isolated cases of crossveinless individuals began to appear among untreated flies of upward selected line. *Up to this stage the population of crossveinless phenotype clearly depends on the environmental stimulus (heat shock) and selection, and a genetic mechanism for the production of crossveinless phenotype has started appearing. This stage is clearly comparable with phase 1 of the classification of neoteny in salamanders observed in A. tigrinum.*

In generation 16 of upward selection there were 1–2% of crossveinless individuals developed in the normal environment without heat shock, and from these a number of pair matings were set up. By selection over a few generations among their progeny a number of different strains were derived, some of which produced high frequencies of crossveinless individuals when reared in the normal environment; that is, canalization of development of the crossveinless phenotype occurred. In some of the best line, in fact, the frequency of crossveinless individuals was 100% at 18° C; it was somewhat lower at 25° C. The crossveinlessness, which was an acquired character exhibited only in abnormal environment, has been converted into an inherited character. During this process genetic assimilation of the phenotype occurred as a result of selection of the genetic mechanism, and this stage is comparable to phases 2 and 3 of genetic fixation of the neotenous morph in salamander species.

In *Drosophila*, experimental structural change did not involve the suppression of metamorphosis as in salamanders. Therefore, the magnitudes of underlying genetic changes in the two cases are not comparable. Yet the process of genetic fixation of characters in question is essentially the same, that is, genetic assimilation.

The above parallel between the evolutionary process of neoteny in salamanders and that of genetic assimilation of the crossveinless phenotype pointed out by Matsuda (1982) was rejected by Ho (1984) on the following grounds:

1. The occurrence of coincidental mutation that results in genetic assimilation is unfounded unless the environmentally induced modification causes coincidental mutations to arise more frequently in some way.
2. Because both somatic modification and the coincidental genetic mutation result in the same phenotype, how could natural selection distinguish between the two?

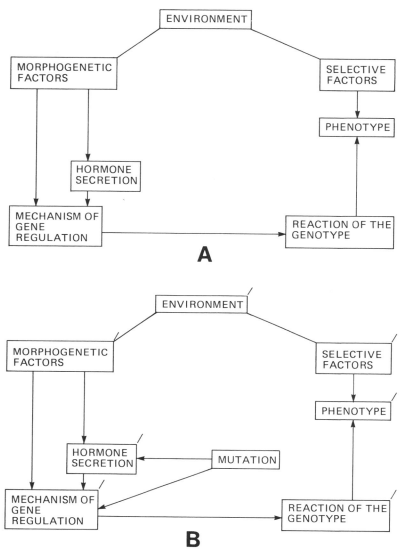

Figure 6. A hypothetical diagram suggesting a more complete process of genetic assimilation of structures through adaptive responses. A given environment consists of the proximate morphogenetic factors (such as temperature and food) that influence the development of animals and ultimate selective factors (such as predation, competition, and some climatic factors that animals have to survive or tolerate). In the original environment (A) proximate morphogenetic factors induce the secretion of morphogenetic hormones (such as ecdysteroids, thyroid hormones) and the mechanism of gene regulation (such as hormone receptors) in target cells responds to the hormones. The hormones, by binding with hormone receptors, induce gene regulation and then the reaction of the genotype and consequent development, leading to the production of the phenotype. The phenotype is adaptive, having been selected for by local selective factors. Because morphogenetic factors would differ considerably both in kind and intensity in a new environment (B) where animals have

3. Organic selection (of Baldwin) proposing coincidental mutation (after the animals have selected new habitats) is untestable.

In answer to objection 1, I would simply point out that the neoteny of *Ambystoma mexicanum* has been nearly completed in laboratories as a result of accumulation of a mutant affecting the pituitary function (see above). Considering the fact that spontaneous metamorphosis of this species could reach 75% of a population in the vicinity of Mexico City, a near complete genetic determination of neoteny achieved in about 100 years can be said to be fast. I (Matsuda 1982) accepted the idea that inadvertent selection for the neotenous form (nonmetamorphosing individuals are easier to rear) contributed to the increase in frequency of the neotenous morph carrying the mutant gene in the offspring. Coincidental mutations that recurred also must have contributed during this process, in the way wing reduction in carabid beetles has become genetically established (Sect. 23D21). Presumably, genetic assimilation could proceed much faster under more stringent selection pressure than in the case of *A. mexicanum*.

Ho's second objection presupposes that natural selection should distinguish genetically and physiologically induced phenotypes with essentially the same morphology and physiology. This is certainly untrue. It is only the phenotype per se that is the direct target of selection, not its genetic background. Quite contrary to what Ho said in her third objection, the Baldwin effect is a very important evolutionary concept which should be explored fully, as discussed in Chap. 5.

Neoteny of *Triturus helveticus* discovered in the congregated population in a pond of Scotland by Dodd and Callan (1955) was unique in that their thyroid glands were goiterous; the enlarged goiterous thyroid glands signify nonsecretion of hormone, which results in neoteny. The reason for this phenomenon was attributed to the effect of kale and turnip cultivated in the vicinity of the pond, which are known to have a goitrogenic effect (the brassica factor). Because the feces of rabbits frequenting the vicinity of water might have been accumulated on the slopes from which water drained into water, Dodd and Callan interpreted that this drainage water contained the brassica factor, and that it might have caused goitrogenous condition of the thyroid glands in the overwintering larvae of *Triturus helveticus*.

---

come to live, each step of the sequence of morphogenesis may be altered and a profound phenotypic modification may occur. If a modified phenotype thus produced is adaptive enough, the number of individuals producing such an adaptive phenotype would increase as a result of selection, and eventually all individuals would respond adaptively to the new environmental stimuli (phase 1 of genetic assimilation). Later, under continued selection pressure, a mutation affecting the level of hormone secretion and (or) that of gene regulation (hormone receptor) would appear to stabilize the developmental process for the phenotype that is essentially the same as the physiologically produced phenotype (genocopy). Accumulation of genocopies (by spreading of such mutants in the offspring and by recurrence of the same mutation) would result in phases 2 and 3 of genetic assimilation. Some other (minor) adaptive improvements of structures must accompany the stabilization of the original adaptive response.

As shown by Rose and Armentrout (1976), the tiger salamander (*Ambystoma tigrinum*) inhabiting permanent sewage sedimentation lagoons (playas) in Estacado, Texas, becomes large and neotenous. Few individuals metamorphose, although some individuals can be induced to metamorphose with thyroxine. In one locality in Lubbock County, when sewage water was used to cool the generator of power station in April 1971, all 13 larvae collected were small morph larvae (which can metamorphose). However, in 3 years the larval size increased by 22%, and none of the larvae collected in 1974 metamorphosed within 60 days, showing how fast they would lose the ability to metamorphose in such a habitat. Knopf (1962) reported that 9 out of 51 larvae from Reese Air Force Base playas failed to metamorphose even after they were injected with triiodothyronine. This indicated that the immediate cause of neoteny is malfunction at the level of thyroid hormone receptors. The large size in this neotenous morph most probably means a prolonged period of prolactin secretion, which in turn delays the time for action of thyroid hormones. This change in the balance between the two antagonistic hormones must have occurred in the sewage.

Rose and Armentrout (1976) contended that in the presence of adequate water, paedomorphic larvae will have a selective advantage, for they can grow to large size, can produce more eggs, and do not face the vicissitudes of the terrestrial environment. When the water is inadequate, there are no such selective advantages. In fact, Rose (1977) found that approximately one-third of a neotenous population inhabiting a small isolated lagoon that was heavily polluted with secondary treated domestic sewage developed neoplastic lesions inducing cancer.

In North America three species of *Gyrinophilus* occur. Of these *G. porphyriticus* develops in springs, seepages, and headwater streams of moist, montane forests (Bruce 1979). It has at least 3 years of larval stage, achieving a relatively large body size, and then metamorphoses within a narrow range of sizes. Two other species are triglobites: *G. palleucus*, a paedomorph (Brandon 1971), and *G. subterraneus*, a species (or an extreme of a highly variable population of *G. porphyriticus*, Blaney and Blaney 1978) approaching paedomorphosis, as witnessed by its very large larval size relative to adult size (Besharse and Holsinger 1977).

Presumably, larval metagenetic neoteny in *G. palleucus* has been induced by continuous darkness, which has affected the pattern of thyroid hormone secretion. This interpretation is supported by the experiments by Doetsch (1949) and Milne (1950), which showed that the tadpoles of *Rana* spp. do not metamorphose when they are kept in darkness. The influence of light by way of the TRH–TSH–TH axis is known. Presumably, in the darkness a sufficient amount of thyroid hormones for metamorphosis is not released. In this species metamorphosis can be induced by thyroxine treatment (Dent et al. 1955, Dent and Kirby-Smith 1963).

According to Bruce (1979), metamorphosing *G. porphyriticus* feed largely on aquatic invertebrates as larvae. However, as adults they feed heavily on other species of salamanders. Cave-dwelling, neotenous species of *Gyrinophilus*, on the other hand, feed on available invertebrates in the lack of other species of salamanders. Thus in this habitat even transformed adults must utilize invertebrate resources. Bruce (1979) therefore contended that the cost of metamorphosis might outweigh any benefit, and that selection would thereby act toward prolongation of the larval phase. Similarly, Brandon (1971) suggested that neoteny in *G. palleucus* is the response to lower food supply. Most probably, however, the cave neoteny here arose initially as the physiological response of the animals to darkness. The resultant larviform phenotype and physiology (for food requirement) were incidentally adaptive (adaptive response). Presumably, the kind of selective pressure Bruce proposed has reinforced or improved the physiological mechanism for neoteny.

Following the initial metamorphosis from the larva to the adult, some salamanders undergo yet another, second metamorphosis. The best-known example of second metamorphosis is that of *Notophthalmus viridescens*, in which the larval form is aquatic, with external gills, a smooth skin, green pigmentation, and a laterally compressed tail. During the initial metamorphosis the larva transforms into a bright orange, terrestrial juvenile called the "eft." The eft, after a period of growth which lasts for 3–4 years, reenters water (water drive), where it completes the second metamorphosis and becomes sexually mature. Although the external gills are not re-formed, the adult assumes many larval characteristics and the structural changes include the disappearance of the thick reddish and water-repellent epidermis and the appearance of olive-colored smooth and shiny skin, a functional lateral line, and the tail keel (Chadwick 1940, Grant 1961, Grant and Cooper 1964, 1965), as well as synthesis of porphyropsin visual pigments characteristic of aquatic vertebrates (Grant 1961, Crim 1975). Thus the consequence of two metamorphoses is the reversal to a neoteny without gills.

It has now been well established since the earlier works by Chadwick (1940, 1941), Grant and Cooper (1964, 1965), Crim (1975), and others that prolactin plays an important role in inducing the water drive of the red eft and the consequent physiological and structural changes suited for the aquatic life. The experiment of Gona et al. (1970) indicated a synergistic action of the thyroid hormone; second metamorphosis appears to be brought about by a reversal of the prolactin level of the eft phase to a high prolactin–low thyroid level. Hurlbert (1969) found that when migrating efts reach breeding ponds they move in and out from water to land and from pond to pond, suggesting that actually prolactin may stimulate initially heightened locomotor wandering between breeding ponds and land, rather than an immediate and clear-cut aquatic habitat preference. This field observation was supported by the experiment with *Ambystoma tigrinum* by Duval and Norris (1978). Prolactin also regulates permeability of the skin in *Notophthalmus* and *Triturus* (Mazzi et al. 1980), and appears to play a role in the male sexual behavior in the aquatic environment (Giorgio et al. 1982).

With reference to the environmental triggering of the water drive, Chadwick

(1941) speculated that temperature, humidity, day length, and the availability or deficiency in mineral salts are concerned with the release of the water drive factor. The experiment of Meier et al. (1971) with *N. viridescens* showed that daily injections of prolactin to the eft late during a 16-hr photoperiod are more effective in promoting the water drive than are injections of prolactin given early or midday. Smith's (1972) study showed the temperature-induced delays in prolactin-initiated water drive in *N. viridescens*; placing newts at 4° C inhibited prolactin-initiated water drive, but when they were returned to 20° C they underwent the second metamorphosis. Thus these studies still did not elucidate the mechanism of the reversal of the hormonal balance during first metamorphosis to the high prolactin – low thyroid hormones level necessary for the water drive.

High morphogenetic plasticity of *N. viridescens* is reflected further by the fact that the adult is occasionally branchiate, especially on the coastal plains of the eastern United States, where the terrain is dry and sandy and ponds lack fish (Bishop 1941), and in southern Illinois, where ponds are permanent and fish are absent (Brandon and Bremer 1966); Brandon and Bremer called such a branchiate adult "neoteny." Healy (1970) observed that as permanent bodies of water gradually disappeared during a drought on a local coastal plain, the incidence of such a neoteny in *N. viridescens* populations decreased. This fact appears to mean that the amount of water available to sustain the development of neotenous individuals became insufficient.

References

Abdel-Wahab, M. F., K. S. Warren, and R. R. Levy. (1971). Function of the thyroid and host–parasite relation in marine *Schistosomiasis mansoni, J. Infect. Dis.,* **124,** 161–171.

Abele, L. G., T. Gilmour, and S. Gilchrist. (1983). Size and shape in the phylum Phoronida, *J. Zool. Soc. Lond.,* **200,** 317–323.

Addis, C. J. (1946). Experiments on the relation between sex hormones and the growth of tapeworm *(Hymenolepis diminuta), J. Parasitol.,* **32,** 574–580.

Adiyodi, K. G., and R. G. Adiyodi. (1970). Endocrine control of reproduction in decapod Crustacea, *Biol. Rev.,* **45,** 121–165.

Ae, S. A. (1957). Effects of photoperiod on *Colias eurytheme, Lepid. News,* **11,** 207–214.

Aizenshtadt, T. B. (1978). Study of oogenesis in *Hydra.* Communication III. Growth and function of oocytes, *Sov. J. Dev. Biol.,* **9,** 95–105.

Aizenshtadt, T. B., and D. G. Polteva. (1982). Vitellogenesis in the hydroid polyp, *Sov. J. Dev. Biol.,* **13,** 23–30.

Åkesson, B. (1958). *A Study of the Nervous System of the Sipunculidae with Some Remarks on the Development of Two Species,* Phascolion strombi *Montagu and* Golfingia minuta *Kieferstein,* G. W. K. Gleerup, Lund, 249 pp.

Alberch, P. (1981). Convergence and parallelism in foot morphology in the neotropical salamander genus *Bolitoglossa.* I. Function, *Evolution,* **35,** 84–100.

Alberch, P., and J. Alberch. (1981). Heterochronic mechanism of morphological diversification and evolutionary change in the neotropical salamanders, *Bolitoglossa occidentalis* (Amphibia: Plethodontidae), *J. Morphol.* **167,** 249–263.

Alberch, P., S. J. Gould, G. F. Oster, and D. B. Wake. (1979). Size and shape in ontogeny and phylogeny, *Paleobiology,* **5,** 296–317.

Albrecht, F. O. (1964). Etat hygrométrique, coloration, et résistance chez l'imago de *Locusta migratoria migratorioides* R. & F., *Experientia,* **20,** 97.

Albrecht, F. O., and J. Lauga. (1978). Influence du photopériodisme et de la température d'élevage sur la morphologie et la phase de *Locusta migratoria migratorioiodes* (R. & F.) (Orthoptère, Acridiens), *C. R. Acad. Sci. Ser D.,* **286,** 1799–1801.

Albrecht, F. O., M. Verdier, and R. E. Blackwith. (1959). Maternal control of ovariole number in the progeny of the migratory locust, *Nature* **184,** 103–104.

Amerasinghe, F. P. (1978). Effects of juvenile hormone 1 and juvenile hormone 3 on yellowing sexual activity and pheromone production in allatectomized male *Schistocerca gregaria, J. Insect Physiol.,* **24,** 603–612.

Ammar, E. D. (1973). Factors related to the two wing forms in *Javesella pellucida* (Fabr.) (Homoptera: Delphacidae), *Z. Angew. Entomol.,* **74,** 211–216.

Ananthakrishnan, T. N. (1969). *Indian Thysanoptera,* CSIR Zoological Monograph No. 1, New Delhi.

Ananthakrishnan, T. N. (1984). *Bioecology of Thrips,* Indian Publishing House, Oak Park, MI.

Anderson, D. T. (1972a). "The development of hemimetabolous insects," in *Developmental Systems: Insects,* Vol. 1. S. J. Counce and C. H. W. Waddington, Eds., Academic, New York, pp. 95–163.

Anderson, D. T. (1972b). "The development of holometabolous insects," in *Developmental Systems: Insects,* Vol. 1. S. J. Counce and C. H. W. Waddington, Eds., Academic, New York, pp. 165–242.

Anderson, D. T. (1973). *Embryology and Phylogeny in Annelid and Arthropods,* Pergamon, Oxford.

Anderson, D. T., and S. M. Manton. (1972). Studies on the Onychophora VIII: The relationship between the embryos and the oviduct in the viviparous onychophorans, *Epiperipatus trinidadensis* (Bouvier) and *Macroperipatus torquatus* (Kennel) from Trinidad, *Phil. Trans. R. Soc. Lond. Ser. B.,* **264,** 161–189.

Anderson, W. W. (1966). *The shrimp and shrimp fishery of the southern United States,* U.S. Fish and Wildlife Service, Fish. Leaflet 589.

André, F., F. Barbe, and S. Rivière. (1971). Mécanismes endocrines du dépôt des cocons chez *Eisenia, Bull. Soc. Zool. Fr.,* **96,** 309–404.

Andries, J. C. (1979). Effect of exogenous JH 1 on imaginal determination in *Aeshna cyanea. J. Insect Physiol.,* **25,** 621–627.

Angel, M. V. (1967). "A histological experimental approach to neurosecretion in *Daphnia magna,*" in *Neurosecretion,* F. Stutinsky, Ed. Springer, Berlin, pp. 229–237.

Aoki, S. (1977). *Colophina clematis* (Homoptera, Pemphigidae) an aphid species with soldiers, *Kontyu,* **45,** 276–282.

Aoki, S. (1982). "Soldiers and altruistic dispersal in aphids," *The Biology of Social Insects,* M. D. Breed et al., Eds., Westview Press, Boulder, CO, pp. 154–158.

Applebaum, S. W., B. Raccah, and R. Leiserowitz. (1975). Effects of juvenile hormone and β-ecdysone on wing determination in the aphid, *Myzus persicae, J. Insect Physiol.,* **21,** 1279–1281.

Arai, T. (1978). Effects of environmental conditions on the wing form and growth in *Gryllodes sigillatus* Walker (Orthoptera: Gryllidae), *Jap. J. Ecol.,* **28,** 135–142.

Arnaud, J., M. Brunet, and J. Mazza. (1982). Etude de l'ovogénèse chez *Centropages typicus* (Copepoda, Calanoida), *Reprod. Nutr. Dev.,* **22,** 537–555.

Arnaud, P. M. (1974). Contribution à la bionomie marine benthique des régions antarctiques et subantarctiques, *Tethys,* **3**, 465–656.

Asencot, M., and Y. Lensky. (1984). Juvenile hormone induction on the female honey bee (*Apis mellifera* L.) larvae reared on worker jelly and on stored royal jelly, *Comp. Biochem. Physiol.,* **78B**, 109–117.

Ashley, H., P. Katti, and E. Frieden. (1968). Urea excretion in the bullfrog tadpole; effects of temperature, metamorphosis and thyroid hormones, *Dev. Biol.,* **17**, 293–307.

Askew, R. R. (1971). *Parasitic Insects,* Elsevier, New York.

Aubert, J. (1945). Le microptérisme chez les Plécoptères (Perlariés), *Rev. Suisse Zool.,* **52**, 395–398.

Avise, J. C. (1976). Genetics of plate morphology in an unusual population of threespine sticklebacks *(Gasterosteus aculeatus),* *Genet. Res.,* **27**, 33–46.

Ax, P. (1963a). "Relationships and phylogeny of the Turbellaria," in *The Lower Metazoa. Comparative Biology and Phylogeny,* E. C. Dougherty, Ed., University of California Press, Berkeley, CA, pp. 191–224.

Ax, P. (1963b). Die Ausbildung eines Schwanzfadens in der interstitiellen Sandfauna und die Verwertbarkeit von Lebensformcharacteren für die Verwandtschaftsforschung, *Zool. Anz.,* **171**, 51–76.

Ax, P. (1966). Die Bedeutung der interstitiellen Sandfauna für allgemeine Probleme der Systematik, Ökologie und Biologie, *Veroeff. Inst. Meeresforsch. Bremerhaven,* **2**, 15–66.

Ax, P. (1967). *Diurodrilus ankeli* nov. spec. (Archiannelida) der nordamerikanischen Pazifikküste. Ein Beitrag zur Morphologie, Systematik and Verbreitung der Gattung *Diurodrilus, Z. Morphol. Oekol. Tiere,* **60**, 5–16.

Axelson, J. (1961). On the dimorphism in *Cyclops scutifer* (Sars) and cyclomorphosis in *Daphnia galeata* (Sars). *Rep. Inst. Freshwater Res. Drottningholm,* **42**, 169–182.

Ayala, F. J. (1977). "The genetic structure of population," in *Evolution,* T. Dobzhansky et al. Eds., New York, pp. 20–56.

Badonnel, A. (1938). Sur la biologie de *Psyllipsocus ramburi* Selys-Longchamps, *Bull. Soc. Zool. Fr.,* **43**, 153–158.

Badonnel, A. (1948). L'effet de groupe chez *Psyllipsocus ramburi* Selys-Longchamps (Psocoptères), *Bull. Soc. Zool. Fr.,* **73**, 80–83.

Badonnel, A. (1951). "Ordre des Psocoptères," in *Traité de Zoologie,* Vol. 10, P.-P. Grassé, Ed., Masson, Paris, pp. 1301–1340.

Badonnel, A. (1959). Sur le déterminisme des ailes de *Psyllipsocus ramburi* Selys-Longchamps, *Bull. Soc. Zool. Fr.,* **84**, 91–98.

Badonnel, A. (1970). Sur les glandes ecdysiales des Psocoptères, *Bull. Soc. Zool. Fr.,* **95**, 861–868.

Baehr, J.-C., P. Cassier, C. Caussanel, and P. Porcheron. (1982). Activity of corpora allata, endocrine balance and reproduction in female *Labidura riparia* (Dermaptera), *Cell Tissue Res.,* **225**, 267–282.

Baer, J. G. (1951). *Ecology of animal parasites,* University of Illinois Press, Urbana, IL.

Bährmann, R. (1973). Anatomisch-morphologisch und histologische Untersuchungen an der Saison-formen von *Aleurochiton complanatus* (Baerensprung) (Homoptera, Aleyrodina) unter besonderer Berücksichtigung der Dormanzentwicklung, *Zool. Jahrb. Syst.,* **100**, 107–169.

252   REFERENCES

Bährmann, R. (1974a). Anatomisch-morphologische und ökologische Untersuchungen an den Intermediärformen von *Aleurochiton complanatus* (Baerensprung) (Homoptera, Aleyrodina) unter besonderer Berücksichtigung der Dormanz, *Zool. Jahrb. Syst.*, **101**, 269–293.

Bährmann, R. (1974b). Zur Entwicklung der Ökomorphosen von *Neobemisia paveli* Zahradnik (Homoptera, Aleyrodina), *Zool. Anz.*. **193**, 336–349.

Bährmann, R. (1978). Rasterelektronenmikroskopische Untersuchungen an den Ökomorphosen (Subitan- und Latenz Puparien) von *Aleurochiton complanatus* (Baerensprung) (Homoptera, Aleyrodina), *Zool. Jahrb. Syst.*, **105**, 474–485.

Bährmann, R. (1979). Ökomorphosen und Dormanz- Nondormanzentwicklung am Beispiel von *Aleurochiton complanatus* (Baerensprung) (Homoptera, Aleyrodina), *Biol. Zentralbl.* **98**, 553–571.

Baid, I. (1964). Neoteny in the genus *Artemia, Acta Zool.*, **45**, 167–177.

Baker, T. C., and G. C. Eickwort. (1975). Development and bionomics of *Chrysomelobia labidomerae* (Acari: Tarsonemina: Podapolipidae), a parasite of the milkweed leaf beetle (Coleoptera: Chrysomelidae), *Can. Entomol.*, **106**, 627–638.

Baldwin, J. M. (1896). A new factor in evolution, *Am. Nat.*, **30**, 441–451, 536–553.

Baldwin, J. M. (1902). *Development and evolution,* Macmillan, New York.

Ball, J. N. (1981). Hypothetical control of the pars distalis in fishes, amphibians, and reptiles, *Gen. Comp. Endocrinol.*, **44**, 135–170.

Balon, E. K. (1975a). Terminology of intervals in fish development, *J. Fish. Res. Bd. Can.*, **32**, 1663–1670.

Balon, E. K. (1975b). Reproductive guilds of fishes, a proposal of definition, *J. Fish. Res. Bd. Can.*, **32**, 821–864.

Balon, E. K. (1977). Early ontogeny of *Labeotropheus* Ahl. 1927 (Mbuna, Cichlidae, Lake Malawi), with a discussion on advanced protective styles in fish reproduction and development, *Environ. Biol. Fish*, **2**, 147–176.

Baltzer, F. (1912). Über die Entwicklungsgeschichte von *Bonellia, Verh. Dtsch. Zool. Ges.*, **33**, 252–261.

Baltzer, F. (1914). Die Bestimmung und der Dimorphismus des Geschlechtes bei *Bonellia, Sber. Phys-med. Ges. Wuerzb.*, **43**, 1–4.

Baltzer, F. (1925). Untersuchungen über die Entwicklung und Geschlechtsbestimmung der *Bonellia, Publ. Stn. Zool. Napoli*, **6**, 223–287.

Barber, H. G. (1911). Descriptions of some new Hemiptera–Heteroptera, *J. N.Y Entomol. Soc.,*19, 23–31.

Barber, H. S. (1913a). Observation on the life history of *Micromalthus debilis* Lec. (Coleoptera), *Proc. Entomol. Soc. Wash.*, **15**, 31–38.

Barber, H. S. (1913b). The remarkable life history of a new family (Micromalthidae) of beetles, *Proc. Biol. Soc. Wash.*, **26**, 185–190.

Barker, J. F. (1978). Neuroendocrine regulation of oocyte maturation in the imported fire ant *Solenopsis invicta, Gen. Comp. Endocrinol.*, **35**, 234–237.

Barrington, E. J. W. (1978). "Evolutionary aspects of hormonal structure and function," in *Comparative Endocrinology*, P. J. Gaillard and H. H. Boer, Eds., Elsevier/North Holland, Amsterdam, pp. 381–396.

Bartok, P. (1944). A *Bathynella chappuisi* fejlodes morfologiaja, *Acta Sci. Math. Nat. Univ. Francisco-Josephina Kolozsvar*, **21**, 1–46.

Beck, S. D. (1971a). Growth and retrogression in larvae of *Trogoderma glabrum* (Coleoptera: Dermestidae). 1. Characteristics under feeding and starvation conditions *Ann. Entomol. Soc. Am.,* **64,** 149–155.

Beck, S. D. (1971b). Growth and retrogression in larvae of *Trogoderma glabrum* (Coleoptera: Dermestidae). 2. Factors influencing pupation, *Ann. Entomol. Soc. Am.,* **64,** 946–949.

Beck, S. D. (1972). Growth and retrogression in larvae of *Trogoderma glabrum* (Coleoptera: Dermestidae). 3. Ecdysis and form determination. *Ann. Entomol. Soc. Am.,* **65,** 1319–1325.

Behrens, W., and K. H. Hoffmann. (1983). Effects of exogenous ecdysteroids on reproduction in crickets, *Gryllus bimaculatus, Int. J. Invertebr. Reprod.,* **6,** 149–159.

Beier, M. (1968a). "Mantodea (Fangheuschrecken)", in *Handbuch der Zoologie,* Vol. 4, Section 2, Part 12, J. G. Helmcke et al., Eds., W. de Gruyter, Berlin, pp. 1–47.

Beier, M. (1968b). "Phasmida," in *Handbuch der Zoologie,* Vol. 4, Part 2, J. G. Helmcke et al., Eds., W. de Gruyter, Berlin, pp. 1–56.

Bell, B. M. (1975). Ontogeny and systematics of *Timeischytes casteri* n. sp.: An enigmatic Devonian edriasteroid, *Bull. Am. Paleontol.,* **67**(287), 33–56.

Bell, B. M. (1976). Phylogenetic implications of ontogenetic development in the class Edriesteroidea (Echinodermata), *J. Paleontol.,* **50,** 1001–1019.

Bell, M. A. (1974). Reduction and loss of the pelvic girdle in *Gelasterosteus* (Pisces): A case of parallel evolution, *Nat. Hist. Mus. Los Ang. Cty. Contrib. Sci.,* **257,** 1–36.

Bell, M. A. (1979). Persistence of ancestral sister species, *Syst. Zool.,* **28,** 85–88.

Bell, M. A. (1981). Lateral plate polymorphism and ontogeny of the complete plate morph of threespine sticklebacks *(Gasterosteus aculeatus), Evolution,* **35,** 67–74.

Belles, X., and M. I. Baldellou. (1983). Precocious metamorphosis induced by precocene on *Oxycarenus lavaterae, Entomol. Exp. Appl.,* **34,** 129–133.

Bemis, W. E. (1981). Studies on dipnoan skulls, *Am. Zool.,* **21,** 1022.

Bemis, W. E. (1984). Paedomorphosis and the evolution of the Dipnoi, *Paleobiology,* **10,** 293–307.

Benazzi, M. (1974). "Fissioning in planarians from a genetic standpoint," in *Biology of the Turbellaria,* N. W. Riser and M. P. Morse, Eds., McGraw-Hill, New York, pp. 476–492.

Bentley, M. G. (1982). Gonadotropic hormone in the polychaete *Nephthys hombergii* and *Nephthys caeca,* an in vitro approach, *Gen. Comp. Endocrinol.,* **46,** 369.

Bentley, M. G., and P. J. W. Olive. (1982). An in vitro assay for gonadotrophic hormone in the polychaete *Nephthys hombergii* Sav. (Nephthyidae), *Gen. Comp. Endocrinol.,* **47,** 467–474.

Bergerard, J. (1975). Cycle sexuel saisonnier dans une population naturelle de *Littorina saxatilis* (Olivi) (Gastropode Prosobranche), *Bull. Soc. Zool. Fr.,* **100,** 133–145.

Bergerard, J., and D. Caugant. (1981). Cycle sexuel saisonnier de *Littorina saxatilis* (Mollusque Prosobranche) et son déterminisme, *Bull. Soc. Zool. Fr.,* **106,** 277–282.

Berlese, A. (1913). Intorno alle metamorphosis degli insetti, *Redia,* **9,** 121–136.

Bern, H. A. (1983). Functional evolution of prolactin and growth hormone in lower vertebrates, *Am. Zool.,* **23,** 663–671.

Bern, H. A., C. S. Nicol, and R. C. Strohman. (1967). Prolactin and tadpole growth, *Proc. Soc. Exp. Biol. Med.,* **126,** 518–520.

Berrill, M. H. (1977). Dwarfism on a sabellid polychaete, a study of an interstitial species, *Biol. Bull.,* **153,** 113–120.

Berrill, N. J. (1931). Studies in tunicate development II. Abbreviation of development in the Molgulidae, *Phil. Trans.,* **219,** 281–341.

Berrill, N. J. (1949). Developmental analysis of Scyphystomae, *Biol. Rev.,* **24,** 393–410.

Berrill, N. J. (1955). *The Origin of Vertebrates,* Clarendon Press, Oxford.

Berrill, N. J. (1975). "Chordata: Tunicata," in *Reproduction of Marine Invertebrates,* A. C. Giese and J. S. Pearse, Eds., Academic, New York, pp. 241–282.

Berry, E. G. (1943). The Amnicolidae of Michigan: Distribution, ecology and taxonomy, *Misc. Publ. Mus. Zool. Univ. Mich.,* **57,** 1–68.

Bertelsen, E. (1951). *The Ceratioid Fishes,* The Carlsberg Foundation Dana-report **37,** Copenhagen, pp. 1–276.

Berthold, G. (1973). Der Einfluss der Corpora allata auf die Pigmentierung von *Carausius morosus* Br., *Wilhelm Roux Arch.,* **173,** 249–262.

Berven, K. A. (1982). The genetic basis off altitudinal variation in the wood frog *Rana sylvatica.* 1. An experimental basis of life history traits, *Evolution,* **36,** 962–983.

Besharse, J. C., and J. R. Holsinger. (1977). *Gyrinophilus subterraneus,* a new triglobitic salamander from southern West Virginia, *Copeia,* **1977,** 624–634.

Betsch, J.-M. (1975). Existence de deux phases juvéniles chez les Collemboles, Symphypleones, *C. R. Acad. Sci.,* **281,** 1601–1603.

Betsch, J.-M., and G. Vannier. (1977). Caractérisation des deux phases juvéniles d'*Allacma fusca* (Collembola Sympleona) par leur morphologie et leur écophysiologie, *Z. Zool. Syst. Evolutions forsch.,* **15,** 124–141.

Beveridge, M. (1982). Taxonomy, environment and reproduction in freshwater triclads (Turbellaria: Tricladida), *Int. J. Inverteb. Reprod.,* **5,** 107–113.

Bezzi, M. (1916). Riduzione e scomparsa delle ali nengli insetti ditteri, *Natura,* **7,** 85–182.

Bhaskaran, G., and G. Jones. (1980). Neuroendocrine regulation of corpus allatum activity in *Manduca sexta*: The endocrine basis for starvation-induced supernumerary larval molt, *J. Insect Physiol.,* **26,** 431–440.

Bierne, J. (1964). Maturation sexuelle anticipée par décapitation de la femelle chez l'hétéronémerte *Lineus ruber* Müller, *C. R. Acad. Sci.,* **259,** 4841–4843.

Bierne, J. (1966). Localisation dans les ganglions cérébroïdes du centre régulateur de la maturation sexuelle chez la femelle de *Lineus ruber* Müller (Hétéronémertes), *C. R. Acad. Sci.,* **262,** 1572–1575.

Bierne, J. (1970). Recherches sur la differenciation sexuelle au cours de l'ontogénèse et de la régénération chez le némertien *Lineus ruber* Müller, *Ann. Sci. Nat. Zool. Biol. Anim.,* **12,** 181–298.

Bierne, J. (1973). Contrôle neuroendocrinien de la puberté chez le mâle de *Lineus ruber* (Hétéronémerte), *C. R. Acad. Sci.,* **276,** 363–366.

Bierne, J., and J. Rué. (1979). Endocrine control in two rhynchocoelan worms, *Int. J. Inverteb. Reprod.,* **1,** 109–120.

Birky, C. W. (1969). The developmental genetics of polymorphism in the rotifer *Asplanchna.* III Quantitative modification of developmental responses to vitamin E, by the genome, physiological state, and population density of reproductive females, *J. Exp. Zool.,* **170,** 437–448.

Bishop, S. C. (1941). The salamanders of New York, *N.Y. State Mus. Bull.*, **324**, 1–365.

Bizer, J. H. (1978). Growth rates and size at metamorphosis of higher elevation populations of *Ambystoma tigrinum, Oecologia,* **34**, 175–184.

Blackburn, D. G. (1984). From whale toes to snake eyes: Comments on the reversibility of evolution, *Syst. Zool.,* **33**, 241–245.

Blackman, R. L. (1972). The inheritance of life cycle differences in *Myzus persicae* (Sulz.) (Hem., Aphididae), *Bull. Entomol. Res.,* **62**, 281–294.

Blackman, R. L. (1974). Life cycle variation of *Myzus persicae* (Sulz.) (Hom. Aphididae) in different parts of the world, in relation to genotype and environment, *Bull. Entomol. Res.,* **63**, 595–607.

Blackman, R. L. (1978). Early development of the parthenogenetic egg in three species of aphids (Homoptera: Aphididae), *Int. J. Insect Morphol. Embryol.,* **7**, 33–44.

Blackman, R. L. (1981). "Species, sex and parthenogenesis in aphids," in *The Evolving Biosphere*, P. L. Forey, Ed., Cambridge University Press, pp. 75–85.

Blanchet-Tournier, M.-F. (1982). Quelques aspects des interactions hormonale entre la mue et vitellogenèse chez le crustacé amphipode *Orchestia gammarellus, Reprod. Nutr. Dev.,* **22**, 325–344.

Blanchet-Tournier, M. F., J.-J. Meusy, and H. Junera. (1980). Mue et vitel logenese chez le crustace Amphipode *Orchestia gammarella* (Pallas). Etude des éffets de la destruction de la région antéro-médiane du protocérébron sur la synthèse de la vitellogénine, *C. R. Acad. Sci.,* **291**, 829–833.

Blaney, R. M., and P. K. Blaney. (1978). Significance of extreme variation in a cave population of the salamander *Gyrinophilus porphyriticus, Proc. Acad. Sci. W.Va.,* **50**, 23.

Blankespoor, H. D. (1974). Host induced variation in *Plagiorchis nobeli* Park, 1936 (Plagiorchidae: Trematoda), *Am. Midl. Nat.,* **92**, 415–433.

Bliss, D. E. (1954a). Light inhibition of regeneration and growth in the crab *Gecarcinus lateralis, Anat. Rec.,* **120**, 742–743.

Bliss, D. E. (1954b). Inhibition of regeneration and growth in *Gecarcinus lateralis* by prolonged exposure to constant darkness, *Anat. Rec.,* **120**, 799.

Bliss, D. E. (1968). Transition from water to land in decapod crustaceans, *Am. Zool.,* **8**, 355–392.

Bocquet-Verdine, J. (1961). Monographie de *Chthamalophilus delagei* J. Bocquet-Verdine. Rhizocéphale parasite de *Chthamalophilus malophilus stellatus* (Poli), *Cah. Biol. Mar.,* **2**, 455–593.

Bocquet-Verdine, J. (1969). La larve du rhizocéphale *Boschmaella balani, Arch. Zool. Exp. Gen.,* **110**, 279–287.

Bocquet-Verdine. J. (1972). Le parasitisme multiple du cirripède operculé *Balanus improvisus* Darwin par le rhizocéphale *Boschmaella balani* (J. Bocquet-Verdine), *Arch. Zool. Exp. Gen.,* **113**, 239–244.

Boelsterli, U. (1975). Notes on oogenesis in *Tubularia crocea* Agassiz. (Athecata, Hydrozoa), *Publ. Stn. Zool. Napoli,* **39**, Suppl. 1, 53–66.

Bohlken, S. (1977). "The influence of daylength on body growth and female reproductive activity in the pond snail (*Lymnaea stagnalis*)," in *Abstracts of the 6th European Malacological Congress,* Amsterdam, p. 98.

Bohlken, S., and J. Josse. (1982). The effect of photoperiod on female reproductive activity of the freshwater pulmonate snail *Lymnaea stagnalis* kept under laboratory breeding conditions, *Int. J. Inverteb. Reprod.,* **4**, 213–222.

Boletzky, S. (1981). Réflexion sur les stratégies de reproduction chez les céphalopodes, *Bull. Soc. Zool. Fr.,* **106**, 293–305.

Bonar, D. B. (1978). "Morphogenesis at metamorphosis in opistobranch molluscs," in *Settlement and Metamorphosis of Marine Invertebrate Larvae,* F. S. Chia and M. Rice, Eds., Elsevier, New York, pp. 177–196.

Bonaric, J. C., and M. De Reggi. (1977). Changes in ecdysone level in the spider *Pisaura mirabilis* nymphs (Araneae, Pisauridae), *Experientia,* **33**, 1664–1665.

Bonnemaison, L. E. (1951). Contribution à l'étude des facteurs provoquent d'apparition des formes ailées et sexuées chez les Aphidinae, *Ann. Epiphyt.,* **2**, 1–380.

Bonnemaison, L. E. (1952). Remarques sur les migrations chez les Aphidinae, *Trans. Ninth Int. Congr. Entomol.,* **1**, 400–403.

Bonnemaison, L. E., and J. Missonnier. (1955). Recherches sur le déterminisme des formes estivales ou hivernales de la diapause chez le psylle des Poiriers (*Psylla pyri* L.), *Ann. I. N. R. A. Ser. Epiphyt.,* **4**, 417–528.

Börner, C. (1910). Parametabolie und Neotenie bei Cocciden, *Zool. Anz.,* **35**, 553–561.

Borradaile, L. A., et al. (1961). *The Invertebrata,* 4th ed., Cambridge University Press.

Boss, K. J. (1982). "Molluscs," in *Synopsis and Classification of Living Organisms,* S. P. Parker et al., Eds., McGraw-Hill, New York, pp. 945–1166.

Botticelli, C. R., F. L. Hisaw, Jr., and W. D. Roth. (1963). Estradiol 17β, estrone, and progesterone in the ovaries of lamprey *(Petromyzon marinus), Proc. Soc. Exp. Biol. Med.,* **114**, 255–257.

Bouligand, Y. (1966). "Recherches récentes sur les copépodes, associés aux Anthozoaires," in *Cnidaria and their evolution,* Symposium of the Zoological Society of London, Vol. 16, pp. 267–306.

Bounhiol, J.-J. (1970). La formation de l'imago chez les lépidoptères. Les facteurs déterminants en particulier ceux d'origine endocrinienne, *Arch. Zool. Exp. Gen.,* **112**, 591–623.

Bousfield, E. (1968). Terrestrial adaptation in Crustacea, *Am. Zool.,* **8**, 393–398.

Bowers, W. S., T. Ohta, J. S. Cleere, and P. A. Marsella. (1976). Discovery of insect anti-juvenile hormones in plants, *Science,* **193**, 542–547.

Boyce, M. S. (1984). Restitution of *r*- and *K*- selection as a model of density-dependent natural selection, *Ann. Rev. Ecol. Syst.,* **15**, 427–447.

Boycott, A. E. (1934). The habitats of land Mollusca in Britain, *J. Ecol.,* **22**, 1–38.

Boycott, A. E. (1938). Experiments on the artificial breeding of *Limnaea involuta, Limnaea burnetti* and other forms of *Limnaea peregra, Prod. Malac. Soc. Lond.,* **23**, 101–108.

Bradley, J. T., and T. Simpson. (1981). Brain neurosecretion during ovarian development and after ovariotectomy in adult *Acheta domestica* L., *Gen. Comp. Endocrinol.,* **44**, 117–127.

Brandon, R. A. (1971). North American triglobitic salamanders: Some aspects of modification in cave habitat, with special reference to *Gyrinophilus palleucus, Bull. Nat. Speleol. Soc.,* **33**, 1–21.

Brandon, R. A., and D. J. Bremer. (1966). Neotenic genus *Notophthalmus viridescens louisianensis* in southern Illinois, *Herpetologica,* **22**, 213–217.

Bresciani, J., and J. Lützen. (1972). The sexuality of *Aphanodomus* (parasitic copepod) and the phenomenon of cryptogonochorism, *Vidensk. Meddr. Dansk. Naturh. Foren.*, **135**, 7–20.

Bresciani, J., and J. Lützen. (1974). On the biology and development of *Aphanodomus* Wilson (Xenocoelomidae), a parasitic copepod of the polychaete *Telepus cincinnatus, Vidensk. Medd. Dansk. Naturh. Foren.*, **137**, 25–63.

Brewin, B. I. (1956). The growth and development of a viviparous compound ascidians *Hypsistozoa fasmeriana, Ql. J. Microsc. Sci.*, **97**, 435–454.

Brian, M. V. (1959). "The neurosecretory cells of the brain, the corpora cardiaca and the corpora allata during caste determination of ants," in *The Ontogeny of Insects*, J. Hrdy, Ed., Czech. Acad. Sci. Prague, pp. 167–171.

Brian, M. V. (1963). Studies of caste differentiation in *Myrmica rubra* L., *Insect Soc.*, **10**, 91–102.

Brian, M. V. (1965). Caste differentiation in social insects, *Symp. Zool. Soc. Lond.*, **14**, 13–38.

Brian, M. V. (1969). Male production in the ant *Myrmica rubra* L., *Insect Soc.*, **16**, 249–268.

Brian, M. V. (1974). Caste differentiation in *Myrmica rubra*. The role of hormones, *J. Insect Physiol.*, **20**, 1351–1365.

Brian, M. V., and J. Hibbie. (1964). Studies of caste differentiation in *Myrmica rubra* L. 7. caste bias, queen *ahe* and influence, *Insect Soc.*, **11**, 223–238.

Brinck, P. (1949). Studies on Swedish stoneflies, *Opusc. Entomol. Suppl.*, **11**, 1–250.

Brinkhurst, R. O. (1959). Alary polymorphism in Gerroidea (Hemiptera–Heteroptera), *J. Anim. Ecol.*, **28**, 211–230.

Brinkhurst, R. O. (1963). Observation on wing-polymorphism in the Heteroptera, *Proc. R. Entomol. Soc. Lond.*, **38**, 15–32.

Broadhead, E. (1947). The life history of *Embidopsocus enderleini* (Ribaga) (Corrodentia, Liposcelidae), *Entomol. Mon. Mag.*, **83**, 200–203.

Broadhead, E. (1950). A revision of the genus *Liposcelis* Motschulsky, with notes on the position of this genus in the order Corrodentia and on the variability of ten *Liposcelis* species, *Trans. R. Entomol. Soc. Lond.*, **101**, 335–388.

Broadhead, E., and B. M. Hobby. (1944). Studies on a species of *Liposcelis* (Corrodentia, Liposcelidae) occurring in stored products in Britain, *Entomol. Mon. Mag.*, **80**, 163–173.

Broertjes, J. J. S., P. De Waard, and P. A. Voogt. (1984a). On the presence of vitellogenic substances in the starfish, *Asterias rubens* (L.), *J. Mar. Biol. Assoc. U. K.*, **64**, 261–269.

Broertjes, J. J. S., P. De Waard, and P. A. Voogt. (1984b). Purification and characterization of vitellogenic substances in the starfish *Asterias rubens* (L.), *J. Mar. Biol.*, **5**, 99–104.

Bromage, N. R., C. Whitehead, and B. Breton. (1982). Relationships between serum levels of gonadotropin, estradiol-17 C, and vitellogenin in the control of ovarian development in the rainbow trout, *Gen. Comp. Endocrinol.*, **47**, 366–376.

Brooks, J. L. (1966a). Cyclomorphosis in *Daphnia* I. An analysis of *D. retrocurva* and *D. galeala, Ecol. Mongr.*, **16**, 411–447.

Brooks, J. L. (1966b). Cyclomorphosis, turbulence and overwintering in *Daphnia, Verh. Int. Ver. Limnol.*, **16**, 1653–1659.

Brooks, W. K., and C. Grave (1899). *Ophiura brevispina, Mem. Natl. Acad. Sci.,* **8,** 79–100.

Brossut, R. (1973). Evolution du système glandulaire exocrine céphalique des Blattaria et des Isoptera, *Int. J. Insect Morphol. Embryol.,* **2,** 35–54.

Brossut, R. (1976). Etude morphologique de la blatte myrmécophile *Attaphila fungicola* Wheeler, *Insect Soc.,* **23,** 167–174.

Brousse-Gaury, P., F. Goudey-Perriere, P. Binet, and M. Miocque. (1979). Mise en evidence d'une vitellogenèse prematurée chez la blatte *Blabera, C. R. Acad. Sci.,* **288,** 701–703.

Brown, E. (1951). The relation between migration rate and type of habitats in insects, with special reference to certain species of Corixidae, *Proc. Zool. Soc. Lond.,* **121,** 539–545.

Brown, W. L. J. (1982). "Zoraptera," in *Synopsis and Classification of Living Organisms,* Vol. 2, S. P. Parker et al., Eds., McGraw-Hill, New York, p. 393.

Bruce, R. C. (1979). Evolution of paedomorphosis in salamanders of the genus *Gyrinophilus, Evolution,* **33,** 998–1000.

Bullière, F., and D. Bullière. (1975). Hormone de mue et synthèse de la cuticule par les céllules epidermiques d'embryon de blatte en culture in vitro, *C. R. Acad. Sci.,* **281,** 925–928.

Bulycheva, A. I. (1957). Marine fleas of the seas of USSR and surrounding waters (in Russian), *Opred. Faune USSR,* **65,** 1–186.

Bunner, H. C., and K. Halcrow. (1977). Experimental induction of the production of ephippia by *Daphnia magna* Straus (Cladocera), *Crustaceana,* **32,** 77–86.

Burnett, A. L. (1968). "The acquisition, maintenance, and lability of the differentiated state in *Hydra,*" in *The Stability of the Differentiated State,* H. Ursprung, Ed., Springer, New York, pp. 109–127.

Burnett, A. L., and N. A. Diehl. (1964). The nervous system of *Hydra, J. Exp. Zool.,* **157,** 237–250.

Buschinger, A. (1975). Eine genetische Komponente im Polymorphismus der dulotischen Ameise *Harpagoxenus sublaevis, Naturwissenschaften,* **62,** 2395.

Buschinger, A. (1978). Genetisch bedingte Entstehung geflügelter Weibchen bei der Sklavenhaltenden Ameise *Harpagoxenus sublaevis* (Nyl.) (Hym. Form.), *Insect Soc.,* **25,** 163–172.

Bush, G. L. (1969). Sympatric host race formation and speciation in fungivorous flies of the genus *Rhagoletis* (Diptera, Tephretidae), *Evolution,* **23,** 237–251.

Bush, G. L. (1973). "The mechanism of sympatric host race formation in the fruit flies (Tephretidae)," in *Genetic Mechanism of Speciation in Insects,* J. D. White, Ed., Riedl., Dordrecht, Holland, pp. 3–23.

Bush, G. L. (1982). Goldschmidt's follies, *Paleobiology,* **8,** 463–469.

Bush, L. (1968). Characteristics of interstitial sand Turbellaria: The significance of body elongation, muscular development and adhesive organs, *Trans. Am. Microsc. Soc.,* **87,** 244–251.

Buttner, A. (1950). La progenèse chez les trématodes digénétiques, *Ann. Parasitol.,* **25,** 376–434.

Buttner, A. (1951). La progenèse chez les trématodes digénétiques (III), *Ann. Parasitol.,* **26,** 19–66, 138–189, 279–322.

Bychowsky, B. E. (1957). *Monogenetic Trematodes, Their Classification and Phylogeny,* Acad. Sci. USSR, Moscow (in Russian; cf. Kearn 1967).

Byers, G. W. (1969a). Evolution of wing reduction in craneflies (Diptera: Tipulidae), *Evolution,* **23,** 346–354.

Byers, G. W. (1969b). A new family of nematocerous Diptera, *J. Kans. Entomol. Soc.,* **42,** 366–371.

Byers, G. W. (1976). A new Appalachian *Brachypanorpa* (Mecoptera: Panorpodidae), *J. Kans. Entomol. Soc.,* **49,** 433–440.

Byers, G. W. (1982). A new subapterous craneflies from Hawaii (Diptera: Tipulidae), *Mem. Entomol. Soc. Wash.,* **10,** 37–41.

Byers, G. W. (1983). The cranefly genus *Chionea* in North America, *Univ. Kans. Sci. Bull.,* **56,** 59–195.

Byers, G. W., and R. Thornhill. (1983). Biology of the Mecoptera, *Ann. Rev. Entomol.,* **28,** 203–228.

Calabrese, D. M. (1980). Zoogeography and cladistic analysis of the Gerridae (Hemiptera: Heteroptera), *Misc. Publ. Entomol. Soc. Am.,* **11**(5), 1–119.

Calabrese, D. M. (1982). "Wing polymorphism and cladogenesis in the Gerridae," in *Evolutionary Significance of Insect Polymorphism,* University of Idaho, pp. 19–24.

Calow, P. (1978). The evolution of life cycle strategies in freshwater gastropods, *Malacologia,* **17,** 351–364.

Calow, P., M. Beveridge, and R. Sibly. (1979). Head and tail. Adaptational aspects of sexual reproduction in freshwater triclads, *Am. Zool.,* **19,** 715–727.

Cals, P., and J. Cals-Usciati. (1982). Développement postembryonnaire des Crustacés Mystacocarides. Le problème des différences présumées entre les deux espèces voisines *Derocheilocaris Remanei* Delamare et Chappuis et *Derocheilocaris typicus* Pennak et Zinn, *C. R. Acad. Sci.,* **294,** 505–510.

Camenzind, R. (1982). Das Follikelepithel während der paedogenetischen Entwicklung der Gallmücke *Heteropeza pygmaea* (Cecidomyiidae: Diptera), *Rev. Suisse Zool.,* **89,** 851–858.

Carpenter, F. M. (1941). A new genus of Mecoptera from Tasmania, *Pap. Proc. R. Soc. Tasmania,* **1940,** 51–53.

Carr, F. E., P. J. Jacobs, and R. C. Jaffe. (1981). Changes in specific prolactin binding in *Rana catesbeiana* tadpole tissues during metamorphosis and following prolactin and thyroid hormone treatment, *Mol. Cell. Endocrinol.,* **23,** 65–76.

Carter, A. (1976). Wing polymorphism in the insect species *Agonum retractum* Leconte (Coleoptera: Carabidae), *Can. J. Zool.* **54,** 1375–1382.

Cassagnau, P. (1955). L'influence de la température sur la morphologie d'*Hypogastrura purpurascens* (Lubbock), collembole poduromorphe, *C. R. Acad. Sci.,* **240,** 1483–1485.

Cassagnau, P. (1958). Quelques données histologiques sur les écomorphoses, *C. R. Acad. Sci.,* **246,** 3379–3381.

Cassagnau, P., and G. Raynal. (1964). Contribution à l'étude des écomorphoses. I Développment comparé de deux races d'*Hypoastrura tullbergi* (Collembole, Poduromorphe), *Rev. Ecol. Biol. Sol.,* **1,** 1–20.

Cassagnau, P., and H. Dalens. (1976). Cycle phénologique et analyse experimentale de quelques caractères histologiques dans trois populations d'*Hypogastrura tullbergi* (Collembole), *Vie et Milieu Ser. C,* **26,** 163–178.

Cassagnau, P., and G. Fabres. (1968). Contribution à l'étude des écomorphoses III. Cycle phénologique et étude expérimentale chez deux espèces du genre *Isotoma* (Collembola Isotomidae), *Rev. Ecol. Biol. Sol.,* **5,** 445–491.

Cassagnau, P., and C. Juberthie. (1983). *Neurohemal Organs of Arthropods,* A. P. Gupta, Ed., Charles C. Thomas, Springfield, IL, pp. 281–318.

Cassier, P., and M. A. Fain-Maurel. (1970). Contrôle plurifactoriel de l'évolution des glandes ventrales chez *Locusta migratoria* L. données expérimentales et infrastructurales, *J. Insect Physiol.,* **16,** 301–318.

Caullery, M. (1908). Recherches sur le Liriopsidae, Epicarides cryptonisciens parasites des Rhizocéphales, *Mitt. Zool. Stat. Neapel,* **18,** 583–643.

Caussanel, C., J.-C. Baehr, P. Cassier, F. Dray, and P. Porcheron. (1979). Correction humorales et ultrastructurales au cours de la vitellogenèse et de la période de soin aux oeufs chez *Labidura riparia* (Insecta Dermaptera), *C. R. Acad. Sci.* **285,** 513–516.

Chadwick, C. S. (1940). Identity of prolactin with water drive factor in *Triturus viridescens, Proc. Soc. Exp. Biol. Med.,* **45,** 335–337.

Chadwick, C. S. (1941). Further observations on the water drive in *Triturus viridescens, J. Exp. Zool.,* **86,** 175–188.

Chaix, J.-C., and M. De Reggi. (1982). Ecdysteroid levels during ovarian development and embryogenesis in the spider crab *Acanthonyx lunulatus, Gen. Comp. Endocrinol.,* **47,** 7–14.

Chang, E. S., and M. J. Bruce. (1980). Ecdysteroid titers of juvenile lobster following molt induction, *J. Exp. Zool.,* **214,** 157–160.

Chang, E. S., and M. J. Bruce. (1981). Ecdysteroid titers of larval lobsters, *Comp. Biochem. Physiol.,* **70A,** 239–241.

Chapman, A. (1961). The terrestrial ostracod of New Zealand, *Mesocypris audax* sp. nov., *Crustaceana,* **2,** 255–261.

Chapman, D. M. (1966). Evolution of the Scyphozoa, *Zool. Soc. Lond. Symp.,* **16,** 51–75.

Chapman, R. F., A. G. Cook, G. A. Mitchell, and W. W. Page. (1978). Wing dimorphism and flight in *Zonocerus variegatus* (L.) (Orthoptera, Pyrgomorphidae), *Bull. Entomol. Res.,* **68,** 229–242.

Chappuis, P. A. (1948). Le développement larvaire de *Bathynella, Bull. Soc. Sci. Cluj,* **10,** 305–309.

Chappuis, P. A., and C. Delamare-Deboutteville. (1954). Remarques sur le développement des Bathynelles, *Arch. Zool. Exp.. Gen.,* **91,** 74–82.

Charlesworth, B. (1982). Hopeful monster cannot fly, *Paleobiology,* **8,** 469–474.

Charlet, M., F. Goltzene, and J. A. Hoffman. (1979). Experimental evidence for a neuroendocrine control of ecdysone biosynthesis in adult females of *Locusta migratoria, J. Insect Physiol.,* **25,** 463–466.

Charniaux-Cotton, H. (1972). "Recherches récentes sur la différenciation sexuelle et l'activité génitale chez divers crustacés supérieurs," in *Hormones et différenciation sexuelle chez les invértébres,* E. Wolff, Ed., Gordon & Breach, Paris, pp. 127–178.

Charniaux-Cotton, H. (1975). "Hermaphroditism and gynandromorphism in malacostracan Crustacea," in *Intersexuality in the Animal Kingdom,* R. Reinboth, Ed., Springer, New York, pp. 91–105.

Charniaux-Cotton, H. (1976a). "Contrôle endocrine de la différenciation sexuelle et du maintien des gonies chez les crustacés," in *Activité sur les hormones d'invertébrés, Colloq. Int., C. N. R. S.,* **251,** 235–246.

Charniaux-Cotton, H. (1976b). L'ovogenèse, la vitellogenèse et leur contrôle chez le crustacé amphipode *Orchestia gammarellus* (Pallas). Comparaison avec d'autres malacostracés, *Arch. Zool. Exp. Gen.,* **119,** 365–397.

Charniaux-Cotton, H. (1982). Secondary folliculogenesis and secondary vitellogenesis in Malacostraca Crustacea, *Gen. Comp. Endocrinol.,* **46,** 383.

Chatani, F., and E. Ohnishi. (1976). Effect of ecdysone on the ovarian development of *Bombyx mori, Dev. Growth Differ.,* **18,** 481–484.

Chen, T. T., P. W. Strahlendorf, and G. R. Wyatt. (1978). Vitellin and vitellogenin from locusts *(Locusta migratoria).* Responses and post-translational modification in the fat body, *J. Biol. Chem.,* **253,** 5325–5331.

Chen, T. T., P. Couble, R. Abu-Hakim, and G. R. Wyatt. (1979). Juvenile hormone-controlled vitellogenin synthesis in *Locusta migratoria* fat body, *Dev. Biol.,* **69,** 59–72.

Cheng, T. C. (1968). The compatibility and incompatibility concepts as related to trematodes and molluscs, *Pac. Sci.,* **22,** 141–160.

Cherbas, P., L. Cherbas, G. Demetri, M. Manteuffel-Cymborowska, C. Savakis, C. D. Younger, and C. M. Williams. (1980). "Ecdysteroid hormone effect on a *Drosophila* cell line," in *Steroid Hormones,* A. K. Roy and J. H. Clark, Eds., Springer, New York, pp. 278–308.

Chernin, E. (1970). Behavioral responses of mirecidia of *Schistosoma mansoni* and other trematodes to substances emitted by snails, *J. Parasitol.,* **56,** 287–296.

Chia, F.-S. (1966). Development of a deep-sea cushion star, *Pteraster tesselatus, Proc. Calif. Acad. Sci.,* **34,** 505–510.

Chia, F.-S. (1978). "Perspectives: Settlement and metamorphosis of marine invertebrate larvae," in *Settlement and Metamorphosis of Marine Invertebrate Larvae,* F.-S. Chia and M. E. Rice, Eds., Elsevier, New York, pp. 283–285.

Chia, F.-S. and M. E. Rice, Eds. (1978). *Settlement and Metamorphosis of Marine Invertebrate Larvae,* Elsevier, New York.

Chopard, L. (1938). *La Biologie des Orthoptères,* M. P. Lechevalier, Ed., Jouve, Paris.

Chopard, L. (1949a). "Ordere des Orthoptères," in *Traité de Zoologie,* Vol. 9, P.-P. Grassé, Ed., Masson, Paris, pp. 617–722.

Chopard, L. (1949b). "Ordre des Dermaptères," in *Traité de Zoologie,* Vol. 9, P.-P. Grassé, Ed., Masson, Paris, pp. 745–770.

Choudhuri, D. K., B. Bhatta, P. Mukherjee, and T. Pande. (1979). The effects of various physical factors on the biology of *Lobella (Lobella) maxillaris* Yosii 1966 (Collembola: Insecta), *Rev. Ecol. Biol. Sol.,* **16,** 241–257.

Christensen, A. M. (1981). The geographical and bathymetrical distribution of the Fecampidae (Turbellaria), *Hydrobiologia,* **84,** 13–16.

Christiansen, K. (1961). Convergence and parallelism in cave Entomobryinae, *Evolution,* **15,** 288–301.

Chudakova, I. V. (1981). Acceleration of larval development of the house cricket *Acheta domestica* on introduction of an analog of the juvenile hormone, *Sov. J. Dev. Biol.,* **12,** 229–233.

Chudakova, I. V., and J. P. Delbecque. (1983). Juvenile hormone action on the last larval instar in the house cricket *Acheta domestica, Acta Entomol. Bohemosl.,* **80,** 344–351.

Chun, C. (1982). Die Dissogonie, eine neue Form der geschlechtlichen Zeugung, *Festschrift zum siebzigsten Geburstage Rudorf Leuckarts,* pp. 77–108.

Clark, B. (1979). "Environmental determination of reproduction in polychaetes," in *Reproduction and Ecology of Marine Invertebrates,* S. E. Stancyk, Ed., University of South Carolina, Columbia, SC, pp. 107–121.

Clark, G. R. (1974). Calcification on an unstable substrate: marginal growth in the mollusk *Pecten diegensis, Science,* **183,** 968–970.

Clark, K. B., and A. Goetzfried. (1979). Geographic influence on development pattern of North Atlantic Ascoglossa and Nudibranchia, with a discussion of factors affecting egg size and number, *J. Molluscan Studies,* **44,** 283–294.

Clark, K. B., and K. R. Jensen. (1981). A comparison of egg size and development pattern in the order Ascoglossa (Sacoglossa) (Mollusca: Opisthobranchia), *Int. J. Inverteb. Reprod.,* **3,** 57–64.

Clark, K. B., M. Busacca, and H. Stirts. (1979). "Nutritional aspects of development of the ascoglossan, *Elysia cauze,*" in *Reproductive Ecology in Marine Invertebrates,* S. E. Stancyk, Ed., University of South Carolina Press, Columbia, SC, pp. 11–24.

Clark, R. B. (1961). The origin and formation of the heteronereis, *Biol. Rev.,* **36,** 199–236.

Clark, R. B. (1969). "Systematics and phylogeny: Annelida, Echiura, Sipuncula," in *Chemical Zoology,* Vol. 4, M. Florkin and B. Scheer, Eds., Academic, New York, pp. 1–68.

Clark, R. B. (1978). "Compositions and relationships," in *Physiology of Annelids,* P. J. Mill, Ed., Academic, New York, pp. 1–32.

Clark, W. C. (1976). The environment and the genotype in polymorphism, *Zool. J. Linn. Soc.,* **58,** 252–262.

Clarke, A. (1979). On living in cold water: K-strategies in Antarctic benthos, *Mar. Biol.* **55,** 111–119.

Clarke, A. (1980). A reappraisal of the concept of metabolic cold adaptation in polar marine invertebrates, *Biol. J. Linn. Soc.,* **14,** 77–92.

Clarke, A. (1982). Temperature and embryonic development in polar marine invertebrates, *Int. J. Inverteb. Reprod.,* **5,** 71–82.

Clarke, B., W. Arthur, D. T. Horsley, and D. T. Parkin. (1978). "Genetic variation and natural selection in pulmonate molluscs," in *Pulmonates,* Vol. 2A, V. Fretter and J. Peake, Eds., Academic, New York, pp. 220–270.

Clausen, C. (1971). Interstitial Cnidaria: Present status of their systematics and ecology, *Smiths. Misc. Contrib. Zool.,* **76,** 1–8.

Clausen, C. (1977). The species problem in Halammohydridae (Cnidaria), *Mikrofauna Meeresbondens,* **61,** 303–304.

Clausen, C. P. (1940). *Entomophagous Insects,* McGraw-Hill, New York.

Clay, T. (1970). The Amblycera (Phthiraptera: Insecta), *Bull. Brit. Mus. Nat. Hist. (Entomol.)*, **25**, 75–98.

Clement, P., and R. Pourriot. (1972). Photopériodisme et cycle hétérogonique chez rotifères monogentes I. Observations preliminaires chez *Notommata copeus, Arch. Zool. Exp. Gen.*, **113**, 41–50.

Clement, P. and R. Pourriot. (1975). Influence du groupement et de la densité de population sur le cycle de reproduction de *Notommata copeus* Ehrle (Rotifère) I. Mise en évidence et essai d'interprétation, *Arch. Zool. Exp. Gen.*, **116**, 375–421.

Clement, P., A. Luciani, and R. Pourriot. (1981). Influences exogènes sur le cycle reproducteur des rotifères, *Bull. Soc. Zool. Fr.*, **106**, 255–262.

Cleveland, L. R., S. R. Hall, E. P. Sanders, and J. Collier. (1934). The wood-feeding roach *Cryptocercus*, its Protozoa, and the symbiosis between Protozoa and roaches, *Mem. Am. Acad. Arts Sci.*, **17**, 185–342.

Cloney, R. A. (1978). "Ascidian metamorphosis: Review and analysis," in *Settlement and Metamorphosis of Marine Invertebrate Larvae*, F.-S. Chia and M. Rice, Eds., Elsevier, New York, pp. 252–282.

Cloney, R. A. (1982). Ascidian larvae and events of metamorphosis, *Am. Zool.*, **22**, 817–826.

Cloudsley-Thompson, J. L. (1957). On the habit and growth stages of *Arixenia esau* Jordan and *A. jacobsoni* Burr (Dermaptera: Arixenioidea), with description of the hitherto unknown adults of the former, *Proc. R. Entomol. Soc. Lond., A*, **32**, 1–12.

Cloudsley-Thompson, J. L. (1958). *Spiders, Scorpions, Centipedes and Mites*, Pergamon, Oxford.

Coker, R. E., and H. H. Addelstone. (1938). Influence of temperature on cyclomorphosis of *Daaphnia longispina, J. Elisha Mitchell Sci. Soc.*, **54**, 45–75.

Cornford, E. M. (1974). *Schistosomatium douthitti:* Effects of thyroxine, *Exp. Parasitol.*, **36**, 210–221.

Cornwell, P. B. (1968). *The cockroach*, Vol. 1, Hutchinson, London.

Costlow, J. D., C. G. Bookhout, and R. Moore. (1980). The effect of salinity and temperature on larval development of *Sesarma cinereum* (Bosc.) reared in the laboratory, *Biol. Bull.*, **188**, 183–202.

Cousin, G. (1938). La neotenie chez *Gryllus caampestris* et ses hybrides, *Bull. Biol. Fr. Belg.*, **72**, 79–117.

Cox, G. W., and D. G. Cox. (1974). Subtrate color matching in the grasshopper, *Circotettix rabula* (Orthoptera, Acrididae), *Great Basin Nat.*, **34**, 60–70.

Cox, J. (1983). An experimental study of morphological variation in mealybugs (Homoptera: Coccoidea: Pseudococcidae), *Syst. Entomol.*, **8**, 361–382.

Crampton, G. C. (1916). The lines of descent of the lower pterygotan insects, with notes on the relationships of the other forms, *Entomol. News*, **27**, 244–258.

Crampton, G. C. (1919). Remarks on the origin and significance of metamorphosis among insects, *Brooklyn Entomol. Soc.*, **14**, 33–40, 93–101.

Cranston, P. S. (1985). *Eretmoptera murphyi* Schaeffer (Diptera: Chironomidae), an apparently parthenogenetic antarctic midge, *Brit. Antarct. Surv. Bull.* **66**, 35–45.

Crawford, M. A., and K. L. Webb. (1972). An ultrastructural study of strobilation in

Chrysaora quiniquecirrha with special reference to neurosecretion, *J. Exp. Zool.,* **182,** 251–270.

Creed, E. R. (1971). "Melanism in the two-spot ladybird, *Adalia bipunctata* in Great Britain," in *Ecological Genetics and Evolution,* E. R. Creed, Ed., Blackwell, Oxford, pp. 131–151.

Crim, J. W. (1975). Prolactin induced modification of visual pigment in the eastern red-spotted newt *Notophthalmus viridescens, Gen. Comp. Endocrinol.,* **26,** 233–242.

Croisille, Y., and H. Junera. (1980). Recherche du lieu de synthèse de la vitellogenèse chez le crustacé amphipode *Orchestia gammarella* (Pallas). Démonstration à l'aide d'anticorps spécifiques, de la présence de vitellogénine dans le tissu adipeux sousépidermique des femêlles en vitellogénèse secondaire, *C. R. Acad. Sci.,* **290,** 1487–1490.

Crowson, R. A. (1955). *The Natural Classification of the Families of Coleoptera,* Nathaniel Lloyd, London.

Curtis, A. T., M. Hori, J. M. Green, W. J. Wolfgang, K. Hiruma, and L. M. Riddiford. (1984). Ecdysteroid regulation of the onset of cuticular melanization in allatectomized and black mutant *Manduca sexta* larvae, *J. Insect Physiol.* **30,** 597–606.

Curtis, M. A. (1977). Life cycle and population dynamics of marine benthic polychaetes from the Disko bay area area of West Greenland, *Ophelia,* **16,** 9–58.

Curtis, W. C. (1902). The life history, the normal fission, and the reproductive organs of *Planaria maculata, Proc. Boston Soc. Nat. Hist.,* **30,** 515–559.

Curtis, W. C., and L. M. Schulze. (1924). Formative cells of planarians, *Anat. Rec.,* **29,** 105.

Custance, D. R. N. (1966). The effect of a sudden rise in temperature on strobilae of *Aurelia aurita, Experientia,* **30,** 588–589.

Dalens, H., and G. Vannier. (1983). Comparaisons biométriques et écophysiologiques entre individus normaux et ecomorphiques de deux populations du collembole *Hypogastrura tullbergi, Pedobiology,* **25,** 199–206.

Dales, R. P. (1962). The polychaete stomodaeum and the interrelationships of the families of Polychaeta, *Proc. Zool. Soc. Lond.,* **139,** 289–328.

Darchen, R., and B. Delage-Darchen. (1971). Le déterminisme des castes chez les Trigones (Hyménoptères apides), *Insect Soc.,* **18,** 121–134.

Darchen, R., and B. Delage-Darchen (1974a). Sur le déterminisme des castes chez les Meliponés (Hyménoptères apides), *Bull. Biol. Fr. Belg.,* **11,** 91–109.

Darchen, R., and B. Delage-Darchen. (1974b). Nouvelles expériences concernant le déterminisme des castes chez les Meliponés (Hyménoptères apides). *C. R. Acad. Sci. Ser. D.,* **278,** 907–910.

Darchen, R., and B. Delage-Darchen. (1975). Contribution à l'étude d'une abeille du Mexique *Melipona beecheii* B., *Apidologie,* **6,** 295–339.

Darchen, R., and B. Delage-Darchen. (1977). Sur le déterminisme des castes chez les Meliponés (Hyménoptères apides), *Bull. Biol. Fr. Belg.,* **111,** 91–109.

Darlington, P. J. (1936). Variation and atrophy of flying wings of some carabid beetles, *Ann. Entomol. Soc. Amer.,* **29,** 136–176.

Darlington, P. J. (1943). Carabidae of mountains and islands: Data on the evolution of island fauna, and on atrophy of wings, *Ecol. Monogr.,* **13,** 39–61.

Darlington, P. J. (1971). The carabid beetles of New Guinea. Part IV. General consideration: analysis and history of fauna: taxonomic supplement, *Bull. Mus. Comp. Zool. Harvard,* **142,** 129–337.

Darwin, C. (1859). *The Origin of Species by Means of Natural Selection,* Harvard Facsimile, Cambridge, MA.

Darwin, C. (1872). *The Origin of Species by Means of Natural Selection,* 6th ed., Collier Books, New York.

Davey, K. G. (1976). "Hormones in nematodes," in *The Organization of Nematodes,* N. A. Croll, Ed. pp. 273–291.

Davydova, E. D. (1967). Effects of ablation and implantation of corpora allata and cardiaca on wing development and metamorphosis in *Lampyris noctiluca* (Coleoptera, Lampyridae) (in Russian), *Dokl. Akad. Nauk SSSR,* **172,** 1218–1221.

Dawydoff, C. (1959). "Classe des echiuriens," in *Traité de Zoologie,* Vol. 5, P.-P. Grassé, Ed., Masson, Paris, pp. 855–907.

Dearn, J. M. (1981). Latitudinial cline in a color pattern polymorphism in the Australian grasshopper *Phaulacridium vittatum, Heredity,* **47,** 111–119.

De Beer, G. R. (1958). *Embryos and Ancestors,* Clarendon, Oxford.

De Camargo, C. A., M. G. de Almeida, M. G. N. Parra, and W. E. Kerr. (1976). Genetics of sex determination in bees, IX. Frequencies of queens and workers from larvae under controlled conditions, *J. Kans. Entomol. Soc.,* **49,** 120–125.

De Coninck, E. (1983). *Gobersa leleupi* n.g. n. sp. a brachypterous sphaerocerid from the Uluguru mountains, Tanzania, *Rev. Zool. Afr.,* **97,** 337–344.

Dees, W. H., D. E. Sonenshine, and E. Breidling. (1984). Ecdysteroids in the American tick, *Dermacentor variabilis* (Acari: Ixodidae), during different periods of tick development, *J. Med. Entomol.,* **21,** 514–523.

Delage, Y. (1884). Evolution de la Sacculine (*Sacculina carcini* Thomps.), *Arch. Zool. Exp. Gen. Ser. 2,* **2,** 417–736.

Delamare-Deboutteville, C. (1948). Observation sur l'écologie et l'éthologie des zoraptères. La question de leur vie sociale et leur prétendus rapports avec les termites, *Rev. Entomol.* (Rio de Janeiro), **19,** 347–352.

Delamare-Deboutteville, C. (1960). *Biologie des eaux souterraines littorales et continentales,* Paris.

De la Paz, A. R., J.-P. Delbecque, J. Bitsch, and J. Delachambre. (1983). Ecdysteroids in the haemolymph and the ovaries of the firebrat *Thermobia domestica* (Packard) (Insecta, Thysanura): Correlations with integumental and ovarian cycles, *J. Insect Physiol.,* **29,** 323–329.

Delbecque, J.-P., P. A. Diehl, and J. D. O'Connor. (1978). Presence of ecdysone and ecdysterone in the tick *Amblysomma hebraeum* Koch., *Experientia,* **34,** 1379–1381.

Delbecque, J.-P., B. Lanzrein, C. Bordereau, C. Imboden, M. Hirn, J. D. O'Connor, C. Noirot, and M. Luscher. (1978). Ecdysone and ecdysterone in physogastric termite queens and eggs of *Macrotermes bellicosus* and *Macrotermes subhyalinus, Gen. Comp. Endocrinol.,* **36,** 40–47.

De Leersnyder, M., A. Dhainaut, and P. Porcheron. (1980). La vitellogenèse chez le crab *Eriocheir sinensis, Bull. Soc. Zool. Fr.,* **105,** 413–419.

Deleurance, S., and M. P. Charpin. (1972). Aspects comparatifs des corps allates chez les Bathysciinae (Coléoptères cavernicoles). Imago, *C. R. Acad. Sci. Ser. D,* **247,** 405–408.

Deleurance-Glacon, S. (1963). Recherches sur les Coléoptères troglobies de la sous-famille des Bathysciinae, *Ann. Sci. Nat. Zool. 12 ser.,* **5**, 1–172.

Delisle, J., C. Clouthier, and J. N. McNeil. (1983). Precocene II-induced alate production in isolated and crowded alate and apterous virginoparae of the aphid, *Macrosiphum euphorbiae, J. Insect Physiol.,* **29**, 477–484.

Dell, R. K. (1972). "Antarctic benthos," in *Advances in Marine Biology,* F. S. Russell and M. Yonge, Eds., Vol. 10, Academic, New York, pp. 1–216.

Demange, J. M. (1968). La réduction métamérique chez les chilopodes et les diplopodes chilognathes (Myriapodes), *Bull. Mus. Natl. Hist. Nat. Paris,* **40**, 532–538.

Demange, J. M. (1974). Réflexions sur le développement de quelques diplopodes, *Symp. Zool. Soc. Lond.,* **1974**, 273–287.

Den Boer, P. J., T. H. P. Huizen, W. den Boer-Daanje, B. Aukema, and C. F. M. den Bieman. (1980). Wing polymorphism and dimorphism in ground beetles as stages in an evolutionary process (Coleoptera: Carabidae), *Entomol. Gen.,* **6**, 107–134.

Denno, R. F. (1978). The optimum population strategy for planthoppers (Homoptera: Delphacidae) in stable marsh habitats, *Can. Entomol.,* **110**, 135–142.

Dent, J. N. (1942). The embryonic development of *Plethodon cinereus* as correlated with the differentiation and functioning of the thyroid gland, *J. Morphol.,* **71**, 577–601.

Dent, J. N. (1968). "Survey of amphibian metamorphosis," in *Metamorphosis,* W. Etkin and L. I. Gilbert, Eds., Appleton-Century-Crofts, New York, pp. 271–311.

Dent, J. N., and J. S. Kirby-Smith. (1963). Metamorphic physiology and morphology of the cave salamander *Gyrinophilus palleucus, Copeia,* **1963**, 119–130.

Dent, J. N., J. S. Kirby-Smith, and D. L. Craig. (1955). Induction of metamorphosis in *Gyrinophilus palleucus, Anat. Rec.,* **121**, 429.

Deroux-Stralla, D. (1948). Recherches expérimentales sur le rôle des "glandes ventrales" dans le mue et la metamorphose chez *Aeschna cyanea* Müll (Odonata), *C. R. Acad Sci.,* **277**, 1277–1288.

Descamps, M. (1981). Influence des facteurs externes sur la spermatogénèse chez *Lithobius forficatus* L. (Myriapoda Chilopoda), *Bull. Soc. Zool.,* **106**, 362.

De Silva, P. K., and M. De Silva. (1980). An ecological study of *Dugesia mannophalus* (Ball) (Turbellaria, Tricladida) in Sri Lanka, *Arch. Hydrobiol.,* **88**, 364–377.

Dickhoff, W. W., and L. C. Folmar (1978). Changes in thyroid hormones during the early development of coho salmon, *Oncorhynchus kisutch, Am. Zool.,* **18**, 652.

Dickhoff, W. W., L. C. Folmar, and A. Gorbman. (1978). Changes in plasma thyroxine during smoltification of coho salmon *Oncorhynchus kisutch, Gen. Com. Endocrinol.,* **36**, 229–232.

Dickhoff, W. W., L. C. Folmar, J. L. Mighell, and C. V. W. Mahnken. (1982). Plasma thyroid hormones during smoltification of yearling and underyearling coho salmon and yearling chinook salmon and steelhead trout, *Aquaculture,* **28**, 39–48.

Diehl, P. A., J. E. Germond, and M. Morici. (1982). Correlations between ecdysteroid titers and integument structure in nymphs of the tick, *Amblyomma hebraeum* Koch (Acarina: Ixodiae), *Rev. Suisse Zool.,* **89**, 859–868.

Dieleman, S. J., and H. J. N. Schoenmakers. (1979). Radioimmunoassay to determine the presence of progesterone and estrone in the starfish *Asterias rubens, Gen. Comp. Endocrinol,* **39**, 534–542.

Dierl, W., and J. Reichholf. (1977). Die Flügelreduktion bei Schmetterlingen als Anpassungsstrategie, *Spexiana,* **1,** 27–40.

Dietz, A., H. R. Hermann, and M. S. Blum. (1979). The role of exogenous JH I and JH III and anti JH (precocene II) on queen induction of 4.5 days old worker honey bee larvae, *J. Insect Physiol.,* **25,** 503–512.

Dingle, H., Ed. (1978). *Evolution of Insect Migration and Diapause,* Springer, New York.

Dinnik, J. A., and N. N. Dinnik. (1964). The influence of temperature on the succession of redial and cercarial generations of *Fasciola gigantica* in a snail host, *Parasitology,* **54,** 59–65.

Dirsch, V. M. (1953). Morphological studies on phases of the desert locust (*Schistocerca gregaria* Forskal), *Anti-Locust Bull.,* **16,** 1–34.

Dirsch, V. M. (1965). *The African Genera of Acridoidea,* Cambridge University Press.

Dixon, K. E., and E. H. Mercer. (1965). The fine structure of the liver fluke *Fasciola hepatica* L., *J. Parasitol.,* **51,** 967–976.

Dobkins, S. (1969). Abbreviated larval development in caridean shrimps and its significance in the artificial culture of these animals, *FAO Fish. Rep.,* **57,** 935–946.

Dobzhansky, T. (1970). *Genetics of the Evolutionary Process,* Columbia University Press, New York.

Dodd, J. M., and H. G. Callan. (1955). Neoteny with goitre in *Triturus helveticus, Q. J. Microsc. Sci.,* **96,** 121–128.

Dodd, M. H. I., and J. M. Dodd. (1976). "The biology of metamorphosis," in *Physiology of the Amphibia,* B. Lofts, Ed., Academic, New York, pp. 467–599.

Dodson, S. I. (1974). Adaptive change in plankton morphology in response to size-selective predation, a new hypothesis of cyclomorphosis, *Limnol. Oceanogr.,* **19,** 721–729.

Doetsch, H. (1949). Experimentelle Untersuchungen über den Einfluss des Lichtes und der ultravioletten Strahlen auf Wachstum mit Entwicklung von Amphibien-larven, *Wilhelm Roux Arch. Entwicklungsmech. Org.,* **144,** 25–30.

Dogterom, A. A., and T. Jentjens. (1980). The effect of the growth hormone of the pond snail *Lymnaea stagnalis* on periostracum formation, *Gen. Comp. Endocrinol.,* **66A:** 687–690.

Dogterom, A. A., H. Van Loenhout, and R. C. Van den Schors. (1979). The effect of the growth hormone of *Lymnaea stagnalis* on shell calcification, *Gen. Comp. Endocrinol.,* **39,** 63–68.

Dohle, W. (1967). Zur Morphologie und Lebensweise von *Ophryotrocha gracilis* Huth 1934 (Polychaeta, Eunicidae), *Kiel. Meeresforsh.,***23,** 68–74.

Donald, D. B., and R. A. Mutch. (1980). The effect of hydroelectric dams and sewage on the distribution of stoneflies (Plecoptera) along the Bow River, *Quaest. Entomol.,* **16,** 657–669.

Donald, D. B., and D. E. Patriquin. (1983). The wing length of lentic Capniidae (Plecoptera) and its relationship to elevation and Wisconsin glaciation, *Can. Entomol.,* **115,** 921–926.

D'Or, R. K., and M. J. Wells. (1973). Yolk protein synthesis in the ovary of *Octopus vulgaris* and its control by the optic gland gonadotropin, *J. Exp. Biol.,* **59,** 665–674

D'Or, R. K., and M. J. Wells. (1975). Control of yolk protein synthesis by *Octopus* gonadotropin in vivo and in vitro (Effects of *Octopus* gonadotropin), *Gen. Comp. Endocrinol.,* **27,** 129–135.

D'Or, R. K., R. D. Durward, and N. Balch. (1977). Maintenance and maturation of squid *(Ilex illecebrosus)* in a 15 meter circular pool, *Biol. Bull.,* **153,** 322–335.

Douglas, M. M., and J. W. Grula. (1978). Thermoregulatory adaptation all owing ecological range expansion by the pierid butterfly, *Nathalis iole* Boisduval, *Evolution,* **32,** 776–783.

Doutt, R. L., and C. M. Yoshimoto. (1970). Hymenoptera: Chalcidoidea: Mymaridae of South Georgia, *Pac. Ins. Monogr.,* **23,** 293–294.

Dowling, H. G., and W. E. Duellman. (1978). *Systematic Herpetology. A Synopsis of Families and Higher Categories,* Hiss, New York.

Downes J. A. (1965). Adaptation of insects in the Arctic, *Ann. Rev. Entomol.,* **10,** 257–284.

Drewry, G. E., and K. L. Jones. (1976). A new ovoviviparous frog, *Eleutherodactylus jasperi* (Amphibia, Anura, Leptodactylidae) from Puerto Rico, *J. Herpetol.,* **10,** 161–165.

Dundee, H. A. (1961). Response of the neotenic salamanders *Haideo triton wallacei* to a metamorphic agent, *Science,* **135,** 1060–1061.

Dunn, A. D. (1980a). Studies of iodoprotein and thyroid hormones in ascidians, *Gen. Comp. Endocrinol.,* **40,** 473–483.

Dunn, A. D. (1980b). Properties of an iodinating enzyme in the ascidian endostyle, *Gen. Comp. Endocrinol.,* **40,** 484–493.

Dupuis, C. (1984). Willi Hennig's impact on taxonomic thought, *Ann. Rev. Ecol. Syst.,* **15,** 1–24.

Durchon, M. (1952). Recherches expérimentales sur deux aspects de la reproduction chez les Annelides polychetes. L'épitoque et la stolonisation. *Ann. Sci. Nat. Zool. Biol. Anim.,* **14,** 119–206.

Durchon, M. (1955). Sur le polymorphisme présenté par quelques Néréidiens (Annélides Polychètes) au moment de la reproduction, *Bull. Soc. d'Hist. Nat. Afr. Nord.,* **46,** 180–191.

Durchon, M. ₁1965). Sur l'évolution phylogénétique et ontogénétique de l'épitoquie chez les Néréidiens (Annélides Polychètes), *Zool. Jahrb. Syst.,* **92,** 1–12.

Durchon, M., and A. Richard. (1967). Etude, en culture organotypique, du rôle endocrine de la glande optique dans la maturation ovarienne chez *Sepia officinalis* (Mollusque Céphalopode), *C. R. Acad. Sci.,* **264,** 1497–1500.

Duval, D., and D. O. Norris. (1978). Prolactin and substrate stimulation of locomotor activity in adult tiger salamanders, *J. Exp. Zool.,* **200,** 103–106.

Dyadechko, N. P. (1977). *Thrips or Fring-Winged Insects (Thysanoptera) of the European part of USSR,* USDA, Washington, D.C.

Dybas, H. (1966). Evidence for parthenogenesis in the featherwing beetles, with taxonomic review of a new genus and eight new species (Coleoptera: Ptiliidae), *Fieldiana Zool.,* **51,** 11–52.

Dybas, H. S. (1978). Polymorphism in featherwing beetles, with a revision of the genus *Ptinellodes* (Coleoptera: Ptiliidae), *Ann. Entomol. Soc. Am.,* **71,** 659–714.

Eagleson, G. W. (1976). Comparison of the life histories and growth patterns of populations of the salamander *Ambystoma gracile* (Baird) from permanent low altitudes and montane lakes, *Can. J. Zool.,* **54,** 2098–2111.

Eason, E. H. (1979). "The effect of environment on the number of trunk-segments in the Geophilomorpha with special reference to *Geophilus carpophagus* Leach," in *Myriapod Biology,* M. Camatini, Ed., Academic, New York, pp. 233–240.

Eastop, V. B. (1973). "Biotypes of aphids," in *Perspectives in Aphid Biology,* A. D. Lowe, Ed., Entomological Society of New Zealand, Auckland, pp. 40–51.

Ebeling, W. (1938). Host-determined morphological variations in *Lecanium cornii, Hilgardia,* **11,** 613–631.

Eckelbarger, K. J. (1983). Evolutionary radiation in polychaete ovaries and vitellogenic mechanisms: their possible role in life history pattern, *Can. J. Zool.,* **61,** 487–504.

Edmunds, G. F. (1956). Exuviation of subimaginal Ephemeroptera in flight, *Entomol. News,* **67,** 91–93.

Edmunds, G. F., L. T. Nielsen, and J. R. Larsen. (1956). The life history of *Ephron album* (Say) (Ephemeroptera: Polymitarcidae), *Wasmann J. Biol.,* **14,** 145–153.

Edmunds, G. F., Jr., S. L. Jensen, and L. Berner. (1976). *The Mayflies of North and Central America,* University of Minnesota Press, Minneapolis.

Edney, E. B. (1960). "Terrestrial adaptation," in *The Physiology of Crustacea,* T. H. Waterman, Ed., Academic, New York, pp. 367–393.

Edney, E. B. (1968). Transition from water to land in isopod crustaceans, *Am. Zool.,* **8,** 309–326.

Efford, I. E. (1967). Neoteny in sand crabs of the genus *Emerita* (Anomura, Hippidae), *Crustaceana,* **13,** 81–93.

Ehlers, U. (1979). *Drepanilla limophila* gen. n., sp. n. (Turbellaria, Dalyelloidea) aus dem H_2S- Horizont des marinen Sandrückensystems, *Zool. Scripta,* **8,** 19–24.

Eickwort, G. C. (1976). A new species of *Chrysomelobia* (Acari: Tarsonemina; Podapolipidae) from North America and the taxonomic position of the genus, *Can. Entomol.,* **107,** 613–623.

Elder, H. (1979). Studies on the host parasite relationship between the parasitic prosobranch *Thyca crystalina* and the asteroid *Linckia laevigata, J. Zool. Lond.,* **187,** 369–391.

Eldredge, N., and S. J. Gould. (1972). "Punctuated equilibria; an alternative to phyletic gradualism," in *Models in Paleobiology,* T. Schopf, Ed., Freeman Cooper, San Francisco, pp. 82–115.

Elgmork, K., and A. L. Langeland. (1970). The number of naupliar instars in Cyclopoida (Copepoda), *Crustaceana,* **18,** 277–282.

Elliott, J. M. (1967). The life histories and drifting of the Plecoptera and Ephemeroptera in a Dartmoor stream, *J. Anim. Ecol.,* **36,** 343–362.

Emberton, L. R. B., and S. Bradbury. (1963). Transmission of light through shells of *Cepaea nemoralis* (L.), *Proc. Malac. Soc. Lond.,* **35,** 211–219.

Emig, C. C. (1974). The systematics and evolution of the phylum Phoronida, *Z. Zool. Syst. Evolutions-forsch.,* **12,** 128–151.

Emig, C. C. (1982). "The biology of Phoronida," in *Advances in Marine Biology,* J. H. S. Blaxter et al., Eds. pp. 1–89.

Endo, K. (1972). Activation of the corpora allata in relation to ovarian development in the seasonal forms of the butterfly, *Polygonia c-aureum, Dev. Growth Differ.,* **15,** 1–10.

Engelmann, F. (1970). *The Physiology of Insect Reproduction,* Pergamon, Oxford.

Eriksson, S. (1934). Studien über die Fangapparate der Branchipoden nebst einigen phylogenetischen Bemerkungen, *Zool. Bidr. Uppsala,* **15,** 23–287.

Etkin, W., and A. G. Gona. (1967). Antagonism between prolactin and thyroid hormone in amphibian development, *J. Exp. Zool.,* **165,** 249–258.

Etkin, W. (1968). "Hormonal control of amphibian metamorphosis," in *Metamorphosis,* W. Etkin and L. Gilbert, Eds., Appleton-Century-Crofts, New York, pp. 313–348.

Fain, A. (1962). Les acariens psoriques parasites des chauves-souris. XXIII. Un nouveau genre hexapode à tous les stades du développement (Teinocoptidae: Sarcoptiformes), *Bull. Ann. Soc. R. Entomol. Belg.,* **98,** 404–412.

Fain, A. (1963). Chaetotaxie et classification des Spéléognathinae, *Bull. Inst. R. Sci. Nat. Belg.,* **39,** 1–80.

Fain, A. (1969). Adaptation to parasitism in mites, *Acarologia,* **11,** 429–449.

Fain, A. (1972). Développement postembryonnaire chez les acariens de la sous-famille Spéléognathinae (Ereynetidae: Trombidiformes), *Acarologia,* **13,** 607–614.

Fain, A. (1977). Observations sur la spécificité des acariens de la famille Myobiidae. Corrélation entre l'évolution des parasites et leur hôtes, *Ann. Parasitol.,* **52,** 339–351.

Fain, A. (1979). "Specificity, adaptation and parallel host parasitic evolution in acariens, especially Myobiidae, with a tentative explanation for regressive evolution caused by the immunological reactions of the host," in *Recent Advances in Acarology,* Vol. 11, Academic, New York, pp. 321–327.

Fain- Maurel, M. A., and M. P. Cassier. (1969). Etude infrastructurale des corpora allata de *Locusta migratoria migratoripides* (R. et F.), phase solitaire au cours de la maturation sexuelle des cycles ovariens, *C. R. Acad. Sci.,* **268,** 2721–2723.

Faubel, A. (1976). Populationsdynamik und Lebenszyklus interstitieller Acoela und Macrostomida, *Mikrofauna Meeresbodens,* **56,** 354–359.

Fauchald, K. (1974). Polychaete phylogeny: A problem in prostome evolution, *Syst. Zool.,* **23,** 493–506.

Faure Y., C. Bellon-Humbert, and H. Charniaux-Cotton. (1981). Folliculogénèse et vitellogenèse secondaires chez le crevette *Palaemon serratus* (Pennault); contrôle par les pédoncules oculaires et l'organe X de la médulla externe (Mex.), *C.R. Acad. Sci.,* **293,** 461–466.

Fell, H. B. (1941). The direct development in a New Zealand ophiuroid, *Q. J. Microsc. Sci.,* **82,** 377–441.

Fell, H. B. (1945). A revision of the current theory of echinoderm embryology, *Trans. R. Soc. N. Z.,* **75,** 73–101.

Fell, H. B. (1946a). Echinoderm embryology and the origin of chordates, *Biol. Rev.,* **23,** 81–107.

Fell, H. B. (1946b). The embryology of the viviparous ophiuroid *Amphipholis squamata* Delle Chiaje, *Trans. R. Soc. N. Z.,* **75,** 419–464.

Ferris, G. F. (1920). *Scale Insects of Santa Cruz Peninsula,* Stanford University Press, Stanford, CA.

Fioroni, P. (1982). Allgemeine Aspekte der Mollusken-Entwicklung, *Zool. Jahrb. Anat.,* **107,** 85–121.

Fisher, R. A. (1930a). The evolution of dominance in certain polymorphic species, *Am. Nat.,* **64,** 385–406.

Fisher, R. A. (1930b). *The Genetical Theory of Natural Selection,* Clarendon, Oxford.

Fisher, R. A. (1939). Selective forces in wild population of *Paratettix texanus, Am. Eugen.,* **9,** 109–122.

Fize, A. (1963). Contribution à l'étude de la microfaune des sables littoraux du Golfe d' Aigues-Mortes, *Vie Milieu,* **14,** 669–774.

Fjellberg, A. (1976). Cyclomorphosis in *Isotoma hiemalis* Schött 1893 (*mucronata* Axelson 1900), syn. nov. (Collembola Isotomidae), *Rev. Ecol. Biol. Sol.,* **13,** 381–384.

Fjellberg, A. (1978). Genetic switch-over in *Isotoma nivea* Schäffer 1896. A new case of cyclomorphosis in Collembola, *Norw. J. Entomol.,* **25,** 221–222.

Fluri, P., A. G. Labatini, M. A. Vecchi, and H. Wille. (1981). Blood juvenile hormone, protein and vitellogenin titers in laying and non-laying queen honeybees, *J. Apicult. Res.,* **20,** 221–225.

Folmar, I. C., and W. W. Dickhoff. (1980). The parr-smolt transformation (smoltification) and seawater adaptation in salmonids, *Aquaculture,* **21,** 1–37.

Folsom, J. W. (1902). The identify of the snow-flea (*Achorutes nivicola* Fitch), *Psyche,* **9,** 315–321.

Ford, E. B. (1940). "Polymorphism and taxonomy," in *The New Systematics,* J. Huxley, Ed., Clarendon, Oxford, pp. 493–513.

Ford, E. B. (1965). *Genetic polymorphism,* Faber and Faber, London.

Francke, O. E. (1982). Parturition in scorpions (Arachnida Scorpiones): A review of the ideas, *Rev. Arachnol.,* **4,** 27–37.

Fraser, J., and P. Pipa. (1977). Corpus allatum regulation during the metamorphosis of *Periplaneta americana:* Axon pathways, *J. Insect Physiol.,* **23,** 975–984.

Frayha, G. J., and D. Fairbairn. (1969). Lipid metabolism in helminth parasites. VI. Synthesis of 2-cis,6-trans farnesol by *Hymenolepis diminuta* (Cestoda), *Comp. Biochem. Physiol.,* **28,** 1115–1124.

Frayha, G. J. (1974). Synthesis of certain cholesterol precursors by hydatid protoscoleces of *Echinococcus granulosus* and cysticerci of *Taenia hydatigena, Comp. Biochem. Physiol.,* **49,** 93–98.

Fredriksson, G., L. E. Ericsson, and R. Olsson. (1984). Iodine binding in the endostyle of larval *Branchiostoma lanceolatum* (Cephalochordata), *Gen. Comp. Endocrinol.,* **56,** 177–184.

Freeman, B. E., and K. Ittyeipe. (1982). Morph determination in *Melittobia,* a eulophid wasp, *Ecol. Entomol.,* **7,** 355–363.

Freeman, R. (1973). Ontogeny of cestodes and its bearing on their phylogeny and systematics, *Adv. Parasitol.,* **11,** 481–557.

Frey, D. G. (1980). The non-swimming chydroid Cladocera of wet forest with description of a new genus and two new species, *Int. rev. gesammten Hydrobiol.,* **65,** 613–641.

Frieden, E., and J. J. Just. (1970). "Hormonal responses in amphibian metamorphosis," in *Actings of Hormones on Molecular Processes,* G. Litwack, Ed., Vol. 1, New York, pp. 1–53.

Frieden, E., A., Wahlborg, and E. Howard. (1965). Temperature control of the response of tadpole to triiodothyronine, *Nature,* **205,** 1173–1176.

Frison, T. H. (1935). The stoneflies, or Plecoptera, of Illinois, *Bull. Ill. Nat. Hist. Surv.,* **20,** 281–471.

Fujita, H. (1980). "Evolution of the thyroid gland," in *Hormones, Adaptation and Evolution,* S. Ishii et al., Eds., Jap. Sci. Soc. Press, Tokyo, pp. 231–239.

Fukuda, S., and K. Endo. (1966). Hormonal control of the development of seasonal forms in the butterfly *Polygonia c-aureum* L., *Proc. Jap. Acad.,* **42,** 1082–1087.

Fukuda, S., and S. Kondo. (1965). Endocrine control of ovarial maturation in *Papilio machaon* (in Japanese), *Zool. Mag.,* **74,** 293.

Furtado, A. (1977). Hormones cérébrales, ecdysones et leurs implications dans le contrôle des mitoses goniales et de la méiose chez la femelle de *Panstrongylus megistus* (Hemiptera Reduviidae), *C.R. Acad. Sci. Ser. D,* **284,** 2377–2380.

Furtado, A. (1979). The hormonal control of mitosis and meiosis during oogenesis in the blood-sucking bug *Panstrongylus megistus, J. Insect Physiol.,* **25,** 561–570.

Furth, D. G. (1979). Wing polymorphism, host plant ecology and biogeography of *Longitarsus* in Israel (Coleoptera, Chrysomelidae), *Isr. J. Entomol.,* **13,** 125–148.

Fuzeau-Braesch, S. (1960). Etude biologique et biochimique de la pigmentation d'un insecte *Gryllus bimaculatus* de Geer, *Bull. Biol. Fr. Belg.,* **94,** 525–625.

Fuzeau-Braesch, S. (1961). Variations dans la longueur des ailes en fonction de l'effet de groupe chez quelques espèces de Gryllides, *Bull. Soc. Zool. Fr.,* **86,** 785–788.

Gabbutt, P. D., and M. Vachon. (1963). The external morphology and life history of the pseudoscorpion *Chthonius ischnocheles* (Hermann), *Proc. Zool. Soc. Lond.,* **140,** 75–98.

Gadeau de Kerville, H. (1930). Observations sur le *Pseudochelidura sinuata* Germ. (Dermaptera), *Bull. Soc. Entomol. Fr.,* **1930,** 61–63.

Gallien, L. (1935). Recherches expérimentales sur le dimorphisme évolutif et la biologie de *Polystomum integerrium* Fröhl, *Trav. Stn. Zool. Wimereux,* **12,** 1–181.

Galton, V. A. (1979). Thyroid hormone receptors hepatic nuclei of premetamorphic tadpoles, *Fed. Proc. Am. Soc. Exp. Biol.,* **38,** 1029.

Galton, V. A. (1984). Putative nuclear triiodothyronine receptors in tadpole erythrocytes: Regulation of receptor number by thyroid hormone, *Endocrinology,* **114,** 735–742.

Gande, A. R., E. D. Morgan, and I. D. Wilson. (1979). Ecdysteroid levels throughout the life cycle of the desert locust, *Schistocerca gregaria, J. Insect Physiol.,* **25,** 669–675.

Gardiner, B. G. (1983). Gnathostome vertebrae and the classification of the Amphibia, *Zool. J. Linn. Soc.,* **79,** 1–59.

Garen, A., L. Kauvar, and J. A. Lepesant. (1977). Roles of ecdysone in *Drosophila* development, *Proc. Natl. Acad. Sci. U.S.A.,* **74,** 5099–5103.

Garstang, S. L. (1928). The morphology of the Tunicata, and its bearing on the phylogeny of the Chordata, *Q. J. Microsc. Sci.,* **72,** 51–187.

Gause, G. F. (1947). Problems of evolution, *Trans. Conn. Acad. Arts Sci.,* **37,** 17–68.

Geraerts, W. P. M. (1976a). Control of growth by the neurosecretory cell hormone in the light green cells in the freshwater snail *Lymnaea stagnalis, Gen. Comp. Endocrinol.,* **29,** 61–71.

Geraerts, W. P. M. (1976b). The role of the lateral lobes in the control of growth and reproduction in the hermaphroditic freshwater *Lymnaea stagnalis, Gen. Comp. Endocrinol.,* **29,** 97–108.

Geraerts, W. P. M., and L. H. Alegra. (1976). The stimulating effect of the dorsal body hormone on cell differentiation in the female accessory sex organs of the hermaphrodite freshwater snail *Lymnaea stagnalis, Gen. Comp. Endocrinol.,* **29,** 109–118.

Germond, J-E., P. A. Diehl, and M. Morici. (1982). Correlations between integument structure and ecdysteroid titers in fifth stage nymph of the tick, *Ornithodoros moubata* (Murray 1877, sensu Walton 1962), *Gen. Comp. Endocrinol.,* **46,** 255–266.

Gharib, B., A. Girardie, and M. De Reggi. (1981). Ecdysteroids and control of embryonic diapause: Changes in ecdysteroid levels and exogenous hormone effects in the egg of cochineal *Lepidosaphes, Experientia,* **37,** 1107–1108.

Ghilyarov, M. S. (1949). *The Characteristics of Soil as a Living Medium and its Importance in the Evolution of Insects* (in Russian), Akad. Nauk U.S.S.R., Moscow.

Ghilyarov, M. S. (1957). Evolution of the postembryonic development and the types of insect larvae (in Russian), *Zool. Jahrb.,* **36,** 1683–1697.

Ghilyarov, M. S. (1969). Die Bedeutung von Larvenmerkmalen für die phylogenetische Systematik der Insekten, *WanderVersamml. Dtsch. Entomol. Ber. 10, Tagesber.* **80,** Teil 1, pp. 37–54.

Ghouri, A. S. K., and J. E. McFarlane. (1958). Occurrence of macropterous form of *Gryllodes sigillatus* (Walker) (Orthoptera: Gryllidae) in laboratory culture, *Can. J. Zool.,* **36,** 837–838.

Gibbs, R. H. (1964). "Family Idiacanthidae," in *Mem. Sears Foundation for marine research,* Number 1. *Fishes of the Western North Atlantic,* pp. 512–521.

Gibson, R. (1982). "Nemertea," in *Synopsis and Classification of Living Organisms,* S. P. Parker et al., Ed., McGraw-Hill, New York, pp. 823–846.

Gibson, R., and J. Moore. (1976). Freshwater nemerteans, *Zool. J. Linn. Soc.,* **58,** 177–218.

Gilbert, J. J. (1967). Control of sexuality in the rotifer *Asplanchna brightwelli* by dietary lipids of plant origin, *Proc. Natl. Acad. Sci.,* **57,** 1218–1225.

Gilbert, J. J. (1968). Dietary control of sexuality in the rotifer *Asplanchna brightwelli* Gosse, *Physiol. Zool.,* **41,** 14–43.

Gilbert, J. J. (1980). Developmental polymorphism in the rotifer *Asplanchna sieboldi, Am. Sci.,* **68,** 636–645.

Gilbert, J. J. (1983). Control of sexuality in *Asplanchna brightwelli;* Threshold levels of dietary tocopherol and modification of tocopherol response by exogenous and endogenous factors, *Hydrobiologia,* **104,** 167–173.

Gilchrist, B. M. (1960). Growth and form of the brine shrimp *Artemia salina, Proc. Zool. Soc. Lond.,* **134,** 221–235.

Giles, E. T. (1961). Further studies on the growth of *Arixenia esau* Jordan and *Arixenia merus* Burr (Dermaptera: Hemimeridae), with a note on the first instar antennae of *Hemimerus talpoides* Walker (Dermaptera: Hemimeridae). *Proc. R. Entomol. Soc. Lond. A,* **36,** 21–26.

Giles, E. T. (1974). The relationships between Hemimerina and the other Dermaptera: a case for reinstating the Hemimerina within the Dermaptera, based upon numerical procedure, *Trans. R. Entomol. Soc. Lond.,* **126,** 189–206.

Gillett, S. D. (1983). Primary pheromones and polymorphism in the desert locust, *Anim. Behav.,* **31,** 221–230.

Gillett, S. D., and M. Philips. (1977). Faeces as a source of a locust gregarisation stimulus. Effects on social aggregation and on cuticular color of nymphs of desert locust *Schistocerca gregaria* (Forsk), *Acrida,* **6,** 279–286.

Giorgi, F., and F. Macchi. (1980). Vitellogenesis in the stick insect *Carausius morosus.* I. Specific protein synthesis during ovarian development, *J. Cell Sci.,* **46,** 1–16.

Giorgio, M., C. Giacoma, C. Vellano, and V. Mazzi. (1982). Prolactin and sexual behaviour in the crested newt (*Triturus cristatus* Laur.), *Gen. Comp. Endocrinol.,* **47,** 139–147.

Girardie, A. (1967). Contrôle neuro-hormonal de la métamorphose et de la pigmentation chez *Locusta migratoria cinerascens* (Orthoptère), *Bull. Biol. Fr. Belg.,* **107,** 79–114.

Girardie, A. (1976). Le polymorphisme phasaire des acridiens et son contrôle endocrine, *Mem. Soc. Sci. Phys. Nat. Bordeaux,* **1975–1976,** 13–17.

Glätzer, K. H. (1971). Die Ei- und Embryonalentwicklung von *Corydendrium parasiticum* mit besonderer Berücksichtigung der Oocyten feinstruktur während der Vitellogenese, *Helgol. Wiss. Meresunters.,* **22,** 213–280.

Gokan, N., T. Nagashima, S. N. Visscher, and H. Ando. (1982). "Fine structure of the eye of *Galloisiana nipponensis* (Caudell and King)," in *Biology of the Notoptera,* H. Ando, Ed., Kashiyo-Insatsu Co. Ltd. Nagano, Japan, pp. 159–172.

Goldschmidt, R. (1938). *Physiological Genetics,* McGraw-Hill, New York.

Goldschmidt, R. (1940). *The Material Basis of Evolution,* Yale University Press, New Haven, CT.

Gona, A. G., T. Pearlman, and W. Etkin. (1970). Prolactin-thyroid interaction in the nest, *Diemictylus viridescens, J. Endocrinol.,* **48,** 585–590.

Gonse, P. (1956a). L'ovogenèse chez *Phascolosoma vulgare.* I. Definition cytologique des stades de croissance des ovocytes, *Acta Zool.,* **37,** 193–214.

Gonse, P. (1956b). L'ovogenèse chez *Phascolosoma vulgare.* II. Recherche biométriques sur les ovocytes, *Acta Zool.,* **37,** 225–233.

Gorbman, A. (1983). "Reproduction in cyclostome fishes and its regulation," in *Fish Physiology,* W. S. Hoar, D. J. Randall, and E. M. Donaldson, Eds., Vol. 9, part A, pp. 1–29.

Gorbman, A., W. W. Dickhoff, J. Michael, E. F. Prentice, and W. Waknitz. (1982). Morphological indices of developmental progress in the parr-smolt coho salmon, *Oncorhynchus kisutch, Aquaculture,* **28,** 1–19.

Gordon, M. S., I. Boetius, D. Evans, R. McCarthy, and L. C. Oglesby. (1969). Aspects of the physiology of terrestrial life in amphibious fishes. I. The mudskipper, *Periophthalmus sobrinus, J. Exp. Biol.,* **50,** 141–149.

Gordon, M. S., W. Wilson, S. Ng, and A. Y. W. Yip. (1978). Aspects of the physiology of terrestrial life in amphibious fishes. III. The Chinese mudskipper *Periophthalmus cantonensis, J. Exp. Biol.,* **72,** 57–75.

Gore, R. H. (1979). Larval development of *Galathea rostrata* under laboratory conditions, with a discussion of larval development in the Galatheidae (Crustacea Anomura), *Fish. Bull.,* **76,** 781–805.

Gosliner, T. M., and M. T. Ghiselin. (1984). Parallel evolution in opisthobranch gastropods and its implications for polyphyletic methodology, *Syst. Zool.*, **33**, 255–274.

Goto, A. (1980). Geographic distributioin and variationis of two types of *Cottus nozawae* in Hokkaido, and morphological characteristics of *C. amblystomopsis* from Sakhalin, *Jap. J. Ichthyol.*, **27**, 97–105.

Goto, A. (1982). Reproductive behavior of a river sculpin, *Cottus nozawae, Jap. J. Ichthyol.*, **28**, 453–457.

Gotto, R. V. (1979). The association of copepods with marine invertebrates, *Adv. Mar. Biol.*, **16**, 1–109.

Götze, E. (1938). Bau und Leben von *Caecum glabrum* (Montagu), *Zool. Jahrb. Syst.*, **71**, 55–122.

Gould, S. J. (1977). *Ontogeny and Phylogeny,* Belknap Harvard Press, Cambridge, MA.

Gould, S. J. (1982). "The uses of heresy: An introduction to Richard Goldschmidt's 'The material basis of evolution,'" in The Material Basis of Evolution by R. Goldschmidt (replica), Yale University Press, New Haven, CT, pp. xiii–xlii.

Gould, S. J., and N. Eldredge. (1977). Punctuated equilibria: The tempo and mode of evolution reconsidered, *Paleontology* **2**, 115–151.

Gould-Somero, M. (1975). "Echiura," in *Reproduction of Marine Invertebrates,* A. C. Giese and J. S. Pearse, Eds., Academic, New York, pp. 277–311.

Grandison, A. G. C. (1978). The occurrence of *Nectophrynoides* (Anura Bufonidae) in Ethiopia. A new concept of the genus with a description of a new species, *Monit. Zool. Ital. N.S. Suppl.*, 120–172.

Granger, N. A., and W. E. Bollenbacher. (1981). "Hormonal control of insect metamorphosis," in *Metamorphosis,* 2nd ed., L. I. Gilbert and E. Frieden, Eds., Plenum, New York, pp. 105–137.

Grant, V. (1963). *The Origin of Adaptations,* Columbia University Press, New York.

Grant, V. (1982). Punctuated equilibria: A critique, *Biol. Zentralbl.*, **101**, 175–184.

Grant, W. C. (1961). Special aspects of the metamorphic process: Second metamorphosis, *Am. Zool.*, **1**, 163–171.

Grant, W. C., and G. Cooper. (1964). Endocrine control of metamorphic and skin changes in *Diemictylus viridescens, Am. Zool.*, **4**, 413–414.

Grant, W. C., and G. Cooper. (1965). Behavioral and integumentary changes associated with induced metamorphosis in *Diemictylus, Biol. Bull.*, **129**, 510–522.

Grau, E. G., W. W. Dickhoff, R. S. Nishioka, H. A. Bern, and L. C. Folmar. (1981). Lunar phasing of the thyroxine surge preparatory to seaward migration of salmonid fish, *Science,* **211**, 607–609.

Grau, E. G., L. H. Specker, R. S. Nishioka, and H. A. Bern. (1982). Factors determining the occurrence of the surge in thyroid activity in salmon during smoltification, *Aquaculture,* **28**, 49–57.

Grau, E. G., P. Prunet, T. Gross, R. S. Nishioka, and H. A. Bern. (1984). Bioassay for salmon prolactin using hypophysectomized *Fundulus heteroclitus, Gen. Comp. Endocrinol.*, **53**, 78–85.

Green, J. (1963). Seasonal polymorphism in *Scapholebris mucronata* (O. F. Muller) (Crustacea: Cladocera), *J. Anim. Ecol.*, **32**, 425–439.

Green, J. (1967). The distribution and variation of *Daphnia lumholtzi* in relation to fish predation in Lake Albert, East Africa, *J. Zool. Lond.*, **151**, 181–197.

Green, J. (1971). Association of Cladocera in the zooplankton of the lake sources of the White Nile, *J. Zool. Lond.*, **165**, 373–414.

Greenberg, S. L. W. (1979). Neotenic development and its control in the primitive termite *Zootermopsis angusticollis* (Hagen), Ph.D. thesis, University of Massachusetts.

Greenberg, S. L. W., and A. M. Stuart. (1982). Precocious reproductive development by larvae of a primitive termite *Zootermopsis angusticollis* (Hagen), *Insect Soc.*, **29**, 535–547.

Greenberg, S. L. W., J. G. Kunkel, and A. M. Stuart. (1978). Vitellogenesis in a primitive termite *Zootermopsis angusticollis* (Hagen) (Hodotermitidae), *Biol. Bull.*, **155**, 336–346.

Gressitt, J. L. (1970). Subantarctic entomology and biogeography, *Pac. Insects Monogr.*, **23**, 295–374.

Griswold, M. D., M. S. Fisher, and P. P. Cohen. (1972). Temperature-dependent intracellular distribution of thyroxine in amphibian liver, *Proc. Natl. Acad. Sci. U.S.A.*, **69**, 1486–1489.

Grün, G. (1972). Über den Eidimorphismus und die Oogenese von *Dinophilus gyrociliatus* (Archiannelida), *Z. Zellforsch.*, **130**, 70–92.

Günther, K. (1953). Über den taxonomische Gliederung und die geographi schen Verbreitung der Insektenordnungen der Phasmatodea, *Beitr. Entomol.*, **3**, 541–563.

Gurkewitz, S., M. Chow, and R. D. Campbell. (1980). *Hydra* size and budding rate: Influence of feeding, *Int. J. Inverteb. Reprod.*, **2**, 199–201.

Gurney, A. B. (1938). A synopsis of the order Zoraptera, with notes on the biology of *Zorotypus hubbardi* Caudell, *Proc. Entomol. Soc. Wash.*, **40**, 57–87.

Gurney, R. (1942). *Larvae of decapod Crustacea,* The Royal Society of London.

Gustafson, M. K. S., and M. C. Wikgren. (1981). Peptidergic and aminergic neurons in adult *Diphyllobothrium dendriticum* Nitzch, 1924, *Z. Parasitenkd.*, **64**, 121–134.

Guyard, A. (1971). Etude de la différenciation de l'ovotestis et des facteurs contrôlant l'orientation sexuelle des gonocytes de l'escargot *Helix aspersa* Müller. These de Sciences, Besancon No. 56, 187 pp.

Hackman, W. (1964). On reduction and loss of wings in Diptera, *Not. Entomol.*, **44**, 73–93.

Hackman, W. (1966). On wing reduction and loss of wings in Lepidoptera, *Not. Entomol.*, **46**, 1–16.

Hafez, M., and L. El-Said. (1970). On the bionomics of *Orgyia dubia* Judaea (Lepidoptera: Lymantridae), *Bull. Soc. Entomol. Egypte*, **53**, 161–183.

Hagan, H. R. (1951). *Embryology of the Viviparous Insects,* Ronald, New York.

Hagedorn, H. H. (1980). "Ecdysone, a gonadal hormone in insects," in *Invertebrate Reproduction,* W. H. Clark and T. S. Adams, Eds., pp. 997–1070.

Hagen, D. W., and L. G. Gilbertson. (1973). The genetics of plate morphs in freshwater threespine sticklebacks, *Heredity*, **31**, 75–84.

Haldane, J. B. S. (1932). *The Cause of Evolution,* Longman Green, London.

Hale, W. G. (1965). Postembryonic development in some species of Collembola, *Pedobiologia* **5**, 228–243.

Hales, D. F. (1976). "Juvenile hormone and aphid polymorphism," in *Phase and Caste Determination,* M. Lüscher, Ed., Pergamon, Oxford, pp. 105–115.

Hales, D. F., and T. E. Mittler. (1981). Precocious metamorphosis of the aphid *Myzus persicae* induced by the precocene analogue 6-methoxy–7-ethonoxy–2.2-methylchromene, *J. Insect Physiol.,* **27**, 333–337.

Halkka, O., M. Raatkainen, and J. Vilbaste. (1975). Clines in the colour polymorphism of *Philaenus spumarius* in eastern central Europe, *Heredity,* **35**, 303–309.

Halkka, O., J. Viblaste, and M. Raatkainen. (1980). Colour gene allele frequencies correlated with altitude of habitat in *Philaenus* populations, *Hereditas,* **92**, 243–246.

Hall, B. K. (1984). Developmental mechanisms underlying the formation of atavism, *Biol. Rev.,* **59**, 89–124.

Hand, C. (1959). On the origin and phylogeny of the coelenterates, *Syst. Zool.,* **8**, 191–202.

Handlirsch, A. (1906–1908). *Die fossilen Insekten und die Phylogenie der rezenten Formen,* W. Engelmann, Leipzig.

Hanström, B. (1940). Inkretorische Organe, Sinnesorgane und Nervensystem des Kopfes einiger niederen Insektenordnungen. *K. Svensk Vetenskapsakad. Handl.* Ser. III, **18**(8), 1–266.

Hardie, J. (1980). Juvenile hormone mimics the photoperiodic apterization of the alate ɩvnopara of aphid, *Aphis fabae, Nature,* **286**, 602–604.

Hardie, J. (1981). Juvenile hormone and photoperiodically controlled polymorphism in *Aphis fabae:* Postnatal effects on presumptive gynoparae, *J. Insect Physiol.,* **27**, 347–355.

Hardie, J., and A. D. Lees. (1983). Photoperiodic regulation of the development of winged gynoparae in the aphid, *Aphis fabae, Physiol. Entomol.,* **8**, 385–391.

Hardie, J., A. D. Lees, and S. Young. (1981). Light transmission through the head capsule of an aphid, *Megoura viciae, J. Insect Physiol.,* **27**, 773–777.

Harding, J. P. (1953). The first known example of terrestrial ostracod, *Ann. Natal Mus.,* **12**, 359–365.

Hargis, W. J. (1953). Monogenetic trematodes of Westhampton lake fishes III, part 2. A discussion of host specificity, *Proc. Helminthol. Soc.* (Washington, DC), **20**, 98–104.

Hargis, W. J. (1957). The host specificity of monogenetic trematodes, *Exp. Parasitol.,* **6**, 610–625.

Harms, J. W. (1934). *Wandlungen der Artgefüges,* Tübingen.

Harrison, A. G. (1982). Return of the hopeful monster, *Paleobiology,* **8**, 459–463.

Harrison, L. (1914). The Mallophaga as a possible clue to bird phylogeny, *Aust. J. Zool.,* **1**, 1–5.

Harrison, R. G. (1980). Dispersal polymorphisms in insects, *Ann. Rev. Ecol. Syst.,* **11**, 95–118.

Hartmann, G. (1973). Zum gegenwärtigen Stand der Erforschung der Ostracoden interstitieller Systeme, *Ann. Speleol.,* **28**, 417–426.

Hartmann-Schroeder, G. (1964). Zum Problem der Anpassung von Polychaeten an das Leben im Küstengrundwasser, *Mitt. Ham. Zool. Mus. Kosswig-Festschrift,* 67–78.

Hartnoll, R. C. (1963). The freshwater graspid crabs of Jamaica, *Proc. Linn. Soc. London,* **175**, 145–169.

Hasegawa, Y. and Y. Katakura. (1981). Androgenic gland hormone and development of oviducts in the isopod crustacean, *Armadillidium vulgare., Dev. Growth Differ.,* **23**, 59–62.

Hashimoto, H. (1971). Females of *Clunio* (in Japanese). *Makunagi*, **6**, 217–226 (Osaka Pref. Univ., Japan).

Hashimoto, H. (1981). Ecology of marine chironomids (in Japanese), *Kontyu to Shizen*, **16**, 6–11.

Haupt, H. (1934). Neues über die Homoptera-Aleurodina, *Dtsch. Entomol. Z.*, **1934**, 127–141.

Haverty, M. I. (1977). The proportion of soldiers in termite colonies, *Sociobiology*, **2**, 199–217.

Hayashi, R., and M. Komatsu. (1971). On the development of the seastar *Certonardoa semiregularis* (Muller & Troschel) I, *Proc. Jap. Soc. Syst. Zool.* **7**, 74–80.

Hazelwood, D. H. (1966). Illumination and turbulence effects on relative growth in *Daphnia, Limnol. Oceanogr.*, **11**, 212–216.

Healy, W. R. (1970). Reduction of neoteny in Massachusetts populations of *Notophthalmus viridescens., Copeia*, **1970**, 578–581.

Heath, D. J. (1975). Colour, sunlight and internal temperature in the land snail *Cepaea nemoralis* (L.), Oecologia, **19**, 29–38.

Hebard, M. (1942). The Dermaptera and orthopterous families, Blattidae, Mantidae and Phasmidae of Texas, *Trans. Am. Entomol. Soc.*, **68**, 239–310.

Helfert, B. (1977). Quantitative Untersuchungen über den Ommochromgehalt im Integument von *Oedipoda coerulescens* L. (Orthoptera, Acrididae), *Zool. Anz.*, **198**, 269–286.

Helfert, B. (1978). Über die experimentelle Beeinflussung von Farbvari anten von *Chorthippus biguttulus* L. (Orthoptera, Acrididae) im Zusammenhang mit dem Ommochromgehalt des Integument, *Zool. Anz.*, **200**, 41–52.

Heller, J. (1975). The taxonomy of some British *Littorina* species, with notes on their reproduction (Mollusca: Prosobranchia: Littornidae), *Zool. J. Linn. Soc.*, **56**, 131–151.

Hendler, G. (1975). Adaptational significance of the patterns of ophiuroid development, *Am. Zool.*, **15**, 691–715.

Hendler, G. (1979). Sex-reversal and viviparity in *Ophiolepis kieri* n. sp., with notes on viviparous brittle stars from the Caribbean (Echinodermata: Ophiuroidea), *Proc. Biol. Soc. Wash.*, **92**, 783–795.

Hendler, G. (1982). An echinoderm vitellaria with a bilateral larval skeleton: Evidence for the evolution of ophiuroid vitellaria from ophioplutei, *Biol. Bull.*, **163**, 431–436.

Hennig, W. (1969). *Die Stammesgeschichte der Insekten*, Waldemar Kramer, Frankfurt am Main.

Hennig, W. (1981). *Insect Phylogeny*, Wiley, New York.

Henry, L. M. (1937). Biological notes on *Timema californica* Scudder (Phasmoidea: Timemidae), *Pan-Pac. Entomol.*, **13**, 137–141.

Hentschel, E. (1964). Zum neurosekretorischen System der Anostraca, Crustacea (*Artemia salina* Leach and *Chirocephalus grubei* Dybowski), *Zool. Anz.*, **170**, 187–190.

Herbaut, C. (1975). Etude expérimentale de la régulation endocrinienne de l'ovogenèse chez *Lithobius forficatus* L. (Myriapode Chilopode). Rôle de la pars intercerebralis, *Gen. Comp. Endocrinol.*, **27**, 34–42.

Herbaut, C. (1976). Etude expérimentale de la régulation endocrinienne de l'ovogènese chez *Lithobius forficatus* L. (Myriapode Chiolopode), Rôle du complexe: "cellules neurosécrétrices protocérébrales-glandes cérébrales," *Gen. Comp. Endocrinol.,* **28,** 264–276.

Herbert, P. D. N. (1978). The adaptive significance of cyclomorphosis in *Daphnia:* More possibilities, *Freshwater Biol.,* **8,** 313–320.

Herlant-Meewis, H. (1966). Evolution de l'appareil génital d' *Eisenia foetida* au cours du jeune de la régénération posterieure et a la suite de l'ablation de ganglion nerveux, *Ann. Soc. R. Zool. Belg.,* **96,** 189–240.

Herlant-Meewis, H. (1975). "Neurosecretory phenomena during reproduction in Oligochaeta," in *Intersexuality in the Animal Kingdom,* R. Reinboth, Ed., Springer, New York, pp. 57–63.

Herman, W. S., and D. C. Bennett. (1975). Regulation of oogenesis, female specific protein production, and male and female reproductive gland development by juvenile hormone in the butterfly *Nymphalis antiopa, J. Comp. Physiol.,* **99,** 331–338.

Herman, W. S., and S. H. Dallmann. (1981). Endocrine biology of the painted lady butterfly *Vanessa cardui, J. Insect Physiol.,* **27,** 163–168.

Hermans, C. O. (1979). "Polychaete egg sizes. life histories and phylogeny, in *Reproductive Ecology of Marine Invertebrates,* S. E. Stancyk, Ed., University Southern California Press, Los Angeles, pp. 1–9.

Herring, P. J. (1974). Size, density and lipid content of some decapod eggs, *Deep-Sea Res.,* **21,** 91–94.

Hertwig, I. and M. Hundgen. (1984). Gonophorenbildung und Keimzellentwicklung bei *Hydractinia echinata* Fleming 1928 (Hydrozoa, Athecata), *Zool. Jahrb. Anat.,* **112L,** 113–136.

Heslop-Harrison, J. W. (1956). Melanism in the Lepidoptera, *Entomol. Rec. J. Var.,* **68,** 172–181.

Hessler, R. R. (1971). Biology of the Mystacocarida, a prospectus, *Smiths. Contrib. Zool.,* **76,** 87–90.

Hessler, R. R., and W. A. Newman. (1975) A trilobitomorph origin for the Crustacea, *Fossil Strata,* **4,** 437–459.

Heymons, R. (1909). Eine Plazenta bei einem Insekt (*Hemimerus*), *Verh. Dtsch. Zool. Ges.,* **19,** 97–107.

Heymons, R. (1912). Über den Genitalapparat und die Entwicklung von *Hemimerus talpoides* Walk., *Zool. Jahrb. Suppl.,* **14,** 141–184.

Hickman, V. V. (1937). The embryology of the syncarid crustacean, *Anaspides tasmaniae* Rep., *Proc. Roy. Soc. Tasmania,* **1936**(April), 1–35, 13 plates.

Highnam, K. C., and L. Hill. (1967). *The Comparative Endocrinology of the Invertebrates,* 2nd ed., Arnold, London.

Hille Ris Lambers, D. (1966). Polymorphism in Aphididae, *Ann. Rev. Entomol.,* **11,** 47–78.

Hincks, W. D. (1949). Dermaptera and Orthoptera, *R. Entomol. Soc. Handb. Brit. Insects,* **1**(5), 1–20.

Hinton, H. E. (1941). The immature stages of *Acrotrichis fascicularis* (Herbst) (Col. Ptiliidae), *Entomol. Mon. Mag.,* **77,** 245–250.

Hinton, H. E. (1946). Correlated phase in the metamorphosis of insects, *Nature,* **157,** 552–553.

Hinton, H. E. (1955). On the structure, function and distribution of the prolegs of the Panorpoidea, with a criticism of the Berlese-Imms theory, *Trans. R. Entomol. Soc. Lond.,* **106,** 455–556.

Hinton, H. E. (1963). The origin of the pupal stage, *Proc. R. Entomol. Soc. A,* **38,** 77–85.

Hinton, H. E. (1981). *Biology of Insect Eggs,* Vol. 1, Pergamon, New York.

Hintze-Podufal, C. (1975). The effects of juvenile hormone and analogues on pupae and imagines of *Sphinx ligusti* after application to mature larvae, *Dtsch. Entomol. Z.,* **22,** 219–227.

Hiraiwa, Y. K. (1936). Studies on a bopyrid, *Epepenaeon japonica* Thienemann III. Development and life cycle, with special reference to the sex differentiation in the bopyrid, *J. Sci. Hiroshima Univ. (Zool.),* **4,** 101–141.

Ho, M.-W. (1984). "Environment and heredity in development and evolution," in *Beyond Neo-Darwinism,* M-W. Ho and P. T. Saunders, Eds., Academic, New York, pp. 267–289.

Hoar, W. S. (1939). The thyroid gland of the Atlantic salmon, *J. Morphol.,* **65,** 257–295.

Hoar, W. S. (1976). Smolt transformation: evolution, behavior, and physiology. *J. Fish. Res. Bd. Can.,* **33,** 1233–1252.

Hodkova, M., and R. Socha. (1982). Why is *Pyrrhocoris apterus* insensitive to precocene II?, *Experientia,* **38,** 977–979.

Hoeppli, R. S. C. (1926). Studies of free-living nematodes from the thermal water of Yellowstone Park, *Trans. Am. Microsc. Soc.,* **45,** 234–254.

Hoffmann, K. H., W. Behrens, and W. Ressin. (1981). Effects of daily temperature cycle on ecdysteroids and cyclic nucleotide titers in adult female crickets, *Gryllus bimaculatus, Physiol. Entomol.,* **6,** 375–385.

Hoffmann, K. H., and W. Behrens. (1982). Free ecdysteroids in adult male crickets, *Gryllus bimaculatus, Physiol. Entomol.,* **7,** 269–279.

Hoffmann, R. J. (1973). Environmental control of seasonal variation in the butterfly *Colias eurytheme* I. Adaptive aspects of a photoperiodic response, *Evolution,* **27,** 387–397.

Hofmann, D. K., R. Neumann, and K. Henne. (1978). Strobilation, budding and initiation of scyphistoma morphogenesis in the rhizostome *Cassiopea andromeda* (Cnidaria: Scyphozoa), *Mar. Biol.,* **47,** 161–176.

Holland, G. P. (1964). Evolution, classification, and host relationships of Siphonaptera, *Ann. Rev. Entomol.,* **9,** 123–146.

Honek, A. (1974). Wing polymorphism in *Pyrrhocoris apterus* (L.). (Heteroptera: Pyrrhocoridae); influence of photoperiod, *Vestn. Cesk. Spol. Zool.,* **38,** 241–242.

Honek, A. (1976). Factors influencing the wing polymorphism in *Pyrrhocoris apterus* (Heteroptera, Pyrrhocoridae), *Zool. Jahrb. Syst.,* **103,** 1–22.

Honek, A. (1981). Wing polymorphism in *Notiophilus biguttatus* in Bohemia (Coleoptera, Carabidae), *Vestn. Cesk. Spol. Zool.,* **45,** 81–86.

Horsfall, W. R. (1943). Biology and control of common blister beetles in Arkansas, *Univ. Arkansas Agric. Exp. Stn. Bull.,* **436,** 1–55.

Hovasse, R. (1943). *De l'Adaptation par la Sélection,* Hermann, Paris.

Hovasse, R. (1950). *Adaptation et Evolution,* Hermann, Paris

Hubbs, C. R. (1971). *Lampetra (Entosphenus) leptocephala,* new species, the non-parasitic derivatives of the Pacific lamprey, *Trans. San Diego Soc. Nat. Hist.,* **16,** 125–163.

Hubschman, J. H. (1975). Larval development of the freshwater shrimp *Palaemonetes kadiakensis* Rathbun under osmotic stress, *Physiol. Zool.,* **48,** 97–104.

Huettel, M. D., and G. L. Bush. (1972). The genetics of host selection and its bearing on sympatric speciation in *Procecidochares* (Diptera; Tephretidae), *Entomol. Exp. Appl.,* **15,** 465–480.

Hughes, A. (1966). The thyroid and development of the nervous system in *Eleutherodactylus martinicensis:* An experimental study, *J. Embryol. Exp. Morphol.,* **16,** 401–430.

Hughes, A., and P. Reier. (1972). A preliminary study on the effects of bovine prolactin on the embryos of *Eleutherodactylus ricordii, Gen. Comp. Endocrinol.,* **19,** 304–312.

Hunter-Jones, P. (1958). Laboratory studies on the inheritance of phase characters in locusts, *Anti-Locust Bull.,* **29,** 1–32.

Hurlbert, S. H. (1969). The breeding migrations and interhabitat wandering of the vermillion spotted newt *Notophthalmus viridescens* (Raffinesque), *Ecol. Monogr.,* **39,** 465–488.

Hurley, D. E. (1959). Notes on the ecology and environmental adaptations of the terrestrial Amphipoda, *Pac. Sci.,* **13,** 107–128.

Hurley, D. E. (1968). Transition from water to land in amphipod crustaceans, *Am. Zool.,* **8,** 327–353.

Hutchinson, G. E. (1963). A note on the polymorphism of *Philaenus spumarius* (L.) (Homoptera, Cercopidae) in Britain, *Entomol. Mon. Mag.,* **99,** 175–178.

Hutton, J. C., P. J. Schofield, and W. R. McManas. (1972). Metabolic activity of *Fasciola hepatica* to mammalian hormones in vitro, *Comp. Biochem. Physiol.,* **42,** 49–56.

Huxley, J. S. (1929). Thyroid and temperature and cold blooded animals, *Nature,* **123,** 712.

Huxley, J. S. (1948). *Evolution. The Modern Synthesis,* Allen & Unwin, London.

Hyman, L. H. (1940). *The Invertebrata.* Vol. 1, *Protozoa through Ctenophora.* McGraw-Hill, New York.

Hyman, L. H. (1941). Environmental control of sexual reproduction in a planarian, *Anat. Rec.* **81.** Suppl., 108.

Hynes, H. B. N. (1941). The taxonomy and ecology of the nymph of British Plecoptera, with notes on the adults and eggs, *Trans. R. Soc. Lond.,* **91,** 459–557.

Hynes, H. B. N. (1976). Biology of Plecoptera, *Ann. Rev. Entomol.,* **21,** 135–153.

Ibrahim, I. A., and A. M. Gad. (1975). The occurrence of paedogenesis in *Eristalis* larvae, *J. Med. Entomol.,* **12,** 268.

Ichikawa, A., and R. Yanagimachi. (1958). Studies on the sexual organization of the Rhizocephala. I. The nature of the "testis" of *Peltogasterella socialis* Kruger, *Annot. Zool. Jap.,* **31,** 82–96.

Ichikawa, A., and R. Yanagimachi. (1960). Studies on the sexual organization of the Rhizocephala. II. The reproductive function of the larval (cypris) males of *Peltogaster* and *Sacculina, Annot. Zool. Jap.,* **33,** 42–56.

Idler, D. R., and C. M. Campbell. (1980). Gonadotropin stimulation of estrogen and yolk precursor synthesis in juvenile rainbow trout, *Gen. Comp. Endocrinol.,* **41,** 384–391.

Ikemoto, H. (1983). The role of juvenile hormone in the density-related color variation in larvae of *Cephanodes hylas* L. (Lepidoptera: Sphingidae), *Appl. Entomol. Zool.,* **18,** 57–61.

Illies, J. (1965). Phylogeny and zoogeography of the Plecoptera, *Ann. Rev. Entomol.,* **10,** 117–140.

Imms, A. D. (1937). *Recent Advances in Entomology,* 2nd ed., J. & A. Churchill, London.

Inger, R. F. (1960). Notes on toads of the genus *Pelophryne, Fieldiana Zool.,* **39,** 415–418.

Inglis, W. G. (1965). Patterns of evolution in parasitic nematodes, *Third Symp. Brit. Soc. Parasitol.,* 79–124.

Injeyan, H. S., and S. S. Tobe. (1981a). Phase polymorphism in *Schistocerca gregaria:* Reproductive parameters, *J. Insect Physiol.,* **27,** 97–102.

Injeyan, H. S., and S. S. Tobe. (1981b). Phase polymorphism in *Schistocerca:* Assessment of juvenile hormone systhesis in relation to vitellogenesis, *J. Insect Physiol.,* **27,** 203–210.

Ishii, S., and Y. Kuwahara. (1967). An aggregation pheromone of the German cockroach, *Blattella germanica* (L.) 1. Site of pheromone production, *Appl. Entomol. Zool.,* **2,** 207–213.

Ishii, S., and Y. Kuwahara. (1968), Aggregation of German cockroach *(Blatella germanica)* nymphs, *Experientia,* **24,** 88–89.

Ivanova-Kazas, O. M. (1965). Trophic connections between the maternal organism and the embryo in paedogenetic Diptera (Cecidomyiidae), *Acta Biol. Hung.,* **16,** 1–24.

Iwao, S. (1962). Studies of the phase variation and related phenomena in some lepidopterous insects, *Mem. Coll. Agrio. Kyoto Univ.,* **84,** 1–80.

Iwao, S. (1968). Some effects of grouping in lepidopterous insects, *Colloq. Int. CNRS No. 173. L'effet de groupe chez les animaux,* pp. 185–212.

Jablonski, D., J. J. Sepkoski, Jr., D. J. Bottjer, and P. M. Sheehan. (1983). Onshore–offshore patterns in evolution of phanerozoic shelf communities, *Science,* **222,** 1123–1125.

Jackson, D. J. (1928). The inheritance of long and short wings in the weevil, *Sitona hispidula,* with a discussion of wing reduction in beetles, *Trans. R. Soc. Edinburgh,* **55,** 665–735.

Jacobi, H. (1954). Biologie, Entwicklungsgeschichte und Systematik von *Bathynella natans, Zool. Jahrb. Syst.,* **83,** 1–62.

Jacobi, H. (1969). Contribucao a ontogenia de *Bathynella* Veld, e *Brasillibathynella* Jacobi 1958 (Crustacea), *Bol. Univ. Fed. Parana, Zool.,* **3,** 131–142.

Jacobs, J. (1961). Cyclomorphosis in *Daphnia galeata mendotae* Birge, a case of environmentally controlled allometry, *Arch. Hydrobiol.,* **58,** 7–71.

Jaenike, J., and R. T. Selander. (1979). Evolution and ecology of parthenogenesis in earthworms, *Am. Zool.,* **19,** 729–737.

Jägersten, G. (1939). Zur Kenntnis der Larventwicklung bei *Myzostomum, Ark. Zool.,* **31**A(11), 1–21.

Jägersten, G. (1940a). Die Abhängigkeit der Metamorphose vom Substrat des Biotopes bei *Protodrilus, Ark. Zool.,* **32**(17), 1–12.

Jägersten, G. (1940b). Zur Kenntnis der äusseren Morphologie, Entwicklung and Ökologie von *Protodrilus rubropharyngus* n. sp., *Ark. Zool.,* **32**(16), 1–19.

Jägersten, G. (1952). Studies on morphology, larval development and biology of *Protodrilus, Zool. Bidr. Uppsala,* **29,** 425–512.

Jägersten, G. (1955). On the early phylogeny of the Metazoa. The bilaterogastraea theory, *Zool. Bidr. Uppsala,* **30,** 321–354.

Jägersten, G. (1959). Further remarks on the early phylogeny of the Metazoa, *Zool. Bidr. Uppsala,* **33,** 79–108.

Jägersten, G. (1972). *Evolution of the Metazoan Life Cycle,* Academic, New York.

Jannone, G. (1939). Studio morfologico, anatomico e istologico del *Dociostaurus maroccanus* (Thunb.) nelle sue fasi transiens congregans, gregaria e solitaria, *Boll. Lab. Entomol. Agric. Portici,* **4,** 1–443.

Jennings, J. B. (1971). Parasitism and commensalism in the Turbellaria, *Adv. Parasitol.,* **9,** 1–31.

Jentsch, S. (1939). Beiträge zur Überordnung Psocoida 7. Vergleichend entwicklungsbiologische und oekologische Untersuchungen an einheimischen Psocopteren unter besonderer Berücksichtigung der Art *Hyperetes guestfalicus* Kolbe 1880, *Zool. Jahrb. Syst.,* **73,** 1–46.

Jepsen, G. G., E. Mayr, and G. G. Simpson. (1949). *Genetics, Paleontology and Evolution,* Princeton University Press, Princeton, N.J.

Jeschikov, J. J. (1929). Zur Frage über die Entstehung der volkommenen Verwandlung, *Zool. Jahrb. Abt. 2,* **50,** 601–650.

Johno, S. (1963). Analysis of the density effect as a determining factor of the wing-form in the brown planthopper, *Nilaparvata lugens, Jap. J. Appl. Zool. Entomol.,* **7,** 48.

Johnson, B. (1956). Wing polymorphism in aphids. III. The influence of host plant, *Entomol. Exp. Appl.,* **9,** 213–222.

Johnson, B. (1959). Effect of parasitization by *Aphidius platensis* Brethes on the developmental physiology of its hosts *Aphis craccivorae* Koch, *Entomol. Exp. Appl.,* **2,** 82–99.

Johnson, B. (1965). Wing polymorphism in aphids. II Interaction between aphids, *Entomol. Exp. Appl.,* **9,** 213–222.

Joly, L., and P. Joly. (1974). Comparaison de la phase grégaire et de la phase solitaire de *Locusta migratoria migratorioides* (Orthoptère) du point de vue de la teneur de leur haemolymphe en hormone juvénile, *C. R. Acad. Sci. Paris* **279,** 1007–1009.

Joly, P. (1962) Rôle joué par les corpora allata dans la réalisation du polymorphisme de phase chez *Locusta migratoria* L., *Coll. Int. CNRS* no 114: 77–87.

Joly, P. (1972). Environmental regulation of endocrine activity, *Gen. Comp. Endocrinol. Suppl.,* **3,** 459–465.

Joly, R. (1964). Action de l'ecdysone sur le cycle de la mue de *Lithobius forficatus* L. (Myriapode, Chilopode), Soc. Biol. Lille, Seance du 14 Fevrier 1964, pp. 548–550.

Joly, R. (1966). Etude expérimentale du cycle de mue et de la régulation endocrine chez les Myriapodes Chilopodes, *Gen. Comp. Endocrinol.,* **6,** 519–533.

Joly, R. (1977). Influence de quelques facteurs externes sur l'activité sécretoire des glandes cérébrales chez *Lithobius forficatus* L. (Myriapode Chilopode). Etude en microscopies photoniques et électronique, *Gen. Comp. Endocrinol.,* **32,** 167–178.

Joly, R., and C. Jamault-Navaro. (1978). Rôle de la pars intercerebralis sur l'activité sécrétoire des glandes cérébrales chez *Lithobius forficatus* L. (Myriapode Chilopode) Etude ultrastructurale, *Arch. Zool. Exp. Gen.,* **119,** 487–496.

Jones, J. S., B. H. Leith, and P. Rawlings. (1977). Polymorphism in *Cepaea:* A problem with too many solutions, *Ann. Rev. Ecol. Syst.,* **8,** 109–143.

Jouin, C. (1962). Le développement larvaire de *Protodrilus chaetifer* Remane (Archiannelida), *C. R. Acad. Sci.,* **255,** 3065–3067.

Jouin, C. (1968). Sexualité et biologie de la reproduction chez *Mesonerilla* Remane (Archiannelides Nerrillidae), *Cah. Biol. Mar.,* **9,** 31–52.

Joyeux, C., and J. G. Baer. (1961). "Classe des cestodes," in *Traite de Zoologie,* P.-P. Grassé, Ed., Vol. 4, No. 1, Masson, Paris, pp. 347–560.

Jucci, C., and A. Springhetti. (1952). Evolution of seminal vesicles in Isoptera, *Trans. 9th Int. Congr. Entomol.,* **1,** 130–132.

Junera, H. C., C. Zerbib, M. Martin, and J.-J. Meusy. (1977). Evidence for control of vitellogenin synthesis by an ovarian hormone in *Orchestia gammarella* (Pallas), Crustacea, Amphipoda, *Gen. Comp. Endocrinol.,* **31,** 457–462.

Kabata, Z. (1981). Copepoda (Crustacea) parasitic on fishes: Problems and perspectives, *Adv. Parasitol.,* **19,** 1–71.

Kabata, Z., and B. Cousens. (1973). Life cycle of *Salminicola californiensis* (Dana 1852) (Copepoda: Lernaeopodidae), *J. Fish. Res. Bd. Can.,* **30,** 881–903.

Kaestner, A. (1963). *Lehrbuch der speziellen Zoologie,* Vol. 1, Gustav Fischer, Jena.

Kaestner, A. (1967). *Lehrbuch der speziellen Zoologie,* Vol. 1, part 2, *Crustacea,* G. Fischer, Stuttgart.

Kaiser, H. (1978). Licht und Elektronenmikroskopische Untersuchung der Ventraldrüsen von *Ephemera danica* Muell. (Ephemeroptera: Ephemeridae) während der Metamorphose, *Int. J. Insect Morphol. Embryol.,* **7,** 377–385.

Kaiser, H. (1980). Licht- und Elektronenmikroskopische Untersuchung der Corpora allata der Eintagsfliege *Ephemera danica* Mull. (Ephemeroptera: Ephemeridae) während der Metamorphose, *Int. J. Insect Morphol. Embryol.,* **9,** 395–403.

Kaiser, P. (1969). Welche Bedingungen steuern den Generationswechsel der Gallmücke *Heteropeza* (Diptera: Itonididae), *Zool. Jahrb. Physiol.,* **75,** 17–40.

Kaiser, P. (1974). Über die Entwicklungsumkehr der Imagolarven von *Heteropeza pygmaea* Winnertz und deren hormonale Regelung, *Zool. Jahrb. Physiol.,* **78,** 199–218.

Kalmus, H. (1945). Correlations between flight and vision, and particularly between wings and ocelli in insects, *Proc. R. Entomol. Soc. Lond. A,* **20,** 84–96.

Kamm, J. A. (1972). Environmental influence on reproduction, diapause, and morph determination of *Anaphothrips obscurus* (Thysnoptera: Thripidae), *Environ. Entomol.,* **1,** 16–19.

Kamp, J. W. (1979). Taxonomy, distribution, and zoogeographic evolution of *Grylloblatta* in Canada, *Can. Entomol.,* **111,** 27–38.

Karlinsky, A. (1967). Corpora allata et vitellogenèse chez les Lépidoptères, *Gen. Comp. Endocrinol.,* **9,** 511–512.

Kat, P. W. (1984). Parasitism and the Unionacea (Bivalvia), *Biol. Rev.,* **59,** 189–207.

Kats, T. S. (1984). Neuroendocrinal system in various morphs of *Megoura viciae, Entomol. Rev.,* **63,** 10–19.

Kearn, G. C. (1967). Experiments on host-finding and host specificity in the monogenean skin parasite *Entobdella soleae, Parasitology,* **57,** 585–605.

Kearn, G. C. (1981). In workshop no 4. Biology of monogeneans, *Parasitology,* **82,** 66.

Kéler, S. v. (1957). Über die Deszendenz und die Differenzierung der Mallophagen, *Z. Parasitenkd.,* **18,** 55–160.

Kenk, R. (1937). Sexual and asexual reproduction in *Euplanaria tigrina* (Girard), *Biol. Bull.,* **73,** 280–294.

Kennedy, J. S., and H. L. G. Stroyan. (1959). Biology of aphids, *Ann. Rev. Entomol.,* **4,** 139–160.

Kerfoot, W. C. (1974). Egg-size cycle of a cladoceran, *Ecology,* **55,** 1259–1270.

Kerfoot, W. C. (1975). The divergence of adjacent populations, *Ecology,* **56,** 1298–1313.

Kerr, W. E. (1950). Evolution of the mechanism of caste determination in the genus *Melipona,* Evolution, **4,** 7–13.

Kerr, W. E., Y. Akahira, and C. A. de Camargo. (1975). Genetic control of juvenile hormone production in *Melipona quadrifasciata* (Apidae), *Genetics,* **81,** 749–756.

Kessel, R. G. (1968). Electron microscope studies on developing oocytes of a coelenterate medusa with special reference to vitellogenesis, *J. Morphol.,* **126,** 211–248.

Kethley, J. B. (1974). Developmental chaetotaxy of a paedomorphic calaenopsoid, *Neotenogynium malkini* n.g. n. sp. (Acari: Parasite formes; Neotenogyniidae, n. fam.) associated with millipeds, *Ann. Entomol. Soc. Am.,* **67,** 571–579.

Kettlewell, B. (1973). *The Evolution of Melanism,* Clarendon, Oxford.

Kevan, D. K. McE. (1973). The place of classical taxonomy in modern systematic entomology, with particular reference to orthopteroid insects, *Can. Entomol.,* **105,** 1211–1222.

Kevan, D. K. McE. (1982). "Phasmatoptera," in *Synopsis and Classification of Living Organisms,* S. P. Parker et al., Eds., Vol. 2, McGraw-Hill, New York, pp. 379–383.

Kevan, D. K. McE. (1982). "Orthoptera," in *Synopsis and Classification of Living Organisms,* S. P. Parker et al., Eds., Vol. 2, McGraw-Hill, New York, pp. 352–379.

Kezer, J. (1952). Thyroxine induced metamorphosis by neotenic salamanders *Eurycea tyrenensis* and *Eurycea neotenes, Copeia,* **1952,** 234–237.

Khoo, S. G. (1964). Studies on the biology of *Capnia bifrons* (Newman) and notes on the diapause in the nymph of this species. *Verh. 3 Intn. Symp. über Plecopteren. Limnol. Sch.,* **34/35,** 23–31.

Khouaidjia, D., and S. Fuzeau-Braesch. (1982). Comparaison de la reproduction de souches d'origine géographique distinctes élévées sous régimes thermiques differents en isolement et en groupement chez *Locusta migratoria* (Orthoptères), *C. R. Acad. Sc.,* **294,** 827–831.

Killington, F. J. (1946). On *Psectra diptera* (Burm.) (Neur. Hemerobiidae), including an account of its life history, *Entomol. Mon. Mag.,* **62,** 161–176.

Kim, K. C., and H. W. Ludwig. (1978). Phylogenetic relationships of parasitic Psocodea and taxonomic position of the Anoplura, *Ann. Entomol. Soc. Am.,* **71,** 910–922.

Kimura, T., and S. Masaki. (1977). Brachypterism and seasonal adaptation in *Orgyia thysellina* Butler (Lepidoptera, Lymantridae), *Kontyu,* **45,** 97–106.

Kinzelbach, R. (1971a). Morphologische Befunde an Fächerflüglern und ihre phylogenetische Bedeutung, *Zoologica* (Stuttgart) **119**, 1–256.

Kinzelbach, R. (1971b) Ordnung Strepsiptera (Fächerflügler), *Handb. Zool., Vol 4, Arthropoda,* Section 2, *Insects,* **2**(24), 1–61.

Kirsteurer, E. (1972). The interstitial nemertean fauna of marine sand, *Smiths. Contrib. Zool.,* **76**, 17–19.

Kisimoto, R. (1956a). Factors determining the wing-form of adult, with special reference to the effect of crowding during the larval period of the brown planthopper, *Nilaparvata lugens* Stål. Studies on the polymorphism in the planthopper (Homoptera Araeopidae) (in Japanese) *J. Appl. Zool. Entomol.,* **12**, 105–111.

Kisimoto, R. (1956b). Effect of crowding during the larval period on the determination of the wing-form of an adult planthopper, *Nature,* **178**, 641–642.

Kisimoto, R. (1957). Studies on the polymorphism in plant hoppers (Homoptera, Araeopidae) III. Differences in several morphological and physiological characters (in Japanese), *Appl. Zool. Entomol.,* **1**, 164–172.

Kisimoto, R. (1975). *Unka umio wataru* (Migration of the planthopper; in Japanese), Chuo-Koron-sha, Tokyo.

Kistler, A., K. Yoshizato, and E. Frieden. (1975). Binding of thyroxine and triiodothyronine by nuclei of isolated liver cells, *Endocrinology,* **97**, 1036–1042.

Klausner, E., E. R. Miller, and H. Dingle. (1981). Genetics of brachyptery in a lygaeid bug island population, *J. Hered.,* **72**, 288–289.

Klie, W. (1943). Ostracoden aus dem Kenia-Gebiet, vornehmlich von dessen Hochgebirgen, *Int. Rev. Hydrobiol.,* **39**, 99–161.

Klier, E. (1956). Zur Konstruktionsmorphologie des männlichen Geschlechts-apparates der Psocopteren, *Zool. Jahrb. Anat.,* **75**, 207–286.

Knopf, G. H. (1962). Paedogenesis and metamorphic variation in *Ambystoma tigrinum mavortium, Southwest Nat.,* **7**, 75.

Koba, K. (1936). Preliminary notes on the development of *Geotelphusa dehaani* (White), *Proc. Imp. Acad. Japan,* **12**, 105–107.

Kobayashi, H., T. Ichikawa, T. Suzuki, and M. Sekimoto. (1972). Seasonal migration of the hagfish, *Pap. J. Ichthyol.,* **19**, 191–194.

Kobayashi, M. (1956). Effect of the brain on the spread of the wings in the silkworm, *Bombyx mori, J. Seric. Sci. Japan,* **25**, 341–343.

Kohler, H.-J. (1976). Embryologische Untersuchungen an Copepoden: Die Entwicklung von *Lernaeocora branchialis* L. 1767 (Crustacea, Copepoda, Lernaeidae), *Zool. Jahrb. Anat.,* **95**, 448–504.

Königsmann, E. (1960). Zur Phylogenie der Parametabola, *Beitr. Entomol.,* **10**, 705–744.

Köppa, P. (1970). Studies on the thrips (Thysanoptera) species most commonly occurring in cereals in Finland, *Ann. Agric. Fenn.,* **9**, 191–265.

Kristensen, R. M. (1983). Loricifera, a new phylum with Aschelminthes characters from the meiobenthos, *Z. Zool. Syst. Evolutions-forsch.,* **21**, 163–180.

Kühne, H. (1972). Entwicklungsverlauf und Studien von *Micromalthus debilis* Le-Conte (Col. Curculionidae) aus einer Laboratoriums-population, *Z. Angew. Entomol.,* **72**, 157–168.

Kulakovsky, E. E. (1976). Neurosecretory cells and their cycles in the brain of *Artemia salina* (in Russian). *Zool. Zh.*, **55**, 354–362.

Kulkarni, O. K. and R. Nagabhushnam. (1980). Role of brain hormone in oogenesis of the Indian freshwater leech *Poecilobdella viridis* during the annual reproductive cycle, *Hydrobiologia*, **69**, 225–228.

Kunigelis, S. C., and A. S. M. Saleuddin. (1978). Regulation of shell growth in the pulmonate gastropod *Helisoma duryi*, *Can. J. Zool.*, **56**, 1975–1980.

Kunkel, G. (1981). "A minimal model of metamorphosis-fat body competence to respond to juvenile hormone," in *Current Topics in Insect Endocrinology and Nutrition*, G. Bhaskaran, S. Friedman, and J. G. Rodriguez, Eds., Plenum, New York, pp. 107–129.

Lacassagne, M. (1968). Anatomie et histologie d'Hydromeduse benthique *Armorhydra janowiczi* Swedmark and Teissier, *Cah. Biol. Mar.*, **9**, 187–200.

La Greca, M. (1946). Osservazioni sul brachitterismo degli ortotteri in rapporto al sesso, *Moni. Zool. Ital.*, **55**, 138–141.

La Greca, M. (1954). Riduzione e scomparsa delle ali negli insetti pterigoti, *Arch. Zool. Ital.*, **39**, 361–440.

Lagueux, M., M. Hirn, and J. A. Hoffmann. (1977). Ecdysone during ovarian development in *Locusta migratoria*, *J. Insect Physiol.*, **23**, 109–113.

Lagueux, M., C. Hetru, F. Goltzene, C. Kappler, and J. A. Hoffmann (1979). Ecdysone titre and metabolism in relation to cuticulogenesis in embryos of *Locusta migratoria*, *J. Insect Physiol.*, **25**, 700–723.

Lamb, R. J. (1976). Polymorphisms among males of the European earwig *Forficula auricularia* (Dermaptera: Forficulidae), *Can. Entomol.* **108**, 69–75.

Lambert, F. J. (1935–1936). Jellyfish. The difficulties of the study of their life cycle and other problems, *Essex Naturalist,* **25**, 70–87.

Lamberti, F. I., and C. E. Taylor. (1979). *Root-Knot Nematodes* (Meloidogyne *species*), Systematics, Biology and Control, Academic, New York.

Lamotte, M., and F. Xavier. (1972). Les amphibiens anoures à développement direct d'Afrique. Observation sur la biologie de *Nectophrynoides tornieri* (Roux), *Bull. Soc. Zool. Fr.,* **97**, 413–428.

Lamotte, M. (1977). Tendances adaptives à l'affranchissement du milieu aquatique chez les amphibiens anoures, *La terre et la vie*, **31**, 225–311.

Lande, R. (1978). Evolutionary mechanism of limb loss in Tetrapods, *Evolution,* **32**, 73–92.

Landowski, J. (1938). Der Einfluss der Einzelhaltung und des gemeinschaftlichen Lebens auf die Entwicklung und das Wachstum der Larven von *Periplaneta orientalis* L., *Biol. Zentralbl.*, **58**, 512–515.

Lanzrein, B. (1979). The activity and stability of injected juvenile hormones (JH I, JH II, JH III) in last instar larvae and adult females of the cockroach *Nauphoeta cinerea*, *Gen. Comp. Endocrinol.*, **39**, 69–78.

Lasserre, P. (1971). Oligochaeta from the marine meiobenthos: Taxonomy and ecology, *Smiths. Contrib. Zool.*, **76**, 71–86.

Lattaud, C. (1971). Evolution des testicules et des vésicules séminales chez les oligochaetes *Eisenia foetida* et *Lumbricus terrestris* au cours du jeune suivi ou non de renutrition. *C. R. Acad. Sci.*, **272**, 319–322.

Lattaud, C. (1975). "Study of sex control of gametogenesis by organ culture in the oligochaete annelid *Eisenia foetida* f. *typica* Sav.," in *Intersexuality in the Animal Kingdom,* R. Reinboth, Ed., Springer, Berlin, pp. 64–71.

Lattaud, C. (1980). Demonstration by organ culture of the cerebral hormone stimulating the secretion of testicular androgen in the oligochaete annelid, *Eisenia foetida* f. *typica* Sav., *Int. J. Inverteb. Reprod., 2,* 23–36.

Lattaud, C. (1982). Stimulation in vivo de l'androgène testiculaire par l'hormone cérébrale chez l'annélide oligochète *Eisenia foetida* f. *typica* Sav., *Int. J. Inverteb. Reprod., 4,* 233–237.

Laubier, L. (1967). Adaptions chez les Annélides Polychètes interstitielles, *Année biol.* **6,** 1–16.

Laubier, L. (1975). Adaptations morphologiques et biologiques chez un Aphroditien interstitiel *Pholoe swedmarki* sp. n., *Cah. Biol. Mar., 16,* 671–683.

Laufer, H., and H. Greenwood. (1969). The effects of juvenile hormone on larvae of the dipteran, *Chironomus thummi., Am. Zool., 9,* 603.

Lauga, J. (1977a). Nature et détermination du polymorphisme phasaire morphologique des larves nouveau-nées de *Locusta migratoria migratorioides (R. & F.), Acrida,* **6,** 239–247.

Lauga, J. (1977b). Le problème de la mesure de la phase chez les acridiens migrateurs: Historique et définition d' échelles phasaires chez *Locusta migratoria* L. (Insecte, Orthoptère), *Arch. Zool. Exp. Gén., 118,* 247–272.

Lauga-Reyrel, F. (1979). Etude histologique du cycle saisonnier d'*Hypogastrura tullbergi* (Collemboles) et des conséquences de l'écomorphose, *Arch. Zool. Exp. Gen.,* **120,** 195–218.

Lauga-Reyrel, F. (1984). Analyse expérimentale du déterminisme endocrinien de l'écomorphose chez *Hypogastrura tullbergi* (Collemboles), *C. R. Acad. Sci.,* **298,** 61–64.

Lees, A. D. (1961). "Clonal polymorphism in aphids," *Insect polymorphism, Symp. R. Entomol. Soc. Lond.,* **1,** pp. 68–69.

Lees, A. D. (1966). The control of polymorphism in aphids, *Adv. Insect Physiol.,* **3,** 207–277.

Lees, A. D. (1967). The production of the apterous and alate forms in the aphid *Megoura viciae* Buckton, with special reference to the role of crowding, *J. Insect Physiol.,* **13,** 289–318.

Lees, A. D. (1983). "The endocrine control of polymorphism in aphids," in *Endocrinology of Insects,* R. G. H. Downer and H. Laufer, Eds., Liss, New York, pp. 369–377.

Lees, D. R., and C. S. Dent. (1983). Industrial melanism in the spittle bug *Philaenus spumarius* (L.) (Homoptera: Aphrophoridae), *Biol. J. Linn. Soc., 19,* 115–129.

Lees, D. R., C. S. Dent, and P. L. Gait. (1983). Geographic variation in the color pattern polymorphism in British *Philaenus spumarius* I. Homoptera Aphorophoridae populations, *Biol. J. Linn. Soc., 19,* 99–114.

Lefeuvre, J.-C. (1971). Hormone juvénile et polymorphisme alaire chez les Blattaria, *Arch. Zool. Exp. Gen., 112,* 653–666.

Lefeuvre. J.-C., and R. Sellier. (1970). Influence d'une privation prématurée en hormone juvénile sur la morphologie tégumentaire de *Blabera craniifer* Burm. 1938 (Insectes Dictyoptère); Étude en microscopie électronique à balayage, *C. R. Acad. Sci., 271,* 2342–2345.

REFERENCES **289**

Le Gall, S. (1981). Etude expérimentale du facteur morphogénétique contrôlant la différenciation du tractus génital mâle externe chez *Crepidula fornicata* (mollusque hermaphrodite protandre), *Gen. Comp. Endocrinol.*, **43**, 51–62.

Le Gall, S., and C. Feral. (1982). Etude expérimentale de l'évolution in vitro du tractus génital mâle externe chez *Crepidula fornicata* L. (mesogasteropode hermaphrodite protandre), *Int. J. Inverteb. Repr.*, **5**, 31–42.

Le Gall, S., and W. Streif. (1975). "Protandric hermaphroditism in prosobranch gastropods," in *Intersexuality in the Animal Kingdom*, R. Reinboth, Ed., Springer, Berlin, pp. 170–178.

Leinaas, H. P. (1981a). Cyclomorphosis in the furca of winter active Collembola *Hypogastrura socialis* (Uzel), *Entomol. Scand.*, **12**, 35–38.

Leinaas, H. P. (1981b). Cyclomorphosis in *Hypogastrura lapponica* (Axelson, 1902) (=*H. frigida* [Axelson, 1905] syn. nov.) (Collembola Poduridae), *Zeits. Zool. Syst. Evolutionsforsch.*, **19**, 278–285.

Lender, T. (1974). "The role of neurosecretion in freshwater planarians," in *Biology of the Turbellaria*, W. Riser and M. P. Morse, Eds., McGraw-Hill, New York, pp. 460–475.

Lender, T. (1980). Endocrinologie des planaires, *Bull. Soc. Zool. Fr.*, **105**, 173–191.

Lensky, Y., J.-C. Baehr, and P. Porcheron. (1978). Dosage radio-immunologique des ecdysones et des hormones juvéniles au cours du développement postembryonnaire chez les ouvrières et les reines d'abeille (*Apis mellifera* L. var. *ligustica*), *C. R. Acad. Sci.*, **287**, 821–824.

Leonard, J. W., and F. A. Leonard. (1962). *Mayflies of Michigan Trout Streams*, Cranbrook Institute of Science, Bloomfield Hills, MI.

Leutert, R. (1974). Zur Geschlechtsbestimmung und Gametogenese von *Bonellia viridis* Rolands, *J. Embryol. Exp. Morphol.*, **32**, 169–193.

Levita, B. (1970). Etude de l'homochromie chez *Oedipoda coerulescens*. L. (Acridien, Orthoptère), *Bull. Biol. Fr. Belg.*, **104**, 149–213.

Lienhard, C. (1975). Entdeckung des Männchen von *Psoculus neglectus* (Roesler) in Tunisien (Psocoptera, Mesopsocidae), *Mitt. Schweiz. Entomol. Ges.*, **48**, 239–245.

Lillehammer, A. (1974). Norwegian stoneflies I. Analysis of the variations in morphological and structural characters used in taxonomy, *Norsk. Entomol. Tidskr.*, **21**, 59–107.

Lillehammer, A. (1976). Norwegian stoneflies V. Variations in morphological characters compared to differences in ecological factors, *Norw. J. Entomol.*, **23**, 161–172.

Lindenmann, W. (1950). Untersuchungen zur postembryonalen Entwicklung schweizerischer Orchesellen, *Rev. Suisse Zool.*, **57**, 353–428.

Lindquist, E. E. (1965). An unusual new species of *Hoploseius* Berlese (Acarina: Blattisociidae) from Mexico, *Can. Entomol.*, **97**, 1121–1131.

Lindroth, C. H. (1946). Inheritance of wing dimorphism in *Pterostichus anthracinus* Ill., *Hereditas*, **32**, 37–40.

Lindroth, C. H. (1949). Die Fennoskandischen Carabidae. Eine tiergeographische Studie. III. Allgemeiner Teil, *Meddel. Göteborgs Mus. Zool. Adv.*, **122**, 1–911.

Lintlop, S. P., and J. H. Youson. (1983). Concentration of triiodothyronine in the sera of the sea lamprey, *Petromyzon marinus*, and the brook lamprey, *Lampetra lamottenii*, *Gen. Comp. Endocrinol.*, **49**, 187–194.

Llewellyn, J. (1981). Evolution of viviparity and invasion by adults, *Parasitology,* **82,** 64–66.

Lloyd Morgan, C. (1896). *Habitat and Instinct,* E. Arnold, London.

Lloyd Morgan, C. (1900). *Animal Behaviour,* E. Arnold, London.

Loher, W., W. Ruzo, F. C. Baker, C. A. Miller, and D. A. Schooley. (1983). Identification of the juvenile hormone from the cricket *Teleogryllus commodus* and juvenile hormone titer changes, *J. Insect Physiol.* **29,** 585–589.

Lombardi, J., and E. E. Ruppert. (1982). Functional morphology of locomotion in *Derocheilocaris typica* (Crustacea, Mystacocarida), *Zoomorphology,* **100,** 1–10.

Loomis, W. F. (1957). Sexual differentiation in hydra: Control by carbon dioxide tension, *Science,* **126,** 735–739.

Loomis, W. F. (1959). Control of sexual differentiation in *Hydra* by PCo_2, *Ann. N. Y. Acad. Sci.,* **77,** 73–86.

Lüscher, M. (1958). Experimentelle Erzeugung von Soldaten bei der Termite *Kalotermes flavicollis* (Fabr.), *Naturwissenschaften,* **45,** 69–70.

Lüscher, M. (1963). Function of the corpora allata in the development of termites, *Proc. 16th Int. Congr. Zool.* Washington D.C., **4,** 244–250.

Lüscher, M. (1972). Environmental control of juvenile hormone (JH) secretion and caste differentiation in termites, *Gen. Comp. Endocrinol.,* **3,** 509–519.

Lüscher, M. (1975). Pheromones and polymorphism in bees and termites, *Symp. Int. Union Stud. Soc. Insects,* **1975,** 123–141.

Lüscher, M. (1976). "Evidence for an endocrine control of caste determination in higher termites," in *Phase and Caste Determination in Insects. Endocrine Aspects,* M. Lüscher, Ed., Pergamon, Oxford, pp. 91–103.

Lutz, B. (1948). Ontogenetic evolution in frogs, *Evolution,* **2,** 29–39.

Lützen, J. (1968). Unisexuality in the parasitic family Entoconchidae (Gastropoda, Prosobranchia), *Malacologia,* **7,** 7–15.

Lützen, J. (1979). Studies on the life history of *Enteroxenos bonnevie,* a gastropod endoparasitic in aspidochirote holothurians, *Ophelia,* **18,** 1–51.

Lyal, C. H. C. (1985). Phylogeny and classification of the Psocodea, with particular reference to the lice (Psocodea: Phthiraptera), *Syst. Entomol.,* **10,** 145–165.

Lynn, W. G. (1942). The embryology of *Eleutherodactylus nubicola,* an anuran which has no tadpole stage, *Carnegie Inst. Wash. Contrib. Embryol.,* **190,** 27–62.

Lynn, W. G. (1947). Effects on thiourea and phenylthiourea upon the development of *Plethodon cinereus, Biol. Bull.,* **92,** 199.

Lynn, W. G. (1961). Types of amphibian metamorphosis, *Am. Zool.,* **1,** 151–161.

Lynn, W. G., and A. M. Peadon. (1955). The role of the thyroid gland in direct development in the anuran *Eleutherodactlus martinicensis, Growth,* **19,** 263–286.

Maa, T. C. (1964). A review of the Old World Polyctenidae (Hemiptera: Cimicoidea), *Pac. Insects,* **6,** 494–516.

Macbeth, N. (1980). Reflection on irreversibility, *Syst. Zool.,* **29,** 402–404.

Macdonald, J. D., P. B. Pike, and D. I. Williamson. (1957). Larvae of the British species of *Diogenes, Pagurus, Anapagurus* and *Lithodes* (Crustacea, Decapoda), *Proc. Zool. Soc. Lond.,* **128,** 209–257.

Mackiewicz, J. S. (1981). Caryophyllidea (Cestoidea). Evolution and classification, *Adv. Parasitol.*, **19**, 139–206.

Mackiewicz, J. S. (1982). Caryophyllidea (Cestoidea). perspectives, *Parasitology*, **84**, 397–417.

MacKinnon, B. M., and M. D. B. Burt. (1982). Development of the embryos of *Paravortex cardii* (Turbellaria: Rhabdocoela) from the intestine of *Cardium edule*, *Parasitology*, **84**, xix.

Madhavan, K., T. Ohta, W. S. Bowers, and H. A. Schneiderman. (1981). Identification of juvenile hormone of a primitive insect, the firebrat, *Thermobia domestica* (Thysanura), *Am. Zool.*, **21**, 733–735.

Maekawa, K., and A. Goto. (1982). *History of River Fishes* (in Japanese), Chuo-Koron sha, Tokyo.

Maggenti, A. (1981). *General Nematology*, Springer, New York.

Mahmud, F. S. (1980). Alary polymorphism in the small brown planthopper *Laodelphax striatellus* (Homoptera: Delphacidae), *Entomol. Exp. Appl.*, **28**, 47–53.

Makarov, R. R. (1968). The abbreviation of larval development in decapods (Crustacea, Decapoda) (in Russian), *Zool. Zh.*, **47**, 358–359.

Malacinski. G. M. (1978). The Mexican axolotl, *Ambystoma mexicanum:* Its biology and developmental genetics, and its autonomous cell-lethal genes, *Am. Zool.*, **18**, 195–206.

Malaquin, A. (1901). Le parasitisme évolutif des Monstrillides (Crustacés Copépodes), *Arch. Zool. Exp. Gen. ser* 3, **9**, 81–232.

Mamaev, B., and W. Mohrig. (1975). Zur Kenntnis flügelreduzierter Dipteren der Bodenstreu. VI Beitrag: Gattungen *Microcordylomyia, Aprionus* und *Trisopsis, Zool. Anz.*, **194**, 125–132.

Marcel, R. (1980). Recherches sur le facteur clitellogène chez *Eisenia foetida* Sav. (Annélide Oligochète), *Bull. Soc. Zool. Fr.*, **105**, 127–132.

Margalef, R. (1949). Importancia de la neotenia en la evolucion de los crustaceos de agua dulce, *Publ. Inst. Biol. Apl.* (Barcelona), **6**, 41–51.

Marsh, E. (1984). Egg size variation in central Texas populations of *Etheostoma spectabile* (Pisces: Percidae), *Copeia*, **1984**, 291–301.

Marshall, N. B. (1953). Egg size in arctic, antarctic and deep-sea fishes, *Evolution*, **7**, 328–341.

Masaki, S., and N. Oyama (1963). Photoperiodic control of growth and wing form in *Nemobius yezoensis* Shiraki (Orthoptera: Gryllidae), *Kontyu*, **31**, 16–26.

Mashiko, K. (1982). Differences in both the egg size and the clutch size of the freshwater prawn *Palaemon paucidens* De Haan in the Sugami river, *Jap. J. Ecol.*, **32**, 445–451.

Masner, P., W. S. Bowers, M. Kalin, and T. Muhle. (1979). Effect of precocene II on the endocrine regulation of development and reproduction in the bug, *Oncopeltus fasciatus, Gen. Comp. Endocrinol.*, **37**, 156–166.

Mason, P. R. (1977). Stimulation of the activity of *Schistosoma mansoni* miracidia by snail conditioned water, *Parasitology*, **75**, 325–338.

Mathad, S. B., and J. E. McFarlane. (1968). Two effects of photoperiod on wing development in *Gryllodes sigillatus* (Walk.), *Can. J. Zool.*, **46**, 57–60.

Mathad, S. B., and J. E. McFarlane (1970). Histological studies of the neuroendocrine system of *Gryllodes sigillatus* (Walk.) in relation to wing development, *Ind. J. Exp. Biol.,* **8,** 179–181.

Matsaki, I. 1970. On the neurosecretory cells of *Opisthodiscus diplodiscoides* (Trematoda), and their structural changes during the day, *Folia Parasitol.* (Praha), **17,** 25–30.

Matsuda, R. (1960). Morphology, evolution and classification of the Gerridae (Hemiptera-Heteroptera), *Univ. Kans. Sci. Bull.,* **41,** 25–632.

Matsuda, R. (1965). Morphology and evolution of the insect head, *Mem. Am. Entomol. Inst.,* **4,** 1–334.

Matsuda, R. (1970). Morphology and evolution of the insect thorax, *Mem. Can. Entomol.,* **76,** 1–431.

Matsuda, R. (1976). *Morphology and Evolution of the Insect Abdomen,* Pergamon, New York.

Matsuda, R. (1979). "Abnormal metamorphosis and arthropod evolution," in *Arthropod Phylogeny,* A. P. Gupta, Ed., Van Nostrand Reinhold, New York, pp. 137–256.

Matsuda, R. (1981). The origin of insect wings (Arthropoda: Insecta), *Int. J. Insect Morphol. Embryol.,* **10,** 387–398.

Matsuda, R. (1982). Evolutionary process of talitrid amphipods and salamanders in changing environments, with a discussion of genetic assimilation and some other evolutionary concepts, *Can. J. Zool.,* **60,** 733–749.

Maury, M. (1962). Etude biométrique des ailés dans deux races de *B. mori.* Effet de la décérébration (Diplôme d'étude supérieure, cited by Bounhiol 1970).

Mayr, E. (1959a). "The emergence of evolutionary novelties," in *The Evolution of Life,* S. Tax, Ed., University of Chicago Press, pp. 349–380.

Mayr, E. (1959b). Where are we? *Cold Spring Harbor Symp. Quant. Biol.,* **24**(1959), 409–440.

Mayr, E. (1963). *Animal Species and Evolution,* Harvard University Press, Cambridge, MA.

Mayr, E. (1970). *Population, Species and Evolution,* Harvard University Press, Cambridge, MA.

Mayr, E. (1976). *Evolution and the Diversity of Life,* Belknap, Cambridge, MA.

Mazzi, V., G. Lodi, and A. Guardabassi. (1980). "Prolactin in the transition from water to land environment. Evidence from amphibians," in *Animal Models in Human Reproduction,* M. Serio and M. Martini, Eds., Raven, New York, pp. 35–46.

McCaffery, A. R., and W. W. Page. (1978). Factors influencing the production of long-winged *Zonocerus variegatus, J. Insect Physiol.,* **24,** 465–472.

McConaugha, J. R. (1980). Identification of the Y-organ in the larval stages in the crab *Cancer anthonyi* Rathbun, *J. Morphol.* **164,** 83–88.

McFarlane, J. E. (1964). Factors affecting growth and wing polymorphism in *Gryllodes sigillatus* (Walk.) dietary protein level and a possible effect of photoperiod, *Can J. Zool.,* **42,** 767–771.

McIntyre, A. D. (1969). Ecology of marine meiobenthos, *Biol. Rev.,* **44,** 245–290.

McKenzie, H. L. (1967). *Mealybugs of California,* University of California Press, Berkeley, CA.

McLaughlin, P. A. (1983). Hermit crabs—Are they really polyphyletic?, *J. Crustacean Biol.,* **3,** 608–621.

McPherson, J. E. (1974). Photoperiodic effects in a southern Illinois population of the *Euschistus tristigmus* complex (Hemiptera: Pentatomidae), *Ann. Entomol. Soc. Am.,* **67,** 943–952.

McPherson, J. E. (1978). Effects of various photoperiods on color and pubescence in *Thyanta calceata* (Hemiptera: Pentatomidae), *Great Basin Naturalist,* **11,** 155–158.

McPherson, J. E. (1979). Effects of various photoperiods on morphology in *Euschistus tristigmus tristigmus* (Hemiptera: Pentatomidae), *Great Basin Naturalist,* **12,** 23–26.

Meade, T. G., and I. Pratt. (1966). Changes in the redia and metacercariae of *Metagonimoides oregonensis* Price, 1931, transplanted from infected to uninfected snails, *Proc. Helminthol. Soc.,* **33,** 35–37.

Meglitsch, P. A. (1967). *Invertebrate Zoology,* Oxford University Press, New York.

Meier, A. H., L. E. Garcia, and M. M. Joseph. (1971). Corticosterone phases. A cercadian water-drive response to prolactin in the spotted newt *Notophthalmus viridescens, Biol. Bull.,* **141,** 331–336.

Melhorn, H., B. Becker, P. Andrews, and H. Thomas. (1981). On the nature of proglottids of cestodes: A light and electron microscopic study on *Taenia, Hymenolepis,* and *Echinococcus, Z. Parasitenkd.,* **65,** 243–259.

Mendis, A. H. W., M.-E. Rose, and T. W. Goodwin. (1983). Ecdysteroids in adults of the nematode, *Dirofilaria immitis, Molc. Biochem. Parasitol.,* **9,** 209–226.

Menzel, R. (1946). Zum Vorkommen von Harpacticoiden in Fallaule, *Rev. Suisse Zool.,* **53,** 524–529.

Mesnier, M. (1980). Study of oocyte growth within the ovariole in a stick-insect *Clitumnus extradentatus, J. Insect Physiol.,* **26,** 59–65.

Messing, C. G. (1984). Brooding and paedomorphosis in the deep-water feather star *Comatilia iridometriformis* (Echinodermata: Crinoidea), *Mar. Biol.,* **80,** 83–91.

Meusy, J.-J. (1980). Vitellogenin, the extraovarian precursor of the protein yolk in Crustacea: A review, *Reprod. Nutr. Dev.,* **20(1A),** 1–21.

Michener, C. D. (1974). *The Social Behaviour of the Bees,* Belknap, Cambridge, MA.

Mileikovsky, S. A. (1971). Types of larval development in marine bottom invertebrates, their distribution and ecological significance: A re-evaluation, *Mar. Biol.,* **10,** 193–213.

Mileikovsky, S. A. (1975). Types of larval development in Littorinidae (Gastropoda: Prosobranchia) of the World Ocean, and ecological patterns of their distribution, *Mar. Biol.,* **30,** 129–135.

Millar, R. H. (1962). The breeding and development of the ascidian *Polycarpa tinctor, Q. J. Microsc. Sci.,* **103,** 399–403.

Millar, R. H. (1971). The biology of ascidians, in *Adv. Mar. Biol.,* **9,** 1–100.

Miller, B. B. (1978). Non-marine molluscs in quarternary paleoecology, *Malacol. Rev.,* **11,** 27–38.

Miller, D. R., and M. Kosztarab. (1979). Recent advances in the study of scale insects, *Ann. Rev. Entomol.,* **24,** 1–27.

Miller, E. M. (1969). "Caste differentiation in the lower termite," in *Biology of Termites,* K. Krishna and F. M. Weesner, Eds., Vol. 1, Academic, New York, pp. 283–310.

Milne, R. (1950). Influence de la lumière sur la morphogénèse, *Med. Arh.,* **25,** 34.

Mittler, T. E. (1973). "Aphid polymorphism as affected by diet," in *Perspectives in Aphid Biology,* A.D. Lowe, Ed., Entomological Society of New Zealand, pp. 65–75.

Miura, Y., and Y. Morimoto. (1953). Larval development of *Bathynella morimotoi* Ueno, *Annot. Zool. Soc. Jap.,* **26,** 238–245.

Mivart, St. G. (1871). *The Genesis of Species,* Macmillan, New York.

Mochida, O. (1973). The characters of the two wing forms of *Javesella pellucida* (F.) (Homoptera: Delphacidae), with special reference to reproduction, *Trans. R. Entomol. Soc. Lond.* **125,** 177–225.

Mockford, E. L. (1956). Life history studies on some Florida insects of the genus *Archipsocus* (Psocoptera), *Bull. Fla. State Mus. Biol. Sci.,* **1,** 253–273.

Mockford, E. L. (1965). Polymorphism in the Psocoptera, *Proc. North Cent. Branch E. S. A.,* **20,** 82–86.

Mohrig, W. (1978). Zur Kenntnis flügelreduzierter Dipteren IX Beitrag. Gattungen *Corynoptera, Bradysia, Plastosciara* (Sciaridae), *Zool. Anz.,* **201,** 424–432.

Mohrig, W., and B. Mamaev. (1970a). Zur Kenntnis flügelreduzierter Dipteren der Bodenstreu II. Beitrag. Gattungen *Bradysia, Corynoptera, Lycoriella* und *Trichosia* (Sciaridae), *Zool. Anz.,* **184,** 349–359.

Mohrig, W., and B. M. Mamaev. (1970b). Neue flügelreduzierte Dipteren der Familien Sciaridae und Cecidomyiidae, *Dtsch. Entomol. Z. N. F.,* **17,** 315–336.

Mohrig, W., and B. Mamaev. (1974). Zur Kenntnis flügelreduzierter Dipteren der Bodenstreu V. Beitrag. Sciaridae (Gattungen *Plastosciara* und *Pnyxiopsis*), *Zool. Anz.,* **193,** 269–275.

Mohrig, W., and B. Mamaev. (1978). Zur Kenntnis flügelreduzierter Dipteren der Bodenstreu VIII Beitrag. Gattungen *Pnyxia, Pnyxiopsis* und Lycoriella (Sciaridae), *Zool. Anz.,* **201,** 129–135.

Mohrig, W., B. M. Mamaev, and L. Matile. (1975). Zur Kenntnis flügelreduzierter Dipteren der Bodenstreu VII Beitrag. Gattung *Hesperinus* (Diptera Hesperinidae), *Zool. Anz.,* **194,** 339–344.

Mohrig, W., R. Schuster, and K. Thaler. (1978). Flügelreduzierte Trauermücken (Fam. Sciaridae, Diptera) der Bodenstreu aus Oesterreich, *Carinthia,* **168**/188, 393–402.

Mohrig, W., B. Mamaev, and W. Spungis. (1980). Zur Kenntnis flügelreduzierten Dipteren der Bodenstreu X Beitrag: Cecidomyiidae (Gattungen *Chastomera, Micropteromyia*), Sciaridae (Gattung *Plastosciara*), *Zool. Jahrb. Syst.,* **107,** 148–153.

Monaco, F., R. Dominici, M. Andreoli, R. De Pirro, and J. Roche. (1981). Thyroid hormone formation in thyroglobulin synthesized in the Amphioxus (*Branchiostoma lanceolatum* Pallas), *Comp. Biochem. Physiol.,* **70B,** 341–343.

Monchenko, V. I. (1981). *Cycloporella eximia* gen. et sp. n. (Crustacea, Copepoda) (in Russian), *Zool. Zh.,* **60,** 984–990.

Monniot, F. (1966). Ascidies interstitielles, *Veroleff. Inst. Meeresforsch. Bremerhaven, Sonderb. II,* 161–164.

Monniot, F. (1971). Les Ascidies littorales et profondes des sediments meubles, *Smiths. Contrib. Zool.,* **76,** 119–126.

Monod, T. (1926). Les Gnathiidae, *Mem. Soc. Sci. Nat. Maroc.*, **13**, 668 pp.

Monteith, G. B. (1982). Biogeography of the New Guinea Aradidae, *Monogr. Biol.*, **42**, 645–657.

Mordue, W., K. C. Highnam, L. Hill, and J. Lutz. (1970). "Environmental effects on endocrine-mediated processes in locusts," in *Hormones and the Environment*, G. K. Benson and J. G. Philips, Ed., Cambridge University Press, pp. 111–136.

Morii, H., K. Nishikata, and A. Tamura. (1978). Nitrogen excretion of mudskipper fish *Periophthalmus cantonensis* and *Boleophthalmus pectinirostris* in water and on land, *Comp. Biochem. Physiol.*, **60A**, 189–193.

Morii, H., and K. Nishikata, and O. Tamura. (1979). Ammonia and urea excretion from mudskipper fishes, *Periophthalmus cantonensis* and *Boleophtalmus pectinirostris* transplanted from land to water, *Comp. Biochem. Physiol.*, **63A**, 23–28.

Morino, H. (1978). Studies on the Talitridae (Amphipoda, Crustacea) in Japan. III. Life history and breeding activity of *Orchestia platensis* Kroyer, *Publ. Seto Mar. Biol. Lab.* **24**, 245–267.

Morse, M. P. (1976). *Hedylopsis riseri* sp. n. a new interstitial mollusc from the New England coast (Opisthobranchia Acochilidiacea), *Zool. Scr.*, **5**, 221–229.

Morteau, B. (1975). Fonction chromatrope de la pars intercerebralis chez l'acridien *Oedipoda coerulescens*, *J. Insect Physiol.*, **21**, 1407–1413.

Morteau-Levita, B. (1972a) Rôle des lobes optiques dans la réalisation de l'homochromie d'*Oedipoda coerulescens* L. (Acridien, Orthoptères), *C. R. Acad. Sci.*, **274**, 2690–2691.

Morteau-Levita, B. (1972b). Les cellules neurosécrétrices médianes de la pars intercerebralis du cerveau d'*Oedipoda coerulescens* L. (Acridien, Orthoptère). *C. R. Acad. Sci.*, **274**, 2779–2781.

Mortensen, T. (1936). Report on Echinoidea and Ophiuroidea, *Discovery Rep.*, **12**, 199–348.

Morton, J. E. (1955). The evolution of the Ellobiidae with a discussion on the origin of the Pulmonata, *Proc. Zool. Soc. Lond.*, **125**, 127–168.

Morton, J. E. (1958). *Molluscs*, Hutchinson University Library, London.

Mound, L. (1963). Host-correlated variation im *Bemisia tabaci* (Gennadius) (Homoptera: Aleyrodidae), *Proc. R. Entomol. Soc. Lond. A*, **38**, 171–180.

Mueller, J. F. (1959). The laboratory propagation of *Spirometra mansonoides* (Mueller 1935) as an experimental tool. II. Culture and infection of copepod host, and harvesting procercoid, *Trans. Am. Microsc. Soc.*, **78**, 245–255.

Muftic, M. (1969). Metamorphosis of miracidia into cercariae of *Schistosoma mansoni* in vitro, *Parasitology*, **59**, 365–371.

Muggleton, J., D. Lonsdale, and B. R. Benham. (1975). Mechanism in *Adalia bipunctata* L. (Col. Coccinellidae) and its relationship to atmospheric pollution, *J. Appl. Ecol.*, **12**, 451–464.

Müller, F. P. (1966). Schädliche Blattläuse in den Tropen und Subtropen unter besonderer Berucksichtigung von Rassendifferenzierungen, *Z. Angew. Entomol.*, **58**, 76–82.

Müller, G. J. (1968). Betrachtungen über die Gattung *Ototyphlonemertes* Diesing 1863 nebst Bestimmungsschlüssel der validen Arten, *Senckenbergiana*, **49**, 461–468.

Müller, H. J. (1954). Saisondimorphismus bei Zikaden der Gattung *Euscelis* Brulle, *Beitr. Entomol.*, **4**, 1–56.

Müller, H. J. (1957). Die Wirkung exogener Faktoren auf die zyklische Formbildung der Insekten, insbesondere der Gattung *Euscelis* (Hom. Auchenorrhyncha), *Zool. Jahrb. Syst. Ökol.*, **85**, 317–430.

Müller, H. J. (1962a). Zur Biologie und Morphologie der Saisonformen von *Aleurochiton complanatus* (Baerensprung 1849) (Homoptera Aleyrodidae), *Z. Morphol. Ökol. Tiere*, **51**, 345–374.

Müller, H. J (1962b). Über die Induktion der Diapause und der Ausbildung der Saisonformen bei *Aleurochiton complanatus* (Homoptera), *Z. Morphol. Ökol. Tiere*, **51**, 575–610.

Müller, H. J. (1962c). Über den saisondimorphen Entwicklungszyklus und die Aufhebung der Diapause bei *Aleurochiton complanatus* (Barensprung) (Homoptera, Aleurodidae), *Entomol. Exp. Appl.*, **5**, 124–138.

Müller, K., and H. Mendl. (1978). Development of wings in *Capnia atra* in the Abisko area (Plecoptera) (in Swedish), *Entomol. Tidskr.*, **99**, 111–113.

Müller, U. and P. Ax (1971). Gnathostomulida von der Nordseeinsel Sylt mit Beobachtungen zur Lebensweise und Entwicklung von *Gnathostomula paradoxa* Ax, *Microfauna des Meeresbodens*, Vol. 9, Akad. Wiss. Lit., Mainz, pp. 313–349.

Munzing, J. (1963). The evolution of variation and distributional patterns in European populations of the threespined sticklebacks, *Gastrerosteus aculeatus*, *Evolution*, **17**, 320–332.

Murray, J. (1975). "The genetics of the Mollusca," in *Handbook of Genetics*, R. C. King, Ed., Plenum, New York, pp. 3–31.

Murray, J., and B. Clarke. (1976). Supergenes in polymorphic landsnails I. *Partula taeniata*, *Heredity*, **37**, 253–269.

Mustafa, T. M., and G. L. Hodgson. (1984). Observations on the effect of photoperiod on the control of polymorphism in *Psylla pyricola*, *Physiol. Entomol.*, **9**, 207–213.

Nabert, A. (1913). Die Corpora allata der Insekten, *Z. Wiss. Zool.*, **104**, 181–358.

Nabours, R. K. (1929). *The Genetics of Tettigidae*, M. Nijhoff, The Hague.

Naef, A. (1923). Die Cephalopoden, *Fauna Flora Golf Neapel*, **35**, 1–863.

Naef, A. (1928). Die Cephalopoden, *Fauna Flora Golf Neapel*, **35**, 1–357.

Nagashima, T., H. Ando, and G. Fukushima. (1982). "Life history of *Galloisiana nipponensis*," in *Biology of the Notoptera*, H. Ando, Ed., Kashiyo-Insatsu, Nagano, Japan, pp. 43–59.

Nagel, M. G., and W. H. Cade. (1983). On the role of pheromones in aggregation formation in camel cricket, *Ceuthophilus secretus* (Orthoptera: Gryllacrididae), *Can. J. Zool.*, **61**, 95–98.

Nair, V. S. K. (1981). The probable neurosecretory control of vitellogenesis in millipeds, *Jonespeltis splendidus* Verhoeff (Diplopoda: Myriapoda), *Entomon.*, **6**, 7–130.

Naisse, J. (1966a). Contrôle endocrinien de la différenciation sexuelle de *Lampyris noctiluca* (Coléoptère Malacoderme). I. Rôle androgène des testicules, *Arch. Biol. (Liège)*, **77**, 139–201.

Naisse, J. (1966b). Contrôle endocrinien de la différenciation sexuelle chez *Lampyris noctiluca* (Coléoptère Lampyridae) II. Phéromones neurosécrétoires et endocrines au cours du développement postembryonnaire chez le mâle et la femelle, *Gen. Comp. Endocrinol.,* **7,** 85–104.

Naisse, J. (1966c). Contrôle endocrinien de la différenciation chez *Lampyris noctiluca* (Coléoptère Lampyridae) III. Influence des hormones de la pars intercerebralis, *Gen. Comp. Endocrinol.* **7,** 105–110.

Naisse, J. (1969). Rôle des neurohormones dans la différenciation sexuelle de *Lampyris noctiluca, J. Insect Physiol.,* **15,** 877–892.

Najt, J. (1979). Modifications morphophysiologiques en relation avec l'écomorphose chez *Isotoma olivacea, Bull. Soc. Hist. Nat. Toulouse,* **115,** 211–221.

Najt, J. (1983). Modifications morphologiques liées à l'écomorphose chez les Collemboles Isotomidae, *Pedobiologia,* **25,** 337–348.

Nakata, S. and T. C. Maa. (1974). A review of the parasitic earwigs, *Pac. Insects,* **16,** 307–374.

Nakayama, Y., C. Suto, and N. Kumada. (1984). Further studies on the dispersion-inducing substances of the German cockroach, *Blattella germanica* (Linne) (Blattaria: Blattellidae), *Appl. Entomol. Zool.,* **19,** 227–236.

Nasu, S. (1969). "Vectors of rice viruses in Asia," in *Proc. Symp. Int. Rice Res. Inst.,* Johns Hopkins Press, Baltimore, pp. 93–109.

Nebeker, A. V., and A. R. Gaufin. (1967). Factors affecting wing length and emergence in the winter stonefly *Capnia nana, Entomol. News,* **73,** 85–92.

Nebeker, A. V. (1971). Effects of temperature at different altitudes on the emergence of aquatic insects from a single stream, *J. Kans. Entomol. Soc.,* **44,** 26–35.

Nelsen, O. E. (1934). The development of the ovary in the grasshopper *Melanoplus differentialis* (Acridide: Orthoptera), *J. Morphol.,* **55,** 515–543.

Neumann, D. (1976). Adaptations of chironomids to intertidal environments. *Ann. Rev. Entomol.,* **21,** 387–414.

Nicholas, W. L. (1971). The evolutionary origins of the Acanthocephala, *J. Parasitol.,* **57,** 84–87.

Nicolas, G., R. A. Farrow, and J. D. Dowse. (1982). Influence de la densité de populations sur le dimorphisme alaire et la morphométrie du *Phaulacridium vittatum* Sjöst (Acrididae, Catantopidae), *C. R. Acad. Sci.,* **294,** 429–432.

Nijhout, H. F., and D. E. Wheeler. (1982). Juvenile hormone and the physiological basis of insect polymorphism, *Q. J. Biol.,* **57,** 109–123.

Nikolei, E. (1961). Vergleichende Untersuchungen zur Fortpflanzung der heterogenen Gallmücken unter experimentellen Bedingungen, *Z. Morphol. Oekol. Tiere,* **50,** 281–329.

Nishikawa, K., T. Hirashima, S. Suzuki, and M. Suzuki. (1979). Changes in circulating L-thyroxine and L-triiodothyronine in the masu salomon, *Onchorhynchus masou* accompanying the smoltification, measured by radioimmunoassay, *Endocrinol. Jap.,* **26,** 731–735.

Noble, G. K. (1931). *The Biology of Amphibia,* McGraw-Hill, New York.

Nogrady, T. (1982). "Rotifera," in *Synopsis and Classification of Living Organisms,* S. P. Parker et al., Eds., Vol. 1, McGraw-Hill, New York, pp. 865–872.

Noirot, C. (1969). "Formation of castes in the higher termites," in *Biology of Termites,* K. Kumar and F. M. Weesner, Eds., Academic, New York, pp. 311–350.

Nolte, D. J. (1968). The chiasma-inducing pheromone of insects, *Chromosoma,* **23,** 346–358.

Nolte, D. J. (1974). The gregarisation of locusts, *Biol. Rev.,* **49,** 1–14.

Nolte, D. J., I. R. May, and B. B. Thomas. (1970). The gregarisation pheromone in locusts, *Chromosoma,* **29,** 462–473.

Nolte, D. J., S. H. Eggers, and R. May. (1973). A locust pheromone, *J. Insect Physiol.,* **19,** 1547–1554.

Noodt, W. (1974). Anpassung an interstitielle Bedingungen: Ein Faktor in der Evolution höherer Taxa der Crustacea, *Faun. Oekol. Mitt.,* **4,** 445–452.

Nordberg, S. (1936). Biologisch-ökologische Untersuchungen über die Vogelnidicolen, *Acta Zool. Fenn.,* **21,** 168.

Norris, D. O. (1978). "Hormonal and environmental factors involved in the determination of neoteny in urodeles," in *Comparative Endocrinology,* P. J. Gaillard and H. H. Boer, Eds., Elsevier/North Holland, Amsterdam, pp. 109–112.

Norris, D. O. (1983). Evolution of endocrine regulation of metamorphosis in lower vertebrates, *Am. Zool.,* **23,** 709–718.

Norris, D. O., and J. E. Platt. (1974). T_3 and T_4 induced rates of metamorphosis in immature and sexually mature larva of *Ambystoma tigrinum* (Amphibia, Caudata), *J. Exp. Zool.,* **189,** 303–310.

Novak, M. (1975). Gonadectomy, sex hormones and the growth of *Tetrathyridial* populations of *Mesocestoides corti* (Cestoda: Cyclophyllidea) in mice, *Intn. J. Parasitol.,* **5,** 269–274.

Novak, V. J. A. (1966). *Insect Hormones,* Methuen, London.

Nussbaum, R. (1960). Der Thorax von *Basilia nana* (Diptera Nycteribiidae), *Zool. Jahrb. Anat.,* **78,** 313–368.

Oberlander, H. (1969). Effects of ecdysone, ecdysterone, and inkosterone on the *in vitro* initiation of metamorphosis of wing disks of *Galleria mellonella, J. Insect Physiol.,* **15,** 297–304.

Oberlander, H. (1972). L-ecdysone induced DNA synthesis in cultured wing disks of *Galleria mellonella*: Inhibition by 20-hydroxyecdysone and 22-isoecdysone, *J. Insect Physiol.,* **18,** 223–228.

Ockelmann, K. W. (1964). *Turtonia minuta* (Fabricius), a neotenous veneracean bivalve, *Ophelia,* **1,** 121–146.

O'Connor, J. D., P. Maroy, C. Beckets, R. Dennis, C. M. Alvarez, and B. A. Sage. (1980). "Ecdysteroid receptors in cultured *Drosophila* cells," in *Steroid Hormones,* A. K. Ray and J. H. Clark, Eds., Springer, New York, pp. 263–277.

Odening, K. (1967). Die Lebenszyklus von *Strigea falconispalumbi* (Viborg), *S. strigis* (Schrank) und *S. sphaerula* (Rudolphi) (Trematoda falconis, Strigeida) im Raum Berlin, *Zool Jahrb.,* **94,** 21–36.

Odhner, N. H. (1937). *Hedylopsis suecia* n. sp. und die Nacktschneckengruppe Acochilidiacea (Hedylacea), *Zool. Anz.,* **120,** 51–64.

Oguro, C., T. Shosaku, and M. Komatsu. (1982). "Development of the brittle star, *Amphipholis japonica* Matsumoto," in *International Echinoderms Conference.,* J. M. Lawrence, Ed., Balkema, Rotterdam, pp. 491–496.

Ohtaki, T. (1966). On the delayed pupation of the fleshfly, *Sarcophaga peregrina* Robineau-Desvoidy, *Jap. J. Med. Sci. Biol.,* **19,** 97–104.

Okasha, A. Y. K. (1968). Effects of sublethal high temperature on an insect *Rhodnius prolixus* (Stål), *J. Exp. Biol.,* **48,** 455–463.

Okot-Kotber, B. M. (1980). The influence of juvenile hormone analogue on soldier differentiation in the higher termite, *Macrotermes michaelsoni, Physiol. Entomol.,* **5,** 407–416.

Okot-Kotber, B. M. (1983). Ecdysteroid levels associated with epidermal events during worker and soldier differentiation in *Macrotermes michaelsoni* (Isoptera, Macrotermitinae), *J. Insect Physiol.,* **52,** 409–417.

Okugawa, K. I (1957). An experimental study of sexual induction in the asexual form of Japanese freshwater planarians *Dugesia gonocephala* (Duģes), *Bull. Kyoto Gakugei Univ. Ser. B,* **11,** 8–27.

Oldfield, G. N. (1970). Diapause and polymorphism in California populations of *Psylla pyricola* (Homoptera: Psyllidae), *Ann. Entomol. Soc. Am.,* **63,** 180–184.

Olive, P. J. W. (1976). Further evidence of vitellogenesis promoting hormone and its activity in *Eulalia viridis* (L.) (Polychaeta: Phyllodocidae), *Gen. Comp. Endocrinol.,* **30,** 397–403.

Olive, P. J. W. (1979). "Endocrine adaptation in Annelida," in *Hormones and Evolution,* E. J. W. Barrington, Ed., Vol. 1, Academic, New York, pp. 73–118.

Olive, P. J. W., and M. G. Bentley. (1980). Hormonal control of oogenesis, ovulation and spawning in the annual reproductive cycle of the polychaete, *Nephtys hombergii* Sav. (Nephtyidae), *Intn. J. Inverteb. Reprod.,* **2,** 205–221.

Olive, P. J. W., and R. B. Clark. (1978). "Physiology of reproduction," in *Physiology of Annelida,* P. J. Mill, Ed., Academic, New York, pp. 271–367.

Oliver, C. (1976). Photoperiodic regulation of seasonal polyphenism in *Phyciodes tharos* (Nymphalidae), *J. Lepid. Soc.,* **30,** 260–263.

Oliver, D. R. (1981). Redescription and systematic placement of *Oreadomyia albertae* Kevan and Cutten-Ali-Khan (Diptera: Chironomidae), *Quaest. Entomol.,* **17,** 121–128.

Ollason, J. G. (1972). A statistical description of structural variation in the cerci of the common earwig (*Forficula auricularia*), *J. Zool. Lond.,* **167,** 153–160.

Onbe, T. (1978). The life cycle of marine cladocerans (in Japanese), *Bull. Jap. Plankton Soc.,* **25,** 41–54.

Oosterhoff, L. M. (1977). Variation in growth rate as an ecological factor in the land snail *Cepaea nemoralis* (L.), *Neth. J. Zool.,* **27,** 1–132.

Orrhage, L. (1974). Über die Anatomie, Histologie und Verwandtschaft der Apistobranchidae (Polychaeta Sedentaria) nebst Bemerkungen über die systematische Stellung der Archianneliden, *Z. Morphol. Tiere,* **79,** 1–45.

Orton, G. L. (1949). Larval development of *Nectophrynoides tornieri* (Roux), with comments on direct development in frogs, *Ann. Carnegie Mus.,* **31,** 257–277.

Osborn, H. F. (1896). A mode of evolution requiring neither natural selection nor the inheritance of acquired characters, *Trans. N. Y. Acad. Sci.,* **15,** 141–142, 148.

Osborn, H. F. (1897). Organic selection, *Science,* Oct. 15, 1897, 583–587.

Osche, G. (1953). Systematik und Phylogenie der Gattung *Rhabditis* (Nematoda). *Zool. Jahrb. Syst.,* **81,** 190–280.

Osche, G. (1956). Die Präadaptation freilebender Nematoden an den Prasitismus, *Verh. Dtsch. Zool. Ges. Zool. Anz. Suppl.,* **19,** 391–396.

Osche, G. (1963). "Morphological, biological, and ecological consideration in the phylogeny of parasitic Nematodes," in *The lower Metazoa,* E. C. Dougherty, Ed., University of California Press, Berkeley, CA, pp. 283–302.

Oster, G. F., and E. O. Wilson. (1978). *Caste and Ecology in the Social Insects,* Princeton University Press, Princeton, NJ.

Ott, J., G. Rieger, R. Rieger, and F. Enders. (1982). New mouthless interstital worms from the sulfide system: symbiosis with prokaryotes, *Mar. Ecol.,* **3,** 313–333.

Otte, W., and K. Williams. (1972). Environmentally induced color dimorphism in grasshoppers, *Syrbula admirabilis, Dichromorpha viridis* and *Chortophaga viridifasciata, Ann. Entomol. Soc. Am.,* **65,** 1154–1161.

Ozeki, K. (1958a). Effect of corpus allatum hormone on development of male genital organs of the earwig, *Anisolabis maritima, Tokyo Univ. Coll. Gen. Educ. Sci. Papers,* **8,** 69–75.

Ozeki, K. (1958b). Effects of the corpus allatum hormone on the postembryonic development of the female of the earwig, *Anisolabis maritima, Tokyo Univ. Coll. Gen. Educ. Sci. Papers,* **8,** 187–200.

Ozeki, K. (1959). Further studies of the effects of the corpus allatum hormone on the development of the genital organs in males of the earwig, *Anisolabis maritima, Tokyo Univ. Coll. Gen. Educ. Sci. Papers,* **9,** 127–134.

Packard, A. (1972). Cephalopoda and fish: The limits of convergence, *Biol. Rev.,* **47,** 241–307.

Palevody, C., and A. Grimal. (1976). Variations cytologiques des corps allates au cours de cycle reproducteur du collembole *Folsomia candida, J. Insect Physiol.,* **22,** 63–72.

Palevody, C., J.-P. Delbecque, and J. Delachambre. (1977). Variations du taux des ecdysteroides en relation avec les cycles de mue et les cycles ovariens, *C. R. Acad. Sci.,* **285,** 1323–1326.

Palmén, E. (1944). Die Anemohydrochore Ausbreitung der Insekten als zoogeographischer Faktor, *Ann. Soc. Zool. Bot. Fenn. "Vanamo,"* **10,** 1–262.

Palmén, E. (1953). Hatching of *Acentropus niveus* (Oliv.) (Lep. Pyralidae) in the brackish waters of Tvärminne, S. Finland, *Ann. Entomol. Fenn.,* **19,** 181–186.

Papillon, M., P. Porcheron, and J.-C. Baehr. (1980). Effets de la température d'élevage sur la croissance et l'equilibre hormonal de *Schistocerca gregaria* au cours des deux derniers stades larvaires, *Experientia,* **36,** 419.

Parshad, V. R., and D. W. T. Crompton. (1981). Aspects of acanthocephalan reproduction, *Adv. Parasitol.,* **19,** 73–138.

Parsons, P. A. (1981). "Habitat selection and speciation in *Drosophila,*" in *Evolution and Speciation,* W. R. Atchley and D. Woodra, Eds., Cambridge University Press, Cambridge, pp. 219–240.

Passera, L. (1974). Différenciation des soldats chez la fourmi *Pheidole pallidula* Nyl. (Formicidae, Myrmicinae), *Insect Soc.,* **21,** 71–86.

Passera, L. (1980). La fonction inhibitrice des reines de la fourmi *Plagiolepis pygmaea* Latr.: Rôle des phéromones, *Insect Soc.,* **27,** 212–225.

Passera, L., and J. P. Suzzoni. (1979). Le rôle de la reine de *Pheidole pallidula* (Nyl.) (Hymenoptera: Formicidae) dans la sexualisation de couvain après traitement par l'hormone juvénile, *Insect Soc.,* **26,** 343–353.

Patricolo, E., G. Ortolani, and A. Cascio. (1981). The effect of L-thyroxine on the metamorphosis of *Ascidia malaca, Cell Tissue Res.,* **214**, 289–301.

Patzner, R. A. (1978). Cyclical changes in the ovary of the hagfish *Eptatretus burgerii* (Cyclostoma), *Acta Zool. Stockh.,* **59**, 57–61.

Paul, H. 1937. Transplantation und Regeneration der Flügel. Zur Untersuchung ihrer Formbildung bei einem Schmetterling mit Geschlechtsdimorphismus, *Orgyia antiqua* L., *Arch. Entwickl.,* **136**, 64–111.

Pawson, D. L. (1969). Holothuroidea. *Am. Geogr. Soc. Antarctic Map. Folio series,* **11**, 38–41.

Pearson, J. C. (1959). Observations on the morphology and life cycle of *Strigea elegans* Chandler and Rausch 1947 (Trematoda: Strigeidae), *J. Parasitol.,* **45**, 155–174.

Pearson, J. C. (1972). A phylogeny of life cycle patterns of the Digenea, *Adv. Parasitol.,* **10**, 153–189.

Pechnik, J. A. (1979). Role of encapsulation in invertebrate life histories, *Am. Nat.,* **114**, 859–870.

Pener, M. P. (1976). The differential effect of the corpora allata on yellow coloration in crowded and isolated *Locusta migratoria migratorioides* (R. & F.) males, *Acrida,* **5**, 189–206.

Pener, M. P. (1983). "Endocrine aspects of phase polymorphism in locusts," in *Endocrinology of Insects,* R. G. H. Downer and H. Laufer, Eds., Liss, New York, pp. 379–394.

Pennak, R. W., and D. J. Zinn. (1943). Mystacocarida, a new order of Crustacea from interstitial beaches in Massachusetts and Connecticut, *Smiths. Misc. Coll.,* **103**(9), 1–11.

Pescador, M. L., and W. L. Peters. (1974). The life history and ecology of *Baetisca rogersi* Berner (Ephemeroptera: Baetiscidae), *Bull. Fla. State Mus.,* **17**, 151–209.

Pesson, P. (1951). "Ordre des Thysanoptera," in *Traité de Zoologie,* Vol. 10, P.-P. Grassé, Ed., Masson, Paris, pp. 1805–1869.

Pestarino, M. (1864). Immunohistochemical demonstration of prolactin-like activity in the neural gland of the ascidian *Styela plicata, Gen. Comp. Endocrinol.,* **54**, 444–449.

Peters, W. L., and J. G. Peters. (1977). Adult life and emergence of *Dolania americana* in northwestern Florida (Ephemeroptera: Behningiidae), *Int. Rev. Ges. Hydrobiol.,* **62**, 409–438.

Petit, L. (1940). The effect of isolation on growth in the cockroach *Blattella germanica* (L.) (Orthoptera Blattidae), *Entomol. News,* **51**, 293.

Pettibone, M. H. (1957). Endoparasitic polychaetous annelids of the family Arabellidae, with description of new species, *Biol. Bull.,* **113**, 170–187.

Pettibone, M. H. (1982). "Annelida," in *Synopsis and Classification of Living Organisms,* Vol. 2, P. Parker et al., Eds., McGraw-Hill, New York, pp. 1–61.

Pflugfelder, O. (1936). Vergleichend–anatomische, experimentelle und embryologische Untersuchungen über das Nervensystem und die Sinnesorgane der Insekten, *Zoologica (Stuttgart),* **34**(5–6), 1–56.

Pflugfelder, O. (1937a). Weitere experimentelle Untersuchungen über die Funktion der Corpora allata von *Dixippus morosus* Br., *Z. Wiss. Zool,* **151**, 149–191.

Pflugfelder, O. (1937b). Bau, Entwicklung und Funktion der Corpora allata und cardiaca von *Dixippus morosus* Br., *Z. Wiss. Zool.,* **149**, 477–512.

Piaget, J. (1949). L'adaptation de la *Limnaea stagnalis* aus milieu lacustres de la Suisse romande. Etude biométrique et génétique, *Rev. Suisse Zool.,* **36**, 263–531.

Pianka, H. D. (1974). "Ctenophora," in *Reproduction of Marine Invertebrates,* A. C. Giese and J. S. Pearse, Eds., Academic, New York, pp. 201–265.

Picaud, J-L. (1980). Vitellogenin synthesis by the fat body of *Porcellio dilatatus* Brandt (Crustacea, Isopoda), *Intn. J. Invertebr. Reprod.,* **2**, 341–349.

Picken, G. B. (1979). Non-pelagic reproduction of some antarctic prosobranch gastropod from Signy island, South Orkney Island, *Malacologia,* **19**, 109–128.

Pickford, G. E., and J. G. Philips. (1959). Prolactin, a factor in promoting survival of hypophysectomized killifish in freshwater, *Science,* **130**, 454–455.

Pilger, J. (1978). "Settlement and metamorphosis in the Echiura: A review," in *Settlement and Metamorphosis of Marine Invertebrate larvae,* F. S. Chia and M. E. Rice, Eds., Elsevier, New York, pp. 103–112.

Poenicke, W. (1969). Über die postlarvale Entwicklung von Flöhen (Insecta, Siphonaptera) unter besonderer Berücksichtigung der sogenannten "Flügelanlagen, *Z. Morphol. Tiere,* **65**, 143–186.

Poisson, R. (1924). Contribution à l'étude des Hémiptères aquatiques, *Bull. Biol. Fr. Belg.,* **58**, 49–305.

Popescu, C. (1979). Natural selection in the industrial melanic psocids *Mesopsocus unipunctatus* (Mull.) (Insecta Psocoptera) in northern England, *Heredity,* **42**, 133–142.

Popham, E. J. (1973). Is *Hemimerus* an earwig?, *Entomologist,* **106**, 193–195.

Porchet, M. (1976). Données actuelles sur le contrôle endocrine de la maturation génitale des néréidiens (Annelides Polychètes), *Ann. Biol. 4 ser.,* **15**, 329–377.

Pourriot, R. (1963). Influence du rhythme nycthéméral sur le cycle sexuel de quelques rotifères, *C. R. Acad. Sci.,* **256**, 5216–5219.

Pourriot, R., and P. Clement. (1973). Photopériodisme et cycle hétérogonique chez *Notommata copeus* (Rotifère Monogononte) II. Influence de la qualité de la lumière. Spectre d'action, *Arch. Zool. Exp. Gen.,* **114**, 227–300.

Pourriot, R., P. Clement, and A. Luciani. (1981). Perception de la photopériode par un rotifère: hypothese sur les méchanismes, *Arch. Zool. Exp. Gen.,* **122**, 317–327.

Pourriot, R., and C. Rougier. (1977). Effets de la densité de population et du groupement sur la reproduction de *Brachionus calyciflorus* (Pallas), *Ann. Limnol.,* **13**, 101–113.

Pourriot, R., and C. Rougier. (1979). Influences conjuguées du groupement et de la qualité de la nourriture sur la reproduction de *Brachionus plicatilis* O. F. Muller, *Netherlands J. Zool.,* **29**, 242–264.

Powell, J. A. (1977). A remarkable new genus of brachypterous moth from coastal sand dunes in California (Lepidoptera: Gelechioidea, Scythrididae), *Ann. Entomol. Soc. Am.,* **69**, 325–339.

Price, E. W. (1937). North American monogenetic trematodes I. The superfamily Gyrodactyloidea, *J. Wash. Acad. Sci.,* **27**, 114–130.

Prossor, C. L. (1973). "Water: osmotic balance: hormonal regulation," in *Comparative Physiology,* C. L. Prossor, Ed., Saunders, New York, pp. 1–78.

Rabalais, N. N., and J. N. Cameron. (1983). Abbreviated development of *Uca subcylindrica* (Simpson 1859) (Crustacea, Decapoda, Ocypodidae) reared in laboratory, *J. Crustacean Biol.,* **3**, 519–541.

Radwan, W., and F. Sehnal. (1974). Inhibition of metamorphosis by juvenoids in *Nauphoeta cinerea* (Olivier), *Experientia,* **30**, 615–618.

Raffaeli, D. G. (1979). The taxonomy of the *Littorina saxatilis* specifies complex, with particular reference to the systematic status of *Littorina patula* Jeffrys, *Zool. J. Linn. Soc.,* **65**, 219–232.

Raimond, R., and P. Juchault. (1983). Masculinisation des femelles prépubères de *Sphaeroma senatum* Fabr. Crustaće Isopode Flabellifère) par implantation d'une glande androgène de mâle pubère, *Gen. Comp. Endocrinol.,* **50**, 146–155.

Ramamurty, P. S., and W. Engels. (1977). Allatektomie und Juvenilhormonwirkungen auf Synthese und Eilagerung von Vitellogenin bei der Bienenkönigin *(Apis mellifera), Zool. Jahrb. Physiol.,* **81**, 165–176.

Ramme, W. (1931). Verlust oder Herabsetzung der Fruchtbarkeit bei macropteren Individuen sonst brachypterer Orthopterenarten; *Biol. Zentralbl.,* **51**, 533–540.

Ramme, W. (1951). Die parallele Farbungsvariation (Parallelochromie) der Acrididae; ihre genetische und phylogenetische Bedeutung (Orthoptera), *Eos, Tom. extraordinairio,* **1950**, 249–266.

Rankin, M. A., and H. Jackle. (1980). Hormonal control of vitellogenin synthesis in *Oncopeltus fasciatus, J. Insect Physiol.,* **26**, 671–684.

Rankin, S. M., and M. A. Rankin. (1980). The hormonal control of migratory flight behaviour in the convergent ladybird beetle, *Hippodemia convergens, Physiol. Entomol.,* **5**, 175–182.

Rasmussen, E. (1944). Faunistic and biological notes on marine invertebrates I. The eggs and larvae of *Brachystoma rissoides* (Hanl.), *Eulinella nitidissima* (Mont.), *Retusa truncatula* (Berg) and *Embletonia pallida* (Alder & Hancock) (Gastropoda Marina), *Vidensk. Meddr. Dansk. Naturh. Forening, Kbn. Havn.,* **107**, 207–223.

Rasmussen, E. (1951). Faunistic and biological notes on marine invertebrates. II, *Vidensk. Meddr. Dansk. Naturhist. Foren. Kbn. Havn.,* **113**, 201–249.

Rass, T. S. (1941). Analogous or parallel variations in structure and development of fishes in northern and arctic seas (in Russian), *Jubilee Publ. Moscow Soc. Naturalists, 1805–1940*, 1–60.

Rass, T. S. (1977). Geographical pattern of reproduction and development in fishes (in Russian), *Tr. Akad. Nauk. SSSR. Inst. Okeanol.,* **109**, 7–41.

Raven, C. P. (1975). "Development," in *Pulmonate,* V. Fretter and J. Peake, Eds., Vol. 1, Academic, New York, pp. 367–400.

Reeve, M. R. (1970). Complete cycle of development of a pelagic chaetognath in culture, *Nature,* **227**, 381.

Regenfuss, H. (1968). Untersuchungen zur Morphologie, Systematik und Oekologie der Podapolipidae (Acarine, Tarsonemini), *Z. Wiss. Zool.,* **177**, 183–282.

Regenfuss, H. (1973). Beinreduktion und Verlagerung des Kopulationsappa rates in der Milbenfamilie Podapolipidae, ein Beispiel für verhaltengesteuerte Evolution morphologischer Strukturen, *Z. Zool. Syst. Evolutions-forsch.,* **11**, 173–195.

Reid, J. A. (1941). The thorax of wingless and short winged Hymenoptera, *Trans. R. Entomol. Soc. Lond.,* **91**, 367–446.

Reid, P. C., and T. T. Chen. (1981). Juvenile hormone-controlled vitellogenin synthesis in the fat body of the locust *(Locusta migratoria):* isolation and characterization of vitellogenin polysomes and their induction in vivo, *Insect Biochem.,* **11,** 297–305.

Reinhard, E. G. (1942). The reproductive role of the complemental males of *Peltogaster, J. Morphol.,* **70,** 389–402.

Reinhard, E. G. (1949). Experiments on the determination and differentiation of sex in the bopyrid *Stegophryxus hyptius* Thompson, *Biol. Bull.,* **96,** 17–31.

Reinhard. E. G., and J. T. Evans. (1951). The spermiogenic nature of the "mantle bodies" in the aberrant rhizocephalid *Mycetomorpha, J. Morphol.* **89,** 59–69.

Reinhardt, H. (1941). Entwicklungsgeschichte der *Prostoma, Vierteljahrschr. Nat. Ges. Zur.,* **86,** 3–4.

Reisa, J. J. (1973). "Ecology," in *Biology of Hydra,* L. Allison and L. Burnett, Eds., Academic, New York, pp. 60–105.

Reish, D. J. (1957). The life history of the polychaetous annelid *Neanthes caudata* (della Chiaje) including a summary of development in the family Nereidae, *Pac. Sci.,* **11,** 216–228.

Reisinger, E. (1924). Die Gattung *Rhynchoscolex, Z. Morphol. Oekol. Tiere* **1,** 1–37.

Remane, A. (1927). *Halammohydra,* ein eigenartiger Hydrozoon der Nord- und Ostsee, *Z. Morphol. Ökol. Tiere,* **7,** 82–92.

Remane, A. (1932). "Archiannelida," in *Tierwelt Nord und Ostsee,* Vol. 22, Part 6A, Akademie Verlag, Leipzig.

Remane, A. (1933). Verteilung und Organisation der benthonischen Mikrofauna der Kieler Bucht, *Meeresunters. Helgoland,* **21,** 161–221.

Remane, A. (1954). "Die Geschichte der Tiere," in *Die Evolution der Organismen,* G. Heberer, Ed., Vol. 2, pp. 340–422.

Remane, A. (1956). *Die Grundlagen des natürlichen Systems der vergleichenden Anatomie und Phylogenetik,* Akademie Verlag, Leipzig.

Remane, A. (1963). "The systematic position and phylogeny of the pseudo-coelomates," in *The Lower Metazoa, Comparative Biology and Phylogeny,* E. C. Dougherty, Ed., University of California Press, Berkeley, CA, pp. 247–255.

Rembold, H. (1976). "The role of determinator in caste formation in the honey bee," in *Phase and Caste Determination in Insects,* M. Lüscher, Ed., Pergamon, Oxford, pp. 21–34.

Rembold, H., B. Lackner, and I. Geistbeck. (1974a). The chemical basis of honey bee, *Apis mellifera,* caste formation, partial purification of queen bee determinator from royal jelly, *J. Insect Physiol.,* **20,** 307–314.

Rembold, H., C. Czoppelt, and P. J. Rao. (1974b). Effect of juvenile hormone treatment on caste differentiation in the honey bee, *Apis mellifera, J. Insect Physiol.,* **20,** 1193–1201.

Renaud-Mornant, J. and N. Coineau. (1978). Etude anatomique des isopodes interstitiels *Angeliera phreaticola* Chappuis et Delamare, 1952. Données générales, *C. R. Acad. Sci.,* **286,** 1249–1252.

Renaud-Mornant, J., and C. Delamare-Deboutteville. (1976). L'originalité de la sous-Classe des mystacocarides (Crustacea) et le problème de leur répartition, *Ann. Speleol.,* **31,** 75–83.

Rensch, B. (1959). *Evolution above the Species Level,* Columbia University Press, New York.

Rentz, D. C. F. (1978). A new parthenogenetic *Timema* from California, *Pan-Pac. Entomol.,* **54,** 173–177.

Rentz, D. C. F. (1980). A new family of ensiferous Orthoptera from the coastal sands of southwest Queensland, *Mem. Queensland Mus.,* **20,** 49–63.

Rentz, D. C. F. (1982). "A review of the systematics, distribution and bionomics of the North American Grylloblattidae," in *Biology of the Notoptera,* H. Ando, Ed., Kashiyo-Insatsu, Nagano, Japan, pp. 1–18.

Renucci, M., and A. Strambi. (1981). Evolution des ecdysteroïdes ovariens et hémolymphatiqes au cours de la maturation ovarienne chez *Acheta domestica* L. (Orthoptera), *C. R. Acad. Sci.,* **293,** 825–830.

Renucci, M., and C. Strambi. (1983). Juvenile hormone levels, vitellogenin and ovarian development in *Acheta domestica, Experientia,* **39,** 618–620.

Reverberi, G. (1947). Ancora sulla trasformazione sperimentale del sesso nei Bopiridi. La trasformazione delle femmine giovanili in maschi, *Publ. Stn. Zool. Napoli,* **21,** 81–91.

Reverberi, G., and M. Pitotti. (1942). Il ciclo biologico e la determinazione fenotypica del sesso di *Ione thoracica* Montagu, Bopiride parassita di *Callianassa laticauda* Otto, *Publ. Stn. Zool. Napoli,* **19,** 111–184.

Reynoldson, T. B. (1983). The population biology of Turbellaria with special reference to the freshwater triclads of the British Isles, *Adv. Ecol. Res.,* **13,** 235–326.

Rice, M. E. (1973). Gametogenesis in three species of Sipuncula: *Phascolosoma agassizii, Golfingia pugettensis,* and *Themiste pyroides, La Cellule,* **70,** 295–313.

Rice, M. E. (1975). Observations on the development of six species of Caribbean Sipuncula with a review of development in the phylum, *Proc. Int. Symp. Biol. Sipuncula and Echiura,* Vol. 1, M. E. Rice and M. Todorovic, Eds., Kotor, pp. 141–160.

Rice, M. E. (1976). Larval development and metamorphosis in Sipuncula, *Am. Zool.,* **16,** 563–571.

Rice, M. E. (1978). "Morphological and behavioral changes at metamorphosis in the Sipuncula," in *Settlement and Metamorphosis of Marine Invertebrate Larvae,* F. S. Chia and M. E. Rice, Eds., Elsevier, New York, pp. 83–102.

Rice, M. E. (1981). Larvae adrift:Patterns and problems in life histories of sipunculans, *Am. Zool.,* **21,** 605–619.

Richard, A. (1966). Action de la température sur l'évolution génitale de *Sepia officinalis, C. R. Acad. Sci.,* **263,** 1998–2001.

Richard, A. (1967). Rôle de la photopériode dans le déterminisme de la maturation génitale femelle du céphalopode *Sepia officinalis, C. R. Acad. Sci.,* **264,** 1315–1318.

Richard, A. (1970a). Differenciation sexuel des céphalopodes en culture vitro, *Ann. Biol.,* **9,** 169–175.

Richard, A. (1970b). Analyse du cycle sexuelle chez les céphalopodes: Mise en evidence expérimentale d'un rhythme conditionné par les variations des facteurs externes et internes, *Bull. Soc. Zool. Fr.,* **95,** 461–469.

Richards, O. W. (1954). Two new wingless species of Diptera, Sphaeroceridae (Borboridae), from Ethiopia, *J. Linn. Soc. Lond. Zool.,* **42,** 387–391.

Richards, O. W. (1957). On apterous and brachypterous Sphaeroceridae from Mt. Elgon in the collection of the Musee royal du Congo belge, Tervuren, *Rev. Zool. Bot. Afr.,* **15**, 374–388.

Richards, O. W. (1963). The genus *Mesaptilotus* Richards (Diptera: Sphaeroceridae) with distribution of new species, *Trans. R. Entomol. Soc. Lond.,* **115**, 165–179.

Richards, O. W., and R. G. Davies. (1964). A General Textbook of Entomology (A. D. Imms), 9th ed., Methuen, London.

Riedl, R. (1969). Gnathostomulida from America. First record of the new phylum from North America, *Science,* **163**, 445–452.

Riegel, G. T., and S. J. Eytalis. (1974). Life history studies on Zoraptera, *Proc. North-Central Branch E. S. A.,* **29**, 106–107.

Rieger, R. M. (1980). A new group of interstitial worms, Labatocerebridae nov. fam. (Annelida) and its significance for metazoan phylogeny, *Zoomorphology,* **95**, 41–84.

Rieger, R. M., and M. Mainitz. (1977). Comparative fine structure study of the body wall in Gnathostomulida and their phylogenetic position between Platyhelminthes and Aschelminthes, *Z. Zool. Syst. Evolutionsforsch,* **15**, 9–35.

Rieux, R. (1975). La spécificité alimentaire dans le genre *Matsucoccus* (Homoptères: Margarodidae) avec reference speciale aux planteshotes de *M. pini* Green, Classement de *Matsucoccus* d'apres leur hotes, *Ann. Sci. Forest,* **32**, 157–168.

Rivault, C. (1983). Influence de groupement sur le développement chez *Eublaberus distanti* (Dictyoptère, Ins.), *Ins. Soc.,* **30**, 210–220.

Robert, A. (1979). Les premiers stades de l'ovogenèse et les variations de la neurosécrétion cérébrale chez deux espèces sympatriques *Roscius elongatus* et *R. brazzavillensis* Robert (Heteroptera: Pyrrhocoridae), *Int. J. Ins. Morphol. Embryol.,* **8**, 11–21.

Roberts, T. M., S. Ward, and E. Chermin. (1979). Behavioral responses of *Schistosoma mansoni* miracidia in concentration gradients of snail conditioned water, *J. Parasitol.,* **65**, 41–49.

Rogers, W. P., and R. I. Sommerville. (1968). The infectious process and its relation to the development of early parasitic stages in nematodes, *Adv. Parasitol.,* **6**, 327–348.

Roháček, J. (1975). Die Flügelpolymorphie bei der europäischen Sphaeroceridenarten und Taxonomie der *Limosina heteroneura*–Gruppe (Diptera), *Acta. Entomol. Bohemoslov.,* **72**, 196–207.

Rohde, K. (1977). A non-competitive mechanism responsible for restricting niches, *Zool. Anz.,* **199**, 164–172.

Rohde, K. (1979). A critical evaluation of intrinsic and extrinsic factors responsible for niche restriction in parasites, *Am. Nat.,* **114**, 648–671.

Rohdendorf, B. B. (1961). Die Palaeontologie in der USSR, *Verh. Int. Kongr. Entomol. 11th Vienna,* **1**, 313–318.

Rolston, L. H. (1982). A brachypterous species of *Alathetus* from Hawaii (Hemiptera: Pentatomidae), *J. Kans. Entomol. Soc.,* **55**, 156–158.

Romanes, G. J. (1896). *Darwin and after Darwin I. Post-Darwinian Questions. Heredity and Utility,* Open Court, Chicago.

Romer, F. (1979). Ecdysteroids in snails, *Naturwissenschaften,* **66**, 471–472.

Romer, F., and I. Eisenbeis. (1978). DNA content and synthesis in several tissues and variation of molting hormone-level in *Gryllus bimaculatus* Deg. (Ensifera, Insecta), *Z. Naturforsch. C.,* **38**, 112–125.

Rose, F. L. (1977). Neoplastic and possibly related skin lesions in neotenic tiger sala-manders from sewage lagoon, *Science*, **196**, 315–316.

Rose, F. L., and D. Armentrout. (1976). Adaptive strategies of *Ambystoma tigrinum* Green inhabiting the Llano estacado of west Texas, *Jr. Anim. Ecol.*, **45**, 713–729.

Röseler, P. F. (1970). Unterschiede in der Kastendetermination zwischen den Hummel-arten *Bombus hypnorum* und *Bombus terrestris*, *Z. Naturforsch.* **25b**, 543–548.

Röseler, P. F. (1977). Juvenile hormone control of oogenesis in bumble bee workers, *Bombus terrestris*, *J. Insect Physiol.*, **23**, 985–992.

Röseler, P. F., and I. Röseler. (1974). Morphologische und physiologische Differenzie-rung der Kasten bei den Hummelarten *Bombus hypnorum* (L.) und *Bombus terres-tris* (L.), *Zool. Jahrb. Physiol.*, **78**,175–198.

Röseler, P. F., and I. Röseler. (1978). Studies on the regulation of the juvenile hormone titer in bumblebee workers, *Bombus terrestris*, *J. Insect Physiol.*, **24**, 707–713.

Röseler, P. F., I. Röseler, and C. G. J. van Honk. (1981). Evidence for inhibition of corpora allata activity in workers of *Bombus terrestris* by a pheromone from the queen's mandibular glands, *Experientia*, **37**, 348–351.

Rosenberg, J. (1979). "Fine structures of the lymphatic tissue of *Cryptops hortensis* (Chilopoda Scolopendromorpha). General organization and intercellular junc-tions," in *Myriapod Biology*, M. Camatini, Ed., Academic, New York, pp. 287–294.

Rosenkilde, P. (1972). Hypothalamic control of thyroid function in Amphibia, *Gen. Comp. Endocrinol.*, **3**, 32–40.

Ross, E. S. (1970). Biosystematics of the Embioptera, *Ann. Rev. Entomol.*, **15**, 157–171.

Ross, E. S. (1984). A classification of the Embidodina of Mexico, with description of new taxa, *Occas. Pap. Calif. Acad. Sci.*, **140**, 1–54.

Ross, H. H. (1944). The caddisflies, or Trichoptera of Illinois, *Ill. Nat. Hist. Surv.*, **23**(1), 1–326.

Rossi, L. (1961). Morfologia e riproduzione vegetative di un Madrepora rio nuova per il Mediterraneo, *Boll. Zool.*, **28**, 261–272.

Rothschild, N. C. (1917). Convergent development among certain ectoparasites (presi-dential address), *Proc. Entomol. Soc. Lond.*, **1916**, 141–156.

Roubos, E. W., W. P. M. Geraerts, G. H. Boerrigter, and G. P. J. Van Kampen. (1980). Control of the activities of the neurosecretory light green and caudo-dorsal cells and of the endocrine dorsal bodies by the lateral lobes in freshwater snail *Lymnaea stagnalis* (L.), *Gen. Comp. Endocrinol.*, **40**, 446–454.

Rounsefell, G. A. (1958). Anadromy of North American Salmonidae, *Fish. Bull. Fish Wildl. Serv.*, **58**, 171–185.

Rowe, V. L., and D. R. Idler. (1977). In vitro stimulation of protein synthesis in squid ovary by optic gland extract, *Gen. Comp. Endocrinol.*, **32**, 248–251.

Rowell, C. H. F. (1971). The variable coloration of the acridoid grasshoppers, *Adv. Insect Physiol.*, **8**, 145–198.

Rubiliani, C., Y. Turquier, and G. G. Payen. (1982). Recherche sur l'ontogenèse des rhizocéphales: I. Les stades precoces de l'endo endoparasitaire chez *Sacculina carcini* Thompson, *Cah. Biol. Mar.*, **23**, 287–297.

Rué, G., and J. Bierne. (1979). Effets du facteur cérébral gonadoinhibiteur (FGI) sur la morphologie et le metabolisme des cellules sexualisées germinales et somatiques des nemertiens, *Bull. Soc. Endocrinol.*, **40**, 81–82.

Rué, G., and J. Bierne. (1980). Contrôle endocrinien de l'oogenèse chez l'hoplonémerte *Amphiporus lactiflores, Bull. Soc. Zool. Fr.,* **105,** 155–163.

Rühm, W. (1955). Spiegeln die ipidenspezifischen Nematoden die Verwandtschaft ihrer Wirte wider? *Wanderversamml. Dtsch. Entomol. Ber.* **7,** 81–90.

Ruppert, L. E. (1978). "A review of metamorphosis of turbellarian larvae," in *Settlement and Metamorphosis of Marine Invertebrate Larvae,* F. S. Chia and M. E. Rice, Eds., Elsevier, New York, pp. 65–82.

Russell, L. M. (1948). The north American species of whiteflies of the genus *Trialeurodes, Misc. Publ. U. S. Dep. Agr.,* **635,** 85 pp.

Russell, L. M. (1957). Synonym of *Bemisia tabaci* (Gennadius) (Homoptera, Aleyrodidae), *Bull. Brooklyn Entomol. Soc.,* **52,** 122–123.

Russell, L. M. (1979). A new genus and a new species of Boreidae from Oregon (Mecoptera), *Proc. Entomol. Soc. Wash.,* **81,** 22–31.

Russell-Hunter, W. D., M. L. Apley, and R. Douglas-Hunter. (1972). Early life history of *Melampus* and the significance of semilunar synchrony, *Biol. Bull.,* **143,** 623–656.

Ryland, J. S. (1976). Physiology and ecology of marine bryozoans, *Adv. Mar. Biol.,* **14,** 285–443.

Saeki, H. (1966a). The effect of the day-length on the occurrence of the macropterous form in a cricket, *Scapsipedus aspersus* Walker (Orthoptera, Gryllidae), *Jap. J. Ecol.,* **16,** 49–52.

Saeki, H. (1966b). The effect of the population density on the occurrence of the macropterous form in a cricket, *Scapsipedus aspersus* Walker (Orthoptera, Gryllidae), *Jap. J. Ecol.,* **16,** 1–4.

Saigusa, T. (1961). On some basic concepts of evolution of psychid moths from the viewpoints of comparative ethology and morphology (in Japanese), *Tyo to Ga,* **12,** 120–143.

Saleuddin, A. S. M. (1979). "Shell formation in molluscs with special reference to periostracum formation and shell regeneration," in *Pathways in Malacology,* S. Van der Spoel et al. Eds., W. Junk, Utrecht, pp. 47–137.

Saleuddin, A. S. M., and S. C. Kunigelis. (1984). Neuroendocrine control mechanisms in shell formation, Am. Zool. **24,** 911–916.

Sall, C., G. Tsoupras, C. Kappler, M. Lagueux, D. Zachary, B. Luu, and J. A. Hoffmann. (1983). Fate of maternal conjugated ecdysteroids during embryonic development in *Locusta migratoria, J. Insect Physiol.,* **29,** 491–507.

Salt, G. (1937). The egg-parasite of *Sialis lutaria:* a study of the influence of the host upon a dimorphic parasite, *Parasitology,* **29,** 539–553.

Salt, G. (1940). Experimental studies in insect parasitism VII. The effect of different hosts on the parasite *Trichogramma evanescens* Westw. (Hym. Chalcidoidea), *Proc. R. Ent. Soc. Lond. A,* **15,** 81–95.

Salt, G. (1952). Trimorphism in the ichneumonid parasite *Gelis corruptor, Q. J. Microsc. Sci.,* **93,** 453–474.

Salvini Plawen, L. (1966). Zur Kenntnis der Cnidaria des nordadriatischen Mesopsammon, *Veroeffentl. Inst. Meeresunters. Bremerhaven Sonder.* **2,** 165–186.

Sams, G. R., and W. J. Bell. (1977). Juvenile hormone initiation of yolk deposition *in vitro* in the ovary of the cockroach, *Periplaneta americana, Adv. Inverteb. Reprod.,* **1,** 404–413.

Samuel, H. H., and S. Tsai. (1973). Thyroid hormone action in cell culture: demonstration of nuclear receptors in intact cells and isolated nuclei, *Proc. Natl. Acad. Sci. U.S.A.*, **70**, 3488–3492.

Sandor, T., and A. Z. Mehdi. (1979). "Steroids and evolution," in *Hormones and Evolution*, E. J. W. Barrington, Ed. Academic, New York, pp. 1–72.

Sänger, K. (1976). Zur vergleichenden Morphologie dreier Flügelformtypen der Laubheuschrecke *Tessellana vittata* (Orthoptera: Tettigoniidae), *Entomol. Germ.*, **2**, 262–276.

Sänger, K. (1984). Die Populationsdichte als Ursache makropter Ökomorphosen von *Tessellana vittata* (Charp.) (Orthoptera, Tettigoniidae), *Zool. Anz.*, **213**, 63–76.

Sano, I. (1967). Density effect and environmental temperature as the factors producing the active form of *Callosobruchus maculatus*, *J. Stored Prod. Res.*, **2**, 187–195.

Sawada, N. (1975). An electron microscopic study on the oogenesis of sipunculan worms. *Proc. Int. Symp. Biol. Sipuncula Echiura*, Vol. I, M. E. Rice and M. Todorovic, Eds., Kotor, pp. 169–175.

Saxena, R. C., S. H. Okech, and N. J. Liquido. (1981). Wing morphism in the brown planthopper, *Nilaparvata lugens*, *Insect Sci. Appl.*, **1**, 343–348.

Schaefer, C. W. (1975). The mayfly subimago: A possible explanation, *Ann. Entomol. Soc. Am.*, **68**, 183.

Schaller, F., and A. Defossez. (1974). Inhibition de la métamorphose de larves d'*Aeshna cyanea* Mull (Insects, Odonate) par un mimetique de l'hormone juvénile, *Wilhelm Roux's Arch.*, **174**, 20–32.

Schaller, H. C., T. Schmidt, K. Flick, and C. J. P. Grimmelikhuijzen. (1977a). Analysis of morphogenetic mutant, *Wilhelm Roux's Arch.*, **183**, 207–214.

Schaller, H. C., T. Schmidt, K. Flick, and C. J. P. Grimmelikhuijzen. (1977b). Analysis of morphogenetic mutants of *Hydra* I. The aberrant, *Wilhelm Roux's Arch.*, **183**, 193–206.

Schaller, H. C., T. Schmidt, K. Flick, and C. J. P. Grimmelikhuijzen. (1977c). Analysis of morphogenetic mutants of *Hydra* III. Maxi and mini. *Wilhelm Roux's Arch.*, **183**, 215–222.

Schaller, H. C., T. Schmidt, and C. J. P. Grimmelikhuijzen. (1979). Separation and specificity of action of four morphogens from *Hydra, Wilhelm Roux's Arch.*, **186**, 139–149.

Scheffel, H. (1969). Untersuchungen über die hormonale Regulation von Häutung und Anamorphose von *Lithobius forficatus* (L.) (Myriapoda, Chilopoda), *Zool. Jahrb. Physiol.*, **74**, 436–505.

Scheffel, H. (1977). Zur Temperaturabhängigkeit des Häutungszyklus bei Larven des 2 Stadiums von *Lithobius forficatus* (L.) (Chilopoda), *Zool. Anz.*, **198**, 287–294.

Scheffel, H., C. Wilke, and W. Pollak. (1974). Die Wirkung von exogenen Ecdysteron auf Larven des Chilopoden *Lithobius forficatus*, *Acta Entomol. Bohemoslov.*, **71**, 233–238.

Scheller, K., and T. A. Wohlfahrt. (1981). Different ecdysteroid titers in spring and summer generations of swallowtail *Iphiclides podalirius*, *Naturwissenschaften*, **68**, 45.

Schindewolf, O. H. (1936). *Paläontologie, Entwicklungslehre und Genetik. Kritik und Synthese*, Gebr. Borntraeger, Berlin.

Schleibung, R. E., and J. M. Lawrence. (1982). Differences in reproductive strategies of morphs of the genus *Echinaster* (Echinodermata: Asteroidea) from the eastern Gulf of Mexico, *Mar. Biol.,* **70,** 51–62.

Schmalhausen, I. I. (1949). *Factors of Evolution,* Blakiston, Philadelphia.

Schmid, F. (1951). Le groupe de *Enoicyla* (Trichopt. Limnophil.), *Tijdschr. Entomol.,* **94,** 207–226.

Schmidt, G. A. (1934). Ein zweiter Entwicklungstypus von *Lineus gesserensis-ruber, Zool., Jahrb. Anat.,* **58,** 607–660.

Schmidt, G. D. (1973). Early embryology of the acanthocephalan *Mediorhynchus grandis* Van Cleave, 1916, *Trans. Am. Microsc. Soc.,* **92,** 512–516.

Schmieder, R. G. (1933). The polymorphic forms of *Melittobia chalybii* Ashmead and the determining factors involved in their production (Hymenoptera: Chalcidoidea, Eulophidae), *Biol. Bull.,* **65,** 338–354.

Schminke, H. K. (1978). Die phylogenetische Stellung der Stygocarididae (Crustacea Syncarida)—unter besonderer Berücksichtigung morphologischer Ähnlichkeiten mit Larven Eucaridea, *Z. Zool. Sys. Evolutionsforsch.,* **16,** 225–239.

Schminke, H. K. (1981). Adaptation of Bathynellacea (Crustacea, Syncarida) to life in the interstitial (zoea theory), *Int. Rev. Gesammten Hydrobiol.,* **66,** 575–637.

Schneider, N. (1977). Réflexions sur l'évolution des psocoptères domicoles, *L'entomologiste,* **33,** 221–228.

Schoener, A. (1972). Fecundity and possible mode of development of some deep-sea ophiuroids, *Limnol. Oceanogr.,* **17,** 193–199.

Schoenmakers, H. J. N. (1979). In vitro biosynthesis of steroid from cholesterol by the ovaries and pyloric caeca of the starfish *Asterias rubens, Comp. Biochem. Physiol.,* **63,** 179–184.

Schoenmakers, H. J. N., and P. A. Voogt. (1980). Stimulation of vitellogenesis in starfish, *Gen. Comp. Endocrinol.,* **40,** 363.

Schoenmakers, H. J. N., and S. J. Dieleman. (1981). Progesterone and estrone levels in the ovaries, pyloric ceca and perivisceral fluid during the annual reproductive cycle of starfish, *Asterias rubens, Gen. Comp. Endocrinol.,* **43,** 63–70.

Scholtz, C. H. (1981). Aptery in *Trox* (Coleoptera: Trogidae); morphological changes and their relationship to habitat, *J. Entomol. Soc. S. Afr.,* **44,** 83–87.

Schultheiss, H. (1980). Isolation of pituitary proteins from Mexican axolotl (*Ambystoma mexicanum* Cope) by polyacrylamide gel electrophoresis, *J. Exp. Zool.,* **213,** 351–358.

Schulz, E. (1950a). Zur Ökologie von *Protohydra leuckarti* Greef (Studien an Hydrozoa, I), *Kiel. Meeresunters.,* **8,** 53–57.

Schulz, E. (1950b). *Psammohydra nanna,* ein neues solitäres Hydrozoon in der westlichen Beltsee, *Kiel. Meeresunters,* **8,** 122–137.

Schulz, J. K. R., and G. E. Lesh. (1970). Evidence for a temperature and ionic control of growth in *Hydra viridis, Growth,* **34,** 31–55.

Schwartz, S. S. (1984). Life history strategies in *Daphnia:* A review and prediction, *Oikos,* **42,** 114–122.

Scott, A. C. (1936). Haploidy and aberrant spermatogenesis in a coleopteran, *Micromalthus debilis* Le Conte, *J. Morphol.,* **59,** 485–515.

Scott, A. C. (1938). Paedogenesis in the Coleoptera, *Z. Morphol. Oekol. Tiere,* **33,** 633–653.

Scott, A. C. (1941). Reversal of sex-production in *Micromalthus, Biol. Bull.,* **81,** 420–431.

Scudder, G. G. E. (1971). The postembryonic development of the indirect flight muscles in *Cenocorixa bifida* (Hung.) (Hemiptera: Corixidae), *Can. J. Zool.,* **49,** 1387–1398.

Sehnal, F., M. M. Metwally, and I. Gelbic. (1976). Reactions of immature stages of noctuid moths to juvenoids, *Z. Angew. Entomol.,* **81,** 85–102.

Seifert, G. (1966). Häutung verursachende Reize bei *Polyxenus lagurus* L. (Diplopoda, Pselaphiognatha), *Zool. Anz.,* **177,** 258–263.

Seifert, G., and J. Rosenberg. (1974). Elektronenmikroskopische Untersuchungen der Häutungsdrüsen (Lymphstränge) von *Lithobius forficatus* L. (Chilopoda), *Z. Morphol. Tiere,* **78,** 263–279.

Sekiguchi, K. (1970). On the inner egg membrane of the horse-shoe crab (in Japanese), *Zool. Mag.,* **79,**115–118.

Sekiguchi, K., S. Yamamichi, H. Seshita, H. Sugita, and T. Ito. (1984). "Development," in *Biology of the Horseshoe Crab* (in Japanese), K. Sekiguchi, Ed., Science House, pp. 123–178.

Selander, R. B., and J. M. Mathieu. (1964). The ontogeny of blister beetles (Coleoptera, Meloidae). I. A study of three species of the genus *Pyrota, Ann. Entomol. Soc. Am.,* **57,** 711–732.

Selander, R. B., and R. C. Weddle. (1969). The ontogeny of blister beetle (Coleoptera, Meloidae) II. The effects of age of triungulin larvae at feeding and temperature on development in *Epicauta segmenta, Ann. Entomol. Soc. Am.,* **62,** 27–39.

Selman, K., and J. M. Arnold. (1977). Ultrastructural and cytochemical analysis of oogenesis in the squid, *Loligo pealei, J. Morphol.,* **100,** 381–400.

Selman, K., and R. A. Wallace. (1978). An autoradiographic study of vitellogenesis in the squid, *Loligo pealei, Tissue & Cell,* **10,** 599–608.

Serban, M. (1960). La néoténie et le problème de la taille chez les copépodes, *Crustaceana,* **1,** 77–83.

Sexton, E. W. (1924). The moulting and growth stages of *Gammarus,* with descriptions of the normals and intersexes of *G. chevreuxi, J. Mar. Biol. Assoc. U.K.,* **13,** 340–401.

Sexton, O. J., and J. R. Bizer. (1978). Life history patterns of *Ambystoma tigrinum* in montane Colorado, *Amer. Midl. Nat.,* **99,** 101–118.

Shakuntala, K., and S. R. Reddy. (1982). Crustacean egg size as an indicator of egg fat/protein reserves, *Int. J. Inverteb. Reprod.,* **4,** 381–384.

Shapiro, A. M. (1975). Genetics, environment, and subspecies differences; the case of *Polites sabuletti* (Lepidoptera: Hesperiidae), *Great Basin Nat.,* **35,** 33–38.

Shapiro, A. M. (1976). Seasonal polymorphism, *Evol. Biol.,* **9,** 259–333.

Shapiro, A. M. (1977). Evidence for obligate monophenism in *Reliquia santamarta,* a neotropical alpine pierine butterfly (Lepidoptera: Pieridae), *Psyche,* **84,** 183–190.

Shapiro, A. M. (1978). Developmental and phenotypic responses to photoperiod and temperature in an equatorial montane butterfly, *Tatochila xanthodice* (Lepidoptera: Pieridae), *Biotropica,* **10,** 297–301.

Shapiro, A. M. (1980a). Physiological and developmental responses to photoperiod and temperature as data in phylogenetic and biogeographic inference, *Syst. Zool.,* **29,** 335–341.

Shapiro, A. M. (1980b). Convergence in pierine polyphenism (Lepidoptera), *J. Nat. Hist.*, **14**, 781–802.

Shapiro, A. M. (1981). Phenotypic plasticity in temperature and subarctic *Nymphalis antiopa* (Nymphalidae): Evidence for adaptive canalization, *J. Lepid. Soc.*, **35**, 124–131.

Sharif, M. (1935). On the presence of wing buds in the pupa of Aphaniptera, *Parasitology*, **27**, 461–464.

Sharif, M. (1937). On the internal anatomy of the larva of the rat flea *(Nosopsyllus fasciatus)*, *Phil. Trans. R. Soc. Lond. Ser. B.*, **227**, 465–538.

Sharov, A. G. (1966). *Basic Arthropodan Stock,* Pergamon, Oxford.

Shetlar, D. J. (1978). Biological observations on *Zorotypus hubbardi* Caudell (Zoraptera), *Entomol. News,* **89**, 217–223.

Shine, R. (1983). Reptilian reproductive modes: The oviparity–viviparity continuum, *Herpetologica,* **39**, 108.

Shostak, S. (1981). Variation in hydra's tentacle numbers as a function of temperature, *Int. J. Inverteb. Reprod.*, **3**, 321–331.

Shuster, C. N., Jr. (1960). Horse shoe crab. Estuarine, *Bull. Univ. Delaware Marine Lab.*, **5**, 1–9.

Shute, S. L. (1980). Wing polymorphism in British species of *Longitarsus* beetles (Chrysomelidae: Alticinae), *Syst. Entomol.*, **5**, 437–448.

Sieber, R. (1982). The role of juvenile hormones in the development of physogastry in *Macrotermes michaelsoni* (Isoptera, Macrotermitidae), *Gen. Comp. Endocrinol.,* **46L**; 405.

Sieber, R., and R. H. Leuthold. (1982). Development of physogastry in the queen of the fungus growing termite *Macrotermes michaelsoni* (Isoptera: Macrotermitidae), *J. Insect Physiol.*, **28**, 979–985.

Silén, L. (1954). Developmental biology of Phoronida of the Gullmar Fiord area (west coast of Sweden), *Acta Zool.*, **35**, 215–256.

Silk, M. H., and I. M. Spence. (1969). Ultrastructural studies of the blood-fluke *Schistosoma mansoni* III, *S. Afr. J. Med. Sci.*, **34**, 93–104.

Silverstone, M., V. A. Galton, and S. H. Imgbar. (1978). Observations concerning the metabolism of iodine by polyps of *Aurelia aurita, Gen. Comp. Endocrinol.*, **34**, 132–140.

Silvestri, F. (1905). Descrizione di un nuovo genere di Rhipiphoridae, *Redia,* **3**, 315–324.

Simpson, G. G. (1953a). *The Major Features of Evolution,* Columbia University Press, New York.

Simpson, G. G. (1953b). The Baldwin effect, *Evolution,* **7**, 110–117.

Simpson, R. D. (1977). The reproduction of some littoral molluscs from Macquarie Island (Subantarctic), *Mar. Biol.,* **44**, 125–142.

Skowerska, K. (1977). Neurosecretory system in *Polystoma integerrimum* Monogenoidea, Polystomatidae, *Prace Naukowe Kotowicach,* **189**, 56–63.

Slama, K. (1964). Die Einwirkung des Juvenilhormons auf die Epidermiszellen der Flügelanlagen bei künstlich beschleunigter und verzögerter Metamorphose von *Pyrrhocoris apterus* L., *Zool. Jahrb. Physiol.*, **70**, 427–454.

Slama, K., (1965). Effect of hormones on growth and respiratory metabolism in the larvae of *Pyrrhocoris apterus* L., *J. Insect Physiol.,* **11,** 113–122.

Slama, K. (1975). Some old concepts and new findings on hormonal control of insect metamorphosis, *J. Insect Physiol.,* **21,** 921–955.

Slama, K., and C. M. Williams. (1965). Juvenile hormone activity for the bug *Pyrrhocoris apterus, Proc. Natl. Acad. Sci.,* **54,** 411–414.

Slater, J. A. (1975). On the biology and zoogeography of Australian Lygaeidae (Hemiptera: Heteroptera) with special reference to the southwest fauna, *J. Aust. entomol. Soc.,* **14,** 47–64.

Slater, J. A. (1977). The incidence and evolutionary significance of wing polymorphism in lygaeid bugs with particular reference to those of South Africa, *Biotropica,* **9,** 217–229.

Slater, J. A. (1982). "Hemiptera, " in *Synopsis and Classification of Living Organisms,* S. P. Parker et al., Eds., Vol. 2, McGraw-Hill, New York, pp. 417–447.

Sluiters, J. F., and W. P. M. Geraerts. (1984). Normal development of *Trichobilharzia ocellata* in *Lymnaea stagnalis* in the absence of the female gonadotropic hormone producing dorsal bodies, *Proc. K. Ned. Akad. Wet. Ser. C,* **87,** 231–234.

Smeeton, L. (1980). Male production in ant *Myrmica rubra* L., unpublished Ph.D. thesis, University of Southampton.

Smit, F. G. A. M. (1972). On some adaptive structures in Siphonaptera, *Folia Parasitol.,* **19,** 5–17.

Smit, F. G. A. M., and G. M. Dunnet. (1962). A new genus and species of flea from Antarctica, *Pac. Insects,* **4,** 895–903.

Smith, C., and C. S. Rand. (1975). *Latimeria,* the living coelacanth, is ovoviviparous, *Science,* **190,** 1105–1106.

Smith, C. J. V. (1972). Temperature-induced delays in prolactin-initiated second metamorphosis of the newt *(Notophathalmus viridescens), Comp. Biochem. Physiol.,* **43A,** 233–237.

Smith, G. (1906). Rhizocephala, *Fauna Flora Golfes Neapel, Monogr.* **29,** 123 pp.

Smith, G. (1909). On the Anaspidacea, living and fossil, *Q. J. Microsc. Sci.,* **53,** 487–578.

Smith, R. I. O. (1958). On reproductive pattern as a specific characteristic among nereid polychaetes, *Syst. Zool.,* **7,** 60–63.

Smith, W. A., and H. F. Nijhout. (1981). Effects of a juvenile hormone analogue on the duration of the fifth instar in the milkweed bug *Oncopeltus fasciatus, J. Insect Physiol.,* **27,** 169–173.

Smithers, C. N. (1972). The classification and phylogeny of the Psocoptera, *Aust. Mus. Mem.,* **14,** 1–349.

Smyth, J. D. (1971). Development of monozoic forms of *Echinococcus granulosus* during in vitro culture, *Int. J. Parasitol.,* **1,** 121–124.

Smyth, J. D., and Z. Davies. (1975). In vitro suppression of segmentation in *Echinococcus multiocularis* with morphological transformation of postscoloces into monozoic adults, *Parasitology,* **71,** 125–135.

Snodgrass, R. E. (1937). The male genitalia of orthopteroid insects, *Smiths. Misc. Coll.,* **96**(5), 1–107.

Snodgrass, R. E. (1952). *A Textbook of Arthropod Anatomy,* Comstock, Ithaca, New York.

Snodgrass, R. E. (1954a). Insect metamorphosis, *Smiths. Misc. Coll.,* **122**(9), 1–124.

Snodgrass, R. (1954b). The dragonfly larvae, *Smiths. Misc. Coll.,* **123**(2), 1–38.

Snodgrass, R. E. (1956). Crustacean metamorphosis, *Smiths. Misc. Coll.,* **131**(10), 1–78.

Snodgrass, R. (1961). The caterpillar and the butterfly, *Smiths, Misc. Coll.,* **143**(6), 1–51.

Snyder, J., and P. W. Bretsky. (1971). Life habits of diminutive bivalve molluscs in the Maquoketa formation (Upper Ordovician), *Am. J. Sc.,* **271,** 227–251.

Snyder, R. C. (1956). Comparative features of the life histories of *Ambystoma gracile* (Baird) from populations at low and high altitudes, *Copeia,* **1956,** 41–50.

Socha, R. (1974). The action of juvenoids on metamorphosis, gonadal development and blood proteins pattern in *Dixippus morosus* (Phasmoidea), *Acta Entomol. Bohemoslov.,* **71,** 1–10.

Solomon, J. M., B. Sandler, M. A. Cocchia, and A. Lawrence. (1977). Effect of environmental illumination on nymphal development, maturation rate, and longevity of *Periplaneta americana, Ann. Entomol. Soc. Am.,* **70,** 409–413.

Southwood, T. R. E. (1961). A hormonal theory of the mechanism of wing polymorphism in Heteroptera, *Proc. R. Ent. Soc. Lond. A,* **36,** 63–66.

Southwood, T. R. E. (1962). Migration of terrestrial arthropods in relation to habitat, *Biol. Rev.,* **37,** 171–214.

Southwood, T. R. E. (1977). Habitat, the templet for ecological strategies, *J. Anim. Ecol.,* **46,** 337–365.

Spangenberg, D. B. (1966). A study of strobilation in *Aurelia aurita* under controlled conditions, *J. Exp. Zool.,* **160,** 1–10.

Spangenberg, D. B. (1968). Recent studies of strobilation in jellyfish, *Oceanogr. Mar. Biol. Ann. Rev.,* **6,** 231–247.

Specian, R. D., R. D. Lumsden, J. E. Ubelaker, and V. F. Allison. (1979). A unicellular endocrine gland in cestodes, *J. Parasitol.,* **65,** 569–578.

Spight, T. M. (1977). Latitude, habitat and hatching type for muricacean gastropods, *Nautilus,* **91,** 67–71.

Spracklin, B. M. (1978). Correlated light and electron microscopic study of oogenesis in *Tubularia larynx* (Hydrozoa, Athecata), *Am. Zool.,* **18,** 646.

Springhetti, A. (1964). Sulla strutura delle vesicole seminali delle Termiti, *Atti Accad. Naz. Ital. Entomol. Rendiconti,* **11,** 212–219.

Springhetti, A. (1970). Influence of king and queen on the differentiation of soldiers in *Kalotermes flavicollis* Fabr. (Isoptera), *Monitore Zool. Ital. (n. s.),* **4,** 99–105.

Springhetti, A. (1971). Il controllo dei reali sulla differenziazione degli alati in *Kalotermes flavicollis* Fabr. (Isoptera), *Boll. Zool.,* **38,** 101–110.

Sprinkle, J., and B. M. Bell. (1978). Paedomorphosis in edriasteroid echinoderms, *Paleobiology,* **4,** 82–88.

Sprules, W. G. (1974a). The adaptive significance of paedogenesis in North American species of *Ambystoma* (Amphibia: Caudata), an hypothesis, *Can. J. Zool.,* **52,** 393–408.

Sprules, W. G. (1974b). Environmental factors and the incidence of neoteny in *Ambystoma gracile* (Amphibia: Caudata), *Can. J. Zool.,* **52,** 1545–1552.

Srihari, T., M. Breuzet, and C. Caussanel. (1975). Effet d'un mimétique de l'hormone juvenile sur le developpement postembryonnaire de *Labidura riparia* (Dermaptere: Labiduridae), *C. R. Acad. Sci.,* **280,** 1107–1110.

Srivastava, U. S., and S. S. Prasad. (1982). A study of pupal–adult intermediates produced with juvenoid treatment of *Spodoptera litura* Fabr. pupae, *Proc. Ind. Acad. Sci. (Anim. Sci.),* **91,** 337–348.

Sroka, P., and L. I. Gilbert. (1974). The timing of juvenile hormone release for ovarian maturation in *Manduca sexta, J. Insect Physiol.,* **20,** 1173–1180.

Stancyk, S. E. (1973). Development of *Ophiolepis elegans* (Echinodermata; Ophiuroidea) and its implications in the estuarine environment, *Mar. Biol.,* **21,** 7–12.

Stannard, L. J. (1965). Polymorphism in the Putnam's scale, *Aspidiotus ancylus* (Homoptera: Coccoidea), *Ann. Entomol. Soc. Am.,* **58,** 573–576.

Stebbins, G. R. (1982). "Modal theme: A new framework for evolutionary synthesis," in *Perspectives on Evolution,* R. Milkman, Ed., Sinauer Associates, Sunderland, MA. pp. 1–14.

Steel, C. G. H. (1976). Photoperiodic regulation of neurosecretory cells controlling polymorphism in the aphid *Megoura viciae, Gen. Comp. Endocrinol.,* **29,** 265–266.

Steel, C. G. H. (1978). "Nervous and hormonal regulation of neurosecretory cells in the insect brain," in *Comparative Endocrinology,* P. J. Galliard and H. H. Boer, Eds., Elsevier-North Holland, Amsterdam, pp. 327–330.

Steel, C. G. H., and A. D. Lees. (1977). The role of neurosecretion in the photoperiodic control of polymorphism in the aphid *Megoura viciae, J. Exp. Biol.,* **67,** 117–135.

Steele, D. H., and V. J. Steele. (1973). The biology of *Gammarus* (Crustacea, Amphipoda) in the northwestern Atlantic. VII. The duration of embryonic development in five species at various temperatures, *Can. J. Zool.,* **51,** 995–999.

Steele, D. H., and V. J. Steele. (1977). The biology of *Gammarus* (Crustacea, Amphipoda) in the northwestern Atlantic XI. Comparison and discussion, *Can. J. Zool.,* **53,** 1116–1125.

Steffan, W. A. (1973). Polymorphism in *Plastosciara perniciosa, Science,* **182,** 1265–1266.

Steffan, W. A. (1975). Morphological and behavioral polymorphism in *Plastosciara perniciosa* (Diptera: Sciaridae), *Proc. Entomol. Soc. Wash.,* **77,** 1–14.

Stein, W. (1973). Zur Vererbung des Flügeldimorphismus bei *Apion virens* Herbst (Col. Curculionidae), *Z. Angew. Entomol.,* **74,** 62–63.

Stephens, E. J. (1955). Induction of mating in the crayfish *Cambarus by* modification of daily photoperiod, *Biol. Bull.,* **108,** 235–241.

Stephenson, W. (1942). On the culturing of *Rhabditis terrestris* n. sp., *Parasitology,* **34,** 246–252.

Sterrer, W. (1972). Systematics and evolution within the Gnathostomulida, *Syst. Zool.,* **21,** 151–173.

Sterrer, W. (1974). "Gnathostomulida," in *Reproduction of Marine Invertebrates,* Vol. 1, A. C. Giese and J. S. Pearse, Eds., Academic, New York, pp. 345–357.

Sterrer, W., and R. Rieger. (1974). "Retronectidae — a new cosmopolitan marine family of Catenulida," in *Biology of the Turbellaria*, N. W. Riser and M. P. Morse, Eds., McGraw-Hill, New York, pp. 63–92.

Sterrer, W. E. (1982). "Gnathostomulida," in Synopsis and Classification of Living Organisms, S. P. Parker et al., Eds., Vol. 1, McGraw-Hill, New York, pp. 847–851.

Stock, J. H. (1973). The existence of interstitial members of *Gammarus* group (Amphipoda), *Crustaceana*, **24**, 339–341.

Stock, J. H. (1979). New data on taxonomy and zoogeography of ingolfiellid Crustacea, *Bijd. Dierk.*, **49**, 81–96.

St. Quentin, D. (1969). Probleme des Wachstums und der Körpergrösse an zwei Libelluliden, *Vgl. Unters. Beitr. Ent.*, **19**, 267–271.

Strathmann, R. R. (1978). Egg size, larval development, and juvenile size in benthic marine invertebrates, *Am. Nat.*, **11**, 373–376.

Streif, W., and J. Le Breton. (1970). Etude endocrinologique des facteurs régissant la morphogenèse et la régression du pénis chez un mollusque prosobranche gonochorique *Littorina littorea* L., *C. R. Acad. Sci.*, **270**, 547–549.

Strenger, A., and W. Erber. (1983). Zur Larvalentwicklung bei Asteroidea und Kritik am systematischen Begriffspaar Pelmatozoa—Eleutherozoa bei Echinodermen, *Z. Zool. Syst. Evolutionsforsch.*, **21**, 235–239.

Strohecker, H. F. (1966). New *Timema* from Nevada and Arizona, *Pan-Pac. Entomol.*, **42**, 25–26.

Strong, D. R., and P. D. Stiling. (1983). Wing dimorphism changed by experimental density manipulation in a planthopper *(Prokelisia marginata)* Homoptera Delphacidae, *Ecology*, **64**, 206–209.

Stross, R. G. (1965). Termination of summer and winter diapause in *Daphnia, Am. Zool.*, **5**, 701.

Stross, R. G. (1969a). Photoperiod control of diapause in *Daphnia* 2. Induction of winter diapause in the Arctic, *Biol. Bull.*, **136**, 264–273.

Stross, R. G. (1969b). Photoperiod control of diapause in *Daphnia* 3. Two stimuli control of long and short day induction, *Biol. Bull.*, **137**, 359–374.

Stross, R. G., and J. C. Hill. (1968). Photoperiod control of winter diapause in the freshwater crustacean, *Daphnia, Biol. Bull.*, **134**, 176–198.

Stunkard, H. W. (1957). Intraspecific variation in parasitic flatworms, *Syst. Zool.*, **5**, 7–18.

Stunkard, H. W. (1959a). Induced gametogenesis in a monogenetic trematode, *Polystoma stellai* Viggeras 1955, *J. Parasitol.*, **45**, 389–394.

Stunkard, H. W. (1959b). Progenetic maturity and phylogeny of digenetic trematodes, *J. Parasitol.* **45** (Section 2), 15.

Stunkard, H. W. (1967). Platyhelminthic parasites of invertebrates, *J. Parasitol.*, **53**, 673–682.

Subramoniam, T. (1981). Protandric hermaphroditism in a mole crab *Emerita asiatica.* Decapoda-Anomura, *Biol. Bull.*, **160**, 161–174.

Sugg, P., J. S. Edwards, and J. Baust. (1983). Phenology and life history of *Belgica antarctica*, an Antarctic midge (Diptera: Chironomidae), *Ecol. Entomol.*, **8**, 105–113.

Sugimoto, K., and H. Watanabe. (1980). Studies on reproduction in the compound ascidian *Symplegma reptans.* Relationship between neural complex and reproduction, *Biol. Bull.,* **159,** 219–230.

Sugita, H., and K. Sekiguchi. (1982). "Horseshoe crab developmental studies II. Physiological adaptation of horseshoe crab embryos to the environment during embryonic development," in *Physiology and Biology of Horse-Shoe Crabs,* J. Bonaventura et al., Eds., Liss, New York, pp. 75–82.

Sugiura, Y. (1965). On the life history of rhizostome medusae. III. On the effects of temperature on the strobilation of *Mastigias papua, Biol. Bull.,* **128,** 493–496.

Sugiura, Y. (1966). On the life history of rhizostome medusae. IV. *Cephea cephea, Embryologia,* **9,** 105–122.

Sutherland, O. R. W. (1969). The role of crowding in the production of winged forms by two strains of the pea aphid *Acyrthosiphon pisum, J. Insect Physiol.,* **15,** 1385–1410.

Suto, C., and N. Kumada. (1981). Secretion of dispersion-inducing substance by the German cockroach, *Blattella germanica* L. (Orthoptera: Blatellidae), *Appl. Entomol. Zool.,* **16,** 113–120.

Sutton, R. D. (1983). Seasonal colour changes, sexual maturation and oviposition in *Psylla peregrina* (Homoptera: Psylloidea), *Ecol. Entomol.,* **8,** 195–201.

Suzuki, S. (1982). Plasma thyroid hormone levels before and after metamorphosis of the lamprey, *Dev. Growth Differ.,* **24,** 416.

Suzzoni, J. P., and H. Cagniant. (1975). Etude histologique des voies génitales chez l'ouvrière et la reine de *Cataglyphis cursor* Fonscolombe (H. F. F.) (Hymenoptera Formicidae, Formicinae). Arguments en faveur d'une parthénogenèse thélytoque chez cette espèces, *Insect Soc.,* **22,** 83–92.

Suzzoni, J. P., L. Passera, and A. Strambi. (1980). Ecdysteroid titre in the ant, *Pheidole pallidula* (Nyl.) (Hymenoptera: Formicidae), *Experientia,* **36,** 1228–1229.

Swedmark, B. (1954). Etude du développement larvaire et remarques sur la morphologie de *Protodrilus symbioticus* Giard (Archiannélides), *Ark. Zool.,* **6,** 511–522.

Swedmark, B. (1955). Recherches sur la morphologie, le développement et la biologie de *Pammodrilus balanoglossoides.* Polychète sédentaire de la microfaune des sables, *Arch. Zool. Exp. Gen.,* **92,** 141–220.

Swedmark, B. (1958). *Psammodriloides fauveli* n. g. et n. sp. et la famille des Psammodrilidae (Polychaeta Sedentaria), *Ark. Zool.,* **12,** 55–64.

Swedmark, B. (1964). The interstitial fauna of marine sand, *Biol. Rev.,* **39,** 1–42.

Swedmark, B. (1968). The biology of interstitial Mollusca, *Zool. Soc. Lond. Symp.,* **22,** 135–149.

Swedmark, B. (1971). A review of Gastropoda, Brachiopoda and Echinodermata in marine meiobenthos, *Smiths. Misc. Contrib. Zool.,* **76,** 41–45.

Swedmark, B., and G. Teissier. (1950). Développement d'un Hydrozoaire aberrant *Halammohydra schulzei* Remane, *C. R. Acad. Sci.,* **231,** 173–174.

Swedmark, B., and G. Teissier. (1957a). *Halammohydra vermifrons* n. sp. et la famille des Halammohydridae Remane, *Bull. Soc. Zool. Fr.,* **82,** 38–49.

Swedmark, B., and G. Teissier. (1957b). Organisation et développement des *Halammohydra* (Hydrozoaires), *C. R. Acad. Sci.,* **244,** 501–504.

Swedmark, B., and G. Teissier. (1958a). *Otohydra vagans* n.g. n. sp. Hydrozoaires des sables apparentés aux Halammohydridées, *C. R. Acad. Sc.,* **247,** 238–240.

Swedmark, B., and G. Teissier. (1958b). *Armorhydra janowiczi* n.g. n. sp. Hydroméduse benthique, *C. R. Acad. Sci.,* **247,** 133–135.

Swedmark, B., and G. Teissier. (1966). The Actinulida and their evolutionary significance, *Zool. Soc. Lond. Symp.,* **16,** 119–133.

Sweet, M. H. (1964). The biology and ecology of the Rhyparochrominae of New England (Heteroptera: Lygaeidae). Part 1 and part II, *Entomol. Am.,* **43,** 1–124; **44,** 1–201.

Sweet, M. H. (1977). The systematic position of the seedbug genus *Neosuris* Barber, 1924 (Hemiptera: Lygaeidae) and a discussion of the zoogeographical significance of the genus and notes on the distribution and ecology of *N. castanea* (Barber, 1911) and *N. fulgida* (Barber 1918), *J. Kans. Entomol. Soc.,* **50,** 569–574.

Szidat, L. (1956). Über den Entwicklungszyklus mit progenetischen Larvenstadien (Cercariacen) von *Genarchella genarchella* Travassos 1928 (Trematoda, Hemiuridae), *Z. Tropenmed. Parasitol.,* **7,** 132–152.

Szidat, L. (1959). Hormonale Beeinflussung von Parasiten durch ihren Wirt, *Z. Parasitkd.,* **19,** 503–524.

Tannert, W. (1958). Die Flügelgelenkung bei Odonaten, *Dtsch. Entomol. Z. (N. F.),* **5,** 393–445.

Tarjan, A. C. (1967). Variability of diagnostic characters among some plant and soil nematodes, *Prace Naukowe Instytutu Ochrony Roslin,* **9,** 105–116.

Tasch, P. (1963). Evolution of the Branchipoda, *Mus. Comp. Zool. Spec. Publ. Phylogeny Evol. Crustacea,* pp. 145–162.

Tata, J. R. (1970). Simultaneous acquisition of mechanism of metamorphic receptors and hormone binding in *Xenopus* larvae, *Nature,* **237,** 686–689.

Tata, J. R. (1976). The expression of vitellogenin gene, *Cell,* **9,** 1–14.

Tata, J. R., and D. F. Smith. (1979). Vitellogenesis: A versatile model for hormonal regulation of gene expression, *Recent Progr. Hormone Res.,* **13,** 47–95.

Taurog, A. (1974). Effects of TSH and long-acting thyroid stimulator in thyroid 131 I-metabolism and metamorphosis of the Mexican axolotl *(Ambystoma mexicanum),* *Gen. Comp. Endocrinol.,* **24,** 257–266.

Taurog, A. C., C. Oliver, R. L. Eskay, J. C. Porter, and J. M. Mackenzie. (1974). The role of TRH in the neoteny of the Mexican axolotl *(Ambystoma mexicanum), Gen. Comp. Endocrinol,* **24,** 267–279.

Taylor, V. A. (1981). The adaptive and evolutionary significance of wing polymorphism and parthenogenesis in *Ptinella* Motschulsky (Coleoptera: Ptiliidae), *Ecol. Entomol,* **6,** 89–98.

Tchernavin, V. (1939). The origin of salmon, *Salmon Trout Mag.,* **95,** 1–21.

Templeton, A. R. (1982). Why read Goldschmidt?, *Paleobiology,* **8,** 474–481.

Thanh-Xuan, N. (1972). Etude de la diapause imaginale de *Psylla pyri* L. (Homoptera: Psyllidae), *Ann. Zool. Ecol. Anim.,* **4,** 281–309.

Thew, T. B. (1957). Observations on the oviposition of a species of *Baetis* (Ephemeroptera), *Mus. Q., Davenport Publ. Mus.,* **2**(2), 6.

Thiel, H. (1962). Untersuchungen über die Strobilisation von *Aurelia aurita* Lam. an einer Population der Kieler Fjorder, *Kiel. Meeresforsch.,* **8,** 198–230.

Thiel, H. (1963a). Untersuchungen über die Entstehung abnormer Scyphistomae, Strobilae und Ephyrae von *Aurelia aurita* Lam. und ihre theoretische Bedeutung, *Zool. Jahrb. Anat.,* **81,** 311–358.

Thiel, H. (1963b). Teil und Spiralephyren von *Aurelia aurita* und ihre Regulation, *Zool. Anz.,* **171,** 303–327.

Thiel, H. (1966). "The evolution of Scyphozoa. A review," in *The Cnidaria and Their Evolution,* W. J. Rees, Ed., *Zool. Soc. Lond. Symp.,* **16,** 77–117.

Thompson, K. S. (1969). The biology of the lobe-finned fishes, *Biol. Rev.,* **44,** 91–154.

Thompson, T. E. (1967). Direct development in a nudibranch, *Caldina laevis,* with a discussion of developmental processes in Opisthobranchia, *J. Mar. Biol. Assoc. U.K.,* **47,** 1–22.

Thorne, B. L., and C. Noirot. (1982). Ergatoid reproductives in *Nasutitermes corniger* (Motschulsky) (Isoptera: Termitidae), *Int. J. Insect Morphol. Embryol,* **11,** 213–226.

Thorne, G., and M. W. Allen. (1959). "Variation in nematodes," in *Plant Pathology, Problems and Progress 1908–1958,* C. H. Holton et al., Eds., University of Wisconsin Press, Madison, pp. 412–418.

Thorpe, A., M. C. Thorndike, and E. J. Barrington. (1972). Ultra-structural and histochemical features of the endostyle of the ascidian *Ciona intestinalis,* with special reference to the distribution of bound iodine, *Gen. Comp. Endocrinol.,* **19,** 559–571.

Thorpe, A., and M. C. Thorndike. (1975). The endostyle in relation to iodine binding, *Symp. Zool. Soc. Lond.,* **36,** 159–177.

Thorpe, W. H. (1930). Biological races in insects and allied groups, *Biol. Rev.,* **5,** 177–212.

Thorpe, W. H. (1940). "Ecology and the future of systematics," in *The New Systematics,* J. Huxley, Ed., Oxford University Press, New York, pp. 341–364.

Thorson, G. (1936). The larval development, growth and metabolism of Arctic marine bottom invertebrates, etc., *Medd. Grønland,* **100,** 1–155.

Thorson, G. (1950). Reproductive and larval ecology of marine bottom invertebrates, *Biol. Rev.,* **25,** 1–45.

Tiegs, W. (1947). The development and affinities of the Pauropoda, based on a study of *Pauropus silvaticus, Q. J. Microsc. Sci.,* **88,** 165–267 and 275–336.

Tinkle, D. W., and N. F. Hadley. (1975). Lizard reproductive effort: Caloric estimates and comments on its evolution, *Ecology,* **56,** 427–434.

Tinkle, D. W., and J. W. Gibbons. (1977). The distribution and evolution of viviparity in reptiles, *Misc. Publ. Mus. Zool. Univ. Mich. No.* **154,** 1–55.

Tobe, S. S., and C. S. Chapman. (1979). The effects of starvation and subsequent feeding on juvenile hormone synthesis and oocyte growth in *Schistocerca americana gregaria, J. Insect Physiol.,* **25,** 701–708.

Tofts, J., and E. Meerovitch. (1973). The effect of farnesylmethylether, a mimic of insect juvenile hormone, on *Hymenolepis diminuta* in vitro, *Int. J. Parasitol,* **3,** 863–868.

Tompkins, R. (1978). Genic control of axolotl metamorphosis, *Am. Zool.,* **18,** 313–319.

Traub, R. (1980). "Some adaptive modifications in fleas," in *Fleas,* R. Traub and H. Starcke, Eds., Balkema, Rotterdam, pp. 33–67.

Travé, J. (1976). Les prelarves d'Acariens. Mise au point et données récentes, *Rev. Ecol. Biol. Sol.,* **13,** 161–171.

Treiblmayr, K., K. Pohlhammer, E. Rieske, and H. Adam. (1981). Exstirpation der Prothorakaldrüsen bei Larven der paedogenetischen Gallmücke *Heteropeza pygmaea* (Insecta, Curculionidae) mit Lasermikrostrahl, *Mikroskopie,* **38,** 97–102.

Truman, J. W. (1972). Physiology of insect rhythms. I. Circadian organisation of the endocrine events underlying the moulting cycle of the larval tobacco hornworm, *J. Exp. Biol.* **57,** 805–820.

Truman, J. W., and L. M. Riddiford. (1974). Physiology of insect rhythms III. The temporal organization of the endocrine events underlying pupation of the tobacco hornworm, *J. Exp. Biol.,* **60,** 371–382.

Truman, J. W., L. M. Riddiford, and L. Safranek. (1973). Hormonal control of cuticle coloration in the tobacco hornworm. *Manduca sexta:* Basis of an ultrasensitive bioassay for juvenile hormone, *J. Insect Physiol.,* **19,** 195–203.

Tsuji, H., and T. Mizuno. (1972). Retardation of development and reproduction in four species of cockroaches, *Blattella germanica, Periplaneta americana, P. fuliginosa* and *P. japonica* under various temperature conditions, *Jap. J. Sanit. Zool.,* **23,** 101–111.

Turner, R. L., and M. Lawrence. (1979). "Volume and composition of echinoderm eggs: Implication for the use of egg size in life history models," in *Reproductive Ecology of Marine Invertebrates,* S. E. Stancyk, Ed., University of South Carolina Press, Columbia, pp. 25–40.

Turner, R. T., W. W. Dickhoff, and A. Gorbman. (1981). Estrogen binding of hepatic nuclei of hagfish *Eptatretus stouti, Gen. Comp. Endocrinol.,* **45,** 26–29.

Tyler, P. A., and J. D. Gage. (1984). The reproductive biology of echithuriid and cidarid sea urchin from the deep sea (Rockall Trough, North East Atlantic Ocean), *Mar. Biol.,* **80,** 63–74.

Uchida, T. (1963). "On the interrelationships of the Coelenterata, with remarks on their symmetry," in *Lower Metazoa,* E. C. Dougherty, Ed., University of California Press, Berkeley, pp. 169–177.

Ude, J. (1962). Neurosekretorische Zelle im Cerebralganglion von *Dicrocoelium lanceatum* St. u. H. (Trematoda-Digenea), *Zool. Anz.,* **169,** 455–457.

Ulrich, H. (1936). Experimentelle Untersuchungen über den Generationswechsel der heterogenen Cecidomyide *Oligarces paradoxus, Z. Indukt. Abstamm. Vererbungsl.,* **71,** 1–60.

Ulrich, W. (1943). Die Mengeniden (Mengenillini) und die Phylogenie der Strepsipteren, *Z. Parasitkd.,* **13,** 62–101.

Underwood, A. J. (1974). On models for reproductive strategies in marine benthic invertebrates, *Am. Nat.,* **108,** 874–878.

Unnithan, G. C., and K. K. Nair. (1979). The influence of corpus allatum activity on the susceptibility of *Oncopeltus fasciatus* to precocene 1, 2, 3, *Ann. Entomol. Soc. Am.,* **72,** 38–40.

Usinger, R., and R. Matsuda. (1959). *Classification of the Aradidae (Hemiptera-Heteroptera),* British Museum (Natural History), London.

Usinger, R. L. (1966). *Monograph of Cimicidae (Hemiptera–Heteroptera),* Thomas Say Foundation, Vol. 7, Entomological Society of America, College Park, MD.

Utida, S. (1954). Presumed two phases in *Callosobruchus quadrimaculatus* (in Japanese), *J. Appl. Zool.,* **13,** 129–134.

Utida, S. (1956). Differential effects of temperature, humidity and population density upon some ecological characters of the two phases, *Res. Popul. Ecol. Kyoto Univ.,* **3,** 93–104.

Utida, S. (1970). Secular change of percent emergence of flight form in the population of southern cow pea weevil. *Callosobruchus maculatus* (in Japanese), *Jap. J. Appl. Zool. Entomol.,* **14,** 71–78.

Utida, S. (1972). Density dependent polymorphism in the adult of *Callosobruchus maculatus* (Coleoptera, Bruchidae), *J. Stored Prod. Res.* **8,** 111–126.

Uvarov, B. P. (1921). A revision of the genus *Locusta* L. (= *Pachytylus* Fieb.), with a new theory as to the periodicity and migrations of locusts. *Bull. Entomol. Res. Lond.,* **12,** 135–163.

Valentine, J. W., and C. A. Campbell. (1975). Gene regulation and the fossil record, *Am. Sci.,* **63,** 673–680.

Van Bohemen, J. G. D., H. J. Lambert, Th. Goos, and P. G. W. Van Gordt. (1982). Estrone and estradiol participation during exogenous vitellogenesis in the female rainbow trout, *Salmo gairdneri, Gen. Comp. Endocrinol.,* **46,** 91–92.

Vance, R. R. (1973). On reproductive strategies in marine benthic invertebrates, *Am. Nat.,* **107,** 339–352.

Vance, R. R. (1974). Reply to Underwood, *Am. Nat.,* **108,** 879–880.

Vandel, A. (1943). Essai sur l'origine, l'évolution et la classification des Oniscoidea (Isopodes terrestres), *Bull. Biol. Fr. Belg.,* **30,** 1–136.

Vandel, A. (1965a). *Biospeleology,* Pergamon, Oxford.

Vandel, A. (1965b). Sur l'existence d'oniscoïdes et sur le polyphylétisme des isopodes terrestres, *Ann. Speleol.,* **20,** 489–518.

Van den Bosch de Aguilar, P. (1969). Nouvelles données morphologiques et hypothèse sur le rôle du système de neurosécretion chez *Daphnia pulex* (Crustacea: Cladocera), *Ann. Soc. R. Zool Belg.,* **99,** 27–44.

Van den Bosch de Aguilar, P. (1972). Les caractérisations tinctoriales des cellules neuro-sécrétrices chez *Daphnia pulex* (Crustacea: Cladocera). *Gen. Comp. Endocrinol.,* **18,** 140–145.

Van den Bosch de Aguilar, P. (1976). Neurosécrétion et régulation hydroélectrolytique chez *Artemia salina, Experientia,* **32,** 228–229.

Van den Broek, E. (1978). The occurrence of a progenetic stage of *Asymphylodora tincae* in relation to environmental temperature, *Parasitology,* **77,** VI–VII.

Van der Plas, A. J., A. H. L. Koenderman, and G. J. Deibel van Schindel. (1982). Effects of estradio 17β on the synthesis of RNA, proteins, and lipids in the pyloric caeca of the female starfish *Asterias rubens, Comp. Biochem. Physiol.,* **73B,** 965–970.

Van de Vyver, G. (1980). "A comparative study of embryonic development of Hydrozoa Athecata," in *Developmental and Cellular Biology of Coelenterates,* P. Tardent and R. Tardent, Eds., Elsevier-North Holland, New York, pp. 109–120.

Van Huizen, T. H. P. (1977). The significance of flight activity in the life cycle of *Amara plebeja* Gyll. (Coleoptera, Carabidae), *Oecologia,* **29,** 27–41.

Van Minnen, J., and D. Reichelt. (1980). Effects of photoperiod on the activity of neurosecretory cells in the lateral lobes of the cerebral ganglia of the pond snail *Lymnaea stagnalis,* with particular reference to the canopy cells, *Proc. K. Ned. Akad. Wet., Ser. C,* **83,** 15–24.

Vayssiere, A. (1934). Etude anatomique des larves nymphales des *Baetisca obesa* et *carolina, Ann. Sci. Nat. Zool. Ser. 10,* **17,** 381–406.

Veillet, A. (1962). Sur la sexualite de *Sylon hippolites* M. Sars. Cirripède de crevettes, *C. R. Acad. Sci.,* **254,** 176–177.

Velthuis, H. H. W. (1976). "Environmental genetics and endocrine influences in stingless bee caste determination," in *Phase and Caste Determination in Insects,* M. Lüscher, Ed., Pergamon, pp. 35–53.

Velthuis, H. H. W., and F. M. Velthuis-Kluppel. (1975). Caste differentiation in a stingless bee, *Melipona quadrifasciata* Lep. influenced by juvenile hormone application, *Proc. K. Ned. Akad. Wet. Ser C,* **78,** 81–94.

Vepsälainen, K. (1971). The role of gradually changing daylength in determination of wing length, alary dimorphism and diapause in *Gerris odontogaster* (Zett.) population (Gerridae, Heteroptera) in South Finland, *Ann. Acad. Sci. Fenn. A, IV Biol.,* **183,** 1–25.

Vepsälainen, K. (1973). The distribution and habitats of *Gerris* Fabr. species (Heteroptera, Gerridae) in Finland, *Annales Zool. Fenn.,* **10,** 419–444.

Vepsälainen, K. (1974). The life cycles and wing lengths of Finnish *Gerris* Fabr. species (Heteroptera, Gerridae), *Acta Zool. Fenn.,* **141,** 1–73.

Vepsälainen, K., and S. Krajewski. (1974). The life cycle and alary dimorphism of *Gerris lacustris* (L.) (Heteroptera, Gerridae) in Poland, *Not. Entomol.,* **54,** 85–89.

Verrier, M. L. (1950). Poecilogonie, écologie et répartition geographique chez les Ephemères, *C. R. Acad. Sci.,* **230,** 1794–1796.

Vieau, F., and D. Lebrun. (1981). Hormone juvénile, vitellogenèse et ponte des jeunes imagos femelles de *Kalotermes flavicollis* Fabr., *C. R. Acad. Sci.,* **293,** 399–402.

Vladykov, V. D., and E. Kott. (1979). Satellite species among the holarctic lampreys (Petromyzonidae), *Can. J. Zool.,* **57,** 860–867.

Voge, M. (1963). "Observation on the habitats of platyhelminths, primarily Turbellaria," in *The Lower Metazoa,* E. C. Dougherty, Ed., University of California Press, Berkeley, pp. 455–470.

Voronov, P. M. (1979). Salt composition of water and variability of *Artemia salina* (in Russian), *Zool. Zh.,* **58,** 175–179.

Voronov, P. M. (1982). Effect of temperature on growth and maturation of *Artemia salina* (in Russian), *Zool. Zh.,* **61,** 1594–1596.

Waddington, C. H. (1953). Genetic assimilation of an acquired character, *Evolution,* **7,** 118–126.

Waddington, C. H. (1961). Genetic assimilation, *Adv. Genet.,* **10,** 257–293.

Waddington, C. H. (1975). *The evolution of an evolutionist,* Cornell University Press, Ithaca, NY.

Wake, D. B. (1966). Comparative osteology and evolution of the lungless salamanders, family Plethodontidae, *Mem. South. Calif. Acad. Sci.,* **4,** 1–111.

Wake, D. B., and A. H. Brame. (1969). Systematics and evolution of Neotropical salamanders of the *Bolitoglossa helmrichi* group, *Los Ang. Cty. Mus. Contrib. Sci.,* **175,** 1–40.

Wake, D. B., and J. F. Lynch. (1976). The distribution, ecology and evolutionary history of plethodontid salamanders, *Nat. Hist. Mus. Los Ang. Cty. Sci. Bull.,* **25,** 1–65.

Wake, M. H. (1980). The reproductive biology of *Nectophrynoides malcolmi* (Amphibia: Bufonidae), with comments on the evolution of reproductive modes in the genus *Nectophrynoides, Copeia* **1980,** 198–209.

Wake, T. A., D. B. Wake, and M. H. Wake. (1983). The ossification sequence in *Aneides lugubris,* with comments on heterochrony, *J. Herpetol.,* **17,** 10–22.

Wakiya, Y., and N. Takahashi. (1937). Study on fishes of the family Salangidae, *J. Coll. Agric. Tokyo Imp. Univ.,* **14,** 265–296.

Walker, E. M. (1937). *Grylloblatta,* a living fossil, *Trans. R. Soc. Can. Sec. V Ser. III,* **26,** 1–10.

Walsh, S. J., and B. M. Burr. (1981). Distribution, morphology and life history of the Least Brook lamprey, *Lampetra aepyptera* (Pisces Pteromyzontidae), in Kentucky, *Brimleyana,* **6,** 83–100.

Walvig, F. (1963). "The gonads and the formation of sexual cells, "in *The Biology of Myxine,* A. Brodal and R. Fanger, Eds., Grondahl & Son, Oslo, pp. 530–580.

Wanyonyi, K. (1974). The influence of the juvenile hormone analogue ZR 512 (zoecon) on caste development in *Zootermopsis nevadensis* (Hagen) (Isoptera), *Insect Soc.,* **21,** 35–44.

Wardle, R. A., J. A. McLeod, and S. Radinovsky. (1974). *Advances in the Zoology of Tapeworms, 1950–1970,* University of Minnesota Press, Minneapolis.

Wasserthal, W. (1973). Zur Ei- und Embryonalentwicklung des Hydroid-Polypen *Eudendrium armaturum.* Eine licht- und elektronenmikroskopische Untersuchung, *Helgol. Wiss. Meeresunters.,* **25,** 93–125.

Watson, J. A. L., and J. J. Sewell. (1981). The origin and evolution of caste systems in termites, *Sociobiology,* **6,** 101–118.

Watt, W. B. (1968). Adaptive significance of pigment polymorphism in *Colias* butterflies I. Variation of melanin pigment in relation to thermoregulation, *Evolution,* **22,** 437–458.

Watt, W. B. (1969). Adaptive significance of pigment polymorphism in *Colias* butterflies. II Thermoregulation and photoperiodically controlled melanin variation in *Colias eurytheme, Proc. Nat. Acad. Sci. U.S.A.,* **63,** 767–774.

Webb, R. A. (1976). Putative neurosecretory cells of the cestode *Hymenolepis microstoma, J. Parasitol.,* **62,** 756–760.

Webb, R. A. (1980). Spermatogenesis in leeches I. Evidence for a gonad otropic peptide hormone produced by the supraoesophageal ganglion of *Erpobdella octoculata, Gen. Comp. Endocrinol.,* **42,** 401–412.

Webb, R. A., and K. G. Davey. (1976). The fine structure of the nervous tissue of the metacestode of *Hymenolepis microstoma, Can. J. Zool.,* **54,** 1206–1222.

Webb, R. A., and T. Friedel. (1979). Isolation of a neurosecretory substance which stimulates RNA synthesis in regenerating planarians, *Experientia,* **15,** 657–658.

Webb, R. A., and F. E. Omar. (1981). Spermatogenesis in leeches 2. The effect of supraoesophageal ganglion and ventral nerve cord ganglia on spermatogenesis in the north American medicinal leech *Macrobdella decora, Gen. Comp. Endocrinol.,* **44,** 54–63.

Wehling, W. E. (1978). Observation on the reproductive biology of *Protohydra leuckarti, Am. Zool.,* **18,** 643.

Weismann, A. (1892). *The Germ Plasm. A Theory of Heredity.* Scribner's, New York.

Weismann, A. (1896). New experiments on the seasonal dimorphism of Lepidoptera, *Entomologist,* **29,** 29–39, 74–80, 103–113, 153–157, 173–185, 203–209, 240–253.

Weismann, A. (1904). *The Evolution Theory,* E. Arnold, London.

Wells, M. J., and J. Wells. (1959). Hormonal control of sexual maturity in octopus, *J. Exp. Biol.,* **36,** 1–33.

Went, D. F. (1979). Paedogenesis in the dipteran insect *Heteropeza pygmaea:* An interpretation, *Int. J. Inverteb. Reprod.,* **1,** 21–30.

Went, D. F., V. Gentinetta, and B. Lanzrein. (1984). Ecdysteroid titers during larval reproduction of the dipteran insect *Heteropeza pygmaea, Experientia,* **40,** 998–1000.

Werner, B. (1963). Effect of some environmental factors on differentiation and determination in marine Hydrozoa, with a note on their evolutionary significance, *Ann. N. Y. Acad. Sci.,* **105,** 461–688.

Werner, B. (1980). "Life cycles of the Cnidaria," in *Developmental and Cellular Biology of Coelenterates,* P. Tardent and R. Tardent, Eds., Elsevier North Holland, New York, pp. 3–10.

Wesenberg-Lund, C. (1908). *Plankton Investigation of the Danish Lakes. General Part,* Nordisk, Copenhagen.

Wesenberg-Lund, C. (1943). *Biologie der Süsswasserinsekten,* Springer, Berlin.

Westblad, E. (1929). Über die Geschlechtsorgane und die systematische Stellung von *Protohydra leuckarti* Greef, *Ark. Zool,* **21**A(23), 1–13.

Westblad, W. (1971). Interstitial Polychaeta (excluding Archiannelida), *Smiths. Contrib. Zool.,* **76,** 57–70.

Westheide, W. (1981). Interstitial fauna of Galapagos Equador 26, Questidae, Cirratulidae, Acrocirridae, Ctenodrillidae, *Mikrofauna Meeresbodens,* **82,** 59–80.

Westheide, W. (1982). *Ikosipodus carolensis* gen. et sp. n., an interstitial neotenic polychaete from North Carolina, U. S. A., and its phylogenetic relationships within Dorvilleidae, *Zool. Scripta,* **11,** 117–126.

Westheide, W. (1984). The concept of reproduction in polychaetes with small body size; adaptation in interstitial species, *Fortschr. Zool.,* **29,** 265–287.

Westheide, W., and N. W. Riser. (1983). Morphology and phylogenetic relationships of the neotenic interstitial polystitial polychaete *Apodotrocha pragenerans* n. gen., n. sp., *Zoomorphology,* **103,** 67–87.

Weygoldt, P. (1969). *The Biology of Pseudoscorpions,* Harvard University Press, Cambridge, MA.

Wharton, D. R. A., J. E. Lola, and M. L. Wharton. (1968). Growth factors and population density in the American cockroach, *Periplaneta americana, J. Insect Physiol.,* **14,** 637–654.

Wheeler, D. E., and H. F. Nijhout. (1981). Soldier determination in ants: New role for juvenile hormone, *Science,* **213,** 361–363.

Wheeler, D. E., and H. F. Nijhout. (1984). Soldier determination in *Pheidole bicarinata:* inhibition by adult soldiers, *J. Insect Physiol.,***30,** 127–135.

Wheeler, W. M. (1900). A new myrmecophilic from the mushroom gardens of the Texas leaf cutting ant, *Am. Nat.,* **34,** 851–862.

White, B. A., and N. E. Henderson. (1977). Annual variation in the circulating levels of thyroid hormones in the brook trout, *Salvelinus fontinalis.* as measured by radio immunoassay, *Can. J. Zool.,* **55,** 475–481.

White, B. A., and C. S. Nicoll. (1979). Prolactin receptors in *Rana catesbeiana* during development and metamorphosis, *Science,* **204,** 851–853.

White, B. A., G. S. Lebovic, and C. S. Nicoll. (1981). Prolactin inhibits the induction of its own renal receptors in *Rana catesbeiana* tadpoles, *Gen. Comp. Endocrinol.,* **43,** 30–38.

White, M. J. D. (1948). The chromosomes of the parthenogenetic mantid *Brunneria borealis, Evolution,* **2,** 90–93.

Whitehead, D. L., and K. Sellheyer. (1982). The identification of ecdysterone (20 hydroxyecdysone) in 3 species of molluscs (Gastropoda: Pulmonata), *Experientia,* **38,** 1249–1251.

Wickstead, J. H. (1964). On the status of the 'amphioxides' larva, *J. Linn. Soc. (Zool.),* **45,** 261–269.

Wickstead, J. H. (1967). *Branchiostoma lanceolatum* larvae; some experiments on the effect of thyrouracil on metamorphosis, *J. Mar. biol. Assoc. U. K.,* **47,** 49–59.

Wickstead, J. H. (1975). "Chordata: Acrania (Cephalochordata)," in *Reproduction of Marine Invertebrates.* A. C. Giese and J. S. Pearse, Eds., Academic, New York, pp. 283–319.

Wigglesworth, V. B. (1934). The physiology of ecdysis in *Rhodnius prolixus* II. Factors controlling moulting and metamorphosis, *Q. J. Microsc. Sci.,* **77,** 191–222.

Wigglesworth, V. B. (1952). Hormone balance and the control of metamorphosis in *Rhodnius prolixus* (Hemiptera), *J. Exp. Biol.,* **29,** 620–631.

Wigglesworth, V. B. (1954). *The Physiology of Insect Metamorphosis.* Cambridge University Press, Cambridge.

Wijdenes, J., and N. W. Runham. (1976). Studies on the function of the dorsal bodies of *Agriolimax reticulatus* (Mollusca, Pulmonata). *Gen. Comp. Endocrinol.,* **29,** 545–551.

Wilbur, K. M. (1976). "Recent studies of invertebrate mineralization," in *The Mechanism of Mineralization in the Invertebrates and Plants,* N. Watabe and K. M. Wilbur, Eds., University of South Carolina Press, Columbia, pp. 79–108.

Wilczynski, J. (1960). On the egg dimorphism and sex determination in *Bonellia viridis, J. Exp. Zool.,* **143,** 61–76.

Wilczynski, J. (1968). On the sex in *Bonellia viridis, Acta Biotheor.,* **18,** 338–360.

de Wilde, J. (1976). "Juvenile hormone and caste differentiation in the honey bee (*Apis mellifera* L.)," in *Phase and Caste Determination in Insects,* M. Lüsher, Ed., Pergamon, Oxford, pp. 5–20.

Wildish, D. J. (1972). Postembryonic growth and age in some littoral *Orchestia* (Amphipoda, Talitridae), *Crustaceana Suppl.* **3,** 267–274.

Wildish, D. J. (1979). Reproductive consequences of terrestrial habitat in *Orchestia* (Crustacea Amphipoda), *Int. J. Inverteb. Reprod.,* **1,** 9–20.

Williams, A. B. (1965). Marine decapod crustaceans of the Carolinas, *U. S. Fish. Wildl. Serv. Fish Bull.,* **65,** 1–298.

Williams, C. M., and F. C. Kafatos. (1971). Theoretical aspects of action of juvenile hormone, *Mitt. Schweiz. Entomol. Ges.,* **44,** 151–162.

Williams, D. H. C., and D. T. Anderson. (1975). The reproductive system, embryonic development, and metamorphosis of the sea urchin *Heliocidaris erythrogramma* (Val.) (Echinoidea, Echinometridae), *Aust. J. Zool.,* **23,** 371–403.

Williams, J. B. (1961). The dimorphism of *Polystoma integerrimum* (Fröhlich) Rudolphi, and its bearing on relationship within the Polystomatidae. Part III, *J. Helminthol.,* **35,** 181–202.

Williams, W. D. (1965). Ecological notes on Tasmanian Syncarida (Crustacea: Malacostraca), with a description of a new species of *Anaspides, Rev. Gesammt. Hydrobiol.,* **50,** 95–126.

Williamson, D. I. (1951). On the mating and breeding of some semiterrestrial amphipods, *King's Coll. Dove Mar. Lab. Rep.,* **3,** 46–92.

Wilson, E. O. (1953). The origins and evolution of polymorphism in ants, *Q. Rev. Biol.,* **28,** 136–156.

Wilson, E. O. (1971). *The Insect Societies,* Harvard University Press, Cambridge, MA.

Wilson, F. H. (1934). The life cycle and bionomics of *Lipeurus heterographus, Nitzch J. Parasitol.,* **20,** 304–311.

Wilson, T. G. (1981a). Expression of phenotypes in a temperature-sensitive allele of the apterous mutation in *Drosophila melanogaster, Dev. Biol.,* **85,** 425–433.

Wilson, T. G. (1981b). A mosaic analysis of the apterous mutation in *Drosophila melanogaster, Dev. Biol.,* **85,** 434–445.

Winget, R. R., and W. S. Herman. (1976). Occurrence of ecdysone in the blood of the chelicerate arthropod, *Limulus polyphemus, Experientia,* **32,** 1345–1346.

Wirtz, P. (1973). Differentiation in the honeybee larva, *Meded. Landbouwhoogesch. Wageningen,* **73(5):** 1–151.

Wirtz, P., and J. Beetsma. (1972). Induction of caste differentiation in the honey bee *(Apis mellifera)* by juvenile hormone, *Entomol. Exp. Appl.,* **15,** 517–520.

Woltereck, R. (1934). Artdifferenzierung (insbesondere Gestaltänderung) bei Cladoceren, *Z. Indukt. Abstamm. Vererbungsl.,* **67,** 173–196.

Wong, C. K. (1981). Cyclomorphosis in *Bosmina* and copepod predation, *Can. J. Zool.,* **59,** 2049–2052.

Wood, E. A., and K. J. Starks. (1975). Incidence of paedogenesis in the greenbug, *Environ. Entomol.,* **4,** 1001–1002.

Woodhead, A. P., and C. R. Paulson. (1983). Larval development of *Diploptera punctata* reared alone and in groups, *J. Insect Physiol.,* **29,** 665–668.

Wourms, J. P. (1981). Viviparity: The maternal-fetal relationship in fishes, *Am. Zool.,* **21,** 473–515.

Wrenn, S. L. (1972). Daily increment formation and synchronizataion in the shell of the bay scallop, *Am. Zool.,* **12,** 32.

Wright, G. M., and J. H. Youson. (1976). Transformation of the endostyle of the anadromous sea lamprey *Petromyzon marinus* L. during metamorphosis I. Light microscopy and autoradiography with ^{125}I, *Gen. Comp. Endocrinol.,* **30,** 243–257.

Wright, G. M., and J. H. Youson. (1980). Transformation of the endostyle of the anadromous sea lamprey *Patromyzon marinus* L., during metamorphosis II. Electronmicroscopy, *J. Morphol.,* **166,** 231–257.

Wright, S. (1931). Evolution in Mendelian population, *Genetics,* **16,** 97–157.

Wyatt, I. J. (1961). Pupal paedogenesis in the Cecidomyiidae (Diptera) I, *Proc. R. Entomol. Soc. Lond. A*, **36**, 133–143.

Wyatt, I. J. (1963). Pupal paedogenesis in the Cecidomyiidae (Diptera) II, *Proc. R. Entomol. Soc. Lond. A*, **38**, 136–144.

Wyatt, I. J. (1964). Immature stages of Lestremiinae (Diptera: Cecidomyiidae) infesting cultivated mushrooms, *Trans. R. Entomol. Soc. Lond.*, **116**, 15–27.

Wyatt, I. J. (1967). Pupal paedogenesis in the Cecidomyiidae (Diptera) 3 — A reclassification of Heteropezini, *Trans. R. Entomol. Soc. Lond.*, **119**, 71–98.

Yamaguti, S. (1968). *Monogenetic Trematodes of Hawaiian Fishes*, University of Hawaii Press, Honolulu.

Yamasaki, T. (1978). A new genus and species of cave-dwelling cricket from Luzon, the Philippines, *J. Speleol. Soc. Jap.*, **3**, 14–19.

Yamasaki, T. (1979). Discovery of the second species of the mangrove cricket, *Apteronemobius* (Orthoptera, Gryllidae), in the Ryukyus, *Annot. Zool. Jap.*, **52**, 79–85.

Yamasaki, T. (1982). Grylloblattid insects as natural environmental indicators (in Japanese), *Iden* **36**, 13–17.

Yanagimachi, R., and N. Fujimaki. (1967). Studies on the sexual organization of the Phizocephala IV. On the nature of the "testis" in *Thompsonia, Annot. Zool. Jap.*, **40**, 98–104.

Yin, C.-M., and C. Gillott. (1975). Endocrine control of caste differentiation in *Zootermopsis angusticollis* Hagen (Isoptera), *Can. J. Zool.*, **53**, 1701–1708.

Yoshimoto, C. M. (1964). Insects of Campbell Island. Hymenoptera: Cynipoidea: Eucolinae, *Pac. Insects Monogr.*, **7**, 509–512.

Young, E. C. (1965a). Teneral development in British Corixidae, *Proc. R. Entomol. Soc. A*, **40**, 159–168.

Young, E. C. (1965b). The incidence of flight polymorphism in British Corixidae and description of the morphs, *J. Zool.*, **146**, 567–576.

Young, E. C. (1965c). Flight muscle polymorphism in British Corixidae: Ecological observation, *J. Anim. Ecol.*, **34**, 353–389.

Young, E. C. (1970). Seasonal changes in populations of Corixidae and Notonectidae (Hemiptera: Heteroptera) in New Zealand, *Trans. R. Soc. N. Z.*, **12**, 113–130.

Youson, I. H. (1980). Morphology and physiology of lamprey metamorphosis, *Can. J. Fish. Aquat. Sci.*, **37**, 1687–1710.

Yu, J. Y.-L., W. Dickhoff, Y. Inui, and A. Gorbman. (1980). Sexual patterns of protein metabolism in liver and plasma of hagfish, *Eptatretus stouti*, with special reference to vitellogenesis, *Comp. Biochem. Physiol.*, **65B**, 111–117.

Yu, J. Y.-L., W. W. Dickhoff, P. Swanson, and A. Gorbman. (1981). Vitellogenesis and its hormonal regulation in the Pacific hagfish, *Eptatretus stouti* L., *Gen. Comp. Endocrinol.*, **43**, 492–502.

Zakhvatkin, A. A. (1953). Studies on morphology and postembryonic development of tirogliphids (Sarcoptiformes, Tyroglyphoidea). Sbornik nauch. rabot Moskousk. universit., pp. 19–120 (in Russian).

Zakhvatkin, Y. A. (1975). Embryology of insects. M.: High school, pp. 1–328 (in Russian).

Zanandrea, G. (1957). Neoteny in a lamprey, *Nature*, **179**, 925–926.

Zaret, T. M. (1969). Predation-balanced polymorphism of *Ceriodaphnia cornuta* Sars, *Limnol. Oceanogr.*, **14**, 301–303.

Zaret, T. M. (1972). Predators, invisible prey, and the nature of polymorphism in the Cladocera (Class Crustacea), *Limnol. Oceanogr.*, **17**, 171–184.

Zdarek, J., and G. Fraenkel. (1970). Overt and covert effects of endogenous and exogenous ecdysone in puparium formation in flies, *Proc. Natl. Acad. Sci.*, **67**, 331–337.

Zdarek, J., and O. Haragsim. (1974). Action of juvenoids on metamorphosis of the honey bee, *Apis mellifera, J. Insect Physiol.*, **20**, 209–221.

Zera, A. J., D. J. Innes, and M. E. Saks. (1983). Genetic and environmental determinants of wing polymorphism in the waterstrider *Limnoporus canaliculatus, Evolution*, **37**, 513–523.

Zerbib, C., and J.-J. Meusy. (1981). Etude ultrastructurale du tissu adipeux chez un crustacé l'amphipode talitride *Orchestia gammarellus, C. R. Acad. Sci.*, **293**, 73–77.

Zerbib, C., and J. J. Mustel. (1984). Incorporation de la vitellogénine tritiée dans les ovocytes des crustacé amphipodes *Orchestia gammarelus* (Pallas), *Int. J. Inverteb. Reprod.*, **7**, 63–68.

Zeve, V. H. and D. E. Howell. (1963). The comparative external morphology of *Trichobius carynorrhini, T. major* and *T. sphaeronotus* (Diptera, Strebliidae) II. The thorax, *Ann. Entomol. Soc. Am.*, **56**, 2–17.

Zlotorzycka, J. (1967). Parasitophyletische Probleme der bei den Mallophagen, Passeres und Pici, *Angew. Parasitol.*, **8**, 45–53.

Author Index

329

Subject Index

Generic Name Index